---◇---

"*Revelation* is a game changer for both teachers and students of the prophetic biography. It is a contribution to the library of Islamic studies in English that will undoubtedly be celebrated by future generations."

USAMA CANON, TA'LEEF COLLECTIVE

"Looking over this text was akin to seeing the internet for the first time. This is something that may change the way the life of the Prophet is understood in the English-speaking world."

UBAYDULLAH EVANS, AMERICAN LEARNING INSTITUTE FOR MUSLIMS

"I have been developing and reviewing Islamic curricula for over 15 years and I can say, without a doubt, that with the book *Revelation*, Meraj Mohiuddin has set a new standard for Islamic studies in the English language. The book is not only rich in information, but organized in a way that helps a teacher present the material, a student review it and assists a self-learner who does not have access to a teacher.

Mohiuddin's extensive research and amazing use of the English language brings the stories of the Sirah to life with eloquent imagery to make you feel as though you are there, watching the events occur."

RAMI NSOUR, TAYBA FOUNDATION

"Many biographies of the Prophet Muhammad (peace be upon him) have appeared in recent years. None, however, display the scholarly depth, methodological precision and factual clarity of Meraj Mohiuddin's, *Revelation: The Story of Muhammad (pbuh)*. Relying on ancient and modern sources, graphs, charts, marginal notes and a moving narration, Mohiuddin rigorously chronicles the life of Muhammad (peace and blessings be upon him) in a uniquely engaging and informative manner."

IMAM ZAID SHAKIR, ZAYTUNA COLLEGE

"This is a fresh and fascinating approach towards learning and teaching the Sirah of Allah's last Messenger. The author has given us a new methodology to appreciate the life and message of Prophet Muhammad and also to learn a great deal about the context, environment and people surrounding the Sirah ... We are grateful to the author for his labor of love."

DR. MUZAMMIL H. SIDDIQI, THE FIQH COUNCIL OF NORTH AMERICA

"*Revelation: The Story of Muhammad (pbuh)* is the first biography of the Prophet that I've read that brings it all together—there is something in it for everyone; as an instructor, I use it for teaching, and as a student, I use it for study. It is the most important work on the Prophet's life I've come across in the English language. I'm proud to announce that it is the official biography of the Prophet used by the Ella Collins Institute for training future faith providers in the USA."

SUHAIB WEBB, ELLA COLLINS INSTITUTE

---◇---

REVELATION

The Story of Muhammad
Peace and blessings be upon him

———

Meraj Mohiuddin

WHITEBOARD
PRESS

Revelation: The Story of Muhammad

Editor: Arifa Chaudhry
Cover Design: Nermin Moufti
Layout Design: Nermin Moufti and Hafsa Farooqui
Illustrations: Meraj Mohiuddin (adapted by Hafsa Farooqui and Nermin Moufti)

———

———

Information for retail and special orders can be found at www.whiteboardpress.com.

Published by: Whiteboard Press, LLC—Scottsdale, AZ

ISBN-13: 978-0-9896288-0-8

10 9 8 7 6 5 4 3 2

First Edition, second reprint with revisions.
Printed in USA.

Whiteboard Press, LLC, is dedicated to green practices and technologies. This book is printed according to Forest Stewardship Council® (FSC®) standards. Inks used are vegetable based and contain non-toxic linseed oils low in Volatile Organic Compounds (VOCs) to help leave a smaller footprint in our world.

For you, the reader.

"Here I am, back in Mecca. I am still traveling, trying to broaden my mind, for I've seen too much of the damage narrow-mindedness can make of things, and when I return home to America, I will devote what energies I have to repair the damage."

MALCOLM X (1925-65)

TABLE OF CONTENTS

EARLY MECCA

YEAR 1: PRIVATE INVITATION

YEAR 2: PRIVATE INVITATION: THE PROPHET'S INNER CIRCLE

YEAR 3: PRIVATE INVITATION: THE PROPHET'S EXTENDED FAMILY

YEAR 4: PUBLIC INVITATION: THE CITY OF MECCA

YEAR 5: ABYSSINIA

YEAR 6: HAMZAH & 'UMAR

LATE MECCA

———

YEAR 7: THE BAN

YEAR 8: THE BAN

YEAR 9: THE BAN

YEAR 10: THE LONG YEAR OF SADNESS

YEAR 11: THE ISRA' & ME'RAJ

YEAR 12: THE 'AQABAH PLEDGE

EARLY MEDINA

YEAR 13: THE HIJRAH

YEAR 14: THE CARAVAN RAIDS

YEAR 15: BADR 1

YEAR 16: UHUD

YEAR 17: BADR 2

YEAR 18: THE TRENCH

LATE MEDINA

———

YEAR 19: HUDAYBIYAH

YEAR 20: THE CONQUEST OF MECCA

YEAR 21: TABUK

YEAR 22: THE DELEGATIONS

LIST OF ILLUSTRATIONS

FOREWORD

The Qur'an is among the most widely read books in the world today. It is also among the most misunderstood. This gulf between reading and understanding is not simply a function of language; native speakers of Arabic are just as likely to draw a blank in the face of the Qur'an's non-linear style as are those who don't know Arabic or who learned it as full-grown adults. Beyond religious devotion, however, three historical facts ensure that the Qur'an will continue to grow in readership. The first is what some scholars refer to as the "de-secularization of the world." The second is the spread of Islam outside the traditional Muslim world. The third is the growing perception in the West of Islam as a civilizational contagion and an existential threat. For all of these reasons, the Qur'an is likely to become a much more widely read document than it has ever been in its history, as non-Muslims join Muslims in an attempt to apprehend the meaning and power of this sacred text.

It is precisely in this context, however, that the profound importance and timeliness of the present work, *Revelation: The Story of Muhammad,* is thrown into bold relief. For the real key to understanding the Qur'an—indeed, Islam as a whole—is a basic grasp of the life and career of the man who served as its delivery system. Muhammad (SAWS) brought life, meaning, depth, human tragedy and human triumph to the Qur'anic adventure. He showed that Islam is not an event that abruptly imposes itself onto human history as a fully constituted fact. Nor is God a divine Santa Claus who immediately damns the naughty and rewards the nice in accordance with some mechanical calculus of good and bad deeds. Rather, Muhammad demonstrated that Islam is a process in which both our ups and our downs expose us to the layers of self-knowledge and spiritual epiphany that surround life's most profound truth: *There is no god except God.*

Muhammad showed us that humans must struggle to make Islam, Islam. And even in possession of unwavering faith, they must be careful not to fall into the idolatry of assuming that good deeds always bring the results they want. As God reminds Muhammad, His faithful servant and "beloved confidant" *(khalil)*:

> *Say, I have no power over whether good or harm should come to me, except as God wills. And if I had knowledge of the unseen I would augment all good for myself and misfortune would never touch me. I am but a warner and a bringer of good tidings for those whose conscience is tied to God.* —Al A'raf (The Heights, 7:188)

Reminders such as this enabled Muhammad to face every challenge and every tragedy—including the loss of reputation, friends and family members—with dignity, hope and resolve.

But Muhammad's life is not merely about him as an individual. It captures the realities of an entire society brought face to face with divine revelation. And here the lessons of his life become especially important today. For Muhammad's career teaches us that Islam negotiates not with abstract concepts of society but with real society, in all its virtues and all its flaws. Even an idol-worshipping, infanticidal society like seventh-century Arabia could be recognized for the good qualities (ma'ruf) it displayed alongside its various evils. Muhammad never disowned his society. Indeed, his career provides a fascinating demonstration of how, while upholding its core commitments, Islam seeks to accentuate society's positives while minimizing its negatives, all the while enabling society itself to retain a collective dignity and a healthy sense of self. Muhammad's struggles in this regard, especially his unwillingness to write his society off, should bring comfort to those Muslims who secretly nurse the fear that for them to have any honest, serious commitment to Islam would bind them to reject America—and Americanness—as a lost cause.

If Islam is to be successfully "translated" into modern Western society, it will not be able to dispense with the life of Muhammad as "translator." Western Muslims will have to be reminded that just as Muhammad did not confront "society" in the abstract, neither should they. And just as he did not assume some cookie-cutter model to which all societies are to be held, neither should they. Western Muslims live in American society, British society, or French society. And all of these societies have their unique virtues and flaws. Muslims must internalize and follow the example of Muhammad and, again, even as they seek to uphold the core values of Islam, try to accentuate their societies' virtues and minimize their flaws. And rather than hide behind such religious categories as "good" and "evil" in the abstract (or even in terms of what these might have meant in seventh-century Arabia) they must confront the real, concrete, specific goods (e.g., religious freedom, economic opportunity) and evils (e.g., racism, police corruption) that define the societies in which they live, just as the Prophet did in his time and place.

I would like to close with a word on Islam in America and a final insight into the implications of an adequate understanding of the life of Muhammad for the future of Islam in the United States. Of all the major Western democracies, America is unique in that a major contingent of its Muslim population consists of native-born converts, Blackamericans, whose roots in this country are centuries old. Among the keys to the success of Islam in Blackamerica is the early proto-Islamic pioneers taking Islam as an instrument for addressing a real American evil: racism. This ultimately earned those associated with Islam a positive place in the collective psyche of Blackamericans as a whole. At the very least, Blackamericans continued to see Blackamerican Muslims as an integral part of the black community united in the struggle against America's most intractable disease. And this had the effect of placing Islam in general in a positive light.

Now, anyone who is familiar with the life of Muhammad knows that his very survival in the early period was due to the support he received from his blood-clan of Banu Hashim, the majority of whom had not converted to Islam but still refused to abandon him as one of their own. Despite their difference in religion, in other words, they continued to recognize their ties of blood, which brought them to see any physical attack on Muhammad as an offense to their collective sense of pride. Notably, this consideration extended not only to Muhammad as a member of Banu Hashim but at critical times to the Muslim community at large, including members of other clans. It should not take much to recognize that the Blackamerican community in America has functioned in many ways as American Muslims' Banu Hashim. Yet, ignorance and inattentiveness have allowed this connection to go unrecognized and thus deteriorate to the point that a Blackamerican candidate for president in 2015 could publicly deny American Muslims the right to serve as president!

Revelation: The Story of Muhammad should go a long way in empowering Muslims in America to recognize these kinds of mistakes. And it should aid them in preventing the recurrence of such missteps and oversights. The book is clear, eminently accessible, and based on some of the best Western scholarship on the life of the Prophet. I can only hope that it will attract the readership it so richly deserves. And I pray that through it God will open our hearts and minds to the miracle that was the life of the Prophet Muhammad.

Sherman A. Jackson, PhD

King Faisal Chair in Islamic Thought and Culture
Professor of Religion and American Studies and Ethnicity
University of Southern California

PREFACE

All my life I have struggled to connect with the Qur'an. I have seen others moved to tears by its words, yet somehow I have always felt a certain distance, separated by its language and historical context. As a non-Arabic-speaking Muslim, I felt that the English translations were keeping the Qur'an's meaning and majesty out of my reach. My understanding of the Qur'an's historical context was no different. Growing up in suburban America, I encountered a huge gap between my world and seventh-century Arabia.

I am neither an Islamic scholar nor an amateur historian. The son of immigrants, I was born and raised in New Jersey and grew up in the American public school system. While education was foremost in our house, my siblings and I never attended Sunday school. At that time, Islamic schools, immersion programs, and podcasts were not widely available. My parents raised us with a solid foundation in the Qur'an and Islamic history. However, as we grew older, most of the books in our house were limited to English translations of traditional Urdu and Arabic texts … not the kind of material most teenagers wanted to read.

I was frustrated because my pursuit of the Qur'an had stalled while I continued to excel at advanced coursework in high school and college. Unable to attend a language immersion program in college, I felt as though the prospect of learning Arabic was out of my immediate reach. Meanwhile I also struggled to learn the historical context of the Qur'an. The Islamic books I read at home were completely different from the textbooks I studied in school. Having learned to use diagrams, tables, and glossaries, I was struggling to remember Islamic history from page after page of translated English text. The books felt devotional rather than scholastic. Meanwhile books on Islam written by Western authors were limited—many lacked academic authority and others were mired in Orientalism.

Life in America doesn't leave much in the way of free time, and medical school took that to the extreme. Four years later, I was feeling lopsided and restless. What I lacked during those formative years was an efficient study guide of classical texts. Something that could present the historical context of the Qur'an in a format that I could study, analyze, memorize, and master.

How does a non-Arabic-speaking Muslim even begin to understand the Qur'an? After struggling with this question for years, I imagined what it would be like to be a companion of the Prophet Muhammad (peace be upon him[1]). After all, his first followers did not read the Qur'an, but experienced it—rich in context—as it unfolded in front of them. To be a companion, I realized, meant immersing myself in the life of Muhammad, or what is traditionally known as the Sirah.

By the time I began residency, weekend intensive programs and audio lectures by Muslim-American scholars were just starting to blossom. Hamza Yusuf, a young American convert who had studied in Mauritania, was gaining popularity in the West as an American voice of classical scholarship. I purchased a copy of his 24-CD audio collection, *The Life of the Prophet*, and began listening to his lectures while commuting to work. Rich with authentic narrations and Qur'anic references, Yusuf provides a classical exposition of Martin Lings' renowned biography, *Muhammad: His Life Based on the Earliest Sources*. On the fifth CD, Yusuf pauses in the middle of his lecture and exposes the very problem that I, as an American Muslim, had been facing:

> This book ... a lot of people find it difficult because of the names ... it is a problem ...and you know what would be really nice? If somebody actually went through the book, wrote down all the names, and then had a glossary of names. You could kind of keep that with you as you read the book. That would be really useful.[2]

I took Yusuf's suggestion to heart. I revisited Lings' book and started writing down all the names I encountered: names of people, their ancestors, parents, and offspring, and various tribes, clans, battles, treaties, and towns. As I worked my way through the text, the long list of names grew unmanageable. I needed a better system. So I employed techniques I used in medical school to consolidate multiple sources of information, reduce them down to succinct notes and diagrams, organize them into an efficient study guide, and use that guide to master the original texts. Over the years, what started as a list of names slowly evolved into an extensive examination of the Prophet's life. Urged by family and friends, I have compiled my notes into a professionally edited textbook to share with others.

THE APPROACH

So how does one approach the history of the Qur'an?

There is a wealth of information on the life of the Prophet and sorting through the literature can be daunting. Biographies of the Prophet vary in size and authenticity.[3] After careful consideration, I decided to limit my primary sources to the works of three scholars who are widely respected for their expertise in the field: Safiur Rehman Al-Mubarakpuri, Martin Lings, and William Montgomery Watt.

SAFIUR REHMAN AL-MUBARAKPURI is a renowned Islamic scholar who wrote the widely acclaimed biography *Ar-Raheeq al-Makhtum (The Sealed Nectar)*. His book was first written in Arabic and Urdu in the late 1970s, and subsequently was translated into numerous languages after winning first prize at the Muslim World League biography competition in 1979. Not surprisingly, it is a standard text throughout most of the Muslim world.

MARTIN LINGS (Abu Bakr Siraj Ad-Din) was an English Sufi Muslim writer and scholar who passed away in 2005. His book, *Muhammad: His Life Based on the Earliest Sources*, was originally published in 1983 and is based on the works of the four earliest biographers of the Prophet: Ibn Ishaq, Ibn Hisham, Ibn Sa'd and Waqidi (see Appendix B). It is exactly because of this loyalty to the earliest sources that his book has earned such high praise and is considered to be one of the most authoritative biographies of the Prophet in the English language. The book stands out because of its rich descriptions and sizeable information about the Companions.

WILLIAM MONTGOMERY WATT was a Scottish historian and professor of Arabic and Islamic studies at the University of Edinburgh. He is best known for his exhaustive biographies of the Prophet, *Muhammad in Mecca* (1953) and *Muhammad in Medina* (1954). A professional historian, Watt painstakingly researched the earliest historical sources and chronicled many details of the Prophet's life that are not found in the other two texts. Watt wrote an abridged follow-up biography, *Muhammad: Prophet and Statesman* (1974), that highlights many essential themes in his previous two books. I would categorize his writings as evenhanded and academic. Although Watt never embraced Islam in its entirety, he is widely respected in the Muslim world because of his persuasive arguments against early Western Orientalists who maligned the Prophet without any historical or sociological foundations.

While there exists overlapping material between the scholars, each author approaches the life of the Prophet from a slightly different angle: Al-Mubarakpuri is devotional, Lings is literary, and Watt is academic. In my attempt to be concise yet complete, I included information mentioned by at least two of the three scholars, if not all three. On rare occasions, I have included important details mentioned by only one of the three sources. I felt it was necessary to include these events because they were significant enough to be mentioned in the Qur'an. (For example, Lings never mentions the Mosque of Dissension cited in Surah At-Tawbah while Al-Mubarakpuri omits the Prophet's separation from his wives mentioned in Surah At-Tahreem.)

When I began this project, the sheer volume of names, places, and dates left me feeling hopelessly resigned that I would never truly master the material. After all, how does one keep track of 20 men who are all named 'Abd Allah? In addition, I have also struggled with certain aspects of the Prophet's life that stemmed from my background as a Western-educated reader—namely my unfamiliarity with seventh-century Arabian customs and my unsophisticated understanding of tribal history and politics.

Given these challenges, I decided to divide the project into six manageable tasks:

1) INTEGRATED TIMELINE: My first step was to compile the biographies into a comprehensive timeline of events. Given that there are differences of opinion on when certain events happened (especially during the Meccan period), I first cross-checked every event making sure it followed the most established timeline (see Appendix A for more details). As I delved deeper into the subject matter, I started feeling overwhelmed by the particulars. In the summer of 2010, I decided to come up with a simpler way of remembering when everything happened. After a period of trial and error, I developed a schematic of the Prophet's life that forever changed how I approached the Qur'an and Sirah. So much so, that I have organized this entire book around that idea (please read the Introduction for more information).

2) CONCISE REVIEW OF EVENTS: After creating a timeline of major events, I sifted through the primary sources and wrote a concise synopsis of each event. My objective was to extract only the most essential information while making sure not to ignore important facts and oversimplify complex material.

3) GLOSSARY OF NAMES: As I studied the Prophet's life, I kept a running list of over 350 names mentioned in the biographies. Because tribal alliances and family ties play such a crucial part of the narrative, I tried my best to include a brief description of each person's kinship ties and their relationship to the Prophet, where applicable. In addition, I have tried to summarize the most salient features of each person's involvement in the bigger story of the Prophet's life.

4) FAMILY TREES: In seventh-century Arabia, where you came from defined who you were. Having a basic understanding of family relationships helps explain why people behaved the way they did. For this reason, I tried my best to re-create family trees based on information available in the texts.

5) MAPS: I have included maps of Arabia and the surrounding empires. Where necessary, I have also created renderings of major expeditions and military confrontations (Badr, Uhud, Trench, etc.) to help visualize the movements of individuals, caravans, and armies.

6) DIAGRAMS: There are a few instances where I have found it easier to illustrate complex ideas, concepts, and relationships through visual aides.

As you can see, what started as a few pages of review notes slowly transformed into a deeper examination of the Prophet's life. As I started to get a handle on the basic storyline, a number of questions occurred to me that I simply could not ignore. For example:

> *Why did young Muhammad feel so disillusioned with Mecca?*

> *Why did he condone caravan raiding?*

> *Why did he marry so many women?*

> *Why did he command his Companions to take captives?*

> *Why didn't he stop the execution of the Jewish tribe of Qurayzah?*

> *Why did he forgive his fiercest opponents?*

> *Why was he worried if he knew he would ultimately succeed?*

To be sure, I've found that the most difficult questions were always the most personal:

> *Why does this bother me?*

> *Why can't I come to terms with this?*

Although there are several places where Al-Mubarakpuri and Lings take it upon themselves to explain certain events or behaviors, for the most part, they simply relate the story as it had been recorded by the earliest Muslim biographers. In contrast, Watt attaches a fair amount of analysis, hypotheses, and explanation to his narrative. In my ongoing search for answers, I started investigating a number of other commentaries about the Prophet's life. My search led me to the following authors:

1) KAREN ARMSTRONG: *Muhammad: A Prophet for our Time*

2) TARIQ RAMADAN: *In the Footsteps of the Prophet*

3) REZA ASLAN: *No god but God*

4) HAMZA YUSUF: *The Life of the Prophet (audio lectures)*

5) ADIL SALAHI: *Muhammad: Man and Prophet*

I began with **KAREN ARMSTRONG** (born 1944) for a number of reasons. Firstly, she is a widely respected author of numerous works on comparative religion. In 1991, she authored her own abridged biography of the Prophet, targeted to non-Muslims and Muslims alike. This was followed in 2006 by the current book, *Muhammad: A Prophet for our Time,* which was largely in response to the events of 9/11 and the growing curiosity about Islam. As an American, I've found her approach simple, respectful, and illuminating. I felt that she already knew what topics I was struggling with and did not waste time getting to the heart of the discussion. In addition, her eloquent description of pre-Islamic Arabia has been pivotal in helping contextualize many issues that surfaced in my study.

TARIQ RAMADAN is a professor of Contemporary Islamic Studies at Oxford University. His book *In the Footsteps of the Prophet* is a work of deep contemplation. Emphasizing the heterogeneous nature of Western Muslims, he strongly advocates the study and re-interpretation of Islamic texts. I've found his tone encouraging; he pushes readers to free themselves from traditional religio-cultural biases, and extract new and fuller meanings from the Prophet's life that are relevant today.

REZA ASLAN is an Iranian-American writer and Associate Professor of Creative Writing at the University of California, Riverside, who came into prominence with his first book, *No god but God*. Published in 2005 and translated into 13 languages, it is a response to the challenges of a post-9/11 world. I have included his book for a number of reasons. First, he has a unique background as a young Iranian-born, American-raised Muslim. Furthermore, I've found his analysis to be quite critical (and in rare instances uncomfortable). He is not afraid to challenge classical dogma with well-researched opinions. "There are those who will call it apology, but that is hardly a bad thing," he writes. "An apology is a defense, and there is no higher calling than to defend one's faith, especially from ignorance and hate." I included him in this discussion because he may represent the voice of a younger generation of Muslims that respect traditional teaching, but have become increasingly unsatisfied with its lack of critical analysis.

I consider **HAMZA YUSUF'S** audio set *The Life of the Prophet* an American classic. As a co-founder of Zaytuna College, Yusuf is one of America's leading proponents of classical Islamic education. The approach of his lectures can be inspiring to many, but runs the risk of alienating others. For example, in his introduction, Yusuf unapologetically states that if audience members are struggling to understand the Prophet's actions, it is not the Prophet's problem but their own. While this may be true, his words had an initial sting that left me feeling quite defensive. I silently wondered, "What's wrong with me that I am bothered by polygamy?" The truth, I later learned, is that the Western-minded Muslim has a lot to sort out, and it takes time and patience to bridge that gap. I am deeply grateful to Hamza Yusuf for inspiring me to tackle this project.

Just when I thought I had studied all the best modern Sirah commentaries, a young Texan imam suggested that I take a look at **ADIL SALAHI'S** book, *Muhammad: Man and Prophet*. Salahi's biography is the work of a seasoned journalist who combines convincing research with persuasive commentary. I included him in this manuscript because of his unique approach to several controversial topics such as 'A'ishah's young age and the execution of Bani Qurayzah. In his preface, Salahi explains, "I became increasingly aware that many misunderstandings of Islam by the West could be cleared up if the West could get to know the personality and the life of the Prophet Muhammad better ... This book is a humble attempt to make such a task easier. It makes no pretense of being 'objective', or trying to evaluate events in a detached manner. ... On the contrary, I believe that there is much that the West could learn about Islam if it is able to look at it through the eyes of a Muslim."

In summary, I have gathered excerpts from four contemporary voices (Muslim, non-Muslim, American, and European) and have tried to balance that with a voice from the classical tradition. Considering that everything we know about the Prophet has come to us from traditional sources, any contemporary analysis ought to be approached with a profound respect for classical scholarship.

HOW TO USE THIS BOOK

Undoubtedly, the most challenging part of this project was arranging the vast array of material in a well-organized and reader-friendly format. With so many perspectives to sift through, I decided that the best way to present all of this information is to imagine that we are sitting in a classroom. Our professors (Al-Mubarakpuri, Lings, and Watt) are summarizing the essentials and citing relevant Qur'anic text on the chalkboard. They are surrounded by five "teaching assistants" (Armstrong, Ramadan, Aslan, Salahi, and Yusuf) who are chiming in with unique insights that serve to enrich the lecture material in one of the following ways:

a) Contextualizing history for modern readers,
b) Providing moral insight into events and themes,
c) Explaining challenging or controversial topics,
d) Eloquently reinforcing ideas, descriptions, or behaviors, or
e) Challenging readers with a sound yet innovative perspective.

Because the details can be intimidating, I have incorporated a network of elaborations that highlight social, political, and historical subtleties that tend to fall through the cracks. These memos will help you remember how people and events are related through time, and also provide background information, mnemonics, and suggested readings from the primary sources.

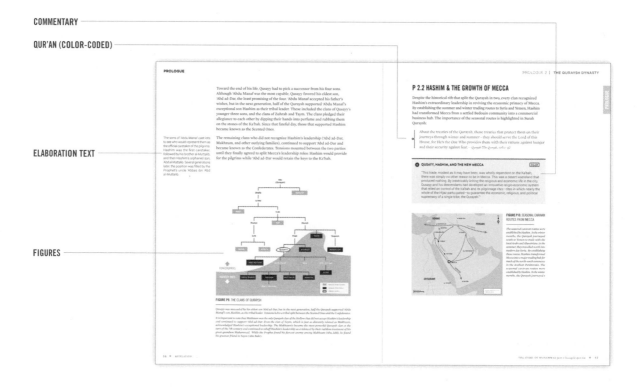

COMMENTARY
QUR'AN (COLOR-CODED)
ELABORATION TEXT
FIGURES

As stated earlier, the ultimate purpose of this book is to help you learn the historical context of the Qur'an by reliving the story of revelation. To that end, I have tried my best to tell the Prophet's story through the verses of the Qur'an whenever possible. For the sake of consistency and clarity, each scholar's translation of the Qur'an is replaced with Yahiya Emerick's translation. I have chosen his work, *The Holy Qur'an in Today's English*, because it is widely regarded as one of the most engaging and accessible translations in the English language.

Each verse is color-coded to indicate if it was revealed in Mecca (blue) or Medina (green). Along the side of the page you will also find short introductions to each surah when it is first mentioned or usually around the time it was revealed. When you encounter these surah introductions, I encourage you to read the entire surah before continuing with your study of the Prophet's life.

I purposely wrote this book in a casual style and did not include any Arabic text so that you will not have to treat it with ceremonial care. This text is designed to be highlighted, questioned, discussed, and debated. In short, my goal is to help you learn the material, inside-out.

If you really engage with this material, I think you will find some topics difficult, perhaps even unsettling. You may need to take a break from this text for a while to clear your head. There were several times during this project when I could not reconcile my pre-existing understanding of Islam with what I was reading. In retrospect, I've found that these difficult moments of inner conflict and struggle yielded illuminating truths not just about Muhammad as a Prophet, but also about myself as a believer.

At the turn of the 12th century, the great Islamic renewer Muhammad Al-Ghazali re-questioned all that he had learned in philosophy, only to discover a deeper mysticism devoid of cultural accretions. He subsequently re-invigorated Islamic thought. I similarly encourage you to contemplate and question the various perspectives herein. I expect that not everything will resonate with you, and I strongly urge you to seek guidance from qualified scholars and their primary sources.

If it is true that the Prophet's character was the Qur'an,[4] my only hope is that, in time, by understanding the Messenger, we can begin to truly understand his Message.

Meraj Mohiuddin
December 2015

---

[1] Islam makes no distinction between its prophets (i.e., Adam, Noah, Abraham, Moses, David, Solomon, Joseph, John, Jesus, or Muhammad) peace be upon them all. As is the Islamic convention, they are all treated with utmost respect, and their names are followed by the praise ("God's peace be upon them"). For the sake of accomodating readers from all backgrounds, I have omitted this convention in the present book. I encourage Muslim readers to recite this prayer whenever they speak, hear, or read about a prophet.

Furthermore, I have taken the liberty to refer to the Prophet Muhammad as "Muhammad" when describing his life before revelation. After his first revelation, he is referred to as "the Prophet."

[2] Yusuf, CD 5:1

[3] The science of Islamic hagiography is not held to the same level of scrutiny as other fields of Islamic scholarship such as *hadith* methodology (the collected sayings of Prophet Muhammad).

[4] Hadith by al-Bukhari

INTRODUCTION

The Battle of Hunayn had just ended, and the Muslims had routed the Hawazin tribe and relocated the captives and spoils to the nearby settlement of Ji'ranah. Just as the celebration was getting underway, two lone riders slowly made their way through neighboring foothills.

One of the men, Safwan ibn Umayyah, never imagined he would have fought on the side of the Muslims. In fact, just a few weeks ago, he was one of only three men who refused to surrender to the Prophet's army in Mecca. As Safwan rode in silence, he tried to figure out why, after 20 years of bitterly opposing the Muslims, he was granted four months of amnesty by the Prophet and was allowed to fight alongside the Prophet's closest Companions.

The truth is that all these years, Safwan had never attempted to get to know the Prophet. At each stage of his life, he found ample reason to oppose him. As a child, he grew up watching his influential father, Umayyah, torture the family's Abyssinian slave, Bilal, for converting to Islam. After learning that Bilal had killed his father at Badr, Safwan hatched a clever scheme to assassinate the Prophet. But the plan backfired when the assassin, 'Umayr (his own cousin no less) ended up embracing the Prophet instead of killing him.

If 'Umayr's conversion was a blow to Safwan's pride, 'Ikrimah ibn Abi Jahl's betrayal knocked the wind out of him. 'Ikrimah was the son of the Prophet's archenemy, Abu Jahl, and like Safwan, grew up with an intense hatred for the Prophet.

As the two riders crested the next hill, Safwan remembered how just a few months ago, another friend, Khalid ibn al-Walid, unexpectedly fell for the Prophet and begged Safwan to come with him to Medina. "Even if every other man of Quraysh were to follow Muhammad," Safwan had declared, "I would never follow him!"

The rolling hills and tranquil pastures gave no indication of the contradictions swirling in Safwan's soul. After 20 years of hostility, why did the Prophet just award him 100 camels from the spoils of Hunayn but not give anything to his closest Companions?

As Safwan descended into the next ravine, he slowed to marvel at the abundance of livestock that had been abandoned by the fleeing Hawazin army.

"Is it pleasing to you?" whispered a voice by his side.

Safwan didn't know how to respond, but his eyes gave him away. "It's yours," the Prophet said smiling, "the valley and everything in it."

At that moment, the proud Qurayshi felt a sudden tightness in his throat as tears trickled past his trembling lips. Twenty years of heated exchanges, bitter opposition, and several attempts on the Prophet's life. Safwan's reward? Four months of amnesty, 100 camels, and a ravine full of livestock?

For the first time in his life, Safwan stopped to look into the Prophet's eyes. "I bear witness," he wept, "I bear witness that no soul could have such goodness as this, if it were not the soul of a Prophet..."

This single incident in the Prophet's life demonstrates one of the most remarkable features of the Sirah—that each Companion traveled along a unique path, and at some magical moment, fell into the Prophet's orbit. If Safwan's journey was at one end of the spectrum, Salman al-Farisi's represented the other. Salman was born to a Zoroastrian family near the Persian city of Isfahan. As a young man, he converted to Christianity and dedicated his youth to finding an Abrahamic prophet whose imminent arrival had been prophesized by the Eastern churches. His search took him from Persia to Syria to Iraq. After an unfortunate turn of events, he was sold into slavery to a Jewish merchant in Yathrib, but even then, Salman never gave up on his dream of finding the Prophet. Ultimately, Salman ended up in the remote valley of Quba, where he embraced the Prophet the moment he laid eyes on him.

The Sirah is as much about the journey of the Companions as it is about the life of the Prophet. Safwan was an insider who spent 20 years evading the Prophet, while Salman was an outsider who waited 20 years to find him. Regardless of the path they took, the moment they opened their hearts to the Prophet, their lives were dramatically altered. This remarkable phenomenon occurred at every stage of the Prophet's life. We see it in the benevolence of Halimah, tenderness of Khadijah, allegiance of 'Ali, loyalty of Hamzah, trustworthiness of Abu Bakr, bravery of Talhah, wisdom of Umm Salamah, patience of Ja'far, transformation of 'Abd Allah ibn Mas'ud, and of course, the selflessness of the Helpers.

But why did the Companions gravitate toward the Prophet in the first place? What made Muhammad so irresistible? That question was put to Zayd ibn Harithah, the adopted son of the Prophet. At an early age, Zayd was kidnapped from his family in northern Arabia and sold into slavery. His journey led him to Mecca where, as a 10-year-old boy, he served in Muhammad's household. Zayd's father, Harithah, never gave up looking for his missing child, and after many years, learned that Zayd was still alive and in Mecca. But when Harithah came to retrieve his son, Zayd refused to leave. "What made Muhammad so irresistible?" Harithah asked. Zayd responded that he had a special feeling about this man. Little did he know that many years later, the Prophet would not only entrust him to command the entire Muslim army, but also teach him how to raise an exemplary son, Usamah, who would eventually outshine his father.

All these stories point to one of the timeless truths of the Sirah—that the Companions were attracted to the Prophet because of how he touched their lives and inspired them to achieve greatness. If they were with us today, the Companions would likely explain that their greatest achievements did not come because they happened to be a part of the Prophet's life, but because the Prophet was an integral part of theirs.

For the past 13 years, I've been trying to unlock the secret to this relationship. In the end I realized something remarkable—the Sirah is a love story. It is about taking your heart and making it bigger. The bigger it gets, the more it gives. The more it gives, the bigger it gets. This is the story of the Prophet and his Companions, and it's the singular reason they are considered to be the greatest generation. It wasn't about following rules; it was about falling in love.

And if we can learn anything from Safwan's story—it's never too late to start.

THE ROADMAP

When I first started studying the Sirah, I felt hopelessly lost in the long list of dates in the Prophet's life. To complicate matters, half my sources used the Gregorian calendar while the remainder used the Hijri system. Even when two scholars used the same calendar, they often differed on when certain events transpired.

I was convinced that there had to be an easier way to memorize the Sirah, and after several failed attempts, came up with the Qur'anic Year (QY) system. Not only has the QY approach allowed me to remember every important event in the Sirah, I have found it much more useful than the Hijri or Gregorian systems in understanding the chronological development of Qur'anic revelation.

This book is designed to help readers remember the smallest details of the Prophet's life without losing sight of the big picture. As you will see below, learning the QY system is the first step toward mastering the story of Qur'anic revelation.

The simplest way to depict the Prophet's life is to divide it into discrete periods of time. For example, we can approach his life in two phases: the "Prologue" (the first 40 years before revelation) and the "Prophethood" (the 23 years thereafter).

Alternately, we can separate the periods of his life by location. Using the Hijrah (emigration to Medina) as the turning point, we can create a timeline representing 52 years in Mecca followed by 11 years in Medina.

If we combine both timelines, we can represent his life in three periods:

Since it is impossible to appreciate the significance of the Prophet's life without beginning a few thousand years earlier, our Prologue will begin with the story of Abraham and the ancient history of Mecca. It will end on the eve of revelation when Muhammad, who after 40 years of searching, is abruptly thrust into the divine spotlight. The story of the Qur'an begins from there and, over the next 23 years, Muhammad the Prophet begins a tireless mission to reclaim the legacy of Abraham.

Now that we have clearly defined the various parts of our timeline, let's redraw it as a divinely scripted Prologue that leads into the "clock" of Qur'anic revelation. The clock begins with the first Qur'anic revelation and ends with the Prophet's death.

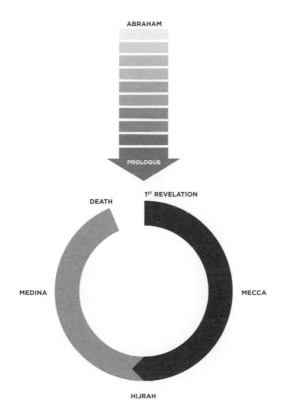

As demonstrated in the below, the circular timeline will help you remember key moments in the Prophet's life.

1   Draw a circle, then two intersecting lines that cut it into four equal pieces.

2   Imagine the circle represents a 24-year clock. Starting from the top, label the four points: 0, 6, 12, and 18.

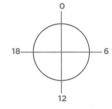

3   Write the letter "H" at 0, 6, 12, 18 (be sure to place the H's above the line next to the 6 and 18 positions.)

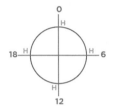

4   At the top (0), write "Hira." At the bottom (12), write "Hijrah." These points will split the clock down the middle. The right side is Mecca (blue) the left side is Medina (green).

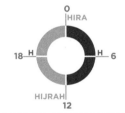

5   At 6 (above the line), write "Hamzah & 'Umar." Above the line at 18, write "Hudaybiyah."

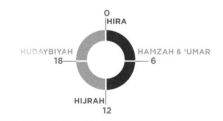

6   Remove the last year from the clock so it ends at year 23.

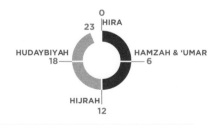

7   Label the quadrants clockwise as "Early Mecca," "Late Mecca," "Early Medina," and "Late Medina."

Now take a step back and review your new Qur'anic Year timeline. By committing this to memory, you should not only be able to remember the most significant events in the Prophet's life, but tackle the minutest details without ever losing sight of the big picture.

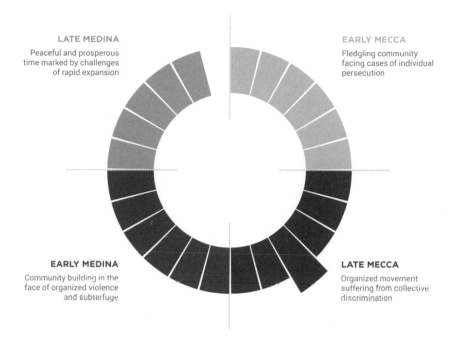

LATE MEDINA
Peaceful and prosperous time marked by challenges of rapid expansion

EARLY MECCA
Fledgling community facing cases of individual persecution

EARLY MEDINA
Community building in the face of organized violence and subterfuge

LATE MECCA
Organized movement suffering from collective discrimination

THE ROADMAP: PERIODS OF QUR'ANIC REVELATION

After the Prologue, we can divide Muhammad's prophethood into four distinct periods: Early Meccan, Late Meccan, Early Medinan, and Late Medinan. The Early Meccan Period begins with the first Qur'anic revelation. Aside from cases of individual persecution, the earliest Muslims are mostly ridiculed for their outlandish beliefs and viewed as a nuisance by the rest of the Quraysh. The early period ends in the sixth year when the Prophet's prominent uncle, Hamzah, and the Prophet's most flagrant enemy, 'Umar, both accept Islam. Their conversions draw attention to the fledgling community, transforming it into a serious political threat. During the next six years of the Late Meccan Period, the Prophet and his followers are collectively persecuted for threatening the institutions of wealth and power in Mecca. The persecution is relentless, and 12 years after the first revelation, the Muslim community migrates to Medina in search of protection (Hijrah). The Early Medinan Period begins with community building but is quickly overshadowed by a stretch of battles and revolts. The tense six-year period ends after the 18th year with the Treaty of Hudaybiyah. The treaty ushers in the relatively peaceful and prosperous Late Medinan Period, which ends with the Prophet's death five years later.

With the Sirah represented as a circular timeline divided into quadrants, we can explore each section in greater detail and assign useful mnemonics to remember the major events that happened in each of the 23 years of Qur'anic revelation.

EARLY MECCA

After the initial revelation, the small Muslim community remains private, not openly preaching their message until the fourth year. That is when the small community publicly invites the Quraysh to Islam, and are mocked and humiliated. The abuse becomes so difficult to endure that in the fifth year, several Muslims migrate to Abyssinia. The fledgling community does not have the strong support it needs until the conversions of Hamzah and 'Umar in the sixth and final year of this period.

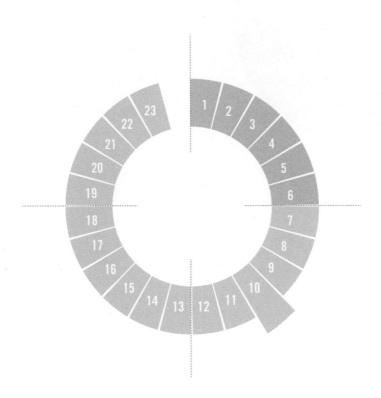

1-2-3 PRIVATE ASSEMBLY

The first three years of the Prophet's message are limited to private gatherings. Only after assembling a core group of supporters is the message ready to go public.

Imagine the core group of believers saying, "On the count of 3, let's spread the word...1-2-3!"

4 PUBLIC INVITATION

The Prophet opens up his message to his extended family and the rest of Quraysh.

The Prophet called a public "for-um" in year four.

5 ABYSSINIA

Several early converts migrate to Abyssinia seeking political asylum.

Imagine the emigrants waving goodbye as they leave Mecca (a hand with 5-fingers).

6 CONVERSIONS OF HAMZAH & 'UMAR

Hamzah & 'Umar become two pivotal supporters who come to the Prophet's aide.

As discussed earlier, their conversions marked the turning point between the Early and Late Meccan periods.

LATE MECCA

The conversions of Hamzah and 'Umar force the Quraysh to rethink their strategy. They decide to impose sanctions against the Prophet's clan, which lasts two to three years. The ban is followed by "The Year of Sadness," a long, difficult year in which the Prophet loses his uncle and wife, and also suffers humiliating rejection at Ta'if. The year of difficulty is soon followed by a heavenly experience—the *Isra' & Me'raj*. With renewed vigor, the Prophet migrates with his followers to the northern settlement town of Yathrib (later renamed *Medina*).

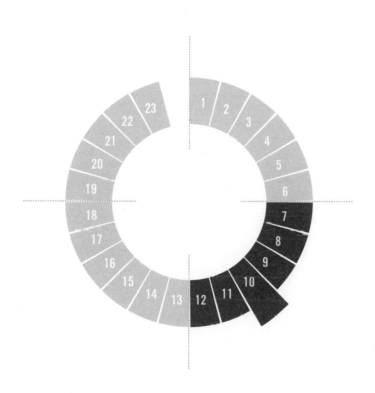

7-8-9 BAN ON HASHIM

The Quraysh impose a difficult three-year socio-economic ban on the Prophet's clan of Hashim.

Just like the 1–2–3 count in Early Mecca, we have another 1–2–3 count here. This time, write the letters B–A–N across the 3 years.

10 THE YEAR OF SADNESS

This is a long year for the Prophet—he loses his wife and uncle, and is persecuted by the people of Ta'if.

The ban is followed by a very long year, hence QY 10 is stretched out. Also you can remember that 10 is two digits, and therefore "longer" than 9.

11 ISRA' & ME'RAJ

The Prophet takes a miraculous journey to Jerusalem and then up to heaven in a single night.

Eleven rhymes with heaven.

12 FIRST 'AQABAH PLEDGE

Twelve pilgrims pledge to protect and obey the Prophet when he arrives in Medina.

Twelve men pledge allegiance in QY 12.

EARLY MEDINA

The Early Medinan Period begins after the Hijrah and is marked by expeditions, battles, and sieges. You can remember these events by using the mnemonic "the Hijrah Resulted in Battle Upon Battle Till Hudaybiyah." Leaving one **H** in Hijrah and Hudaybiyah, write the remaining six letters **(R-B-U-B-T)** in each of the five remaining years.

NOTE *Each major battle (Badr 1, Uhud, and Trench) is followed by an incident with one of the Jewish tribes in Medina (Qaynuqa, Nadir, and Qurayzah respectively). You can remember the order* **Q-N-Q**, *because alphabetically, Qaynuqa comes before Qurayzah.*

18 BATTLE OF THE TRENCH

The Quraysh and their allies converge on Medina and lay siege to the city, but return home defeated.

'Till" = Trench

17 BATTLE OF BADR 2

The Prophet marches to Badr for a rematch, but the Quraysh never show up.

"Battle" = Badr 2

16 BATTLE OF UHUD

The Quraysh march to just north of Medina and inflict serious damage to the Muslim army.

"Upon" = Uhud

15 BATTLE OF BADR 1

Far outnumbered, the Muslims march to Badr and pull off a stunning upset against the Quraysh.

"Battle" = Badr 1

14 RAIDS

This is a year of caravan raids directed against the Quraysh.

"Resulted in" = Raids

13 HIJRAH

The Prophet migrates to Medina and begins building a new community.

Hijrah, as discussed earlier, begins the Early Medinan Period.

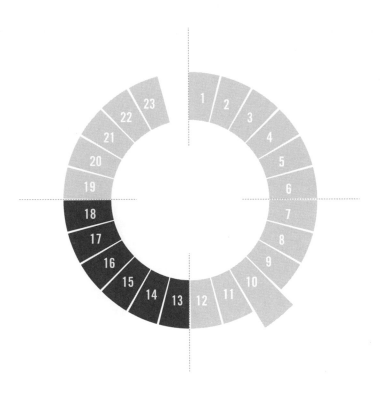

LATE MEDINA

Late Medina starts with the Treaty of Hudaybiyah, which brings peace and prosperity to the Muslims. As the community grows, the Prophet is finally able to return to Mecca with a conquering army and reclaim the city of Abraham. While the peaceful victory establishes Medina's dominance in central Arabia, it also brings unwelcome challenges like the threat of a Roman invasion from the north. One year after the Conquest of Mecca, the Prophet leads his largest expedition to the border city of Tabuk to confront the advancing Roman army. Word of the Tabuk expedition quickly spreads throughout Arabia, and the following year, delegations from all over the peninsula come to Medina to pledge allegiance to the Prophet. The subsequent spread of Islam in Arabia marks the end of the Prophet's mission. The final year of the Prophet's life is highlighted by the Farewell Pilgrimage, a time to reflect on the tremendous achievements of the past 23 years and articulate a clear direction for future generations.

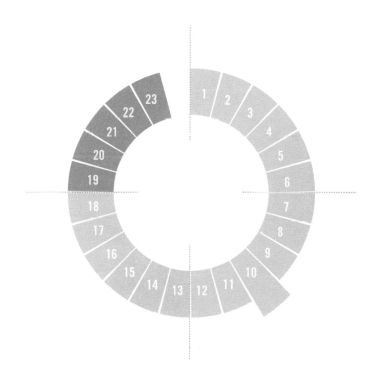

23 FAREWELL HAJJ

The Prophet leads his first and only Hajj pilgrimage, in the footsteps of Abraham.

Farewell marks the final year of the Prophet's journey.

22 YEAR OF DELEGATIONS

Once-hostile tribes from all over Arabia come to form peaceful alliances with Medina.

Imagine previously hostile tribes waving signs of peace (two fingers on both hands) as they enter Medina.

21 TABUK

The Prophet leads the largest Arabian army ever assembled to confront the Romans at the border city of Tabuk.

Twenty-one is considered the age of full-grown adulthood. In QY 21, the Muslim community is full-grown and ready to take on the Romans at Tabuk.

20 CONQUEST OF MECCA

The Prophet marches with 10,000 followers and peacefully reclaims Mecca.

The Qur'an (28:85) gave the Prophet a clear vision (20/20) that he would return to Mecca one day (QY 20).

19 HUDAYBIYAH

The Muslims sign a peace treaty that ends hostilities with Mecca.

As discussed earlier, Hudaybiyah marks the beginning of the relatively peaceful Late Medinan Period.

The QY calendar is the system that will be used throughout this book. It differs from the traditional Hijri calendar in several ways. The Hijri calendar begins in the middle of Qur'anic revelation (the Hijrah) and proceeds in both directions. Because the Hijri system is bi-directional and skips year "zero," it often confuses readers who are trying to understand how much time elapsed between Meccan and Medinan events. For example, how do we calculate the number of years between the Year of Sadness and Badr?

	SADNESS			HIJRAH		BADR
QUR'ANIC YEAR	QY 10	QY 11	QY 12	QY 13	QY 14	QY 15
HIJRI YEAR	3 BH	2 BH	1 BH	1 AH	2 AH	3 AH

Using the Hijri system, we have: 3 AH - 3 BH = ?

Using the QY system: QY 15 - QY 10 = 5 years

Another notable difference is that the QY system is based on the solar calendar while the Hijri system is lunar. This difference adds a layer of complexity in determining equivalent dates between the two calendars, and is addressed in Appendix A.

As far as assigning Gregorian dates to any given event, the only year you need to remember is 609 CE—the year before the first revelation. To determine the corresponding Gregorian year of any event, just add the Qur'anic Year to 609. For example, the Hijrah (QY 13) took place in 609+13 or 622 CE, while Badr (QY 15) took place in 609+15 or 624 CE. Additionally, if you want to determine the Prophet's approximate age at any given time, simply add 39 to the Qur'anic Year. For example, at Badr (QY 15) the Prophet was 39+15 or 54 years old.

	SADNESS			HIJRAH		BADR
QUR'ANIC YEAR	QY 10	QY 11	QY 12	QY 13	QY 14	QY 15
GREGORIAN YEAR (ADD 609)	619	620	621	622	623	624
PROPHET'S AGE (ADD 39)	49	50	51	52	53	54

THE QUR'ANIC YEAR (QY) TIMELINE

If my experience is any indication, I hope that the QY timeline will be the breakthrough you need to navigate the Sirah without getting lost along the way. You will find it used throughout the text and also along the side of every page, orienting you to your final destination.

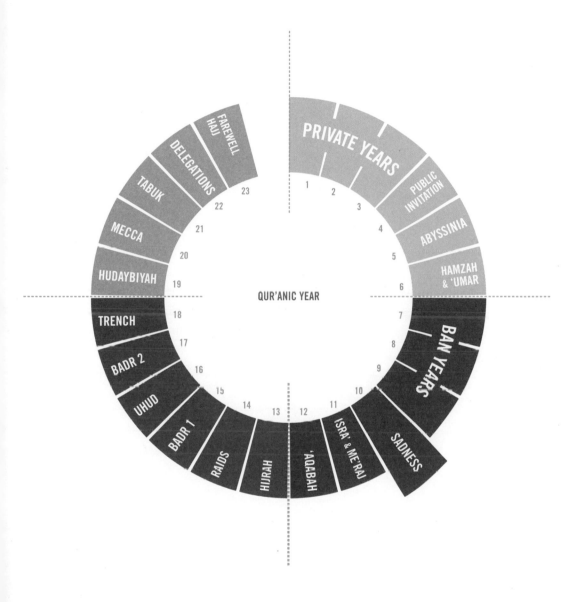

PROLOGUE

P1   The Early History of Mecca
P2   The Quraysh Dynasty
P3   The 7th Century before Muhammad
P4   Muhammad before Revelation

PROPHETIC APPEARANCE

———◇———

'Abdullah ibn al-Harith narrated: "I never saw a person who smiled more than the Messenger of Allah (peace be upon him)."

———

Ibrahim ibn Muhammad (who is from the grandchildren of Ali ibn Abi Talib) reported that whenever Ali used to describe the Prophet (peace be upon him), he would say: " The Messenger of Allah was neither very tall nor very short, but of a medium stature amongst the people. His hair was neither very curly nor completely straight; rather it was in between these two descriptions.

———

He did not have a fleshy body or a [fully] round face, his face was slightly round. His skin colour was white with some redness. He had extremely black eyes with long eyelashes. He had large joints and broad shoulders. There was no hair [more than normal] on his body and he had a thin line of hair running from the chest to the navel. He had thick hands and feet. When he walked, he lifted his legs with vigour and his steps were firm and strong as if he was descending down a slope. When he wished to look behind, he would turn his whole body, and not just the face. The seal of prophethood was situated between his shoulders. He was the seal of the Prophets, and he had the most generous of hearts and the most truthful tongue. He was the most kind-hearted and tolerant person ever. He was the best to spend time with due to his awe-inspiring character and kind treatment; anyone who came across him unexpectedly would become awestruck; and whoever came in close contact with him would love him. One who describes him can only state, 'I have never seen anyone comparable to him.' "

———

Taken from A Commentary on the Depiction of Prophet Muhammad,
by Imam al-Tirmidhi (#227, #7)

PROLOGUE 1: THE EARLY HISTORY OF MECCA

P1.1 THE FIRST ARABS

Arabs can be classified into three distinct categories: the Perished Arabs, the Pure Arabs, and the Arabized Arabs. All three groups are mentioned in the Qur'an and play a significant role in Islamic history.

THE PERISHED ARABS

The Perished Arabs are considered descendants of Noah (*Nuh*). They include the ancient tribes of 'Ad and Thamud, which the Qur'an refers to numerous times. Surah Fussilat describes how both tribes perished for rejecting their messengers:

> As for the (people of) 'Ad, they acted arrogantly throughout the land against all right. They boasted, "Who is stronger in power than we are?" Didn't they see that God, the One Who created them, was infinitely mightier than they (could ever be)? They worked against Our signs with determination, so We sent a terrible sandstorm against them, causing many days of disaster, in order to give them a taste of the most degrading punishment this life can offer. The punishment of the next life will be even more degrading still, and they'll have no one to help them.
>
> As for the (people of) Thamud, We offered them guidance, but they preferred blindness over guidance, so a sudden humiliating disaster overtook them as a consequence of what they earned. However, We saved those who believed and who were mindful (of God among both nations).

— *Fussilat (Clear Explanation, 41:15–18)*

The term *surah* can be read as "chapter." There are 114 surahs in the Qur'an, ranging from 3 to 286 verses in length.

TRIBE	PROPHET	DEMISE
'Ad	Hud	Wind
Thamud	Saleh	Thunderbolt

Many scholars consider Prophet Hud to be Noah's great-grandson, Eber. For more descriptions of 'Ad and Thamud in the Qur'an, refer to Surahs Al A'raf (7:73-79), Hud (11:50-68), and Al Ahqaf (46:21-25).

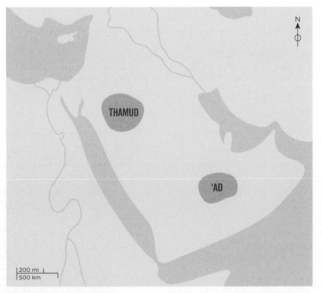

FIGURE P1. THE ANCIENT TRIBES OF 'AD AND THAMUD

The extinct tribes of 'Ad and Thamud are an integral part of early Arabian history. The 'Ad settled in the area between current-day Yemen and Oman. According to the Qur'an, they were destroyed after ignoring the warnings of Prophet Hud. The Thamud succeeded 'Ad and inhabited an area farther north, known as al-Hijr (currently known as Mada'in Saleh). The Thamud are commonly mentioned in the Qur'an as a people who were destroyed for ignoring the fate of their predecessors ('Ad) and the warnings of their own prophet, Saleh. In fact, during the march to Tabuk (QY 21.1) when the Muslim army passed by al-Hijr, the Prophet urged his men not to stop until the ancient carved dwellings of Thamud were well behind them. (Similar to the famous carvings at Petra, these dwellings can still be seen today.)

THE PURE ARABS

Qahtan is considered to be the founder of the Pure Arabs. Contrary to popular misconception, *Sheba* is not the name of the historic Queen of Sheba. Rather Sheba is the name of Qahtan's great-grandson. The empire that Sheba established took his name. Arab texts refer to the Queen of Sheba as *Bilqis*.

Frankincense and **myrrh** are aromatic resins derived from the sap of trees native to southern Arabia and the Horn of Africa. They were often used in religious ceremonies and are best known from a single passage in the Gospel of Matthew regarding the nativity scene of Jesus.

SURAH AN-NAML (The Ant) will be revealed during the Early Meccan Period and includes several lessons from the lives of Prophets Moses, Solomon, Saleh, and Lot. The surah describes how Solomon was given the power to communicate with nature and understand the speech of ants. After relating these stories, the surah concludes, "This Qur'an addresses most of that over which the Children of Israel disagree, and it's a guide and a mercy for those who believe."

The Pure Arabs (also known as the *Qahtanian Arabs*) settled in Yemen and founded the empire of Sheba (*Saba*) as far back as 2500 BCE. Between 1300 and 650 BCE, they built the Dam of Ma'rib, which they used to cultivate two adjacent valleys. The dam's complex irrigation systems allowed the empire to grow into a prosperous civilization that controlled the surrounding areas by land and water, and flourish for centuries. Their main export crops included frankincense and myrrh, which were transported through Becca to the lands of Canaan.

The queen who ruled over the empire is specifically mentioned in Surah An-Naml, when Prophet Solomon's (*Suleiman*) messenger returned to his court to describe the Arabs of Yemen:

…"I'm coming to you with a report about something of which you're unaware. I've just come back from (the land of) Sheba, and I have an accurate report."

"I found a woman there who was ruling over them with every necessary resource of authority, and she also had a magnificent throne."

"I found her and her people worshipping the sun in place of God. Satan has truly made their actions seem dazzling to their eyes… *—An-Naml (The Ant, 27:22-24)*

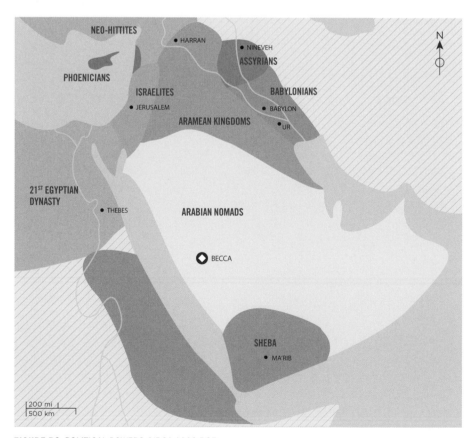

FIGURE P2. POLITICAL POWERS CIRCA 1000 BCE

Hebrew texts suggest that Solomon ruled around 1000 BCE. Jewish and Islamic texts suggest that the Queen of Sheba ruled at the same time as Solomon and visited him in Jerusalem.

The passage from Surah An-Naml continues to narrate how the queen accepted Solomon's invitation to Jerusalem and returned to Yemen to spread Islam.

Over the next few centuries, the empire deteriorated until the descendants of Sheba split into two competing tribes: Himyar and Kahlan. Shortly after 100 CE, the Himyarites gained control of Yemen and forced their brethren out. Ultimately the Kahlan tribes spread north, and settled in various parts of the Arabian Peninsula.

We will pick up the story of the Himyarites later in the Prologue (P3.2).

THE ARABIZED ARABS

The Arabized Arabs are considered the direct descendants of Ishmael (*Isma'il*). Their story, however, begins with Ishmael's father and the founding of Mecca.

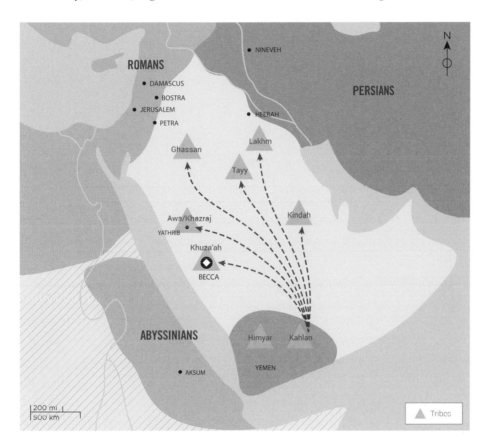

FIGURE P3. THE PURE ARABIAN DIASPORA

Two-thousand years after they founded the Empire of Sheba, the Pure Arabs split apart (100-200 CE). The Himyarites remained in the region while the Kahlanis were forced to settle in the northern parts of the peninsula. Among the Kahlanis, Ghassan and Lakhm formed large kingdoms that bordered the Romans and Persians. The Aws and Khazraj settled in Yathrib. Meanwhile, the Khuza'ites expelled the Jurhumites and took control of Becca. Each of these tribes will play a significant role in the Sirah and will be revisited in future chapters.

	PERISHED ARABS	PURE ARABS*	ARABIZED ARABS*
DESCRIPTION	Little is known of these ancient Arabs except that they are considered to be the descendants of Noah who inhabited the Southern Arabian peninsula as well as an area in the north of the peninsula known as *al-Hijr*.	Also called *Qahtanian Arabs*, they originated from Yemen and gave rise to the Empire of Sheba. Around the 2nd century CE, they divided into two main branches, Himyar and Kahlan. The Himyar stayed in Yemen, while the Kahlan spread north and settled throughout the peninsula (Fig P3).	These are the descendants of Ishmael and his wife, a pure Arab from the tribe of Jurhum. 'Adnan was a descendant of Ishmael and became the namesake of the *'Adnanian Arabs*, who remained in the central Arabian Peninsula (Hijaz and Nejd regions).
NOTABLE TRIBES	**'AD** *(tribe of Prophet Hud)* **THAMUD** *(tribe of Prophet Saleh)*	**JURHUM** *(ancient Mecca)* **HIMYAR** *(Yemen)* **KAHLAN** ▪ KHUZA'AH** *(Mecca)* ▪ AWS*** *(Yathrib)* ▪ KHAZRAJ*** *(Yathrib)* ▪ GHASSAN*** *(Syria)* ▪ LAKHM *(Iraq)*	**NABETEANS** *(Petra)* **'ADNANIANS** ▪ HAWAZIN *(Hijaz)* ▪ GHATAFAN *(Nejd)* ▪ THAQIF *(Ta'if)* ▪ QURAYSH *(Mecca)*

FIGURE P4. CLASSIFICATION OF THE ARABS

*   According to Al-Mubarakpuri, another scholar—Al-Hafiz ibn Hajar—believed that the Pure Arabs were actually Arabized Arabs who were descendants of Ishmael's son Nabet.

**   Lings describes the Khuza'ah as Arabized Arabs who had moved to Yemen and later returned to Mecca. However, according to Al-Mubarakpuri, they were Pure Arabs, not the descendants of Ishmael.

***   Some scholars, including Imam Bukhari, believe that the Aws, Khazraj, and Ghassan were not Pure Arabs but in fact Nabeteans (descendants of Ishmael's son Nabet) who remained in the region (Bukhari 3507).

P1.2 ABRAHAM: THE ARCHETYPAL MUSLIM

> Abraham was neither a Jew nor a Christian. Rather, he was a natural monotheist, submissive (to God's will), and he certainly wasn't an idol-worshipper.
>
> The first among the people (of this world) who resemble Abraham the most are those who follow (his example), like this prophet (Muhammad) and his followers. God is the protector of all who believe (in Him)! —*Ali 'Imran (3:67-68)*

Abraham (*Ibrahim*) was born into a family of staunch polytheists, possibly around 1800 to 1600 BCE. He was raised in the town of Ur (near present day Kufah, Iraq) on the banks of the Euphrates River. According to Genesis 11:32, Abraham, along with his father, Terah (*Azar*), and his nephew Lot (*Lut*), set out for Canaan through the town of Harran, near the present Turkish-Syrian border (Fig. P5). As a young man, Abraham was uneasy about following the pagan religion of his forefathers. Surah Maryam relates the beginning of Abraham's prophethood when he first confronted his father:

> Mention in the Book (something about) Abraham, for he was an honest man and a prophet.
>
> He said to his father, "My father! Why are you worshipping things that can neither hear nor see nor bring you any benefit at all? My father! Some teachings have come to me that haven't reached you, so follow me, and I'll guide you to an even path."
>
> "My father! Don't be in the service of Satan, for Satan is a rebel against the Compassionate. My father! I'm afraid that a punishment might befall you from the Compassionate that might cause you to be included among Satan's allies."
>
> "Are you talking against my gods?" (his father) demanded. "Abraham! If you don't back off, then I'll stone you! Now get yourself away from me!"
>
> "So peace (and good bye) to you then." (Abraham) answered. "However, I'm still going to pray to my Lord for your forgiveness, because He's always been kind to me."
>
> "Now I'm going to turn away from you and from those whom you call upon besides God. All I can do is call upon my Lord and hope my prayer to my Lord doesn't go unanswered." —*Maryam (Mary, 19:41-48)*

Abraham left his father in Harran, and continued on to Canaan with Sarah (*Sara*) and Lot. By the time Abraham was 85 and Sarah 76, they still remained childless. Despite his advanced age, he wished for children:

> (In later years, Abraham prayed,) "My Lord! Grant me a righteous son!" Then We gave him the good news of a resolute boy. —*As-Saffat (The Rows, 37:100-101)*

In Hebrew, **Canaan** refers to the area encompassing modern-day Palestine, Israel, Lebanon, and western Syria and Jordan. The Europeans later introduced the term *Levant* to describe this general area (levant means "rising" in French, hence the place where the sun rises). In Arabic, this region is referred to as *ash-Sham*. Sham means "left" just as *yamin* means "right." So when an Arab faces East, ash-Sham (Syria) is to his left and al-Yamin (Yemen) is to his right.

The **BOOK OF GENESIS** is the first section of the Hebrew Bible and Christian Old Testament. It begins with the story of creation, describes the great flood and the ascent of Abraham, and ends on the eve of the Israelite escape from Egypt under the leadership of Prophet Moses.

The Bible confirms that God heard Abraham's prayer and spoke to him:

> "Look now towards heaven, and count the stars if thou art able to number them ... So shall thy seed be."— *Genesis 15:5*

Abraham wandered throughout Canaan and eventually entered Egypt, where he came face to face with the Pharaoh (Genesis 12:10). The Pharaoh attempted to seduce Sarah, but quickly withdrew when he realized she was a God-fearing woman who was already married to Abraham. Instead the Pharaoh offered the services of his daughter, Hagar (*Hajira*), to Sarah. So that Abraham might have children, Sarah welcomed Hagar into her household, and her addition to the family soon proved to be a blessing.

In Genesis, Hagar is told:

> "I will multiply thy seed exceedingly, that it shall not be numbered for multitude. ... Behold, thou art with child, and shalt bear a son, and shalt call his name Ishmael; because the Lord has heard thy affliction."— *Genesis 16:10-11*

---

① WAS HAGAR A SLAVE GIRL? `AL-MUBARAKPURI`

"It is popularly believed that Hagar was a slave girl, but the great scholar and writer Qadi Muhammad Sulaiman Mansurpuri has indeed verified that she was not a slave but in fact the daughter of Pharaoh. ... When he [Abraham] went to Egypt, the Pharaoh tried to do evil to his wife Sarah, but Allah saved her and the Pharaoh's wicked scheme recoiled on him. He thus came to realize her strong attachment to Allah, and, in acknowledgement of her grace, the Pharaoh rendered his daughter Hagar at Sarah's service."[1]

- -

② WAS ISHMAEL AN ILLEGITIMATE SON OF ABRAHAM? `YUSUF`

"We reject the modern Christian and Jewish view that Ishmael is an illegitimate son. This is the way it is presented in the West. If you read the Bible, it is clear that Ishmael is honored, and not deemed an illegitimate son. In the Islamic point of view, it is impossible for prophets [to father illegitimate children] because prophets are impeccable. They cannot commit major sins, according to all of our scholars, and they cannot commit minor sins, according to the majority of scholars."[2]

According to biblical tradition, when Abraham was 100 years old and Sara 90, God also promised a son to Sarah, named Isaac (*Is'haq*).

> "As for Ishmael, I have heard thee, Behold, I have blessed him ... and I will make him a great nation. But My covenant will I establish with Isaac, which Sarah shall bear unto thee at this set time in the next year." — *Genesis 17:20-21*

❸ DOES THE BIBLE CONFIRM ISHMAEL'S PROPHETHOOD?   YUSUF

"It is important to note that God said, 'I will make him a great nation.' Now it is impossible for God to say that about a nation that would not be a righteous nation. In the eyes of God, the only thing that is great is piety, taqwa, toward Allah. That means that it is very clear in the Bible itself that Ishmael, peace be upon him, would be the father of a spiritual nation, a nation following prophetic teaching, which is a clear indication from the Bible that the Arabs would have a religious nation and would be chosen by God."[3]

This account in Genesis is echoed in Surah Hud, which describes how Sarah could not believe the news:

> His wife just stood there and laughed when We gave her the good news of (a son named) Isaac and (a grandson named) Jacob. "Misfortune is mine!" she sighed. "How could I bear a child now, seeing that I'm an old woman and my husband here is an old man? That would be something amazing, indeed!"
> —Hud (11:71-72)

Abraham was deeply grateful for God's provision. His prayer in Surah Ibrahim reads:

> "Our Lord! You know what we conceal and what we reveal, for nothing at all can ever be hidden from God, neither on the earth nor in the sky. Praise be to God Who has given me my sons, Ishmael and Isaac, even in my old age, for My Lord hears all requests! My Lord! Make me a prayerful person, and make my descendants prayerful, as well. Our Lord! Hear my request. Our Lord! Forgive me and my parents and all those who believe on the Day of Account."
> — Ibrahim (Abraham, 14:39-41)

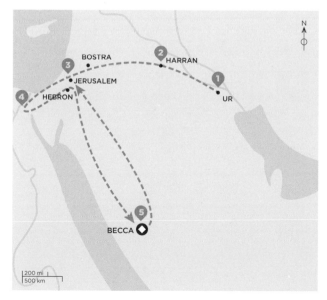

FIGURE P5. ABRAHAM'S ROUTE

Abraham was born in Ur (1) possibly between 1800-1600 BCE. He traveled with his father, Terah, and nephew Lot to Harran (2). Terah stayed behind, while Abraham and Lot moved farther west to Canaan (3). At some point, Abraham and Sarah traveled to Egypt and returned to Canaan with Hagar (4). Later, Abraham brought Hagar and Ishmael to the valley of Becca, 40 camel days south of Canaan (5). He returned often to visit them and built the Ka'bah with Ishmael. Many years later, he was buried in Hebron by his two sons, Ishmael and Isaac.

P1.3 ISHMAEL, MECCA & THE ARABIZED ARABS

According to biblical tradition, Sarah became jealous of Hagar and asked her to leave. With God's guidance, Abraham left with Hagar and Ishmael and traveled to the desolate valley of Becca, 40 camel days south of Canaan. The Book of Genesis picks up the story of how Abraham left them in the valley, and explains the discovery of the well of Zamzam:

> And God heard the voice of the lad; and the angel of God called to Hagar out of heaven and said to her: "What aileth thee, Hagar? Fear not, for God hath heard the voice of the lad where he is. Arise and lift up the lad and hold him in thy hand, for I will make him a great nation." And God opened her eyes, and she saw a well of water. — *Genesis 21:17-20*

---

④ WHY DID HAGAR LEAVE CANAAN? 　　　　　　　　　　　　YUSUF

"According to our tradition, Ibrahim, peace be upon him, was commanded to take Hajar to this place [Becca] for a reason. Here Lings says that we don't really know how Hajar was guided there. According to our tradition, however, Ibrahim, peace be upon him, took her there and made dua [supplication] for her. And she became nervous and said to Ibrahim, peace be upon him, 'Why are you leaving me here? Did Allah tell you to do this?' And he said, 'Yes.' ... This woman [Hajar] is a mu'mina [believer]. She said, 'If Allah told you to do this, then go.' "[4]

The **BOOK OF PSALMS** is mostly credited to the Prophet David and is part of the Hebrew Bible and Christian Old Testament. The Qur'an celebrates several divinely revealed books, including the Scrolls of Abraham (Suhuf), Torah of Moses (Taurat), Psalms of David (Zabur), the Gospel of Jesus (Injeel), and of course the Qur'an of Muhammad. While all of these books are considered sacred, Muslims believe that only the Qur'an has been preserved through time, in its originally revealed form.

The word "**Ka'bah**" is Arabic for "cube." It is a simple structure that the Qur'an also describes as the "Sacred House." The Ka'bah is the site of the annual Hajj pilgrimage as well as the focal point for the direction of prayer (*qibla*) for Muslims around the world. The story of the Ka'bah will be revisited later in the Prologue and throughout the Sirah.

The remainder of the Hebrew Bible deals with the descendants of Isaac, except for a few references to Ishmael:

> And God was with the lad; and he grew and dwelt in the wilderness and became an archer. — *Genesis 21:21*

> Blessed is the man whose strength is in Thee; in whose heart are the ways of them who, passing through the valley of Baca, make it a well. — *Psalm 84:5-6*

Abraham lived for an additional 75 years after the discovery of the Zamzam well. He visited Becca several times and erected the Ka'bah with Ishmael as God had commanded him. He instructed his followers to perform the pilgrimage to Becca's holy sanctuary and to repeat Hagar's steps between the hills of Safa and Marwa.

> When We showed Abraham where to build the (Sacred) House, (We told him), "Don't take anything as a partner in My divinity. Purify My House for those who walk around it, stand (near it) or bow down in prostration."
>
> "Declare the pilgrimage ritual to all people. They're going to come to you on foot and on every type of well-worn transportation, traveling from every deep canyon (on earth), so they can bear witness to things that will benefit them, and so they can remember the name of God during the (ten) appointed days (of Hajj)..." — *Al Hajj (The Pilgrimage, 22:26-28)*

While living in the fertile land of Canaan, Abraham fervently prayed for the progeny of Ishmael whom he had left in the remote and barren valley. In Surah Ibrahim, we hear his prayer:

> Recall when Abraham said, "My Lord! Make this settlement (of Mecca) tranquil and secure, and keep me and my descendants away from idol-worship. My Lord! So many people have been led astray by them. Whoever follows me is of the same mind as me, and whoever disobeys me– well, You're forgiving and merciful."
>
> "Our Lord!" (he continued,) "I've settled some of my descendants in this barren valley next to Your Sacred House, so they can, our Lord, establish prayer. So make some people sympathetic towards them, and supply them with fruits so they can learn to be thankful." — *Ibrahim (Abraham, 14:35-37)*

❧ SURAH IBRAHIM (Abraham) is named after several verses, which recall Abraham's prayer in the valley of Mecca. The surah, which was revealed shortly before the Hijrah, also recounts the challenges of previous prophets who, like the Prophet and his Companions, faced nearly insurmountable opposition. After reminding listeners about the fate of those who ignored God's messengers, the revelation poignantly asks, "Don't you see that God created the heavens and the earth for a true purpose?"

---

⑤ WHAT IS THE ROLE OF SELF-DOUBT IN DEVELOPING TRUST? [RAMADAN]

"In the course of those trials, beyond his human grief and in fact through the very nature of grief, Abraham develops a relationship with God based on faithfulness, reconciliation, peace, and trust. God tries him but is always speaking to him, inspiring him and strewing his path with signs that calm and reassure him. Such signs [see Qur'an 37:101-9], expressing the presence of the divine at the heart of the trial, have an essential role in the experience of faith and shape the mode of being with oneself and with God. Doubt about self is thus allied to deep trust in God."[5]

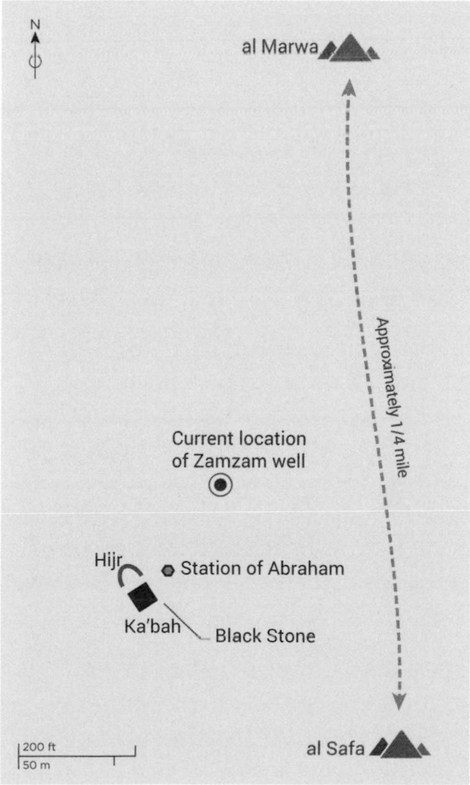

FIGURE P6. THE KA'BAH AND ITS SURROUNDINGS

When Abraham left his family in Becca, Hagar searched back and forth between the hills of Safa and Marwa frantically looking for water for her crying son. (The Ka'bah was built several years later by Abraham and Ishmael). About 2,000 years later, the Prophet Muhammad commemorated the event by retracing Hagar's steps (QY 23.1) as part of his pilgrimage after the Conquest of Mecca. Muslims have been walking in Hagar's footsteps ever since.

The **Creed of Abraham** is Emerick's translation of the Arabic term *millatu Ibrahim*. "Millat" can also be described as "way" or "path." The Qur'an uses the term 15 times (10 times in direct or indirect reference to Abraham) and emphasizes that Islam is nothing more than Abraham's Way. In fact, for most of the Prophet's life, it is unlikely that the term "Islam" was used to denote the religion (see QY23.1). Although we will use the terms "Islam" and "Muslim" throughout this book, it is important to remember that for the majority of the Prophet's career, the Companions may have identified themselves as followers of Haneefism, *tazzaki* (purification/righteousness), or possibly, Millatu Ibrahim. As seen in the verses from surahs An-Nisa and Al Hajj, the Prophet's call to monotheism was not a novel doctrine, but simply a return to the pure religion of Abraham. "What could be better?" the Qur'an asks.

According to the Book of Genesis (25:9), Ishmael and Isaac later came together to bury their father in Hebron. The Bible and Qur'an reserve the highest praise for Abraham. The Qur'an describes him as the archetypal Muslim, and Muslims everywhere are instructed to reverently bless him and his family during each of the five daily prayers.

> Whose way of life can be better than the one who submits himself to God, does what's morally right and follows the creed of Abraham, the natural monotheist? Indeed, God even took Abraham as a friend...
> — *An-Nisa (The Women, 4:125)*

> Strive in His cause with honest effort, for He's chosen you and hasn't made any difficult (regulations) for you to follow. This way of life is no less than the creed of your forefather Abraham. (God) is the One Who has named you Submitters, both before and in this (revelation), so that the Messenger could be a witness for you, and so you could be witnesses (to your faith) before all people. Establish prayer, give in charity, and hold firmly to God. He is your protector, and (He's) the best for defense and the best for giving help!
> — *Al Hajj (The Pilgrimage, 22:78)*

 ABRAHAM: THE ARCHETYPAL MUSLIM   `RAMADAN`

"From the outset, the Quran points to this particular link with Abraham through the insistent and continuous expression of pure monotheism, of human consciousness's adherence to the divine project, of the heart's access to His recognition and to His peace through self-giving."[6]

P1.4 THE JURHUM DYNASTY

The Jurhumites were Pure Arabs from Yemen who had passed through Becca (sometime later known as Mecca) long before Hagar and Ishmael's arrival. They had settled in the surrounding valleys and later, with Hagar's permission, relocated to the central part of the valley of Mecca.

Al-Mubarakpuri mentions that Nabet's descendants, the **Nabeteans**, settled in Petra, Jordan. Despite the same name and location, there is no historic evidence linking the descendants of Nabet (who lived well before 1000 BCE) with the Nabateans who inhabited Petra during the first century CE. The latter are credited for the extraordinary rock carvings in Petra.

Ishmael married the daughter of the Jurhumite chief and had 12 sons who settled throughout Arabia, Syria, and Egypt (Fig. P7). He maintained custodianship of the Ka'bah until his death at the age of 137 (Genesis 25:13) and was succeeded by his eldest sons, Nabet and Qidar. The Nabeteans ultimately settled in northern Arabia, making Petra their capital. While the majority of Ishmael's descendants spread throughout Arabia, Qidar's offspring settled in the central region of the peninsula known as the *Hijaz*. Among Qidar's descendants was a man named 'Adnan, who remained in Mecca and founded an exceptional group of tribes collectively known as the *'Adnanian Arabs*.

Isaac's descendants used to visit the Ka'bah and regarded it as an outlying Abrahamic temple. The annual pilgrimage brought prosperity to Mecca, but as centuries passed, idols from neighboring tribes were gradually introduced into the Ka'bah. Not surprisingly, as the Holy Sanctuary slowly transformed into a pantheon, the Jews gradually ceased to visit.

---

7 **WAS THE KA'BAH A UNIQUE SANCTUARY?** ARMSTRONG

"Despite the claims of the Arabic sources, both historical evidence and basic geographical sense clearly indicated that Mecca was not situated on any known trading route in the Arabian Peninsula ... There was no reason either to travel to Mecca or for that matter, to settle there. No reason, that is, but the Ka'bah. Unlike the other sanctuaries dotting the desert landscape of the Hijaz—each dedicated to a local deity—the Ka'bah was unique in that it claimed to be a universal shrine."[7]

Much to the 'Adnanians' dismay, Mecca's scarce resources and harsh living conditions led the Jurhumites to abuse their position as keepers of the Holy Sanctuary. Their injustices toward visitors did not sit well with the 'Adnanians who, with the help of the neighboring tribe of Khuza'ah, chased the Jurhumites out of the valley. However, before relinquishing nearly 2,000 years of Meccan rule (since the time of Ishmael), the Jurhumites razed the sanctuary and buried the well of Zamzam. They ultimately resettled in Yemen, and the Khuza'ah became the rulers of Mecca.

Remember that the **Khuza'ah** were one of the Kahlan branches from Sheba that were forced out of Yemen by their Himyarite brethren (Fig. P3).

P1.5 THE KHUZA'AH DYNASTY & THE DECLINE OF THE ABRAHAMIC WAY

The Khuza'ah did not bother searching for Zamzam because other wells had since sprung up in the valley. Far from upholding Abraham's religion, their leader, 'Amr bin Luhai, imported an idol from the Syrian Moabites named Hubal and established it as the chief deity of Mecca.

Aside from the usual forms of idol worship, the Khuza'ites introduced a number of unusual religious practices explicitly referred to in the Qur'an. Examples include:

- Dedication of certain portions of food, drink, cattle, and crops to the idols and to Allah (Qur'an 6:136).

- Dedication of certain animals to the idols by sparing them from domesticated work (Qur'an 6:138).

- Shortening Abraham's rites of pilgrimage by not going out to the plain of 'Arafah with the rest of the visiting pilgrims (Qur'an 2:199).

- Innovated acts of worship such as following restricted diets during the pilgrimage and circumambulating the Ka'bah with little to no clothing (Qur'an 7:31).

- Entering their houses from the back door when in a state of ritual piety (Qur'an 2:189).

Surahs Az-Zumar and Yunus explain how such innovations were cloaked in the guise of pleasing God:

> ...Those who take protectors other than God (say), "We're only serving (the idols) so they can bring us closer to God..." — *Az-Zumar (The Crowds, 39:3)*

> Who's more wrong than the one who invents a forgery and then attributes it to God or who denies (the truth of) His (authentic) verses? The wicked will never succeed!
>
> They serve in place of God things that can neither harm them nor benefit them, but then they (try to justify their idol-worship by) saying, "These (idols) intercede for us with God."
>
> So ask them, "Are you really informing God about something in the heavens and the earth about which He doesn't know?" Glory be to Him! He's so high above the partners they're assigning to Him! — *Yunus (Jonah, 10:17-18)*

Over the centuries, Mecca continued to fall further away from the Abrahamic Way By the time Jesus was preaching about reclaiming Abraham's legacy in Jerusalem, the Abrahamic Way was barely recognizable in Mecca.

> The polytheists, who faked Abrahamism, were detached from its principles and inherent good manners. They were indulged into disobedience, ungodliness and certain peculiar superstitions that managed to leave a serious impact on the religious and socio-political life in the whole of Arabia.[8]

With the Khuza'ah in control of Mecca, Ishmael's direct descendants, the 'Adnanian Arabs, remained a marginalized minority. While many 'Adnanians left Mecca to settle in nearby regions of the Hijaz, one man by the name of Fihr (also known as *Quraysh*) remained near the sacred precinct. Fihr's descendants became a fixed part of Meccan society and collectively came to be known as the tribe of Quraysh.

According to scholars like Armstrong, it is possible that the name Quraysh may have been derived from *taqarrush,* which means "accumulation" or "gaining."

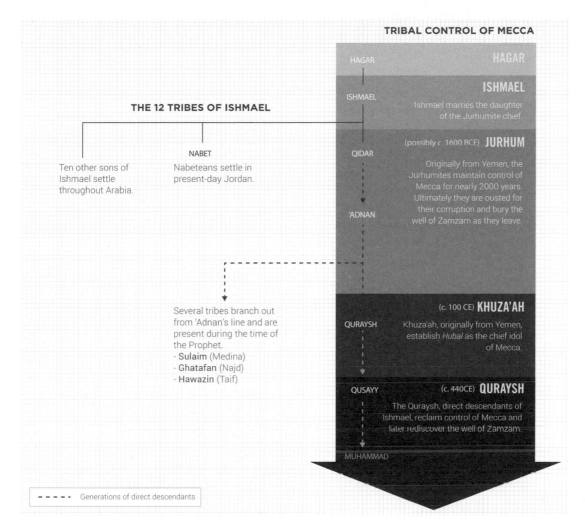

FIGURE P7. THE CONTROL OF MECCA

Mecca was founded by Hagar and Ishmael. Ishmael married into the Jurhumite tribe and had 12 sons. While most of his sons settled throughout Arabia, the 'Adnanian Arabs stayed in and around Mecca. 'Adnan was the forefather to many of the tribes that we will encounter in this book, including the Quraysh. One of his descendants, a remarkable man by the name of Qusayy, married into the Khuza'ah tribe and reclaimed Mecca for the descendants of Abraham. The Prophet Muhammad was a direct descendant of 'Adnan by 21 generations and Qusayy by five. (A simple mnemonic for remembering the control of Mecca is "H-I-J-K" or Hagar-Ishmael-Jurhum-Khuza'ah.)

PROLOGUE 2: THE QURAYSH DYNASTY

P2.1 QUSAYY & THE RECLAMATION OF MECCA

About 400 years after the birth of Jesus, a Qurayshi named Qusayy married the daughter of Hulayl ibn Hubshiyah, the chief of Khuza'ah. Hulayl preferred his son-in-law—a non-Khuza'ah—over his own sons as the keeper of the Ka'bah. After Hulayl's death, a fierce power struggle ensued. Ultimately, Qusayy established himself as the ruler of Mecca in 440 CE and brought his closest relatives to live beside the Sanctuary. This group, the Quraysh of the Hollow, included the families of Qusayy, Zuhrah, Taym, and Makhzum. Qusayy's more remote tribesmen were pushed to the surrounding areas and became known as the Quraysh of the Outskirts.

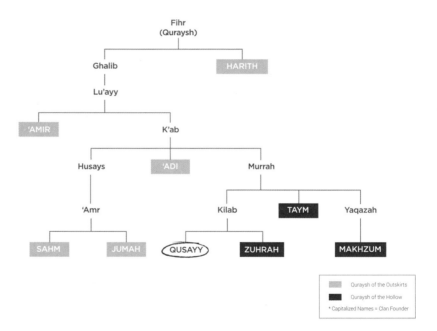

FIGURE P8. QUSAYY AND THE QURAYSH OF THE HOLLOW

Qusayy was credited with winning control of Mecca from the Khuza'ites and restoring it to the descendants of Ishmael. Upon taking control, Qusayy and his closest relatives settled in the area around the Holy Sanctuary and became known as the "Quraysh of the Hollow." Qusayy's distant kinsmen were pushed to the surrounding areas and were subsequently called the "Quraysh of the Outskirts."

Toward the end of his life, Qusayy had to pick a successor from his four sons. Although 'Abdu Manaf was the most capable, Qusayy favored his eldest son, 'Abd ad-Dar, the least promising of the four. 'Abdu Manaf accepted his father's wishes, but in the next generation, half the Quraysh supported 'Abdu Manaf's exceptional son Hashim as their tribal leader. These included the clans of Qusayy's younger three sons and the clans of Zuhrah and Taym. The clans pledged their allegiance to each other by dipping their hands into perfume and rubbing them on the stones of the Ka'bah. Since that day, those who supported Hashim became known as the Scented Ones.

The remaining clans who did not recognize Hashim's leadership ('Abd ad-Dar, Makhzum, and other outlying families), continued to support 'Abd ad-Dar and became known as the Confederates. Tensions mounted between the two parties until they finally agreed to split Mecca's leadership roles: Hashim would provide for the pilgrims while 'Abd ad-Dar would retain the keys to the Ka'bah.

The sons of 'Abdu Manaf cast lots to see who would represent them as the official caretaker of the pilgrims. Hashim was the first caretaker, followed by his brother Muttalib, and then Hashim's orphaned son, Shaybah ('Abd al-Muttalib). Later, the position was filled by the Prophet's uncle 'Abbas ibn 'Abd al-Muttalib.

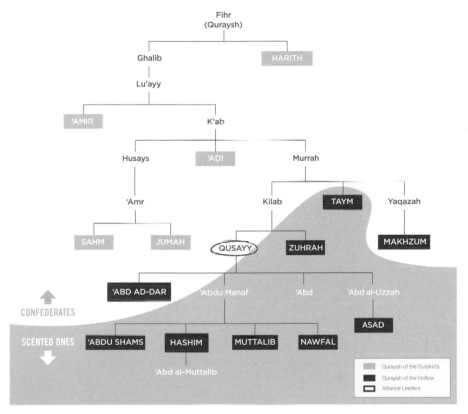

FIGURE P9. THE CLANS OF QURAYSH

Qusayy was succeeded by his eldest son 'Abd ad-Dar, but in the next generation, half the Quraysh supported 'Abdu Manaf's son Hashim as the tribal leader. Tensions led to a tribal split between the Scented Ones and the Confederates.

It is important to note that Makhzum was the only Quraysh clan of the Hollow that did not accept Hashim's leadership and continued to support 'Abd ad-Dar. Even the clan of Taym, which is just as distantly related as Makhzum, acknowledged Hashim's exceptional leadership. The Makhzumis became the most powerful Quraysh clan at the turn of the seventh century and continued to rebuff Hashim's leadership as evidenced by their ruthless treatment of his great-grandson Muhammad. While the Prophet found his fiercest enemy among Makhzum (Abu Jahl), he found his greatest friend in Taym (Abu Bakr).

P2.2 HASHIM & THE GROWTH OF MECCA

Despite the historical rift that split the Quraysh in two, every clan recognized Hashim's extraordinary leadership in reviving the economic primacy of Mecca. By establishing the summer and winter trading routes to Syria and Yemen, Hashim had transformed Mecca from a settled Bedouin community into a commercial business hub. The importance of the seasonal routes is highlighted in Surah Quraysh:

SURAH QURAYSH (The Quraysh) is an early Meccan surah that was revealed to Hashim's great-grandson, Muhammad. The short surah (shown in its entirety here) reminds listeners that God is in complete control of all worldly affairs.

> About the treaties of the Quraysh, those treaties that protect them on their journeys through winter and summer - they should serve the Lord of this House, for He's the One Who provides them with their rations against hunger and their security against fear. — *Quraysh (The Quraysh, 106:1-4)*

① QUSAYY, HASHIM, AND THE NEW MECCA　　ASLAN

"This trade, modest as it may have been, was wholly dependent on the Ka'bah; there was simply no other reason to be in Mecca. This was a desert wasteland that produced nothing. By inextricably linking the religious and economic life in the city, Qusayy and his descendants had developed an innovative religio-economic system that relied on control of the Ka'bah and its pilgrimage rites—rites in which nearly the whole of the Hijaz participated—to guarantee the economic, religious, and political supremacy of a single tribe, the Quraysh."[1]

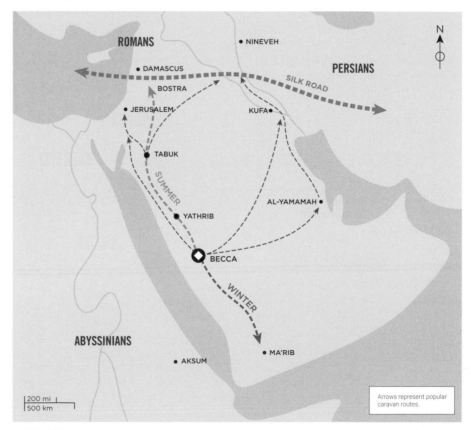

FIGURE P10. SEASONAL CARAVAN ROUTES FROM MECCA

The seasonal caravan routes were established by Hashim. In the winter months, the Quraysh journeyed south to Yemen to trade with the local Arabs and Abyssinians. In the summer, they traveled north into modern-day Syria. By establishing these routes, Hashim transformed Mecca into a major trading hub for much of the north-south commerce in the Arabian Peninsula.

The summer caravan route passed through the oasis settlement of Yathrib, a predominantly agricultural community comprised of Jewish and Arab villages.

While Hashim was on a caravan trip to Syria, he stopped in Yathrib, and proposed to Salma' bint 'Amr, one of the most influential women from the Khazraj sub-clan of Najjar. Salma' agreed to the marriage on the condition that any child of theirs would remain with her in Yathrib. The couple was soon blessed with a son they named Shaybah.

Several years later (in 497 CE), Hashim died in Gaza, while on a caravan expedition to Syria. He had three brothers—'Abdu Shams, Nawfal (a half-brother), and Muttalib—but since the first two were busy merchants, the leadership of the Scented Ones fell to the third (Fig. P9).

After the Prophet's emigration to Yathrib, the settlement was renamed *Medina Al-Munawwarah* (The City of Radiant Light) or *Medina* (The City) for short.

> ② **WHAT WAS THE SIGNIFICANCE OF HASHIM'S MARRIAGE TO SALMA?** [YUSUF]
>
> "Salma' was from the clan of Najjar, and the people of Bani Najjar are the ones who greeted the Prophet, God's peace and blessings be upon him, when he came into Medina. You can see the divine work here. These people were going to be related to the Prophet, God's peace and blessings be upon him, through blood!"[2]

P2.3 'ABD AL-MUTTALIB & THE RECOVERY OF ZAMZAM

Many years after assuming leadership of Quraysh, Muttalib had to choose his own successor. He recognized Shaybah's extraordinary potential and passed up his own sons in favor of his orphaned nephew who was still in Yathrib.

Muttalib set out for Yathrib and, after persuading Salma' to let her son live among the Quraysh, returned to Mecca with Shaybah riding behind him. The Quraysh had never seen Shaybah before, and thinking he was a servant of Muttalib, began calling him *'Abd al-Muttalib* (the servant of Muttalib).

'Abd al-Muttalib lived with his uncle until the latter died during a caravan journey in Yemen. After Muttalib's death, his brother Nawfal forcefully seized control of Bani Hashim, thereby blocking 'Abd al-Muttalib from succeeding his uncle. When the rest of Quraysh refused to arbitrate the matter, 'Abd al-Muttalib wrote to his maternal uncles in Yathrib asking for support. Eighty men from the Khazraj clan of Najjar responded—they entered Mecca and demanded that Nawfal hand over the leadership of Hashim to 'Abd al-Muttalib.

'Abd al-Muttalib will give rise to some of the most important individuals in the Sirah, including Muhammad.

Although Nawfal relented, his entire clan allied with the clan of his brother 'Abdu Shams against the clans of Hashim and Muttalib. Meanwhile, the nearby tribe of Khuza'ah watched the developments unfold in Mecca. They had a vested interest in seeing 'Abd al-Muttalib succeed (even though all three clans were equally related to Bani Khuza'ah through Qusayy's wife). After 'Abd al-Muttalib came to power, the Khuza'ah entered an alliance with the clan of Hashim against Nawfal and 'Abdu Shams.

These shifting clan alliances will play a critical role during the life of the Prophet. During the initiation of the ban against Hashim, Muttalib will be the only clan standing by their brethren while 'Abdu Shams and Nawfal remain indifferent to Hashim's suffering (QY 7.1). Furthermore, the alliance between Khuza'ah and Hashim will resurface several decades later and give way to the Prophet's Conquest of Mecca (QY 20.7).

'Abd al-Muttalib was widely regarded as a better leader than his celebrated father, Hashim. He enjoyed spending time in the Sanctuary and used to sleep in a special area next to the Ka'bah—above the tombs of Ishmael and Hagar—known as the *Hijr* (Fig. P6). On several occasions he dreamt about Zamzam and one night received clear instructions to dig up the long forgotten well:

> *"Dig her, thou shalt not regret,*
> *For she is thine inheritance*
> *From thy greatest ancestor.*
> *Dry she never will, nor fail*
> *To water all the pilgrim throng."*[3]

With the help of his only son, Harith, 'Abd al-Muttalib began unearthing centuries of packed dirt until he uncovered buried Jurhumite treasures and the sacred spring. As the official caretakers of the pilgrims, 'Abd al-Muttalib's clan of Hashim naturally assumed control of the well.

Although 'Abd al-Muttalib enjoyed a position of authority in Mecca, he was not content with having only one son. He vowed that if God blessed him with 10 sons, he would sacrifice one in God's honor. After his 10th son, 'Abd Allah, came of age, 'Abd al-Muttalib came face to face with the oath he made many years ago. Through the customary practice of divination, his favorite son 'Abd Allah was chosen to be sacrificed.

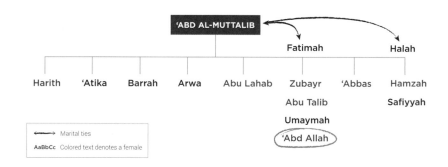

FIGURE P11. NOTABLE CHILDREN OF 'ABD AL-MUTTALIB

'Abd al-Muttalib had many children through different wives (not all children are shown here). His wife Fatimah bint 'Amr was from the clan of Makhzum and was the mother of Zubayr, Abu Talib, Umaymah, and 'Abd Allah. Although Hamzah, Safiyyah, and 'Abbas are shown in this figure, they were many years younger than 'Abd Allah and were born after 'Abd al-Muttalib sacrificed 100 camels in lieu of his son.

'Abd Allah's mother Fatimah bint 'Amr was from the clan of Makhzum. Not surprisingly, before 'Abd al-Muttalib could carry out his plan, Mughirah—the powerful chief of Makhzum—pleaded with him to find an alternative solution and spare Fatimah's son.

'Abd al-Muttalib was desperate to find a way out of his oath. His search for alternatives led him north to the Jewish settlement of Khaybar. On the advice of a respected elder, he began casting lots between 'Abd Allah and 10 camels, adding an additional 10 camels each time the arrow pointed toward his son. After 10 failed attempts, 'Abd al-Muttalib was able to save his son's life at the cost of 100 camels.

Having fulfilled his oath, 'Abd al-Muttalib was determined to get his son married to Aminah bint Wahb from the Quraysh clan of Zuhrah. Aminah's father had passed away and she was under the guardianship of her uncle Wuhayb ibn 'Abdi Manaf. 'Abd al-Muttalib approached Wuhayb and asked for the hand of his niece. Not only did Wuhayb agree to the union, he also consented to the marriage of his own daughter Halah to 'Abd al-Muttalib on the same day.

"Fatimah" is a common name in the Sirah. Not only is it the name of the Prophet's grandmother (Fig. P11), but also Abu Talib's wife (who will care for Muhammad as an orphan) and much later, the Prophet's youngest daughter.

On the day of his wedding, 'Abd Allah was approached by Qutaylah bint Nawfal, who saw a radiance in the young man, and asked to marry him on the spot. 'Abd Allah declined as he was on his way to marry Aminah. Many years later, Qutaylah's first cousin, Khadijah, will see the same glimmer in 'Abd Allah's only son, Muhammad, and offer a similar proposal (Fig. P23). *(Keep in mind that Qutaylah bint Nawfal was from the Quraysh clan of Asad, not the clan of Nawfal that was at odds with Bani Hashim.)*

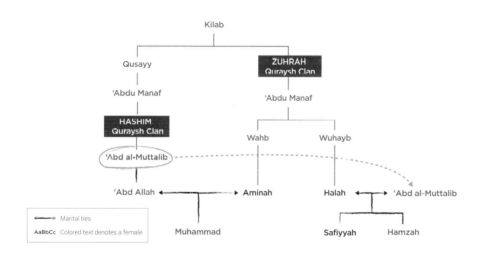

FIGURE P12. 'ABD ALLAH MARRIES AMINAH

'Abd al-Muttalib married his son 'Abd Allah to Aminah, and married Aminah's first cousin, Halah, the very same day. Muhammad was born to Aminah, while Hamzah and Safiyyah were born to Halah. Thus Hamzah was Muhammad's uncle through 'Abd al-Muttalib and a second cousin through Halah. Given their strong family ties, it is not surprising that Hamzah and Safiyyah were among the Prophet's most loyal supporters.

PROLOGUE 3: THE 7TH CENTURY BEFORE MUHAMMAD

P3.1 RELIGIONS IN & AROUND MECCA

PAGANISM   Pagan rituals and beliefs were widespread throughout Arabia and, over the centuries, had slowly crept into Meccan society as well. The Ka'bah, which was erected as a testament to unwavering monotheism, had been reduced to a pantheon of statues and figures. Not only did Mecca have a chief idol named *Hubal*, it was also surrounded by three sister idols—*al-Lat, al-Uzzah,* and *al-Manat*—that the Arabs referred to as the "daughters of God." All three are mentioned by name in Surah An-Najm:

> Have you seen (the idols named) Al-Lat and Al-'Uzza, and the third one named Manat? What! For you, (you prefer) males (as sons), but then you assign to (God) females (for children)! That's hardly a fair deal!
>
> In fact, they're nothing more than names you've made up - you and your ancestors. God sent down no permission for (you to do) that. They're only following their own opinions and what they themselves (foolishly) desire. And so it is that guidance has now come to them from their Lord, (so see if they will obey God now, as they always claimed they would)!
> — *An-Najm (The Star, 53:19-23)*

The people of Ta'if (known as Bani Thaqif) were very proud of al-Lat and had developed a strong rivalry with Mecca. The Quraysh, however, were satisfied with their preeminent position in the Hijaz, and considered themselves superior to the rest of the Arabs. They welcomed anyone who wanted to honor the Sanctuary of Abraham, and were receptive to Christian pilgrims who passed through. In their estimation, adding the likenesses of Mary and Jesus to their collection of idols would only increase the number of pilgrims who might visit Mecca.

FIGURE P13. MAP OF THE SISTER IDOLS

———

Hubal was the chief idol of Arabia. The Khuza'ah chief, 'Amr bin Luhai, had brought it from Syria sometime in the first century CE. The three "sister" idols were subsequently established around the Holy Precinct and are specifically mentioned in the Qur'an.

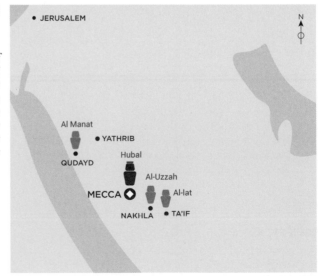

1 **HOW DID THE ARABS VIEW MONOTHEISM?** ARMSTRONG

"Arabs did not understand the idea of a closed system of beliefs, nor would they have seen monotheism as incompatible with polytheism. They regarded Allah, who was surrounded by the rings of idols in the Ka'bah, as lord of a host of deities, in much the same way as some of the biblical writers saw Yahweh as 'surpassing all other gods.'"[1]

----

2 **WHAT MADE MECCA UNIQUE?** ARMSTRONG

"The world passed through Mecca, but did not stay long enough to interfere ... They [the Quraysh] were not pressured to convert to an alien religion or conform to official orthodoxy. The closed circle of both the trade cycle and the hajj rituals symbolized their proud self-sufficiency, which as the years passed, would become a mark of their urban culture."[2]

For an excellent discussion on pre-Islamic Meccan society, read Armstrong (p.17-23).

ZOROASTRIANISM Zoroastrianism was the dominant religion of the Persian Empire. Founded by the prophet Zarathustra in the 10th or 11th century BCE, it began as a fairly monotheistic religion that subsequently developed into a dualistic theology, pitting good against evil. While the vast majority of Persia was Zoroastrian, the empire also served as a refuge for many Jews and Nestorian Christians.

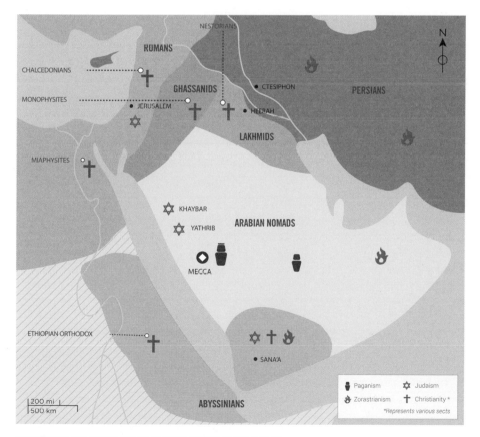

FIGURE P14. RELIGIONS IN AND AROUND ARABIA CIRCA 600 CE

Many religious traditions surrounded Arabia but never made significant headway into the peninsula. Although Mecca had become a sanctuary for pagan worship, the Quraysh continued to welcome a wide variety of beliefs if it meant more pilgrims coming to Mecca.

JUDAISM   The Jews traced their ancestry from Abraham through his second son, Isaac (Fig. P16). Isaac's son Jacob (also known as *Israel*) had 12 sons, including the Prophet Joseph. Thus Jacob's sons formed the 12 tribes of Israel, which spread throughout Canaan and gave rise to the great Hebrew prophets mentioned in the Bible and Qur'an. The Jews experienced a number of successive diasporas from their lands in Canaan. The most recent occurred after the Roman occupation of Jerusalem in 70 CE, which forced a number of Jewish tribes to seek refuge in the Arabian Peninsula. By the end of the sixth century, Jewish tribes had spread all over the Middle East, not to mention a number of enclaves in Arabia.

One of these enclaves was known as Yathrib, a collection of Jewish settlements roughly 200 miles north of Mecca. The Aws and Khazraj Arabs came to live with the Jews of Yathrib in the first or second century CE. Initially the Jews maintained their religious identity, however over time, they began to adopt pagan superstitions such as belief in black magic and divination.

---

3 **WHO WERE THE JEWS OF ARABIA?**   ASLAN

"For the most part, the Jews were a thriving and highly influential diaspora whose culture and traditions had been thoroughly integrated into the social and religious milieu of pre-Islamic Arabia. Whether Arab converts or immigrants from Palestine, the Jews participated in every level of Arab society ... And while some of these Jews may have spoken Aramaic, their primary language was Arabic.

The relationship between the Jews and pagan Arabs was symbiotic in that not only were the Jews heavily Arabized, but the Arabs were also significantly influenced by Jewish beliefs and practices. One need look no further for evidence of this influence than to the Ka'bah itself, whose origin myths indicate that it was a Semitic sanctuary with its roots dug deeply in Jewish tradition.

In sixth-century Arabia, Jewish monotheism was in no way an anathema to Arab paganism, which, as mentioned, could easily absorb a cornucopia of disparate religious ideologies. The pagan Arabs would likely have perceived Judaism as just another way of expressing what they considered to be similar sentiments."[3]

Refer to Appendix C for a closer look at the evolution of Christian theology.

CHRISTIANITY   By the fifth century, Christianity had evolved significantly from its simple origins. Within a few hundred years after Jesus, what began as a small Jewish sect had become the state religion of the Roman Empire. In 325 CE, Jesus was formally recognized as both fully man and fully God. By 451, the majority of Roman Christians had officially adopted the concept of the trinity. By this time, Trinitarian Christianity had also penetrated the Himyarite kingdom in Yemen as well as the northern Arab tribes of Ghassan and Tayy.

Meanwhile, Christian theology at the edge of the Roman Empire (i.e. closer to Mecca) remained at the borders of the newest developments in Christian theology. A central point of contention among these outlying areas was their understanding of the basic nature of Jesus—specifically, how they chose to resolve his dual attributes as human and divine. Ironically, the original belief that Jesus was a Jewish prophet like other biblical messengers was largely abandoned. A few minority Christian sects like the Ebionites may have still practiced this early form of Christianity, but only in small pockets of Palestine and Arabia. The Ebionites were followers of Jesus who upheld Mosaic Law and believed that Jesus was the Messiah. Translated as "the poor ones" in Hebrew, the Ebionites practiced voluntary poverty as a means of attaining God-consciousness.

Like many Jews, these Christians believed that the coming of a prophet was imminent. Perhaps this was due to their interpretation of what was later known as the miracle of the Pentecost:

> He shall not speak of himself, but whatsoever he shall hear, that shall he speak. — *St. John 16:13*

This belief may not have been widespread, but it was supported by one or two venerable dignitaries of eastern churches, and also by the astrologers and soothsayers. As to the Jews, for whom such a belief was easier, since for them the line of Prophets ended only with the Messiah, they were almost unanimous in their expectancy of a Prophet ... He would, of course, be a Jew, for they were the chosen people. The Christians, Waraqah amongst them, had their doubts about this; they saw no reason why he should not be an Arab. The Arabs stood in need of a Prophet even more than the Jews.[4]

'Abd al-Muttalib was acquainted with **Waraqah** ibn Nawfal, a Christian from the Quraysh clan of Asad (possibly an Ebionite). Waraqah was Khadijah's cousin and will soon confirm Muhammad as the prophet he had been expecting (QY 1.1)

---

4 **WHY DID INNOVATIVE PRACTICES DEVELOP IN MECCA?**   ASLAN

"The relative distance that these three major religions [Christianity, Judaism, Zoroastrianism] enjoyed from their respective centers gave them the freedom to develop their creeds and rituals into fresh, innovative ideologies."[5]

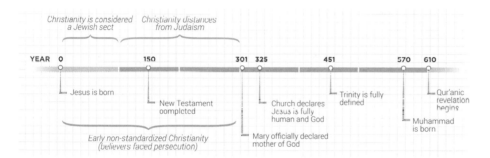

FIGURE P15. MAJOR MILESTONES IN CHRISTIAN THEOLOGY

In the five centuries that followed the birth of Jesus, Christian theology went through several non-linear transformations. Each turning point redefined mainstream Christian thought and pushed non-conformist teachings to the fringes of the Roman Empire. (See Appendix C for a closer look at the non-linear development of early Christian theology.)

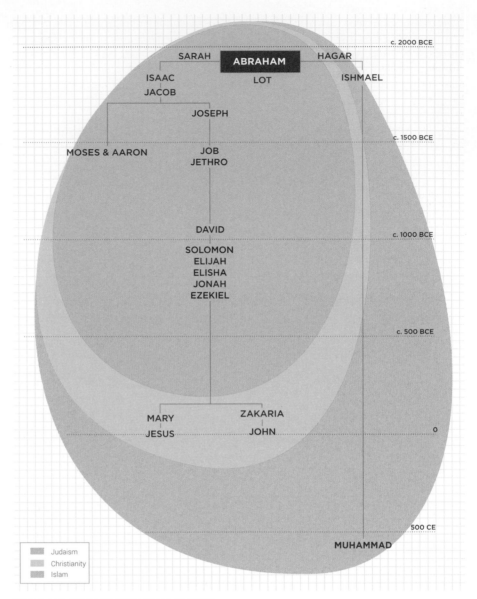

FIGURE P16. THE PROPHETIC LINE OF ABRAHAM

The shaded areas represent similarities and differences between Judaism, Christianity, and Islam (dates are approximations). Muslims consider all of these prophets as followers of Abraham's religion of Islam. Although Mary is not considered a prophet, she is included because of her unparalleled historical and spiritual significance in Islam.

HANEEFISM   Haneefism was a form of primitive monotheism that dates back to the fifth and sixth centuries CE. It was a reaction to the growing prevalence of idolatry—the Haneef shunned idols in exchange for a simpler life devoid of pagan rituals. The Haneef were scattered around Arabia, including a handful who lived among the Quraysh in Mecca.

5   WHO WERE THE HANEEF?   ASLAN

"Especially in Mecca, the center of the Jahiliyyah religious experience, this vibrant pluralistic environment became a breeding ground for bold new ideas and exciting religious experimentation, the most important of which was an obscure Arab monotheistic movement called Hanifism, which arose some time around the sixth century C.E. … At the heart of the movement was a fervent commitment to absolute morality. It was not enough merely to abstain from idol worship; the Hanifs believed one must strive to be morally upright."

6   WHAT IS THE MEANING OF 'HANEEF'?   YUSUF

" 'Haneef' in Arabic means 'to incline towards what is straight.' In Greek, you would probably say 'orthodox.' They comprised a group of people who did not believe in the idols. Most of them did not condemn the idols. They just stayed out of it. They prayed to Allah."

7   WHAT DID THE 'HANEEF' SYMBOLIZE?   ARMSTRONG

"Instead of creating something new, they simply withdrew from the mainstream. They had a clearer idea of what they did not want than a positive conception of where they were going. But the movement was a symptom of the spiritual restiveness in Arabia at the beginning of the seventh century…"

P3.2 EMPIRES SURROUNDING THE QURAYSH

By the turn of the seventh century, central Arabia was surrounded by three empires—the Romans, Persians, and Abyssinians—and three Arab border kingdoms—the Ghassanids, Lakhmids, and Himyarites.

The inhabitants of the Roman Empire were originally known as *Romans*, not **Byzantines**. The empire was named Byzantine much later in European history to distinguish it from the Western Roman Empire, which emerged after the Dark Ages. The Qur'an refers to the Romans by their historically correct name, *ar-Rum*. For the remainder of this book, we will refer to them as the Romans as well. The Roman Emperor Heraclius ruled from 610-641 CE, spanning the entire period of Qur'anic revelation.

THE ROMANS   The Romans ruled a vast territory from the great city of Constantinople. Several centuries earlier they had officially adopted Trinitarian Christianity as the state religion and had successfully pushed all competing theologies to the borders of the empire. By the time of Muhammad's birth in 570 CE, the Romans had amassed a huge territory encompassing modern-day Italy, Greece, Turkey, Lebanon, Egypt, and North Africa. As detailed below, several Roman territories were later conquered by the Persians, only to be taken back by Emperor Heraclius during the Prophet's lifetime.

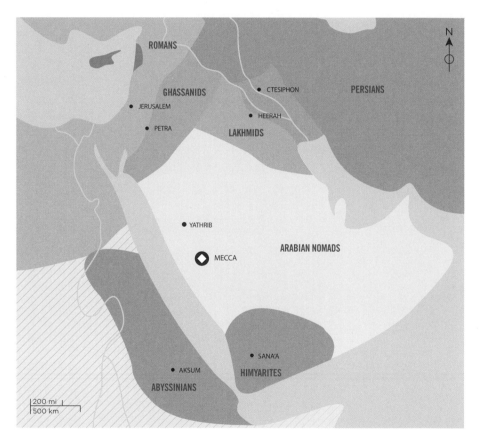

FIGURE P17. POLITICAL POWERS CIRCA 600 CE

The Arabian Peninsula was surrounded by three powerful empires and three border kingdoms. Arabia itself had never been consolidated into a single empire, and was ruled by several competing tribes that lacked the political and military organization of its neighbors.

THE PERSIANS   The Persian (Sassanid) Empire was known to its inhabitants as Eran or Eranshahr. They came to power in 224 CE and retained their dominance until the mid-seventh century. Their territory included modern-day Iraq, Iran, Afghanistan, Pakistan, eastern Syria and Turkey, parts of the Caucusus, and the Persian Gulf. In 602 CE, King Chosroes II (who ruled for much of Muhammad's lifetime) led his armies against the Roman territories in Turkey, Syria, Jordan, and Egypt. By the time the Prophet began publicly inviting the Quraysh to Islam, the Persians had gained control of Damascus, Jerusalem, and Egypt. Initially the Roman Empire was unable to stop the advancing Persian army and faced the possibility of total collapse. Then under the leadership of Emperor Heraclius, the Romans mobilized a successful campaign to reclaim their losses. Heraclius' assault began in 622 CE (the year of the Prophet's migration to Medina) and culminated with the surrender of the Persian capital, Ctesiphon, in 627 CE. Two years later, the Romans regained control of Jerusalem (one year after the Treaty of Hudaybiyah).

Surah Rum foretells the unthinkable victory of the Romans over the Persians during the Late Medinan Period (QY 21.1). In time, the Persian Empire will finally succumb to the rapidly expanding Islamic civilization under Caliph 'Umar in 641 CE.

THE GHASSANIDS   The Ghassanids were Pure Kahlan Arabs who settled in northern Arabia after being expelled by the Himyarites in Yemen (Fig. P3). They had become Hellenized Christians who, after establishing their own kingdom, helped the Romans against the Persians and Lakhmid Arabs. Their capital was Jabiyah in the Golan Heights, and their territory encompassed parts of modern-day Syria, Jordan, Israel, Palestine, and Lebanon. Most Ghassanids were Miaphysite Christians who believed that Jesus had one nature—divine and human at the same time.

THE LAKHMIDS   The Lakhmids were also Pure Kahlan Arabs from Yemen who settled farther east in present-day Iraq. They were mostly Nestorian Christians who believed that Jesus had two loosely defined but distinct natures (human and divine). In the fourth century, the Romans persecuted Nestorian Christians who lived in their territories and forced them to settle in northern Arabia and Persia where they could freely practice their faith. For the most part, the Lakhmids enjoyed the support of the Persians against the Ghassanids and Romans. However in 602, Chosroes II invaded the territory, assassinated the Lakhmid king, and annexed the Arab dynasty into his rapidly expanding Persian Empire.

Scholars suggest that Chosroes' betrayal ultimately led the Lakhmids to turn on the Persians and help Khalid ibn al-Walid conquer the Persian Empire many years later.

THE ABYSSINIANS   Formally known as the Kingdom of Aksum, the Abyssinians were the third major empire bordering Arabia. The empire was established as early as 400 BCE, and later embraced Christianity in the third century CE. Recognized for their seaworthiness, they progressively gained control over the Horn of Africa, Red Sea coast, and occasionally Western Arabia. They exerted intermittent control over Yemen from where they were finally pushed out by Persian forces shortly after 570 CE.

THE HIMYARITES The description of the Pure Arabs left off with the Himyarites in Yemen (P 1.1). After expelling the Kahlan Arabs, the Himyarites controlled Yemen from 115 BCE until 450 CE. However, the fractured empire was never able to regain its control over Arabia and was intermittently invaded by the Abyssinians, Persians, and Romans. In 450 CE, cracks appeared in the ancient Ma'rib Dam that ultimately led to the Great Flood (*Sayil Arim*) described in Surah Saba':

> And so it was that there was a sign for the people of Sheba in their vicinity. There were two expansive gardens to the right and to their left (along every canal). "Eat of the bounty of your Lord and be thankful to Him! (Your) land is a fine one, and (your) Lord is a forgiving One."
>
> However, they turned away (from their Lord), so We sent a flood against them that breached their dams and transformed their two (luxurious) gardens into gardens (of ruin), where only mustard trees, tamarisks and thorny bushes grew.
>
> That was what they deserved, for they were utterly thankless (for Our favors and did wrong). Would We ever bring such a payback against anyone else besides the thankless? — *Saba' (Sheba, 34:15-17)*

SURAH SABA' (Sheba) will be revealed during the Early Meccan Period with lessons from the lives of David, Solomon, and the people of Sheba from Yemen. In addition, the surah will specifically coach the Prophet on how to address his many skeptics.

The flood effectively ended millennia of continuous Arabian autonomy in Yemen. After the destruction of the Himyarite stronghold, Yemen was invaded by the Abyssinian Empire.

Prior to the Great Flood in 450 CE, Christianity appeared in Yemen in 340 when Roman forces conquered the area and helped Abyssinian Christian missionaries settle in Najran. The Abyssinians remained in control of Yemen for 38 years until the local Himyarite Arabs regained their independence. Later, in the fifth century, many of the Himyarite kings turned to Judaism and converted a number of subjects to their faith. In 523, the Yemeni king Yusuf Dhu Nawas attempted to force the Christians in Najran to convert to Judaism. When they refused, entire communities were exterminated. Tens of thousands of faithful Christians were thrown into a ditch of fire—a massacre that scholars believe is referenced in Surah Al Buruj:

> By the sky filled with constellations, by the Promised Day and by the witness and all that it witnesses, (by these same tokens know that) the pit-diggers will be ruined, (for they tried to destroy the faithful) with a well-fed fire. They gathered around it and witnessed what they were doing to the faithful.
>
> They persecuted them for no other reason than that they had faith in God, the Exalted and Praiseworthy, the One Whose dominion extends over the heavens and the earth, and God is a witness to everything.
> — *Al Buruj (The Constellations, 85:1-8)*

SURAH AL BURUJ (The Constellations) is named after its opening verse, and will be revealed during the Early Meccan Period. The short surah will warn the Quraysh about persecuting the faithful, by narrating the story of the pit-diggers who similarly prevented dedicated Christians from practicing their faith.

Backed by Roman forces, Christian Abyssinians reconquered Yemen two years after the massacre. In the aftermath, Abraha, an Abyssinian general who had fought against the Himyarites, quickly maneuvered into the role of governor of Yemen.

P3.3 THE YEMENI ATTACK ON MECCA

Shortly after Abraha assumed control, he erected a grand cathedral in Sana'a called *Yemeni Al-Ka'bah*. His ambitious plan to lure pilgrims away from Mecca did not sit well with some Arabs, and a man from Bani Kinanah (just south of Mecca) traveled to Sana'a and defiled Abraha's cathedral. In response, the Abyssinian general swiftly assembled 60,000 soldiers and several elephants, and set out to destroy the Ka'bah in Mecca.

---

8 **WHAT WAS ABRAHA'S TRUE MOTIVATION?** ASLAN

"The Abyssinians tried to destroy the Ka'bah … not because the Ka'bah was a religious threat, but because it was an economic rival."[9]

Abraha's army first stopped at Ta'if. The Thaqif feared that they had been misidentified as the Quraysh, and quickly redirected Abraha toward Mecca. Two miles outside the city, Abraha's army stopped at Mughammis, plundered the area, and stole 200 camels belonging to the Quraysh. Before attacking the Holy Sanctuary, Abraha asked to meet with the chief of Quraysh. Ever since the split of the Scented Ones and the Confederates, the Quraysh had no official chief, and so the Quraysh sent one of their leading representatives, 'Abd al-Muttalib.

When Abraha met 'Abd al-Muttalib, he was so impressed by the Qurayshi that he told him he would grant him one favor. 'Abd al-Muttalib simply asked that his camels be returned to him. As to the imminent destruction of the Ka'bah, he explained:

> *"I am the lord of the camels, and the temple likewise has a Lord who will defend it."*[10]

---

9 **DID 'ABD AL-MUTTALIB REALLY REPRESENT ALL OF QURAYSH?** WATT

"While certain features of the story (e.g. the statement that 'Abd al-Muttalib was then the kabir and sayyid of Quraysh) are doubtless due to a desire to glorify the clan of Hashim, it is probable that the fact of the negotiations is correctly stated, but ought to be interpreted as a party move of a small group of Quraysh … from which the main body of Quraysh stood aloof. If that is so, 'Abd al-Muttalib was presumably trying to get support from the Abyssinians against his rivals among Quraysh, such as the clans of 'Abd Shams, Nawfal, and Makhzum."[11]

Abraha's army resumed its march to Mecca. However, as it neared the Ka'bah, the sky turned ominously dark and the lead elephant, Mahmud, refused to go farther:

> Suddenly it was too late: the western sky grew black, and a strange sound was heard; its volume increased as a great wave of darkness swept upon them from the direction of the sea, and the air above their heads, as high as they could see, was full of birds. Survivors said that they flew with a flight like that of swifts, and each bird had three pebbles the size of dried peas, one in its beak and one between the claws of each foot. They swooped to and fro over the ranks, pelting as they swooped, and the pebbles were so hard and launched with such velocity that they pierced even coats of mail.[12]

Sixty years from now, during the march to Hudaybiyah, the Prophet will refer to God's hold on Mahmud when the Prophet's camel also refuses to approach the city of Mecca (QY 19.1).

Abraha's army was decimated and the few remaining survivors fled back to Yemen. Surah Al Feel recalls the incident succinctly:

SURAH AL FEEL (The Elephant) is an early Meccan surah that was revealed at least 40 years after Abraha's failed attack on Mecca. The tone of the surah (shown in its entirety here) suggests that the Quraysh were already quite familiar with what happened to Abraha's army.

Haven't you seen how your Lord dealt with the army of the elephant? Didn't He foil their evil plans?

He let loose upon them a horde of fliers (carrying a plague), which struck them down with stone-smacked (wounds), leaving their ranks like barren fields - harvested and razed. — *Al Feel (The Elephant, 105:1-5)*

⑩ IS THE STORY OF THE ELEPHANT REALLY TRUE?   YUSUF

"The important thing about this story is that it is a story that goes under the category in hadith of mutawatir. In other words, so many people witnessed the event and then transmitted it to so many other people that it becomes mutawatir amongst the Arabs. In other words, it wasn't a lie. They saw birds come. And they saw these birds fling stones that killed many soldiers. The important thing to remember is that at the time when [Surah Al Feel] was revealed, there were still people alive who had seen that event. None of them said, 'It's a fairy tale.' None of them said, 'This didn't happen.' They knew this was true, and they were being reminded by Allah, 'Don't you remember that sign that Allah showed you? This house is really Allah's house.'"[13]

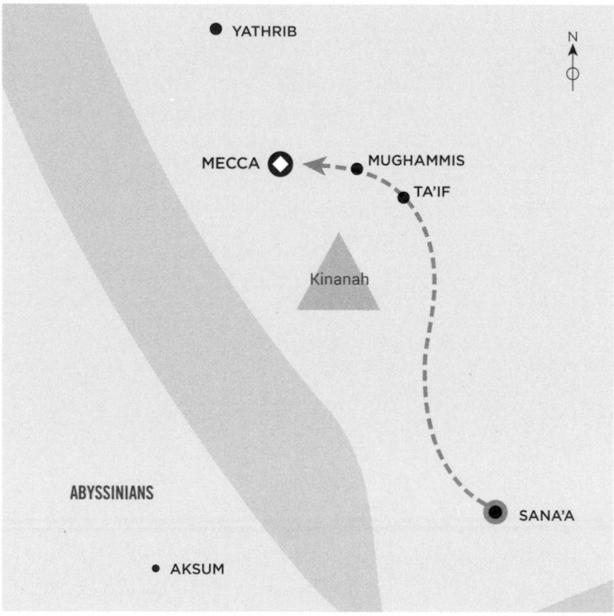

FIGURE P18. ABRAHA'S ROUTE TO MECCA

In the year 570 CE, Abraha marched 500 miles north to Mecca with an army of up to 60,000 troops and 9 to 13 elephants. He first stopped in Ta'if, then turned west toward Mecca traveling through the outlying town of Mughammis. Abraha's unsuccessful attempt to destroy the Ka'bah is chronicled in Surah Al Feel.

After Abraha's defeat, the Yemeni Arabs, backed by Persian forces, overthrew their Abyssinian rulers and established a Persian governorship in Yemen. Back in Mecca, the miraculous victory over Abraha's army further highlighted the widespread regard that the rest of the Arabs held for the Quraysh as the *People of God*.

---

⑪ WHAT DID ABRAHA'S FAILED INVASION DO FOR THE QURAYSH? YUSUF

"[This was] an extremely significant year for the Arabs. After that, the Quraysh were called by the other Arabs, 'the people of Allah.' In other words, their respect went way up. 'Don't mess with Quraysh!' That was the message to the other Arabs. 'These are special people and they live in a special place, and don't mess with them!' That was the message to the rest of the Arabs."[14]

'Abd al-Muttalib's son, 'Abd Allah, never witnessed Abraha's miraculous defeat as he was on a trading expedition to Syria and Palestine. On the way home, 'Abd Allah fell seriously ill in Yathrib and died shortly thereafter. Back in Mecca, the news of his death was especially difficult for his young bride Aminah, who was expecting their first child. If there was any comfort to be found in the few remaining months leading up to her delivery, perhaps it came from a voice she heard, telling her to name the baby *Muhammad* (the praiseworthy).

PROLOGUE 4: MUHAMMAD BEFORE REVELATION

P4.1 EARLY CHILDHOOD

The Quraysh held a special regard for the nomadic lifestyle of the Bedouin Arabs, and customarily entrusted their boys to the care of Bedouin foster-families. They believed that Bedouins lived a freer, healthier, and nobler lifestyle, in contrast to city-dwellers who were unnaturally confined to places of sickness, sloth, greed, and decline:

> A high level of solidarity is needed for success in the life of the desert, and that is linked up with a high level of respect for personality and appreciation of human worth. In the furnace of the desert the dross of inferior attitudes and actions was burned out and the pure gold left of a high morality, a high code and tradition of human relationships, and a high level of human excellence.[1]

---

1 WHAT CAN BE LEARNED FROM THE NOMADIC LIFESTYLE?   `RAMADAN`

"For nomads, forever on the move, finitude in space is allied to a sense of freedom blended, here again, with the experience of fleetingness, vulnerability, and humility... Such is the experience of the believer's life, which the Prophet was later to describe to young Abdullah ibn Umar in terms reminiscent of this dimension: 'Be in this world as if you were a stranger or wayfarer.' "[2] (Ramadan citing Bukhari)

---

2 WHAT CAN BE LEARNED FROM THE NATURAL WORLD?   `RAMADAN`

"This relationship with nature was so present in the Prophet's life from his earliest childhood that one can easily come to the conclusion that living close to nature, observing, understanding, and respecting it, is an imperative of deep faith.
... [B]eing close to nature, respecting what it is, and observing and meditating on what it shows us, offers us, or takes (back) from us requirements of a faith that, in its quest, attempts to feed, deepen, and renew itself. Nature is the primary guide and the intimate companion of faith.
Far removed from the formalism of soulless religious rituals, this sort of education, in and through its closeness to nature, fosters a relationship to the divine based on contemplation and depth that will later make it possible, in a second phase of spiritual education.
Cut off from nature in our towns and cities, we nowadays seem to have forgotten the meaning of this message to such an extent that we dangerously invert the order of requirements and believe that learning about the techniques and forms of religion (prayers, pilgrimages, etc.) is sufficient to grasp and understand their meaning and objectives. This delusion has serious consequences since it leads to draining religious teaching of its spiritual substance, which actually ought to be at its heart."[3]

PRACTICALITY: THE RELIGION OF THE NOMAD   `ASLAN`

3

"The nomadic lifestyle is one that requires a religion to address immediate concerns: Which god can lead us to water? Which god can heal our illnesses?"[4]

The clan of Sa'd ibn Bakr was part of the great Hawazin tribe that controlled the city of Ta'if and the central Hijaz. Halimah bint Abi Dhu'ayb and her husband Harith ibn 'Abd al-'Uzzah belonged to this desert community and had come to Mecca looking for a nursling to take back with them. They were the poorest from their clan and were unable to persuade a single Qurayshi family to entrust them to care for their child. In an equally desperate situation, Aminah could not find any Bedouin foster-couple willing to take care of her orphaned son, Muhammad.

Halimah knew that a young widow like Aminah could not afford her services, but agreed to take Muhammad because she did not want to return to her people empty-handed. Her decision proved to change the young couple's life, as the boy's presence soon brought numerous blessings to their household.

---

4 **WHY WOULD HALIMAH TAKE AN ORPHAN?**   YUSUF

"Halimah says to her husband, as they're about to leave, 'Why don't we just take this orphan?' This is amazing because her name 'Halimah' means someone who shows concern and compassion for others. This is definitely part of her nature. There was no material gain here but she recognizes, 'We're being charitable and maybe we'll get some *ihsan* [something better, blessing] from Allah.' She has a pure intention."[5]

Halimah and Harith lovingly raised Muhammad as their own son, and would regularly return to Mecca to let Aminah see her son's progress. After several years in the desert, Halimah returned to Mecca to tell Aminah about a miraculous incident involving the little boy. The Prophet later narrated the incident from his early childhood:

> *"Two men in white clothes came to me with a golden basin full of snow. They took me and split open my body, then they took my heart and split it open and took out from it a black clot which they flung away. Then they washed my heart and my body with that snow until they made them pure..."*[6]

This is not the last time the Prophet encountered the people of Sa'd ibn Bakr. Sixty years later, following the Conquest of Mecca and the Battle of Hunayn, he will rekindle several relationships from his earliest childhood days (QY 20.8).

Aminah had been apart from her son for three to four years and now decided to keep him in Mecca, where he grew up around his new playmates Hamzah and Safiyyah.

Hamzah and Safiyyah were the children of 'Abd al-Muttalib and Halah, who married the same day as 'Abd Allah and Aminah (Fig. P12).

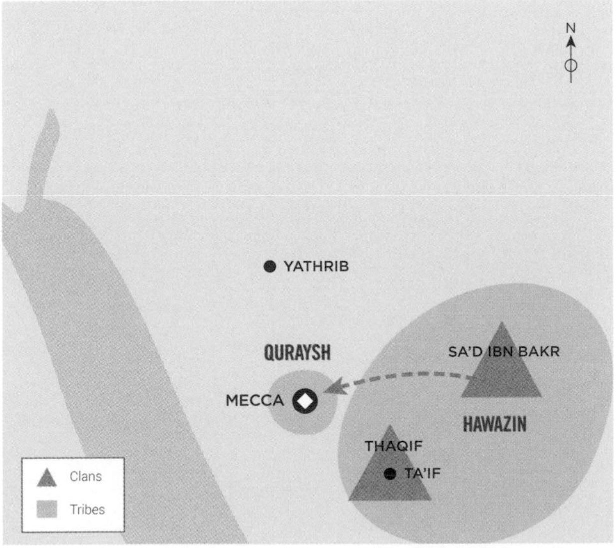

FIGURE P19. HALIMAH COMES FROM SA'D IBN BAKR

Halimah was from the Hawazin clan of Sa'd ibn Bakr. Like the Quraysh, the Hawazin were 'Adnanian Arabs (Fig. P4) who had settled east of Mecca.

Recall that 'Abd al-Muttalib (aka Shayba) left Yathrib for Mecca after losing his father, Hashim, in Gaza. The boy was welcomed into the city by his uncle Muttalib, and later rose to prominence in Mecca. Decades later, 'Abd al-Muttalib welcomed his orphaned grandson Muhammad who just like himself, entered Mecca under the guardianship of his extended family.

In the next several years **Fatimah bint Asad** will give birth to some of Muhammad's closest companions, including Ja'far, 'Ali, and Umm Hani. Fatimah will later become one of Prophet Muhammad's earliest supporters.

At the age of six, Muhammad traveled to Yathrib with his mother to visit their Khazraji relatives. In Yathrib he enjoyed the company of his distant kinsmen and learned how to swim and fly kites. The happy memories, however, were interrupted on the return journey, when Aminah fell ill and passed away in the town of Abwa'. Twice orphaned, Muhammad returned to Mecca where his adoring grandfather, 'Abd al-Muttalib, was waiting to take care of him.

'Abd al-Muttalib was inseparable from young Muhammad, and took him everywhere he went. In fact, he would take his grandson to nap in the Hijr where none of his sons and grandsons dared venture. The remarkable relationship however, was short lived. Two years after Aminah's death, 'Abd al-Muttalib passed away at age 81.

Before he died, 'Abd al-Muttalib entrusted Muhammad's guardianship to 'Abd Allah's full brother—Abu Talib. He and his wife Fatimah bint Asad loved their nephew dearly, leaving little doubt in the boy's mind that they sacrificed for him as much, if not more than their own children.

---

5 **WHAT DID IT MEAN TO BE AN ORPHAN FROM THE CLAN OF HASHIM?** [WATT]

"In the old nomadic way of life it had been understood that the head of a clan or family had a certain responsibility for the weaker members. But at Mecca in a mad scramble for more wealth every man was looking after his own interests and disregarding the responsibilities formerly recognized. Muhammad's guardians saw that he did not starve to death, but it was difficult for them to do more for him, especially as the fortunes of the clan of Hashim seem to have been declining at this time."[7]

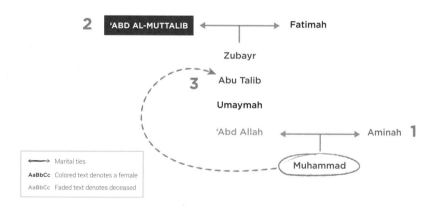

FIGURE P20. GUARDIANS OF MUHAMMAD

'Abd Allah never lived to see the birth of his son. After the death of Aminah, 'Abd al-Muttalib took care of his grandson, preferring him over his own sons and other grandsons. Two years later, after his grandfather's death, Muhammad moved into the house of Abu Talib—his father's full brother.

P4.2 MUHAMMAD'S TEENS & THE PACT OF CHIVALRY

'Abd al-Muttalib did not leave his children much inheritance when he died. His son Abu Talib was not nearly as well off as Abu Lahab and his other brothers. Therefore it was necessary for young Muhammad to help support his uncle's family by herding sheep along the hills surrounding Mecca.

At the age of 12, Muhammad accompanied his uncle on a commercial caravan to Syria. As the men neared the city of Bostra, a Christian monk named Bahira observed that the clouds seemed to follow the approaching caravan, shading it from the intense sunlight. When the men stopped to rest, Bahira was amazed to see a tree move to shade the mysterious travelers. He was determined to find out if there was someone special traveling with the caravan, and invited the entire group to dine with him that day.

According to sacred manuscripts that had been passed down from earlier generations, Bahira knew of several telltale marks of prophethood. He carefully studied the faces of his guests, but could not identify the face of a prophet. He asked if anyone from the party had been excluded, and they admitted to leaving their youngest boy behind to safeguard their camels and cargo. Upon Bahira's request, the men sent for Muhammad, and Bahira quickly recognized him as the much-anticipated Arabian prophet. Before the party departed, Bahira urged Abu Talib to take care of his nephew and protect him from evil.

---

6 **THE BIRTHS OF DAVID, JESUS, AND MUHAMMAD**   ASLAN

"The story of the pregnant Amina is remarkably similar to the Christian story of Mary, who when pregnant with Jesus, heard the angel of the Lord declare, 'You will be with child and will give birth to a son, and you are to give him the name Jesus. He will be great and will be called the Son of the Most High' (Luke 1:31-32). The story of Bahira resembles the Jewish story of Samuel, who, when told by God that one of Jesse's sons would be the next king of Israel, invited the entire family to a feast in which the youngest son, David, was left behind to tend the sheep. 'Send for him,' Samuel demanded when the rest of Jesse's sons were rejected. 'We will not sit down until he arrives.' The moment David entered the room, he was anointed king (1 Samuel 16:1-13)

...What matters is what these stories say about our prophets, our messiahs, our kings: that theirs is a holy and eternal vocation, established by God from the moment of creation."[8]

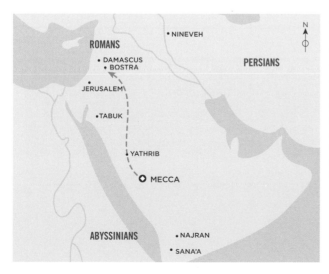

FIGURE P21. THE ROUTE FROM MECCA TO BOSTRA

Young Muhammad accompanied his uncle Abu Talib on a northbound trading caravan through Bostra, where a Christian monk named Bahira met the boy and confirmed his suspicion that Muhammad was the Arabian Prophet he had been expecting.

For most of his early childhood, Muhammad led the solitary life of a shepherd. As he grew older he began some military training and excelled in archery like his great ancestor Ishmael.

---

7 A NEARLY INSURMOUNTABLE CHILDHOOD `RAMADAN`

"At the age of eight, young Muhammad had experienced fatherlessness, poverty, solitude, and the death of his mother and then of his grandfather ... As a shepherd, young Muhammad learned solitude, patience, contemplation, and watchfulness."[9]

Muhammad was approximately 20 years old at the time. Al-Mubarakpuri states that he did not fight in these battles, but only collected arrows for the Quraysh.

During Muhammad's teens, there was an ongoing intertribal skirmish known as *Harb al-Hijar* (The Sacrilegious War) because it started during one of the four sacred months when violence was strictly prohibited (see Appendix A). The Quraysh were not directly involved in the dispute, but were pulled into the fighting because of a pre-existing intertribal alliance. The war lasted several years, during which Muhammad was praised for his valor.

The Sacrilegious War was yet another example of the endless cycle of retaliation in Arabia. The costs were high and it was becoming increasingly apparent to the Arabs that, unlike the surrounding empires, they had no regulated system of justice.

---

8 WHY DID THE ARABS RESORT TO RETRIBUTION? `ASLAN`

"In a society with no concept of an absolute morality as dictated by a divine code of ethics—a Ten Commandments, if you will—the Shaykh had only one legal recourse for maintaining order in his tribe: the Law of Retribution ... Yet far from being a barbaric legal system, the Law of Retribution was actually meant to limit barbarism."[10]

- -

9 CHIVALRY GONE BAD? `ARMSTRONG`

"Muruwah was an inspiring ideal, but by the end of the sixth century, its weaknesses were becoming tragically apparent. Tribal solidarity ('asbiyyah) encouraged bravery and selflessness, but only within the context of the tribe. There was no concept of universal human rights. He [tribal member] had no concern for outsiders, whom he regarded as worthless and expendable. If he had to kill them to benefit his own people, he felt no moral anguish and wasted no time in philosophical abstractions or ethical considerations."[11]

- -

10 ARABIA'S GANG CULTURE `YUSUF`

"They were really a nomadic people that had only recently settled. They didn't have a civilization like other people, and for that reason, their laws were not developed. They had pretty crude tribal laws. In a lot of ways, it is not that dissimilar from the laws of the street in some communities in America. In gang culture, the gang is tight, and a gang's members defend each other irrespective of whether they are right or wrong. This is a jahiliya phenomenon called *fa'ar* in the Arab tradition."[12]

Terms defined by Armstrong:
Badawah: Nomadic life
'Asbiyyah: Tribal solidarity
Hasab: Ancestral honor
Istighna': Haughty self-reliance
Muruwah: Chivalric code of courage, patience, and endurance

Shortly after the end of the Sacrilegious War, a visiting Yemeni merchant agreed to sell some of his goods to a local Meccan from the Confederate clan of Sahm. However, when the Meccan refused to pay the predetermined price, the visiting merchant had no legal recourse. Alone and helpless, he publicly challenged the Quraysh to arbitrate the matter. Muhammad's uncle, Zubayr ibn 'Abd al-Muttalib, heard the merchant's cry and conveyed his concern to the leaders of Quraysh.

---

(11) WHAT RIGHTS DID INDIVIDUALS HAVE OUTSIDE THE TRIBE? | ASLAN |

"Crimes committed against those outside the tribe were not only unpunished, they were not really crimes. Stealing, killing, or injuring another person was not considered a morally reprehensible act per se, and such acts were punished only if they weakened the stability of the tribe.
… It was often the case that an individual had no legal protection, no rights, and no social identity whatsoever outside his own tribe."[13]

THE QURAYSH

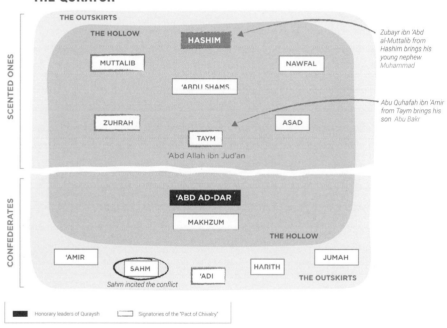

FIGURE P22. THE PACT OF CHIVALRY

The clan of Sahm had unjustly treated the visiting merchant. Not surprisingly, none of the Confederate clans supported the pact except for 'Adi (the clan of 'Umar ibn al-Khattab). 'Abdu Shams and Makhzum may have been on opposing sides of the rift, but they shared one thing in common: as the two wealthiest clans of Quraysh, both refused to change the status quo. Abu Bakr's clan of Taym was the first to respond to the cry for justice. Later, Abu Bakr will be the first (outside the Prophet's family) to respond to the Prophet's call to Islam.

Though the Quraysh may have wanted to appear united, tensions continued to run deep between the Confederates and Scented Ones. As expected, none of the Confederate clans spoke up to challenge Bani Sahm. Instead, a number of individuals among the Scented Ones felt compelled to resolve the matter. 'Abd Allah ibn Jud'an, a man from the clan of Taym, called an open meeting at his house to address the complaint and develop a code of justice. Only five of the 14 Quraysh clans accepted 'Abd Allah's invitation. The attendees agreed to a simple code of ethics—that each clan would stand for the oppressed, against the oppressor, regardless of who was oppressing.

---

12 **WHY DID THE QURAYSH LOSE THEIR BEDOUIN NOBILITY?** ARMSTRONG

"The old communal spirit had been torn apart by the market economy ... Instead of sharing their wealth generously, people were hoarding their money and building private fortunes ... The principles of muruwah [tribal ethic of chivalry] seemed incompatible with market forces, and many felt thrust into a spiritual limbo. The old ideals had not been replaced by anything of equal value, and the ingrained communal ethos told them that this rampant individualism would damage the tribe, which could only survive if its members pooled all their resources."[14]

The **Black Stone** (al Hajar al Aswad) is the eastern cornerstone of the Ka'bah, which Muslims believe fell from heaven when Adam and Eve were sent down from Paradise. Centuries later it was recovered by Abraham who used it to erect the Ka'bah with Ishmael.

After ratifying the Pact of Chivalry (Hilf al-Fudul), each dignitary pledged his allegiance by drinking from hallowed water poured over the Black Stone. Two teenagers sat among the adults and witnessed the important proceedings—Abu Bakr and his best friend, Muhammad. Many years later, the Prophet reflected on the occasion:

"I witnessed a confederacy in the house of 'Abdullah bin Jad'an. It was more appealing to me than herds of cattle. Even now in the period of Islam, I would respond positively to attending such a meeting if I were invited."[15]

---

13 **WAS THE PACT OF CHIVALRY BORN OUT OF ALTRUISM OR SURVIVAL?** WATT

"It aimed at upholding commercial integrity, but beyond this it was probably interested in preventing the exclusion of Yemenite merchants from the Meccan market, and the clans which formed it seem to have been those which were themselves incapable of sending caravans to the Yemen, or which had specialized trade between Mecca and Syria."[16]

- -

14 **WHAT WAS THE LASTING SIGNIFICANCE OF THE PACT OF CHIVALRY?** WATT

"It is unfortunate that we do not know more about the League of the Virtuous, since it seems to have played an important part in the life of Mecca, and in large part to have been directed against the men and policies to which Muhammad later found himself opposed. In particular his clan of Hashim came to have a leading role in the League of the Virtuous. Apart from the religious questions the political attitude of Hashim and the clans in alliance with it would make them tend to support Muhammad."[17]

15 HOW COULD THE PACT OF CHIVALRY ADDRESS THE ERODING BEDOUIN ETHIC? ASLAN

"The problem in Mecca was that the concentration of wealth in the hands of a few ruling families had not only altered the social and economical landscape of the city, it had effectively destroyed the tribal ethic. The sudden tide of personal wealth in Mecca had swept away tribal ideals of social egalitarianism. No longer was there any concern for the poor and marginalized; no longer was the tribe only as strong as its weakest members. The Shaykhs of Quraysh had become far more interested in maintaining the apparatus of trade than in caring for the dispossessed.
How could the Law of Retribution function properly when one party in a dispute was so wealthy and so powerful as to be virtually untouchable?"[18]

- -

16 WHAT CAN WE LEARN FROM THE PACT OF CHIVALRY? ASLAN

"This implies acknowledging the act of laying out those principles is prior to and transcends belonging to Islam, because in fact Islam and its message came to confirm the substance of a treaty that human conscience had already independently formulated.
...[T]he Prophet clearly acknowledges the validity of adhering to principles of justice and defending the oppressed, regardless of whether those principles come from inside Islam or outside it.
...The third teaching is a direct consequence of this reflection: the message of Islam is by no means a closed value system at a variance or conflicting with other value systems.
...Islam does not establish a closed universe of reference but rather relies on a set of universal principles that can coincide with the fundamentals and values of other beliefs and religious traditions. Islam is a message of justice that entails resisting oppression and protecting the dignity of the oppressed and the poor, and Muslims must recognize the moral value of a law or contract stipulating this requirement, whoever its authors and whatever the society, Muslim or not."[19]

- -

17 WHAT CAN WE LEARN FROM THE PACT OF CHIVALRY? YUSUF

"This is an indication that Muslims should be on the side of the truth even if it is coming from non-Muslims. It teaches the Muslim that we should not be in a jahili framework. A Muslim must stand up for the truth and not support a fellow Muslim against a Jew or a Christian when it's clearly the case that the Jew or the Christian is oppressed and the Muslim is oppressing.'
...This is a radical change from the psychology of the Arab. And the Prophet, God's peace and blessings upon him, is letting us know that Islam is no different. 'Don't make the Muslims into a tribe where you take vengeance for your Muslim brother if he is an oppressor against an oppressed.' There are some really interesting stories in the sirah literature about the Prophet, God's peace and blessings upon him, supporting the non-Muslim against the Muslim."[20]

P4.3 MUHAMMAD'S TWENTIES

Abu Talib had several sons by now
including Talib (20s), 'Aqil (13), and
Ja'far (4). His daughters included
'Atika, Bara, and Fakhitah. Fakhitah
(better known as Umm Hani) will
remain a close friend of the Prophet
throughout his lifetime and will be
the first to hear about his miraculous
Night Journey (QY 11.4).

The Qurayshi *clan* of Asad should
not be confused with the Arabian
tribe of Asad which settled northeast
of Mecca. For the remainder of the
book, *Asad* will refer to the Qurayshi
clan unless otherwise specified.

It is possible that **Nestor** was a
Nestorian Christian. Nestorians
believed that Jesus had both human
and God-like natures that were
distinct entities in the same person.

By his mid-20s, Muhammad had become fairly involved in the caravan business
and was soon asked to take full charge of other merchants' goods. When
Muhammad reached financial independence, he asked Abu Talib for permission
to marry his daughter, Fakhitah. Abu Talib declined and, rather than limit her
prospects to the poorer clan of Hashim, married his daughter to his maternal
cousin Hubayrah ibn Abi Wahb from the wealthy clan of Makhzum.

Meanwhile, Khadijah bint Khuwaylid (from the Quraysh clan of Asad) arranged
for Muhammad to take charge of her caravan to Syria. He was paid twice the usual
rate and given a young servant named Maysarah for the trip. They stopped at
Bostra, where another Christian monk, Nestor, observed Muhammad and confided
in Maysarah that the young merchant was destined to be a prophet. Nestor
believed that Muhammad was the fulfillment of the prophecy of Shiloh:

> And Jacob called unto his sons and said, Gather yourselves together, that I
> may tell you that which shall befall you in the last days. ... The scepter shall
> not depart from Judah, nor a lawgiver from between his feet, until Shiloh
> come; and unto him shall the gathering of the people be. — *Genesis 49:1,10*

---

18 **DID THE PROPHECY OF SHILOH REFER TO JESUS OR MUHAMMAD?** `YUSUF`

"Although the Christians interpret Shiloh to mean Christ, if you look at the verses in
Genesis, Jacob is a prophet from Bani Israel foretelling of a prophet who will not be
from Bani Israel. The verse doesn't make any sense if it is Jesus because Jesus is a
direct descendant of Dawud [David] according to their own tradition. Jesus is from
the children of Jacob, and so he does not fit into this category."[21]

Upon returning to Mecca, Maysarah told Khadijah about Nestor's prediction.
Khadijah approached her cousin Waraqah, who corroborated the monk's
premonition. She also consulted her friend Nufaysah about marrying a man 15
years younger than her. When Nufaysah approached Muhammad with Khadijah's
proposal, he welcomed the offer, and soon after, Khadijah spoke to Muhammad directly:

> *"Son of mine uncle, I love thee for thy kinship with me, and for that thou art ever
> in the center, not being a partisan amongst the people for this or for that; and
> I love thee for thy trustworthiness and for the beauty of thy character and the
> truth of thy speech."*[22]

---

19 **WAS KHADIJAH REALLY 15 YEARS OLDER THAN MUHAMMAD?** `WATT`

"The age of Khadijah has perhaps been exaggerated. The names of seven children
whom she bore to Muhammad are mentioned in the sources ... Even if, as Ibn Sa'd's
authorities say, they came at regular intervals, that would make her forty-eight
before the last was born. This is by no means impossible, but one would have
thought it sufficiently unusual to merit comment; it is even the sort of thing that
might well have been treated as miraculous. Yet no single word of comment occurs
in the pages of Ibn Hisham, Ibn Sa'd, or at-Tabari."[23]

The clans of Hashim and Asad had several preexisting ties, most recently was the marriage of Hamzah's sister, Safiyyah, to Khadijah's brother, 'Awwam. Naturally, Hamzah was chosen to accompany his 25-year-old nephew to Khadijah's uncle's house to officially ask for her hand in marriage.

Prior to his marriage, Muhammad had inherited a servant from his father named Barakah. On his wedding day to Khadijah, Muhammad freed Barakah so that she could marry a man from Yathrib.

Khadijah also had a servant at the time—a 15-year-old boy named Zayd ibn Harithah—whom she gave to Muhammad as a wedding gift. Zayd was from the northern tribe of Kalb, between Syria and Iraq, where he had been abducted and sold into servitude. Shortly after the marriage, Zayd encountered visiting pilgrims from Bani Kalb and sent word to his family that he was safe and happy in Mecca. Upon hearing the news, his father Harithah ibn Sharahil came to Mecca to pay for Zayd's freedom. Muhammad empathized with the boy's father, but when he told Zayd he was free to return to his family, Zayd replied:

> *"I would not choose any man in preference to thee. Thou art unto me as my father and mother ... I have seen from this man such things that I could never choose another above him."*

Barakah later had a son named Ayman, and was thereafter known as Umm Ayman. Several years later, she will marry Zayd and become the mother of Usama ibn Zayd.

---

20 **WHAT DID IT MEAN TO BE A SLAVE IN ARABIA?**   WATT

"The attitude of the Qur'an to slavery is not unlike that of the New Testament. Both accept the fact of slavery and do something to mitigate it...
There were obvious advantages in removing slaves far from their original region. On the whole, however, slaves seem to have been well treated. Despite their inferior status they had a recognized position in the family and clan, and shared to a large extent in its good fortune and bad fortune ... The freedmen (muwali) also stuck closely to their patrons, on whom they were dependent for protection according to the pre-Islamic security system. Zayd b. Harithah, after receiving his freedom, chose to remain with Muhammad rather than return to his own family."[24]

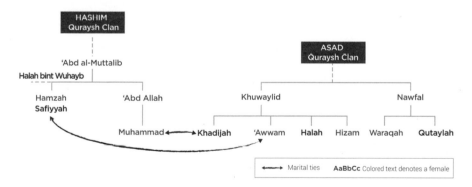

FIGURE P23. KHADIJAH MARRIES MUHAMMAD

Recall that Khadijah's first-cousin Qutaylah had seen a radiance in Muhammad's father, 'Abd Allah, and sought to marry him the day he was set to marry Aminah (P 2.3). Khadijah's brother 'Awwam married Hamzah's sister, Safiyyah. It comes as no surprise then that Hamzah accompanied Muhammad when he made his official proposal to Khadijah's uncle, 'Amr ibn Asad.

After hearing those words, Muhammad invited Zayd's father and uncle to join him at the Ka'bah, where he publicly proclaimed:

> *"All ye who are present, bear witness that Zayd is my son; I am his heir and he is mine."*[25]

From that day, Zayd ibn Harithah became known as *Zayd ibn Muhammad*. He remained in Mecca with his adoptive father, and Harithah returned home without any bitterness in his heart.

㉑ AS A PROPHET, SHOULD MUHAMMAD HAVE DONE MORE TO ABOLISH SLAVERY? `WATT`

"The critics may say that, in view of his political power towards the end of his life, Muhammad could have done more to alleviate the lot of the slaves. Such a criticism rests on a false appreciation of the situation in which he found himself. There were many things which urgently required to be set right but this was not one of them. On the whole the slaves were not too badly treated. The chief disability in being a slave was that one could not of one's own will leave the group to which one was attached. In the Arabia of the early seventh century, however, this was much less of a disadvantage than it would be in a more individualistic society. Though the connexion of Islam with the rise of individualism has been emphasized throughout this study of the life of Muhammad, it should also be realized that individualism was only at its beginnings."[26]

FIGURE P24. HARITHAH COMES FROM BANI KALB

When Zayd ibn Harithah was a child, he was kidnapped from his tribe of Bani Kalb. He was later purchased by Khadijah's nephew Hakim ibn Hizam, and subsequently given to Khadijah as a servant. Upon hearing that his son was in Mecca, Zayd's father, Harithah ibn Sharahil, traveled to Mecca to find his son. Upon Harithah's arrival, Zayd was given the option of returning to his family or remaining in Mecca under the care of Muhammad. Zayd chose the latter.

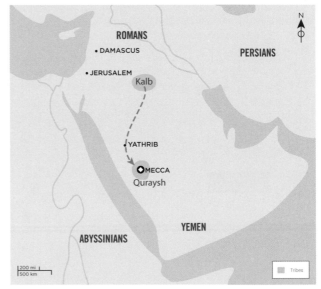

P4.4 MUHAMMAD'S THIRTIES

Over the next several years, Muhammad and Khadijah had six children: Qasim—who died before he was two, Zaynab, Ruqayyah, Umm Kulthum, Fatimah, and 'Abd Allah—who died in infancy.

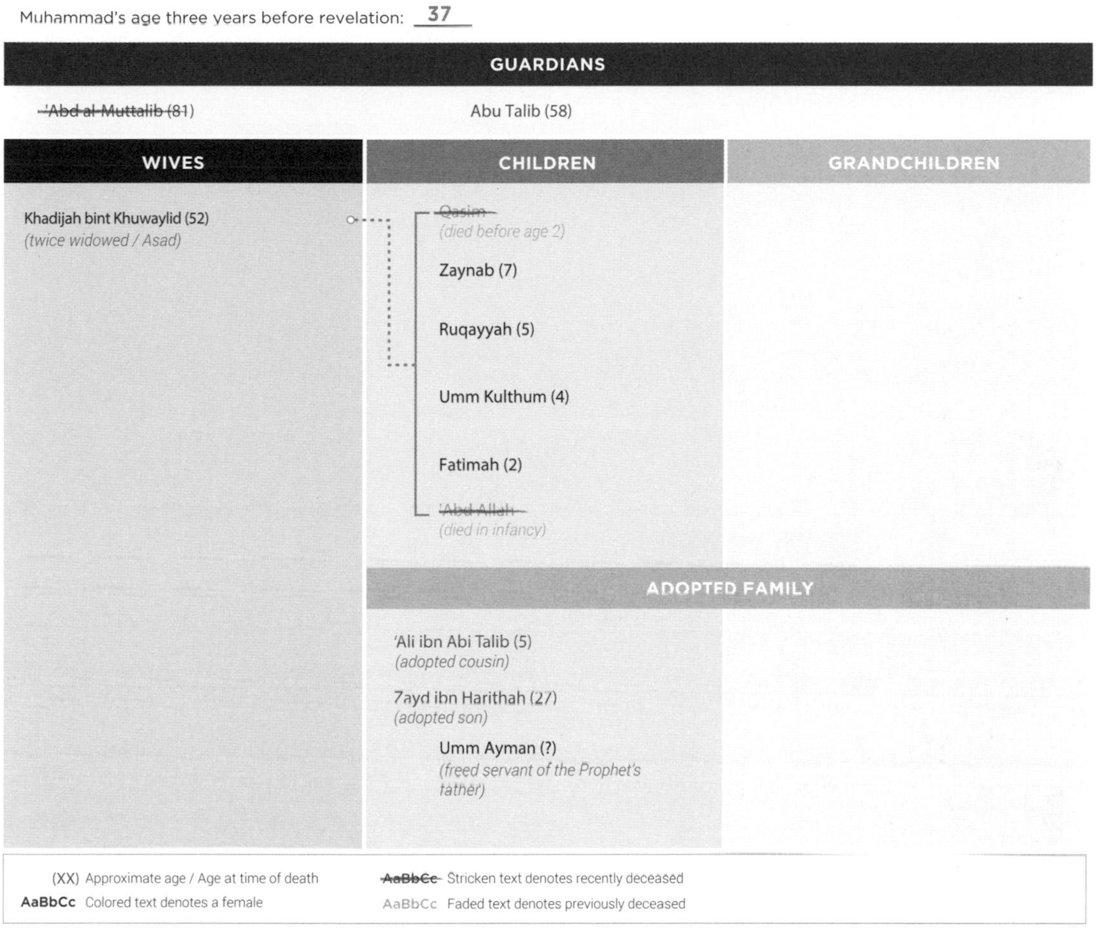

Muhammad's age three years before revelation: __37__

GUARDIANS		
~~'Abd al-Muttalib (81)~~	Abu Talib (58)	

WIVES	CHILDREN	GRANDCHILDREN
Khadijah bint Khuwaylid (52) *(twice widowed / Asad)*	~~Qasim~~ *(died before age 2)*	
	Zaynab (7)	
	Ruqayyah (5)	
	Umm Kulthum (4)	
	Fatimah (2)	
	~~'Abd Allah~~ *(died in infancy)*	

ADOPTED FAMILY	
'Ali ibn Abi Talib (5) *(adopted cousin)*	
Zayd ibn Harithah (27) *(adopted son)*	
Umm Ayman (?) *(freed servant of the Prophet's father)*	

(XX) Approximate age / Age at time of death	~~AaBbCc~~ Stricken text denotes recently deceased
AaBbCc Colored text denotes a female	AaBbCc Faded text denotes previously deceased

FIGURE P25. MUHAMMAD'S HOUSEHOLD BEFORE REVELATION

Ever since 'Abd al-Muttalib's death at 81 years of age, Muhammad was under the watchful guardianship of his uncle Abu Talib. At the age of 25, Muhammad married Khadijah who bore him six children, of which only four daughters survived. Despite his first son's untimely death, Muhammad was well known in Mecca as Abu l-Qasim (the father of Qasim).

In a way, the Prophet's two sons were replaced by two others. Zayd was approximately 10 years younger than the Prophet and was much older than the rest of the children. 'Ali was adopted as a young child and was about the same age as Ruqayyah.

Given her close relationship with the Prophet, Umm Ayman is also included in the diagram above. She was 'Abd Allah's servant who continued to serve in the Prophet's household. After Muhammad's marriage, Umm Ayman left to marry a man from Yathrib, only to return for unclear reasons.

By the turn of the seventh century, Abu Talib was struggling to support his large family. Muhammad approached his uncle 'Abbas, and suggested that they each take charge of one of Abu Talib's children. Ja'far, 15, went to live with 'Abbas. 'Ali, who was no older than five, went to live with Muhammad, whose household now consisted of Khadijah, Zayd, Zaynab, Ruqayyah, Umm Kulthum, Fatimah, and 'Ali.

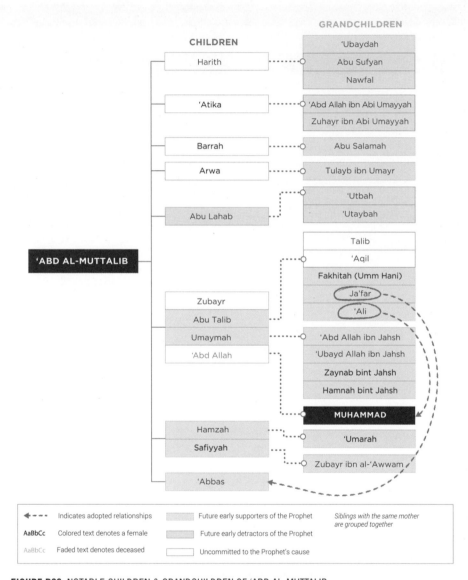

FIGURE P26. NOTABLE CHILDREN & GRANDCHILDREN OF 'ABD AL-MUTTALIB

'Abd al-Muttalib's descendants represent some of the most preeminent individuals in the Sirah. During the Early Meccan Period, Muhammad's first revelations divided his extended family into supporters, detractors, and onlookers. The figure above also shows how the guardianship of Ja'far and 'Ali were transferred to 'Abbas and Muhammad.

Khadijah was keen on marrying her daughters to suitable men from the family, so when her eldest daughter, Zaynab, came of age, Khadijah arranged her marriage to her favorite nephew, Abu l-'As ibn ar-Rabi'. As for Ruqayyah and Umm Kulthum, Abu Lahab had high expectations that his nephew would be the leader of the next generation and approached Muhammad on behalf of his sons 'Utbah and 'Utaybah. Muhammad and Khadijah agreed to both engagements.

Although **Abu l-'As ibn ar-Rabi'** will not embrace Islam until after the Battle of Badr (over 14 years later), he will remain loyal to his wife and in-laws when they face intense persecution at the hands of the Quraysh during the Early and Late Meccan periods.

---

22 **WHAT WAS THE SIGNIFICANCE OF ABU LAHAB'S PROPOSALS?**   YUSUF

"There is a recognition in Bani Hashim now that the Prophet, God's peace and blessings upon him, is a leader, even though he is not somebody who is asking for this position. He did not rally Bani Hashim or intend to take leadership of the Quraysh. However, they all recognize that there is something extraordinary about this person: the sagacity of his intellect, his wisdom, the eloquence of his speech, though he spoke very little. Everyone recognized that he had an eloquence that was unmatched in Quraysh.

Abu Lahab obviously tries to get in, because to marry his children to the daughters of the Prophet, God's peace and blessings upon him, will benefit him, since in their culture, one marries also for social positioning."[27]

Around this time, Barakah—'Abd Allah's servant whom Muhammad had inherited and freed—returned to Mecca without her husband. Muhammad warmly accepted her back into his household as she was the only living connection he had to his father.

Although **Barakah** (Umm Ayman) is several years older than Zayd, the Prophet soon encourages the two to marry. Their son Usamah will become a pivotal member of the Prophet's growing family in Medina.

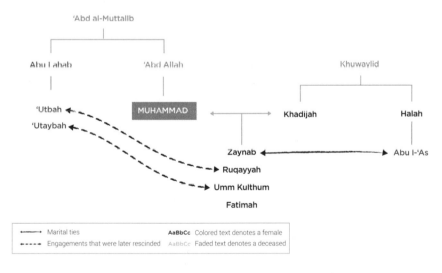

FIGURE P27. MUHAMMAD'S SONS-IN-LAW

Abu Lahab approached Muhammad seeking to bring their families together. He later rescinded the offer after Muhammad began preaching in Mecca. Meanwhile, Zaynab was married to Khadijah's nephew, Abu l-'As.

Recall that 'Abd al-Muttalib and his eldest son **Harith** had uncovered the well of Zamzam several years ago. Despite their childhood friendship, Harith's son Abu Sufyan will oppose the Prophet for most of his life.

There are two **Abu Sufyans** in the Sirah, and both opposed the Prophet until the Conquest of Mecca. The other, more recognized individual, Abu Sufyan ibn al-Harb, was from the clan of 'Abdu Shams and will be the Prophet's main rival for most of his life. You can remember the latter by thinking *Harb* caused the most *harm* to the Prophet.

Aside from his nuclear family, Muhammad enjoyed the support of his close relatives. One of his closest friends was his first cousin Abu Sufyan ibn al-Harith, son of 'Abd al-Muttalib's eldest son, Harith (Fig. P26). Not only was Abu Sufyan similar in age and likeness to Muhammad—the two were foster brothers nursed by Halimah.

Another group of close relatives included Muhammad's four beloved cousins from his paternal aunt Umaymah. She had married a man from the distant tribe of Asad named Jahsh ibn Ri'ab. Although Jahsh was not a Qurayshi, he was given honorary membership by the clan of 'Abdu Shams when he settled in Mecca. Throughout their childhood, the Jahsh children formed a close bond with their first cousin, Muhammad.

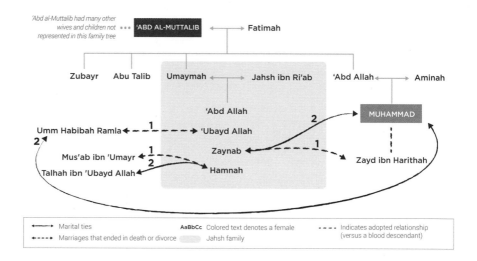

FIGURE P28. THE JAHSH FAMILY

The Jahsh family played a significant role during Muhammad's prophethood. All four children supported the Prophet during the first years of revelation, and continue to reappear throughout the Sirah. 'Abd Allah and 'Ubayd Allah were two of the first migrants to Abyssinia. 'Abd Allah was named after Muhammad's father. 'Ubayd Allah was a Christian prior to converting to Islam. He married Abu Sufyan ibn al-Harb's daughter Umm Habibah and later died in Abyssinia. After 'Ubayd Allah's death, Umm Habibah married the Prophet as his ninth wife.

Upon the Prophet's advice, Zaynab bint Jahsh reluctantly married Zayd. They divorced several years later and she married the Prophet as his seventh wife. Meanwhile, Zaynab's sister Hamnah married two of the Prophet's closest Companions (she married Talhah after the death of Mus'ab).

In the years before revelation, the Quraysh decided to rebuild the Ka'bah. Walid ibn al-Mughirah, the newest chief of Makhzum, was one of the men who took the lead in removing its stones. When it came to rebuilding the foundation, the nobles of Quraysh began to argue over who should have the honor of setting the sacred Black Stone in its proper place.

They finally agreed that the next man who entered the sanctuary should arbitrate the matter. By his mid-30s, Muhammad had earned the title of *Al-Ameen* (the trustworthy) for his reputation as one of the most honest and upright men in Mecca:

> The Prophet was distinguished among his people for his modesty, virtuous behavior and graceful manners. He proved himself to be the ideal of manhood, and to possess a spotless character. He was the most obliging to his compatriots, the most honest in talk and the mildest in temper. He was the most gentle-hearted, chaste, and hospitable. He always impressed people by his piety-inspiring expressions. He was the most truthful and the best to keep covenant. His fellow citizens gave him the title of Al-Ameen.[28]

Not surprisingly, when Muhammad entered the premises, the Meccan chiefs were happy to let Al-Ameen arbitrate the matter. After listening to all sides of the debate, Muhammad decided that the stone should be placed on a cloak and raised by all. Once it was lifted to the correct level, he would position it himself. They agreed with his decision and supported him as he set the stone in its appropriate place.

---

23 HOW WAS MUHAMMAD A UNIFIER? | YUSUF |

"This characteristic feature of his [Muhammad's] mind was to be often illustrated by his ability to maintain the first Muslim community's unity despite the presence of very strong personalities with widely differing temperaments ... teach the heart not to give way to proud emotions and arrogant thinking; bring the mind to heart-soothing solutions that make it possible to control oneself gently and wisely."[29]

EARLY MECCA

———

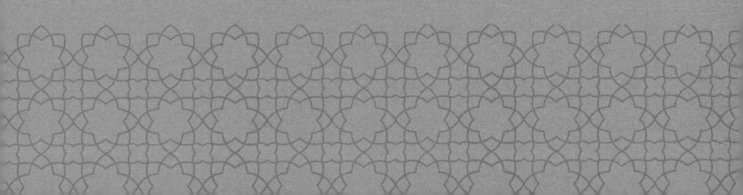

PROPHETIC CHARACTER

◆

Al-Hasan ibn Ali narrated that al-Hussain ibn Ali said: "I inquired from my father regarding the conduct of the Prophet (peace be upon him) with his company. He replied, 'The Messenger of Allah (peace be upon him) maintained a cheerful countenance and he was easy mannered. He was soft-natured; neither rude nor harsh, and neither stone-hearted nor loud or offensive in his speech. He did not mention the faults of anything and he was not narrow-minded or argumentative. If he heard or saw something he disliked he would turn his attention away as if he did not notice it. He did not make people fall into despair or feel disheartened, and he did not respond negatively to the requests that he disliked. He refrained from three traits related to himself: stubbornness in arguments (in some versions: pretension), excessiveness (in some versions: pride), and that which did not concern him. He refrained from three traits related to people: he did not disgrace or insult anyone, nor look for the hidden faults of others; he only spoke that from which reward was hoped.

———

When he spoke, those present bowed their heads in such a manner, as if birds were perched upon them. When he was silent, the others would begin speaking. They would not dispute in his presence regarding anything and whenever a person spoke to him the others would keep quiet and listen until he would finish. They would speak in order (i.e. the first person to arrive would be the first person to speak and so forth). When those around him laughed due to some reason, he would laugh as well and he would show surprise at the things that surprised the people. He exercised patience at the crude and indecent questions of the traveller and his companions would bring travellers to his assemblies. He used to say to his companions, 'When you see a person in need, always help that person.' If someone praised him, he would detest it unless it came from someone, who in the process of giving thanks praised him. He did not interrupt someone speaking. However , if one exceeded the limits he would stop him or would get up and leave."

———

Taken from A Commentary on the Depiction of Prophet Muhammad,
by Imam al–Tirmidhi (#351)

YEAR 1: PRIVATE INVITATION

1.1 READ!

By his late 30s, Muhammad was accustomed to the Haneef practice of extended meditation known as *tahannuth*:

> This meditative temperament helped to widen the mental gap between him and his compatriots. He used to provide himself with saweeq (barley porridge) and water and then directly head for the hills and ravines in the neighborhood of Makkah ... His heart was restless about the moral evils and idolatry that were widespread among his people; he was as yet helpless because no definitive course or specific approach had been available for him to follow.[1]

Be sure to review the **Qur'an Year** system in the Introduction before proceeding with the remainder of this book.

1   **WHAT IS THE ORIGIN OF "TAHANNUTH?"**   `WATT`

"The precise meaning and derivation of tahannuth is uncertain, though it is evidently some sort of devotional practice. The best suggestion is perhaps that of H. Hirschfeld that it comes from the Hebrew tehinnoth, meaning prayers for God's favour. The meaning may have been influenced by the Arabic root, however. Hinth is properly the violation of or failure to perform an oath, and so more generally sin; and tahannuth is accordingly said to mean 'doing some work so as to escape from sin or crime.' "[2]

2   **WHAT WAS MUHAMMAD RETREATING FROM?**   `RAMADAN`

"It was indeed a quest for truth: dissatisfied with the answers offered by those around him, driven by the intimate conviction that he must search further, he decided to isolate himself in contemplation."[3]

As he approached his 40th year, Muhammad had found success in his worldly affairs, but his achievements had not calmed the restlessness in his heart. He sought solace in the cave of Hira, less than three miles from the city-center, where he could search for meaning above the din of city life.

3   **WHAT WAS TROUBLING MUHAMMAD?**   `ASLAN`

"He seemed to be acutely aware of his complicity in Mecca's religio-economic system, which exploited the city's unprotected masses in order to maintain the wealth and power of the elite. For fifteen years he struggled with the incongruity between his lifestyle and his beliefs; by his fortieth year, he was an intensely troubled man."[4]

4   **MUHAMMAD DIAGNOSES THE MALAISE OF MECCA**   `ARMSTRONG`

"We know very little about these early years. But from his later career it is clear that he had accurately diagnosed the malaise that was particularly rife among the younger generation, who felt ill at ease in this aggressive market economy. The Quraysh had introduced class distinctions that were quite alien to the muruwah ideal ... They had abandoned the badawah virtue of generosity and become niggardly, except that they called this shrewd business sense ... Increasingly, it seemed to Muhammad that the Quraysh had jettisoned the best and retained only the worst aspects of muruwah: the recklessness, arrogance, and egotism that were morally destructive and could bring the city to ruin. He was convinced that social reform must be based on a new spiritual solution, or it would remain superficial."[5]

The archangels **Gabriel** and **Michael** are recognized in all three Abrahamic faiths. Gabriel is mentioned once in the Old Testament and once in the New Testament. In the Gospel of Luke, as in the Qur'an, Gabriel comes to Zachariah (Zakariya) and Mary (Maryam) to give news of the birth of John the Baptist (Yahya) and Jesus ('Isa) respectively. The Qu'ran says: "Whoever is an enemy to God, and His angels, and His messengers—and [especially to angels] Gabriel and Michael—then [let it be known that], most surely, God is an enemy to [all] the disbelievers." Al Baqarah (The Cow, 2:98)

Sometimes, as he hiked to the surrounding foothills, he would hear an unidentifiable voice greeting him with the words:

> *"Peace be on thee, O Messenger of God."* [6]

During one of his retreats, in the month of Ramadan in 610 CE, his years of searching are finally answered. While sitting in meditation, he is visited by the angel Gabriel (Jibreel), who appears to him on the horizon in the form of a man and commands him:

> *"Read!"*

Muhammad responds:

> *"I cannot read."*

---

5 DID MUHAMMAD ASPIRE TO BE A PROPHET? [SALAHI]

"Modern authors and biographers in particular have tried to show him trying to find a way out of the total darkness that enshrouded his people. This may bring us very close to saying that Muhammad was in search of an idea or a belief. This is true only in as much as it means that Muhammad rejected all beliefs which were known to him and were practised in Makkan society. He certainly did not aspire to the role that was later assigned to him. Addressing the Prophet, God says in the Qur'an: *'You had not entertained any hope that Scriptures would be given you, but this was an act of grace by Your Lord.'* " (Qur'an 28: 86)[7]

- -

6 HOW DID PROPHETHOOD BEGIN? [ASLAN]

"Obviously, no one but the Prophet can describe the experience of revelation, but it is neither irrational nor heretical to consider the attainment of prophetic consciousness to be a slowly evolving process."[8]

- -

7 WAS MUHAMMAD AN ILLITERATE PROPHET OR A PROPHET FOR THE ILLITERATE? [ASLAN]

"An-nabi al-ummi is traditionally understood as 'the unlettered Prophet.' But while Muhammad's illiteracy may enhance the miracle of the Quran, there is no historical justification for it. As Kenneth Cragg and many others have demonstrated, an-nabi al-ummi should more properly be understood as 'the Prophet for the unlettered' (that is, the Scripture-less), a translation consistent both with the grammar of the sentence and with Muhammad's view that the Quran is the Revelation for a people without a sacred book."[9]
"However, we never sent them any books to study nor any messengers to warn them before you, (Muhammad), and their predecessors (in the region) denied (their prophets, as well)."[Qur'an, 34:44]

≋ **SURAH AL 'ALAQ** (The Clinging Thing) is also known as Surah Iqra' (Read). It takes its name from the second verse, which details how humans are created from a single embryo. Of the surah's 19 verses, the first five verses were revealed here, while the remaining were sent down a short while after surahs Al Muzzamil (73) and Al Muddathir (74).

He later describes the experience:

> *"Once again he squeezed me and let go until I was exhausted. Then he said, 'Recite.' I said I cannot recite. He squeezed me for a third time and then let go of me and said:"*[10]

◇ Read in the name of your Lord Who created—created human beings from a clinging thing. Read, for your Lord is Most Generous. He taught with the pen; He taught human beings what they didn't know before. —*Al 'Alaq (The Clinging Thing, 96:1-5)*

The experience is physically and emotionally overwhelming, and he runs back to Khadijah crying:

"Cover me! Cover me!"

---

8 **WHAT DID IT MEAN TO TEACH THE ARABS WHAT THEY DIDN'T KNOW BEFORE?** ARMSTRONG

"It [revelation] identified the proud self-sufficiency of muruwah as a delusion, because humans are entirely dependent on God. ... Instead of approaching God in a spirit of prideful istighna', they must bow before Him like a lowly slave."[11]

---

9 **WHAT DID THE PROPHET FEEL IN THOSE FIRST MOMENTS?** YUSUF

"The angel takes the Prophet, God's peace and blessings upon him, and squeezes him until he thought his sides were going to burst. The ulema [scholars] say one of the indications of this is recognizing the difficulty of the Qur'an. The Qur'an is not an easy book. It's literally going to squeeze the *nafs* [self]. It's going to completely take you to a point where your nafs can't bear it anymore."[12]

---

10 **WHAT MUST IT HAVE FELT LIKE TO RECEIVE REVELATION?** ARMSTRONG

"Muhammad would have understood the German historian Rudolf Otto, who described the sacred as a mystery that was both *tremendum* and *fascinans*. It was overpowering, urgent, and terrible, but it also filled human beings with 'delight, joy, and a sense of swelling harmony and intimate intercourse.' Revelation cannot be described in a simple manner, and the complexity of his experience made Muhammad very cautious of telling anybody about it."[13]

---

11 **WAS KHADIJAH SURPRISED BY THE PROPHET'S REVELATION?** YUSUF

"She was aware that at some point, this was going to happen. This is what she has been waiting for. When he has doubts about the authenticity of his experience, she reminds him, 'You take care of the orphan. You look after the widow. You give charity to people in need. And you help the oppressed. How could your Lord abandon you?' "[14]

Terrified that he is possessed, the Prophet finds refuge with Khadijah who urges him not to doubt God's mercy. She reminds him that he is an extraordinary individual who has nothing to fear. The two approach Khadijah's cousin Waraqah, who confirms Muhammad's prophethood and warns:

"I wish I were younger. I wish I could live up to the time when your people would turn you out ... Anyone who came with something similar to what you have brought was treated with hostility: and if I should be alive till that day, then I would support you strongly."[15]

---

12 **HOW PIVOTAL WAS KHADIJAH'S ROLE?** ASLAN

"Eventually God relieved Muhammad's anxiety by assuring him of his sanity. But it is safe to say that if it were not for Khadija, Muhammad might have gone through with his plan to end it all, and history would have turned out quite differently."[16]

Iqrah is the first revealed word of the Qur'an, and is commonly translated as either "read" or "recite." Yahiya Emerick uses the first in his translation of the Qur'an, while Al-Mubarakpuri and Lings use the latter.

For a detailed account of the Prophet's first revelation, read Chapter 15 in Lings and listen to CD 5 of Yusuf. Review Al-Mubarakpuri p.72-73 for a description of the seven different ways revelation came to the Prophet.

Waraqah ibn Nawfal was a Christian Haneef who anticipated the coming of an Arabian prophet. Recall that many years ago, his sister Qutaylah had proposed to the Prophet's father, 'Abd Allah, on his wedding day to Aminah (P2.3)

1.2 SILENCE & DOUBT

The first revelation is followed by a brief period of silence, which leads the Prophet to doubt his own sanity. On several occasions he nearly throws himself off mountain cliffs, but each time he is greeted by Gabriel, who reminds him that he is, indeed, God's messenger.

Shortly thereafter, the Prophet's second revelation, Surah Al Qalam, erases his initial misgivings:

> Nun.
>
> By the pen and what (the scribes of destiny) record, by the grace of your Lord, you're not crazy (as the Meccans claim).
>
> On the contrary, you're going to have an unfailing reward, for you have a most excellent character. Soon you and your critics will see who it was that was really being challenged the most. — *Al Qalam (The Pen, 68:1-6)*

≫ **SURAH AL QALAM** (The Pen) is also known as Surah Nun (the Arabic letter pronounced "noon"). It begins with a defiant tone that instructs the Prophet not to listen to the harsh abuse of his detractors. The Late Meccan surahs have a less defiant, and more psychologically supportive tone in the face of public persecution.

---

13 **DIVINE REVELATION OR EPILEPSY?** WATT

"He would be gripped by a feeling of pain, and in his ears there would be a noise like the reverberation of a bell. Even on a cold day the bystanders would see great pearls of sweat on his forehead as the revelation descended upon him. Such accounts led some Western critics to suggest that he had epilepsy, but there are no real grounds for such a view. Epilepsy leads to physical and mental degeneration, and there are no signs of that in Muhammad; on the contrary he was clearly in full possession of his faculties to the very end of life."[17]

- -

14 **THE LETTER "NUN"** RAMADAN

"The dignity of humankind, conferred by knowledge, cannot be devoid of the humility of reason aware of its own limits and thereby recognizing the necessity of faith. Accepting, and accepting not to understand, the mysterious presence of the letter nun requires faith; understanding and accepting the mysterious statements of the verses that follow require use of a reason that is active but necessarily—and indeed naturally—humbled."[18]

- -

15 **WHAT WAS THE FOCUS OF THE EARLY SURAHS?** ASLAN

"The fact that there are dozens of verses in the Quran refuting the accusation that Muhammad was a Kahin [a jinn-inspired soothsayer] indicates how important the issue was for the early Muslim community. As Muhammad's movement expanded throughout the region, the Revelation gradually became more prosaic and ceased to resemble the oracular style of the early verses. However, in the beginning, Muhammad knew exactly what would be said of him, and the thought of being considered a Kahin by his contemporaries was enough to bring him to the edge of suicide. Eventually God relieved Muhammad's anxiety by assuring him of his sanity."[19]

The initial surahs are followed by another, even longer period of silence. The abrupt break in revelation triggers a second wave of uncertainty and self-doubt. In those moments of despair, he returns to Khadijah who once again reassures him that he has done nothing to incur God's displeasure.

The timing and duration of this period of silence is a point of disagreement among scholars. Some suggest it lasted for days while others argue that it extended for several years. Read Watt's *Muhammad in Mecca* (p.48-49) and Al-Mubarakpuri (p.69) for details.

16 WHAT WAS THE PURPOSE OF SILENCE AND DOUBT?   RAMADAN

"He was actually undergoing the same experience as Abraham: in the ordeal of this silence, he doubted himself, his capacities, and his power, but God was constantly strewing his path with signs and visions that prevented him from doubting God. Revelation had verbally told him about the necessity of humility, but God's silence was now teaching it to him practically."[20]

Khadijah's role is so integral to the Prophet's well-being, that on one occasion, while she is sitting next to him, the Prophet informs her that Gabriel has just relayed God's greeting to her.

Khadijah is stunned, and simply answers:

"God is Peace, and from Him is Peace, and on Gabriel be Peace."[21]

Finally, Surah Ad-Duha breaks the protracted silence. The revelation releases the Prophet from fear and doubt, and establishes the first blueprints of social change:

By the brilliance of daybreak and by the still of the night, your Lord hasn't forsaken you (Muhammad) nor is He displeased. Your future is brighter than your present situation, for your Lord will soon grant you (what you truly seek), and you will be well-pleased.

Didn't He find you an orphan and shelter you? Didn't He find you lost and show you the way?

Didn't He find you in need and make you independent?

Therefore, don't be mean to the orphan nor scoff at the requests (of the poor), and continue to declare (the mercy) and blessings of your Lord.

— *Ad-Duha (The Early Dawn, 93:1-11)*

 SURAH AD-DUHA (The Early Dawn) is named after its opening verse. Here God swears by the brilliance of daybreak that he has not forsaken the Prophet, and commands him not to abandon those in need around him.

17 WHAT WERE THE FIRST LESSONS?   RAMADAN

"The first teaching is obviously the vulnerability and humility he must naturally have felt from his earliest childhood ... This left him utterly dependent on God, but also close to the most destitute among people.
The second spiritual teaching emanating from these verses is valid for each human being: never to forget one's past, one's trials, one's environment and origin, and to turn one's experience into a positive teaching for oneself and for others. Muhammad's past, the One reminds him, is a school from which he must draw useful, practical, and concrete knowledge to benefit those whose lives and hardships he has shared, since he knows from his own experience, better than anyone else, what they feel and endure."[22]

⑱ WHY STRESS PURIFICATION?   `ARMSTRONG`

"The new karim [noble] was no longer a person who gave away his entire fortune in a single night, but one who tirelessly practiced the 'works of justice.' At this stage the new faith was called tazakkah ('purification'). By looking after the poor and needy, freeing slaves, performing small acts of kindness on a daily, hourly basis, the Muslims learned to cloak themselves in the virtue of compassion and would gradually acquire a responsible, caring spirit, which imitated the generosity of Allah himself. If they persevered, they would purge their hearts of pride and selfishness and achieve a spiritual refinement."[23]

⑲ WHAT WAS THE QUR'AN'S RESPONSE TO THE NEW RELIGION OF WEALTH IN MECCA?   `WATT`

"In Mecca there was a new ideal, supereminence in wealth instead of honour, and to this ideal many besides the wealthy subscribed. This was an ideal and a religion which might satisfy a few people for a generation or two, but it is not likely to satisfy a large community for long. People soon discover that there are things which money cannot buy. At best they can only find meaning and significance in being wealthy by shutting their eyes to unpleasant facts such as disease and death, especially early death. In a community of any size some unpleasant facts are bound to thrust themselves forcibly even upon certain of the wealthy, quite apart from the poor who have difficulty in forgetting their financial inferiority. The tensions due to the inadequacy of this religion of wealth and material prosperity are perhaps felt most keenly by those who have some wealth, but are only on the fringes of the very wealthy; they have some leisure for reflection and some degree of awareness of the limitations of the power of money. It is against all this background that we must try to understand the insistence on acts of generosity. Such acts had a social and economic effect, but that was almost certainly not the most important aspect ... They were a practical exercise in detachment from wealth, an outward expression of the new inner attitude which should serve to strengthen it."[24]

1.3 THE VERY FIRST COMPANIONS

The Prophet's disciples are classically referred to as the *sahabah* or Companions (in this book they are denoted by a capital "C"). The word sahaba comes from the verb *sa-ha-ba*, which means "to accompany/to rub together." By definition, a Companion is any individual who embraced Islam, interacted with the Prophet, and died a Muslim. The Companions who emigrated to Medina are specifically referred to as the *Muhajireen* (the Emigrants), while those who lived in Medina and gave refuge to the Prophet and the Emigrants became known as the *Ansar* (the Helpers).

Read Ramadan (p. 39-44) for a synopsis of the Prophet's earliest message:

(1) Oneness of God (*tawhid*)
(2) Status of the Qur'an
(3) Significance of Prayer
(4) Final judgment and the Hereafter

By the turn of the seventh century, Mecca and its inhabitants had evolved significantly from the days of 'Abdu Manaf and Hashim:

> Mecca was more than a mere trading centre, it was a financial centre ... The leading men of Mecca in Muhammad's time were above all financiers, skillful in the manipulation of credit, shrewd in their speculations, and interested in any potentialities of lucrative investment from Aden to Gaza or Damascus. In the financial net that they had woven not merely were all the inhabitants of Mecca caught, but many notables of the surrounding tribes also. The Qur'an appeared not in the atmosphere of the desert, but in that of high-finance.[25]

Against this backdrop, the Prophet begins cultivating a group of loyal supporters from among his close family and friends. His message calls for *tawhid* (belief in the absolute unity of God) coupled with a pressing need for social justice. Despite the urgency of his early message, the Prophet is careful to tread lightly:

> It is well known that Makkah was the religious center for the Arabs, and housed the custodians of Al-Ka'bah. Protection and guardianship of the idols and stone carved images that were honored by all the Arabs, lay in the hands of the Makkans. Hence the difficulty of hitting the target of reform and goodness in a place considered the center of idolatry. Working in such an atmosphere no doubt requires unshakable will and determination, that is why the initial call to Islam assumed a limited form so that the Makkans should not be enraged by the unexpected surprise.[26]

20 **WHAT IS TAWHID?** ARMSTRONG

"The principle of tawhid became the crux of Muslim spirituality. It was not simply an abstract metaphysical affirmation of the singularity of the divine, but, like all Qur'anic teaching, a call to action. Because Allah was incomparable, Muslims must not only refuse to venerate the idols, but must also ensure that other realities did not distract them from their commitment to God alone: Wealth, country, family, material prosperity, and even such noble ideals as love or patriotism must take second place."[27]

21 **FAITH, KNOWLEDGE, AND DEEDS** RAMADAN

"Faith in God and knowledge, in the light of the divine, must have as their immediate consequence a behavior, a way of acting, that respects an ethic and promotes good."[28]

The first converts include Khadijah, 'Ali ibn Abi Talib, Zayd ibn Harithah, and Abu Bakr ibn Abi Quhafah. They are soon followed by others including 'Abdu 'Amr ibn 'Awf (who subsequently changed his name to 'Abd ar-Rahman) and Abu 'Ubaydah ibn al-Jarrah.

22 **WHO WAS THE FIRST MALE MUSLIM CONVERT?** WATT

"It is universally agreed that Khadijah was the first to believe in her husband and his message but there is hot dispute about the first male. At-Tabari has a large selection of source material, and leaves the reader to decide for himself between the three candidates, 'Ali, Abu Bakr, and Zayd b. Harithah. 'Ali in a sense may be true, but for the Western historian it cannot be significant, since 'Ali was admittedly only nine or ten at the time and a member of Muhammad's household. The claim made for Abu Bakr may also be true in the very different sense that, at least from the time of the Abyssinian affair, he was the most important Muslim after Muhammad; but his later primacy has probably been reflected back to the early records. As a matter of sheer fact Zayd b. Harithah has probably the best claim to be regarded as the first male Muslim, since he was a freedman of Muhammad's and there was a strong mutual attachment; but his humble status means that his conversion has not the same significance as that of Abu Bakr."[29]

During the first days of revelation, a successful young merchant by the name of 'Uthman ibn 'Affan was on his way home from trading in Syria when he is awoken in the desert by the words:

"Sleepers, awake, for verily Ahmad hath come forth in Mecca."[30]

23 **WHO WAS ASLEEP IN MECCA?** ARMSTRONG

"The Quraysh, however, were busily amassing private fortunes, without giving a thought to the plight of the 'weak.' They did not seem to realize that their deeds would have long-lasting consequence. To counter this heedlessness, the Qur'an taught that individuals would have to explain their behavior to God."[31]

'Abd ar-Rahman ibn 'Awf is one of the most ardent supporters of the Prophet, and 18 years from now, will be one of five men to sign the Treaty of Hudaybiyah. On the march to Tabuk, 'Abd ar-Rahman will lead the congregational prayer with the Prophet praying behind him. He is one of the 10 Companions whom the Prophet will promise Paradise.

Abu 'Ubaydah ibn al-Jarrah will become another prominent Companion. He will fight valiantly at Badr and Uhud, and will lead one of four battalions at the Conquest of Mecca. He is also one of the 10 Companions whom the Prophet will promise Paradise. So great is his standing that after the Prophet's death, Abu Bakr will nominate Abu 'Ubaydah and 'Umar as the first caliph of the Muslim community.

'Uthman ibn 'Affan is from the same clan of 'Abdu Shams as Abu Sufyan ibn al-Harb. One of the most trusted of the Prophet's Companions, 'Uthman will marry two of the Prophet's daughters, both of whom pass away during 'Uthman's lifetime. 'Uthman is one of the 10 Companions whom the Prophet will promise Paradise.

1
2
3
4
5
6

Ahmad (highly praised) derives from the same root as *Muhammad* (h-m-d), and is one of the Prophet's many names, as mentioned in Surah As-Saff:

> Remember that Jesus, the son of Mary, (also faced a similar challenge) when he announced, "Children of Israel! I'm the Messenger of God sent to you. I confirm the truth of the Torah that came before me, and I bring you the good news of a messenger who will come after me, whose name will mean 'praise'."
>
> However, when (the foretold prophet) came to them with clear evidence (of the truth), they scoffed, "This (message he brings) is obviously some kind of magic!" — *As-Saff (The Formations, 61:6)*

≽ **SURAH AS-SAFF** (The Formations) is named after its fourth verse, which describes God's love for those who struggle in His cause in tight formations of solidarity. The surah was revealed in the Early Medinan Period and addresses the disobedience of the Uhud archers (QY 16.6) by recalling the trials of Moses and Jesus.

Talhah ibn 'Ubayd Allah is from the same clan as Abu Bakr and will play a prominent role in the Prophet's life. He fights gloriously at Uhud where he deflects a death-blow meant for the Prophet. He is also one of the 10 Companions whom the Prophet will promise Paradise.

Before reaching Mecca, 'Uthman runs into Abu Bakr's cousin, Talhah ibn 'Ubayd Allah, who tells 'Uthman that he was recently asked about the very same Ahmad by a monk in Syria. The two return to Mecca and approach their friend Abu Bakr with the news. Abu Bakr explains what has transpired during their absence and that he has embraced Muhammad as one of God's chosen prophets. 'Uthman and Talhah visit the Prophet and join his cause.

---

24 WHO WERE THE EARLIEST CONVERTS?　　WATT

"It is therefore misleading to say that his followers consisted of the 'plebeians' or 'members of the lower social strata', as is often asserted…
The simplest way of describing the main body of Muhammad's followers is to say that they were the strata of society immediately below this topmost stratum. Since the majority of Meccans did not follow him, it may be inferred that they either were deeply involved in the commercial operations of the topmost stratum or else in some other way were its hangers-on. Those who followed Muhammad would be those with a certain measure of independence from the topmost stratum. The younger brothers and cousins of the chief merchants must have been wealthy young men, while the men from other clans, like Abu Bakr, were probably struggling to retain such an independence as still remained to them…
Thus we see that, while the nascent Islamic movement was a movement of 'young men', it was by no means a movement of 'down-and-outs.'"[32]

- -

25 WHAT DROVE YOUNG PROFESSIONALS TO THE PROPHET?　　ARMSTRONG

"Many of the younger generation, who were disturbed by the aggressive capitalism of Mecca, came to him [Muhammad] for advice. Some of the young felt an urgent sense of personal peril, a torpor of depression from which they longed to wake, and a frightening alienation from their parents.
Any society divided against itself would be destroyed, because it was going against the very nature of things. This was a frightening period … There was an apocalyptic sense of impending catastrophe. Muhammad was convinced that unless the Quraysh reformed their attitudes and behavior, they too would fall prey to the anarchy that threatened to engulf the world."[33]

YEAR 2: PRIVATE INVITATION: THE PROPHET'S INNER CIRCLE

2.1 THE EARLIEST REVELATIONS

The Prophet shares the newest revelations with his closest family members, and teaches them how to pray and perform *wudu* (ritual cleansing). Despite their fairly inconspicuous gatherings, the Prophet and his Companions start feeling pressure from the outside. In this context, the latest revelations—Al Muzzammil and Al Muddathir—convey a sense of urgency and warning:

> O (Prophet), covered up (in a cloak)! Stand up (in prayer) at night, but not all night—half of it or a little less or more. Recite the Qur'an in slow, measured tones, for soon We're going to send you weighty teachings.
>
> Rising at night is truly a powerful (way) for taming (the soul), and it's the best (time) for composing words (of praise). You're far too busy in the day with ordinary duties (to be able to concentrate).
>
> Remember the name of your Lord, and devote yourself completely to Him. (He's) the Lord of the East and the West; there is no god but He! So look upon Him as the One Who can take care of (your) affairs.
>
> Have patience with what the (Meccans) are saying, and distance yourself from them in an amiable way. Let Me (deal with) those deniers who have the finest things in life. Bear with them—just for a little while longer.
>
> — *Al Muzzammil (Enfolded, 73:1-11)*

> O (Prophet), wrapped up (in a blanket)! Arise and warn! Magnify your Lord! Keep your clothes clean and shun the idols. Don't give (in charity) with the expectation of receiving anything back. For your Lord's sake, be patient.
>
> — *Al Muddathir (Enwrapped, 74:1-7)*

According to Al-Mubarakpuri (p. 75), the five daily prayers were not established until after the Isra' (Night Journey) approximately nine years later (QY 11.3). At this time, it is believed that there were two prayers, one before sunrise and one after sunset.

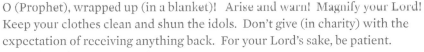 **SURAH AL MUZZAMMIL** (Enfolded) is named after the Prophet who, in a state of despondency, enfolded himself in his cloak, awaiting further instructions. The surah establishes the night prayer as a powerful method of achieving spiritual equilibrium, and also reminds him to bear patiently with the abuse he was suffering. God has plans for his critics.

SURAH AL MUDDATHIR (Enwrapped) is named after the Prophet who, in a state of fear and anxiety, enwrapped himself in his cloak for comfort. The first five verses are some of the very first instructions given to the Prophet. The second and third parts of the surah deal with the arrogance of Walid ibn al-Mughirah (Makhzumi chief and early detractor of the Prophet) and introduce the concept of personal accountability.

2.2 AR-RAHMAN & AR-RAHIM

Surahs Al Muzzammil and Al Muddathir are followed by surahs with a gentler tone that reassure the Prophet of his mission and remind him of God's all-encompassing mercy. They stress the names of God, focusing on his mercy (*ar-Rahman*) and benevolence (*ar-Rahim*):

> Amongst the most striking features of the Revelation were the two Divine Names ar-Rahmán and ar-Rahím. The word rahím, an intensive form of ráhim, merciful, was current in the sense of very merciful or boundlessly merciful. The still more intensive rahmán, for lack of any concept to fit it, had fallen into disuse. The Revelation revived it in accordance with the new religion's basic need to dwell on the heights of Transcendence. Being stronger even than ar-Rahím (the All-Merciful), the name ar-Rahmán refers to the very essence or root of Mercy, that is, to the Infinite Beneficence or Goodness of God, and the Koran expressly makes it an equivalent of Allah.[1]

> "Call upon God, or call upon the Compassionate, for regardless of whatever name you use to invoke Him, the most beautiful names belong to Him..."
> *— Al–Isra' (The Night Journey, 17:110)*

---

❶ WHAT WAS THE PROPHET'S COACHING STYLE?   `RAMADAN`

"This natural initiation into morals, remote from any obsession with sin and fostering of guilt, greatly influenced the kind of education the Prophet was to impart to his Companions. With a teaching method relying on gentleness, on the common sense of individuals, and on their understanding of commands, the Prophet also strove to teach how to put their instincts to sleep, so to speak, and how to resort to diversion to escape evil temptations.

... [This] reminds us that a moral sense should be developed not through interdiction and sanction but gradually, gently, exactingly, understandingly, and at a deep level."[2]

- -

❷ WHAT WAS THE MISSION OF EARLY ISLAM?   `ARMSTRONG`

"Muhammad wanted every man, woman, and child in Mecca to develop within themselves the humble thankfulness that should characterize the human condition ... Muhammad was not content simply to work for social reform; he believed that without an interior transformation, a purely political program would be superficial."[3]

YEAR 3: PRIVATE INVITATION: THE PROPHET'S EXTENDED FAMILY

3.1 INVITING THE CLANS OF HASHIM AND MUTTALIB

After a few years of private gatherings, the Prophet is instructed by Surah Ash-Shu'ara' to broaden the invitation to his extended family:

> ...Warn your nearest relatives, and lower your wing (in kindness) to the believers who follow you. If they ever disobey you, then say, "I'm not responsible for what you've done." — *Ash-Shu'ara' (The Poets, 26:214-216)*

He calls together 45 men from the clans of Hashim and Muttalib for a feast of mutton and milk. But before he can explain the reason for the gathering, his uncle, Abu Lahab, disperses the crowd. The very next day, the Prophet renews his invitation and promptly addresses his family before his uncle can intervene:

"I celebrate Allah's praise, I seek His help, I believe in Him, I put my trust in Him, bear witness that there is no god to be worshipped but Allah with no associate. A guide can never lie to his people. I swear by Allah that there is no god but He, that I have been sent as a Messenger to you in particular, and to all the people in general. I swear by Allah that you will die just as you sleep, and you will be resurrected just as you wake up. You will be called to account for your deeds. It is then either Hell forever or the Garden (Paradise) forever."[1]

> ❶ **WHY WAS THE INITIAL MESSAGE IGNORED?** `ASLAN`
>
> "Muhammad was not yet establishing a new religion; he was calling for sweeping social reform. He was not yet preaching monotheism; he was demanding economic justice. And for this revolutionary and profoundly innovative message, he was more or less ignored."[2]
>
> -
>
> ❷ **WHAT WAS THE FIRST MESSAGE REALLY ABOUT?** `ARMSTRONG`
>
> "In his desire to avoid a serious dispute, Muhammad did not, at this stage, emphasize the monotheistic content of his message ... It was more important to practice the 'works of justice' than to insist on a theological position that would offend many of the people he was trying to win over.
> Nobody criticized his social message ... it was one thing to be selfish and greedy, but quite another to defend these attitudes."[3]

SURAH ASH-SHU'ARA' (The Poets) is named after the hostile Arabian poets who used to slander God and his Prophet. The surah opens as a source of encouragement to the Prophet, and reminds him of the challenges faced by Moses, Abraham, Noah, Hud, Saleh, Lot, and Shu'ayb. It is a reminder to trust in the One who sees us at all times.

1
2
3
4
5
6

'Ali ibn Abi Talib is one of the Prophet's dearest supporters and intimate Companions. He will lie in the Prophet's bed when the Prophet escapes to Medina. After the Hijrah, 'Ali marries the Prophet's youngest daughter, Fatimah, and much later prepares the Prophet's body for burial.

Zubayr ibn al-'Awwam is a lifelong supporter of the Prophet. After the Hijrah, he marries Abu Bakr's daughter Asma' and later leads one of the four battalions during the Conquest of Mecca. He will be one of the 10 Companions whom the Prophet will promise Paradise.

Everyone is quiet until 'Ali speaks in support of his older cousin. When the Prophet acknowledges the 13-year-old's allegiance, many of the elders laugh at the spectacle and depart. While Abu Lahab warns the Prophet that his message is bad for the Quraysh, Abu Talib remains cautiously supportive:

> *"Do what you have been ordered. I shall protect and defend you, but I cannot quit the religion of 'Abdul-Muttalib."*[4]

The Prophet's younger uncle 'Abbas remains evasive but his wife, Umm al-Fadl, becomes the second woman after Khadijah to enter Islam. She brings along three of her sisters: Maymunah, Asma', and Salma. By this time, only one of the Prophet's six aunts, Safiyyah, enters Islam with her son Zubayr ibn al-'Awwam.

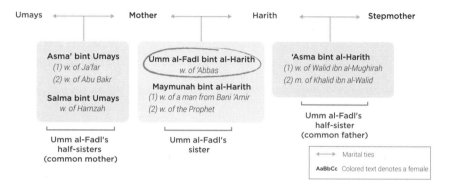

FIGURE 3A. THE SISTERS OF UMM AL-FADL

Umm al-Fadl was a beloved member of the Prophet's inner circle. She was the wife of his uncle 'Abbas and the second woman to enter Islam after Khadijah. She is also credited with the conversion of her sisters Asma', Salma, and Maymunah (who will later become the Prophet's 11th wife). Referring to these women, the Prophet said, "Verily the sisters are true believers."

'Asma bint al-Harith was the wife of Walid ibn al-Mughirah, the chief of Makhzum. Several years later, she converted to Islam and was followed by her son Khalid ibn al-Walid. (All of these women are married to some of the most influential Companions in the Sirah.)

Umm Ayman is another early responder to the Prophet's message. Although the Prophet's adopted son Zayd is much younger than Umm Ayman, he marries her after hearing the Prophet suggest that marrying Umm Ayman would be akin to marrying a woman of Paradise. The newlywed couple is soon blessed with a son, Usamah, who is brought up as the Prophet's own grandson.

Usamah ibn Zayd is about the same age as 'A'ishah and will vigorously defend her when an infidelity scandal erupts in Medina. They are two of the first children born into Islam. Many years later, not only will Usamah help bury the Prophet's son, Ibrahim, he will also help 'Ali prepare the Prophet's body for burial.

FIGURE 3B. AUNTS OF THE PROPHET

Umm al-Fadl was the wife of 'Abbas, and therefore the Prophet's aunt by marriage. The Prophet's notable nieces and nephews are also indicated below their mother's names.

3.2 ABU LAHAB

Having secured Abu Talib's guardianship, the Prophet ascends Mount Safa and calls out to the Quraysh:

> *"You see, if I were to tell you that there were some horsemen in the valley planning to raid you, will you believe me?"*

When the onlookers affirm his trustworthiness, he continues:

> *"I am a warner to you before a severe torment."*

Upon hearing these words, Abu Lahab exclaims:

> *"Perish you all the day! Have you summoned us for such a thing?"*[5]

The Prophet's response from atop Mount Safa is sharp and direct:

> Cut off are (the works) of Abu Lahab's hands—cut off! Neither his money nor his accomplishments will save him, for in a raging blaze he shall soon be. And his woman, who must feed the flame, will have around her neck a twisted fiber chain. — *Lahab (Flame, 111:1-5)*

⪢ SURAH LAHAB (Flame) is named after the Prophet's uncle Abu Lahab, who criticized the Prophet at every stage of his life. The surah also denounces his wife, Umm Jamil, for her equally harsh treatment of the Prophet.

Shortly thereafter, Abu Lahab's wife, Umm Jamil, catches wind of Surah Al-Lahab. In a fit of rage she approaches Abu Bakr, and referring to the Prophet as *Mudhammam* (the belittled one), demands to know his whereabouts. When Abu Bakr does not respond and she storms off in anger, he is amazed that she could not see the Prophet sitting right beside him. True to his nature, the Prophet later muses to his Companions:

> *"Is it not wondrous how God turneth away from me the injuries of Quraysh? They revile Mudhammam, whereas I am Muhammad."*[6]

Like the numerous insults he had suffered since the first revelation, Umm Jamil's remark does not weaken the Prophet's sense of purpose. He continues to decry the very things that troubled him in his 30s: personal aggrandizement, wealth inequality, and social injustice. And yet, despite his earnestness, the Prophet's call to family and friends is met with varying degrees of success. Not surprisingly, Abu Lahab and Umm Jamil dissolve their sons' engagements to Ruqayyah and Umm Kulthum. Their public retraction underscores a troubling new wave of individualism that is splitting Mecca apart:

> In Mecca this tribal solidarity was being replaced by individualism. There may have been some beginnings of individualism among the nomads, but at Mecca the trend to individualism was mainly due to the growth in commerce. The great merchants put business interests before everything else, and would join with business associates against their fellow clansmen. Muhammad suffered from this in his last year or two at Mecca, because his uncle Abu-Lahab had friends among the great merchants who induced him to turn against his nephew. In a sense a new type of unit was being formed by common business interests, but to this unit few of the older social attitudes were attached, and it was incapable of solving the problems of Meccan society.

The breakdown of the tribe or clan led to the oppression of weaker members of the community such as widows and orphans. The successful merchant thought only of increasing his own power and influence. His wealth might originally have come to him as chief of his clan, but he was no longer prepared to carry out the chief's traditional duty of looking after the poorer members of the clan.

Nothing short of a miracle could reverse the growing trend of exploitative individualism that had taken hold of the Quraysh. Against these odds, the Prophet and his earliest followers cling to the growing collection of surahs as their only chance of saving Mecca.[7]

Taken together, the early Meccan surahs start giving shape to a novel solution to Mecca's growing problem:

The conduct of the rich Meccans would have been looked on as dishonourable in the desert, but there was nothing in the atmosphere of Mecca to make them feel ashamed of it. The old ideal had been quietly abandoned.

The problem, however, is not simply a restoration of the old nomadic ideal, but the production of a new moral ideal suited to the needs of settled life. To salvage what can be salvaged is one part of the task, but the smaller part of it. Much that is new will also be required; and this larger part of the task is dealt with in the early passages of the Qur'an by the provision of a source or channel for a new morality, namely, the revealed commands of God and the prophet through whom they are revealed.[8]

---

3 WAS THE EARLY MESSAGE AGAINST PAGANISM OR MATERIALISM? `WATT`

"It is contrary to our preconceived ideas of Islam that this theme of God's goodness and power should be so prominent in the early passages. The preconceptions rest on the later developments of Islamic dogma, when the fact that God is unique was emphasized and idols were declared to be nothing. In other words Muhammad's original message was not a criticism of paganism. It appears to be directed to people who already had a vague belief in God, and to aim at making this belief of theirs more precise by calling attention to particular events and natural processes in which God's agency was to be seen ...

... What, then, is the point of the Qur'an's insistence on God's goodness and power? Against whom is it directed? It is directed against the materialism of the Meccan merchants who thought that, because of their wealth and influence, they were little gods, disposing of Meccan commerce and politics as they pleased."[9]

NAME	RELATIONSHIP TO THE PROPHET	DETAILS
Khadijah bint al-Khuwaylid	First wife	The very first person to accept Islam and the biggest source of comfort for the Prophet after his first revelations.
'Ali ibn Abi Talib	Adopted nephew & first cousin	Marries the Prophet's daughter Fatimah. Carries the standard at Khaybar, later becomes the 4th Caliph.
Zayd ibn Harithah	Adopted son	Leads an army of 3,000 against the Ghassanids in Syria where he is martyred.
Umm Ayman	Father's servant	Marries Zayd ibn Harithah. Mother of Usamah ibn Zayd. Joins the expedition to Khaybar.
Ja'far ibn Abi Talib	Younger first cousin	Leads the migration to Abyssinia. Returns and dies during the attack on the Ghassanids in Syria.
Safiyyah bint 'Abd al-Muttalib	Maternal aunt	Prays with the Prophet over her slain brother, Hamzah. Mother of Zubayr ibn al-'Awwam.
Zubayr ibn al-'Awwam	First cousin	Marries Asma' bint Abi Bakr. Leads one of the battalions at the Conquest of Mecca.
Sa'd ibn Abi Waqqas	Maternal cousin	One of the loyal archers at Uhud. Later is nominated as the 3rd Caliph, and eventually the governor of Kufa.
Umayr ibn Abi Waqqas	Maternal cousin	Pleads with the Prophet to fight at Badr, where he is martyred at age 15.
'Abd Allah ibn Jahsh	First cousin	Immigrates to Abyssinia. Kills a man during the sacred month of Rajab. Martyred at Uhud and buried next to Hamzah.
'Ubayd Allah ibn Jahsh	First cousin	Immigrates to Abyssinia. Later reverts to Christianity and dies abroad. His surviving wife, Umm Habibah, becomes the Prophet's ninth wife.
Zaynab bint Jahsh	First cousin, later seventh wife	Marries Zayd ibn Harithah, and later the Prophet. Known for her generosity. First of Prophet's wives to pass away after his death.
Hamnah bint Jahsh	First cousin	Marries Mus'ab ibn 'Umayr, and later Talhah ibn 'Ubayd Allah.
Umm al-Fadl bint al-Harith	Uncle 'Abbas' wife	As Abbas' wife, she is the second woman to enter Islam and is very dear to the Prophet. She kills Abu Lahab after Badr by striking him on the head.
Maymunah bint al-Harith	Future 11th wife	Brings Islam to her clan of 'Amir. Eleventh wife of the Prophet.
Asma' bint Umays	Cousin's wife	Wife of Ja'far and later Abu Bakr.
Salma bint Umays	Uncle's wife	Wife of Hamzah and half-sister of Umm al-Fadl.

AaBbCc Colored text denotes a female

FIGURE 3C. THE EARLIEST SUPPORTERS

Many of the earliest supporters came from the Prophet's household: his wife, Khadijah, was the first to convert, followed by 'Ali, Zayd, and Umm Ayman. Ja'far soon followed his younger brother, 'Ali, into Islam. Many children of the Prophet's aunts also joined him, including Zubayr ibn al-'Awwam (son of Safiyyah) and the Jahsh family (children of Umaymah). From his mother's side, the Prophet had the support of his two dearest cousins Sa'd and 'Umayr ibn Abi Waqqas. Umm al-Fadl, wife of the Prophet's uncle 'Abbas, joined the cause and brought her sisters with her.

4.1 THE FIRST PUBLIC ENCOUNTER

During the Early Meccan Period, the Companions pray in secret, far from watchful eyes. On one occasion, however, several Meccans discover a congregation of Muslim worshippers and begin harassing the small group. A brawl ensues in which Sa'd ibn Abi Waqqas wounds one of the instigators.

Despite the intensifying opposition, surahs Al Muzzammil and At-Tariq strongly urge the Companions to patiently endure the Meccan assault.

> Have patience with what the (Meccans) are saying, and distance yourself from them in an amiable way. Let Me (deal with) those deniers who have the finest things in life. Bear with them - just for a little while longer.
> — *Al Muzzammil (Enfolded, 73:10-11)*

> (Though the faithless) continue to plot their schemes, I'm making a plan, as well. So give the faithless some time, and leave them alone (for a while).
> — *At-Tariq (The Night Star, 86:17)*

---

1 WHAT DID IT MEAN TO BE AN EARLY CONVERT?   [ASLAN]

"...conversion to Muhammad's movement was not only changing one's faith, but also cutting oneself off from the activities of the tribe; in essence, removing oneself from the tribe."[1]

- -

2 WHAT DID IT MEAN TO PRACTICE "HILM" (FORBEARANCE)?   [ARMSTRONG]

"Men and women of hilm were forbearing, patient and merciful. They could control their anger and remain calm in the most difficult circumstances instead of exploding with rage; they were slow to retaliate; they did not hit back when they suffered injury, but left revenge to Allah. Hilm also inspired positive action: if they practiced hilm, Muslims would look after the weak and disadvantaged, liberate their slaves, counsel each other to patience and compassion, and feed the destitute, even when they were hungry themselves. It must have been very difficult indeed for the Muslims, brought up in the jahili spirit, to practice hilm and turn the other cheek."
"For true servants of the Most Gracious are they who walk gently on the earth, and who, whenever the jahilun address them, reply Peace." Al Furqan (The Criterion, 25:63)[2]

Meanwhile, the Quraysh feel increasingly threatened by the Prophet's growing influence, and ask Abu Talib to intervene. When Abu Talib asks his nephew to concede, the Prophet responds:

"Oh my uncle! By Allah if they put the sun in my right hand and the moon in my left on condition that I abandon this course, I would not abandon it until Allah has made me victorious or I perish therein."

Abu Talib returns the Prophet's oath with his own:

"Go and preach what you please, for by Allah, I will never forsake you."[3]

Sa'd ibn Abi Waqqas is the Prophet's cousin from the same clan as the Prophet's mother, Aminah. For this reason, he is commonly referred to as *Sa'd of Zuhrah*, to differentiate him from two prominent Helpers—Sa'd ibn Mu'adh from Aws and Sa'd ibn 'Ubadah from Khazraj. He will later fight at Badr and Uhud and remain by the Prophet's side through out the Medinan period. He is one of the 10 Companions whom the Prophet will promise Paradise.

SURAH AT-TARIQ (The Night Star) is named after its opening verses. Here God swears by the brightest star in the sky, that each soul will be held accountable for what it's done. It reminds the Prophet and his followers to be patient with their critics, as God has a plan for all of them.

4.2 THE EARLY SURAHS: AN INVITATION TO REFLECT

Millennia of harsh desert life had forced the Arabs to refine and perfect the Bedouin ideals of nobility, honor, generosity, and justice. In the absence of a centralized authority, it was all they had to guard self-preservation. The sudden urbanization of Mecca was quietly changing everything:

> In the Mecca of Muhammad's prime, however, men had ceased to think much about honour. Honour was bound up with the traditional morality of the desert, and much of that had become irrelevant in Mecca. Instead they thought of increasing their own wealth and power. It was in super-eminent wealth that they found the meaning of life. To increase one's wealth and power became the great aim in life, not only for the few very rich men in Mecca, but also for the great majority of the population who aped from the distance.[4]

SURAH AL MU'MINUN (The Faithful) is named after its opening verses, which describe the six characteristics of truly successful people. The surah provides coping advice for the Prophet, and reminds listeners to be mindful of God's signs and His role as Creator and Judge.

In light of this subtle paradigm shift, the Qur'an challenges the Quraysh to take stock of their lives:

> Did you think that We created you just for fun and that you wouldn't be returned to Us? — *Al Mu'minun (The Faithful, 23:115)*

God's answer is clear:

> We didn't create the heavens and the earth and all in between them merely for fun. We didn't create them except for a truthful purpose, but most of them don't know that. — *Ad-Dukhan (The Smoky Haze, 44:38-39)*

SURAH AD-DUKHAN (The Smoky Haze) accurately foretells of a smoky haze that would pass through Mecca during a severe draught in the valley. The surah goes on to predict that despite calling on God to lift the draught, the Meccans would immediately revert to disbelief. Such was the pattern of the Pharaoh who denied Moses' message. The surah reminds us that it's better to be on the side of humility and belief, before it's too late.

Despite asking such penetrating questions, early Meccan surahs fall on mostly deaf ears. Some listeners ignore the warnings, while others brazenly challenge the entire premise of resurrection and personal accountability.

> Then they say, "There's nothing beyond our lives here on earth, nor will we ever be raised to life again." — *Al An'am (Livestock, 6:29)*

Despite such widespread objections, a number of ambivalent Meccans are swayed by the Prophet's charisma and determination:

> A parallel imperative cause for accepting the message was the Messenger himself, a man who was, they were certain, too full of truth to deceive and too full of wisdom to be self deceived.[5]

Regardless of the Quraysh's bitter hostility, the Prophet continually encourages them to embrace the glad tidings from Heaven.

> On the contrary, those who said, "Our Lord is God," and then stood firm, will have angels descending upon them, (strengthening their hearts, inspiring them with messages such as), "Have no fear! Have no sorrow! Accept the good news of the Garden that you've been promised! We're your protectors in this life, as well as in the next life, within which you'll receive everything your souls ever desired and everything you ever asked for!" That's a welcome gift from the (One Who) forgives and shows mercy! — *Fussilat (Clear Explanation, 41:30-32)*

> Ask them, "Is that (fate) better or the Eternal Garden that's been promised to the mindful?" That'll be their reward and also their final destination. They'll have everything within for which they ever wished, and they can dwell within it forever. Now that's a promise from your Lord for which to pray!
> — *Al Furqan (The Standard, 25:15-16)*

He explains that true Muslims are those who wish to meet their Lord, as opposed to:

> Those who don't look forward to their meeting with Us, who are satisfied with the life of this world and who disregard Our (revealed) verses—they're going to have their home in the Fire on account of what they've earned for themselves. — *Yunus (Jonah, 10:7-8)*

Nonetheless, the deceptive glamour of life continues to charm most of the Quraysh. Rather than heed the Prophet's words, they repeatedly challenge him to prove himself as God's prophet. On one occasion, they dare him to split the full moon. But when the moon is cleaved in two, the Quraysh accuse him of sorcery and only increase their aversion to the Prophet's message.

> Such wonders were never allowed to stand in the center, for the revealed Book itself was the central miracle of the Divine intervention now taking place ... functioning ... to reawaken in man his primeval sense of wonderment which, with the passage of time, had become dimmed or misdirected. Therefore when Quraysh ask for marvels, the Koran's main response is to point to those which they have always had before their eyes without seeing the wonder of them.[6]

The Qur'an argues that to be awake to the reality of one's true existence means not only shifting one's hopes from this world to the next, but also marveling at the signs of God in the natural world:

> Don't (the skeptics) ever gaze at the moisture-laden clouds and ponder over their formation or at the sky and how it's been raised up so high or at the mountains and how they've been firmly set or at the earth and how it's been spread out? — *Al Ghashiyah (The Overwhelming, 88:17-20)*

SURAH YUNUS (Jonah) is named after a few verses that mention the Prophet Jonah and how his people were the only community that followed their prophet. The surah recalls the stories of several other prophets and addresses basic theological concepts in Islam. Ultimately each person is responsible for his own fate in the Hereafter.

SURAH AL GHASHIYAH (The Overwhelming) is named after its opening verse, which describes the seriousness of the Day of Judgment, heaven, and hell. It asks listeners to ponder God's creation in the natural world, and reminds the Prophet that he is just a messenger. Whether people listen to him is God's affair.

Blessed be the One Who placed constellations in the sky and Who placed therein a lamp and a lighted moon. He's the One Who made the night and the day to follow each other (as a sign) for any who wish to be reminded or who wish to be thankful.

The (true) servants of the Compassionate are those who walk humbly through the earth. Whenever the ignorant try to engage them (in futile argument), they say to them, "Peace." — *Al Furqan (The Standard, 25:61-63)*

The growing collection of early Meccan surahs is characterized by short, harmonious, and often rhyming verses that stress sincerity and inspire self-reflection. One of the hallmarks of this period is Al Fatihah, a remarkable surah that prescribes humility, sincerity, and hope as the foundation of man's relationship with God.

SURAH AL FATIHAH (The Opening) is the inaugural chapter of the Qur'an (in the Qur'an's final, compiled order). The surah is a concise overview of the essential message contained in the remaining 113 surahs that follow. Unlike the four previous chapters that came down in sections (Al Alaq, Al Qalam, Al Muzammil, and Al Muddathir), Al Fatihah was the first surah to be revealed to the Prophet in its complete form. It is recited at least 17 times each day by practicing Muslims in their prayers.

Praise be to God, Lord of All the Worlds; the Compassionate, the Merciful and Master of the Day of Judgment.

To You alone do we render service and to You alone do we look for aid. Guide us on the straight path: the path of those whom You have favored, not of those who've earned Your anger, nor of those who've gone astray.
— *Al Fatihah (The Opening, 1:1-7)*

③ THE EARLY MECCAN SURAHS ADDRESS WEALTH AND ARROGANCE [WATT]

"If we now turn to the earlier passages of the Qur'an ... the points made there are relevant to the contemporary situation ... It calls on men to acknowledge the power and goodness of God their Creator and to worship Him. Thereby they will be denying the omnipotence and omni-competence of the wealthy man ... The malaise arose from the unscrupulous pursuit of wealth, and the Qur'an tries to curb this."[7]

Taken together, the early Meccan surahs are a return to Abraham's creed—a religion of pure, uncompromising monotheism.

SURAH IKHLAS (Pure Faith) is comprised of only four verses and is the most succinct summary of Islamic theology in the Qur'an. The word *ikhlas* is not used in the surah but rather conveys its basic theme.

Say (to them): "He is only one God—God the Eternal Absolute. He neither begets nor was He begotten, and there is nothing equal to Him."
— *Al Ikhlas (Pure Faith, 112:1-4)*

④ WHAT WAS THE EARLIEST MESSAGE OF THE QUR'AN? (SUMMARIZED) [WATT]

- God's goodness and power (87:1-3; 80:25-31; 93:3-8; 55:26)
- The return to God for judgment
- Man's response—gratitude and worship
- Man's response to God—generosity (93:9-11; 104:1-3)
- Muhammad's own vocation (74:2; 87:9)[8]

4.3 THE EARLY SURAHS: A WARNING AGAINST ARROGANCE

While some Meccans remain skeptical of the Prophet, others are downright obstinate. Had God wanted to send a messenger, they argued, surely He would have sent them an angel:

> Those who think that they're never going to meet Us say, "So why aren't any angels being sent down to us? Why aren't we seeing our Lord (face to face)?" They think so highly of themselves, and their audacity is enormous!
>
> When the day comes that they finally do see the angels, the sinners won't have any good news at all that day! — *Al Furqan (The Standard, 25:21-22)*

SURAH AL FURQAN (The Standard) is named after its opening verse, which refers to the Prophet's revelation as "The Standard." It documents the attacks of the Meccan idolaters and reminds the Prophet that other prophets faced the same pattern of resistance. Like many Meccan surahs, the verses were a source of comfort to the Prophet, who was being attacked on all sides.

---

⑤ WHAT IS THE MEANING OF "KAFIR?" [ARMSTRONG]

"Kafir ... implies a discourteous refusal of something that is offered with great kindness and generosity ... the Qur'an does not berate the kafirun for their lack of religious conviction, but for their arrogance ... The kafirun are bursting with self-importance; they strut around haughtily, addressing others in an offensive, braying manner, and fly into a violent rage if they think that their honor has been impugned. They are so convinced that their way of life is better than anybody else's that they are particularly incensed by any criticism of their traditional lifestyle."[9]

Surah Al Isra' guides the Prophet's response:

> Say to them, "If the earth were populated by angels, going about their business quietly, then We would've certainly sent an angel down from the sky to be a messenger for them." Then say, "God is enough of a witness between you and me, for He's well-informed and watchful over His servants."
> — *Al Isra' (The Night Journey, 17:95-96)*

From the beginning, the Qur'an cautioned the Quraysh against their *istighna'* (haughty self-reliance), reminding them about the terrors of Judgment Day:

> It's the day when people will seem like moths fluttering about, when the mountains will be like tangled tufts of wool. — *Al Qari'ah (The Sudden Disaster, 101:4-5)*

In the latest revelations, the Prophet is instructed to confront the arrogance of the Quraysh head on:

> "How, then, shall you shield yourselves if you disbelieve in a Day [the unthinkable terror of] which shall turn children gray?"
> — *Al Muzzammil (Enfolded, 73:17)*

SURAH AL QARI'AH (The Sudden Disaster) is an early Meccan surah that is named after it's alarming description of the Day of Judgment. On that day, the surah explains, every individual will be rewarded or punished according to whatever good they did during their lifetime.

The formidable tone of the latest verses further polarizes the divided community and pushes a number of fair-minded individuals to the extremes. Surah Al Isra' explains:

> And so it is that We've explained (the issues in) various (ways) in this Qur'an, so they can be reminded, but it only seems to make them distance themselves from it even more! —*Al Isra' (The Night Journey, 17:41)*

> We (only use such symbols) to instill fear in them (so that they'll perhaps be inclined to listen), but it only adds to their immense suppression (of faith). —*Al Isra' (The Night Journey, 17:60)*

Against this backdrop of mounting opposition, a timely revelation about the story of Noah reminds the Prophet not to lose hope. Just as Waraqah had predicted, the Prophet too must follow in the footsteps of all God's prophets.

> (He was ignored, however, and in his despair he cried out to God), saying, "My Lord! I've called to my people through the night and through the day, but my invitation only (seems to) make them drift further away. Every time I've called to them so You could forgive them, they've stuck their fingers in their ears and wrapped themselves up in their cloaks, growing more stubborn and arrogant!" —*Nuh (Noah, 71:5-7)*

SURAH NUH (Noah) describes the distressing way in which Noah's people rejected his message. The surah's timing in the Early Meccan Period must have been a clear reminder to the Messenger that he too was following in the footsteps of every great prophet.

4.4 THE SMEAR CAMPAIGN

Aside from taking an uncompromising stance against idolatry, the early surahs begin to uncover the insidious problem of wealth inequality in Mecca:

> While it seems unlikely that there had been any increase in absolute poverty in Mecca, it is probable that the gap between the rich and poor had widened in the last half-century. The Qur'an implies an increasing awareness of the difference between rich and poor ... apparently too, the rich were showing less concern for the poor and uninfluential, even among their own kin.

> The early passages of the Qur'an have no more than a premonition of the real remedy for this situation, namely, that a new basis for social solidarity is to be found in religion. The insistence on the duties of generosity would bring some alleviation of the troubles; the poor would be helped materially (though this was not the primary purpose of generosity), and money would cease to be so great a social driver in that the rich would admit or reaffirm that they were stewards of their wealth rather than absolute owners.[10]

---

6 WHAT WAS THE PROPHET ATTACKING? ARMSTRONG

"Most hanifs had retained a deep respect for the Haram and had made no attempt to reform the social order. But in attacking the effigies that surrounded the Ka'bah, Muhammad implied that the Haram, on which the Meccan economy depended was worthless ... Overnight, Muhammad became the enemy."[11]

7 WHAT WAS THE QUR'AN'S DIAGNOSIS OF MECCA'S PROBLEMS? | WATT |

"The diagnosis of the Meccan situation by the Qur'an is that the troubles of the time were primarily religious. On the other hand it has been suggested above that the rise of Islam is somehow connected with the change from a nomadic to a mercantile economy. Is there a correlation here, or can the two views be reconciled?
In a word the trouble is the outcome of man's failure to adjust himself to the economic change because of certain pre-existing attitudes. The new economic circumstances lead to a heightening of man's confidence in himself without an awareness of his creatureliness to balance it, to an individualism in social affairs without a new moral ideal to balance it and without a new religious outlook to give the individual significance."[12]

8 WHAT WAS THE PROPHET ATTACKING? | ASLAN |

"As a businessman and a merchant himself, Muhammad understood what the Hanifs could not: the only way to bring about radical social and economic reform in Mecca was to overturn the religio-economic system on which the city was built; and the only way to do that was to attack the very source of the Quraysh's wealth and prestige—the Ka'ba ... And because the religious and economic life of Mecca were inextricably linked, any attack on one was necessarily an attack on the other ... If the Ka'ba was useless, then there was no more reason for Mecca's supremacy as either the religious or the economic center of the Hijaz."[13]

With their commercial interests at risk, Mecca's elite turn to their leader—Walid ibn al-Mughirah, who, as described in Surah Al Muddathir, masterminds a smear campaign against the Prophet. He instructs the Quraysh to warn all visiting pilgrims of the poet-sorcerer who has been sowing discord in Mecca.

He pondered, and he schemed (against Me), so now he's doomed! Oh, how he schemed! Once again, he's doomed! Oh, how he schemed! Then he looked around (and saw the truth of God's signs), but then he frowned and scowled, turning arrogantly away, saying, "This (Qur'an) is no more than some remnant of the magic of ancient days. This is no more than the speech of a mortal man!" — *Al Muddathir (Enwrapped, 74:18-25)*

The malicious smear campaign is well documented in many early Meccan surahs:

(The Meccans) say, "Hey you, the one who's getting this 'revealed message.' (We think) you're crazy! So why aren't you bringing angels down to show us if you're really so honest?" — *Al Hijr (The Stony Ground, 15:6-7)*

So are they surprised that a warner should come to them from their own people? Yet, the faithless only say, "Just a lying wizard! Has he lumped all the gods together into just one God? That's a strange thing, indeed!" — *Sad (38:4-5)*

Indeed, the faithless nearly unsettle you with their venomous stares when they hear this reminder, and they shout, "He's crazy!" However, this is no less than a reminder to all the worlds. — *Al Qalam (The Pen, 68:51-52)*

SURAH AL HIJR (The Stony Ground) is named after the rocky terrain of northern Arabia where an ancient civilization was destroyed for disobeying its messengers. Al Hijr is known for its carved rock dwellings still visible today. The surah contains powerful words of solace and encouragement to the Prophet and his followers who were enduring long years of criticism and abuse.

SURAH AT-TATFEEF (The Shortchanger) is also known as Surah Mutaffifin (The Defrauders). The names come from the first few verses (revealed later in Medina), which begin with a warning to misers who expect exact payment from those who owe them, but shortchange others their fair due. The chapter describes the miserable fate of those who cheat others versus the delight of those who remain honest and righteous.

The wicked used to laugh at those who believed. They winked at each other whenever they passed by, then hurried back to their associates to laugh and joke, and whenever they saw them they would say, "Truly, these are the ones who got it all wrong!"

However, they weren't sent to look after them! Yet, on this day, it will be the believers who will scoff at the faithless from high thrones. Won't the faithless then be fully repaid for (the evil) they did? — *At-Tatfeef (The Shortchanger, 83:29-36)*

The faithless say, "This is all just a pack of lies that he's made up, and some people helped him do it!" They're the ones who've brought an unfair charge and an unsubstantiated accusation.

They say, "It's all just tales from long ago that he's ordered to be written down. They're being dictated to him in the morning and at night."
— *Al Furqan (The Standard, 25:4-5)*

SURAH AN-NAHL (The Bee) is named after a series of verses that prompts listeners to reflect on God's wondrous creation by highlighting the remarkable characteristics of honeybees. The surah warns against the folly of polytheism and underscores God's infinite power to create the natural world from which humans derive so much benefit. The surah also attacks those who accuse the Prophet of inventing the Qur'an, saying, "It is those who don't believe in God's verses who are frauds..." The surah was revealed after the Abyssinian migration and, among other things, commends those who emigrated in God's name.

We know that they're saying, "It's a man who's teaching him," but the tongue of the (foreign slave) to whom they're pointing is not fluent (in Arabic), while this (Qur'an) is in the purest and most precise Arabic. — *An-Nahl (The Bee, 16:103)*

Now they're saying, "What kind of a 'messenger' is this? He eats food (just like we do) and walks around in the markets! Why hasn't an angel been sent down to him to warn us alongside of him? Why hasn't he been given a treasure or a nice garden (like the one he talks about in an afterlife) in which to have his meals?"

Then these same corrupt (critics) say (to the believers), "You're following some kind of lunatic." Do you see, (Muhammad,) how they're making you out to be? However, they're the mistaken ones, and they'll never be able to find a path (to salvation). — *Al Furqan (The Standard, 25:7-9)*

4.5 SURAH 'ABASA: GUIDANCE FOR THE PROPHET

After three years of preaching, the Prophet had not yet secured the support of Mecca's two leading clans, Makhzum and 'Abdu Shams. Although both had been vying for supremacy in Mecca, they remained united against revelations like Surah Al 'Ankabut, which examines the true reality of wealth and power.

> What is there in this world except distractions and games? The realm of the next life is where the real living is, if they only knew. — *Al 'Ankabut (The Spider, 29:64)*

SURAH AL 'ANKABUT (The Spider) is named after verse 41, which likens those who take protectors other than God to spiders that build fragile webs to protect themselves. The surah challenges the faithful to remain steadfast in the face of persecution, and uses examples from past nations to bolster their resolve.

---

9 WHAT WAS THE FOCUS OF THE EARLY REVELATIONS? ASLAN

"In the beginning, Muhammad seemed more concerned with revealing what kind of god Allah was, not how many gods there were … The Quraysh did not need to be told there was only one god; they'd heard that message many times before from the Jews, the Christians, and the Hanifs, and they did not necessarily disagree. At this point in his ministry, Muhammad had a far more urgent message … the demise of the tribal ethic in Mecca. In the strongest terms, Muhammad decried the mistreatment and exploitation of the weak and unprotected. He called for the end to false contracts and the practice of usury that had made slaves of the poor."[14]

In an attempt to break this barrier, the Prophet approaches Walid ibn al-Mughirah, the most influential man in Mecca. In the midst of their conversation, a blind man named 'Abd Allah ibn Umm Makhtum interrupts the Prophet by asking to hear a few verses of revelation. Surprisingly the Prophet brushes him off, and Surah 'Abasa (revealed shortly thereafter) tells the remainder of the story:

> (Muhammad) frowned and turned away when the blind man came (and interrupted his preaching), but for all you knew he could've grown in purity or received a useful reminder.
>
> The one who thought he needed nothing was the one to whom you gave your full attention, though he wasn't your responsibility. So the one who came to you eagerly (in search of knowledge), and who feared (God), you neglected.
> — *'Abasa (He Frowned, 80:1-10)*

Far from a discreet reminder, Surah 'Abasa is a public declaration that the Prophet, like his followers, remains entirely dependent on God's guidance.

Ironically, Walid never converts to Islam while the blind man, **'Abd Allah ibn Umm Makhtum,** becomes a major asset to the Prophet. Several years later, 'Abd Allah will remain in Medina and lead the congregational prayers in the Prophet's mosque, while the Prophet marches out to fight Walid's nephew Abu Jahl at Badr.

SURAH 'ABASA (He Frowned) is named after its opening verse, which describes the Prophet's treatment of 'Abd Allah ibn Umm Makhtum. The surah is a reminder against ingratitude, and warns of the absolute reality of Judgment Day.

---

10 WAS 'ABASA A TURNING POINT? ARMSTRONG

"God reproved Muhammad severely: a prophet must approach all members of the community with the same respect. He must move beyond the aristocratic ethos of muruwah: the Qur'an was for rich and poor alike … Muhammad had now given up hope of converting the Meccan establishment and realized that he must concentrate on the disaffected poorer people, who were eager for his message. This was a poignant turning point, which is recorded poignantly in the Qur'an."[15]

YEAR 5: ABYSSINIA

5.1 SURAH AN-NAJM

During the month of Ramadan, the Prophet enters the Holy Sanctuary where several of his notable opponents had gathered. He approaches the crowd and begins reciting Surah An-Najm.

> By the star when it declines, your companion is not mistaken, nor is he being misled, and he says nothing on his own. It's no less than revelation revealed!
> — *An-Najm (The Star, 53:1-4)*

As expected, the men begin to mock the Prophet, and—as explained in Surah Fussilat—speak over him in order to prevent others from listening to his recitation.

> The faithless say, "Don't listen to this Qur'an! Talk nonsense over it when it's being recited, so you can come out on top!" — *Fussilat (Clear Explanation, 41:26)*

Despite their mockery, the Prophet continues to recite the remainder of the surah.

> This (man Muhammad) is a warner just like the warners of old. (The Day of Judgment) is getting closer and closer, and no one can move it forward save God. So are you amazed at this narrative? Will you laugh and not cry, wasting all your time in useless distractions? Then (know that you should) bow down prostrate before God and serve Him. — *An-Najm (The Star, 53:56-62)*

SURAH AN-NAJM (The Star) is named after its opening verse, which swears by the declining star that the Prophet is not misled, but the recipient of a true revelation. The incident regarding the sister idols is tied to the controversy of the **satanic verses**. A number of Muslim historians relate that Satan had inspired the Prophet to suggest that the three sister idols were intercessors for God, and that the verse was later removed from the Qur'an (53:19). This alternate account does not appear in the earliest biography by Ibn Hisham, but does appear in other respected texts that were written later by al-Waqidi and at-Tabari. The account, as described here, is taken from Al-Mubarakpuri, who cites Sahih al-Bukhari.

The powerful verses catch the crowd off guard, and upon hearing the final stanza, they fall in prostration alongside him. News of the implausible incident quickly spreads through Mecca and the individuals who had prostrated in response to Surah An-Najm quickly fabricate a story, explaining that they had heard the Prophet call upon the sister idols al-Lat, al-'Uzzah, and al-Manat as divine intercessors for God.

Surah An-Najm tackles this allegation head-on:

> Have you seen (the idols named) Al-Lat and Al-'Uzza, and the third one named Manat? What! For you, (you prefer) males (as sons), but then you assign to (God) females (for children)! That's hardly a fair deal!
>
> In fact, they're nothing more than names you've made up—you and your ancestors. God sent down no permission for (you to do) that. They're only following their own opinions and what they themselves (foolishly) desire. And so it is that guidance has now come to them from their Lord, (so see if they will obey God now, as they always claimed they would)!
> — *An-Najm (The Star, 53:19-23)*

5.2 ABYSSINIA

Over the past four years, the Prophet and his followers barely survived the rising tide of persecution in Mecca. In the fifth year, Surah Az-Zumar hints at the possibility of emigrating from their homeland in search of religious asylum.

> (Muhammad), tell them (that I have said), "My believing servants! Be mindful of your Lord! Good is for those who do good in this world. God's earth is wide (so you always have somewhere to go to escape evil)! Those who patiently persevere will certainly be given a reward without limit!"
>
> — *Az-Zumar (The Crowds, 39:10)*

Hoping the benevolent Negus, Ashamah, will protect the small community of Muslims, the Prophet instructs a number of his Companions to emigrate.

SURAH AZ-ZUMAR (The Crowds) is named after its final verses, which describe the fate of humans who will be divided into one of two crowds—one will be led to the gates of Hell, while the other to the gates of Heaven. The surah addresses issues of the Hereafter and how people will be sorted out according to their faith and deeds in this life.

Negus is a title in the Afro-Asiatic languages that means "king."

There is a difference of opinion on whether there were two separate migrations to Abyssinia. Al-Mubarakpuri suggests that the Abyssinian immigration occurred in two distinct waves. The first was a group of 16 Companions, followed by a second migration of 100 individuals (with the aforementioned incident of Surah An-Najm occurring between the two). Other scholars suggest that two parties may have departed at slightly different times but rejoined in Abyssinia around the same time.

---

❶ WERE THERE TWO DISTINCT EMIGRATIONS TO ABYSSINIA? `WATT`

"... it is commonly said by later Muslim historians that there were two hijrahs to Abyssinia, and that certain persons, namely, those on the first list, took part in both. Some returned to Mecca and later took part in the hijrah to Medina; others did not return until the year A.H. 7 when they joined the Messenger of God at Khaybar...
...The main reason for rejecting the two hijrahs is that Ibn Ishaq, as reported by Ibn Hisham and by at-Tabari, does not in fact say that there were two hijrahs. He says, 'The first Muslims to set out were...' and gives a short list; then he continues, 'Then Ja'far b. Abi Talib set out, and the Muslims followed him one after another...' There is no mention of the first list returning in order to go back a second time; and the lists are not in order of priority in travelling to Abyssinia, but follow the order of precedence in which names, we may presume, were arranged in the public registers of the caliphate."[1]

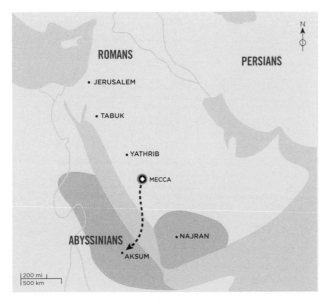

FIGURE 5A. THE MIGRATION TO ABYSSINIA

Led by Ja'far ibn Abi Talib, approximately 80 emigrants left for Abyssinia in the fifth year of the Prophet's career. Most returned a few years later after the ban on Hashim was lifted. Ja'far was one of the last to return 13 years later.

Over 80 emigrants arrive safely in Abyssinia, including notable Companions 'Uthman and Ruqayyah, Ja'far ibn Abi Talib and his wife Asma', and Mus'ab ibn 'Umayr.

The Quraysh immediately dispatch two mercenaries, led by 'Amr ibn al-'As, to bring back the runaways. The two men bribe the Negus' generals before approaching the Negus himself. But the king swears that he will continue to protect the Prophet's followers as long as they ask for his protection. He then summons the Muslim emigrants to his court to hear their case.

Ironically, after the rapid spread of Islam (15 years later), **'Amr ibn al-'As** will try to seek asylum in Abyssinia from the Muslims. He later embraces Islam, and despite his past enmity, the Prophet will choose 'Amr to lead his army of 500 men to the Syrian border. 'Amr's account with the Negus can be found in Salahi (p. 127-128).

② WHY DID THE PROPHET SEND HIS COMPANIONS TO ABYSSINIA? | SALAHI

"Although people often give more prominence to the Prophet's desire to spare his companions the persecution inflicted by the Quraysh, it had some definite objectives. If one analyses the emigration and the whole situation that prevailed in Makkah at that time, one is bound to realize that there were other, far more important reasons, which made this emigration a shrewd strategic move on the part of the Prophet. A close examination of the list of people who travelled to Abyssinia shows that hardly any of the weak and vulnerable elements who were subjected to unbearable torture joined the travellers...

One need only look at these names to realize that the emigrants belonged to most, if not all, the clans of the Quraysh, and many of them belonged to highly placed families in Makkah...

This meant that an all-out confrontation would involve every clan of the Quraysh turning against some of its own people. That was totally unacceptable in that particular place at that particular time.

As the Quraysh watched all those Muslims suddenly move out, across tribal lines, and join an exodus to seek a safer place where they could worship God, the Quraysh realized that their rejection of tribal values was irrevocable and allegiance to the new faith was total. Moreover, the Quraysh realized that Islam was able to gain ground in all sectors of society. Hence, any move to mount a full strike against the Muslims must win support throughout all the clans, because there were a number of Muslims in each and every clan. To unite them all in a determined confrontation with Muslims was impracticable because several clans had not given up hope of the possibility of working out a certain kind of understanding which would be satisfactory to both sides...

The Prophet was keen to emphasize the very concept which the Quraysh wanted to block. He wanted his followers to realize that belonging to Islam meant that they no longer belonged to Hāshim, Umayyah, Sahm, 'Adiy or any other clan. Their only tie of allegiance was to their faith. They were simply Muslims. As long as they were in Makkah, where hostile forces tried hard to play on feelings of tribal loyalty, this particular task was going to be difficult. Those companions of the Prophet also valued their tribal ties very highly until the moment they became Muslims. Living among their own people, where they needed tribal protection, would make it inevitable that they would have to seek some sort of modus vivendi with their own tribes who were still predominantly pagan."[2]

5.3 JA'FAR, 'AMR & THE NEGUS

Upon his arrival, Ja'far pleads the emigrants' case before the Negus:

"Oh king! We were an ignorant people. We worshipped idols and ate the meat of dead carcasses. We were accustomed to lewd behavior, to severing the ties of kinship, neglecting our neighbors, and the strong amongst us consumed the weak. This is how we were, but then Allah sent a Messenger to us. We were aware of his lineage, his truthfulness, that he was trustworthy, and chaste. He began inviting us to Allah, that we single Him out and that we worship Him. So we left the religion of our forefathers that we had been previously following, we left the worship of stones and idols, of all others besides Allah. He also commanded us to be truthful in our speech, fulfill trusts, nurture the ties of kinship, be kind to our neighbor, and to refrain from spilling blood unlawfully. He forbade us from lewd behavior, from bad speech, from consuming the orphan's wealth, and from slandering chaste women. He commanded that we worship Allah alone without associating anything with Him, he commanded us to perform the prayer, give charity, and fast..."

He lists the Islamic injunctions:

"...So we trusted him and believed in him, and followed the religion of Allah that he delivered. We began to worship Allah alone, we would not associate anything with Him, and we began prohibiting what He made unlawful for us, as well as allowing what He had made lawful for us. For this our people rose as enemies against us, punishing us, torturing us to get us to leave our religion and return to worshipping idols instead of worshipping Allah, and they expected us to consider all of the filthy things lawful as we previously did. So when they overpowered us, oppressed us and restricted us, when they came between us and our religion, then we came to your land, we chose you over others besides you, desiring to be your neighbor, and hoping that you—O king—will not wrong us."[8]

When the Negus asks to hear a portion of the Qur'an, Ja'far recites Surah Maryam, retelling the story of the birth of Jesus:

> Mention in the Book (the story of) Mary when she withdrew from her family to a place in the east.
>
> She erected a curtain (to screen herself) off from (her family), and then We sent Our angel to her, who appeared like a mortal man in all respects.
>
> "I seek the protection of the Compassionate from you!" she cried out (when she saw the stranger approaching). "If you're mindful (of God, then you'll leave me alone)!"
>
> "Truly, I am a messenger from your Lord," he answered, "(sent to tell) you about the gift of a pure boy."
>
> "But how can I have a son," she asked (in surprise), "when no man has ever touched me, and I'm not a loose woman?"
>
> "And so it will be," he answered, "for your Lord says, 'That's easy for Me.' (Your son) will be appointed as a sign for people, as well as a (source of) mercy from Us, and thus it's been decided!" — *Maryam (Mary, 19:16-21)*

SURAH MARYAM (Mary) is named after a beautiful collection of verses, which celebrate Mary's exemplary status and describe the miraculous birth of baby Jesus. The surah also tells the story of Zachariah, John the Baptist, Abraham, Moses, and Noah. This is another must-read passage for anyone interested in understanding how Islam fits into the greater Abrahamic tradition.

The revelation leaves the Negus in tears. The next day, when both sides reconvene, 'Amr strategically tells the king to ask Ja'far about Jesus. Ja'far responds:

"We speak about Jesus as we have been taught by our Prophet, that is, he is the servant of Allah, His Messenger, His Spirit and His Word breathed into Virgin Mary."[4]

---

③ WHAT COMPELLED JA'FAR TO TELL THE TRUTH? `SALAHI`

"Some people may argue that in their delicate situation the Muslims' stand might have been foolhardy. The situation called for a somewhat 'diplomatic' stance. People of faith, however, consider such an argument to be short-sighted. Truth, they argue, speaks louder and more frankly. Given a chance, it will always prevail. To the Muslim refugees in Abyssinia, the case was simply stating a fact revealed by God and conveyed by His Messenger. Evasion was unthinkable. Moreover, evasion is alien to the nature of those who follow the truth."[5]

Ja'far continues:

This was Jesus, the son of Mary, and that's an exposition of the truth about which they're arguing. It's not right (to say) that God has taken a son. All glory be to Him! Whenever He decides something, all He has to do is say, "Be," and it is!

(Jesus, himself, said), "God is my Lord and your Lord, so serve Him, for that's the straight path." — *Maryam (Mary, 19:34-36)*

Per the earliest biographer, Ibn Ishaq, the Negus clearly accepted the prophethood of Jesus and Muhammad.

Moved by Ja'far's eloquence, the Negus quickly dismisses 'Amr and returns his gifts. But the Negus' actions trouble his advisers, and when they ask him if he believes in Ja'far's testimony, he vaguely responds to appease them, but in his heart, testifies to the Prophet's message.

---

④ HOW DID THE ABYSSINIAN MIGRATION HELP THE MUSLIMS WHO REMAINED IN MECCA? `SALAHI`

"Those hundred or so Muslim emigrants belonged to no fewer than 15 clans of the Quraysh. Before Islam, these lines of separation could be very prominent. When they went out on their long trip to Abyssinia, every single one of them had in his mind only one tie of allegiance, which required him to give all his loyalty to the nation of Islam. When they faced the threat of extradition, their unity was complete. These same ties of allegiance were also strengthened among those Muslims who remained in Makkah. Now that their number had been much reduced, they were even more keenly aware of their weakness. They were concerned for the safety of their brethren who went on their hazardous journey, and they were worried about their own safety. They trusted to the wisdom of the Prophet in encouraging his companions to leave for Abyssinia. They were now weaker than ever before, and it was only natural that their weakness brought them closer together. Thus the emigration to Abyssinia made the feelings of unity among Muslims even stronger, whether they were among the emigrants or those who stayed behind."[6]

NAME (relationship to the Prophet)	DETAILS
RETURN 13 YEARS LATER	
Ja'far ibn Abi Talib (cousin) & Asma' bint Umays	At 27 years old, Ja'far is entrusted to lead the migration to Abyssinia. Although most of the emigrants return after the ban on Hashim is lifted, Ja'far remains there for 13 years with his wife and three children. He returns to Medina when the Prophet is away at Khaybar, and dies one year later while fighting in Syria. Asma' later marries Abu Bakr and they have a child named Muhammad.
'Ubayd Allah ibn Jahsh (cousin) & Umm Habibah bint Abi Sufyan	While in Abyssinia, 'Ubayd Allah reverts to Christianity and passes away, leaving Umm Habibah a widow. She comes to Medina with Ja'far's party and joins the Prophet's household as his ninth wife.
RETURN SOON AFTER THE BAN ON HASHIM IS LIFTED (APPROXIMATELY 5 YEARS)	
'Uthman ibn 'Affan (son-in-law) & Ruqayyah bint Muhammad (daughter)	'Uthman is one of the foremost Companions, and later becomes the third Caliph after 'Umar. His wife Ruqayyah becomes ill just before Badr and dies while the Prophet is away at battle.
Abu Salamah ibn 'Abd al-Asad (cousin) & Umm Salamah bint Abi Umayyah	Abu Salamah returns after the ban is lifted and is the first Muslim to immigrate to Medina. He dies a few months after Uhud and his wife, Umm Salamah, later becomes the Prophet's sixth wife. She is credited for narrating most of the accounts of the Abyssinian migration.
Abu Sabrah ibn Abi Ruhm (cousin) & Umm Kulthum bint Suhayl	Abu Sabrah is the son of the Prophet's aunt Barrah. His wife Umm Kulthum is the daughter of Suhayl, the chief of 'Amir.
Abu Hudhayfah ibn 'Utbah & Sahlah bint Suhayl	Abu Hudhayfah is the son of 'Utbah, one of the chiefs of 'Abdu Shams. He is married to Sahlah, another daughter of Suhayl, the chief of 'Amir.
Sakran ibn 'Amr al-'Amiri & Sawdah bint Zam'ah	Sakran is the brother of Suhayl, the chief of 'Amir. He dies shortly after returning to Mecca, and his widow, Sawdah, becomes the second wife of the Prophet and a leading figure in his household.
Mus'ab ibn Umayr	Mus'ab returns to Mecca with 'Uthman. After the second 'Aqabah, the Prophet sends him to Yathrib to prepare the community for the Prophet's arrival. Soon after the Hijrah, Mus'ab marries Hamnah bint Jahsh. He is killed on the battlefield at Uhud.
Shammas ibn 'Uthman	Shammas is one of the few Makhzumis to immigrate to Abyssinia. After his return, he fights valiantly at Uhud to protect the Prophet. He dies in Medina a few days after Uhud, and the Prophet orders his body to be buried on the battlefield with the other martyrs.
Zubayr ibn al-'Awwam (cousin)	After the Hijrah, he marries Abu Bakr's daughter Asma'. In Medina, Zubayr remains by the Prophet's side and later leads one of the four battalions at the Conquest of Mecca.
Tulayb ibn 'Umayr (cousin)	Tulayb is the son of the Prophet's aunt Arwa. He entered Islam as a young teenager and successfully persuaded his mother to follow him.
'Abd Allah ibn Jahsh (cousin)	'Abd Allah is 12 years younger than the Prophet. He is martyred at Uhud and buried alongside his uncle Hamzah.
Hatib ibn 'Amr al-'Amiri	Hatib is the brother of Suhayl, the chief of 'Amir. Although he fights valiantly at Badr, many years later, Hatib tries to send a message to Mecca to warn his son about the Prophet's impending Conquest of Mecca. The message is intercepted, but the Prophet forgives him because of his years of unwavering support.
Khunays ibn Hudaifah	Khunays returns from Abyssinia and marries Hafsah bint 'Umar. He dies one year after Badr, and his widow later marries the Prophet as his fourth wife.
Hisham ibn al-'As	The Quraysh had sent Hisham's half-brother 'Amr to persuade the Negus to deny asylum to the Muslims. After returning to Mecca, he is held captive by his family, but finally escapes to Medina.

AaBbCc Colored text denotes a female

FIGURE 5B. NOTABLE EMIGRANTS IN ABYSSINIA

Over 80 emigrants fled to Abyssinia in the fifth year. Most of their accounts have come to us through Umm Salamah. The Quraysh sent 'Amr ibn al-'As, Hisham's half brother, to persuade the Negus to return the Muslims to Mecca. Ironically, just prior to the Conquest of Mecca (15 years later), he returned to Abyssinia to seek asylum from the Muslims. The Negus counseled him to go to Medina and join the Prophet. Later, 'Amr said that when he embraced Islam, he was unable to look up at the Prophet's face out of reverence. Soon thereafter, the Prophet asked 'Amr to lead an army of 500 men to the Syrian border.

5.4 ALLIES & ENEMIES: A SURVEY OF THE 14 CLANS OF QURAYSH

By the end of the Early Meccan Period, the Prophet's message had created a bewildering array of responses. Although clan alliances tended to influence loyalties, several individuals went against their clansmen in supporting or opposing the Prophet:

> The tendency to individualism and away from tribal solidarity was fostered in Mecca by the circumstances of commercial life ... So we frequently find men acting in opposition to their clans. Abu Lahab adopted a different attitude towards Muhammad from most of the rest of Hashim. At the same time there was an interesting new phenomenon in Mecca—the appearance of a sense of unity based on common material interests [i.e. 'Abdu Shams and Makhzum].[7]

CLAN OF HASHIM:

Abu Sufyan ibn al-Harith was the same age and appearance as the Prophet. He will continue to resist the call to Islam until the eve of the Conquest of Mecca.

While the Prophet derives strength from his close family, he is saddened by the aloof and sometimes hostile reactions of many other relatives he was counting on for support. He is especially disappointed by his dear childhood friend Abu Sufyan ibn al-Harith, who is his first cousin and foster-brother through their nursemaid Halimah. Surah Al Qasas, however, reminds the Prophet that guidance is not in his hands.

> You'll never be able to guide all those whom you love, though God guides whomever He wants, and He knows better who it is that accepts guidance.
> —*Al Qasas (The Tales, 28:56)*

The Prophet is also disheartened by Abu Talib's eldest sons, Talib and 'Aqil, who do not follow their younger brothers, Ja'far and 'Ali, into Islam. Elsewhere in the clan of Hashim, Abu Lahab and his wife, Umm Jamil (sister of Abu Sufyan ibn al-Harb), retract their sons' engagements to Ruqayyah and Umm Kulthum. But soon thereafter, Umm Jamil's wealthy cousin 'Uthman ibn 'Affan asks for the beautiful Ruqayyah's hand in marriage, becoming the Prophet's second son-in-law. 'Uthman and Ruqayyah make such a handsome couple, that the Prophet later comments:

> *"God is beautiful and he loveth beauty."*[8]

Meanwhile, the Prophet's aunt Arwa holds out for a while, waiting to see how her sisters will respond to the Prophet's call. Ultimately her 15-year-old son Tulayb is the one who prods her into taking the Prophet seriously. Soon after Arwa's conversion, she rebukes her half-brother Abu Lahab for mistreating their nephew.

THE QURAYSH

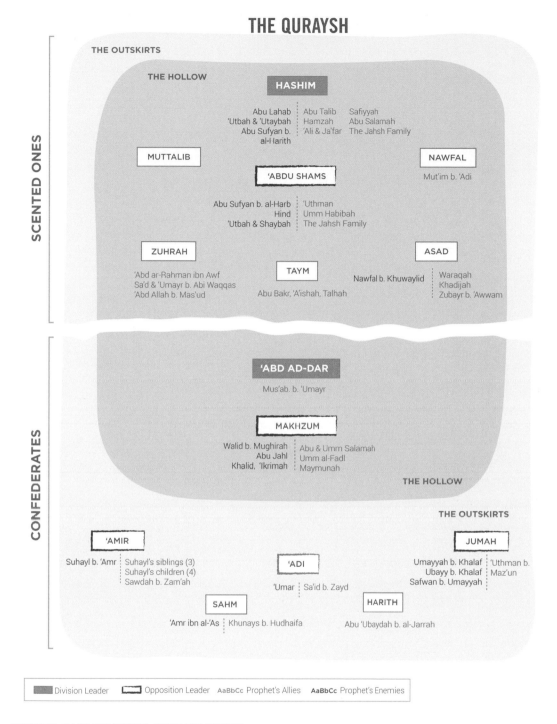

THE OUTSKIRTS

THE HOLLOW

HASHIM

Abu Lahab	Abu Talib	Safiyyah
'Utbah & 'Utaybah	Hamzah	Abu Salamah
Abu Sufyan b. al-Harith	'Ali & Ja'far	The Jahsh Family

SCENTED ONES

MUTTALIB

NAWFAL

Mut'im b. 'Adi

'ABDU SHAMS

Abu Sufyan b. al-Harb	'Uthman
Hind	Umm Habibah
'Utbah & Shaybah	The Jahsh Family

ZUHRAH

'Abd ar-Rahman ibn Awf
Sa'd & 'Umayr b. Abi Waqqas
'Abd Allah b. Mas'ud

TAYM

Abu Bakr, 'A'ishah, Talhah

Nawfal b. Khuwaylid

ASAD

Waraqah
Khadijah
Zubayr b. 'Awwam

'ABD AD-DAR

Mus'ab. b. 'Umayr

MAKHZUM

Walid b. Mughirah	Abu & Umm Salamah
Abu Jahl	Umm al-Fadl
Khalid, 'Ikrimah	Maymunah

CONFEDERATES

THE HOLLOW

THE OUTSKIRTS

'AMIR

Suhayl b. 'Amr : Suhayl's siblings (3)
: Suhayl's children (4)
: Sawdah b. Zam'ah

'ADI

'Umar : Sa'id b. Zayd

JUMAH

Umayyah b. Khalaf : 'Uthman b.
Ubayy b. Khalaf : Maz'un
Safwan b. Umayyah

SAHM

'Amr ibn al-'As : Khunays b. Hudhaifa

HARITH

Abu 'Ubaydah b. al-Jarrah

| ▢ Division Leader | ▢ Opposition Leader | AaBbCc Prophet's Allies | **AaBbCc** Prophet's Enemies |

FIGURE 5C. ALLIES AND ENEMIES AMONG THE QURAYSH

A few generations ago, Qusayy's closest relatives settled in Mecca (the Quraysh of the Hollow), while their remote kinsmen inhabited the surrounding hills (the Quraysh of the Outskirts). In the next generation, the Quraysh split once again into the Scented Ones and Confederates, thereby turning the clans of 'Abd ad-Dar and Makhzum against the Prophet's clan of Hashim and the other six clans of the Hollow (P 2.1).

While historical differences were one reason to oppose the Prophet, another equally compelling reason was purely economic. The clans of 'Abdu Shams and Makhzum were the most wealthy and powerful among the Quraysh. They had the most to lose from the Prophet's repeated warnings about wealth inequality, and naturally led the opposition in Mecca. Even the Prophet's wealthy uncle Abu Lahab turned against his own nephew. Several of the most prominent Meccans—both allies and enemies—are indicated here. Their names will come up repeatedly throughout the Sirah.

CLAN OF MUTTALIB:

The closest clan to Hashim is Muttalib. They have not experienced the same material success as many of the other clans of Quraysh and are in many ways dependent on Hashim for financial and political support. Two notable converts from Muttalib are the elderly 'Ubaydah ibn al-Harith and his younger cousin Mistah ibn Uthathah.

'Ubaydah ibn al-Harith lends his support to the early Muslim community and later migrates to Medina. He fights valiantly at one of the three opening duels at Badr, but is later martyred on the battlefield.

Mistah ibn Uthathah is Abu Bakr's relative and relies on him for financial support. Although Mistah will spread rumors of infidelity about 'A'ishah bint Abu Bakr, he is later forgiven by her father (QY 18.7).

CLAN OF ASAD:

Khadijah's clan of Asad has grown into prominence since the Pact of Chivalry, and has realigned with the powerful clans of Makhzum and 'Abdu Shams. Although Khadijah's half-brother Nawfal remains a violent enemy of Islam, his son Aswad embraces the Prophet and his message. Meanwhile, Khadijah is disappointed that her son-in-law and favorite nephew, Abu l-'As, has not yet embraced Islam. Though the Quraysh pressure Abu l-'As to divorce the Prophet's daughter Zaynab, he adamantly refuses. Similarly, Khadijah's favorite nephew Hakim ibn Hizam (who gave her Zayd) also retains affection for his aunt, but he and his brother Khalid do not enter Islam during her lifetime.

Although **Abu l-'As** will fight against the Prophet at Badr, he always remains a devoted husband and father. He will be separated from his family after Badr, when it is forbidden for a Muslim woman to be married to a non-Muslim man, but arrives in Medina soon after to be with Zaynab and their daughter, Umamah.

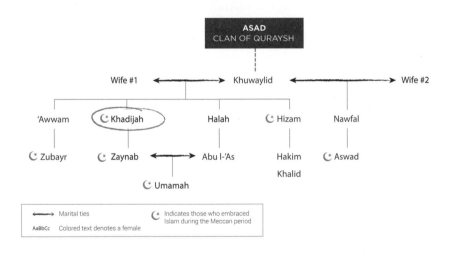

FIGURE 5D. CLAN OF ASAD: KHADIJAH'S EXTENDED FAMILY

Abu l-'As ibn ar-Rabi' was Khadijah's dear nephew and the Prophet's only son-in-law who waited until the Medinan period to enter Islam. Zubayr ibn al-'Awwam was an early convert and constant supporter of the Prophet and his family. His mother, Safiyyah, is Hamzah's sister and the Prophet's aunt. Hakim ibn Hizam used to bring supplies to the Muslims during the ban on Hashim. He entered Islam on the eve of the Conquest of Mecca and was given a large portion of the spoils after Hunayn. Khalid ibn Hizam cared for Khadijah and her household, yet did not embrace Islam in Mecca. Nawfal ibn Khuwaylid, Khadijah's half-brother, was a violent enemy of the Prophet and took part in abusing Abu Bakr and Talhah ibn 'Ubayd Allah. Nonetheless, his son Aswad ibn Nawfal embraced Islam during the Meccan years.

CLAN OF ZUHRAH:

The Prophet's mother, Aminah bint Wahb, belonged to the clan of Zuhrah. In the last few decades, Zuhrah enjoyed an intermediate level of success, greater than Hashim, Muttalib, and Taym, but not like Makhzum and 'Abdu Shams. In recent years the clan leadership has most likely passed over to Akhnas ibn Shariq, who—although a non-Qurayshi confederate—is respected for his leadership qualities.

The two chief Muslim converts during the Early Meccan Period are 'Abd ar-Rahman ibn 'Awf (in his mid-30s) and Sa'd ibn Abi Waqqas (in his late teens). Although Sa'd's younger brother 'Umayr embraces the Prophet's message, his other brother, 'Utbah, remains incalcitrant.

CLAN OF TAYM:

'Abd Allah ibn Jud'an had been the preeminent elder of Taym. Over 20 years ago, he had organized the Pact of Chivalry at his house when the Prophet and Abu Bakr were still teenagers ('Abd Allah most likely died before the first revelations).

Abu Bakr and Talhah ibn 'Ubayd Allah are also from the clan of Taym. Abu Bakr's wife, Umm Ruman, embraces Islam shortly after giving birth to their second child, 'A'ishah. 'Abd Allah and Asma', Abu Bakr's two children from another wife, also join their father's religion. Although he is credited for countless conversions, Abu Bakr is unable to persuade 'A'ishah's older brother, 'Abd al-Ka'bah, to convert to Abraham's Way during the Meccan period.

Five years from now, **Akhnas ibn Shariq** will deny the Prophet's request for protection after the Prophet returns from Ta'if. Nevertheless, Akhnas later persuades his entire clan of Zuhrah not to fight the Prophet's army at Badr (QY 15.2).

Beautiful and devout, **Umm Ruman bint 'Amr** dies shortly after the Treaty of Hudaybiyah and will be buried by the Prophet himself.

Several years from now, **'Abd al-Ka'bah ibn Abu Bakr** will fight against the Prophet at Uhud. After the death of his mother, he arrives in Medina and finally embraces Islam. Upon his conversion, the Prophet will change 'Abd al-Ka'bah's name to 'Abd ar-Rahman.

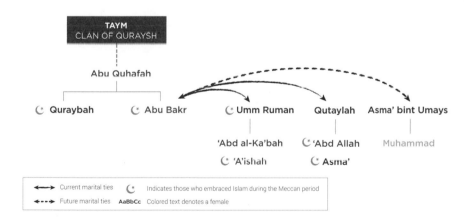

FIGURE 5E. CLAN OF TAYM: ABU BAKR'S FAMILY

Abu Quhafah was present at the Pact of Chivalry and brought Abu Bakr to the meeting. After the Hijrah, Quraybah stays behind in Mecca to take care of her father. 'Abd Allah and Asma' both help the Prophet and Abu Bakr escape Mecca. Asma' later marries the Prophet's nephew, Zubayr ibn al-'Awwam. 'Abd al-Ka'bah first resisted his father's invitation to Islam but later converted in Medina and changed his name to 'Abd ar-Rahman. 'A'ishah was the Prophet's third and favorite wife. After the Conquest of Mecca, Abu Bakr married Asma' bint Umays (after her husband Ja'far was martyred in Syria). Their son, Muhammad, was born during the Prophet's Hajj pilgrimage to Mecca.

CLAN OF MAKHZUM:

Abu Jahl ibn Hisham is the grandson of the late Meccan chief Mughirah, and nephew of Walid ibn al-Mughirah, the current chief of Makhzum (Fig. 20b). As such, he is intent on succeeding his uncle as the next chieftain. Abu Jahl is known for his ruthlessness, which he specifically directs toward the less protected followers of the Prophet. Though his true name is Abu l-Hakam ibn Hisham, his enmity toward the Muslims quickly earns him the name Abu Jahl (the father of ignorance). Several years from now, after the Prophet's escape from Mecca, Abu Jahl will lead the Meccans at the Battle of Badr and be killed.

Just a few generations earlier, Makhzum was the only clan among the Quraysh of the Hollow (aside from 'Abd ad-Dar) that did not recognize the leadership of Hashim (Fig. P9). As the wealthiest and most powerful clan of Quraysh, it also did not support the Pact of Chivalry, which would have disrupted the status quo. Not surprisingly, Makhzum houses some of the Prophet's fiercest enemies—most notably Abu Jahl ibn Hisham. Abu Jahl ruthlessly persecutes the weaker members of his own clan, including Yasir ibn 'Amir, his wife, Sumayyah, and their son, 'Ammar. Abu Jahl's abuse is so relentless that Sumayyah is ultimately martyred for her unshakable faith.

Another young upstart is Abu Jahl's cousin, 'Abd Allah ibn Abi Umayyah, who openly ridicules the Prophet at the start of his public ministry.

Despite Makhzum's fierce opposition, several of the clan's young personalities embrace the Prophet's cause. These include his relatives Abu Salamah, Umm Salamah, Maymunah, and Abu Sabrah, to name a few. Perhaps Makhzum's biggest disappointment is the conversion of Abu Salamah's wealthy cousin, Arqam ibn 'Abdi Manaf. After embracing Islam, Arqam establishes his large house near Mount Safa as a meeting place for the growing Muslim community.

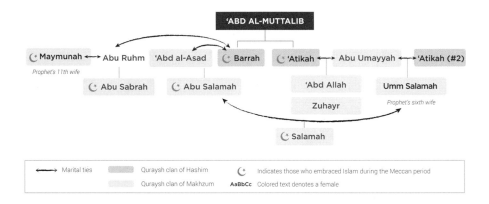

FIGURE 5F. CLAN OF MAKHZUM: THE PROPHET'S MANY COUSINS

Two of the Prophet's aunts, Barrah and 'Atika, were responsible for bringing many members of Makhzum to Islam. Abu Sabrah ibn Abi Ruhm (Sahm clan) migrated to Abyssinia and later returned to Mecca. Abu Salamah ibn 'Abd al-Asad was also one of the Prophet's earliest supporters. He was the son of Barrah, who had married into the clan of Makhzum. He died after the Battle of Uhud, and his 29-year-old widow, Umm Salamah, married the Prophet as his sixth wife. 'Abd Allah ibn Abi Umayyah, named after the Prophet's father, told the Prophet that he would never believe in Islam, even if the Messenger brought angels down from Heaven. However, just before the Prophet's army entered Mecca, he rushed out of the city and testified his faith in Islam. Zuhayr ibn Abi Umayyah also refused to enter Islam until after the Conquest of Mecca. Nonetheless, he was one of the five men who told the Quraysh to lift the ban on Hashim. Maymunah was also from Makhzum. Several years after the death of her husband, she married the Prophet as his 11th wife. She and Umm Salamah were loyal supporters of the Prophet and were a source of strength and reconciliaton against the fierce Makhzum clan.

CLAN OF SAHM:

Although the Sahm clan is one of the more powerful clans in Mecca, it contains few notable allies and enemies other than 'Amr ibn al-'As (who tried to bring the Muslim emigrants back from Abyssinia) and the Prophet's Companion, Khunays ibn Hudhafah, who belongs to a less important branch of Sahm.

Khunays ibn Hudhafah immigrates to Abyssinia and returns soon after to marry Hafsah bint 'Umar. When he dies one year after Badr, Hafsah marries the Prophet and becomes his fourth wife.

CLAN OF 'AMIR:

Although the clan of 'Amir is part of the Quraysh of the Outskirts, its economic and political interests are more in line with the Quraysh of the Hollow. Its chief, Suhayl ibn 'Amr al-'Amiri—a violent enemy of the Prophet—had become incensed by so many conversions within his own family.

Although most of his family joins Islam, **Suhayl ibn 'Amr al-'Amiri** resists the Prophet longer than anyone else in Mecca. In fact, he imprisons his son Abu Jandal for becoming a Muslim, and later represents the Quraysh at the Treaty of Hudaybiyah.

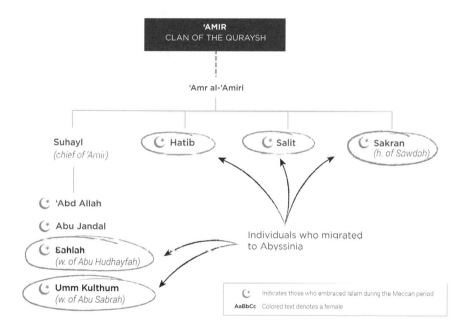

FIGURE 5G. CLAN OF 'AMIR: SUHAYL'S FAMILY OF CONVERTS

Suhayl ibn 'Amr al-'Amiri was the chief of 'Amir and a longstanding enemy of the Prophet. The Meccans sent him to negotiate the Treaty of Hudaybiyah, and he insisted on striking out "Muhammad the Messenger of Allah" on the document and replacing it with "Muhammad the son of 'Abd Allah." After the Conquest of Mecca, he was one of three men who did not enter Islam, but was nonetheless granted temporary amnesty. He finally embraced Islam after the Prophet gave him a generous portion of the spoils after the Battle of Hunayn.

'Abd Allah ibn Suhayl was forced to march out to Badr against the Prophet but managed to escape to the other side. Abu Jandal ibn Suhayl was imprisoned by his father, and as soon as the Treaty of Hudaybiyah was signed, he was paraded out in chains in front of the Muslims. The Prophet advised Abu Jandal to be patient, and he later escaped to Medina. Sahlah and Umm Kulthum bint Suhayl migrated to Abyssinia with their husbands and returned after the ban on Hashim was lifted. Suhayl's brothers Hatib, Salit, and Sakran ibn 'Amr also migrated to Abyssinia and returned with the others. Sakran died shortly after returning to Mecca, and the Prophet married Sakran's widow, Sawdah, a year after Khadijah's death.

CLAN OF 'ABDU SHAMS:

Umm Habibah and 'Ubayd Allah ibn Jahsh migrate to Abyssinia. When 'Ubayd Allah passes away, the Prophet will ask the Negus to officiate his marriage to Umm Habibah as his ninth wife (QY 19.5).

Second only to Makhzum, the clan of 'Abdu Shams enjoyed a seat of power in Mecca. Like Makhzum, it deeply opposes the Prophet's message. In addition to 'Utbah and Shaybah ibn Rabi'ah, Abu Sufyan and his wife, Hind, remain staunch opponents. They are dismayed when several of their children join the Prophet's cause, including Umm Habibah, who follows her husband 'Ubayd Allah ibn Jahsh. 'Ubayd Allah's father, Jahsh ibn Ri'ab, is a confederate of 'Abdu Shams and all four of his children (the Jahsh siblings, see Fig. P28) embrace Islam during the Meccan period.

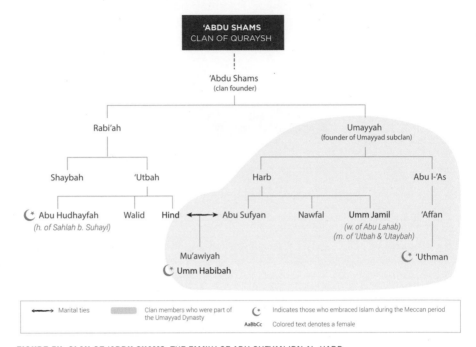

FIGURE 5H. CLAN OF 'ABDU SHAMS: THE FAMILY OF ABU SUFYAN IBN AL-HARB

'Abdu Shams was the brother of Hashim. His son Umayyah was the namesake of the Umayyad dynasty that wrested control of the Islamic empire in 661 CE. Although Shaybah and 'Utbah were enemies of the Prophet, when both were vacationing in Ta'if, they saw the Prophet and sent their servant 'Addas with grapes for him. Both were killed in the Battle of Badr during the opening duels. Abu Hudhayfah was one of the few Muslims from 'Abdu Shams. He married the daughter of Suhayl ibn 'Amr (the chief of 'Amir), and together they migrated to Abyssinia during the years of the ban. Walid ibn 'Utbah continued to be an enemy of the Prophet and was defeated by 'Ali at the opening duel at Badr. Hind was married to Abu Sufyan and was a violent enemy of Islam for the first 20 years. She lost her brother, father, and uncle at Badr and sought violent retribution at Uhud. She finally entered Islam after the Conquest of Mecca. Umm Habibah entered Islam early on and migrated to Abyssinia with her husband 'Ubayd Allah ibn Jahsh. She was later widowed and married the Prophet. Her brother Mu'awiyah later established himself as the founder of the Umayyad Dynasty. Harb ibn Umayyah had given honorary clan membership to Jahsh ibn Ri'ab, the husband of the Prophet's aunt Umaymah. Abu Sufyan was one of the Prophet's biggest enemies. He was married to Hind and led the Quraysh armies during the battles of Uhud and the Trench. He ultimately entered Islam with his wife after the Conquest of Mecca. Nawfal did not play a notable role in the Sirah. (Note, there are four other men named Nawfal in this book.) Umm Jamil was married to Abu Lahab, from the clan of Hashim. She was openly hostile to the Prophet and rescinded the engagements of her two sons to Ruqayyah and Umm Kulthum. 'Uthman ibn 'Affan was the great grandson of Umayyah. He was one of the Prophet's closest Companions and later became the third Caliph in Islam.

CLAN OF 'ADI:

'Adi's position among the Quraysh had been in decline in the last few years. Historically they were Confederates like Makhzum, but they had been drifting toward the Scented Ones (just as their bitter enemy, 'Abdu Shams, was moving toward the Confederates). Nu'aym ibn 'Abd Allah is one of 'Adi's most prominent leaders.

Prior to his conversion at the end of the Early Meccan Period, 'Umar ibn al-Khattab shared his father's staunch loyalty to the pagan traditions of their forefathers and was outraged that most of his close family had just forsaken idolatry.

One year from now, **Nu'aym ibn 'Abd Allah** will prevent 'Umar ibn al-Khattab from trying to kill the Prophet by telling him to first confront his sister, who had recently embraced Islam.

1
2
3
4
5
6

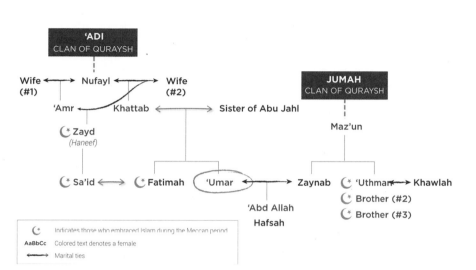

FIGURE 5I. CLAN OF 'ADI: 'UMAR IS SURROUNDED BY MONOTHEISTS

Nufayl had two sons ('Amr and Khattab) by two separate wives. After Nufayl's death, his second wife married her stepson, 'Amr ibn Nufayl. Their child, Zayd ibn 'Amr, could not bring himself to follow his pagan ancestors and became a Haneef. 'Amr's half-brother, Khattab ibn Nufayl, was married to Abu Jahl's sister. He was a staunch pagan who chased Zayd out of Mecca. Zayd later died in Syria and was praised by the Prophet in later years. Zayd's son, Sa'id ibn Zayd, married Fatimah bint Khattab. When the call to Islam reached Sa'id, he and his wife became one of the earliest couples to embrace the new religion. Though they tried to hide their Islam from Fatimah's violent brother, 'Umar, they ultimately played a significant role in his conversion to Islam. 'Umar was also surrounded by monotheists through his wife, Zaynab. Her brother 'Uthman ibn Maz'un was an ardent supporter of the Prophet. He was an ascetic by nature and the Prophet had to guide him toward moderation. Many years later, 'Umar was surprised to see the Prophet weep at 'Uthman's funeral, because 'Uthman had not died a martyr's death. 'Umar later changed his stance when he witnessed the Prophet and Abu Bakr also die of natural causes. 'Uthman's wife, Khawlah, was very close to the Prophet and later suggested Sawdah and 'A'ishah as suitable wives for him. Several years later, Hafsah bint 'Umar married the Prophet in Medina.

CLAN OF JUMAH:

Umayyah ibn Khalaf, the overweight chief of Jumah, will try to avoid marching to Badr, but is eventually goaded by 'Uqbah ibn Abi Mu'ayt into fighting. At the end of the battle, Bilal will find him injured on the battlefield and finish him. Bilal is best known as the muezzin (announcer of the prayer) during the Prophet's lifetime. After the Conquest of Mecca, he climbs atop the Ka'bah to announce the call to prayer.

The clan of Jumah is not as powerful as Makhzum, 'Abdu Shams, or Sahm, yet is more influential than many of the other clans. Despite the early conversion of 'Uthman ibn Maz'un, Bani Jumah contains a number of the Prophet's fiercest enemies. Their chief, Umayyah ibn Khalaf, endlessly tortures his Abyssinian slave Bilal for converting to the new religion. Surah Al Humazah specifically warns Umayyah of his *jahil* (irascible) behavior.

> A warning to every slanderer and backbiter who hoards his money in preparation—is he hoping to buy immortality?
>
> No way! He'll be thrown into the crusher. — *Al Humazah (The Slanderer, 104:1-4)*

⬙ SURAH AL HUMAZAH (The Slanderer) is named after its first verse, which warns the Meccans to consider the serious consequences of engaging in slander, gossip, and miserliness.

---

❺ WHAT IS JAHILIYYA?　　　　　　　　　　　ARMSTRONG

"The chief vice of the kafirun was jahiliyya ... its primary meaning is 'irascibility': an acute sensitivity to honor and prestige; arrogance, excess, and above all, a chronic tendency to violence and retaliation."[9]

Abu Bakr employs **'Amir ibn Fuhayrah** as a shepherd. Several years later, 'Amir will use his flocks to cover the Prophet and Abu Bakr's tracks as they escape Mecca under the cover of night. After Uhud, the Prophet will send 'Amir with a delegation of 40 men to teach Islam to the Hawazin clan of 'Amir (QY 16.11). Along the way, the party is ambushed and massacred. When 'Amir's body is not found among the dead, the Prophet later confirms that 'Amir had been lifted up to heaven.

Abu Bakr lives among the Jumah clan and is alarmed when he hears that Umayyah would place heated boulders on Bilal's chest. He promptly buys the Abyssinian's freedom and subsequently frees countless other servants including 'Amir ibn Fuhayrah and a slave girl who was abused by 'Umar ibn al-Khattab.

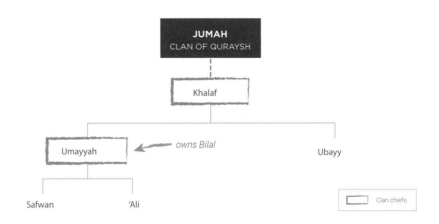

FIGURE 5J. CLAN OF JUMAH: THE FAMILY OF UMAYYAH IBN KHALAF

Umayyah ibn Khalaf was the chief of Jumah and a violent enemy of the Prophet. He and his son 'Ali were killed at Badr at the hands of Bilal and a few other Companions. Umayyah's brother, Ubayy ibn Khalaf, was also a fierce opponent of the Prophet. He later came to Medina to ransom his son after the Battle of Badr. As Ubayy was leaving, he threatened to slay the Prophet at their next meeting. One year later at Uhud, he confronted the Prophet and was slain. Umayyah's son Safwan urged his cousin to assassinate the Prophet in Medina. Safwan also chided Khalid ibn al-Walid when Khalid decided to convert and migrate to Medina. After the Conquest of Mecca, Safwan was one of three men who did not enter Islam, but was given four months of amnesty. After the Battle of Hunayn, he embraced Islam and the Prophet gave him a very generous portion of the spoils.

Umayyah's brother, Ubayy, is no less arrogant, and ridicules the Prophet by crumbling a dry bone and blowing the dust in his face, saying:

"Claimest thou, Muhammad, that God can bring this to life?"

The Prophet answers:

"Even so, that do I claim: He will raise it, and thee too when thou art as that now is; then will He enter thee into the fire."[10]

> Doesn't the human being see that We created him from a drop? Yet, he's clearly defiant. He sets up depictions of Us, all the while forgetting his own creation. He asks, "Who can bring old rotted bones back to life?"
>
> Say to him, "The One Who gave them life the first time will give them life again, for He knows about every type of creation. He's the One who can produce a fire from green trees when you kindle it. Doesn't the One Who created the heavens and the earth have the power to create something like (a human being again)? Definitely! He's the Creator and the Knowing!"
> — *Ya Seen (36:77-81)*

CLANS OF HARITH, 'ABD AD-DAR, AND NAWFAL:

The three lesser clans of Quraysh did not play a considerable role in opposing or supporting the early Muslim community. Nawfal was part of the Scented Ones but had grown apart from Hashim ever since 'Abd al-Muttalib took back control of Mecca from his uncle, Nawfal. 'Abd ad-Dar is the leader of the Confederates and retain the rights to the keys to the Ka'bah. They maintain a historic rivalry with Hashim that goes back several generations.

Two noteworthy personalities from these clans include Mus'ab ibn 'Umayr (from 'Abd ad-Dar) and Abu 'Ubaydah ibn al-Jarrah (from Harith).

SURAH YA SEEN is named after the enigmatic letters that begin the surah. The Prophet once described it as the heart of the Qur'an, as it beautifully encapsulates several fundamental themes presented throughout all of the Meccan surahs.

In the coming years, **Mus'ab ibn 'Umayr** will play a pivotal role in helping the Prophet prepare Medina for the Hijrah. He will remain a loyal supporter until his death at the Battle of Uhud.

Abu 'Ubaydah ibn al-Jarrah is one of the earliest Muslim converts, who will later fight at all the major battles and ride alongside the Prophet at the Conquest of Mecca. He is one of the 10 Companions to whom the Prophet promises Paradise.

YEAR 6: HAMZA & 'UMAR

6.1 THE CONVERSION OF HAMZAH

Despite the ongoing persecution in Mecca, the Prophet continued to visit the Sacred Precinct regularly. One day, as the Prophet is performing *tawaf* (ritual circumambulation) around the Ka'bah, several Meccan leaders begin to slander him out loud.

The *muhstahziyeen* included Abu Jahl, Abu Lahab, and Walid ibn al-Mughirah.

❶ WHO WERE THE MUHSTAHZIYEEN?   YUSUF

Abu Jahl is the leader of a group of people that the Quran calls the muhstahziyeen. The muhstahziyeen are people that make fun of the Prophet, God's peace and blessings upon him. This is very significant because this group is different from the others. Abu Sufyan [Ibn al-Harb] was not a part of this, which indicates some nobility in Abu Sufyan. On the other hand, these people were cruel and were constantly mocking the Prophet, God's peace and blessings upon him, and his people."[1]

In the middle of his third circuit, he unexpectedly turns to the jeering crowd, and exclaims:

> "O people of Quraysh! Listen, I swear by Allah in Whose Hand is my soul, that you will one day be slaughtered to pieces."

The crowd is stunned and finally Abu Jahl responds:

> "You can leave Abul-Qasim, for you have never been foolish."[2]

❷ WHAT WAS THE PROPHET'S PROBLEM WITH THE QURAYSH?   ARMSTRONG

"Muhammad had no quarrel with the beliefs of Abu l-Hakam [Abu Jahl] or Abu Sufyan. In fact, much of their theology was quite correct. They believed without question, for example, that Allah was the creator of the world and the lord of the Ka'bah. The trouble was that they did not translate their beliefs into action."[3]

On a separate occasion, Abu Jahl confronts the Prophet at the Ka'bah and taunts him mercilessly. Unlike the previous encounter, the Prophet returns to his house without saying a word. At the same time his uncle Hamzah had been returning from a hunting expedition. As he enters the Holy Precinct, a former servant of the late 'Abd Allah ibn Jud'an pulls him aside and describes what just transpired between Abu Jahl and the Prophet. Outraged at the abuse suffered by his beloved nephew, Hamzah strides over to Abu Jahl and strikes him with his bow, exclaiming:

> "Ah! You have been abusing Muhammad; I too follow his religion and profess what he preaches."

Abu Jahl recoils from the swift blow. Cowering under Hamzah's looming presence, he confesses to mistreating the Prophet and quickly disperses the astonished crowd.

3 **WHY WAS ABU JAHL SO BITTER?** `WATT`

"It has sometimes been suggested that the Meccan merchants were afraid that the new religion would lead to a disregard of the sacredness of Mecca and so to the reduction or destruction of its trade … There was no attempt to change the sacral character of Mecca and it's shrine … there was nothing to justify the belief that Muhammad's religion would seriously reduce the trade of Mecca.

Deep in the Arab heart was the feeling that the best man to rule a tribe or clan was the man who was outstanding in wisdom, prudence and judgment. If they accepted Muhammad's claim, would they not also have to admit in the long run that he was the man best fitted to direct all the affairs of Mecca? The threat was not an immediate one, but a future one. It was in ten or twenty years' time that Muhammad's power might be irresistible. The men of the previous generation, who still dominated Meccan affairs in the years round 613, were not so bitterly opposed to Muhammad as his contemporary Abu-Jahl."[5]

Hamzah ibn 'Abd al-Muttalib is related to the Prophet in more ways than anyone else. His half-brother 'Abd Allah was the Prophet's father (Fig. P10) and his mother Halah is a first cousin to the Prophet's mother Aminah (Fig. P11). Finally, his full sister Safiyyah is married to the Prophet's brother-in-law 'Awwam (Fig. P23). Lings describes him as "the most formidable and most unyielding of the Quraysh."

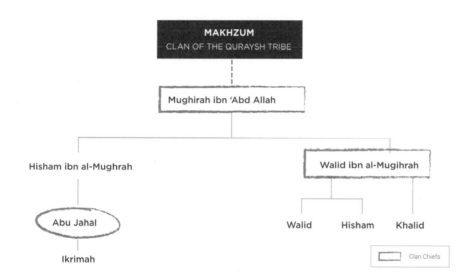

FIGURE 6A. ABU JAHL AND THE LEADERS OF MAKHZUM

Makhzum was the most powerful Quraysh clan during the Prophet's lifetime. At the beginning of the Prophet's mission, Walid ibn al-Mughirah was its chief and also the one whom the Prophet was talking to when he was approached by a blind man looking for guidance (Chapter 22). All three of Walid's sons entered Islam at different points in time. Walid ibn al-Walid was the first to convert after the battle of Badr. His half-brother Khalid converts after the battle of the Trench and soon becomes one of the greatest generals in Islamic history. Hisham is the last to convert, after the conquest of Mecca. Unlike Walid's own sons, Abu Jahl considered himself to be the next leader of Makhzum, and persecuted the Prophet until his own death. His son 'Ikrimah also joined his father's relentless attacks on Islam, and only entered Islam after the Conquest of Mecca.

6.2 THE CONVERSION OF 'UMAR

For the past several years Abu Jahl's brash 26 year-old nephew, 'Umar ibn al-Khattab, had become one of the most outspoken critics of the Prophet. He had previously heard Surah Al Haqqaq, and was convinced that Muhammad was a poet. As if reading 'Umar's mind, the surah responds:

> So now I call to witness what you can see and also what you can't see, (to demonstrate) that this is truly the word of an honored messenger. These aren't the words of a mere poet - oh, how little you believe! Neither are these the words of a fortune-teller - oh, how few reminders you take!
> — *Al Haqqaq (The Reality, 69:40-42)*

SURAH AL HAQQAQ (The Reality) is named after its opening verse, which pointedly asks listeners to reflect on the true reality in which they live.

Although the Qur'an is beginning to speak to 'Umar, his attachment to the tradition of his forefathers prevents him from opening his heart to the Prophet's recitation. After the Quraysh's humiliating failure in Abyssinia, 'Umar quickly realizes that the only way to wipe out the Prophet's movement is to eliminate its leader. He makes his way to the Prophet's house, but is stopped by Nu'aym ibn 'Abd Allah who convinces 'Umar to first confront his sister's family who had secretly joined the new religion.

Sa'id ibn Zayd is 'Umar's close childhood friend and will soon become a very valuable Companion to the Prophet. He is one of the 10 men whom the Prophet later promises Paradise (refer to Fig. 5i for 'Umar's family tree).

When 'Umar approaches Fatimah's house, he overhears the melodic recitation of Surah Ta Ha and is infuriated by her betrayal. He attacks his brother-in-law, Sa'id ibn Zayd, and, in the heat of the moment, strikes Fatimah as well.

But 'Umar's rage quickly turns to remorse when he sees his sister bleeding. He reads a few verses from the surah and is swept away by its nobility.

> I am God. There is no other god than I, so serve Me (alone) and establish prayer, so you can remember Me. — *Ta Ha (20:14)*

SURAH TA HA is named after the enigmatic letters that begin the surah. It details the prophetic career of Moses and the challenges he faced at the hands of Pharaoh and his own people. The surah ends with clear instructions to the young Muslim community to approach God in humble prayer, so as not to be deluded by material distractions.

---

(4) WHAT CAN WE LEARN FROM 'UMAR'S CONVERSION? [RAMADAN]

"The Prophet of course knew that God alone has the power to guide hearts ... the conversions that took the longest were not necessarily the most solid, and the reverse was not true either: when it comes to conversion, the heart's dispositions, faith, and love, there is no logic, and all that remains is the extraordinary power of the divine.
This heart's revolution was a sign, and it carried a twofold teaching: that nothing is impossible for God, and that one should not pronounce final judgments on anything or anybody ... remembering God's infinite power should mean healthy self-doubt as to oneself and suspending one's judgment as to others."[6]

'Umar heads directly to the Prophet's house where Hamzah (who had converted only three days earlier) is armed and ready to defend his nephew. Undeterred, 'Umar marches past Hamzah and declares his wholehearted conversion to the Prophet.

Without a minute to spare, 'Umar immediately goes to the house of the Prophet's fiercest enemy—Abu Jahl. When the Makhzumi answers the knock at his door, 'Umar defiantly proclaims his new affiliation with the Prophet. As expected, his uncle curses his young clansman and slams the door in his face.

Abu Jahl is not only the Prophet's most treacherous enemy, he is also 'Umar's maternal uncle (see Fig. 6a).

'Umar's defiant attitude immediately strengthens the Prophet's cause. Several years later he reminisced:

> "... After I embraced Islam, I asked the Prophet: Aren't we on the right path here and Hereafter? ... Why then do we have to conduct secret activities? I swear by Allah Who has sent you with the Truth, that we will leave our concealment and proclaim our noble cause publicly ... We then went out in two groups, Hamzah leading one and I the other. We headed for the Mosque in broad daylight when the polytheists of Quraysh saw us, their faces went pale and got incredibly depressed and resentful. On that very occasion, the Prophet attached to me the epithet of Al-Farooq [one who can tell right from wrong]."[7]

An example of the power of 'Umar's conversion comes from a diminutive 22-year-old shepherd named 'Abd Allah ibn Mas'ud. A few years earlier, 'Abd Allah had witnessed the Prophet produce milk from a dry ewe, and was so impressed by the miracle, that he embraced Islam. Since 'Abd Allah was only a confederate of Bani Zuhrah, and not Quraysh by blood, he was particularly vulnerable to religious persecution. In fact, only after 'Umar's high-profile conversion, did 'Abd Allah note that he and most of the other Companions finally feel safe praying in public at the Ka'bah:

'Abd Allah ibn Mas'ud is the first person to openly recite the Qur'an at the Ka'bah and will later become one of the most authoritative scholars of the Qur'an and *Hadith* (collected sayings of the Prophet).

> So great and instant was the effect of his conversion on the situation for the believers who had until then worshipped Allah within their four walls in secret, now assembled and performed their rites of worship openly in the Holy Sanctuary itself. This raised their spirits, and anxiety and uneasiness began to seize the Quraysh.[8]

6.3 THE LAST ATTEMPT AT RECONCILIATION

With every new revelation, the leaders of Quraysh grow increasingly frustrated with their inability to stop the Prophet's movement. The untimely conversions of Hamzah and 'Umar only add to their desperation and uncertainty.

In a shift of strategy, 'Utbah ibn Rabi'ah, a leading man of 'Abdu Shams, tries to explain to the Prophet that the revelations are not only dividing the community, but dishonoring their forefathers:

> "O nephew! If you are doing this with a view to getting wealth, we will join together to give you greater riches than any Qurayshite has possessed. If ambition moves you, we will make you our chief. If you desire kingship we will readily offer you that. If you are under the power of an evil spirit which seems to haunt and dominate so that you cannot shake off its yoke, then we shall call in skillful physicians to treat you."[9]

When 'Utbah is finished, the Prophet responds with the rhythmically metered verses of Surah Fussilat:

> Ha. Meem.
>
> (This is) a revelation from the Compassionate and Merciful - a book with clearly explained verses and a recitation in Arabic for people who understand. It gives good news and warnings. Yet, most (people) turn away and fail to listen.
>
> They say, "Our hearts are immune to what you're inviting us, and our ears are deaf (to what you say). There's a veil between us and you, so do (whatever you like), and we'll do whatever we like, as well!"
>
> Say to them, "I'm just a mortal man like you. Revelation has come to me that (compels me to say that) your god is only One God, so stand firmly for Him, and ask for His forgiveness! Ruin to those who make partners (with God) - those who make no effort to cleanse themselves through charity and who reject (the concept of) an afterlife! However, those who believe and do what's morally right will receive a reward that will never end."
>
> — *Fussilat (Clear Explanation, 41:1-6)*

'**Utbah ibn Rabi'ah** is the father of Hind, the wife of Abu Sufyan ibn al-Harb. Despite his warning to the Quraysh, 'Utbah never joins the Prophet and is killed several years later during the opening duels at Badr.

SURAH FUSSILAT (Clear Explanation) is named after the third verse, which describes the Qur'an as a clear explanation written in the Arabic language. Its rhetorical questions and sharp answers are a forceful rebuttal to the Prophet's critics in Mecca.

---

5 **WHY DID THE QURAYSH HAVE A PROBLEM WITH MUHAMMAD?**   ASLAN

"In short, the difference between Muhammad and the Hanifs was that Muhammad was not just preaching 'the religion of Abraham,' Muhammad was the new Abraham (6:83-86; 21:51-93). And it was precisely this self-image that so greatly disturbed the Quraysh. By proclaiming himself 'the Messenger of God,' Muhammad was blatantly transgressing the traditional Arab process through which power was granted. This was not authority that had been given to Muhammad as 'the first among equals.' Muhammad had no equals."[10]

Surah Fussilat continues to narrate the story of creation, the prophets, destruction, and hellfire. The revelation holds no punches:

> The faithless say, "Don't listen to this Qur'an! Talk nonsense over it when it's being recited, so you can come out on top!" — *Fussilat (Clear Explanation, 41:26)*

The Prophet ends by explaining to 'Utbah the attitude of a sincere believer:

> Among His signs are the night and the day and the sun and the moon. Don't bow down to the sun or the moon, but bow down to God Who created them, if you really aim to serve Him. If they're too arrogant (to bow before God, it doesn't matter), because in your Lord's presence (are many who already) glorify Him throughout the night and the day, and they never get bored of it.
> — *Fussilat (Clear Explanation, 41:37-38)*

---

6 HOW DO THE EARLY SURAHS SPEAK TO US? | ARMSTRONG

"In each of the early suras [chapters of revelation], God spoke intimately to the individual, often preferring to pose many of his teachings in the form of a question— 'Have you not heard?' 'Do you consider?' 'Have you not seen?' Each listener was thus invited to interrogate him or herself ... This new religion was not about achieving metaphysical certainty: the Qur'an wanted people to develop a different kind of awareness."[11]

The surah leaves 'Utbah speechless. He returns to the Quraysh warning:

> *"I have never heard words similar to those he recited. They definitely relate neither to poetry nor to witchcraft nor do they derive from soothsaying. O people of Quraysh! I request you to take note of my advice and grant the man full freedom to pursue his goals..."[12]*

---

7 WHAT DOES THE QUR'AN ASK OF US? | ARMSTRONG

"The probing, intimate questioning and use of the present tense obliged listeners to face up to the implications of their behavior on a daily basis. The Qur'an asks insistently: 'Where are you going with your life?' [Al-Takwir (The Enfolding) 81:26] People must, therefore become self-aware, conscious of what they are doing ... They must cultivate the virtue of taqwa' [God consciousness] ... continually guard against selfishness, greed, and arrogance."[13]

Unsatisfied with the Prophet's response, the Quraysh repeat their offers, but the Prophet simply responds:

> *"I am not possessed, neither I seek honour amongst you, nor kingship over you. But God hath sent me to you as a messenger and revealed to me a book and commanded me that I should be for you a teller of good tidings and a warner. Even so I have conveyed to you the message of my Lord, and I have given you good counsel. If ye accept from me what I have brought you, that is your good fortune in this world and the next; but if ye reject what I have brought, then will I patiently await God's judgment between us."*[14]

---

8   **HOW CAN THE PROPHET BE ACCUSED OF WANTING POWER?**   YUSUF

"The naysayers and detractors of the Prophet, God's peace and blessings upon him, say he only wanted power. Why, then, at the time when he was being most persecuted in Mecca, and was offered power, did he refuse it? He was offered so much worldly power, yet he refused it, which is really one of the great proofs of his message."[15]

In response, the Quraysh dig in their heels and demand to see the Prophet perform miracles. When he refuses, they mock the recently revealed verses of Surah Saba' by asking him to make the sky fall down on their heads.

 ...If We wanted, We could make the earth swallow them up or cause a piece of the sky to fall down upon them... — *Saba' (Sheba, 34:9)*

But the Prophet remains unfazed and patiently responds:

> *"That is up to Allah, as He wills, He does."*

'Abd Allah ibn Abi Umayyah was named after the Prophet's father. He is the Prophet's first cousin through his aunt 'Atikah (Fig. 3b). Despite his avowed enmity to Islam, many years later, just before the Prophet's army enters Mecca, he will rush out to meet the Prophet and embrace Islam.

As he gets up to leave the gathering, 'Abd Allah ibn Abi Umayyah declares:

> *"I will not believe in thee ever, nay, not until thou takest a ladder and I see thee mount on it up to heaven, and until thou bringest four Angels to testify that thou art what thou claimest to be, and even then I think I would not believe thee."*[16]

6.4 SURAH AL KAFIRUN: NO COMPROMISE IN FAITH

For the past six years, the Quraysh had failed to produce a rational counterargument to the Qur'an's piercing arguments. While a number of verses from the latest revelations may have penetrated some of the the hardest hearts, for the most part, confusion and malaise keep the Quraysh in a state of disbelief. Surah Hud explains:

> And so it was that We gave the scripture to Moses, but (later generations) differed about it. If it wasn't for the statement (of principle) that went out before from your Lord (that people will have time to make their choice as to whether or not to believe), then the matter would've been decided between them. However, they persist in doubts and misgivings about it. — *Hud (11:110)*

---

9 **WHAT WAS REALLY HOLDING THE MECCANS BACK?** [WATT]

"The grounds of opposition to Islam were thus, besides self-interest, fear of its political and economic implications, and sheer conservatism. The situation which confronted Muhammad was a malaise which had social, economic, political, and intellectual symptoms. His message was essentially religious in that it attempted to remedy the underlying religious causes of the malaise, but it affected the other aspects, and consequently the opposition had many facets."[17]

In a shift in strategy, the Quraysh reason that if Muhammad cannot be stopped, perhaps he could be persuaded to assimilate. Walid ibn al-Mughirah proposes a compromise:

> *"O Muhammad! Come and let us worship what you worship, and you worship what we worship. We can be partners with you in this matter. If the one you worship is better than what we worship then we will get some kind of benefit. Whereas, if what we worship is better than the one you worship then you will get some kind of benefit."*[18]

But the Prophet responds with Surah Al Kafirun, which leaves no room for compromise:

> Say (to them): "O, all you who suppress (your awareness of the truth)! I don't serve what you serve, and you don't serve what I do. And I won't serve what you serve, nor will you serve what I do - to you, your way of life, and to me, mine." — *Al Kafirun (The Faithless, 109:1-6)*

---

10 **WAS AL KAFIRUN A POINT OF NO RETURN?** [WATT]

"He [Muhammad] doubtless accepted the Qur'anic view that he was only a warner, and sought for no more than a religious function. Yet in the circumstances, that is, in view of the Arab conception of what constituted fitness or worthiness to bear rule, this divorce between prophethood and political leadership could not be maintained. How could any secular leader carry out a policy if the word of God, or even the word of His prophet merely, was against it? The mention of the goddesses is thus properly the beginning of the active opposition of Quraysh, and Surat al-Kafirun, which seems so purely religious, made it necessary for Muhammad to conquer Mecca."[19]

SURAH HUD is named after a series of verses that detail the challenges Prophet Hud faced when calling on his people to abandon idolatry. Like other late Meccan surahs, this surah chronicles the fate of several prophets, including Noah and Moses, who were instructed to leave their people in search of a new beginning. Not surprisingly, Surah Hud was revealed shortly before the Hijrah to strengthen the hearts of the faithful.

SURAH AL KAFIRUN (The Faithless) is named after its main subject matter. It had the desired effect of drawing a clear line in the sand between the small Muslim community and its surrounding critics.

1
2
3
4
5
6

6.5 SURAH AL KAHF & THE THREE QUESTIONS

Powerless to refute the verses of the Qur'an, the Quraysh decide to consult the Jewish rabbis of Yathrib, who provide clear instructions:

"Ask him three questions. If he informs you about them then he is indeed a Messenger. Ask him about the children who went away in earlier times; what happened to them? Ask him about a man whose journeys reached the east and west of the earth; what was his prophecy? Ask him about the soul; what is it?"[20]

When the Quraysh relay the three questions to the Prophet, he promises an answer the next day, but does not say, *insha'Allah* (if God wills). For 15 days, the Prophet endures awkward silence, while the Quraysh wait for an answer. Surah Al Kahf later explains:

> Never say of anything, "I'll do it tomorrow," without adding, "If God wills." If you forget (to add this phrase), then remember your Lord (when you recall your lapse) and say, "I hope that my Lord guides me closer to the rightly guided way." — *Al Kahf (The Cave, 18:23-24)*

 SURAH AL KAHF (The Cave) is named after a series of verses that describe the Sleepers of Ephesus who fell asleep in a cave for hundreds of years. The surah also includes the spellbinding travels of Moses and Dhul-Qurnayn (see below).

---

11 WHY SAY "INSHA'ALLAH?"   `RAMADAN`

"It expresses the awareness of limits, the feeling of humility of one who acts while knowing that beyond what he or she can do or say, God alone has the power to make things happen. This is by no means a fatalistic message: it implies not that one should not act but, on the contrary, that one should never stop acting while always being aware in one's mind and heart of the real limits of human power."[21]

The uncomfortable delay creates a difficult situation for the Muslims. Nevertheless, it corroborates the Prophet's role as a conduit of divine revelation:

> Was it conceivable that if Muhammad had invented the earlier Revelations he could have delayed so long before inventing this latest one, especially when so much appeared to be at stake?[22]

The story of the **Seven Sleepers of Ephesus** is related in early Christian and Roman writings. It refers to seven Christian youths who fled from Roman persecution and fell asleep in a cave for hundreds of years. Make sure to revisit all of Surah Al Kahf for detailed answers to the rabbis' questions.

Finally, two of the three long-awaited answers arrive in the form of Surah Al Kahf, which narrates the spellbinding account of the Sleepers of Ephesus (18:9-25) and the story of Dhul-Qurnayn (18:83-98).

> Have you ever considered that the Companions of the Cave and the inscribed writings might be among Our wondrous signs? When the young people fled (from persecution) to the cave, they said, "Our Lord! Be merciful to us, and resolve our situation in the most appropriate way."
>
> Then We drew (a veil) over their ears for a number of years in the cave, (so they would have no news of the outside world). Then, (after some time had passed), We awakened them to test which of the two sides (among them) would be better able to calculate the length of their stay.
>
> We're telling you their story truthfully, for they were young people who believed in their Lord. Therefore, We increased them in guidance.
> — *Al Kahf (The Cave, 18:9-13)*

(Christians differ over the details of the story, with some) saying that there were three (young people in the cave) and that their dog was the fourth among them. (Others) said they were five, with their dog being the sixth, but they're just guessing about what they haven't seen. (Others even assert that) they were seven, with their dog being the eighth.

Say to them, "My Lord knows best what their exact number was, and only a few (people) know for sure (how many they were)." So don't get drawn into arguments with them (on such speculative issues), but rather (talk to them) only on topics that have clear resolutions, and don't consult any of them at all about (such obscure topics). — *Al Kahf (The Cave, 18:22)*

Now they're asking you about the Master of the Two Horns. Say to them, "I'll narrate for you something of his story."

We established him in the earth and gave him the means to reach every (place he wanted). He followed one way until he reached the setting of the sun, and he found it setting (behind) a murky body of water. Near it he found a people (who were given to misbehavior, but who had no power to resist him). We said, "Master of the Two Horns! Either punish them or treat them well."

"The one who does wrong shall be punished," he announced. "Then he'll be sent back to his Lord, and He'll punish him with a harsh penalty. However, the one who has faith and does what's morally right will be well rewarded, and we'll issue easy commands to him." — *Al Kahf (The Cave, 18:83–88)*

Regarding the Spirit, the Prophet responds:

Now they're asking you about the spirit (that resides within each person). Tell them, "The spirit is under the command of my Lord, and no knowledge of it has ever come to you except for a little." — *Al Isra' (The Night Journey, 17:85)*

The rabbis of Yathrib acknowledge the first two answers, but protest the third. When they argue that they have knowledge of all things, the Prophet responds:

"That all is but little in respect of God's Own Knowledge; yet have ye therein enough for your needs, if ye would but practice it."[23]

His words are echoed by the verses of Al Kahf which underscore God's infinite wisdom:

Say to them, "If the ocean was made of ink (and it was used to write out) the words of my Lord, the ocean would run dry first before the words of my Lord would be exhausted, even if we added another ocean just like it to help!"

Say to them: "I'm just a man like yourselves. I've received inspiration (that commands me to inform) you that your God is One God and that whoever expects to meet his Lord, let him do moral deeds and let him not join any partners at all in the service of his Lord." — *Al Kahf (The Cave, 18:109-110)*

Although the exact identity of **Dhul-Qurnayn** (master of the two horns) is not known, many Muslim scholars suggest that he was either Alexander the Great (356−323 BCE) or Cyrus the Great (576 BC−530 BCE). (In his translation, Yahiya Emerick presents intriguing details to support the latter.)

The Prophet's age after 'Umar's conversion: __46__

GUARDIANS		
'Abd al-Muttalib (81/37 yrs ago)	Abu Talib (67)	

WIVES	CHILDREN	GRANDCHILDREN
Khadijah bint Khuwaylid (61) *(twice widowed / Asad)*	Qasim *(died in infancy)*	
	Zaynab (16) *(w. of Abu l-'As)*	
	Ruqayyah (14) *(w. of 'Uthman ibn 'Affan)*	
	Umm Kulthum (13) *(unmarried)*	
	Fatimah (11) *(unmarried)*	
	'Abd Allah *(died in infancy)*	

ADOPTED FAMILY		
	'Ali ibn Abi Talib (14) *(adopted nephew)*	
	Zayd ibn Harithah (36) *(adopted son)*	Usamah ibn Zayd (infant)
	Umm Ayman (?) *(freed servant of the Prophet's father)*	

(XX) Approximate age / Age at time of death	~~AaBbCc~~ Stricken text denotes recently deceased	
AaBbCc Colored text denotes a female	AaBbCc Faded text denotes previously deceased	

FIGURE 6B. THE PROPHET'S HOUSEHOLD AT THE END OF THE EARLY MECCAN PERIOD

During the entire Early Meccan Period, the Prophet continued to enjoy the protection of his uncle Abu Talib. At this time, two of the Prophet's daughters were married. Zaynab had married Khadijah's nephew, Abu l-'As. After Ruqayyah's engagement to 'Utbah ibn Abi Lahab had been annulled, she then married 'Uthman ibn 'Affan. Umm Kulthum's engagement to 'Utbah's brother, 'Utaybah, had also been dissolved, and she and Fatimah were single at this time.

By the time 'Umar (26) had converted to Islam, Zayd was already 36 years old. A few years earlier, Zayd had followed the Prophet's recommendation and married Umm Ayman. The couple had a little boy named Usamah, whom the Prophet raised as his own grandson.

(Refer to Fig. P25 for previous details about the Prophet's household.)

LATE MECCA

PROPHETIC ROUTINE

Al-Hussain ibn Alī ibn Abī Tālib narrated: "I asked my father about what the Prophet (peace be upon him) did when he was at home. He said: "He (peace be upon him) distributed his time into three portions ; one portion for Allāh, another portion for his family and a portion for himself. Then, he distributed his personal portion in two, one for himself and one for the people; in such a manner that he communicated knowledge to the masses through his close companions when they visited him and he did not conceal anything from them. During the portion he dedicated for people, he gave preference to the people of greater piety and status to enter upon him and he distributed this time according to their level of piety . From among those who visited him, some had one need, some had two needs, and some had many needs. He (peace be upon him) sacrificed the time to fulfil all their requirements and busied them in things that would rectify them and the entire nation. When they inquired on matters related to religion, he replied to them in a manner that benefited them and he used to say, 'Those that are present, should convey to those that are absent regarding these beneficial matters.' He also used to say, 'Those people who for some reason cannot bring forth their needs, you should inform me about them. This is because the person who conveys to a ruler the need of another, who is unable to do so himself, Allāh will keep that person firm on the Day of Judgment.' No issues besides those of importance and benefit were presented to him in his gatherings and he did not accept listening except to that which was beneficial and lawful. The companions came to his assemblies for their religious and lawful needs and they did not depart without enjoying the taste of his knowledge, and they left with guidance for the people.' "

‘Amrah reported that someone asked Aisha: "What was the normal routine of the Messenger of Allah (peace be upon him) at home?" She replied: "He was a man from amongst men. He himself removed anything that was attached to his clothing, milked his goats, and did all of his work himself."

Taken from A Commentary on the Depiction of Prophet Muhammad, by Imam al-Tirmidhi (#336, #342)

YEAR 7: THE BAN

7.1 INITIATION OF THE BAN

'Umar's high-profile conversion highlights the Quraysh's inability to halt the growth of Islam in Mecca. In desperation, the leaders of Quraysh arrange a covert meeting to draft crippling sanctions against the Prophet's clan. They forbid all inter-clan trade and marriage with Bani Hashim until the clan outlaws the Prophet or the Prophet abandons his movement. Not surprisingly, Abu Lahab conveniently excuses himself from the meeting and is subsequently exempted from the sanctions.

---

❶ WHAT WAS THE POINT OF THE BAN?　　　　　ASLAN

"If Muhammad and his Companions wished to be separated from the social and religious activities of Mecca, then they must be prepared to be separated from its economy. After all, if religion and trade were inseparable in Mecca, no one could so brazenly deny the former and still expect to participate in the latter."[1]

With the notable exception of Bani Muttalib, who refuse to forsake their close relatives from Hashim, 40 men of Quraysh endorse the ban. Of course, Muttalib's refusal comes at a cost, and it too is boycotted along with Hashim.

The ban is not merely an expression of philosophical differences, but a desperate attempt to preserve Mecca's emerging plutocracy:

> The movement led by Muhammad, though primarily religious, impinged upon economic matters, and in this respect it could perhaps be regarded as continuing the attitude of Hilf al-Fudul of opposition to unscrupulous monopolists. To this extent Muhammad might be regarded as continuing the traditional policy of Hashim, and it would therefore not be surprising if he also received a certain measure of general support from his clan.
>
> ... On the one hand, this was a stage in the campaign against Muhammad; but on the other hand, it was also a stage in the aggrandizement of Makhzum and their associated clans at the expense of the Hilf al-Fudul, for it involved the disruption of the latter.[2]

This is not the first time that the Scented Ones were pitted against each other. Recall that after 'Abd al-Muttalib's rise to power, the clans of Nawfal and 'Abdu Shams had developed an alliance against Hashim (P 2.3).

Remember that the **Hilf al-Fudul** (Pact of Chivalry) was formed over 20 years ago to address economic injustices practiced by the more powerful clans of Quraysh (Fig. P22).

---

❷ WHAT DID THE QUR'AN EMPHASIZE DURING THE PERIOD OF THE BAN?　　　　　RAMADAN

"The purpose of the boycott was not to starve the two clans, but to bring home to them the consequence of removing themselves from the tribe. If Muhammad wanted to withdraw from the religious life of Mecca, he could not continue to benefit from the economy.

During this ban, the Qur'an reminded the Muslims that other Prophets—Joseph, Noah, Jonah, Moses, and Jesus—had also warned their people to reform their behavior, and when they refused, their societies had collapsed, because they were not acting in accordance with the fundamental principles of the universe ... When they oppress the weak and refuse to share their wealth fairly with the poor, this violation of God's law is as unnatural as though a fish were to try to live on dry land. Disaster was inevitable."[3]

YEAR 8: THE BAN

8.1 STARVATION

For the most part, the ban is strictly enforced in Mecca and the clans of Hashim and Muttalib near starvation:

> It was a horrible and deadly siege. The supply of food was almost stopped and the people in confinement faced great hardships ... they had to eat leaves and skins of animals. Cries of little children suffering from hunger used to be heard clearly ... During "the prohibited months"—when hostilities traditionally ceased, they would leave their confinement and buy food coming from outside Makkah. Even then the food stuff was unjustly overpriced so that their financial situation would fall short of finding access to it.[1]

During this difficult period, several non-Hashimites, including Abu Bakr and 'Umar, supply food and necessities for Bani Hashim and Muttalib. Though not yet Muslims, Hisham ibn 'Amr and Khadijah's beloved nephew, Hakim ibn Hizam, also smuggle valuable provisions to the starving families.

Recall that **Hakim ibn Hizam** had purchased Zayd ibn Harithah and gave him to Khadijah many years ago. Several years from now, he will try to persuade the Quraysh not to take up arms against the Prophet at Badr. Despite Hakim's constant support for Khadijah's family, he doesn't embrace Islam until the eve of the Conquest of Mecca.

The following year, **Hisham ibn 'Amr** will initiate a campaign that successfully lifts the ban on Hashim and Muttalib.

8.2 "TALES FROM LONG AGO"

Although the terms of the ban permit the Prophet to enter the Holy Sanctuary during the four sacred months, his visits are often met with jeers and harassment. The Quraysh mock him wherever he goes, whispering to each other that his revelations are merely tales from the distant past.

Despite the constant humiliation, the Prophet remains undeterred, allowing Surah At-Tatfeef to address the Quraysh head-on:

> When Our (revealed) verses are read to one of them, he says, "Tales from long ago!" No way! Not so! Their hearts are rusted by the burden (of the sins) they've earned. — *At-Tatfeef (The Shortchanger, 83:13-14)*

YEAR 9: THE BAN

9.1 LIFTING THE BAN

The clans of Hashim and Muttalib endure nearly three long years of hunger and hardship. Fed up with the cruelty inflicted on their fellow tribesmen, five Meccans led by Hisham ibn 'Amr, challenge the Quraysh to drop the ban. Despite Abu Jahl's opposition, most of the Quraysh finally concede. When they enter the Ka'bah to remove the document on which the sanctions were written, all that is left of the ant-eaten parchment are the words, "In Thy Name, O God."

Despite the miraculous sign, the Quraysh continue to oppose the Prophet and his message. Surah Al Qamar chronicles their senseless opposition, even to the most obvious miracles:

> The Hour (of Judgment) is near, and the moon has split in half. However, if they see a miracle, they turn away and say, "Just some kind of fading magic." They deny (such miracles) and follow their own vain desires...
> — Al Qamar (The Moon, 54:1-3)

〜 **SURAH AL QAMAR** (The Moon) is named after its opening verse, which refers to the miraculous splitting of the moon. It narrates the stories of Noah, Hud, Saleh, and Lot, and asks its listeners, "Will anyone be reminded?"

THE QURAYSH

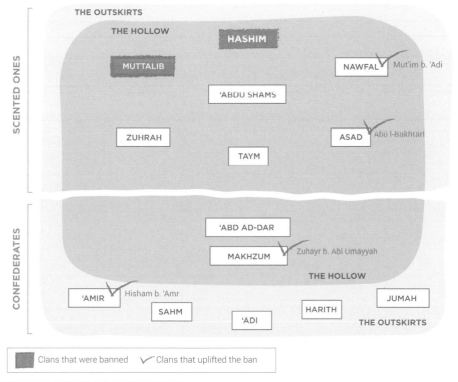

FIGURE 9A. THE BAN AND ITS ANNULMENT

The Late Meccan Period began with the ban on Hashim, which was initiated by Abu Jahl and cosigned by at least 40 other Meccan notables. Bani Muttalib refused to abandon its close kinsmen and was subsequently included in the ban. Abu Lahab (from Hashim) was conveniently excluded from the sanctions. The ban lasted two to three years and, though difficult, had the unintended consequence of bringing more attention to the plight of the Muslims. Finally, Hisham ibn 'Amr (from 'Amir) persuaded four other Meccans from Nawfal, Asad, and Makhzum to support his campaign to successfully lift the ban and release the Prophet and his family from years of isolation and hardship.

> **1** WHAT WERE THE UNDERLYING MOTIVES OF THE BAN-BREAKERS?   WATT
>
> "The absence of the other members of the Hilf al-Fudul is probably not significant except that of 'Abd Shams; but the latter suggests that this clan was now coming to have very close business relations with Makhzum and in consequence common interests, and that these rather than traditional alliances were now molding its policy. If we may hazard a guess about the motives of the boycott-breakers, it would be that with the passage of time they had realized that the grand alliance and the boycott were strengthening the position of the strong clans which aimed at establishing monopolistic controls over Meccan trade, and were consequently weakening the position of the other clans."[1]

9.2 RETURN FROM ABYSSINIA

'Uthman ibn Maz'un is an ascetic by nature and the Prophet will later urge him toward moderation. He is married to Khawlah, a close friend of the Prophet, who later suggests 'A'ishah and Sawdah as suitable wives for him. 'Uthman's sister Zaynab marries 'Umar and is the mother of Hafsah, the Prophet's fourth wife.

With the ban lifted, a relaxed feeling enters Mecca and soon many of the Muslim emigrants, including 'Uthman and Ruqayyah, Abu Salamah and Umm Salamah, and Abu Hudhayfah, return from Abyssinia. When another notable emigrant, 'Uthman ibn Maz'un, returns to Mecca, he arranges for his protection under Walid ibn al-Mughirah. But when he sees other Companions lacking the same security he has been afforded, he absolves Walid as a guardian saying:

> *"I would have the protection of God and I desire not the protection of any but Him."*

Poetry had long been considered the highest form of entertainment in Arabia, and it was not uncommon for the most famous poets to tour the peninsula reciting their poems. One day a group of Meccans is assembled around the renowned poet Labid, as he sings:

> *"Lo, everything save God is naught. And all delights away shall vanish."*[2]

'Uthman ibn Maz'un overhears Labid's words and accuses the poet of lying. In retaliation, Labid strikes 'Uthman over the eye. When the Prophet hears about what happened, he acknowledges the truth of Labid's words. In fact, recently revealed verses from Surahs Al Qasas and Ar-Rahman reinforce the notion that, indeed, all earthly attachments will vanish.

 SURAH AR-RAHMAN (The Compassionate) is named from its opening verses, "The Compassionate taught the Qur'an." This surah is distinguished by its poetic brilliance and probing message. The surah's most notable feature is the refrain, "So which of the favors of your Lord will you deny?" which is repeated 31 times amidst a series of rhyming couplets and tercets.

 Don't call upon any god other than God, for there is no other god besides Him. Everything will pass away except His face. The power to command is His, and you'll all be brought back to Him. —*Al Qasas (The Tales, 28:88)*

All who are on (the earth) shall pass away, but the face of your Lord will last (forever) - full of Majesty and Honor! So which of the favors of your Lord will you deny? —*Ar-Rahman (The Compassionate, 55:26-28)*

YEAR 10: THE LONG YEAR OF SADNESS

10.1 THE LOSS OF ABU TALIB & KHADIJAH

Several months after the lifting of the ban, Abu Talib falls gravely ill. Twenty-five Quraysh notables, led by Abu Sufyan and Abu Jahl, approach the dying chief of Hashim and ask him to make one final attempt to rein in his nephew. When Abu Talib presents their demands and concessions, the Prophet responds to the gathered men:

> *"It is just one word that will give you supremacy over the Arabs and the non-Arabs ... I want you to testify that there is no God worthy to be worshipped but Allah, and then dissociate yourselves from any sort of worship you harbor for any deities other than Allah."*[1]

---

② WHAT WAS THE WISDOM IN THE PROPHET'S RESPONSE? | YUSUF |

This is *hikmat al-dawah* [wisdom in inviting to Islam]. He is speaking to these people according to what they understand. These people are obsessed with prestige and power, and he is asking them if they really want power. This is indicative of the idea that in giving dawah to people, the first and foremost thing to recognize is the blessing of Islam in its worldly sense. Islam is not simply an otherworldly tradition."[2]

The chiefs of Quraysh ridicule the Prophet's counteroffer and abandon all hope for reconciliation. The first verses of Surah Sad capture the moment in detail:

> Sad.
>
> By (this) Qur'an, filled with reminders - but oh, the faithless (persist in boosting their) reputations and fomenting division! How many generations did We destroy before them who cried out (for deliverance) when there was no longer time to be saved?
>
> So are they surprised that a warner should come to them from their own people? Yet, the faithless only say, "Just a lying wizard! Has he lumped all the gods together into just one God? That's a strange thing, indeed!"
>
> Their leaders turn and leave (impatiently, saying), "Let's get out of here. Stay true to your gods. This is what you have to do. We've never heard anything like this from the other (religious) sect of late, so this is no more than an invented (religion)!" — *Sad (38:1-7)*

SURAH SAD is named after the enigmatic letter that begins the surah (pronounced *Sa'ad*). After documenting the interaction between the Prophet and the Meccans, it goes on to describe the patience of David, Solomon, and Job, who persevered despite equally difficult challenges. The surah is a reminder to the Prophet and the believers that they too must follow in the footsteps of the greatest prophets.

With Abu Talib's health failing, the Prophet yearns for his uncle to embrace the religion of Abraham. He pleads with him to testify to the oneness of God, but Abu Talib responds:

"If I did not fear that the Quraysh would think I had but said the words in dread of death, then would I say them..."[3]

SURAH AL QASAS (The Tales) is named after a specific verse that refers to the story of Moses. The majority of the surah describes Moses' journey from his birth to the Jewish exodus from Egypt. Its timely verses (revealed partly in Mecca and partly during the Prophet's Hijrah) remind listeners, that despite incredible odds and ongoing tribulations, the prophets never gave up.

Surah Al Qasas addresses the Prophet's helpless state:

> You'll never be able to guide all those whom you love, though God guides whomever He wants, and He knows better who it is that accepts guidance.
> — *Al Qasas (The Tales, 28:56)*

When his uncle dies, the Prophet disavows 'Abbas' claim that Abu Talib quietly testified to God's oneness in his final hours. Nonetheless, the Prophet continues to pray for Abu Talib's forgiveness until Surah At-Tawbah instructs him otherwise:

> It's not right for the Prophet and the believers to pray for the forgiveness of idol-worshippers, even if they're close relatives, after it's been made clear to them that they're going to be companions of the raging blaze.
>
> Abraham only prayed for his father's forgiveness because of a promise he had made to him. However, when it became clear to him that (his father) was an enemy of God, he distanced himself from him. It was just that Abraham was accustomed to invoking (God frequently), and he was forbearing.
> — *At-Tawbah (Repentance, 9:113-114)*

After Abu Talib's death, the leadership of Hashim passes to his half-brother Abu Lahab. As expected, Abu Lahab offers the Prophet nominal protection.

The order of deaths reported here follows the narration of Al-Mubarakpuri. Lings suggests that Abu Talib died a few months after the death of Khadijah.

Three months after Abu Talib's death, the Prophet's beloved wife Khadijah dies during the month of Ramadan at the age of 65. The couple had been married for 25 years and was blessed with four surviving daughters. Many years later, the Prophet describes what set Khadijah apart from everyone else:

"She believed in me while the people disbelieved in me. And she trusted in me while the people belied me. And she helped and comforted me, in person and wealth, when the people would not. Allah provided me with children by her, and He did not with others."[4]

---

3 WHAT WAS KHADIJAH'S ROLE IN MECCA?   `RAMADAN`

"Khadijah is a sign of God's presence at the heart of Muhammad's trial; she is to the Prophet Muhammad's spiritual experience what Ishmael and Hagar were to Abraham's trial ... she was a woman, independent, dignified, and respected, then a wife, strong, attentive, faithful, and confident; she was a pious Muslim, sincere, determined, and enduring. Muhammad, the Last Prophet of the One, was not alone, and one of the clearest signs of God's bounty and love for him was a woman in his life, his wife."[5]

10.2 ABU BAKR IS DISOWNED

Elsewhere in Mecca, a decade of unwavering support has cost Abu Bakr the esteemed status he once held among the Quraysh. Shortly after Abu Talib's death, two Taymis–Abu Bakr and Talhah ibn 'Ubayd Allah–are mercilessly attacked by Khadijah's half-brother Nawfal ibn Khuwaylid for teaching Islam to Nawfal's son Aswad. Nawfal ambushes the two men and leaves them beaten and bound on the side of the road. When their clan of Taym fails to protect them, Abu Bakr and Talhah realize they are no longer safe in Mecca.

Fearing for his life, Abu Bakr makes plans to migrate to Abyssinia. However, when he reaches the city of Birk al-Ghimad, he is stopped by Ibn ad-Dughannah, an influential man from a confederate tribe of Quraysh. Ibn ad-Dughannah already knew Abu Bakr and is amazed to see the dramatic change in his appearance. Abu Bakr explains:

> *"My people have ill-treated me and driven me out, and all I seek is to travel over the face of the earth, worshipping God."*

Ibn ad-Dughannah responds:

> *"Thou art as an ornament to thy clan, a help in misfortune, a doer of right, ever fulfilling the needs of others. Return for thou art beneath my protection."* [6]

The two men return to Mecca and the Quraysh agree to respect Ibn ad-Dughannah's protection so long as Abu Bakr only prays in the privacy of his house.

---

4   **HOW DID ABU BAKR'S CONDITION CHANGE SO DRAMATICALLY?**   YUSUF

"Abu Bakr was an incredibly gentle soul in his nature. He was somebody like the Prophet, God's peace and blessings upon him, before the advent of Islam. He was not somebody who was out to gain some position of ascendancy amongst the Quraysh. He did not have those types of aspirations. He was somebody whose heart was always with the oppressed. He was always there to help the one in need. This was really the nature of Abu Bakr al-Siddiq. He was a wealthy merchant, but through freeing slaves who were being persecuted, and through helping in other ways during the time of the sanctions against Bani Hashim, he had expended all of his money. By the end of this period, he had nothing. He had lost the support of his own clansmen and could be beaten with impunity by the Quraysh. He was in a dire situation."[7]

- -

5   **WHY DID ABU BAKR NEED A GUARDIAN?**   ARMSTRONG

"Nobody could survive in Arabia without an official protector. A man who had been expelled from his clan could be killed with impunity, without fear of vendetta."[8]

10.3 THE JOURNEY TO TA'IF

'Uqbah ibn Abi Mu'ayt owns the sheep tended by 'Abd Allah ibn Mas'ud. In a few years, he will be captured at Badr and killed by his former shepherd.

After Abu Talib's death, the Quraysh intensify their opposition. Dirt, entrails, and excrement are repeatedly thrown on the Prophet—once even by 'Uqbah ibn Abi Mu'ayt, the stepfather of his son-in-law 'Uthman ibn 'Affan. When the abusive treatment brings the Prophet's daughter to tears, he gently reassures her saying:

> "Do not weep, my daughter. Allah will verily protect your father."[9]

Facing grave danger, and with no other options, the Prophet and Zayd flee to the nearby oasis settlement of Ta'if. Upon his arrival, the Prophet approaches the sons of 'Amr ibn Umayyah, the chief of Bani Thaqif. The first and second swiftly reject his message. When the third son is approached by the Prophet, he declares:

> "I swear by Allah that I will never speak to you. If you are really the Messenger of Allah, then you are too important to be speaking to me. If you are lying against Allah, then I should never speak to you."[10]

Meccan nobles had summer retreats in Ta'if because of its milder climate. The fertile, well-fortified oasis was inhabited by the Thaqif clan of the great Hawazin tribe of central Arabia. Twelve years after the Prophet's visit, Bani Thaqif will enter Islam.

After 10 days of rejection and humiliation, the Prophet and Zayd are chased out of the city by a mob of servants and children. They barely escape under a shower of rocks and curses, stopping to rest several miles away in a private orchard that is owned by the two chiefs of 'Abdu Shams–'Utbah and Shaybah ibn Rabi'ah.

There on the outskirts of Ta'if, the Prophet collapses in a state of complete exhaustion. In the past several months, he had lost his outward protection from Abu Talib and inward security from Khadijah. Then he was forced out of his home only to be rejected by outsiders as well. In a state of complete humility, he turns to his only remaining Protector:

> "O Allah! To You alone I complain of my weakness, my insufficient ability and my insignificance before the people. You are the most Merciful of the mercifuls. You are the Lord of the helpless and the weak. O Lord of mine! Into whose hands would You abandon me: into the hands of an unsympathetic distant relative who would angrily frown at me, or to the enemy who has been given control over my affairs? But if Your wrath does not fall on me, there is nothing for me to worry about.
>
> Your pardon is ample enough for me. I seek protection in the light of Your Face, which illuminates the darkness, fixing the affairs in this world as well as in the Hereafter. May it never be that I should incur Your wrath, or that You should be wrathful to me. And there is no power nor resource, but Yours alone."

6 WHAT IS THE SIGNIFICANCE OF THE PROPHET'S SUPPLICATION IN TA'IF? `YUSUF`

"This is an extraordinary dua [supplication] that the Prophet, God's peace and blessings upon him, makes. This is pure Islam. The Prophet, God's peace and blessings upon him, is, in essence, saying to God, 'If this is what You want—as long as You are not angry with me—I don't care. But if You are upset with me, then I have to do something. But if You are not angry with me, I don't care what You do with me.'"[11]

7 **HOW WAS THIS TRIAL A NECESSARY STAGE IN THE EXPERIENCE OF FAITH?** RAMADAN

"All the messengers have, like Abraham and Muhammad, experienced the trial of faith and all have been, in the same manner, protected from themselves and their own doubts by God, His signs, and His word. Their suffering does not mean they made mistakes, nor does it reveal any tragic dimension of existence: it is, more simply, an initiation into humility, understood as a necessary stage in the experience of faith."[12]

From their vacation residence, 'Utbah and Shaybah recognize the Prophet in the distance. Despite their hostile feelings, they are moved by his tattered condition and send their slave 'Addas with some grapes for him. Before eating, the Prophet whispers, *"In the name of God."*

'Addas overhears his words and muses:

"These are words which people in this land do not generally use."

The two men begin to talk, and when 'Addas explains that he is a Christian from Nineveh, the Prophet responds:

"You belong to the city of the righteous Yunus [Jonah], son of Matta. He is my brother. He was a prophet, and so am I."[13]

Along with 'Addas' presence, Surah Al Anbiya' provides the Prophet with a timely reminder of faith and perseverance:

> And the fish master, (Jonah) - he left in anger and thought We had no power over him, but he cried out in the darkened (belly of the fish), "There is no god besides You! Glory be to You! I was truly wrong!" We listened to him and saved him from his distress. That's how We save those who have faith!
> — *Al Anbiya' (The Prophets, 21:87-88)*

8 **WHAT WAS JONAH'S SIGNIFICANCE AT TA'IF?** YUSUF

"What is really significant about this is that Yunus ibn Matta [Jonah] is somebody whose people rejected him. Allah was sending a reminder to the Prophet, God's peace and blessings upon him, that he was in the tradition of the prophets. They suffered like he did. The people of Yunus ibn Matta in Nineveh wouldn't listen to him: They laughed at him; they mocked him until he finally left the city. But Allah sent him back. Similarly, the Prophet, God's peace and blessings upon him, has to go back to Mecca. This is a very powerful event."[14]

- -

9 **WHAT WAS 'ADDAS' SIGNIFICANCE IN TA'IF?** RAMADAN

"Twice already, in sorrow and isolation, Muhammad had encountered on his path Christians who offered him trust, respect, and shelter: a king welcomed Muslims and granted them security, a slave served their Prophet when everybody else had rejected him and his message."[15]

- -

10 **HOW WAS TA'IF A SUCCESS?** WATT

"The experience of Muhammad at Nakhlah on his return from at-Ta'if, when he received comfort in his mood of depression, might be taken as marking a stage in his weaning from reliance on human companionship."[16]

10.4 AN ENCOUNTER WITH JINN

Jinn are spiritual creatures mentioned numerous times in the Qur'an. Muslims believe that they inhabit an unseen world and exercise free will, much like humans.

🔖 **SURAH AL AHQAF** (The Sand Dunes) is named after a verse describing the people of 'Ad who lived among sand dunes typical of the southeastern portion of the Arabian Peninsula. It is the last of seven surahs that begin with the enigmatic letters Ha-Meem. Among other themes, God declares, "We've made it an obligation upon every human being to show kindness to his parents."

🔖 **SURAH AL JINN** (The Jinn or Hidden Ones) is named after its first verse, which describes a group of jinn that visited the Prophet and were transfixed by his recitation of the Qur'an.

🔖 **SURAH AL ANBIYA'** (The Prophets) is named after its opening verses, which defend all of God's prophets as ordinary humans who were inspired to convey a divine message. This was an entirely new idea to the Arabs who viciously attacked the Prophet for being a poet or even a madman. The surah mentions Noah, Idris, Abraham, Lot, Isaac, Ishmael, Moses, Jacob, Job, David, Solomon, Jonah, Ezekiel, Zachariah, John the Baptist, Mary, and Jesus. God concludes, "Truly, this community of yours is one community, and I am your Lord, so serve me."

Though **Akhnas** fails to protect the Prophet on this occasion, several years later, he will turn his adoptive clan of Zuhrah back to Mecca and refuse to fight the Prophet at Badr.

This is not the first time **Mut'im** helps the Prophet. Just a year ago, Mut'im was one of the five men who lifted the ban on Hashim. The Prophet never forgot Mut'im's gesture, and after the battle of Badr, says: "If Mut'im bin 'Adi were living and had asked me for the release of these rotten people, then I would have given them to him." [17]

Despite Bani Thaqif's merciless persecution, the Prophet prays for their guidance and forgiveness. On his way back to Mecca, he stops to pray at the valley of Nakhlah, where he is visited by several *jinn* from Nasibin, in present-day Turkey. Surah Al Ahqaf describes the encounter:

> It came to pass that We turned a company of hidden ones towards you, (Muhammad), and they listened to the recitation of this Qur'an as they stood by. (After hearing it), they exclaimed (to each other), "Listen quietly!" When the recitation was finished, they returned to their own kind to warn them.
> — *Al Ahqaf (The Sand Dunes, 46:29)*

In another revelation, Surah Al Jinn reminds listeners that the Prophet had been sent for the benefit of all God's creation.

> (Muhammad,) say to them, "It's been revealed to me that a group of hidden ones (jinns) heard (this Qur'an being recited)."
>
> They (listened to it and) said, "We've just heard an amazing presentation! It guided (us) towards the right direction, so now we believe in it. We'll never hold anyone else the equal of our Lord ever again. Exalted is the majesty of our Lord! He hasn't taken any female consort nor any son!"
> — *Al Jinn (The Jinn, 72:1-3)*

That the Prophet was sent for all creation was not a new concept. Surah Ar-Rahman had already been revealed, which from beginning to end, addresses both jinn and men. Surah Al Anbiya' corroborates this notion:

> (Muhammad,) We didn't send you except to be a mercy to all the worlds.
> — *Al Anbiya' (The Prophets, 21:107)*

With the clan of Hashim under the leadership of Abu Lahab, the Prophet is convinced that he will not be protected from the rest of Quraysh. Before returning to Mecca, he tries to arrange his protection under other influential Meccan leaders. Although Akhnas ibn Shariq (a confederate of Zuhrah) and Suhayl ibn 'Amr (the chief of 'Amir) both make excuses as to why they cannot help him, Mut'im ibn 'Adi (the chief of Nawfal) agrees to protect the Prophet from his enemies.

FIGURE 10A. THE JOURNEY TO TA'IF

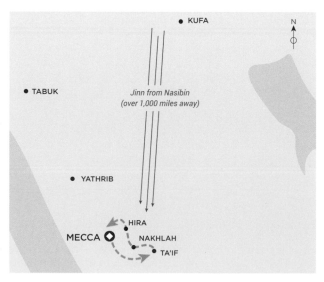

Ta'if was about 60 miles southeast of Mecca. After he was painfully rebuffed in Ta'if, the Prophet was approached by 'Addas, a Christian slave from Nineveh. 'Addas' presence reminded the Prophet that he too was following in the tradition of Jonah (from Nineveh), who turned to his Lord in a moment of despair, only to return to his people and fulfill his mission. In Nakhlah, several jinn from Nasibin in eastern Turkey passed by and heard the Prophet recite the Qur'an. The Prophet ultimately returned to Mecca by way of the cave Hira, after obtaining the protection of Mut'im ibn 'Adi.

10.5 UNLIKELY OUTSIDERS: ABU DHARR & TUFAYL

While the Prophet faces an uphill battle in Mecca, several individuals from distant tribes visit Mecca and unexpectedly join his mission. One account involves a traveler by the name of Abu Dharr ibn Junadah, whose brother Unays tells him about the Prophet. When Abu Dharr enters Mecca, the Quraysh warn him to avoid the poet-sorcerer named Muhammad. Instead, Abu Dharr goes straight to the Prophet's house, and, after hearing a recitation of the Qur'an, formally embraces his cause. When the Prophet learns that Abu Dharr is a highway brigand from the rugged northwest tribe of Ghifar, he muses:

> *"Verily God guideth whom He will."*[18]

Another unlikely convert is Tufayl ibn 'Amr, a visiting poet from the western tribe of Daws. Like Abu Dharr, Tufayl is also warned not to listen to the Prophet's sorcery. At first Tufayl stuffs his ears with cotton to avoid falling under a spell. But when he sees the Prophet praying, he decides to listen to his recitation and is immediately moved by the words. When Tufayl returns home, he garners little support from his people, other than his close family. He comes back to Mecca and vents his frustration to the Prophet, who advises him:

> *"Return to thy people, call them to Islam, and deal gently with them."*[19]

Ultimately **Tufayl** will gather 70-80 of his tribesmen and migrate to Medina shortly after the expedition to Khaybar (QY 19).

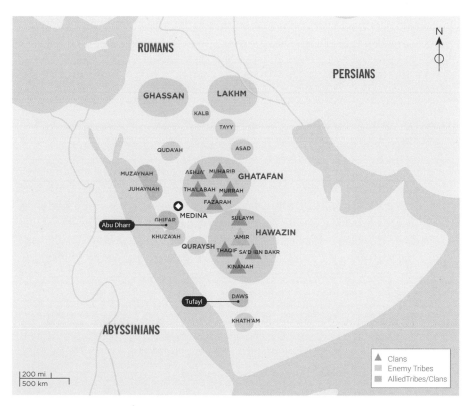

FIGURE 10B. THE TRIBES OF ARABIA

The Arabian peninsula was inhabited by a number of tribes of varying size and power. To the east of Mecca lay the great inland Hawazin tribe. Their clans of Sulaym, Thaqif, 'Amir, Kinanah, and Sa'd ibn Bakr will reappear later in the Sirah. (Recall that the Prophet was nursed by Halimah who belonged to Sa'd ibn Bakr.) Equally impressive were the Bani Ghatafan who inhabited the desert region northeast of Mecca. Both the Ghatafan and Hawazin tribes opposed the Prophet during most of his life. Among a sea of enemies, Medina was able to create alliances with the tribes of Abu Dharr ibn Junadah (Ghifar) and Tufayl ibn 'Amr (Daws).

10.6 NEWS OF THE PROPHET REACHES YATHRIB

While talk of the new movement slowly spreads in Arabia, nowhere is it more hotly discussed than in the northern farming community of Yathrib. The Arabs in Yathrib descended from a common ancestress whose two sons, Aws and Khazraj, had developed a rivalry that recently escalated into a bitter civil war:

> The fundamental trouble underlying the fighting and the tension at Medina was that the nomadic outlook and ethic, to which the men of Medina still adhered, was not suited to the conditions of agricultural life in an oasis. As it became more difficult to gain a livelihood from the soil of Medina for the growing population, quarrels would arise and blood would be shed. To deal with this situation nomadic custom had only the method of the blood-feud ... In the wide spaces of the steppe this method was tolerably successful since contacts were few, but in the restricted area of an oasis it was unsatisfactory. Here there were too many disputes, and therefore too many possibilities of disagreement.[20]

11 WHAT WAS THE SITUATION IN YATHRIB BEFORE THE HIJRAH? `ARMSTRONG`

"Yathrib was not a city like Mecca, but a series of hamlets, each occupied by a different tribal group, and each heavily fortified. The settlement was situated in an oasis, a fertile island of about twenty square miles, surrounded by volcanic rocks and uncultivable stony ground. Some of its inhabitants engaged in trade, but most were farmers, making a living out of their dates, palm orchards, and arable fields. Unlike the Quraysh, they were not wholly dependent upon commerce, and had retained more of the old badawah values, including, unfortunately, an entrenched hostility to other tribal groups."[21]

Along with the hostility they felt for each other, Yathrib's pagan Arabs suffered from an inferiority complex toward the oasis' many Jewish tribes:

> Of the three main tribes Qaynuqa' possessed no agricultural land but had a compact settlement where they conducted a market and practised crafts such as that of the goldsmith. Qurayzah and an-Nadir, on the other hand, had some of the richest lands in the oasis, situated in the higher part towards the south and mostly given over to growing palms. Here, as in several other fertile spots in western Arabia such as Khaybar, the Jews appear to have been pioneers in agricultural development.
>
> The Aws and the Khazraj were allowed to settle, presumably on lands that had not yet been brought under cultivation, and were under the protection of some of the Jewish tribes. One of the marks of their subordinate position was the ius primae noctis [right of the first night] exercised by Fityawn of B. Tha'labah.[22]

12 WHO WERE THE JEWS OF MEDINA? `ARMSTRONG`

"...There were about twenty Jewish tribes in Yathrib, many whose members may have been Arabs who had assimilated to Judaism. They preserved a separate religious identity, but otherwise were almost indistinguishable from their pagan neighbors. Clan and tribal loyalty came first, and there was no united 'Jewish community.' The Jewish tribes formed separate allegiances with Arab groups and were often at war with one another."[23]

Among the Jewish tribe of Qurayzah lived a saintly man named Ibn al-Hayyaban who foretells the coming prophet. Not surprisingly, when the Aws and Khazraj hear of a new Arabian prophet in Mecca, they remember Ibn al-Hayyaban's words and intently listen to the Prophet's message.

In recent years, constant fighting between the Aws and Khazraj had raised tensions throughout the city. In desperation, the Aws send a delegation to Mecca to see if the Quraysh might arbitrate their differences. While the visiting delegation awaits an answer (ultimately the Quraysh decline to get involved), the Prophet approaches the members of the delegation and asks if they would be interested in something better than what they came for. He explains his message and invites them to join his movement. But when one of the Aws' youngest men, Iyas ibn Mu'adh, openly testifies to the Prophet's message, he is berated by his elders.

Ibn al-Hayyaban is originally from Syria. He urges his people to follow the Arabian Prophet, but will not live to see him. After the battle of the Trench, the entire tribe of Qurayzah will be punished for treason against the city of Medina. At that time, Lings notes, they come to recall Ibn al-Hayyaban's words.

Iyas ibn Mu'adh dies soon after his conversion, and is considered the first man of Yathrib to enter Islam. As we will see in the next sections, his brother Sa'd ibn Mu'adh will become one of the Prophet's preeminent Companions amongst the Helpers.

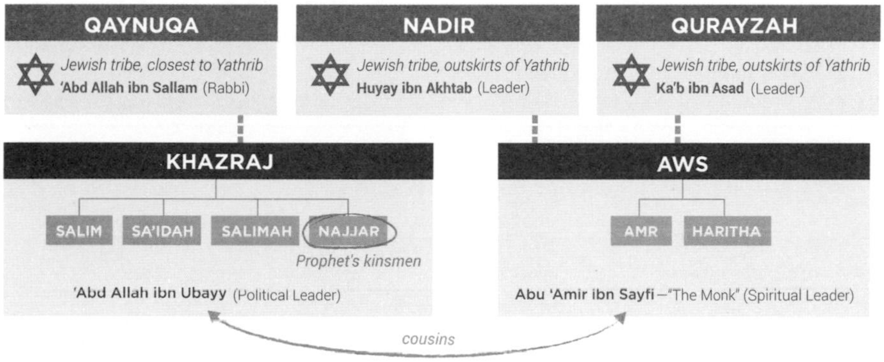

FIGURE 10C. THE MAJOR CLANS OF YATHRIB

Khazraj and Aws were the two Arab clans of Yathrib. Each had alliances with different Jewish tribes in the oasis (indicated by color). Note that 'Abd al-Muttalib's mother, Salma, was from the Khazraj sub-clan of Najjar, which was important when the Prophet immigrated to Yathrib. (The names of each of the clan chiefs are indicated above. All of these names will be revisited later in the Sirah.)

YEAR 11: THE ISRA' & ME'RAJ

11.1 THE PRE-'AQABAH PLEDGE

With the annual pilgrimage to Mecca approaching, Arab pilgrims from all over the peninsula begin arriving to visit the Sacred Precinct. The Prophet, who until now had been rejected by Bani Quraysh and Thaqif, approaches six Khazraj pilgrims from Yathrib and explains his message. The pilgrims have every reason to listen to his call:

> ... Medina was much divided; and the lack of unity, with the suicidal warfare to which it led, meant that the point which had been at the root of opposition in Mecca—Muhammad's position as prophet and its political implications—was the very thing which offered the Medinans some hope of peace. The idea may be present in the verse: "Each community has a messenger, and when their messenger comes, judgement is given between them with justice, and they are not wronged. [Yunus (Jonah, 10:47)]"[1]

---

❶ WHY DID THE PROPHET LOOK TO YATHRIB? `WATT`

"All that could been done in Mecca had been done; therefore the chief hope lay in advances elsewhere. Muhammad had originally regarded himself as a prophet sent solely or primarily to Quraysh, and there is no way of telling whether prior to the death of Abu Talib he had thought of an expansion of his mission to the Arabs in general. The deterioration in his position, however now forced him to look farther afield, and during the last three years in Mecca we hear only of dealings with nomadic tribes and with the citizens of at-Ta'if and Yathrib."[2]

When he explains his mission, they confer with one another saying:

> *"Know surely, this is the Prophet with whom the Jews are ever threatening us; so, let us make haste and be the first to join him."*

Without a moment of hesitation, all six pilgrims accept Islam. They explain:

> *"We have left our community, for no tribe is so divided by hate and enmity as they are. Allah may cement our ties through you. So, let us go and invite them to this religion of yours; and if Allah unites them in it, no man will be dearer than you."*[3]

---

❷ WHY WOULD THE PEOPLE OF YATHRIB WELCOME A FOREIGN ARBITER? `WATT`

"It is easy to see how clans and sub-clans in this position would be attracted by the prospect of an outsider coming to hold the balance in the affairs of Medina. They may have felt that unification was bound to come sooner or later, but have disliked being under a ruler from Ba'l-Hubla or Bayadah [other clans in Yathrib]. A member of any of the Medinan clans would already have his friends and his enemies among the other clans, and was unlikely to be fair to all."[4]

11.2 SAWDAH & 'A'ISHAH

In the year after Khadijah's death, Khawlah bint al-Hakim suggests Sawdah bint Zam'ah and 'A'ishah bint Abi Bakr as suitable wives for the Prophet. Sawdah's husband, Sakran ibn 'Amr, had recently passed away in Abyssinia, and she had returned to Mecca with the other emigrants. At the age of 30, she agrees to the marriage.

Independent of Khawlah's suggestion, the Prophet has a symbolic dream about marrying Abu Bakr's young daughter. 'A'ishah was already engaged to Jubayr ibn Mut'im, but Abu Bakr persuades Jubayr's father to break the engagement so she can marry the Prophet.

For the next 12 years, **Sawdah bint Zam'ah** will become a central personality in the Prophet's household. Not only will she be a maternal figure to 'A'ishah and Hafsah, she will also help prepare the Prophet's eldest daughter Zaynab's body for burial.

Five years from now, **Jubayr ibn Mut'im** will instruct his slave, Wahshi, to avenge his uncle's death by killing Hamzah at Uhud. Four years later, he finally embraces Islam.

---

③ HOW COULD THE PROPHET MARRY 'A'ISHAH AT SUCH A YOUNG AGE? `YUSUF`

"The fact that Khawlah tells him to marry 'A'ishah is very indicative of the fact that this was not an unusual thing in their culture. Obviously in modern Western culture, this would be completely shocking.

In most modern anthropological methodologies, one is expected to try to remove one's social frames of reference when one is examining another culture, because it is unfair to superimpose one's own prejudices upon another culture. Each culture has its own traditions and its own way of doing things. And if you try to force upon it your own ideals, your principles and what you feel is acceptable, then you end up being unjust towards another tradition. This was a normal thing in their society. Nobody was shocked by it. It was just part of their culture.

If you look also in the Oxford Dictionary of the Bible, it says that they think that Mary was probably between 12 and 14 years old [when married]. They recognize that this was the age when a woman got married in that culture. That was also very normal both in the Hebraic and Semitic cultures and in most parts of the world including China and India. It's really modern society that has extended the age of marriage. There's an important book by Neil Postman called *The Disappearance of Childhood*. And one of the things he writes in there is that childhood was in fact an invention of Renaissance Europe. Prior to Renaissance Europe, children became adults at about the age of 7 or 8. Islam extended the age for military service to 15, which in that time was radical because we know that there were children in the Crusades. Obviously now, if we apply those same standards, a 9-year-old to us is a child. But a lot of that has to do with our own socialization—in other words, the expectations we have of them. If you go into a village in Morocco, for instance, responsibilities are given to young people at much earlier ages than they are given to in the cities. You'll find in villages, somebody who is 8 or 9 years old is already having adult responsibilities. So don't try to apply standards we have today for a 9-year-old, to a 9-year-old in seventh century Arabia, because there is actually no comparison. These were very mature people at an early age.

Neil Postman points out that modern education really has extended childhood. The adolescent phase is a creation of the modern world, what postmodernists would call an artificial construct. Adolescents in this culture [seventh century Arabia] were adults. 'Usama ibn Zayd led an army at the age of 17. He was an adult and that's how they viewed him. It was a very different world then."[5]

Read Salahi (p. 808-819) for a detailed examination of whether 'A'ishah was as young as many scholars suggest.

④ WAS 'A'ISHAH REALLY AS YOUNG AS THE SOURCES INDICATE? `SALAHI`

"Much has been said about 'A'ishah, the Prophet's wife, and her age at the time when she married the Prophet... The question that arises here is: could Khawlah, who seems to be a Muslim woman with foresight, recognizing the effects of the loss of his wife on the Prophet, have suggested to him a child aged six, who was several years younger than the youngest of his four daughters?

... Had it been true that 'A'ishah was only six years of age, the very mention of her name in this context at that time would be exceedingly odd. A girl of six would have been in need of looking after, not assigned the task of looking after a man with the most difficult task in history... Another clue to 'A'ishah's age is the time when she adopted the Islamic faith. In his biography of the Prophet, which is the earliest detailed one, Ibn Ishaq lists 51 names under the heading, 'the people who accepted God's Messenger in its early days'. The list does not include any children ... but it is very significant that 'A'ishah is the only young person mentioned in the list. Had she been nine years of age at the time of her wedding, she would have been only one year old at the time we are talking about. We need make no comment. However, there is plenty of evidence that 'A'ishah accepted Islam in its early days. If we say that she was 10 when she adopted Islam, and we put that event in the fifth year of Islam, she would be 19 at the time of her marriage ... The Battle of Uhud took place in the month of Shawwal of the third year of the Prophet's settlement in Madinah, i.e. two years or less after 'A'ishah's marriage. Consider the following hadīth which is related by al-Bukhārī under several headings: Anas reports: "When the Muslim army was in retreat during the Battle of Uhud and people moved away from the Prophet, I saw 'A'ishah and Umm Sulaym ... they were carrying waterskins on their backs and almost running to give people to drink, before going back to refill their containers with water and come back to pour it in people's mouths." [Related by al-Bukhari and Muslim.] Had she been 9 at the time of her marriage, she would be 11, or even younger when that battle took place. Can we imagine that the Prophet, who did not permit young men of 14 to stay with the army, would have allowed a girl of 11 to stay? ... When we take all this evidence into consideration, we are bound to reject the statement that 'A'ishah was as young as nine at the time of her marriage to the Prophet. We say that most probably she was around 20; perhaps one or two years younger or older."[6]

⑤ WHY DID THE PROPHET HAVE NUMEROUS WIVES? `ARMSTRONG`

"Muhammad's harem has excited a good deal of prurient and ill-natured speculation in the West, but in Arabia, where polygamy was more common than the monogamous marriage that Muhammad had enjoyed with Khadijah, it would have been commonplace. These marriages were not romantic or sexual love affairs but were undertaken largely for practical ends. Sawdah seems to have been a rather homely woman, who was past her first youth; but she could take care of Muhammad's domestic needs. Muhammad may also have hoped to win over Suhayl. ... There was no impropriety in Muhammad's betrothal to 'A'isha. Marriages conducted in absentia to seal an alliance were often contracted at this time between adults and minors who were even younger than 'A'isha. This practice continued in Europe well into the early modern period. There was no question of consummating the marriage until 'A'isha reached puberty, when she would have been married off like any other girl. Muhammad's marriages usually had a political aim. He was starting to establish an entirely different kind of clan, based on ideology rather than kinship, but the blood tie was still a sacred value and helped to cement this experimental community."[7]

Recall that when Abu Bakr was trying to migrate to Abyssinia, Ibn ad-Dughannah persuaded him to return to Mecca under his formal protection.

In addition to arranging his daughter's engagement, Abu Bakr busies himself with building a small mosque adjoining his house. According to the terms of Ibn ad-Dughannah's protection, Abu Bakr is not allowed to pray in public. However when he begins to pray in his newly erected mosque, the Quraysh complain that Abu Bakr's neighbors can easily see and hear him recite the Qur'an over the low walls. In response, Abu Bakr forfeits Ibn ad-Dughannah's guardianship, proclaiming that he is content with God's protection. That very day, the Prophet informs Abu Bakr of his plans to migrate to Yathrib.

11.3 THE NIGHT JOURNEY

Abu Talib's wife, Fatimah bint Asad, had entered Islam sometime before or after the death of her husband. Her daughter Umm Hani remained close to the Prophet and, in the year after Abu Talib's death, invites him over to lead the evening prayer in her house. The Prophet accepts his cousin's invitation and, after the prayer, rests at her house.

Like his grandfather 'Abd al-Muttalib, the Prophet used to enjoy spending nights in the Hijr, near the tomb of Hagar and Ishmael. After a short nap at Umm Hani's house, he steps out to visit the Ka'bah and falls asleep in the Hijr. In the midst of his sleep, he is greeted by Gabriel who leads him to a mounted winged beast named *Buraq*. Then, as described in Surah Al Isra', he is carried to Jerusalem (about 760 miles away), where he encounters several biblical prophets and leads them in prayer (the *Isra'*).

> Glory be to the One Who took His servant on a journey by night from the sacred place of prostration (in Mecca) to the faraway place of prostration (in Jerusalem) - to an area that We've specially blessed - so We could show him some of Our signs. — *Al Isra' (The Night Journey, 17:1)*

---

6 **WHAT WAS THE PROPHET'S PRAYER BEFORE THE OTHER PROPHETS?** `YUSUF`

[Yusuf translating into English] "Each prophet praised Allah, the Sublime and Exalted, with some good praise. And then the Prophet, God's peace and blessings upon him, said, 'All of you have praised Allah and now I will praise Allah.

'Praise to the One who sent me as a mercy to all of the worlds, and for all of humanity as a warner and a bringer of good tidings, and who revealed to me the Qur'an. In it is a clarification of everything. And He made my ummah [community of followers] the best ummah that has come out for people. And He made my ummah the first and the last. And He expanded my breast, and He removed the weightiness from me. And He raised up my remembrance. And He made me the opener and the sealer.' "[8]

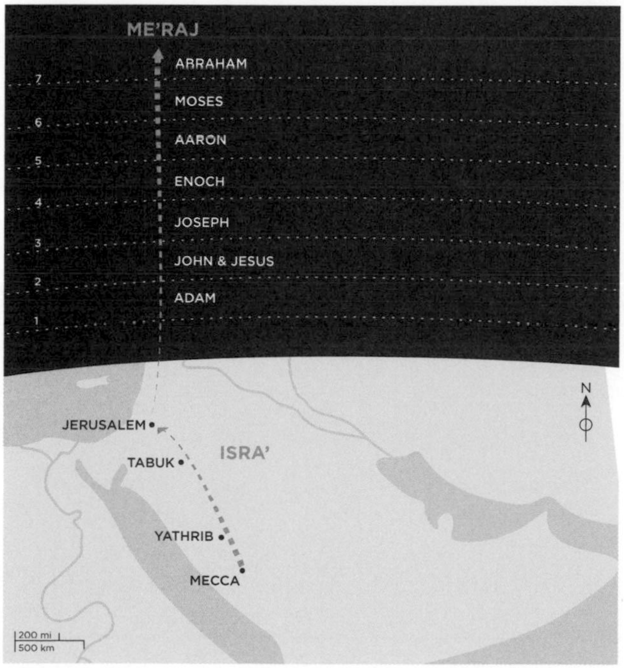

Umm Hani is the full sister of Ja'far and 'Ali ibn abi Talib. Recall that over 20 years ago, the Prophet had asked Abu Talib for Umm Hani's hand in marriage. Instead she was married to a Makhzumi, who resisted Islam but remained hospitable to the Prophet.

SURAH AL ISRA' (The Night Journey) is named after its opening verse, which confirms the Prophet's miraculous journey from Mecca to Medina, and then up into the heavens. The surah was revealed during the Late Medinan Period and covers many topics including personal accountability, acting kindly to one's parents, and sharing wealth with the poor. It also addresses the Prophet's critics head-on. "We know what they're really listening for when they listen to you, (for they merely wish to find something to criticize) so they can talk about it in their private conversations, saying, 'You (Muslims) are following nothing more than a man who's been bewitched!'"

FIGURE 11A. THE NIGHT JOURNEY

Although there is some difference of opinion, the Isra' and Me'raj most likely occured shortly after the Prophet's return from Ta'if. While the miraculous experience was a turning point in the Prophet's 23-year career, it also tested the conviction of his Companions.

There is a difference of opinion on what year the Night Journey took place. Some scholars believe it happened much earlier in Mecca, while others suggest that it must have happened after the Year of Sadness because of the general consensus that Khadijah died before the five daily prayers were established. More details of the Night Journey can be found in Al-Mubarakpuri (p.135-140).

After the congregational prayer, the Prophet ascends through the seven heavens. At each level he encounters different prophets, who collectively endorse his prophethood. Surah An-Najm captures the transcendent moment when, after passing the seventh heaven, the Prophet finally meets his Creator:

> The lote tree was shrouded (in a shimmering light), but his sight never swerved, nor did it fail, for he really saw the greatest sign of his Lord!
> —*An-Najm (The Star, 53:16-18)*

7 HOW WAS THE NIGHT JOURNEY A BLUEPRINT FOR THE REST OF US? [ARMSTRONG]

"The story became the paradigm of Muslim spirituality, outlining the path that all human beings must take, away from their preconceptions, their prejudices, and the limitations of egotism … He had to move beyond his original expectations, and transcend the received ideas of his time … In Muhammad's night journey, these old muruwah values were reversed. Instead of returning to his tribe, the prophet traveled far away from it to Jerusalem; instead of asserting his tribal identity with the arrogant chauvinism of jahiliyyah, Muhammad surrendered his ego. Instead of rejoicing in fighting and warfare, Muhammad's journey celebrated harmony, transcendence of the blood group, and integration with the rest of humanity."[9]

At the height of the *Me'raj* (ascension), the Prophet is commanded to instruct his followers to perform 50 prayers daily. He also receives revelation that contains the creed of his faith:

> The Messenger believes in what his Lord revealed, as do the faithful. Each of them believes in God, His angels, His books and His messengers. (The believers say), "We don't consider one of His messengers as being better than another." (They pray), "We hear, and we obey, (and we seek) Your forgiveness, Our Lord, for we (know that our) final destination is back with You."
> —*Al Baqarah (The Cow, 2:285)*

As the Prophet descends through the heavens, he is approached by Moses who persuades him to return to God and ask Him to make worship easier for his community by decreasing the number of obligatory daily prayers. When the Prophet returns a second time, Moses reiterates his recommendation. They repeat this several more times until the number of daily prayers is reduced to five. Even then Moses encourages him to seek a further reduction, but the Prophet responds:

> *"I feel ashamed now of repeatedly asking my Lord for reduction. I accept and resign to His Will."*[10]

8 **WHAT CAN WE LEARN FROM THE STORY OF MOSES AND MUHAMMAD?** `RAMADAN`

"The fact that this appreciation of other traditions is written into the archetypal myth of Muslim spirituality shows how central this pluralism was to early Islam."

"Say to them, "We believe in God and in what was revealed to us, as well as in what was revealed to Abraham, Ishmael, Isaac, Jacob and the tribes (of Israel), and (we believe) in what was given to Moses and Jesus and to all other prophets from their Lord. We don't claim that one of them was better than another, and to Him we surrender.
Now if anyone looks for a way of life other than submission (to God), it will never be accepted of him, and in the next life he'll be among the losers." —*Ali 'Imran* (The Family of Amran, 3:84-85)

"This verse is often quoted to 'prove' that the Qur'an claims that Islam is the one, true faith and only Muslims will be saved. But 'Islam' was not yet the official name for Muhammad's religion, and when this verse is read correctly in its pluralistic context, it clearly means the opposite."

"We've given to each one of you (differing religious groups) a legal tradition and a clear method (for dealing with legal issues). If God had wanted, He could've made you all into one community, but He tests you in what He's given you, so forge ahead as if you were racing towards everything virtuous. Your ultimate return is back to God, and He's going to show you (the truth) of those things about which you argued." —*Al-Ma'idah* (The Banquet Table, 5:48)[11]

----

9 **WHAT WAS SPECIAL ABOUT THE TIMING OF THE NIGHT JOURNEY?** `YUSUF`

"This was the turning point. One of the things to remember about this is that this happens at a point where the Prophet, God's peace and blessings upon him, is at his lowest point in *dunya* [worldly] terms. Allah is teaching us something extraordinary: The Prophet, God's peace and blessings upon him, has no wealth. His beloved wife [Khadijah] is gone. His protector [Abu Talib] is gone. He is completely in a state of dejection in his own city and Allah is raising him up to this incredible status.
Once you've seen what the Prophet, God's peace and blessings upon him, has seen, what significance does all of that dunya have? He is seeing this whole other realm of reality—the unseen world—and that next to it, dunya just loses all significance."[12]

11.4 THE RESPONSE TO THE NIGHT JOURNEY

The next morning, the Prophet describes his miraculous journey to Umm Hani. Against her counsel, he insists on sharing his experience with the Quraysh. As Umm Hani predicts, the Prophet's enemies are thrilled to hear what sounds like a ludicrous story, while his Companions face an unexpected trial of faith.

> We (only use such symbols) to instill fear in them (so that they'll perhaps be inclined to listen), but it only adds to their immense suppression (of faith).
> — *Al Isra' (The Night Journey, 17:60)*

Those who are nearby ask Abu Bakr, who hadn't yet heard about what had happened, to confirm the Prophet's incredible story. But for Abu Bakr, the news is hardly unbelievable. *"If so he saith, then it is true,"* he calmly responds.

> *"And where is the wonder of it? He telleth me that tidings come to him from Heaven to earth in one hour of the day or night, and I know him to be speaking the truth. And that is beyond what ye cavil at."*[13]

Since the first revelation, Abu Bakr never wavers from his conviction in God and his commitment to the Prophet. Shortly after hearing Abu Bakr's response to the Isra' account, the Prophet honors him with the title *as-Siddiq* (the great witness of truth).

SURAH AL AN'AM (Livestock) is named after several verses that address the pagan superstitions about livestock. It documents the pagan attacks on the Prophet and gives clear responses he should convey to the idolaters. The surah reminds the Prophet that it is not he they are rejecting, but his message. Al An'am also includes the famous exchange between Abraham and his pagan father, as well as the "10 commandments" of Islam. As with all surahs, this is a must-read passage to understand the Early and Late Meccan periods.

While the Night Journey is a unique moment in the Prophet's life, Surah Al An'am explains that it is not unlike the experiences of Muhammad's great forefather:

> That's the result (of Our demonstration) to Abraham, when We showed him that We have all dominion over the heavens and the earth, and thus he was convinced (that the idols were false). — *Al An'am (The Livestock, 6:75)*

---

10 WHY WAS THE PROPHET GIVEN THE PRIVILEGE OF MEETING HIS CREATOR? `AL-MUBARAKPURI`

"The Prophets, after seeing Allah's Signs, will establish their Faith on solid certainty too immune to be parted with. Indeed actual observation is not the equal to mere information. They are in fact eligible for this Divine privilege because they are the ones who will bear burdens too heavy for other ordinary people to carry, and in the process of their mission, they will regard all worldly trials and sufferings too small to care about."[14]

YEAR 12: THE 'AQABAH PLEDGE

12.1 THE FIRST 'AQABAH PLEDGE

In the seemingly endless civil war between the Aws and Khazraj, the Battle of Bu'ath was the fourth and latest clash, and had increasingly polarized the community in the past year. Yathrib's moderate clansmen therefore, propose electing a single leader to unify the city, and 'Abd Allah ibn Ubayy, the chief of Khazraj, positions himself as the leading contender.

Meanwhile, five of the six Khazraj men who had pledged their loyalty to the Prophet one year earlier, return to 'Aqabah along with seven other men, including two men from Aws. They gather around the Prophet and intently listen to his words:

> *"Come here and pledge that you will not associate any with Allah, that you will not steal, nor commit unlawful sexual intercourse, nor kill your children, nor utter slander intentionally forging falsehood, nor disobey me in any good. He who fulfills this, Allah will reward him; and who neglects anything and is afflicted in this world, it may prove redemption for him in the Hereafter; and if the sin remains hidden from the eyes of men and no grief comes to him, then his affair is with Allah. He may forgive him or He may not."*[1]

THE FIRST

'AQABAH PLEDGE

1. Associate nothing with God.
2. Do not steal.
3. Do not fornicate.
4. Do not practice infanticide.
5. Do not slander.
6. Do not disobey the Prophet in that which is right.

FIGURE 12A. THE TERMS OF THE FIRST 'AQABAH PLEDGE

The First 'Aqabah pledge took place in Mina near the area called the Jamaraat, where Muslims perform several rites of the annual Hajj pilgrimage.

Surah Al Fet-h will be revealed approximately six years later, when the Companions are asked to take a pledge of allegiance to the Prophet (known as the Pact of Ridwan) prior to the Treaty of Hudaybiyah (QY 19.2).

All 12 men from Yathrib agree to follow the Prophet's moral code and pledge their loyalty to him in an event known as the First 'Aqabah. Several years later, Surah Al Fet-h will underscore the significance of pledging allegiance to the Prophet:

> Indeed, those who pledge their allegiance to you, (Muhammad,) do no less than pledge their allegiance to God. The hand of God is over their hands! Thereafter, the one who violates his pledge does so to the harm of his own soul, while the one who fulfills what he's promised to God, then God will soon give him a valuable reward. — *Al Fet-h (Victory, 48:10)*

---

2 WHAT WERE THE CONDITIONS OF THE FIRST 'AQABAH?   YUSUF

[Yusuf translates the conditions as narrated by 'Ubada ibn Samit. Here they are presented as a list, and not as a direct quote from Yusuf]
The Ansar agreed to the following five conditions:
1. They will hear and obey the Prophet, God's peace and blessings upon him, in hardship and in ease.
2. They will prefer others over themselves (this was a preparation for the arrival of the Emigrants).
3. They will not fight people who have authority over them.
4. They will speak the truth wherever they are.
5. They will fear only Allah, not the blame of anyone who reproaches them.[2]

- -

3 HOW DID THE FIRST 'AQABAH LAY THE GROUNDWORK FOR THE FUTURE MUSLIM COMMUNITY?   YUSUF

[Referring to the third condition of the oath] "This is really interesting. This was an oath they took with the Prophet, God's peace and blessings upon him, which was that they would not dispute people over political ascendancy. So when the time comes when the Prophet, God's peace and blessings upon him, dies and the Aws and the Khazraj begin to speak about electing a khalifa [leader] from amongst themselves, 'Umar and Abu Bakr come and they say this amr [trust] is Quraysh's. And the other tribes submit to that because they took that baya [oath] that they would not dispute that."[3]

12.2 MUS'AB LEAVES FOR MEDINA

The Prophet accepts the pilgrims' allegiance and sends Mus'ab ibn 'Umayr to Yathrib to teach them the growing collection of Meccan surahs and lead them in prayer. Mus'ab, who had recently returned from Abyssinia, stays with As'ad ibn Zurahah of Khazraj. As'ad's hospitality greatly annoys his cousin Sa'd ibn Mu'adh. As one of the chiefs of Aws, Sa'd sends his friend Usayd ibn Hudayr to break up Mus'ab's gatherings. To Sa'd's dismay, Usayd is captivated by the Meccan surahs and returns a converted man. Sa'd decides to confront Mus'ab himself, but he too is transfixed by the beautiful recitation. Soon after, Sa'd leverages his position in his clan to persuade clan members to embrace the new religion.

By this point, it is possible that nearly 75% of the Qur'an has been revealed.

As'ad ibn Zurahah was the first of six Khazraji men from Yathrib who pledged themselves to to the Prophet.

In the next few years, **Sa'd ibn Mu'adh** will become the unofficial leader of Aws and one of the most prominent men of the Ansar (Helpers from Medina). Recall that his brother Iyas was the first man from Yathrib to enter Islam.

---

4 **WHY DID THE PROPHET SEND MUS'AB TO MEDINA?**   ARMSTRONG

"This was a wise move. Tribal hatred was so intense in the oasis, that neither Aws nor Khazraj could bear to hear a rival leading the prayers or reciting the Qur'an."[4]

Eleven months after leaving Mecca, Mus'ab returns to report on his progress. Though not perfect, Yathrib's sociopolitical climate appears better suited to cultivating the loyal community of Muslims that somehow managed to survive Mecca's rocky and unforgiving terrain:

> Because this new religion or ideology corresponded very exactly to the needs of the non-nomadic communities of Western Arabia, it was capable of being the vehicle of a profound social change. In both Mecca and Medina the nomadic ethics and outlook, however well suited to desert conditions, were proving unsatisfactory for settled communities. In Mecca the chief trouble was probably selfish individualism; in Medina the need for a supreme judicial authority was most prominent. In a sense the great work of Islam was to modify the nomadic ethics for use in settled conditions; and the key to this was a new principle of organization for society. Hitherto the bond of society had been blood-relationship; but this was very weak in the case of larger groups—the common ancestry of the Aws and the Khazraj did not prevent their bitter feud; and group loyalty was proving an insufficient sanction for conduct as individualism grew...

> That Muhammad should have had in mind—albeit in rudimentary form—an ideology capable of being elaborated to form the basis of the great movement of Arab expansion, is a measure of the width of his perception of the needs of his time and the vastness of his achievement during the Meccan period.[5]

With Yathrib ready for his arrival, the Prophet tells 'Abbas and his wife Umm al-Fadl of his plans to emigrate.

Mus'ab ibn 'Umayr is one of the Prophet's dearest Companions. After successfully preparing Yathrib for the Prophet's Hijrah, Mus'ab will later be entrusted to carry the Prophet's banner at the Battle of Badr and later Uhud, where he will be martyred.

7
8
9
10
11
12

EARLY MEDINA

PROPHETIC GATHERINGS

Al-Hussain ibn Alī ibn Abī Tālib narrated: "I then asked him ['Ali ibn Abi Talib] about his interaction with people outside his house. He replied, 'The Messenger of Allāh (peace be upon him) controlled his tongue, only speaking regarding that which concerned him. He brought unity amongst the people and did not alienate them. He honoured the esteemed ones of every group and made them the leaders of their groups. He warned the people and was cautious when dealing with people to preserve his status among them but he never lacked courtesy towards others ... Those who were close to him were the best of people, the best of whom in his eyes were the ones who wished everybody well, and the ones with the highest status in his eyes were the ones with the most compassion, who aided the creation the most.'

———

I then asked my father regarding the gatherings of the Messenger (peace be upon him). He replied, 'The Messenger of Allāh (peace be upon him) began and ended all of his sittings with the remembrance of Allāh. When he came to a gathering, he sat where there was space available, and instructed the people to do the same. He gave every attendee his due respect and rights to a degree that led every individual present to think that he (peace be upon him) was honour-ing him the most. When an individual came to sit with him or came regarding some issue, he (peace be upon him) would remain seated until that person began to rise. Whenever he was asked for something, he would fulfil that request, and did not refuse it; [if he did not possess that which was required] he would advise the person with soft and kind words . His affection and good manners were for all and not restricted to certain people. He was like a father to them and he was just and fair with each one of them.

———

His gatherings were the gatherings of knowledge, humility, patience and trustworthiness. In his gatherings, voices were not raised and vile and unlawful topics were refrained from. If anyone committed a fault, it was not publicised. All were regarded as equals amongst themselves and superiority was according to the piety possessed. Therein the old were respected , the young were loved, the needy were given preference, and strangers and travellers were cared for and his gems were observed attentively and memorised.' "

———

Taken from A Commentary on the Depiction of Prophet Muhammad,
by Imam al-Tirmidhi (#336)

YEAR 13: THE HIJRAH

13.1 THE SECOND 'AQABAH PLEDGE

Shortly after Mus'ab's return, 73 men and two women (62 Khazraj and 11 Aws) travel to Mecca for the annual pilgrimage. Upon their arrival, they agree to meet with the Prophet in secret and help plan his escape. 'Abbas escorts the Prophet to the gathering at 'Aqabah, and is the first to address the audience:

> *"O you people of the Khazraj ... all of you know the position that Muhammad holds among us. We have protected him from our people as much as we could. He is honored and respected among his people. He refuses to join any party except you. So, if you think you can carry out what you promise while inviting him to your town, and if you can defend him against the enemies, then assume the burden that you have taken. But if you are going to surrender him and betray him after having taken him away with you, you had better leave him now because he is respected and well defended in his own place."*

Once again, the pilgrims affirm their allegiance to the Prophet, who addresses the group, beginning with a recitation from the Qur'an and concluding with a final request:

> *"I give you my pledge that you protect me from whatever you protect your women and children from."*

When one of the men asks what might happen to the Helpers if the Prophet immigrates to Medina but later returns to Mecca, the Prophet responds:

> *"Nay, it would never be; your blood will be my blood. In life and death I will be with you and you with me. I will fight whom you fight and I will make peace with whom you make peace."* [1]

Although **'Abbas ibn Abi Talib** is a source of strength for the Prophet, he has not yet entered Islam. In fact, he fights against the Prophet at Badr, and enters Islam after he is captured.

In just a few years, the Prophet will be face to face with the Meccans at the Battle of Badr. Knowing that the Second 'Aqabah Pledge does not obligate the Helpers to assist him (since Badr was not a defensive battle within city limits), he will have to formally ask for their help before marching to the battlefield.

THE SECOND

'AQABAH PLEDGE

1. To listen and obey in all difficulty and ease.
2. To spend in plenty as well as in scarcity.
3. To enjoin good and forbid evil.
4. In Allah's service, you will fear the censure of none.
5. To aid me when I come to you, and protect me from anything you protect yourself, your spouses and children from.

"...Then Paradise is in store for you." – The Prophet

FIGURE 13A. THE TERMS OF THE SECOND 'AQABAH PLEDGE

This was the third time the Prophet met with pilgrims from Yathrib. The first time was a spontaneous gathering with six Khazraj pilgrims. The following year, 12 men came to pledge themselves at the First 'Aqabah. They returned to Yathrib with Mus'ab ibn 'Umayr and began to learn about Islam. Now in the months prior to the Hijrah, 75 pilgrims traveled to Mecca to pledge themselves at the Second 'Aqabah. The terms of the First 'Aqabah later came to be called the "pledge of the women" because it was a pledge of moral conduct, which, unlike the Second 'Aqabah, did not bind them to defend the Prophet in battle. Three years later, Nusaybah bint Ka'b, one of the two women present at the Second 'Aqabah, insisted on keeping their word and defending the Prophet at the Battle of Uhud.

After all 75 pilgrims individually promise to uphold the terms of the pledge, the Prophet requests 12 representatives (9 Khazraj and 3 Aws) to come forward and assume responsibility for their clansmen. The event becomes known as the Second ʿAqabah.

When news of the pledge reaches the Quraysh, they rush to ʿAqabah, but the pilgrims have already departed for Yathrib. They chase the caravan but are only able to catch up to Saʿd ibn ʿUbadah, whom they torture until he is rescued by Mutʿim ibn ʿAdi and a fellow Meccan sympathizer.

Remember that **Mutʿim ibn ʿAdi** was one of only five Meccans who persuaded the Quraysh to end the ban on Hashim. Shortly thereafter, he agreed to protect the Prophet after Taʾif, when no one else would. Just a year ago, he dissolved his son's engagement to ʿAʾishah so the Prophet could marry her.

According to Al-Mubarakpuri, Abu Salamah left for Medina before the Second ʿAqabah.

ʿUthman ibn Talhah will convert to Islam seven years later when he is approached by Khalid ibn al-Walid, who also decides to join the Prophet in Medina. ʿUthman is from the clan of ʿAbd ad-Dar, and after the Conquest of Mecca, the Prophet will honor him with the keys to the Kaʿbah.

13.2 THE FIRST EMIGRANTS TO YATHRIB

Abu Salamah is one of the first Muslims to leave for Yathrib. When he tries to leave Mecca with his entire family, his fellow clansmen intercept the party and force Umm Salamah and her son to stay behind. The separation however, is temporary– she and her son, Salamah, are soon escorted by ʿUthman ibn Talhah to the town of Quba, just south of Yathrib.

---

① WHY WAS THE HIJRAH RISKY?   `ARMSTRONG`

"The hijrah was a risky enterprise, an irrevocable, frightening step. Nobody knew how it would work out, because nothing quite like it had ever happened in Arabia before … The fact remained that even after the hijrah, the Muslims would remain a tiny minority in the oasis, dwarfed in size by the aloof, appraising pagans, hanifs, and Jews."[2]

Several more Muslims begin leaving for Yathrib after the Second ʿAqabah. Among them are ʿUmar ibn al-Khattab and Zaynab bint Mazʾun, and their children Hafsah and ʿAbd Allah; ʿUthman and Ruqayyah; Abu Sabrah and his wife Umm Kulthum bint Suhayl; and Hamzah and Zayd (without their wives).

---

② HOW DID ʿUMAR START HIS HIJRAH?   `SALAHI`

"Umar was the only one to announce his intention to emigrate. He challenged the Quraysh to stop him, telling them: *'I am emigrating. He who wants to leave behind him a bereaved mother, a widow or orphan children can meet me beyond this valley.'* "[3]

Recall that **Hisham ibn al-ʿAs** had previously migrated to Abyssinia and watched his half-brother ʿAmr fail to persuade the Negus to return the Muslims to Mecca. He later renews his faith and joins the Emigrants in Medina. Many years later, he rejoices when ʿAmr finally embraces Islam.

However, not every emigrant makes it safely to Yathrib. On a number of occasions, the Quraysh harass several Companions and block them from leaving. Hisham ibn al-ʿAs and ʿAyyash ibn Abi Rabiʾah are even forced to renounce their faith, for which they are guilt stricken. But Surah Az-Zumar's timely verses reaffirm their faith and increase their resolve to escape.

◇ (Muhammad,) tell (people that I, Myself, have said), "All My servants who
  have acted excessively against their own souls! Don't lose hope of God's
  mercy, for God can forgive all sins. He truly is the Forgiving and the Merciful!"
  — *Az-Zumar (The Crowds, 39:53)*

③ HOW DID THE PROPHET HANDLE HISHAM AND AYYASH'S REVERSION TO IDOLATRY? `RAMADAN`

"During the same period, the Prophet also showed a most understanding attitude
toward those who, under persecution or pressure from their families, had left Islam
… Later on, in Medina, he was to speak out harshly and take firm measures against
those who falsely converted to Islam for the sole purpose of gathering information
about the Muslims, then denied Islam and went back to their tribes to bring them
the information they had managed to obtain. These were in fact war traitors, who
incurred the penalty of death because their actions were liable to bring about the
destruction of the Muslim community."[5]

When almost every other Companion had left Mecca, Abu Bakr finally asks for
permission to emigrate, and the Prophet responds:

"Wait for a while, because I hope that I will be allowed to emigrate also."[4]

13.3 THE DRAMATIC ESCAPE

The untimely death of the Prophet's guardian, Mut'im ibn 'Adi, leaves the Prophet
especially vulnerable and provides a compelling reason for the Prophet to leave
Mecca. Immediately after Mut'im's passing, Abu Jahl assembles the leaders
of Quraysh (minus Abu Lahab, who purposely skips the meeting) and, after
entertaining several options, persuades them to assassinate the Prophet. Hoping
to minimize retribution to any one clan, the conspirators agree to appoint one
assassin from each clan to descend upon the Prophet in unison.

When Gabriel informs the Prophet of the conspiracy, the Prophet goes straight
to Abu Bakr's house and informs him that the time has come to leave for Yathrib.
'A'ishah, who is at home with her half-sister Asma', later stated:

*"I knew not before that day that one could weep for joy until I saw Abu Bakr
weep at those words."*[6]

④ WHY WAS THE PROPHET AMONG THE LAST TO MAKE THE HIJRAH? `WATT`

"Muhammad's reasons for thus waiting until the majority had reached Medina were
probably to ensure that waverers did not abandon the enterprise and to make it
certain that he would be in a strong and independent position when he reached
Medina and would not have to rely solely on the support of the Medinan Muslims."[7]

'Ayyash ibn Abi Rabi'ah migrates to
Medina with 'Umar ibn al-Khattab
but is persuaded to return by his
half-brothers, Abu Jahl and Harith
ibn Hisham, who inform him that
their mother has taken an oath of
self-neglect if he does not return.
Despite 'Umar's warnings, when
'Ayyash enters Mecca, his brothers
make an example out of him by
binding him up and forcing him to
renounce his faith. Despite their
cruel efforts, 'Ayyash will later
return to Islam.

13
14
15
16
17
18

That evening, the assassins surround the Prophet's house. They hear the voices of Sawdah, Umm Kulthum, Fatimah, and Umm Ayman, and decide to attack in the morning when the Prophet usually emerged from the threshold.

That night, the Prophet wraps his cloak around 'Ali and instructs him to sleep in the Prophet's bed. He then exits the house and, while reciting Surah Ya Seen, is able to walk unseen right past the unsuspecting assassins.

> We've put a wall (of uncertainty) in front of them and behind them and covered them (in the darkness of ignorance), so they can't see a thing. It's all the same whether you warn them or don't warn them, for they won't believe.
> — *Ya Seen (36:9-10)*

Shortly after the Prophet's escape, a man passes by his house and informs the assassins that he just saw the Prophet fleeing in the opposite direction. However the men see 'Ali's silhouette through the window, and decide to stick to their original plan and attack at dawn.

Surah Al Anfal captures the dramatic moment:

> Recall how the faithless (idol-worshippers of Mecca) plotted against you, (Muhammad,) either to imprison you, murder you or drive you out (of the city). They were making plans, and God was making plans, and God is the best planner of all! — *Al Anfal (The Spoils of War, 8:30)*

The next morning, when 'Ali comes to the door, the assassins are completely bewildered. They immediately sound the alarm —Muhammad has escaped!

---

5 **WHAT WAS THE IRONY OF THE PROPHET'S ESCAPE?**   ASLAN

"It is a wonder—some would say a miracle—that this same man, who had been forced to sneak out of his home under cover of night to join the seventy or so followers anxiously awaiting him in a foreign land hundreds of miles away, would, in a few short years, return to the city of his birth, not covertly or in darkness, but in the full light of day, with ten thousand men trailing peacefully behind him; and the same people who once tried to murder him in his sleep would instead offer up to him both the sacred city and the keys to the Ka'ba—unconditionally and without a fight, like a consecrated sacrifice."[8]

13.4 THE ROUTE TO YATHRIB

Rather than taking the usual northern route to Medina, the Prophet and Abu Bakr travel five miles south of Mecca to a cave in Mount Thawr. 'Amir ibn Fuhayrah and his flock of sheep strategically follow them to cover their tracks. Meanwhile, Abu Bakr's children, 'Abd Allah and Asma', travel back and forth with provisions for the two men.

6 WHAT WAS THE SOCIOLOGICAL SIGNIFICANCE OF THE HIJRAH? [ARMSTRONG]

"In Arabia, where the tribe was the most sacred value of all, this amounted to blasphemy; it was far more shocking than the Qur'anic rejection of the goddesses … The very word hijrah suggests a painful severance. The root HJR has been translated: 'he cut himself off from friendly or loving communication or intercourse … he ceased … to associate with them.' … This traumatic dislocation was central to their new identity."[9]

7 WHAT WAS THE PSYCHOLOGICAL SIGNIFICANCE OF THE HIJRAH? [RAMADAN]

"Hijrah is primarily this essential teaching at the heart of the Prophet's experience: a trust in God that entails, without arrogance, absolute independence from people, as well as the humble recognition of absolute dependence on God…
Hijrah is the exile of the conscience and of the heart from false gods, from alienation of all sorts, from evil and sins. Turning away from the idols of one's time (power, money, the cult of appearances, etc.); emigrating from lies and unethical ways of life; liberating oneself, through the experience of breaking away, from all the appearances of freedom paradoxically reinforced by our habits—such is the spiritual hijrah.
Their physical journey to Medina was a spiritual exile toward their inner selves; in leaving their city and their roots, they came back to themselves, to their intimacy with God, to the meaning of their lives beyond historical contingencies.
Exile for the sake of God is in essence a series of questions that God asks each individual being: Who are you? What is the meaning of your life? Where are you going? Accepting the risk of such an exile, trusting the One, is to answer: Through You, I return to myself and I am free."[10]

8 HIJRAH: A MIGRATION FROM JAHILIYYA [ARMSTRONG]

"Increasingly the Qur'an would insist that when Muslims found themselves in frightening or disturbing circumstances, they should be serene and tranquil, and should never fall prey to the impetuous rage and vengeful fury of jahiliyya."[11]

9 HIJRAH: PLANNING, WORKING, THEN TRUSTING [RAMADAN]

"Only after making intelligent and thorough use of his human powers had he trusted himself to the divine will, thereby clarifying for us the meaning of at-tawakkul ala Allah (reliance on God) … Indeed, this teaching is the exact opposite of the temptation of fatalism: God will only act after humans have, at their own level, sought out and exhausted all the potentialities of action. That is the profound meaning of this Quranic verse: 'Verily never will God change the condition of a people until they change what is in themselves.' [Qur'an 13:11]
Once again, in spite of their carefully planned strategy, the Prophet and his Companion were going through the trial of vulnerability … When Muhammad emigrated, he took care to owe nothing to anyone (he refused gifts, settled his debts, and gave back the deposits he held), but he also knew that he owed everything to the One, that his indebtedness and obligation to Him were infinite."[12]

'Amir ibn Fuhayrah was a servant who was freed by Abu Bakr several years ago. After the Battle of Uhud, 'Amir will join a peaceful 40-man expedition to visit the Bedouin clan of Banu 'Amr. The group is ambushed and 'Amir is killed along with 37 others. When the survivors return, the Prophet confirms witness reports of those who saw 'Amr's body lifted to heaven.

'Abd Allah and **Asma' bint Abi Bakr** are half-siblings to 'A'ishah. During her father's escape, Asma' rips her girdle in two so she can lash provisions to his saddle, earning the nickname, "she of the two girdles." After the Hijrah, Asma' will marry Zubayr ibn al-'Awwam, the Prophet's first cousin through his aunt Safiyyah.

For an outstanding discussion on the Hijrah and exile, read Ramadan (p. 84-86).

Back in Mecca, the Quraysh are furious that the Prophet has slipped through their fingers. They set a bounty of 100 camels for each of the two fugitives and send out mercenaries. Soon enough, one of the search parties ascends Mount Thawr and approaches the cave where the Prophet and Abu Bakr are hiding. Abu Bakr whispers his concern for the Prophet's safety, and the Prophet responds:

"Abu Bakr! What do you think of those two with whom the Third is Allah?"[13]

Surah At-Tawbah captures the tense moment:

> If you don't help (Muhammad against the Byzantine Romans,) then (you should know that) God helped him when the faithless drove him away (from Mecca and tried to hunt him down). He was just one of two (men hiding out) in a cave when he said to his companion, (Abu Bakr, who was afraid that the Meccans would capture them), "Don't be afraid, for God is with us."
>
> — At-Tawbah (*Repentance, 9:40*)

FIGURE 13B. THE PROPHET'S HIJRAH

_____

Hoping to confuse the Meccans, the Prophet and Abu Bakr first headed south to the cave of Thawr. After three days in hiding, they made their way north, avoiding the usual trade route to Yathrib. As they approached Yathrib, they encountered Abu Bakr's cousin Talhah, who provided them with a new set of white garments to wear. The Prophet and Abu Bakr arrived in Quba on Day 12 and erected the first mosque in Islam. A few days later, the two men arrived in Yathrib—16 days after leaving Mecca—in September 622 CE.

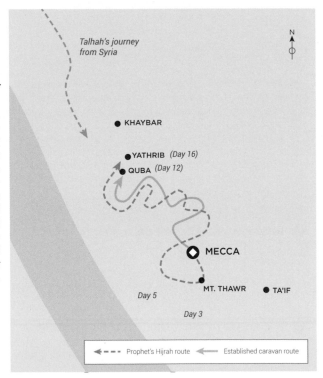

Miraculously, their presence goes unnoticed thanks to a freshly spun spider web over the mouth of the cave and a nesting dove perched overhead, lending the area a deserted and undisturbed appearance. When the two men depart Mount Thawr after three days of hiding, Abu Bakr offers his camel Qaswa to the Prophet, but the Prophet refuses to accept the gift without paying for it.

---

⑩ WHY DID THE PROPHET REFUSE TO ACCEPT ABU BAKR'S GIFT?   YUSUF

"Because this was a hijrah for the sake of Allah, the Prophet (saws) wanted to take every reward in it. And so he refused to take it as a gift because he was expending his wealth to go 'fi sabilillah' [for the sake of God] to Medina. It is important to remember that the Prophet (saws) is a believer. You can forget that because of his maqam [position]. But you have to remember … the commands that are in the Qur'an are commands to him as well as everybody else, and more. … He gave all his wealth away. He never went to bed with any wealth. And that is all fi sabilillah."[14]

Abu Bakr hires a local, non-Muslim guide, 'Abd Allah ibn Uraiqit, to plan their escape route. The three set out for the Red Sea coast and slowly work their way north, trying to avoid the usual route to Medina. With Mecca fading in the distance, Surah Al Qasas reassures the two men that, one day, they will return to their homeland.

Be sure to read Al-Mubarakpuri, p. 158-161 for details of the Hijrah not found in Lings.

 The One Who bestowed the Qur'an upon you will surely bring you back to the destination. — *Al Qasas (The Tales, 28:85)*

---

⑪ HOW COULD THE PROPHET ENTRUST THE HIJRAH TO A NON-MUSLIM GUIDE?   RAMADAN

"The women and men he surrounded himself with might not share his faith, but they were known to him for their moral qualities and/or their human abilities."[15]

As the men near Yathrib, they spot an unidentified caravan approaching from the opposite direction. As the caravan gets closer, the two are relieved to see Abu Bakr's cousin, Talhah ibn 'Ubayd Allah, returning from a trading expedition to Syria. After accepting a gift of fresh garments from Talhah, the Prophet and Abu Bakr continue north.

Twelve days after leaving Mecca, the Prophet and Abu Bakr reach the village of Quba on the southern outskirts of Yathrib. Shortly after his much anticipated arrival, the Prophet addresses the excited crowd assembled around him:

> *"O people, give unto one another greetings of Peace; feed food unto the hungry; honor the ties of kinship; pray in the hours when men sleep. Even so shall ye enter Paradise in Peace."[16]*

Talhah ibn 'Ubayd Allah belongs to Abu Bakr's clan of Taym and was one of the first converts in Mecca. He will fight gloriously at Uhud and will later be named as one of the 10 Companions to whom the Prophet promises Paradise. (According to Al-Mubarakpuri, the Prophet and Abu Bakr encounter a man named az-Zubayr, not Talhah.)

---

⑫ WHY DID THE PROPHET EMPHASIZE PRAYER IN QUBA?   RAMADAN

"Caring for the poor and honoring kinship ties appears as reminders of the ethical basis of the Muslim presence, which each believer must pledge to permanently respect. [Prayer] provides the heart with the strength and serenity in faith that make it possible to fulfill the requirements of respecting ethics and of spreading peace."[17]

13
14
15
16
17
18

The Prophet stays with Kulthum ibn Hidm, from the Aws sub-clan of Bani 'Amr, and Abu Bakr resides with a Khazraj family in the northern village of Sunh.

Having taken care of the Prophet's debts in Mecca, 'Ali ibn Abi Talib reaches Quba a few days after the Prophet's arrival. Meanwhile, Salman al-Farisi, a Persian who had anticipated the coming of a prophet, arrives from Medina to catch a glimpse of the Prophet. Salman was born to a Zoroastrian family near the Persian city of Isfahan. He converted to Christianity when he was young, and dedicated his youth to finding an Abrahamic prophet whose imminent arrival had been prophesized by the eastern churches. His search took him from Persia to Syria to Iraq. After an unfortunate turn of events, he was sold into slavery to a Jewish merchant in Yathrib, but even then, Salman never gave up on finding the Arabian prophet he had spent his entire life searching for. After confirming the Prophet's identity, he returns to Yathrib, hoping to see the Prophet once again.

Five years later, **Salman** will counsel the Prophet to dig a trench around Medina to defend the city from imminent destruction by invading armies. He will become such a popular Companion that both the Helpers and Emigrants will claim he is one of theirs. The Prophet however breaks the tie when he states that Salman is part of his family (Ahl al-Bait).

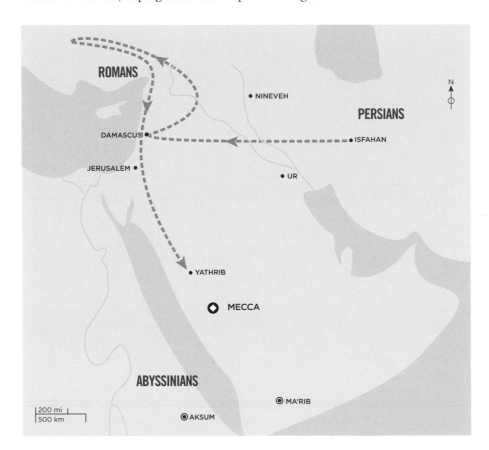

FIGURE 13C. THE JOURNEY OF SALMAN AL-FARISI

Salman al-Farisi's search for the Prophet is one of the most dramatic accounts in the Sirah. His journey led him from his birthplace near present-day Isfahan to Syria, Iraq, Turkey, back to Syria, and finally to Yathrib, where he was wrongfully sold into slavery. Salman dedicated his entire life in search of the Prophet, and when he finally found him, he wept.

Before departing Quba three days later, the Prophet lays the foundations for the very first mosque. He leaves for Yathrib, and reaches the valley of Ranuna' where he leads the Khazraj clan of Salim in the Friday congregational prayer. Then, escorted by a group of about 100 men fully dressed in battle attire, the Prophet enters Yathrib on September 27, 622 CE. As he makes his way through the city, his camel halts a few times before stopping at a courtyard belonging to two orphans, Sahl and Suhayl, who are under the guardianship of As'ad ibn Zurahah. The orphans offer their property as a gift, but the Prophet insists on paying for the land, which becomes the site of the Prophet's mosque. Meanwhile, Abu Ayyub ibn Zayd takes the Prophet's belongings into his house and the Prophet moves into the first floor of Abu Ayyub's apartment.

Shortly after the Prophet's arrival, the Companions begin referring to Yathrib as *Medina al-Munawwarah* (The City of Lights), often abbreviated to just *Medina* (The City).

Remember that **As'ad ibn Zurahah** was the first of six pilgrims from Yathrib who pledged allegiance to the Prophet (prior to the first 'Aqabah), and housed Mus'ab ibn 'Umayr when he arrived in Medina before the Hijrah. As'ad will pass away shortly after the Hijrah.

Lings refers to **Abu Ayyub ibn Zayd** as Abu Ayyub Khalid. He is better known as Abu Ayyub al-Ansari, one of the 12 men to pledge at the Second 'Aqabah. He is a close Companion to the Prophet and will take part in every military expedition during the Prophet's lifetime. Abu Ayyub will later join the Muslim expeditions that advance into Turkey. Seven centuries later, after the Ottoman conquest of Constantinople, Sultan Mehmed II will build a mosque and shrine to commemorate Abu Ayyub al-Ansari's resting place in there.

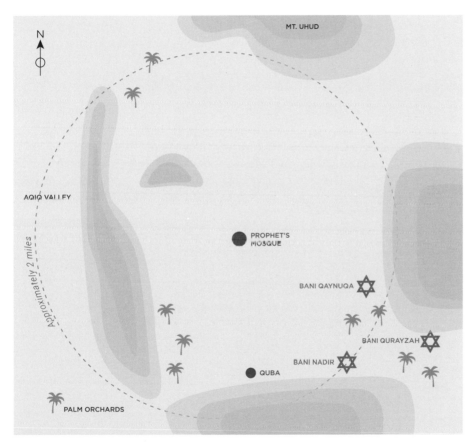

FIGURE 13D. THE CITY OF MEDINA

Medina was a fertile oasis unlike Mecca, and was surrounded by several natural barriers that made it easy to defend. The major Jewish tribes lived in the southeast sector. Bani Nadir and Qurayzah were highly skilled farmers, while Bani Qaynuqa supported themselves as tradesmen and blacksmiths. The many clans of Aws and Khazraj were spread throughout the city. (Note the size of Yathrib compared with the modern city of Medina.)

13.5 THE NEW SOCIAL CONTRACT

Prior to the Hijrah, Yathrib had been a collection of settlements on the verge of civil war. Not only had tensions mounted between the Aws and Khazraj clans—the various Jewish tribes also were divided and had formed separate alliances with the Arabs. At a critical juncture when Yathrib is struggling to survive, the Prophet offers a unique solution:

> The root of the social troubles of the Hijaz in the early seventh century A.D. was that the communal (tribal) system of the desert was breaking down in the settled life of Mecca and Medina. The precise reasons were different in the two places. In Mecca a mercantile economy had fostered the growth of individualism. In Medina the autonomy of each tribe and clan, appropriate to desert conditions, led in the confined space of an oasis to an insecurity of life that had become intolerable. Individualism meant that the strong oppressed the weak and neglected their traditional duties to clan and family. It was present at Medina, but not so noticeable there as at Mecca. The characteristic of the social structure of Medina was a tendency towards the formation of larger groupings, either as alliances or on the basis of kinship, real or artificial. In all this social disintegration most individuals were doubtless painfully aware of their insecurity and isolation...
>
> Against this background it is interesting to see how individualism and communalism were combined by Muhammad...
>
> In one respect it was a community of individuals, for Islam accepted the tendency towards individualism, and even encouraged it (as in the new family structure). The ultimate moral sanction in Islam, punishment in Hell, applies to the individual for his conduct as an individual. On the other hand, the individual was taken out of his isolation and insecurity and made to feel that he belonged to the ummah [community].[18]

⑬ WHAT WAS THE PROPHET'S VISION FOR MEDINA? `ARMSTRONG`

"His goal was to create a society of hilm [forbearance]. Those who kept the faith (mu'min) were not simply 'believers.' Their faith must be expressed in practical actions: they must pray, share their wealth, and in matters that concerned the community, 'consult among themselves' to preserve the unity of the ummah. If attacked, they could defend themselves, but instead of lashing out in the old, uncontrolled jahili way, they must always be prepared to forgive an injury. Automatic, vengeful retaliation—the cardinal duty of muruwah—could be a great evil. 'Hence, whoever pardons [his foe] and makes peace, his reward rests with God,' the Qur'an insisted tirelessly." [19]

⑭ HOW WAS ISLAM'S CURE FOR MECCA JUST AS POTENT FOR MEDINA? `WATT`

"In the growth of all the great world-religions it is found that ideas specially relevant to the situation in one small region are capable of application much more generally. The adaptation of Meccan Islam to circumstances in Medina is a striking example of this phenomenon. The chief feature in the Meccan situation was the increase of commerce and wealth, and, with that, of individualism. There was nothing on a comparable scale at Medina. The one thing they had in common was that in both towns men from a nomadic background, and still retaining much of the social, moral and intellectual outlook of the desert, were attempting to live a settled life. The Islamic religion had been trying, not very successfully, to deal with this problem in its Meccan form. This gave it a certain relevance to the Medinan form of the problem, and this relevance was greatly increased by placing more emphasis on the function of the prophet or messenger."[20]

(15) WHAT WAS THE PROPHET'S FIRST ACTION IN MEDINA?   YUSUF

"The Prophet, God's peace and blessings upon him, does two things. He has the Muslims set up their own marketplace and he sets out building the mosque. That is Islam right there: deen [faith] and dunya [worldly obligations]. We have our own place to worship and we have to maintain economic integrity and independence. And that's the foundation of the strength of a people."[21]

While the situation in Medina presented new challenges for the Prophet and his followers, it also afforded them fresh opportunities:

> The conditions of life in Medinah were totally different from those they [the Muslims] experienced in Makkah. There, in Makkah, they used to strive for one corporate target, but physically, they were scattered, overpowered and abandoned. They were helpless in terms of pursuing their new course of orientation. Their means, socially and materially, fell short of establishing a new Muslim community. In parallel lines, the Makkan Chapters of the Noble Qur'an were confined to describing the Islamic principles, establishing legislations pertaining to the believers individually and enjoining good and piety and forbidding evils and vices.
>
> In Medina, things were otherwise; here all the affairs of their life rested in their hands. Now, they were at ease and could quite comfortably handle the challenges of civilization, construction, means of living, economics, politics, government administration, war and peace, classification of the questions of the allowed and prohibited, worship, ethics and all the relevant issues. Briefly, they were in Medina at full liberty to erect the pillars of a new community not only totally different from that pre-Islamic code of life, but also distinctive in its features in the world as a whole … Allah the All-Knowing of course undertook legislation, and His Prophet Muhammad the explanation, implementation, and reformation.[22]

Upon his arrival, the Prophet immediately sets out to unify the community. Surah Al Jumu'ah describes the divinely guided process:

> He's the One Who raised a messenger from an unschooled nation - a messenger from among their own kind to recite revealed verses from Him, to reform them, to teach them the scripture and to give them wisdom, for they lived in obvious error before. — *Al Jumu'ah (The Congregation, 62:2)*

SURAH AL JUMU'AH (The Congregation) is a shorter Medinan surah that discusses the importance of attending the Friday congregational prayer. Among other things, the surah warns listeners not to fall prey to worldly distractions.

13
14
15
16
17
18

Refer to Salahi (p. 239-242) and Al-Mubarakpuri (p.174-180) for a detailed summary of the new constitution (translated from Ibn Hisham) and further insights into the Prophet's teachings of brotherhood.

The First and Second 'Aqabahs had unified the Aws and Khazraj, and in doing so, dissolved their previous alliances with the Jews. Hoping to bring the entire community together, the Prophet drafts a constitution which the disenfranchised Jewish tribes agree to sign:

1. The Jews are one community with the Muslims, with freedom to practice their own religion.

2. Each shall be responsible for their own expenses.

3. Each shall help the other from outside attack.

4. Each shall confer matters with the other in a mutual relationship based on righteousness.

5. Neither shall commit sins nor prejudice the other.

6. A wronged party will be aided by the other party.

7. Jews will pay for military defense as long as they are fighting alongside the Muslims.

8. The city will be a sacred place for both parties.

9. God and His Messenger will settle disagreements between the two.

10. Both parties will boycott the Quraysh.

11. Both parties will defend Medina from attack.

12. The treaty will not stop either party from seeking lawful retribution for an offense.

---

16 **WHAT WAS THE MINDSET OF YATHRIB'S JEWS?**   ARMSTRONG

"The Jews of seventh century Medina had only a limited knowledge of Torah and Talmud, were not strictly observant, and most were used to seeing their faith as a variant of Arabian religion. The idea of an Arabian prophet was not a strange idea to them: they had a prophet of their own called Ibn Sayyad."[23]

- -

17 **WHAT WAS THE SPIRIT OF THE PROPHET'S PACT WITH THE JEWS?**   RAMADAN

"The principles of justice, equality, and equal dignity for all the signatories (whether Jewish or Muslim, Medina natives or immigrants from Mecca, Aws, or Khazraj) were mentioned in it. Referring to the Jews, the text stipulates: 'They have the same rights and the same duties' which in effect implied that they fully and equally belonged to the local community. It stated that the rights of each person would be defended by all, and should a conflict with the polytheists break out, they were all to stand together and not enter into separate alliances or peace agreements."[24]

13.6 SURAH AL BAQARAH

Construction of the Prophet's house begins immediately after his arrival. The adjoining courtyard becomes a mosque (approximately 70x70 yards) made of stone and adobe walls and a roof of palm leaves. The *qiblah* (direction of prayer) is set toward Jerusalem.

Shortly after the Hijrah, the first few installments of Surah Al Baqarah are revealed. The surah begins with the definition of the *muttaqeen* (the God-fearing):

> Alif. Lam. Meem.
>
> That is the Book in which there is no doubt. It's a guide for those who are mindful (of their duty to God).
>
> (They're the ones) who believe in what's beyond their perception, establish regular prayer and spend in charity out of what We've given to them.
>
> They believe in what's being revealed to you, (Muhammad), even as they believe in what's been revealed before your time, and they're confident of the reality of the next life. They're living by the guidance of their Lord, and they're the ones who will be successful. — *Al Baqarah (The Cow, 2:1-5)*

These first verses are followed by others that hint at the possibility of discord:

> Among people (are some) who say, "We believe in God and the Last Day," but they have no faith. They try to deceive God and those who believe, but they fool no one but themselves – and they don't even realize it!
> — *Al Baqarah (The Cow, 2:8-9)*

The surah warns the Prophet that although the Hijrah distanced him from the *mushrikeen* (polytheists) in Mecca, he will soon confront a more insidious problem the *munafiqeen* (hypocrites) in Medina.

> When they meet the believers they affirm, "We believe, too," but when they're alone with their satanic (friends), they take back what they said by saying, "We're really with you. We were only joking with them."
> — *Al Baqarah (The Cow, 2:14)*

Surah Al Baqarah not only warns the Prophet about the hypocrites among the newly converted in Medina, it also instructs him to be vigilant about the integrity of his newest political alliances:

> Many of the Followers of Earlier Revelation will selfishly try to destroy your faith, even after they know the truth. So pardon them, and pay them no mind until God fulfills His purpose, for God has power over all things.
> — *Al Baqarah (The Cow, 2:109)*

SURAH AL BAQARAH (The Cow) is the longest surah and marks the beginning of the Medinan portion of the Qur'an, which comprises roughly 25% of the Qur'an. The surah is named after a series of verses that describe the obstinacy of the Israelites when Moses instructed them to sacrifice a cow. Instead of willingly submitting to God's command, they repeatedly pestered Moses to ask God for a clearer description of the cow (age, color, and type) that should be sacrificed (this account is also found in Numbers 19:1-4). Surah Al Baqarah covers many far-reaching topics including the nature of hypocrisy, the story of Adam and Eve, and the the trials of Abraham, Moses, and Solomon. In addition, the surah provides broad legislative guidance on a number of issues including (but not limited to) dietary regulations, capital punishment, estate planning, fasting, self-defense, performing the Hajj pilgrimage, giving charity, consuming alcohol, fair treatment of orphans and widows, marriage and divorce, remarriage, childcare, preservation of religious liberty, dowries, alimony, predatory lending, and sound business ethics.

13.7 TROUBLE UNDER THE SURFACE

Undoubtedly, the Prophet's various alliances unify and strengthen the city. Although the Jews share in this strength, the pact also brings unwelcome military obligations (in defense only). Furthermore, some of them may not want to resolve Yathrib's tribal instability, as they had indirectly benefited from the civil war between the Aws and Khazraj. Aside from their economic monopoly over the city, their support had been constantly sought after, and as such, they had gained prominence in the valley as a non-combatant third party.

The latest revelations hardly paint sweeping generalizations of Medina's Jews, but rather they speak to the divided nature of the Jewish clans inhabiting the oasis, highlighting the trustworthiness of some clans over others.

> (There are, of course, honest people) among the Followers of Earlier Revelation. They will return a fortune in gold entrusted to them, while others won't give back a single silver coin with which they've been entrusted - unless you stood there and demanded it! That's because they say, "We're not obligated by our faith (to be fair with those of another religion)." Yet, how terrible do they lie against God, and well they know it!
>
> —Ali 'Imran (The Family of Amran, 3:75)

---

18 **WHAT WAS THE POSITION OF THE JEWS IN YATHRIB?** WATT

"The Jews, however, became increasingly hostile, and used their knowledge of the Old Testament to criticize Muhammad's claim that the Qur'an was the speech of God. In a largely illiterate environment it was easy for them to assert and appear to prove that the Qur'an was mistaken in various matters mentioned in the Old Testament. And the conclusion of the argument, of course, was that the Qur'an was not the speech of God and that therefore Muhammad was not a prophet. In view of the gravity of this matter it must have been one of Muhammad's chief preoccupations during the early months."[25]

- -

19 **WHAT DID THE PROPHET EXPECT FROM THE JEWS?** ARMSTRONG

"Muhammad would not have expected the Jews to convert to his religion, because they had their own revealed din. God had decreed that each community should have its own messenger. But it was natural for Muslims to pray and fast in the same way as the other members of the Abrahamic family."[26]

In an attempt to break the pact between the Aws and Khazraj, an elderly man from the Jewish tribe of Bani Qaynuqa named Shas ibn Qais instructs one of his younger clansmen to recite poems about the Battle of Bu'ath, the most recent skirmish between the Aws and Khazraj. The boy's verses ignite longstanding feelings of animosity and revenge among the Helpers, but before the two sides come to blows, the Prophet swiftly dissipates the situation:

> "O Muslims! By Allah! Have you entered the state of pre-Islamic ignorance while I am still among you, after Allah guided you to Islam, honored you with it, by it He cut the fetters of ignorance from your necks, and delivered you from disbelief and united your hearts?"

20 **HOW DID THE PROPHET WORK WITH THE TRIBAL MINDSET?** | ASLAN |

"But there may be something to this change in terms. Despite its ingenuity, Muhammad's community was still an Arab institution based on Arab notions of tribal society. There was simply no alternative model of social organization in seventh-century Arabia, save for monarchy. Indeed, there are so many parallels between the early Muslim community and traditional tribal societies that one is left with the distinct impression that, at least in Muhammad's mind, the Ummah was indeed a tribe, though a new and radically innovative one ... By enacting a series of radical religious, social, and economic reforms, he was able to establish a new kind of society, the likes of which had never been seen in Arabia ... Because neither ethnicity nor culture nor race nor kinship had any significance to Muhammad, the Ummah, unlike a traditional tribe, had an almost unlimited capacity for growth through conversion."[27]

21 **IS THERE ROOM FOR SECTARIANISM IN ISLAM?** | ARMSTRONG |

"Muslims had been driven out of Mecca because of religious intolerance, so they must avoid all exclusivity ... It was idolatry to take pride in belonging to a particular religious tradition rather than concentrating upon Allah himself."[28]

The event highlights a clear weakness in the new Muslim community and prompts the Prophet to initiate a pact of brotherhood between the Helpers and the Emigrants. In the clearest terms, the Prophet redefines the meaning of brotherhood in Medina:

> Brotherhood-in-faith was holding subordinate every distinction of race and kindred and supporting the Islamic principle: none is superior to the other except on the basis of piety and God-fearing.[29]

Interestingly, the Prophet takes 'Ali as his brother and instructs Hamzah to form a pact with Zayd. Perhaps the Prophet was trying to avoid conflict by choosing 'Ali instead of preferring a man from one Medinan clan over another.

22 **WHAT WAS THE SIGNIFICANCE OF THE PACT OF BROTHERHOOD?** | YUSUF |

"This is an extraordinary thing because you have to see it from the perspective of the jahili [pre-Islamic] Arab where the kinship bond is everything. It's stronger than anything that most of us can understand about a blood brother. We should consider this deeply. This idea of the brotherhood of Islam overrides family, nation and tribe. These are all jahili concepts [nationalism, and so on]. Islam honors blood ties as long as those blood ties do not come into conflict with the deen [faith]. If they come into conflict with the deen, then those blood ties are severed."[30]

23 **WHAT WAS THE SECRET OF THE COMMUNITY'S SUCCESS?** | RAMADAN |

"Those bonds constituted the Muslim community's spiritual and social strength, and in this lay the secret of their success before God and among men: faith in God, love for parents, fraternity among people, and ethics at the service of the universe and of all beings."[31]

13
14
15
16
17
18

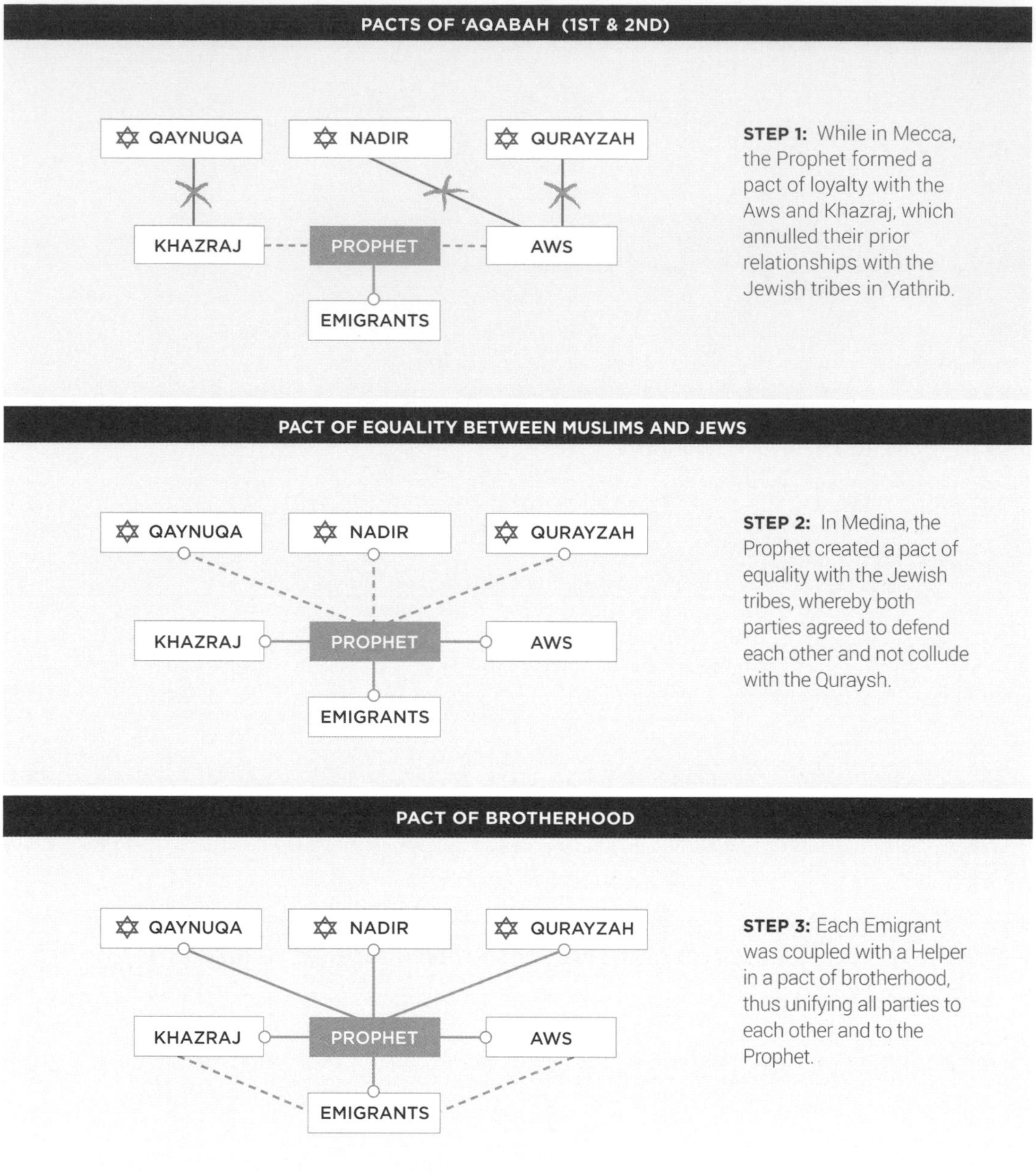
PACTS OF ʻAQABAH (1ST & 2ND)
QAYNUQA
NADIR
QURAYZAH
KHAZRAJ
PROPHET
AWS
EMIGRANTS
STEP 1: While in Mecca, the Prophet formed a pact of loyalty with the Aws and Khazraj, which annulled their prior relationships with the Jewish tribes in Yathrib.
PACT OF EQUALITY BETWEEN MUSLIMS AND JEWS
QAYNUQA
NADIR
QURAYZAH
KHAZRAJ
PROPHET
AWS
EMIGRANTS
STEP 2: In Medina, the Prophet created a pact of equality with the Jewish tribes, whereby both parties agreed to defend each other and not collude with the Quraysh.
PACT OF BROTHERHOOD
QAYNUQA
NADIR
QURAYZAH
KHAZRAJ
PROPHET
AWS
EMIGRANTS
STEP 3: Each Emigrant was coupled with a Helper in a pact of brotherhood, thus unifying all parties to each other and to the Prophet.

FIGURE 13E. PACTS THAT UNIFIED MEDINA

13.8 'ABD ALLAH IBN UBAYY & ABU 'AMIR IBN SAYFI

Before the Prophet arrived in Medina, the foremost leaders of Yathrib included Abu 'Amir ibn Sayfi of Aws and his cousin 'Abd Allah ibn Ubayy of Khazraj (Fig. 10c). Upon the Prophet's arrival, Abu 'Amir, a self-declared "Abrahamic monk," accuses the Prophet of falsifying the true faith of Abraham and taunts him with an ultimatum:

"May God let the liar die a lonely outcast in exile!"[32]

The Prophet acknowledges his words and, within a few years, the monk finds himself disenfranchised, and leaves Medina with only 10 followers.

'Abd Allah ibn Ubayy is no less eager to give up his position of authority to the Prophet. On one occasion, when the Prophet stops to talk to him while he is on his way to visit Sa'd ibn 'Ubadah, 'Abd Allah tells him to limit his preaching to his own house. In turn, 'Abd Allah is scolded by his own friend 'Abd Allah ibn Rawahah. When the Prophet arrives at Sa'd's house, he asks for advice on how to deal with 'Abd Allah's hostility and Sa'd explains:

"Deal gently with him, O Messenger of God, for when God brought thee unto us, even then were we fashioning for him a diadem wherewith to crown him; and he seeth that thou hast robbed him of a kingdom."[33]

24 HOW MUCH SUPPORT DID THE PROPHET FIRST ENJOY IN YATHRIB? [ASLAN]

"That Muhammad came to Yathrib as little more than the Hakam in the quarrel between Aws and Khazraj is certain. And yet the traditions seem to present Muhammad arriving in the oasis as the mighty prophet of a new and firmly established religion, and as the unchallenged leader of the whole of Yathrib ... His movement represented the tiniest fraction of Yathrib's population; the Jews alone may have totaled in the thousands. When Muhammad arrived in the oasis, he had brought fewer than a hundred men, women, and children with him."[34]

Despite **Abu 'Amir's** strong opposition to the Prophet, his own son Hanzalah is a devout follower and will soon die at Badr, fighting alongside the Prophet.

'Abd Allah ibn Ubayy's children are strong supporters of the Prophet. His son, also named 'Abd Allah, will fight at Badr even when his father, a professed Muslim, turns his back on the Prophet. His daughter Jamilah will marry Hanzalah, the son of Abu 'Amir ibn Sayfi.

At the opening of Badr, **'Abd Allah ibn Rawahah** will be the first Companion to challenge the Quraysh to a duel. Seven years later, 'Abd Allah will help Zayd lead a large expedition to the Syrian border where they are martyred.

In the next few months, **Sa'd ibn 'Ubadah** will replace 'Abd Allah ibn Ubayy as the leader of Khazraj and will be left in charge of Medina when the Prophet marches out on his first caravan raid. Sa'd will lead one of four battalions during the Conquest of Mecca. After the Prophet's death, many of the Ansar will nominate him as the first caliph.

13.9 THE END OF THE 13TH YEAR

As'ad ibn Zurahah passes away shortly after the Hijrah, and Salman al-Farisi steals away from work to catch a glimpse of the Prophet at As'ad's funeral. When he identifies the unique prophetic seal on the Prophet's back, Salman embraces the new religion before returning to Bani Qurayzah, where he is contracted to complete four more years of indentured work.

Many years later, **Husayn ibn Sallam** will be one of the few men who will try to ward off the assassins of Caliph 'Uthman ibn 'Affan.

The chief rabbi of Bani Qaynuqa, Husayn ibn Sallam, becomes another notable convert during the first year in Medina. After Husayn's conversion, the Prophet invites the leaders of Qaynuqa to his house and asks them what they think of their leader. Their lavish praise, however, quickly turns to scorn when Husayn steps out and openly endorses the Prophet.

---

25 **WHAT WAS AT THE CENTER OF THE JEWISH-MUSLIM DEBATE IN MEDINA?** [WATT]

"The most important aspect of the break with the Jews was the intellectual. The Jews were attacking the whole set of ideas on which Muhammad's position was based. They declared that some of the things in the Qur'an contradicted the ancient scriptures in their hands, and must therefore be false; in that case they could not be a revelation and Muhammad could not be a prophet. This was very serious. If many of the Muslims thought that what the Jews were saying was true, the whole structure of the community so carefully built by Muhammad would crumble away... The Jews were doing what they could to deprive him of such support, and as the possessors of the scriptures they were able to act effectively. At the centre of Muhammad's attempt to 'contain' the attacks of the Jews was the conception of the religion of Abraham. The Qur'an had all along insisted that its message was identical with that of previous prophets, and notably with the messages of Moses and Jesus, the founders of Judaism and Christianity respectively. This idea could not be excised from Islam. It had been an important part of the claim presented to the pagan Meccans, and was asserted or implied in a great many passages. Yet it was difficult not to admit that the Jews were correct in pointing to the differences. The only alternative to the inference that the Qur'an was false was to show that the differences were due to deviations on the part of the Jews...

This new way of looking at things could be supported by various facts which the Jews could not deny. They could not deny the Muslim assertion that Abraham was not a Jew, for they had to admit that he lived before the Jewish religion was revealed, whether that is made to begin with Jacob or, as the Muslims normally did, with Moses. And when the Muslims argued that there was nothing surprising in the Jewish rejection of Muhammad, since they had rejected many of the prophets sent to them and mentioned in their own scriptures, the Jews could not deny that there was some truth in this latter matter...

The conception of Islam as a restoration of the pure religion of Abraham offends modern Western standards of historical objectivity. Yet from a sociological standpoint it must be admitted that it was effective in its original environment. It enabled Muhammad to maintain with only a slight modification the set of ideas on which his religion was based, and to parry the hostile criticisms of the Jews... Islam is thus a form of the religion of Abraham—a form, too, well suited to the outlook of men whose way of life was closer to Abraham than that of the bulk of Jews and Christians."[35]

After Husayn's conversion, 'Abd Allah ibn Zayd, a Khazraji who was present at the Second 'Aqabah, experiences a dream in which the *adhaan* (call to prayer) is used to gather the prayer congregation. The Prophet confirms his vision and establishes Bilal as the first *muezzin* (one who announces the call to prayer).

Over the next several months, the Muslim community establishes its daily routine. Prayers are conducted five times every day. Fasting is prescribed during the month of Ramadan and many injunctions of what is *halal* (permitted) and *haram* (prohibited) are revealed in the Qur'an. The mosque becomes the center of community affairs in Medina, and soon after its construction, two rooms are added to the side for the Prophet's second and third wives, Sawdah and 'A'ishah.

The Prophet sends Zayd to Mecca to escort Sawdah and the Prophet's daughters Umm Kulthum and Fatimah to Medina. Zayd also brings his family—Umm Ayman and Usamah.

Shortly after Zayd's return, the Prophet persuades his first cousin Zaynab bint Jahsh to marry his adopted son. Around the same time, Zaynab's sister Hamnah bint Jahsh marries Mus'ab ibn Umayr (Fig. P28). The Prophet's aunt Umaymah bint 'Abd al-Muttalib comes to Medina to attend both her daughters' weddings and at that time embraces her nephew's religion.

Abu Bakr sends his son 'Abd Allah to bring Abu Bakr's wife Umm Ruman and daughters Asma' and 'A'ishah. Upon her arrival, 'A'ishah marries the Prophet in a very simple ceremony. Abu Bakr's converted sister Quraybah stays in Mecca to take care of their elderly father, Abu Quhafah, who has not yet entered Islam. Another Qurayshi to arrive in Medina is Abu Bakr's close cousin, Talhah ibn 'Ubayd Allah, who had recently wrapped up his business affairs in Mecca.

Despite the relative security in Medina, life in the oasis presents its own set of challenges. Several months after the Hijrah, an epidemic breaks out and a number of Companions including Abu Bakr and Bilal suffer from a temporarily debilitating fever.

Adhaan translation: *God is Great! I bear witness that there is no god but God! I bear witness that Muhammad is the Messenger of God! Come to Prayer! Come to success! God is Great! There is no god but God!*

According to Al-Mubarakpuri, the obligatory fast *(sawm)* and alms-tax *(zakat)* will be enjoined two years after the Hijrah, after the Battle of Badr.

Read Lings (p.136) for a detailed description of the Prophet's relationship with 'A'ishah.

Remember that **Talhah ibn 'Ubayd Allah** had recently encountered the Prophet and Abu Bakr as he was returning from Syria. In a few years, Talhah will fight gloriously at Uhud, where he deflects a deathblow meant for the Prophet. Later the Prophet remarks, *"He that would behold a martyr walking the face of the earth, let him look on Talhah the son of 'Ubayd Allah."*[36]

13
14
15
16
17
18

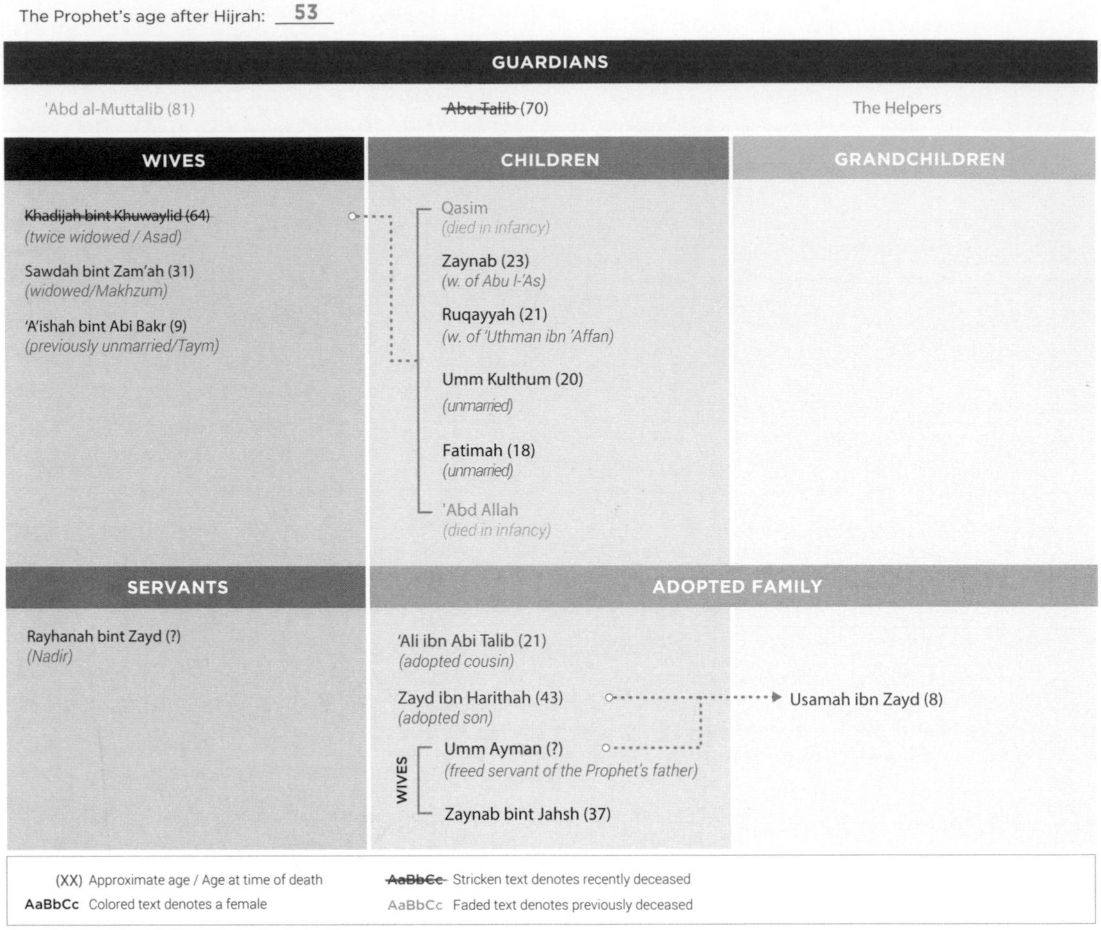

The Prophet's age after Hijrah: __53__

GUARDIANS		
'Abd al-Muttalib (81)	~~Abu Talib~~ (70)	The Helpers

WIVES	CHILDREN	GRANDCHILDREN
~~Khadijah bint Khuwaylid~~ (64) *(twice widowed / Asad)*	Qasim *(died in infancy)*	
Sawdah bint Zam'ah (31) *(widowed/Makhzum)*	Zaynab (23) *(w. of Abu l-'As)*	
'A'ishah bint Abi Bakr (9) *(previously unmarried/Taym)*	Ruqayyah (21) *(w. of 'Uthman ibn 'Affan)*	
	Umm Kulthum (20) *(unmarried)*	
	Fatimah (18) *(unmarried)*	
	'Abd Allah *(died in infancy)*	

SERVANTS	ADOPTED FAMILY	
Rayhanah bint Zayd (?) *(Nadir)*	'Ali ibn Abi Talib (21) *(adopted cousin)*	
	Zayd ibn Harithah (43) *(adopted son)*	▶ Usamah ibn Zayd (8)
	WIVES — Umm Ayman (?) *(freed servant of the Prophet's father)*	
	Zaynab bint Jahsh (37)	

(XX) Approximate age / Age at time of death	~~AaBbCc~~ Stricken text denotes recently deceased
AaBbCc Colored text denotes a female	AaBbCc Faded text denotes previously deceased

FIGURE 13F. THE PROPHET'S HOUSEHOLD AFTER THE HIJRAH

One year after Khadijah's death, the Prophet remarried to Sawdah bint Zam'ah. Sawdah had recently returned from Abyssinia after her husband, Sakran ibn 'Amr, had passed away. Shortly thereafter, the Prophet entered an engagement with Abu Bakr's daughter 'A'ishah. After the Hijrah, rooms were constructed by the mosque for both women so they could join the Prophet's household. By the end of the 13th year, the Prophet instructed his first cousin Zaynab bint Jahsh to marry Zayd ibn Harithah. At first Zaynab hesitated at the idea of marrying a non-Qurayshi but later conceded to the union. A few years later, the two divorced and, according to a command from Surah Al Ahzab, Zaynab became the Prophet's seventh wife.

Note: The Prophet's daughter, Zaynab, stayed behind in Mecca to be with her husband, 'Abu l-'As. She finally came to Medina after the Battle of Badr.

(Refer to Figs. P25 and 6B for previous details about the Prophet's household.)

YEAR 14: THE CARAVAN RAIDS

14.1 THE FIRST CARAVAN RAIDS

Several months after leaving Mecca, the Prophet begins dispatching several teams of Emigrants to intercept Qurayshi caravans. By the fourth expedition, he personally leads 70 men out of Medina, leaving Sa'd ibn 'Ubadah in charge during his absence. The mission is a success and the Prophet forms a non-aggression pact with one of the outlying Bedouin tribes. On the heels of this victory, the Prophet leads another operation, but fails to capture the caravan of Umayyah ibn Khalaf.

Al-Mubarakpuri suggests that this was the Prophet's second mission. He details seven other missions carried out before Badr (p.184-186).

Recall that **Umayyah ibn Khalaf** was the abusive chief of Jumah and former owner of Bilal.

1 HOW COULD THE PROPHET CONDONE CARAVAN RAIDING? [ARMSTRONG]

"At the very least, he had to ensure that the Emigrants did not become a drain upon the economy. But it was difficult for them to earn a living. Most of them were merchants or bankers, but there was very little opportunity for trade in Medina, where the wealthier Arabs and Jewish tribes had achieved a monopoly ... Their aim was not to shed blood, but to secure an income by capturing camels, merchandise, and prisoners, who could be held for ransom. Nobody would have been particularly shocked by this development. The ghazu [raid] was a normal expedient in times of hardship, though some of the Arabs would have been surprised by the Muslims' temerity in taking on the might of the Quraysh, especially as they were clearly inexperienced warriors... He was living in a chronically violent society and he saw these raids not simply as a means of bringing in much-needed income, but as a way of resolving his quarrel with the Quraysh. We have discovered in our own day, that waging a war for the sake of peace is a high-risk venture ... once it has started, a cycle of violence achieves an independent momentum, and can spin tragically out of control."[1]

2 THE RAIDS: OFFENSE OR DEFENSE? [YUSUF]

"This is something that is not alien to the Judeo-Christian tradition. If you read the Old Testament, prophets did take their enemies' property. This is economic warfare. Remember, these were people who had all their houses taken away from them, their wealth taken away from them. They had been oppressed. And now it is time for them to defend themselves and take what was rightfully theirs."[2]

3 WHY WERE ONLY EMIGRANTS SENT ON CARAVAN RAIDS? [RAMADAN]

"Some of the Quraysh went further and even decided, in violation of the honor code respected by all the clans in the peninsula, to seize the property and belongings the emigrants had left behind in Mecca ... they [the Emigrants] would attack the Meccan caravans passing near Medina in order to take back the equivalent of their belongings expropriated in Mecca ... These [raids] included only Muhajirun, since only they were the victims of Quraysh usurpation."[3]

4 WHAT DID CARAVAN RAIDS MEAN TO THE ARABS? [WATT]

"In these little raids, then, he was deliberately challenging and provoking the Meccans. In our peace-conscious age it is difficult to understand how a religious leader could thus engage in offensive war and become almost an aggressor. The first thing to be said in explanation of Muhammad's behaviour is that the raid or razzia was a normal feature of Arab desert life. It was a kind of sport rather than war. The Arabs had their wars indeed, but these were much more serious affairs. The next point to consider is that Muhammad and his contemporaries thought of a religious community in a different way from the modern West. For us a religious body is a group of people who come together for common worship, and perhaps for some other limited purposes; but for Muhammad the religious community was a body of people associated with one another in the whole of their lives, that is, was also a political unit."[4]

The Prophet initially focuses on Mecca's northbound caravans. Several months after the first raid, he decides to send a warning to the Quraysh that nothing is off limits. He learns of a Makhzumi caravan returning from Yemen and sends an eight-person reconnaissance team to verify the news. The group, led by his cousin 'Abd Allah ibn Jahsh, is instructed to proceed to the road that connects Mecca to Ta'if, and watch for a returning Qurayshi caravan. Though the men are instructed to simply observe the caravan, they spot a rare opportunity to attack it near the village of Nakhlah. It is the last day of the sacred month of Rajab, when fighting is strictly forbidden throughout Arabia, but they justify their actions citing a recent revelation from Surah Al Hajj:

⩘ **SURAH AL HAJJ** (The Pilgrimage) is named after several verses that explain the Abrahamic origins of the Hajj. The surah is considered a transitional revelation that has elements from the Meccan and Medinan periods. The surah emphasizes that regardless of opposition, God's plan will always prevail.

> Those who've been attacked now have permission (to fight back) because they've been wronged, and God can provide them with powerful aid.
>
> They're the ones who've been driven from their homes against all right and for no other reason than that they've said, "Our Lord is God." If God didn't use one set of people to check (the ambitions) of another, then there would've been many monasteries, churches, synagogues and mosques, which are used to commemorate the name of God abundantly, pulled down and ruined. God will definitely help those who help Him, for God is strong and powerful!
>
> —*Al Hajj (The Pilgrimage, 22:39-40)*

---

5 **WAS THE QUR'AN CHANGING THE RULES OF WAR?** | ARMSTRONG |

"The Qur'an had begun to develop a primitive just war theory. In the steppes, aggressive warfare was praiseworthy; but in the Qur'an, self-defense was the only possible justification for hostilities and the preemptive strike was condemned (Q 2:190). War was always a terrible evil, but it was sometimes necessary in order to preserve decent values, such as freedom of worship. Even here, the Qur'an did not abandon its pluralism: synagogues and churches as well as mosques should be protected. The Muslims felt that they had suffered a fearful assault; their expulsion from Mecca was an act that had no justification. Exile from the tribe violated the deepest sanction of Arabia; it had attacked the core of the Muslim's identity."[5]

- -

6 **WHY WAS THE QUR'AN GRANTING PERMISSION TO FIGHT?** | RAMADAN |

"Henceforth, the Muslims were no longer required to resist passively; rather, they were to defend themselves against enemy aggression. To the jihad of spirituality and intelligence, which had consisted either in resisting the darkest attractions of the ego-centric, greedy, or violent self ... a new possible form of jihad was now added: al-qital, necessary and armed resistance in the face of armed aggression, self-defense against oppressors ... At the end of the verse, fighting is presented as a necessity in order to resist human beings' natural propensity for expansionism and oppression.
... Hence, the confrontation of forces and resistance to human beings' temptation to war are presented, in an apparent paradox, as the promise of peace among human beings ...The essence of jihad is the quest for peace, and qital is, at times, the necessary path to peace."[6]

The attack is unexpected, and all but two Meccans are taken captive. One man is killed, while the other, Nawfal ibn 'Abd Allah, escapes to Mecca. But when the Emigrants return from Nakhlah, the Prophet condemns their decision to attack during the sacred month and refuses to accept the spoils. The Jews are convinced it is a bad omen for the Muslims; however a revelation from Surah Al Baqarah absolves 'Abd Allah ibn Jahsh and his guilt-stricken companions:

> When they ask you about fighting in a sacred month, tell them, "Fighting in it is indeed wrong, but an even greater wrong in the sight of God is to discourage people from His way, to reject Him, and to keep people out of His Sacred Mosque, even driving out those who were already living there!"
>
> Oppression is worse than death, (and the oppressors, who will never tolerate your existence), will always seek to wage war against you until they make you renounce your faith, if at all possible... — *Al Baqarah (The Cow, 2:217)*

Several months later, **Nawfal ibn 'Abd Allah** will fight in the Battle of Badr and, three years later, participate in the seige on Medina (QY18.1) . He dies in battle, when his horse fails to clear the defensive trench dug by the Muslims.

---

7 **DID THE PROPHET INTEND TO FIGHT DURING RAJAB?** | WATT |

"If we suppose that Muhammad intended the violation of the sacred month (although it is by no means proved that he did so), it does not mean that he was contemplating anything scandalous or dishonourable. The sacredness of the month of Rajab was bound up with the pagan religion which he was denouncing. Violation of the sacred month would be on a par with the destruction of idols. But, on this supposition, what are we to make of Muhammad's hesitation before accepting a fifth of the booty?

... It is tolerably certain that Muhammad himself had few scruples about fighting in the sacred months, but that he had to respect the scruples of an important section of his followers and to guard against repercussions which might weaken his prophetic authority. And it must be insisted that, even if Muhammad intended the raiding party to violate the sacred month, there was in Arab eyes nothing dishonourable or disgraceful about that, especially in view of his general attack on paganism."[7]

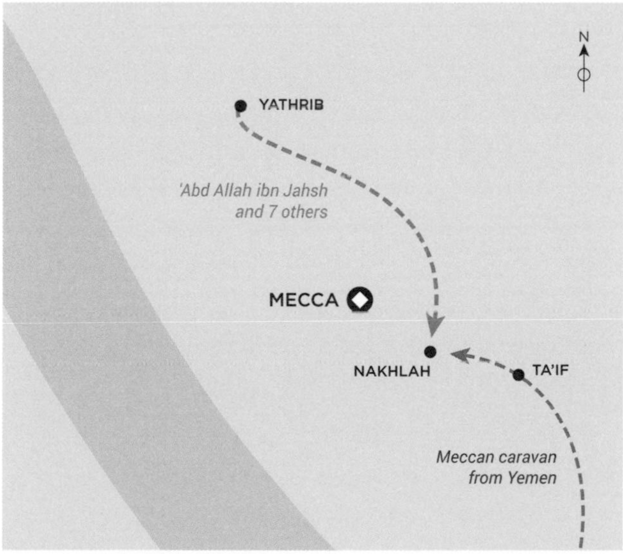

FIGURE 14A. THE ATTACK AT NAKHLAH

The attack at Nakhlah took place during the holy month of Rajab, when Arabs traditionally forbade any form of violence. 'Abd Allah ibn Jahsh and seven others ambushed the Meccan caravan, killing all but one of the unsuspecting Qurayshi men. The Prophet swiftly condemned the attack, but the Qur'an absolved the eight men, saying that oppression and expulsion at the hands of the Quraysh was a far greater sin than what they had committed.

8 **WHAT DID THE EARLIEST EXPEDITIONS ACTUALLY ACCOMPLISH?** `SALAHI`

"The early expeditions achieved considerable results for the Muslims. They enabled them to form a good idea of the geography and topography of the area surrounding Madinah. They identified the routes followed by trade caravans travelling between Makkah and Syria. They also established contacts with several tribes in the area and entered into alliances with some of them. The Muslims also proved that they were powerful enough to defend themselves and their faith against any external or internal threat. They were aware that threats could potentially come from either direction. Internally, the Jews and the Arabs who had not accepted Islam could pose a threat, while externally the Quraysh and her allies were on the lookout for a chance to crush the new Muslim state.

The Prophet also introduced certain new tactics which he employed in these expeditions. Most important among these was secrecy, which helped in taking the enemy by surprise. As a result of these expeditions, the Quraysh recognized that its trade route to Syria was no longer secure. As Makkah relied on trade, such insecurity and the threat of an economic siege were restraining factors against the Quraysh making any rash move against the Muslims in Madinah."[8]

14.2 THE NEW QIBLAH

Throughout the Meccan period, the Prophet had faced Jerusalem whenever he led his followers in prayer. Ever since the Hijrah, however, he longed to return to his birthplace, and more importantly, the Sanctuary that had been erected by Abraham and Ishmael several thousand years ago. In the year after the Hijrah, Surah Al Baqarah pacifies his heart, instructing him to change the direction of prayer from Jerusalem to Mecca.

> We've seen you look to the sky for guidance, so now We'll turn you towards a more pleasing direction. Now you can turn your face towards the Sacred Mosque (in Mecca), so turn your faces towards it wherever you happen to be. The Followers of Earlier Revelation can see the proper reasoning in this from their Lord, and God is not unaware of what they're doing.
>
> — *Al Baqarah (The Cow, 2:144)*

Nearly two years after Al Baqarah's first verses were revealed, the surah is nearly complete. Its tone and subject matter are a departure from the Meccan surahs and address the new challenges of the Muslim community in Medina. Among other things, it instructs Muslims in the way of warfare, treatment of captives, legislation, and justice:

> The prevalent conditions made it a top priority to encourage the Muslims to fight. Any leader with deep insight would order his soldiers to get ready for any sort of emergency, let alone the All-Knowing Exalted Lord.[9]

❾ WHY DIDN'T THE MUSLIMS PRAY TOWARD MECCA FROM THE VERY BEGINNING?   SALAHI

"Arabs revered the Ka'bah before the advent of Islam. To them it was the symbol of their national glory. It was also one of the factors which held the Arab tribes together. Islam, however, requires of its followers total, undivided loyalty. Muslims must dedicate themselves wholly to God and the cause of Islam. The Prophet's companions must, therefore, abandon all their former loyalties, tribal, racial or national. Hence the need to separate their worship from their traditional reverence of the Ka'bah. To accomplish this they were ordered to turn towards Jerusalem when they prayed. After a period of time, when the Muslims had accepted the new situation – moving away, in the process, from the rest of the Arabs – they were taught to regard the Ka'bah in a different light. They were told to face it in their prayers because it was built by the two Prophets, Abraham and Ishmael, as a place wholly devoted to the worship of God alone. Thus it becomes part of the heritage of the Islamic nation, which has come into existence by way of answering Abraham's prayers to raise among his seed a Prophet who would teach them the true religion. Thus, having achieved the objective of making the Muslims turn to Jerusalem in their prayers for a while, it was now time to give them their own distinctive qiblah – the Ka'bah, the first house of worship ever built. This process made the Muslims keenly aware that they were the true heirs of Abraham and his religion, based on total submission to God. To be distinct from others is very important when one speaks of faith and worship, for worship is the visible expression of the beliefs which take root in the soul. If worship is visibly distinct from that of other religions, then it strengthens the perception that the religion itself is unique. The purpose of giving the Muslims their own qiblah must be seen in this light." [10]

YEAR 15: BADR 1

15.1 ABU SUFYAN'S CARAVAN

Sa'id ibn Zayd was 'Umar's cousin and childhood friend (Fig. 5i) who, unlike 'Umar, was raised a monotheist by his father Zayd "the Haneef." He is one of 10 Companions to whom the Prophet later promises Paradise.

Almost two years after the Hijrah, the Prophet learns about a rich caravan belonging to Abu Sufyan ibn al-Harb returning from Syria. He immediately sends Talhah ibn 'Ubayd Allah and Sa'id ibn Zayd to the coastal town of Hawra', just west of Medina, to gather more information.

> ### ❶ WHY WAS THE PROPHET SO FOCUSED ON MECCA? ASLAN
>
> "But while they [the Quraysh] may have been concerned with the growing number of his followers, as long as they remained confined to Yathrib, Mecca was content to forget about Muhammad. Muhammad, however, was not willing to forget about Mecca.
>
> Of course, no matter how popular or successful or large his community became, it could never hope to expand beyond the borders of Yathrib if the religious, economic, and social center of the Hijaz continued to oppose it. Eventually, Muhammad would have to confront and, if possible, convert the Quraysh to his side. But first he had to get their attention … the only effective way to confront the Quraysh was through their pocketbooks."[1]

Not wanting to miss a rare opportunity to surprise Abu Sufyan, the Prophet decides to mobilize the Companions before Talhah and Sa'id return. Leaving his gravely ill daughter Ruqayyah behind, he heads southwest of Medina to intercept the nearby caravan. Unbeknownst to him, news of the ambush leaks out of Medina and Abu Sufyan urgently sends a messenger to Mecca requesting immediate backup.

'Abd Allah ibn Umm Makhtum is one of the few Companions mentioned in the Qur'an. Recall that Surah 'Abasa describes him as the blind man who approached the Prophet in Mecca when the Prophet was busy conversing with Walid ibn al-Mughirah (QY 4.5).

This is not the last time the Prophet will honor the traditions of his people. After the Conquest of Mecca, he will give the keys of the Ka'bah to 'Uthman ibn Talhah of 'Abd ad-Dar. Remember that a few generations earlier, the Quraysh had split into the Scented Ones and Confederates (P2.1). The clan of 'Abd ad-Dar led the Confederates and since then had retained their position as keepers of the Ka'bah.

All but four Emigrants march to the coastal city of Badr: 'Uthman ibn 'Affan stays behind to take care of his wife, Ruqayyah; Talhah and Sa'id return from their scouting mission after the expedition had already left; and 'Abd Allah ibn Umm Makhtum had been left behind to lead the congregational prayers in Medina during the Prophet's absence. The expedition consists of 306 men (74 Emigrants and 232 Helpers), 70 camels, and three horses.

In keeping with Qurayshi tradition, the Prophet awards the white banner to Mus'ab ibn 'Umayr, whose clan of 'Abd ad-Dar had an ancestral right to carry the banner of Quraysh in times of war. Mus'ab is followed by the Prophet, who is followed by two black pennants carried by 'Ali ibn Abi Talib (an Emigrant) and Sa'd ibn Mu'adh (a Helper). Many youngsters also try to join the expedition, but the Prophet insists that they all return home, except for Sa'd ibn Abi Waqqas' younger brother, 'Umayr, who was brought to tears by the idea of missing out on the expedition.

> ### ❷ HOW DID THE PROPHET FEEL ABOUT HONORING PRE-ISLAMIC TRADITIONS? YUSUF
>
> "It is important, because traditionally with the Quraysh, it was the clan of 'Abd ad-Dar that were given the banner in war. Tradition is not always bad. The Prophet, God's peace and blessings upon him, was honoring a tradition of his people there that did not go against Islam."[2]

Every single clan of Quraysh marches out to fight the Prophet except for 'Umar's clan of 'Adi. Abu Lahab also stays behind, sending a hired soldier to fight in his place. In all, the Meccans number over 1,000 soldiers, including 100 horsemen and 600 men in chainmail.

As the two parties near the battlefield, Surah Al Anfal describes the dramatic scene as it unfolds:

> (Remember) how Satan made their actions seem good to them and how he told them, "No people can ever beat you today as long as I'm near you." However, when the two forces came in full view of each other, (Satan) turned on his heels and said, "I'm free of you! I see what you don't see. I'm afraid of God, and God is harsh in punishment!" — *Al Anfal (The Spoils of War, 8:48)*

⬳ SURAH AL ANFAL (The Spoils of War) was revealed in the aftermath of Badr. The surah is named after its opening verse, which explains how to distribute the spoils of war. Surah Al Anfal recalls the Battle of Badr and explains how God helped the faithful achieve an astounding victory. The surah expounds on just war practices and explicitly commands the faithful to pursue the path of peace, whenever possible.

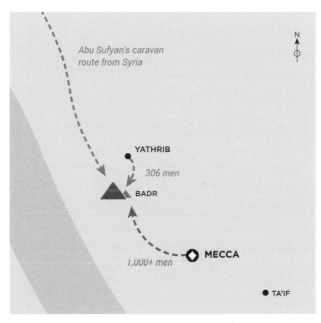

FIGURE 15A. THE MARCH TO BADR

When the Prophet missed the opportunity to attack Abu Sufyan's caravan on its way to Syria, he sent Talhah ibn 'Ubayd Allah and Sa'id ibn Zayd to spy on it as it passed Badr on the way back to Mecca. But before the two men returned to Medina with news of the approaching caravan, the Prophet left for Badr to intercept it.

When Abu Sufyan learned of the Prophet's plans, he immediately sent for help. Within days, over 1,000 Meccans arrived at Badr to defend their property.

13
14
15
16
17
18

15.2 THE DECISION TO FIGHT

Abu Sufyan redirects his caravan toward the coast to avoid the Prophet's men. With the Meccan army fast approaching, the Prophet consults with the Emigrants. They had all left Medina expecting a simple caravan raid, and now, outnumbered three-to-one, some hearts begin to waiver:

> (These different grades in status in God's sight) are evidenced by the fact that when your Lord had ordered you to leave your home, (Muhammad, to make a stand at the wells of Badr) for a true purpose, a segment of the believers didn't like it, and they argued with you (about it), even after the reality (of the situation) was made evidently clear. (Indeed, they made it seem as if) they were being marched off to their own deaths right before their own eyes!
>
> — *Al Anfal (The Spoils of War, 8:5-6)*

---

3 DID THE PROPHET REALLY NEED THE ADVICE OF OTHERS? YUSUF

"The Prophet, God's peace and blessings upon him, was commanded to take counsel from his Companions in order to teach the Muslims. He doesn't need the opinions of others. But this is a teaching event; his whole life was a lesson."[3]

- -

4 WHY DID THE PROPHET CONSULT HIS COMPANIONS BEFORE BADR? SALAHI

"Here, one notes again that the Prophet was always ready to listen to advice and put it into effect. The fact that he himself might have had different ideas was never an obstacle to the implementation of sound advice. Incidents like this one tended to emphasize that he was a human being whose views on matters not related to the faith or to his task of conveying God's message to mankind could be subject to review and amendment. Such incidents were also practical lessons to all future Muslim rulers that no man could always be right."[4]

- -

5 WHY DID THE PROPHET ENCOURAGE CRITICAL THINKING? RAMADAN

"Furthermore, the Prophet had evolved a genuine pedagogy through which he allowed the Muslims to develop their critical faculties, express their talents, and mature in his presence. The Prophet stimulated his Companions' critical sense and their ability to go beyond mere blind obedience or mechanical, mind-destroying imitation. This method developed the intellectual capacities necessary for consultations to be effective. Indeed, if they were to give useful advice, the Companions had to be intellectually awake, bold, and independent, even in the presence of a Prophet whose personality and status must have impressed them. By stimulating their intelligence and giving them opportunities to speak, he exercised a type of leadership that made it possible for his Companions to learn to assert themselves and take initiative. The Messenger's authority in human affairs was neither autocratic nor unrestricted; he allowed his Companions a substantial role in consultation, and his teaching, as we have seen, developed the conditions for acquiring those critical and creative faculties. The Prophet gave his Companions, women and men alike, the means and confidence to be autonomous, to dare to address and contradict him without his ever considering it as a lack of respect for his status. Through this attitude, he showed them his deep respect for their intelligence and for their heart; as for them, they loved their Prophet, their leader, for this attention, this availability, and this demand to use their abilities to the fullest."[5]

Abu Bakr and 'Umar argue that it is time to confront the Meccan army. Miqdad ibn 'Amr, an ally of Bani Zuhrah, adds:

> "O Messenger of Allah! Proceed where Allah directs you to, for we are with you. We will not say as the Children of Israel said to Moses: 'Go you and your Lord and fight and we will stay here [Qur'an 5:24];' rather we shall say: 'Go you and your Lord and fight and we will fight along with you.' "[6]

After the Emigrants have spoken, the Prophet looks for support from the Helpers. Sa'd ibn Mu'adh eloquently responds:

> "O Prophet of Allah! We believe you and we bear witness to what you have granted to us and we declare in clear terms that what you have brought is the Truth. We give you our firm pledge of obedience and sacrifice. We will obey you most willingly in whatever you command us, and by Allah, Who has sent you with the Truth, if you were to ask us to throw ourselves into the sea, we will do that most readily and not a man of us will stay behind. We do not deny the idea of encounter with the enemy. We are experienced in war and we are trustworthy in combat. We hope that Allah will show you through our hands those deeds of bravery which will please your eyes. Kindly lead us to the battlefield in the Name of Allah."[7]

Sa'd's response is a huge boost for Emigrants. Remember that the Helpers were not obligated to fight at Badr. According to the Second 'Aqabah, they had only pledged to protect the Prophet within the confines of Yathrib (QY 13.1).

---

6 WERE THE MUSLIMS PREPARED FOR BADR? [ASLAN]

"For days the two armies surveyed each other from opposite sides of a sizeable valley: the Quraysh arrayed in white tunics, straddling ornately painted horses and tall, brawny camels; the Ummah, dressed in rags and prepared for a raid, not a war. The Quraysh probably assumed their overwhelming numbers would elicit immediate surrender or, at the very least, contrition. And Muhammad, who must have known that fighting the Quraysh under these circumstances would result not only in his own death, but in the end of the Ummah, was anxiously awaiting instructions from God. 'Oh God,' he kept praying, 'if this band of people perishes, you will no longer be worshipped.' "[8]

With more than 1,000 soldiers protecting his caravan from the Prophet's men, Abu Sufyan tells the Quraysh leaders they can now safely return to Mecca. Abu Jahl, however, has greater ambitions and goads the army to march to Badr and destroy the Prophet's renegade force. While Akhnas ibn Shariq persuades his entire clan of Zuhrah to return to Mecca, several of the Prophet's own clansmen from Hashim prepare for battle. The Prophet's opponents include his uncle 'Abbas, and first cousins 'Aqil ibn Abi Talib and Abu Sufyan and Nawfal ibn al-Harith.

The Prophet's men arrive at Badr and prepare to halt at the first well they encounter. But when a Khazraji by the name of Hubab ibn al-Mundhir asks the Prophet whether the decision to stop is a matter of divine revelation or personal opinion, the Prophet acknowledges that it is the latter. Hubab explains that it might be a tactical mistake not to take control of all the wells and persuades him to advance the army to the farthest well. Then, as described in Surah Al Anfal, the Companions have a restful night before the battle.

Recall that **Akhnas ibn Shariq** had refused to protect the Prophet in Mecca when he returned from Ta'if.

'Aqil ibn Abi Talib is about six years younger than the Prophet, and is the older brother of Ja'far and 'Ali. Though he marches out to Badr with the Meccans, he will embrace Islam a few years later.

It is curious that **'Abbas ibn Abi Waqqas** fought against the Prophet at Badr, even though he previously helped him escape Mecca. See Watt's commentary in QY20.2 for an interesting perspective on this matter.

One year later, **Hubab** will carry one of the three banners on the march to Uhud.

> (Remember) how He covered you in a state of rest (just before the eve of battle) to calm your anxiety (as a gift) from Himself, and He made water fall from the sky to cleanse you, to remove the taint of Satan, to strengthen your hearts and to make your stance firm. — Al Anfal (The Spoils of War, 8:11)

15.3 THE BATTLE OF BADR

There is a palpable hesitation among the men in the Meccan army about fighting their own relatives from Quraysh, but Abu Jahl rouses their feelings of vengeance and urges them forward with a prayer:

> *"Our Lord, whichever of the two parties was less kind to his relatives, and brought us what we do not know, then destroy him tomorrow."*[9]

Surah Al Anfal answers Abu Jahl's supplication:

> (All you faithless Meccans!) If you had ever looked for a definitive resolution (in your struggles with the believers), then there you have it! The resolution has come to you, so if you would just stop (opposing God), it would be better for you.
>
> If you ever return (to fight against the believers,) then We'll bring about the same (result). The forces under your command are of no use to you, no matter how numerous they become, for God is with the believers, (and He helps them to achieve victory). —Al Anfal (The Spoils of War, 8:19)

Just before the battle begins, 'Abd Allah ibn Suhayl, who had been coerced by his father to join the Meccan army, escapes to the Prophet's camp.

In the moments before the battle, the Prophet walks among his men inspecting the ragtag group assembled before him. While aligning the ranks, he gently prods a Helper named Sawad ibn Ghaziyyah with the point of his arrow. Sawad feigns discomfort and asks to return the injury. When the Prophet agrees, Sawad chooses to kiss him instead, explaining:

> *"I desired that at my last moment with thee—if so be it—my skin should touch thy skin."*[10]

Within a few hours, Abu Jahl will be slain on the battlefield along with 49 other Meccans.

'Abd Allah's father Suhayl ibn 'Amr (the chief of 'Amir) kept a close eye on his son in Mecca fearing he would flee and join the Prophet. In just a few years, 'Abd Allah will be one of five Companions to co-sign the Treaty of Hudaybiyah while his father sits across from him and negotiates on behalf of the Quraysh.

---

7 **WHAT IS THE SYMBOLISM OF BADR?** | YUSUF |

"This battle is so important because it is the essential reality of truth and falsehood. It's all in Badr. One group fighting for Arab pride, for their tribalism, for glory to be remembered by poets. And the other group is completely masakeen [poor], bereft; they're not interested in the dunya [worldly possessions]."[11]

- -

8 **WAS FIGHTING THE LAST OPTION?** | RAMADAN |

"Muhammad tried to discourage the Quraysh from choosing war. He sent Umar ibn al-Khattab to suggest to the Quraysh that they should turn back and thus avoid confrontation."[12]

- -

9 **HOW SHOULD MUSLIMS BEHAVE IN TIMES OF CONFLICT?** | ARMSTRONG |

"Constantly the Qur'an insists upon the importance of mercy and forgiveness, even during armed conflict. While engaged in hostilities, Muslims must fight with courage and steadfastness in order to bring the conflict to an end as quickly as possible. But the moment the enemy asks for peace, Muslims must lay down their arms (Quran 2:193-4). They must accept any offer of truce, whatever the conditions are imposed, even if they suspect the enemy of double-dealing. And although it is important to fight persecution and oppression, the Qur'an constantly reminds Muslims that it is much better to sit down and solve the problem by courteous discussion (Quran 8:62-63)."[13]

It is a Friday during the month of Ramadan, and with the actual fighting moments away, the Prophet turns to his closest Companion and offers a few words of gentle encouragement:

> "Be of good cheer, Abu Bakr; the help of God hath come to thee. Here is Gabriel and in his hand is the rein of a horse which he is leading, and he is armed for war."[14]

The Meccans send out the most prominent men of 'Abdu Shams for the opening duels: 'Utbah ibn Rabi'ah, his brother Shaybah, and son Walid. Before the Prophet can select three men to respond to the challenge, three Helpers—'Awf and Mu'awwidh ibn al-Harith, and 'Abd Allah ibn Rawahah—run out to fight the Meccans. But the Quraysh refuse to fight the three men from Yathrib. They had envisioned a showdown between the clans of 'Abdu Shams and Hashim, and the Prophet quickly orders 'Ubaydah ibn al-Harith, Hamzah, and 'Ali to evenly match the ages of the challengers. Soon enough, all three Companions defeat their Meccan opponents.

'Ubaydah ibn al-Harith is the son of the Prophet's eldest uncle Harith. He is the oldest man in the army and dies from the injuries inflicted at Badr. His widow, Zaynab bint Khuzaymah, later marries the Prophet after Uhud.

FIGURE 15B. FACE-OFF AT BADR: A QURAYSH AFFAIR

The opening duels at Badr pitted the clan of 'Abdu Shams against Hashim. 'Utbah ibn Rabi'ah (the father of Hind) stepped up first, followed by his brother Shaybah and son Walid. In response, the Prophet sent out his own clansmen from Hashim to fight the challengers. After defeating their opponents, Hamzah and 'Ali helped a wounded 'Ubaydah defeat the last of the three Meccan challengers. The face off at Badr fueled Hind's hatred for the Muslims, and Hamzah in particular.

After the battle, Harithah's mother hears about her son's death and worries that he will not qualify for martyrdom because he died before the actual fighting began. The Prophet allays her fears, reminding her that actions are counted by their intentions.

The opening duels are soon followed by a shower of Meccan arrows, one of which kills a young Khazraji named Harithah ibn Suraqah, who was drinking at one of Badr's wells. The boy's death marks the beginning of the battle, and the Prophet gives the order to charge:

"Ya mansur amit!" ("O thou whom God has made victorious, slay!")[15]

---

10 WHAT IS SIGNIFICANT ABOUT THE PROPHET'S BATTLE CRY?   YUSUF

"This is a negation of self. You're not the nasir [the one who helps yourself], Allah is the Nasir. It's pure tawheed [belief in one God]. It is an acceptance of the asbab [means], but it's also a recognition that Allah is the Nasir. It's an incredible battle cry."[16]

As the battle intensifies, the Prophet remains standing with his arms outstretched in prayer:

"O Allah! Should this group (of Muslims) be defeated today, You will no longer be worshipped."[17]

Be sure to read Aslan (p.75-87) for a deeper discussion on jihad and warfare.

11 DID THE PROPHET CHANGE THE RULES OF WARFARE?   ASLAN

"It is not that Arabia was short on 'rules of war.' A host of regulations existed among the pagan tribes with regard to when and where fighting could take place. But for the most part these rules were meant to contain and limit fighting to ensure the tribe's survival, not to establish a code of conduct in warfare. In the same way that absolute morality did not play a significant role in tribal concepts of law and order, neither did it play a role in tribal notions of war and peace. Muhammad understood that just as the Revelation had forever transformed the socioeconomic landscape of pre-Islamic Arabia, so must it alter the methods and morals of pre-Islamic warfare. At the heart of the doctrine of jihad was the heretofore, unrecognized distinction between combatant and noncombatant ... regulations that ... were eventually incorporated into the modern international laws of war. But perhaps the most important innovation in the doctrine of jihad was its outright prohibition of all but strictly defensive wars ... Badr became the first opportunity for Muhammad to put this theory of jihad into practice ... Muhammad refused to fight until attacked."[18]

Surah Al Anfal answers his call:

(Remember) how you had fervently asked for the help of your Lord (at the Battle of Badr), and He answered you, saying, "I will help you with a regiment of a thousand angels." —*Al Anfal (The Spoils of War, 8:9)*

(Muhammad,) remember also that your Lord inspired the angels (to bring a message of hope to your heart that said), "I'm with you, so steady the believers. I'm going to put terror into the hearts of the faithless, so strike at their necks (with your weapons) and lop off their fingertips (as they brandish their swords against you)!" —*Al Anfal (The Spoils of War, 8:12)*

It wasn't you who struck them down (at the Battle of Badr); it was God. When you threw (a symbolic handful of pebbles at the idol-worshippers as the battle commenced, Muhammad), it wasn't something you did, but God Who did it, so He could test the believers with a fine test from Himself, for God hears and knows (all things). —*Al Anfal (The Spoils of War, 8:17)*

12 **HOW DOES ONE RECONCILE THE QUR'ANIC INJUNCTION TO "SLAY THE POLYTHEISTS?"** ASLAN

"It is true that some verses in the Quran instruct Muhammad and his followers to 'slay the polytheists wherever you confront them' (9:5); to 'carry the struggle to the hypocrites who deny faith' (9:73); and, especially, 'to fight those who do not believe in God and the Last Day' (9:29). However, it must be understood that these verses were directed specifically at the Quraysh and their clandestine partisans in Yathrib—specifically named in the Quran as 'the polytheists' and 'the hypocrites,' respectively—with whom the Ummah [community] was locked in a terrible war. Nevertheless, these verses have long been used by Muslims and non-Muslims alike to suggest that Islam advocates fighting unbelievers until they convert. But this is not a view that either the Quran or Muhammad endorsed. This view was put forth during the height of the Crusades, and partly in response to them, by later generations of Islamic legal scholars who developed what is now referred to as the 'classical doctrine of jihad.' Ibn Taymiyya argued that the idea of killing nonbelievers who refused to convert to Islam—the foundation of the classical doctrine of jihad—not only defied the example of Muhammad but also violated one of the most important principles in the Quran: that 'there can be no compulsion in religion.' " [Qur'an, 2:256][19]

By the end of the battle, only 14 of the Prophet's men are slain, including 'Umayr ibn Abi Waqqas, the 15-year-old brother of Sa'd who begged to join the army. In stark contrast, the Meccans suffer much greater losses: 50 dead and another 50 taken captive. Their humiliating defeat was multifactorial:

> Lack of unity among the Meccans contributed to their defeat ... many of the pagans were men past their prime, whereas the Emigrants were mostly younger men at the height of their physical power. All the Muslims, too, would tend to fight more bravely because of their belief in a future life, while Muhammad's confidence, grounded in his steadfast belief in God, would inspire confidence in his followers.[20]

Al-Mubarakpuri reports 70 Meccans killed and another 70 captured.

15.4 THE CAPTIVES & SPOILS OF WAR

Having won the battle, the Companions are at a loss over what to do with so many captives. Sa'd ibn Mu'adh and 'Umar ibn al-Khattab say the prisoners should be killed. The Prophet and Abu Bakr, however, elect to spare them in the hope that they might eventually embrace Islam. But later that day, 'Umar finds the two men weeping, as a verse from Surah Al Anfal had just ruled against their decision, in favor of his own:

Three years later, when the tribe of Qurayzah is found guilty of treachery, the Prophet will place their fate in the hands of Sa'd, who rules that the men should be executed.

> It's not right for a prophet to start taking prisoners of war (wholesale in order to collect their ransoms) when he hasn't even subdued the land. You (believers) want the temporary goods of this lower world, while God wants (to give you the rewards) of the next life, and God is powerful and wise.
> —*Al Anfal (The Spoils of War, 8:67)*

13 **WHY DID THE PROPHET WANT TO BE LENIENT WITH THE CAPTIVES?** WATT

"Muhammad's decision (contrary to the views of some of his supporters) that in general the prisoners from Badr were to be held to ransom is not simply a mark of leniency of disposition and of the great need for improving the financial position of the Muslims; it is perhaps also the beginning of the realization that, to achieve the distant aims he was beginning to see over the horizon, he required the administrative abilities of the Meccans, and that therefore his task must be not to destroy Quraysh but to win them for his cause."[21]

13
14
15
16
17
18

Nonetheless, the surah instructs the Prophet not to revoke his decision:

> O Prophet! Say to the captives that you're holding, "If God finds any good in your hearts, then He'll give you something better than what's been taken from you, and He'll forgive you, for God is forgiving and merciful." —*Al Anfal (The Spoils of War, 8:70)*

With the fighting over, 'Abd Allah ibn Mas'ud returns to the battlefield in search of Abu Jahl. When the wounded Quraysh commander sees 'Abd Allah standing over him, he cries out:

> *"Thou has climbed high indeed, little shepherd."*[22]

Then, with a swift motion of his sword, 'Abd Allah finishes the Meccan chieftain.

Many years ago, Abu Jahl struck **'Abd Allah ibn Mas'ud** on the face for being the first man to openly recite the Qur'an at the Ka'bah. Remember, 'Abd Allah was not a Qurayshi, but a confederate of Bani Zuhrah. Short in stature, he was considered a lowly shepherd in Mecca, and yet became a preeminent Companion in Medina.

---

14 **WHO WAS 'ABD ALLAH IBN MAS'UD?**   YUSUF

"He is going to become one of the greatest scholars of Islam. He eventually goes to Iraq and Abu Hanifa's madhab [school of thought] is based mostly on his positions."[23]

Similarly, Bilal finds his abusive former master, Umayyah ibn Khalaf, taken captive and insists that he be killed as well.

---

15 **WHAT WAS THE PROPHET'S POLICY ON THE TREATMENT OF CAPTIVES?**   WATT

"Such excesses [killing captives on the battlefield] Muhammad put a stop to. In general his policy was to hold prisoners to ransom, but those belonging to his own clan or in some other way specially related to the Muslims, and those not sufficiently influential or wealthy to be ransomed, he usually set free without ransom."[24]

- -

16 **THE TREATMENT OF PRISONERS AFTER BADR**   ARMSTRONG

"A revelation came down to ensure that the prisoners of war must either be released or ransomed [Quran 47:4]. Even in war, Muslims would abjure the savage customs of the past."[25]

Remember that **Abu Hudhayfah ibn 'Utbah** entered Islam with his wife Sahlah. The two sought asylum in Abyssinia, and returned after the ban on Hashim was lifted.

While the Companions search the battlefield for their fallen brothers, Abu Hudhayfah sees the body of his father, 'Utbah ibn Rabi'ah, and is filled with remorse that his father died before embracing Islam. When the Prophet spots Abu Hudhayfah on the battlefield, he quickly comforts the grieving son.

The Companions gather the remaining captives and assemble them before the Prophet. When they begin to argue over the spoils they had collected, a verse from Surah Al Anfal immediately quells the debate.

> They're asking you about the prizes (collected after a battle). Say to them, "The prizes belong to God and His Messenger, so be mindful of God and maintain good relations among you. Obey God and His Messenger if you're (really true) believers." —*Al Anfal (The Spoils of War, 8:1)*

After hearing the verses from Surah Al Anfal, the Companions immediately return the spoils to the Prophet, who evenly redistributes it to them before the army makes its way back to Medina.

17 **WHY DID THE PROPHET HAVE A CLAIM ON THE SPOILS?** | WATT |

"In the month after Badr, it had been decreed that a fifth (khums) of all spoils taken on a Muslim expedition was to go to Muhammad. This change, moreover, implies several other changes. For one thing it implies that Muhammad had been recognized as in some sense chief of the ummah. It was customary in Arabia for the chief of a tribe to receive a quarter of the spoils, partly for his own use, but partly in order to perform certain functions on behalf of the tribe, such as looking after the poor and giving hospitality. The change from a quarter to a fifth marks off the head of the ummah from tribal chiefs; yet the verse prescribing the fifth (which was perhaps revealed immediately after Badr) indicates that the fifth was in part to be used by Muhammad for these communal purposes."[26]

15.5 THE TRIUMPHANT RETURN TO MEDINA

The victorious party is welcomed into Medina with a festive celebration:

A wonderful and striking coincidence was the establishment of the Shawwal 'Eid (the Festival of the Fast-Breaking) directly after the manifest victory at Badr. It was the finest spectacle ever witnessed of Muslims leaving their houses, praying, acclaiming Allah's Name and entertaining His praise at the top of their voices in recognition of His favor and grace.[27]

The surah captures the exuberant moment:

Remember how you (Muslims) used to be such a small group (in the early days of the Prophet's mission). Everyone in the land thought you were so weak; you were constantly afraid of people robbing or kidnapping you, but He found a place of refuge for you (in Medina) and gave you strength with His help. He also provided wholesome resources for you, as well, so you could be thankful.
— Al Anfal (*The Spoils of War, 8:26*)

18 **HOW WAS THE PROPHET'S VICTORY AT BADR AKIN TO MOSES' DELIVERANCE FROM THE PHARAOH?** | WATT |

"It would be a mistake, however, to think of Badr simply as a political event. For Muhammad and his followers it had a deep religious meaning. There had been those weary years of hardship and opposition at Mecca. Then there had been the long months at Medina when nothing seemed to be going right. Now came this astounding success. It was a vindication of the faith that had sustained them through disappointment. It was God's vindication of their faith in Him, His supernatural action on their behalf. The Qur'an develops this religious interpretation of the event in various passages, e.g. 'You did not kill them, but God killed them; you did not shoot (and strike) when you shot, but God shot, to let the believers experience good from Himself' (8:17).

So the victory at Badr came to be regarded as the great deliverance God had effected for the Muslims, comparable to the deliverance he had effected for the Israelites at the Red Sea. The destruction of Pharaoh and his hosts and the escape of the Israelites was the furqan or 'salvation' given to the prophet Moses (the Arabic word is an adaptation of the Syriac purqana). Similarly the disaster to the Meccans was the Calamity foretold for them in the Qur'an, and the victory granted to Muhammad was his furqan, and a 'sign' confirming his prophethood. In the light of this interpretation the mood of the convinced Muslims was one of great elation."[28]

After Ruqayyah's death, 'Uthman will marry the Prophet's third daughter, Umm Kulthum, and henceforth be known as *Dhul-Noorain* (he of the two moons). Many years later, while 'Uthman and the Prophet are away at Tabuk, Umm Kulthum dies as well. Upon returning, the Prophet prays at her grave and tells 'Uthman that if he had another daughter, he would have given her to him in marriage as well.

In this quote, the Prophet is referring to the Arabian practice of beating one's chest and wailing aloud as public signs of mourning.

The jubilant mood, however, is quickly tempered by news of Ruqayyah's death. At the age of 22, she had died during the Prophet's absence and had already been buried by her grieving husband. The Prophet accompanies Fatimah to her elder sister's grave and dries her tears with the edge of his cloak.

In the days after battle, 'Umar admonishes several families for crying over the martyrs at Badr, but the Prophet reminds him to be gentle:

> " 'Umar, let them weep. What cometh from the heart and from the eye, that is from God and His Mercy, but what cometh from the hand and from the tongue, that is from Satan."[28]

---

19 WHAT WAS DISTINCTIVE ABOUT THE PROPHET'S NATURE ? RAMADAN

"Always his distinctive feature was the combination of strict faithfulness to his principles and human warmth constantly radiating from his presence ... That gentleness and kindness were the very essence of his teaching. He kept saying: 'God is gentle [rafiq] and he loves gentleness [ar-rifq] in everything.' " (Ramadan citing Bukhari and Muslim)[30]

15.6 THE MECCAN RESPONSE TO DEFEAT

Umm al-Fadl was the second woman to enter Islam after Khadijah (well before her husband, 'Abbas). She remains in Mecca for eight years after the Hijrah.

After returning to Mecca, the Prophet's cousin Abu Sufyan ibn al-Harith tells Abu Lahab about the shocking defeat at Badr. Two Muslims, Umm al-Fadl and her servant Abu Rafi', happened to be nearby. Upon hearing of the Prophet's victory, Abu Rafi' rejoices and is subsequently beaten by Abu Lahab. Umm al-Fadl rushes to her servant's rescue and in a fit of rage, smashes a tent post upon his attacker's head. Abu Lahab's condition deteriorates and he dies a few days later.

After the deaths of Abu Jahl and Abu Lahab, Abu Sufyan ibn al-Harb (of 'Abdu Shams) emerges as the only viable leader of Quraysh:

> The loss of trained men was a disaster of the first magnitude for Mecca ... There can hardly have been left alive in Mecca a dozen men of similar ability and experience [to Abu Jahl, 'Uqbah ibn Mu'ayt, Umayyah ibn Khalaf, and a few others]. Abu Sufyan, of course, was safe with the caravan and now became the most prominent man in the city. Suhayl b. 'Amr was a prisoner, but was ransomed, and Hakim b. Hizam and various others managed to escape from the battlefield. There were younger men, too, coming forward. Nevertheless the catastrophe was considerable.[31]

Fueled by the humiliation of Badr, the Quraysh redouble their efforts to raise an army large enough to crush the emerging threat from Medina.

The painful defeat is especially painful for Abu Sufyan's wife, Hind bint 'Utbah, who had lost her uncle, father, and brother in the opening duels (Fig. 15b). Hind resolves to help the Meccans at the next encounter with the Prophet, and vows to eat the raw liver of Hamzah (who had killed her father and uncle) when the Quraysh take their revenge.

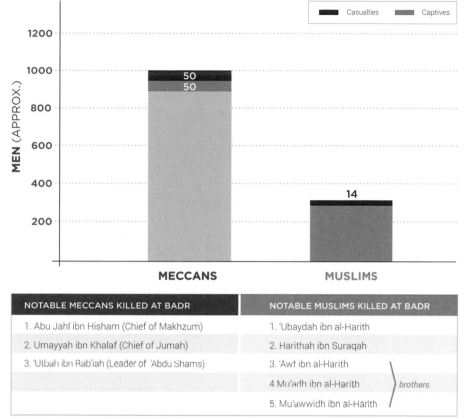

NOTABLE MECCANS KILLED AT BADR	NOTABLE MUSLIMS KILLED AT BADR
1. Abu Jahl ibn Hisham (Chief of Makhzum)	1. 'Ubaydah ibn al-Harith
2. Umayyah ibn Khalaf (Chief of Jumah)	2. Harithah ibn Suraqah
3. 'Utbah ibn Rab'iah (Leader of 'Abdu Shams)	3. 'Awf ibn al-Harith
	4. Mu'adh ibn al-Harith } brothers
	5. Mu'awwidh ibn al-Harith

NOTABLE MECCAN CAPTIVES	NOTABLE MUSLIM CAPTIVES
1. Suhayl ibn 'Amr (Chief of 'Amir)	*none*
2. 'Abbas ibn 'Abd al-Muttalib	
3. Nawfal ibn al-Harith	
4. Aqil ibn Abi Talib	
5. Abu l-'As ibn ar-Rabi'	
6. Walid ibn al-Walid	

FIGURE 15C. LOSSES AT BADR

Before Badr, the Prophet told his Companions, "This Mecca has thrown unto you the best morsels of her liver."[32] As predicted, several of the most prominent Meccan chiefs were killed or taken captive. The captives included four notable relatives of the Prophet: an uncle, two cousins, and his own son-in-law.

13
14
15
16
17
18

15.7 THE FATE OF NOTABLE MECCAN CAPTIVES

Several Meccans come to Medina to ransom their captured relatives according to what their families can afford. Any captive who does not have the resources to buy his freedom is instructed to teach 10 Medinan children how to read and write before returning to Mecca.

One of the most notable captives is the Prophet's uncle, 'Abbas ibn 'Abd al-Muttalib. Despite 'Abbas' loyalty to the Prophet during the Meccan period, the Prophet refuses to show his uncle any leniency and demands that he pay his own ransom if he wishes to return to Mecca. 'Abbas tries to convince his nephew that he has no money, but to his astonishment, the Prophet reminds him of a secret conversation 'Abbas had with his wife Umm al-Fadl about dividing his wealth should he be killed at Badr. 'Abbas exclaims:

> *"By Him who sent thee with the truth, none knew of this but she and I. Now I know that thou art the Messenger of God."*[33]

Meanwhile, Walid ibn al-Walid, son of the late chief of Makhzum, waits for his brothers Khalid and Hisham (Fig. 6a) to pay for his release with their father's famous armor. However, when the three brothers begin their trip back to Mecca, Walid slips away and returns to Medina where he enters Islam. He explains to the puzzled Companions that he did not want people to think he entered Islam to save his family from paying his ransom. After his conversion, however, Walid returns to Mecca to fetch some of his belongings and is quickly imprisoned by his family.

Jubayr ibn Mut'im also arrives to ransom several captives. During his visit, he overhears the Prophet reciting a verse from Surah At-Tur:

> So wait patiently upon the command of your Lord, for you're present in Our sight. Glorify the praises of your Lord whenever you stand up (for prayer), and glorify Him for part of the night, as well, and also after the stars have set.
> — *At-Tur (The Mountain of Tur, 52:48-49)*

Though Jubayr develops a fleeting inclination toward Islam, he returns home and, out of revenge for the death of his uncle, will later instruct his Abyssinian slave Wahshi to kill Hamzah at the Battle of Uhud.

Another notable captive is the Prophet's son-in-law, Abu l-'As ibn ar-Rabi'. To pay his ransom, the Prophet's daughter, Zaynab, sends her mother's jewelry to Medina. But when the Prophet sees Khadijah's necklace, his face turns pale. He agrees to release his son-in-law on the condition that he send Zaynab to Medina (recent revelations had made it clear that a Muslim woman could not be married to a pagan man).

In Mecca, Abu Sufyan hears of the Prophet's offer and permits Zaynab to leave with Abu l-'As' brother, Kinanah ibn ar-Rabi', but only at night when no one can see the weakness of the Quraysh.

Ubayy ibn Khalaf, brother of Umayyah (the slain chief of Jumah), also comes to Medina to ransom his son. Before leaving, he taunts the Prophet saying:

> *"O Muhammad, I have a horse named 'Awd that I feed every day on many measures of corn. I shall slay thee when I am riding him."*[34]

Even though 'Abbas fought with the Meccans at Badr, he always retained a special relationship with his nephew. Before the Hijrah, he escorted the Prophet to the meeting of the Second 'Aqabah. After Badr, he returns to Mecca, and, in the following year, will warn his nephew about the Meccan army marching to Uhud. When the Prophet passes away, it is 'Abbas and 'Ali who will prepare his body for burial.

Other Muslims held against their will in Mecca included Abu Jahl's two half-brothers, Ayyash ibn Rabi'ah and Salamah ibn Hisham. Both were detained by 'Ikrimah ibn Abi Jahl. After Badr, the Prophet continues to pray for the release of all his Companions detained in Mecca.

🦋 SURAH AT-TUR (The Mountain of Tur) is named after its opening verse. Here God swears by Mount Tur (where Moses delivered his people and received God's commandments) of the absolute certainty of Judgment Day, Heaven, and Hell. The surah addresses its naysayers and boldly challenges them to produce a surah like it. The surah coaches the Prophet, who is adrift in a sea of adversity, to wait patiently for God's command.

Jubayr is the son of Mut'im ibn 'Adi, the late chief of Nawfal who had granted protection to the Prophet after Ta'if. Recall that Jubayr was engaged to 'A'ishah bint Abi Bakr, but his father agreed to forgo the marriage so she could marry the Prophet. After the Treaty of Hudaybiyah, Jubayr will come to Medina to embrace Islam.

From the very beginning, **Ubayy ibn Khalaf** had mocked the Prophet. Recall that when the Prophet was warning the Quraysh about the Day of Resurrection, Ubayy ridiculed him by crumbling a dry bone and blowing it into his face. At Uhud, he will charge at the Prophet on his horse and be slain by him.

Fueled by his father's death, Safwan ibn Umayyah (Fig. 5j) persuades his cousin 'Umayr ibn Wahb to assassinate the Prophet. Armed with a poisoned sword, 'Umayr rides out to the mosque in Medina to confront the Prophet. But when the Prophet recounts to 'Umayr his exact conversation with Safwan about their assassination plot, 'Umayr confesses:

> *"We called thee a liar when thou didst bring us tidings from Heaven. But praise be to God who hath guided me unto Islam."*[35]

Not surprisingly, when 'Umayr returns to Mecca to invite others to Islam, Safwan refuses to talk to him.

Several years later, **Safwan** harasses another young Qurayshi—Khalid ibn al-Walid—when Khalid decides to immigrate to Medina. After the Conquest of Mecca, Safwan is one of only three men who does not enter Islam at the moment, but is nonetheless given four months of amnesty. After the Battle of Hunayn, Safwan will finally embrace Islam after witnessing the Prophet's unparalleled generosity (QY 20.9).

15.8 THE AL KUDR INVASION

A few days after Badr, the Prophet receives information that the hostile Bedouin tribes of Sulaym and Ghatafan are planning a raid on Medina. In response, he immediately leads a preemptive strike to neutralize the attack. By the time the expedition arrives at the Bedouin oasis of Al Kudr, their hostile tribes had already heard of its approach and had scattered. Without needing to engage the enemy, the Prophet's men collect 500 camels abandoned by the enemy tribe.

15.9 THE EXPULSION OF BANI QAYNUQA

While most settlements in Medina thrived on agriculture, Bani Qaynuqa consisted of craftsmen and blacksmiths, and their abundance of arms and armor made them the most militarized Jewish colony in the oasis.

Shortly after the Prophet's arrival in Medina, Qaynuqa had signed a pact of allegiance with the Muslims. After the victory at Badr, the Prophet reaches out to the Jewish clan to invite them to Islam. But the Qaynuqa scoff at his offer and challenge the Muslims to a *real* fight:

> *"O Muhammad! Do not deceive yourself, you merely fought a party of the Quraish who were inexperienced at war. But if you want to fight us then know that we are an entire people! And indeed you have not met up with anyone like us before!"*[36]

---

20 **WHY DID THE PROPHET VISIT QAYNUQA AFTER BADR?** | RAMADAN |

"To determine the truth about what was going on, and to avoid letting the Banu Qaynuqa think that they could act as they pleased, Muhammad paid them a visit and invited them to ponder the Quraysh's defeat ... This threatening answer was confirmation of Muhammad's suspicions: they had become hostile to the Muslims."[37]

13
14
15
16
17
18

㉑ WHY DID BANI QAYNUQA THREATEN THE PROPHET? ⸢ASLAN⸣

"To facilitate the new economy, he established his own market, which, unlike the one controlled by Banu Qaynuqa, charged no tax on transactions and no interest on loans. While this tax-free market eventually became a point of conflict between Muhammad and the Banu Qaynuqa, the Prophet's move was not a means of antagonizing the Qaynuqa, but a further step toward alleviating the divide between the ridiculously wealthy and the absurdly poor."[38]

Their mockery leaves no room for misinterpretation:

> It is clear that the Jews did not consider the Prophet's covenant as binding upon them, and that most of them preferred the pagan idolaters to the Muslim worshippers of the One God. While affirming the piety and trustworthiness of individuals amongst the Jews, the Revelations were now full of warnings against the majority ... There could be no doubt that the hopes of the Jews were turning more and more to the Prophet's own tribe as the chief means of obliterating the new religion and restoring the oasis of Yathrib to what it had been in the past."[39]

Despite their obvious betrayal, the Prophet ignores the threat. Surah Ali 'Imran addresses his challengers:

> Say to those who reject (the truth), "You'll soon be defeated and gathered together in Hellfire - and how terrible a resting place!"
>
> You've already been given a sign in the two armies that clashed (at the battle of Badr). One (army) was fighting in the cause of God, while the other was resisting Him.
>
> With their own eyes (your opponents) saw you to be twice their number, (even though you were outnumbered by them), for God reinforces with His help whomever He wants. There's a lesson in this for those who have eyes to see! — *Ali 'Imran (The Family of Amran, 3:12-13)*

> All you who believe! Don't take those from outside your own ranks to be your intimate companions, for they'll try anything to corrupt you, as they only want to ruin you. Stinging hatred issues from their mouths, and what their hearts are hiding is far worse. We're making these verses clear for you, if you would (only use) your sense! — *Ali 'Imran (The Family of Amran, 3:118)*

> If you're doing well, it aggravates them, but if some misfortune befalls you, they're delighted. If you would just remain patient (in adversity) and be ever mindful (of God), then their scheming won't harm you in the least, for God encompasses everything they attempt. — *Ali 'Imran (The Family of Amran, 3:120)*

22 **WHAT WAS BEHIND THE ARABIAN JEWISH RESISTANCE TO ISLAM?**   WATT

"When ideas, such as those of a new religion, prove appropriate not just to one situation, but to a whole series of situations over generations, then they become woven into the texture of the social life and the culture of those who entertain them. When this has happened, ideas that have proved satisfactory over a long period and have become part of the texture of a people's life, cannot easily be changed. That was the case with the Jews. They believed that they were God's chosen people through whom alone He revealed Himself to men. It was difficult for them to see why they should change this idea because of an uneducated upstart (as they considered him) like Muhammad.

The intellectual or ideational conflict between Muhammad and the Jews became as bitter as it did because it threatened the core of the religious ideas of each. If prophets could arise among Gentiles, the Jews were not God's chosen people, and that was tantamount to having no religion left. If Muhammad was not God's prophet and messenger, then in his own eyes he could only be a self-deceived impostor. This was at the root of the quarrel...

Even this, however, is not the whole of the matter. In the relations of individuals and groups, especially in the field of religion, there is often a period when the character of their relationship is indeterminate. Then, either suddenly or gradually, they come to a point at which for one at least the relationship has become determinate. They have decided that they and the others are friends or enemies, belong together or do not belong together. From that point things go either all right or all wrong. The Jews possibly reached this point of no return about the time of the Hijrah, though Muhammad did not reach his till about a year and a half after that. Once they had decided to reject Muhammad, the Jews had to justify this decision at least to themselves, and perhaps this was why they indulged, quite unnecessarily, in mocking criticism of Muhammad. And when, after unavailing efforts to make them change their minds, Muhammad broke with the Jews, the whole sorry train of events was set in motion."[40]

After the Meccan defeat at Badr, Ka'b ibn Ashraf, chief of the Jewish tribe of Nadir, travels to Mecca to recite incendiary poetry about the Prophet and his Companions. He laments the Meccans who died at Badr and urges Quraysh to avenge their humiliating defeat.

In Medina, 'Abd Allah ibn Sallam, the rabbi-turned-Muslim of Bani Qaynuqa, informs the Prophet that his clan is plotting against the small Muslim community. Around the same time, the Prophet receives timely guidance from Surah Al Anfal:

> If you fear treachery from any group, then throw back (their treaty at them) so you'll at least be on an even level with them, for God has no love for the treacherous.
>
> Don't let those who suppress (their inner awareness of the truth) think that they can make progress (against God), for they can't escape (the punishment they deserve).
>
> Keep yourselves prepared against them to the best of your ability, especially with a strong mobile force that can strike fear into God's enemies and your enemies and also other (potential enemies) about whom you know nothing, but about whom God knows. Whatever you spend in the cause of God will be repaid to you, and you won't be treated unfairly. (Remember) that if the enemy leans towards peace, then you also must pursue the path of peace. Trust in God, for He's the Hearing and the Knowing.

— *Al Anfal (The Spoils of War, 8:58-61)*

13
14
15
16
17
18

The growing hostility between Bani Qaynuqa and the Muslims mounts after a marketplace scuffle in which a Muslim Helper comes to the defense of a woman who had been insulted by a Jewish merchant. The scene quickly escalates and the Helper kills the Jewish merchant, whose tribesmen then kill the Muslim. The Companions suggest that the Prophet arbitrate the matter, but the Qaynuqa refuse to abide by the terms of their pact with him and fortify themselves in their garrison.

23 WHY WOULD QAYNUQA BREAK THEIR PACT WITH THE PROPHET? `ASLAN`

"The Banu Qaynuqa's treachery may not have been unfounded … The Banu Qaynuqa suffered especially from the Prophet's tax-free market, which had eradicated their economic monopoly over Medina and greatly reduced their wealth. A war with Mecca would only have worsened the situation of Medina's Jewish clans by permanently severing their economic ties to the Quraysh, who were, after all, the primary consumers of their dates, wines, and arms. Despite their victory at Badr, there was still no reason to believe that Muhammad could actually conquer the Quraysh. Eventually the Meccans would regroup and return to defeat the Prophet. And when that happened, it would be imperative for the Jewish clans to make their loyalties to the Quraysh absolutely clear."[41]

With Hamzah by his side, the Prophet quickly mobilizes a brigade that surrounds the Jewish fortress. Qaynuqa's leaders look for support from their pre-existing alliance with Khazraj via 'Abd Allah ibn Ubayy and 'Ubadah ibn Samit. Despite his own willingness to help them, 'Abd Allah is unable to persuade 'Ubadah to break his pact with the Prophet. The Qaynuqa stronghold is surrounded, and after a two-week standoff, the Jewish tribe surrenders.

In an effort to save face, 'Abd Allah ibn Ubayy grabs the Prophet by the neck of his coat and publicly demands that he let them go. But the Prophet remains steadfast—Surah Al Anfal had already instructed him on how to deal with Qaynuqa's betrayal:

> Therefore, if you ever gain ascendancy over them on the battlefield, scatter them completely, so that those who come after them will have a lesson to consider. — *Al Anfal (The Spoils of War, 8:57)*

They are banished from Medina for breaking several terms of the pact, and ultimately resettle in the oasis of Wadi l-Qura' near the Syrian border.

24 WHY DIDN'T THE OTHER JEWS HELP QAYNUQA? `SALAHI`

"It is interesting to note that the two other main Jewish tribes, namely al-Nadir and Qurayzah, who both lived on the outskirts of Madinah, did not attempt to help the Qaynuqa Jews in their confrontation with the Prophet. This, in itself, could be taken as evidence of the treachery of the Qaynuqa Jews. The other Jews were no less hostile to Islam than the Qaynuqa tribe, although they did not show it at the time. If the case of treachery was not clear cut, the other Jews would at least have mediated between the Prophet and their cousins. The fact that these tribes remained neutral suggests that the Qaynuqa Jews would have lost their case even if it had been put to a Jewish jury."[42]

25 **WHAT KIND OF PUNISHMENT DID QAYNUQA EXPECT?** [ARMSTRONG]

"Muhammad would have been expected to massacre the men and sell the women and children into slavery—the traditional punishment meted out to traitors—but he acceded to Ibn Ubayy's plea for clemency and spared them, provided that the whole tribe left Medina immediately. Qaynuqa' were ready to go. They had taken a gamble, but had underestimated Muhammad's new popularity. Neither their Arab allies nor the other Jews protested ... Bloodshed was avoided."[43]

26 **HOW DID QAYNUQA TAKE THE NEWS OF THEIR EXPULSION?** [ASLAN]

"They were shocked, therefore, when Muhammad rejected traditional law and decided instead to exile the clan from Medina, even going so far as to allow them to take most of their property with them. It was a magnanimous decision on Muhammad's part ... But it was a decision he would be forced to make again a year later, after the disastrous defeat of his overconfident army at Uhud."[44]

27 **HOW DID THE PROPHET DISTINGUISH BETWEEN SITUATIONS AND THE PEOPLE INVOLVED IN THEM?** [RAMADAN]

"Muhammad kept distinguishing between situations and the people involved in them, and he showed the utmost respect toward individuals and their beliefs ... This is Revelation's key message and the heart of its Prophet's action; all the later verses of the Quran that refer to conflicts, killing, and fighting must be read in the context of their Revelation (Muslims being in a situation of war and needing to defend themselves) and by no means alter the essential contents of the message as a whole."[45]

15.10 THE BARLEY INVASION

Smoldering from the loss at Badr, Abu Sufyan promises not to bathe until he exacted revenge on the Muslims. Two months after Badr, he leads 200 men to Medina to fulfill his oath. After obtaining assistance from Bani Nadir, the Meccan party raids one of Medina's suburbs at night. They kill two Muslims and cut down several palm trees before fleeing back to their camp. When the Prophet hears the news, he immediately dispatches a party to capture Abu Sufyan who, unbeknownst to him, had already fled back to Mecca. The Muslims never catch Abu Sufyan's men but recover all the provisions and barley that the Meccans had hastily jettisoned to lighten their load.

13

14

15

16

17

18

15.11 THE DEATH OF 'UTHMAN IBN MAZ'UN

At the time, 'Umar ibn al-Khattab is surprised that a pious man like 'Uthman ibn Maz'un did not die a martyr's death. He will later change his stance when the Prophet and Abu Bakr die from natural causes as well. Recall that 'Uthman is the brother of Zaynab bint Maz'un, 'Umar's wife (Fig. 5i).

In the year after Badr, 'Umar's brother-in-law, 'Uthman ibn Maz'un, passes away of natural causes. From the beginning, 'Uthman was a tireless activist and ardent supporter of the nascent Muslim community, and his departure brings tears to the Prophet's eyes. 'Uthman was an ascetic by nature, and used to fast all day and pray all night. In fact, on several occasions, the Prophet had to guide him toward moderation:

> *"Hast thou not in me an example? ... verily thine eyes have their right over thee, and thy body hath its rights, and thy family have their rights. So pray, and sleep, and fast, and break fast."*[46]

At his funeral, an elderly woman proclaims that 'Uthman will soon enter the doors of Paradise. But when the Prophet overhears her comment, he gently teaches her to avoid speaking on God's behalf, no matter how deserving the individual might appear to be. Instead, the Prophet instructs her to merely say that he loved God and His Messenger.

---

28 **WHAT CAN WE LEARN FROM 'UTHMAN IBN MAZ'UN'S DEATH?** | YUSUF |

"This is an important lesson because what the Prophet, God's peace and blessings upon him, was teaching here is that we do not say about Allah what we don't know. We don't say what we don't know."[47]

15.12 ABU LUBABAH'S TREE

This is not the first time **Abu Lubabah ibn 'Abd al-Mundhir** will disappoint the Prophet. Two years later, he will make an error in judgment regarding Bani Qurayzah (QY 18.4).

Several months after Badr, one of the Prophet's Companions, Abu Lubabah ibn 'Abd al-Mundhir, is falsely accused of taking a palm tree belonging to an orphan. Against the Prophet's advice, however, Abu Lubabah refuses to give his tree to the orphan as an act of charity. Suprisingly, when the Prophet repeats his request, telling him that doing so will earn him a tree in Paradise, Abu Lubabah refuses once more. Thabit ibn ad-Dahdahah, however, overhears the Prophet's offer and trades an entire orchard for Abu Lubabah's one tree so he can give it to the orphan and earn the reward intended for Abu Lubabah.

---

29 **WHAT CAN WE LEARN FROM ABU LUBABAH'S SENSE OF JUSTICE?** | RAMADAN |

"He had gone to such lengths to assert his right of ownership that to concede to this request was inconceivable. This obsession veiled his heart and compassion. Revelation was to recall, on both the individual and collective levels, the singular nature of the spiritual elevation that makes it possible to reach beyond the consciousness of justice, that demands right, to the excellence of the heart, that offers forgiveness or gives people more than their due: 'God commands justice and excellence.' " An-Nahl (The Bee, 16:90)
The Prophet realized that Abu Lubabah's almost blind attachment to one of Islam's recommendations, justice, prevented him from reaching the superior level of justness of the heart: excellence, generosity, giving. ... Muhammad ... did not resent Abu Lubabah's attitude. He later entrusted him with other missions, such as conveying to the Banu Qurayzah the terms of their surrender."[48]

15.13 THE HOUSEHOLD AFTER BADR

At the age of 20, Fatimah remains unmarried. Both Abu Bakr and 'Umar had asked for her hand in marriage, but the Prophet turned them down and instead encourages 'Ali to consider marrying her. At first 'Ali is hesitant on account of his poverty, but ultimately consents to the union. The wedding is simple and the bridal room is sparse. On the night of the wedding, after the guests have left, the Prophet comes to their room and tenderly blesses the young couple.

Be sure to read Lings (p.168) for a detailed description of the wedding.

Shortly after their marriage, Fatimah and 'Ali settle down in a house that is much farther away from the mosque. But Harithah ibn Nu'man, a distant Khazraji relative from the clan of Najjar, senses the Prophet's desire to be near his daughter and son-in-law, and donates his house in Medina to the young couple.

Since the Hijrah, a number of impoverished followers had begun residing in the mosque. Destitute and homeless, a stone platform is erected for their exclusive use next to the Prophet's house. These emigrants, known as the *Ahl as-Suffah* (People of the Bench), become a permanent fixture in the community. Because they devote most of their time to studying and preserving the Prophet's revelations, their daily needs are largely dependent on the generosity of others, most notably, Fatimah.

---

30 **HOW DID THE PROPHET CARE FOR THOSE AROUND HIM?** RAMADAN

"He would listen to them, answer their questions, and look after their needs. One of the characteristics of his personality and of his teachings, as much in regard to the people of the bench as to the rest of his community, was that when asked about matters of spirituality, faith, education, or doubt, he would often offer different answers to the same questions, taking into account the psychological makeup, experience, and intelligence of the questioner."[49]

- -

31 **BENEVOLENCE FOR THE POOR** ASLAN

"Benevolence and care for the poor were the first and most enduring virtues preached by Muhammad in Mecca. Piety, the Quran reminds believers, lies 'not in the turning of your face to the East or West in prayer … but in distributing your wealth out of love for God to your needy kin; to the orphans, to the vagrants, and to the mendicants; it lies in freeing the slaves, in observing your devotions, and in giving alms to the poor.' " [Qur'an, 2:177][50]

- -

32 **WHY WAS THERE SUCH AN EMPHASIS ON CARING FOR THE POOR?** RAMADAN

"The quest for proximity to the One can only be experienced and perfected through proximity to the poor: respecting, caring for, and serving them brings one closer to God."[51]

Given their close contact with the Prophet, it is not surprising that **Anas ibn Malik** and **'Abd Allah ibn Mas'ud** will eventually become two of the most authoritative scholars of the Qur'an and *hadith* (sayings of the Prophet).

Umm Sulaym bint Milhan will be one of only two women to join the Companions at the Battle of Uhud, and later join the expedition to Khaybar.

Nearly two years have passed since the Hijrah, and the Prophet's extended household has grown considerably. In the year after Badr, Umm Sulaym bint Milhan sends her 10-year-old son Anas ibn Malik to serve as the Prophet's personal servant. 'Abd Allah ibn Mas'ud spends a significant time around the house, and 'Uthman ibn Maz'un's widow, Khawlah bint al-Hakim, redoubles her attention to the Prophet's domestic affairs after her husband's death.

Everyone in the Prophet's household assists with daily chores. The work is exhausting, and one day 'Ali (who is a water carrier) suggests to Fatimah that she ask her father for a servant to help them around the house. At first, Fatimah (who would grind corn for the family) is too ashamed to ask, but when they approach the Prophet together, the Prophet tells them that there are others, like the Ahl as-Suffah, who are in greater need of help. Instead of offering material support, he teaches them how to invoke God's praise after each prayer, explaining that it is far more valuable than what they are seeking.

YEAR 16: UHUD

16.1 THE EASTERN DESERT CAMPAIGN

Not only does the Battle of Badr escalate tensions between Mecca and Medina, it begins to divide the Arabian Peninsula into competing sides. In the battle's aftermath, the Prophet forms alliances with several tribes along the Red Sea coast, aimed at blocking Mecca's coastal trade routes. Desperate to preserve their only remaining route to the north, the Quraysh reach out to Bani Ghatafan and Hawazin for help.

In response, the Prophet sets out on several preemptive marches to the east. On one such occasion, as they are chasing Bani Muharib (a sub-clan of Bani Sulaym from the tribe of Hawazin), the Prophet and his Companions stop to rest. Shortly after falling asleep, the Prophet is abruptly awoken by the chief of Muharib, Du'thur ibn al-Harith, who is standing over him brandishing his sword and threatening:

> *"Who would hold me back from killing you now?"*

With the word "Allah" on the Prophet's lips, Gabriel suddenly appears and thrusts Du'thur backward. The Prophet quickly stands over his fallen attacker and asks him:

> *"Who would hold me back from killing you now?"* [1]

The miraculous blow jolts Du'thur—he immediately testifies his faith to the Prophet and returns home to summon his people to Islam.

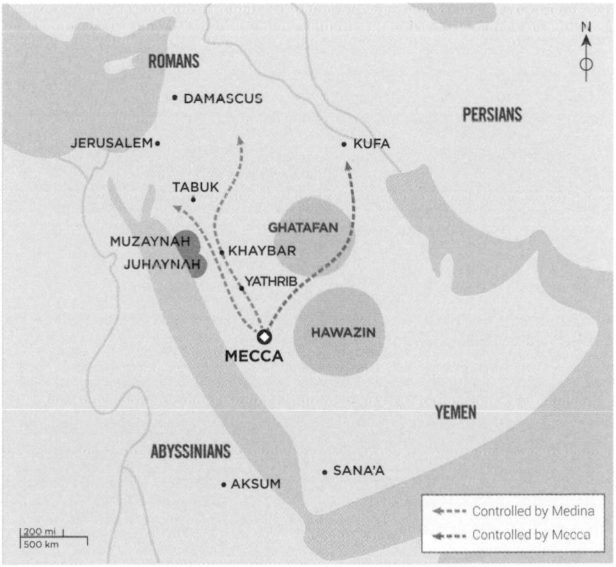

According to Al Mubarakpuri (citing al-Bukhari, Muslim, and al-'Asqalani) the incident involving Du'thur may have occured in QY 19, after the fall of Khaybar.

FIGURE 16A. CONTROL OF THE SUMMER CARAVANS

The Prophet formed strategic alliances with several coastal tribes such as Juhaynah and Muzaynah. To protect their only remaining northern trade route through the Nejd desert, the Quraysh allied themselves with the tribes of Hawazin and Ghatafan. In response, the Prophet set out on several preemptive marches against the two hostile tribes.

16.2 THE ASSASSINATION OF KA'B IBN ASHRAF

Al-Mubarakpuri reports that this event happened after the fall of Khaybar in QY 19.

 SURAH AN-NISA (The Women) is named after numerous verses that relate to the rights of women and their spiritual equality to men. This was a radical idea that flew in the face of traditional Arabian customs. The surah also details inheritance law, danger of the hypocrites, and theological differences between Judaism, Christianity, and Islam.

Many years later, at the Conquest of Mecca, **Muhammad ibn Maslamah** will lead the Prophet's camel as they circle the Ka'bah.

After the Hijrah, Ka'b ibn Ashraf, the Jewish leader of Bani Nadir, became one of the Prophet's most vocal critics, and would write incendiary poetry against the Muslims. After Badr, Ka'b visits Mecca to encourage the Quraysh to seek revenge for their loss. When Abu Sufyan asks Ka'b if he is more inclined to Islam or Meccan paganism, Ka'b indicates the latter. His response is described in Surah An-Nisa:

> Haven't you noticed the case of those (Jews of Medina) who received a portion of the scripture? Yet, they put their faith in idols and superstition! They told the faithless (idolaters of Mecca) that they (the idolaters) were better guided on the way (of truth) than the believers! — *An-Nisa (The Women, 4:51)*

By rallying the Meccans against Medina, Ka'b's actions are tantamount to treason. When Ka'b returns from Mecca, the Prophet asks for volunteers to neutralize the threat from Bani Nadir. Muhammad ibn Maslamah and four others from Aws volunteer to lure Ka'b from his fortress and kill him, and the Prophet approves their strategy.

When the five Companions carry out their plan, Bani Nadir furiously voice their dissatisfaction to the Prophet, who remains unapologetic:

> The Prophet knew well that most of them were as hostile to Islam as Ka'b had been, and with great disappointment he had come to accept this. But it was vital to show them that if hostile thoughts were tolerable, hostile action was not ... He then invited them to make a special treaty with him in addition to the covenant, and this they did.[2]

---

❶ HOW COULD THE PROPHET CONDONE KA'B'S ASSASSINATION? | YUSUF

"You have to see the Prophet, God's peace and blessings upon him, as a prophet and also as a leader of a government. By the nature of governance, you cannot allow certain things to happen without serious punishment as a consequence, because if you do, then it leads to anarchy. Although his dominant characteristic is rahmah [mercy], you'll see that he will show his just side only when it's necessary. In times when it's not necessary, he is always going to forgive. But the times when it is necessary are the times of war. Their security and their lives are based on his judgments and his decisions. He sees the treachery that's going on and he has to stop it. This is a message to Bani Nadir. If you make oaths and you break them, then this is your recompense."[3]

- -

❷ HOW COULD THE PROPHET CONDONE KA'B'S ASSASSINATION? | WATT

"In the gentler or (should we say?) less virile age in which we live men look askance at such conduct, particularly in a religious leader. But in Muhammad's age and country it was quite normal. Men had no claims upon you on the basis of common humanity. Members of your tribe and of allied tribes, and those protected by your tribe, had very definite claims; but outside this circle no one had any claim at all. That is to say, in the case of a stranger or enemy there was no reason why you should not kill him if you felt inclined. The only consideration that might hold you back was the ability of his kinsmen to exact vengeance, or respect for your own word in the case where you had been induced to accept him as a guest before you realized who he was. A man like Ka'b ibn-al-Ashraf was a clear enemy of the Islamic community, and so there was no obligation to consider him in any way. Since those who assassinated him were from a clan in alliance with his and on which his own clan was dependent there was no likelihood of a blood-feud developing ... The other side of this picture is that Muhammad himself had to be constantly on his guard against possible assassins."[4]

16.3 THE PROPHET'S MARRIAGE TO HAFSAH

One year after Badr, 'Umar's son-in-law, Khunays ibn Hudhafah, dies. But when 'Umar starts searching for a new husband for his 18-year-old daughter, he is turned down by Abu Bakr and 'Uthman (who recently lost his wife, Ruqayyah). Not knowing where to turn, 'Umar confides his disappointment to the Prophet, who responds:

> *"Behold, I will show thee a better son-in-law than 'Uthman, and I will show him a better father-in-law than thee."*[5]

The Prophet not only agrees to marry Hafsah, he also arranges the marriage of his daughter Umm Kulthum to 'Uthman. In a few months, Hafsah seamlessly integrates into the Prophet's family and quickly becomes 'A'ishah's close friend.

Muhammad's age before the battle of Uhud: __55__

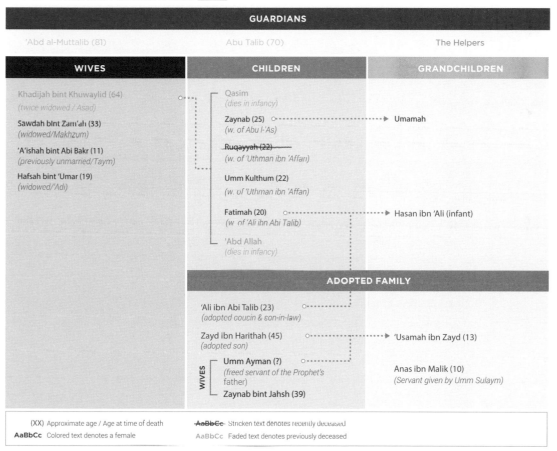

FIGURE 16B. THE PROPHET'S HOUSEHOLD BEFORE UHUD

Several months ago, the Prophet arranged Fatimah's marriage to 'Ali, and within the year, the couple was blessed with a son named Hasan. Shortly after Fatimah's marriage, the Prophet told 'Umar that he would marry 'Umar's widowed daughter, Hafsah, whose husband, Khunays ibn Hudhafah, had passed away after Badr. Around this time, 'Uthman consented to marrying Umm Kulthum. In the year after Badr, Umm Sulaym gave her 10-year-old son, Anas ibn Malik, to the Prophet to serve as his personal attendant.

Note: The Prophet's eldest daughter, Zaynab, never left Mecca during the Hijrah, but later joined the Prophet's household after her father agreed to release her husband, Abu l-'As, a Meccan captive after Badr. Zaynab was accompanied by her daughter Umamah. (Abu l-'As ultimately joined his wife and daughter in Medina, five months after the Battle of the Trench.) (Refer to Figs. P25, 6b, and 13f for previous details about the Prophet's household.)

16.4 ZAYD'S EXPEDITION TO QARADAH

With the summer trading season coming to an end and their usual coastal routes blocked, the Meccans send a heavily laden caravan northeast to Iraq led by Abu Sufyan's chief rival in Mecca, Safwan ibn Umayyah. The Prophet hears of the expedition and dispatches Zayd ibn Harithah at the head of 100 horsemen. The men successfully intercept the caravan near Qaradah and straightaway return to Medina with abundant spoils.

The ambush is a financial disaster for the Quraysh. Having been cut off from all northern commerce, they are forced to make a decision—either make peace or declare war:

> The Makkans were terribly anxious and worried about their prospects of life now at stake with no hope whatsoever for any possible rehabilitation of commercial life or redemption of former prestige at the socio-political level, except through two avenues categorically contrasting: Giving up all symbols of pride and all attitudes of arrogance through reconciliation with the new state of affairs, and peaceableness with the Muslims; or launching a decisive overpowering war with the aim of crushing down the military forces of Madinah. It was apparent through the process of events that the Quraish had opted for the second alternative.[6]

16.5 THE MARCH TO UHUD

Within a year of their marriage, Fatimah and 'Ali have a son, whom the Prophet names Hasan. The news however, is followed by an alarming dispatch from 'Abbas in Mecca—Abu Sufyan has assembled an army of 3,000 men and 200 horses and is heading north to Medina. Unbeknownst to the Prophet, Abu Sufyan's wife, Hind, is accompanying the army and has promised Jubayr ibn Mutim's Abyssinian slave, Wahshi, his freedom if he kills Hamzah in battle.

The Quraysh army marches up the western Arabian coast and encamps north of Medina. They rest at a spot just south of Mount Uhud, where they feed on Medina's unharvested crops. Their arrival prompts several nearby residents to evacuate into Medina with their livestock.

That night, the Prophet experiences a visionary dream. He later explains to his Companions that while he will sustain personal injury and the loss of several followers, the Muslims will nonetheless kill the leader of Quraysh. The Prophet considers fortifying his troops behind the city's natural defenses—a plan backed by 'Abd Allah ibn Ubayy and a number of older Companions. The majority of younger Companions, however, urge the Prophet to take the offensive and attack the Meccans at Uhud.

During the discussion, Khaythamah Abu Sa'd relates a recent dream in which his son beckoned him to Paradise, and Khaythamah argues to attack the Meccans at Uhud so he can join his son Sa'd in the afterlife.

Malik ibn Sinan, a Khazraji Helper, also supports the offensive saying:

> "O Messenger of God, we have before us one of the two good things: either Allah will grant us mastery of them, and that is what we would have; or else Allah will grant us martyrdom. I care not which it may be, for verily there is good in both."[7]

After entertaining all the Companions' arguments, the Prophet elects to attack the Quraysh at the base of Mount Uhud. He returns to his house where Abu Bakr and 'Umar dress him for battle.

One year ago, Khaythamah's son, Sa'd, was martyred at Badr. As foretold in his dream, **Khaythamah Abu Sa'd** will be martyred at Uhud.

Malik ibn Sinan fights valiantly at Uhud and will be too wounded to chase the Quraysh back to Mecca. During the battle, when the Prophet's cheek is bleeding, Malik sucks on the blood to stem the flow. Though he dies a few days later in Medina, the Prophet orders that his body should be returned to the battlefield and buried alongside the other Uhud martyrs.

---

③ THE DEBATE TO ATTACK OR RETREAT   `RAMADAN`

"Nevertheless, during the debates, his opinion was defeated, particularly through the opposition of the younger Companions and those who had not taken part in the Battle of Badr: they hoped to acquire merit similar to that of the Badr fighters in the impending battle."[8]

As the men prepare for the northward march, a number of them fear they have pressured the Prophet into fighting at Uhud when he initially preferred to take a defensive approach. One of the most prominent Companions, Sa'd ibn Mu'adh, suggests that from now on, they should let the Prophet determine military strategy without their interference.

When the Prophet emerges from his house in full battle armor, he learns that several Companions are worried that they dissuaded him from his original plan. With his sword by his side and his shield on his back, he proclaims to his men:

> "It does not suit a Prophet that once he had put on armor, he should take it off, until Allah has decided between him and the enemy."[9]

---

④ WHAT DOES UHUD TEACH US ABOUT BEING STEADFAST?   `RAMADAN`

"Once you've determined to do something, trust in Allah. This is a great lesson in life: once you set out on something, be steadfast and don't waver."[10]

With those words, he mounts his horse and asks for his bow and spear. He distributes three banners to Usayd ibn Hudayr (of Aws), Hubab ibn al-Mundhir (of Khazraj), and Mus'ab ibn 'Umayr (of Quraysh). Before marching out with an army of 1,000 men, the Prophet asks 'Abd Allah ibn Umm Makhtum, the blind Companion from Mecca, to lead prayers in Medina during his absence.

Recall that just a few years ago, the Prophet sent **Mus'ab ibn 'Umayr** to Yathrib to teach Islam and prepare the city for his arrival. Sa'd ibn Mu'adh sent his clansman Usayd ibn Hudayr to drive Mus'ab out, and instead both men embraced Islam.

Remember that just one year ago **Hubab ibn al-Mundhir** had persuaded the Prophet to take control of all the wells at Badr.

13
14
15
16
17
18

Remember that **Hanzalah ibn Abi 'Amir** is the son of Abu 'Amir ibn Sayfi, the self-declared Abrahamic monk from Aws who died in exile. Hanzalah's marriage to 'Abd Allah ibn 'Ubayy's daughter, Jamilah, joins the families of the two powerful ex-leaders of Aws and Khazraj, something that may not have happened prior to Islam (see Fig. 10c). As seen in Jamilah's dream, Hanzalah will be killed on the battlefield later that day.

As predicted, **'Abd Allah ibn 'Amr** will be killed in battle. The added responsibility leaves Jabir with little means of taking care of his seven sisters, let alone starting a family. One year later, the Prophet will buy Jabir's camel from him, only to return the camel as a gift so that Jabir can get married. As we will see, this is not the only time the Prophet lends a generous hand to the young Companion.

The eve of the battle coincides with Hanzalah ibn Abi 'Amir's wedding to Jamilah, the daughter of 'Abd Allah ibn Ubayy. When Hanzalah asks the Prophet for permission to continue with the wedding, the Prophet blesses the couple and instructs Hanzalah not to postpone the marriage. That night Jamilah dreams that the door to heaven opened to let Hanzalah in, and then closed behind him. The next morning, Hanzalah leaves to catch up with the rest of the army, which has already left for Uhud.

Another Companion and recent widower, 'Abd Allah ibn 'Amr experiences a dream that he will be martyred on the battlefield. Before leaving for Uhud, he instructs his only son, Jabir, to stay behind and take care of 'Abd Allah's seven younger daughters.

Jabir is not the only person disappointed to have to stay behind. Several other young boys try to join the expedition, but the Prophet only permits two 15-year-olds, Rafi' ibn Khadij and Samurah ibn Jundub, to join the army.

FIGURE 16C. THE MARCH TO UHUD

When the Prophet heard about the advancing Meccan army, he considered remaining fortified in the city of Medina. He consulted his Companions and 'Abd Allah ibn Ubayy strongly urged them to remain in the city. The younger Companions convinced the Prophet otherwise, and a party of 1,000 men marched north to Uhud. Halfway there, 'Abd Allah ibn Ubayy turned 300 men around and returned to the city, explaining that there would be no actual fighting. The army, now reduced to 700 men, camped between the enemy and Mount Uhud.

Ironically, after the battle, the Quraysh decided not to attack Medina because they had heard that 300 fresh troops were waiting to defend the city.

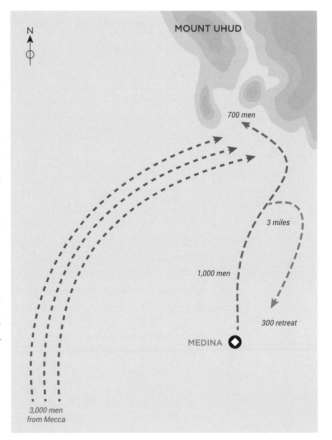

Shortly after setting out with his men, 'Abd Allah ibn Ubayy defects with 300 soldiers and returns to the city. He explains that the Prophet disobeyed his counsel and suggests that his men are not necessary because there will be no actual fighting. Despite 'Abd Allah ibn Ubayy's betrayal, his son, 'Abd Allah, stays to fight alongside the Prophet. Days later, Surah Ali 'Imran addresses the sudden betrayal:

> When they were told, "Come and fight in the cause of God, or at the very least defend yourselves," (they offered) excuses, saying, "If we knew a fight was (really) going to happen, then we would've surely followed you (in the battle)." They were much closer to disbelief than belief that day. They said with their lips the opposite of what was in their hearts, and God knows what they were hiding.
>
> Now they're lamenting, after they've been sitting (in safety all along), "If only (our slain friends) would've listened to us (and not fought in the Battle of Uhud), then they wouldn't have been killed." (Then challenge the hypocrites by) saying, "So save yourselves from death, if you have that power!"
> — *Ali 'Imran (The Family of Amran, 3:167-168)*

'Abd Allah ibn Ubayy's sizeable defection causes confusion in the Muslim army. When two other clans, Bani Salimah of Khazraj and Bani Harithah of Aws, consider withdrawing as well, Jabir ibn 'Abd Allah reminds them of their oath to fight alongside the Prophet.

Surah Ali 'Imran recalls the tense moment before battle:

> Remember that morning, (Muhammad), when you left your family to assign the believers to their battle stations (at the Mountain of Uhud). God was listening, and He knew (all about it).
>
> Remember when two of your regiments almost lost the will to fight. Yet, God was their guardian, and the believers should trust in God!
> — *Ali 'Imran (The Family of Amran, 3:121-122)*

Now reduced to 700 men, the Prophet and his men camp between the enemy and Mount Uhud. After the morning prayer, the Prophet tells his men:

> *"Verily this day, ye are at a station that is rich in reward and rich in treasure, for him who is mindful of what he is about and who devoteth his soul thereunto in patience and certainty and earnestness and effort."[11]*

'Abd Allah ibn Jubayr is chosen to lead 50 archers at a rise to the left of the main army. The Prophet instructs the archers to keep the Meccan cavalry at bay with their arrows, whatever the cost:

> *"Whether we win the battle or lose it, stand steadily in your position and mind that we are not attacked from your side..."[12]*

To further emphasize the point, he adds:

> *"If you see us snatched into pieces by birds, do not leave this position of yours till I send for you. And if you see that we have defeated the enemy and trodden on them do not desert your position till I send for you."[13]*

Remember that **Jabir ibn 'Abd Allah's** father had asked him to stay home and take care of his seven sisters in case their father was killed at Uhud. Jabir's obedience to his father was fortunate because from Medina he is able to persuade Bani Salima and Harithah not to abandon the Prophet. Jabir's contribution may have prevented the Muslim army's annihilation at Uhud.

13
14
15
16
17
18

After putting on a second coat of mail, the Prophet presents a sword to his followers, asking which Companion is most worthy of wielding it against the Quraysh. Although 'Umar ibn al-Khattab and Zubayr ibn al-'Awwam rise to the challenge, the Prophet motions to Abu Dujanah ibn Kharashah. The Khazraji brandishes the sword and uncharacteristically swaggers in front of the ranks. On seeing the display, the Prophet comments:

"This is a sort of walking that Allah hates except in such a situation."[14]

With those words, he then leads his men to the battlefield, closely accompanied by Zayd ibn Harithah, Sa'd ibn Abi Waqqas, and Sa'ib ibn 'Uthman. Unlike the Quraysh, who had brought their wives and daughters to the battlefield, the Prophet had left the women of Medina behind. Nonetheless, two women—Nusaybah bint Ka'b and Umm Sulaym bint Milhan—catch up with the Prophet's forces to lend their support to the wounded.

Sa'ib ibn 'Uthman is the son of 'Uthman ibn Maz'un, the highly revered Companion and 'Umar's ascetic brother-in-law, who had passed away just a few months ago.

Recall that **Nusaybah bint Ka'b** was one of the two women at the Second 'Aqabah who pledged to protect the Prophet under any circumstance. Her husband and two sons fight at Uhud as well. In the coming years, Nusaybah will also join the expeditions to Hudaybiyah and Khaybar.

Umm Sulaym bint Milhan is the mother of the Prophet's servant, Anas ibn Malik. Like Nusaybah, she will later take part in the expedition to Khaybar.

---

⑤ WHY TWO COATS OF ARMOR? [YUSUF]

"On that day, he put on two coats of armor. Sidi Ahmad Zarruq says that this was teaching the sahaba [companions] that despite the fact that Allah was protecting them with angels, when you go out, you take the asbab [means of protection] with you."[15]

16.6 THE BATTLE OF UHUD

The Meccan army consists of three battalions. Abu Sufyan leads from the center while Khalid ibn al-Walid and 'Ikrimah ibn Abi Jahl lead from either side. With the armies facing each other, Abu Sufyan steps out and announces that the Quraysh have no quarrel with the Aws and Khazraj. He asks them to abandon the Prophet's army, but his request is met with jeers. Then, much to Hanzalah's dismay, his father, Abu 'Amir ibn Sayfi, emerges from behind the Meccan infantry and also invites his clan of Aws to leave the Prophet's side. Much to Abu 'Amir's embarrassment, he too is met with a volley of insults.

Al-Mubarakpuri notes that Zubayr ibn al-'Awwam, not 'Ali, is the one who killed Talhah ibn 'Abd Allah.

From the Meccan side, Talhah ibn 'Abd Allah of 'Abd ad-Dar steps forward and challenges anyone in the Muslim army to a duel. Waving the Meccan banner, he is followed by his two brothers and four sons. 'Ali ibn Abi Talib rises to the challenge and kills Talhah in the opening duel, and Hamzah kills Talhah's brother. Then 'Ali, Hamzah, and a few other Companions finish Talhah's other brother and four sons.

As soon as the two armies meet, Abu Dujanah begins wreaking havoc on the battlefield with the sword given to him by the Prophet. He strikes down every man in his path and just stops short of killing Hind when he realizes she is a woman. Amid the clamor, Wahshi gets a clear shot at Hamzah and fatally pierces him with his javelin. Just as Jamilah bint ʿAbd Allah saw in her dream, her newlywed husband, Hanzalah ibn Abi ʿAmir, is martyred at the foot of Mount Uhud.

After a period of intense fighting, the Prophet's forces finally break the enemy line and, sensing imminent victory, 40 archers abandon their post to collect the spoils. They leave ʿAbd Allah ibn Jubayr with only nine other archers to protect the rear of the Muslim army. Khalid and ʿIkrimah spot the opening and circle around the northwest of Uhud to attack the Prophet's forces from behind. Soon enough all 10 archers are martyred, and the rear flanks of the Muslim forces begin to flee up the mountainside.

When you were scrambling up the slopes (of Mount Uhud in full retreat), not even noticing those around you, the Messenger was behind you, calling you to come back (and face the enemy, but you ignored him). So God brought the disappointment (of shame) upon you, even as you disappointed (the Prophet by running away from him).

This added shame) befell you so that you wouldn't feel bad only for the (war prizes) you missed, but also for what you suffered, as well, and God is well-informed of all that you do. — Ali ʿImran (The Family of Amran, 3:153)

♻ SURAH ALI ʿIMRAN (The Family of Amran) is named after two verses which allude to the respected Jewish family of Amran that gave rise to Mary and Jesus. It is the second longest surah in the Qur'an and, among other topics, relates the birth of Mary, the life of Jesus, and the importance of holding on to the religion of Abraham. The latter part of the surah examines several important lessons from Uhud and ends by praising the faithful (Jews, Christians, and Muslims) who follow Revelation and persevere through times of adversity.

6 WHAT CAN WE LEARN FROM KHALID AND THE ARCHERS? [RAMADAN]

"That particular moment of the Uhud encounter is rich with a profound teaching: human beings can never completely overcome the culture and experiences that have fashioned their past, and no final judgment can ever be expressed as to the future of their choices and orientations. The Muslims were caught up by an unfortunate feature of their past customs; Khalid ibn al-Walid was to undergo a future conversion that would wipe out whatever judgments had been pronounced about his past. 'Nothing is ever final,' is a lesson in humility; 'no final judgment should be passed,' is a promise of hope."[16]

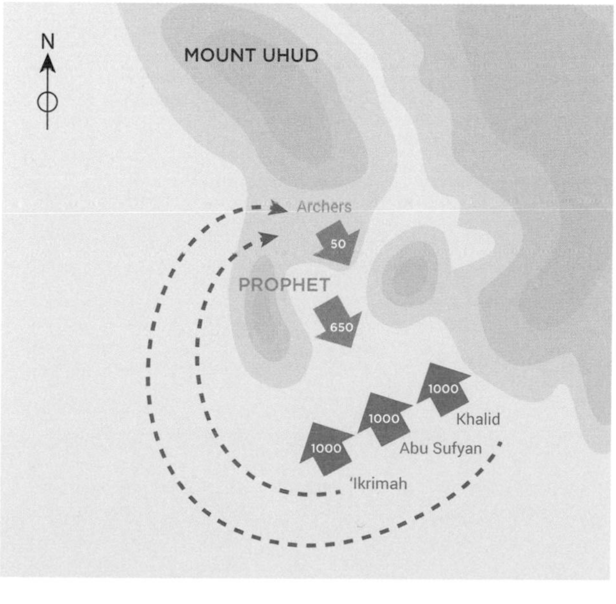

FIGURE 16D. THE BATTLE OF UHUD

The Battle of Uhud took place just northwest of Medina at the base of Mount Uhud. The Prophet had allotted 50 archers to protect the rear flank while he marched into battle with the remaining 650 men.

When the archers sensed imminent victory, 40 of them left their position to gather their portion of the spoils. ʿIkrimah ibn Abi Jahl and Khalid ibn al-Walid spotted the breach and circled around the back of the Muslim army. After killing the 10 remaining archers, the Meccans gained a tactical advantage that quickly swung the battle in their favor.

The shift in momentum catches the Muslims off guard and they find themselves scrambling to avoid certain defeat. In the heat of battle, Wahb al-Muzani, a man of the coastal tribe of Muzaynah, volunteers to protect the Prophet. When the Meccan forces approach, the Prophet and his men watch in awe as Wahb fights them off with incredible valor until he is surrounded and killed by the enemy. After the battle, his body is found punctured with countless wounds, and 'Umar later confesses:

> *"Of all deaths, the one I would most fain have died was the Muzaynite's death."*[17]

'Abd al-Ka'bah was 'A'ishah's full brother. By Uhud, he was the only person in Abu Bakr's immediate family who hadn't followed his father into Islam. After the death of his mother, Umm Ruman, he will come to Medina and convert to Islam. At that time, the Prophet will change his name to 'Abd ar-Rahman.

Amid the clamor and confusion, 'Abd al-Ka'bah ibn Abi Bakr emerges on his horse and challenges the Muslim forces. Abu Bakr rises to fight his eldest son, but the Prophet beckons him to remain by his side.

Abu Dujanah leads 'Ali, Zubayr, and Talhah in pushing back the enemy lines. As the fighting intensifies, the Prophet sustains a heavy blow to his jaw and shoulder. At the last second, Talhah deflects another vicious blow meant for the Prophet. Nevertheless, the impact momentarily stuns the Prophet and he falls to the ground. While Nusaybah and Shammas ibn 'Uthman rush to his defense, word quickly spreads throughout the battlefield that the Prophet has been slain. Sensing the sudden shift in momentum, Anas ibn Nadir cries out to his companions:

Shammas ibn 'Uthman had migrated with the first group of Muslims to Abyssinia. He valiantly protects the Prophet at Uhud and is later described as a living shield. He will die after returning to Medina and the Prophet requests that his body be taken back to Uhud for burial.

> *"What are you waiting for? What do you live for after Muhammad? Come on and die for what Allah's Messenger has died for."*[18]

His battle cry is echoed in Surah Ali 'Imran:

> Muhammad is no more than a messenger. There were many messengers who passed away before him. If he dies or is killed, would you then turn and run away? Anyone who runs away does no harm to God in the least, and God will quickly reward (those who serve Him) in gratitude.
> — *Ali 'Imran (The Family of Amran, 3:144)*

Anas ibn Nadir is later found on the battlefield with more than 80 wounds, and is only recognizable by his fingers. Anas is the uncle of Harithah ibn Suraqah, the young Khazraji who was slain by the first arrow at Badr. Anas is also the uncle of the Prophet's young servant, Anas ibn Malik, who was named after him.

The Prophet regains consciousness and climbs to higher ground. Abu 'Ubaydah ibn al-Jarrah examines the Prophet and uses his teeth to remove a few rings of chain mail embedded in the Prophet's cheek. As blood trickles down his face, the Prophet remarks:

> *"How can a people who cut the face of their Prophet and broke his teeth—he who calls them to worship Allah—how can such people thrive or be successful?"*[19]

Remember that **Abu 'Ubaydah ibn al-Jarrah** was one of the earliest converts to Islam. He will lead one of four battalions at the Conquest of Mecca, and will later be nominated by Abu Bakr to be the first Caliph. He is one of the 10 Companions to whom the Prophet promises Paradise.

Then after a brief pause, he adds:

> *"My Lord, forgive my people for they have no knowledge."*[20]

Malik ibn Sinan sucks the Prophet's blood to stop the bleeding. To Malik's great joy, the Prophet informs him:

"Whose blood hath touched my blood, him the fire cannot reach."[21]

No sooner does morale plummet, than Ka'b ibn Malik announce that the Prophet is still alive. Upon hearing the news, Ubayy ibn Khalaf charges in the Prophet's direction screaming:

"Where is Muhammad? Either I kill him or I will be killed."[22]

The Prophet emerges from the ring of Companions surrounding him and accepts Ubayy's challenge:

He shook himself clear of them as if they had been no more than flies on a camel's back. Then he took a spear from Harith ibn as-Simmah and stepped in front of them all. Not daring to move, they looked on in awe at his grim and deadly earnestness. As one of them said: 'When the Messenger of God made a deliberate effort toward some end, there was no earnestness that could compare with his.' Ubayy approached with drawn sword, but before he could strike a blow the Prophet had thrust him in the neck.[23]

Although severely weakened by his own injuries from the battlefield, Talhah carries the wounded Prophet up to a safe vantage point. The Prophet is too weak to stand on his own and leads the noon prayer seated with his Companions seated behind him. From the safety of their elevated position, the men rest as the battle dies down.

Malik ibn Sinan was one of the men who supported attacking the enemy at Uhud. A few days after returning from the battle, he dies from his wounds and is buried in Medina. But the Prophet insists that his body be exhumed and reburied at Uhud.

Several years later, after the Conquest of Mecca, **Ka'b ibn Malik** will stay behind when the Muslims march to Tabuk (QY 21.2). After 50 days of self-banishment, he will be absolved of his misjudgment (see Qur'an 9:118).

Recall that after Badr, **Ubayy ibn Khalaf** swore that he would kill the Prophet while riding his horse (QY 15.7).

16.7 THE AFTERMATH OF UHUD

The Quraysh bury their dead, while Hind and a few other Meccans walk through the strewn battlefield mutilating the bodies of the martyrs. When Abu 'Amir locates his son Hanzalah's body, he asks that it be spared from mutilation.

Abu Sufyan calls out to the Prophet, and challenges him to a third and final battle next year at Badr. When the Prophet accepts his challenge, Abu Sufyan acknowledges that the Quraysh have mutilated the bodies of many slain Muslims and admits that he neither condoned nor condemned their behavior.

Ironically, these were the 300 men who had deserted the Prophet under the direction of 'Abd Allah ibn Ubayy.

Before returning to Medina, the Prophet instructs Sa'd ibn Abi Waqqas to verify that the Meccans are, in fact, retreating south. To the Muslim's relief, the Quraysh decide to return straight away to Mecca because they heard that 300 fresh soldiers are waiting to defend Medina.

When the Prophet finally descends to the battlefield, he is angered at the sight of the mutilated bodies and vows to mutilate 30 bodies at the next battle. Surah An-Nahl, however, warns him against senseless retribution, and from then on, the Prophet strictly forbids the practice altogether.

> If you can bring consequences against them, don't bring any consequences against them that are worse than what you've suffered. However, if you persevere patiently instead (and suppress the urge to retaliate), then that's the best for those who are patient. — *An-Nahl (The Bee, 16:126)*

---

7 HOW WAS THE QUR'AN REVERSING THE TRADITION OF RETALIATION? `ASLAN`

"While retribution was maintained as a legitimate response to injury, Muhammad urged believers toward forgiveness: 'The retribution for an injury is an equal injury, but those who forgive the injury and make reconciliation will be rewarded by God' (Qur'an 42:40). … a stark reversal of tribal tradition and a clear indication that Muhammad was already beginning to lay the foundations of a society built on moral rather than utilitarian principles."[24]

Recall that **Khaythamah Abu Sa'd** was one of the men who persuaded the Prophet to march out to Uhud so that he could be martyred and join his son in Paradise, as he saw in his dream.

Just a few months ago **Thabit ibn-ad-Dahdahah** had traded an orchard of palm trees for Abu Lubabah's single tree in order to give it to an orphan. After Thabit's death, the Prophet remarked, *"Palms with low-hanging heavy-laden clusters, with a multitude of these hath the son of Dahdahah in Paradise!"*[49]

The losses at Uhud include 22 of 3,000 Meccans and 70 of 700 from Medina (65 Helpers, 4 Emigrants, and 1 Jew). The martyred include Hamzah ibn 'Abd al-Muttalib, 'Abd Allah ibn Jahsh, Hanzalah ibn Abi 'Amir, Khaythamah Abu Sa'd, Mus'ab ibn 'Umayr, and Thabit ibn ad-Dahdahah. Per his father's wishes, Hanzalah's body remains untouched on the battlefield, and the Prophet confirms that his body had, in fact, been washed by angels:

> None passed him [Hanzalah] by who did not give thanks, for in his beauty and his peace he was as a sign from Heaven, to inform the bereaved of the present state of their martyred kinsmen.[25]

The tragic loss of some of the community's most valuable supporters comes as a shock to the Muslims. The Prophet is particularly moved by the casualties and laments:

> *"Would that I had been left abandoned with my Companions at the mountain's foot!"*[26]

8 WHO WON THE BATTLE OF UHUD? [WATT]

"In trying to make an assessment of the battle of Uhud the first question to ask is the purely military one: who won the battle? Who had the advantage in it? Some Western scholars, not without justification from the early Muslim accounts, have thought that it was a very serious defeat for the Muslims and a great victory for the Meccans. From the military standpoint this view is mistaken. The strategic aim of the Meccans was nothing less than the destruction of the Muslim community as such, or—what amounts to the same thing the removal of Muhammad from his position of influence in Medina. This aim they completely failed to achieve … What humiliation for the proud merchant princes of Mecca! It was an intimation that the end of their commercial empire was at hand…

For Muhammad, on the other hand, the purely military result of the battle was not wholly unsatisfactory. The Muslims had shown themselves almost equal to the Meccans. Their infantry was more than a match for their opponents. The Muslim casualties were mostly due to the enemy cavalry, and the Muslims were still too poor to have a cavalry squadron of their own. Despite this weakness, however, Muhammad had managed to hold his own against the Meccans, and that was all he needed to do at the moment."[27]

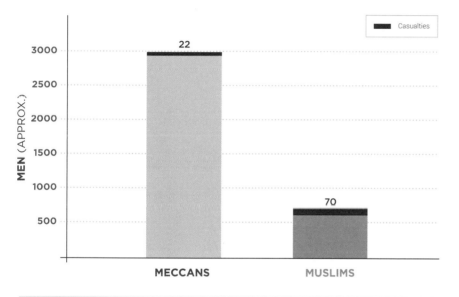

NOTABLE MECCANS KILLED AT UHUD	NOTABLE MUSLIMS KILLED AT UHUD
1. Ubayy ibn Khalaf	1. Hamzah ibn 'Abd al-Muttalib^
2. Talhah ibn 'Abd Allah	2. 'Abd Allah ibn Jahsh*
	3. Mus'ab ibn 'Umayr*
	4. Khaythamah Abu Sa'd
	5. Thabit ibn ad-Dahdahah
	6. Hanzalah ibn Abi 'Amir
	7. 'Abd Allah ibn Jubayr (along with 9 other archers)

Men of Quraysh

FIGURE 16E. LOSSES AT UHUD

A man from Aws named Usayrim ibn Thabit is also found slain on the battlefield. Usayrim had embraced Islam that morning and quickly becomes known as the man who entered Paradise without having prayed a single prayer. Mukhayriq, a rabbi from the Jewish clan of Tha'labah, is also found among the dead. Mukhayriq urged his people to keep their covenant with the Prophet, but they refused. He set off for Uhud, after authorizing all his property to the Messenger if Mukhayriq did not return. After seeing Mukhayriq's body on the battlefield, the Prophet eulogizes him as "the best of the Jews."

When the women approach the frontlines, the Prophet's aunt, Safiyyah, beholds her brother Hamzah's mutilated body and that of her nephew, 'Abd Allah ibn Jahsh. The Prophet escorts Fatimah to the battlefield and together with Safiyyah, they weep over their loved ones. They are soon joined by Hamnah bint Jahsh, who learns that she has just lost her husband (Mus'ab ibn 'Umayr), brother ('Abd Allah ibn Jahsh), and uncle (Hamzah) in a single day.

---

9 **HOW IS UHUD A LESSON IN FRAGILITY?** `RAMADAN`

"Just as there was no room for fatalism in revealed teachings, there was no room either for the airy optimism that their path would be easy just because they struggled for God's sake. On the contrary, faith required additional rigors in terms of respect for the principles, additional feeling in human relations, and additional caution about the risk of complacency. Uhud had been that lesson in fragility..."[28]

The families of the deceased find comfort in the recently revealed verses of Surah Al Baqarah:

> All you who believe! Seek courage with perseverance and prayer, for God is with the persevering. Don't say that those who've been killed in the path of God are dead. No, they're living (in the next realm), though you might not perceive it.
>
> Be sure that We're going to test you in some things like fear, hunger and loss of wealth and self, and also in the fruits (of your labor), but give good news to those who patiently persevere, who say, when stricken with adversity: "To God we belong, and to Him we return."
>
> The prayers and mercy of their Lord are upon them, and they're the ones who are truly guided. — *Al Baqarah (The Cow, 2:153-157)*

Recall that the Prophet had entrusted **Mus'ab ibn 'Umayr** with the monumental task of preparing Yathrib for his arrival in the year before the Hijrah. Mus'ab was from the clan of 'Abd ad-Dar and was given one of the three banners to carry at Badr and Uhud.

The Prophet prays over each martyr, 70 in all, and they are buried together in twos and threes. Hamzah is laid to rest with his nephew, 'Abd Allah ibn Jahsh. After lowering Mus'ab in his grave, the Prophet recites from Surah Al Ahzab:

> There are some men from among the faithful who've been true to their promise with God. Some have completed their oath (by sacrificing their lives in God's cause), while others are still waiting (to prove themselves), and they've never swerved (in their determination) at all.
> — *Al Ahzab (The Allied Forces, 33:23)*

The heavy losses at Uhud bring another unforeseen challenge to the community—with the death of so many husbands and fathers, how would the Muslim community ensure the welfare of its widows and orphans? Surah An-Nisa hints at a solution:

> If any of you (men) fear that you might not be able to treat orphaned (women) with justice, (by being tempted to marry them for their money while they have no guardian to look after their interests), then marry (other) women of your choice, up to two, three, or four.
>
> If you're afraid that you might not be able to treat (multiple wives) equally, then marry only one (woman) or (marry a maid-servant) who is under your authority. This will help keep you from committing injustice.
> — *An-Nisa (The Women, 4:3)*

---

10 WHY DID MEDINA NEED POLYGAMY?   ASLAN

"Essentially, while the individual believer was to strive for monogamy, the community that Muhammad was trying to build in Yathrib would have been doomed without polygyny." (Polygyny is the practice of having more than one wife.)[29]

---

11 POLYGAMY: RIGHT OR RESPONSIBILITY?   ARMSTRONG

"The institution of polygamy has been much criticized as the source of considerable suffering for Muslim women, but at the time of this revelation it constituted a social advance. In the pre-Islamic period, both men and women were allowed several spouses. After marriage, a woman remained at the home of her family, and was visited by all her 'husbands.' It was, in effect, a form of licensed prostitution. Paternity was, therefore, uncertain, so children were usually identified as the descendants of their mothers. Men did not need to provide for their wives and took no responsibility for their offspring. But Arabia was in transition.
The Qur'anic institution of polygamy was a piece of social legislation. It was designed not to gratify the male sexual appetite, but to correct the injustices done to widows, orphans, and other female dependents, who were especially vulnerable. All too often, unscrupulous people seized everything and left the weaker members of the family with nothing. They were often sexually abused by their male guardians or converted into a financial asset by being sold into slavery … The Qur'an bluntly refutes this behavior and takes it for granted that a woman has an inalienable right to her inheritance. Polygamy was designed to ensure that unprotected women would be decently married, and to abolish the old loose, irresponsible liaisons; men could only have four wives and must treat them equitably; it was an unjustifiably wicked act to devour their property…
In a society of scarcity, it took courage and compassion to take financial responsibility for four women and their children … Muhammad led the way."[30]

---

12 WHAT WAS THE MALE RESPONSE TO THE ENHANCED RIGHTS OF WOMEN?   ASLAN

"Women in the Ummah were, for the first time, given the right both to inherit the property of their husbands and to keep their dowries as their own personal property throughout their marriage … As one would expect, Muhammad's innovations did not sit well with the male members of his community … If Muhammad's male followers were disgruntled about the new inheritance laws, they must have been furious when, in a single revolutionary move, he both limited how many wives a man could marry and granted women the right to divorce their husbands."[31]

The Qur'an's recommendation aims squarely at protecting and preserving the rights of the wives and daughters who lost their guardians at Uhud:

> It has commonly been held in Christendom that the distinctive feature of Islamic marriage is the permission to have four wives. The practice is based on a curious verse of the Qur'an (4. 3) …
>
> The interesting point is that the verse is not placing a limit on a previous practice of unlimited polygyny. It is not saying to men who had had six or ten wives "You shall not marry more than four." On the contrary it is encouraging men who had had only one wife (or perhaps two) to marry up to four. It is not the restriction of an old practice but the introduction of something new …
>
> Such a view is in harmony with the traditional account that the verse about plurality of wives was revealed shortly after the battle of Uhud. In that battle some seventy Muslims, mostly Medinans, were killed, so that the number of widows for whom the Islamic community had to care must have been considerable. It was doubtless in order to meet this sudden increase in the number of unattached women that encouragement was given to polygyny. It has also to be noted, however, that the Qur'an connects the matter with just conduct towards orphans (yatama). This suggests that the crux of the problem of excess women was not the widows but the unmarried girls who now came under the guardianship of uncles, cousins, and other kinsmen. With some hints from the sources, we can imagine the treatment women and girls might receive from selfish and unsympathetic guardians; they would be kept unmarried so that the guardian could have unrestricted control of their property, and it would be difficult for them to obtain legal redress against their legal protectors. The matter would be specially irksome in matrilineal Medina if, as seems likely, guardianship now went in the male line. This, then, is the situation the Qur'an tries to meet by encouraging polygyny. It probably did not intend that the guardians should themselves marry their wards, though, where the wards were outside the forbidden degrees, this would be possible. The idea seems rather to be that, if the Muslims generally adopt polygyny, it will be possible for all girls to be properly married as soon as they reach marriageable age.[32]

---

13 HOW WAS THE PROPHET ADVANCING WOMEN'S RIGHTS IN MATRILINEAL ARABIA?   WATT

"We conclude, then, that virilocal polygyny [multiple wives living together with their husband], or the multiple virilocal family, which for long was the distinctive feature of Islamic society in the eyes of Christendom, was an innovation of Muhammad's. There may have been some instances of it before his time, but it was not widespread, and it was particularly foreign to the outlook of the Medinans. It remedied some of the abuses due to the growth of individualism. It provided honourable marriage for the excess women, and checked the oppression of women by their guardians; and it thereby lessened the temptation to enter into the loose unions allowed in the matrilineal society of Arabia. In view of some of the practices hitherto current, this reform must be regarded as an important advance in social organization."[33]

16.8 THE CHASE TO RAWHA

After returning home, the Prophet falls into a deep sleep and misses the call for the congregational night prayer. In the morning, he announces that only those who fought at Uhud may chase after the Quraysh, who have retreated to the nearby settlement of Rawha. Surah An-Nisa explains:

> Don't hesitate in pursuing the enemy. If you're suffering from hardship, (know that) they're suffering similar hardships, too. (Remember that) you have hope in God, while they have hope in nothing. God is full of knowledge and wisdom. — *An-Nisa (The Women, 4:104)*

The Muslims strategically set up a vast array of campfires near the enemy camp, giving the impression that a much larger army is approaching. The strategy works and the Quraysh quickly pack up their belongings and flee back to Mecca. However, before leaving, Abu Sufyan threatens the Prophet that he will return to wipe out the Muslims. To this the Prophet simply replies:

> God is enough for us, and He's the most favorable (One upon Whom) to rely. — *Ali 'Imran (The Family of Amran, 3:173)*

16.9 SURAH ALI 'IMRAN & REFLECTIONS ON UHUD

The Prophet returns to Medina to find that Shammas ibn 'Uthman and Malik ibn Sinan have died from their injuries (both men had fought at Uhud, but were too injured to chase the Quraysh the next day). The Prophet instructs the Companions to take the bodies back to Uhud and bury them alongside the other martyrs.

Meanwhile, 'Abd Allah ibn Ubayy rebukes his son 'Abd Allah for not listening to him and fighting alongside the Prophet at Uhud. He in turn is scolded by several Companions at the following Friday prayer, and the public humiliation compels 'Abd Allah ibn Ubayy to walk out of the congregation.

Nevertheless, the stark contrast between Badr and Uhud leaves many Companions rattled. A number of Jews in Yathrib quickly voice their opinion that the heavy losses at Uhud combined with the Prophet's own injuries are a sign of Muhammad's failure as a prophet. 'Umar is infuriated by the remarks, but the Prophet strictly forbids him from retaliating. Instead, he reassures 'Umar that they are, in fact, destined to win Mecca.

Malik ibn Sinan was one of the men who supported attacking the enemy at Uhud and later helped stop the bleeding from the Prophet's cheek.

Soon after Uhud, the Prophet receives several verses from Surah Ali 'Imran that examine the hearts of those who were martyred and those who disobeyed the Prophet in battle. Part of the expiation of the latter, the surah explains, is their remorse upon hearing the rumor that the Prophet had been slain.

God was certainly fulfilling His promise when, by His leave, you were about to vanquish your foes (at the Battle of Uhud), but then you flinched and argued over your orders (to guard the mountain pass). You disobeyed (the Prophet's orders) after (God) showed you (the war-prizes) that you coveted.

Some among you desired the things of this world, while others desired the next life. He allowed you to be distracted from your enemy so He could test you (in order to discipline you, and even though you failed in your duty), He's forgiven you, for God is limitless in His favor towards those who believe.

When you were scrambling up the slopes (of Mount Uhud in full retreat), not even noticing those around you, the Messenger was behind you, calling you to come back (and face the enemy, but you ignored him). So God brought the disappointment (of shame) upon you, even as you disappointed (the Prophet by running away from him.

This added shame) befell you so that you wouldn't feel bad only for the (war-prizes) you missed, but also for what you suffered, as well, and God is well-informed of all that you do.

Then, after this time of distress, He allowed a feeling of peace and confidence to descend upon a group of you. Even still, another faction (of your people) took to venting their frustrations and spoke out against God, thinking thoughts of pagan ignorance, saying, "Don't we have any say in the matter?"

Say to them, "Surely every command belongs to God." They try to hide their lack of conviction from you by lamenting, "If only we were in charge, there would've been far fewer casualties (from the battle)."

Say to them, "Even if you had remained in your homes (within the city of Medina, like you had wanted from the beginning), those whose time it was to die would still have gone forth to their place of death." This was merely (a test) so God could show your true feelings and purge (any impurities) in your hearts, for He knows the secrets of the mind.

Those who deserted (their posts on the battlefield) on the day the two armies clashed (at Uhud) were made to fail by Satan, (who had some influence over them) because of some (sins) they had earned before. However, God forgave them, for God is forgiving and forbearing. — *Ali 'Imran (The Family of Amran, 3:152-155)*

14 **WHAT CAN WE LEARN FROM THE PROPHET'S TREATMENT OF HIS COMPANIONS AFTER UHUD?**   RAMADAN

"The Prophet had remained composed and understanding towards the Companions who had been carried away by their desire for wealth and had disobeyed him. Revelation relates the event and confirms ... the constant blending of respect for the principles and the strength of gentleness in the Prophet's personality.

'It was by the mercy of God that you were lenient [gentle] with them, for if you had been severe or harsh-hearted, they would have broken away from about you. So pardon them and ask for God's forgiveness for them; and consult them upon the conduct of affairs. Then, when you have taken a decision, put your trust in God. For God loves those who put their trust in Him. [Qur'an 3:159]'

The Quran here confirms the principle of shura, consultation, whatever the result: this Revelation is of crucial importance and states that the principle of deliberation, of majority decision making, is not to be negotiated and must be respected beyond historical contingencies and human mistakes in decisions ... that principle must remain even though the ways in which it is implemented cannot fail to change over time and from place to place.

He was never brutal nor stern, and he did not condemn them for being carried away by the reflexive greed stemming from their past customs. His gentleness soothed their pain and enabled them to draw many lessons from that setback."[34]

The surah continues, foretelling that the established order will soon pass away:

Many ways of life have passed away before your time. So travel all over the world, and see how those (former civilizations) that denied (the truth) came to an end. This is a clear lesson for people and also a source of guidance and admonition for those who are mindful (of God).

Don't lose hope or get despondent, for you must triumph, that is if you really believe. Indeed, if you're injured, know that others have been injured likewise. We alternate days (of triumph and defeat) among (nations) so that God can make known those who believe and also so that He can take for Himself martyrs from among you.

God has no love for oppressors, (and He may use other nations to keep them in check). Even further, God (uses such setbacks) as a way to purge the believers (of any impurities) and to erase the gains of those who suppress (their awareness of the truth). — *Ali 'Imran (The Family of Amran, 3:137-141)*

13

14

15

16

17

18

Unlike Medina's prior victories, Uhud leaves the Muslim community in a state of confusion and unease:

> Yet if the battle of Uhud was not a military defeat for Muhammad, it might almost be called a spiritual defeat ... Because of this intellectual context in which it took place the battle had a devastating effect on most of the Muslims. If Badr was a sign of God's favour, were their casualties at Uhud a sign of his disfavour? Or was he completely neutral with regard to them? The average Muslim must have been seriously troubled by such thoughts.

> The Qur'an gives some indications of how the problem was dealt with. The chief point was to explain how God, without abandoning the Muslims, could allow such misfortunes to befall them ... It was solved by placing the blame on the Muslims themselves ... In other words, the misfortunes of the Muslims at Uhud were permitted by God, partly as a punishment for disobedience and partly as a test of their steadfastness.[35]

Ali 'Imran ends with a succinct explanation of Uhud—it is a test of faith, not just between the Muslims and the Quraysh, but within each Muslim as well.

> God won't leave the believers in the (weak) position that they're now in until He separates what is filthy from what is wholesome, nor will God give you insight into what is beyond human perception. Rather, He chooses from among His messengers as He wills (and assigns each his own level of success). So believe in God and His Messenger, for if you believe and remain mindful (of your duty to God), then this will secure for you a valuable reward.
> —*Ali 'Imran (The Family of Amran, 3:179)*

---

15 QUALITY VERSUS QUANTITY: WHAT WAS THE DOWNFALL AT UHUD?   WATT

"And this decline in the military qualities of the Muslims is no doubt connected with their increase in numbers. During the past year Muhammad had been aware that he would need a far larger force than that at Badr, and he had not turned away men attracted to Islam by prospects of booty. Because of this there was serious indiscipline at Uhud and lack of steadfastness not merely among the archers but in various other ways. This was therefore the point on which he had to concentrate as he prepared for the next round of the struggle."[36]

16.10 THE ATTACK AT RAJI

The northwest Arabian *tribe* of Asad should not be confused with the Quraysh *clan* of Asad—the clan of Khadijah and Zubayr ibn al-'Awwam. Make sure to read Lings (p. 200) for a stirring account of this incident.

Shortly after Uhud, the Prophet sends out 150 men to disperse the tribe of Asad, which had been planning an imminent attack on Medina. He then sends a second campaign led by 'Abd Allah ibn Unays to kill the leader of Bani Hudayl who had been fomenting hostilities toward Medina. In retaliation, the men of Bani Hudayl attack six wayfaring Muslims at Raji near Mecca, killing all but two—Khubayb ibn 'Adi of Aws and Zayd ibn ad-Dathinnah of Khazraj—whom they sell to the Quraysh. Tortured and near death, Khubayb tells his captors that he would not want so much as a thorn hurting the Messenger if he could have it himself. With his last breath, he sends a message of peace to the Prophet. To the Meccan's astonishment, when Zayd is prepared for execution, he reiterates Khubayb's response as well. The Quraysh witness the dramatic scene in wonderment, and Akhnas ibn Shariq later acknowledges:

Although **Akhnas ibn Shariq** had declined to protect the Prophet when the Prophet returned from Ta'if, he later persuaded his entire clan of Zuhrah not to fight the Muslims at Badr, and instead return to Mecca.

"No father so loveth his son as the companions of Muhammad love Muhammad."[37]

16.11 THE MA'UNAH AMBUSH

After the Battle of Uhud, the Prophet marries Zaynab bint Khuzaymah, the widow of 'Ubaydah ibn al-Harith. Zaynab is from the Hawazin clan of 'Amir, and after the marriage, the chief of Zaynab's clan, Abu Bara ibn Malik, invites the Prophet to send teachers to his people. Forty men answer the call, but 38 are slaughtered at Ma'unah by the neighboring Hawazin clan of Bani Sulaym. Abu Bara's power-hungry nephew had instigated the Bani Sulaym to attack the travelers after failing to find support in his own clan for the offensive. One of the two men who survive the initial onslaught, Harith ibn as-Simmah, insists on fighting the attackers, and kills four before he is slain. The other, 'Amr ibn Umayyah ad-Damri, is left to identify the bodies of his companions. To his surprise, 'Amir ibn Fuhayrah is among those killed, but his body is not found. 'Amir's attacker, Jabbar, relates how 'Amir declared victory when Jabbar's spear pierced his chest. Then 'Amir's body was lifted in the air and carried away. The miraculous incident spurs Jabbar and many of his tribesmen (who had attacked the Muslim envoy) to enter Islam.

When 'Amr ibn Umayyah is released, he is misled to believe that the attack was instigated by Bani 'Amir, not Bani Sulaym. On his way back to Medina, he tries to avenge the deaths of his companions by killing two men from Bani 'Amir. When the Prophet hears the news, he insists that blood money be paid to the innocent victims' families.

Recall that **Zaynab's** husband, 'Ubaydah ibn al-Harith, was the Prophet's first-cousin and the oldest man to fight at the opening duels at Badr where he was martyred. His brother Abu Sufyan took the opposite stance to Islam.

Be sure to read Lings (p. 202) for a rich narrative of the Ma'unah ambush. Recall that **'Amir ibn Fuhayrah** was a slave freed by Abu Bakr. He helped the Prophet and Abu Bakr escape Mecca by following them with his flock of sheep to cover their tracks. After the Ma'unah ambush, the Prophet will confirm Jabbar's observation that 'Amir had been raised to Heaven. (Of note, Al-Mubarakpuri notes that 70 Companions were killed at Ma'unah.)

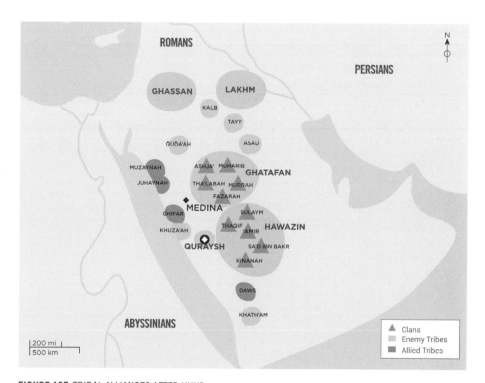

FIGURE 16F. TRIBAL ALLIANCES AFTER UHUD

The Battle of Uhud left the Muslim community in a state of confusion and uncertainty. Shortly thereafter, the Prophet sent out a force of 150 men to disperse another hostile group—this time the northeast tribe of Asad—that was planning to attack Medina. To the southeast, the Prophet formed an alliance with the Hawazin clan of 'Amir through his marriage to Zaynab bint Khuzaymah. Unlike 'Amir, the rest of the Hawazin clans remained hostile to Medina and joined the Quraysh one year later at the Battle of the Trench. Bani Daws and Ghifar had preexisting alliances with Medina through the early conversions of Tufayl ibn 'Amr and Abu Dharr ibn Junadah (QY 10.5) while the coastal tribes of Juhaynah and Muzaynah had allied themselves with Medina after the Battle of Badr.

16.12 THE EXPULSION OF BANI NADIR

Because the Bani Nadir had a preexisting alliance with Bani ʿAmir, the Prophet requests their assistance in paying blood money for the two men killed by ʿAmr ibn Umayyah.

They ostensibly agree to the Prophet's request and invite him and his Companions to dinner. Shortly after being seated, the Prophet receives inspiration that his hosts are planning to kill him by dropping a stone on his head. He immediately leaves the gathering and Abu Bakr and the other Companions leave shortly thereafter.

---

16 WHY PAY BANI ʿAMIR BLOOD MONEY?   `RAMADAN`

"The Banu ʿAmir had been faithful to Abu Bara's pledges and were therefore not responsible for his men's death; the Prophet, scrupulously respectful of the terms of his pacts, immediately decided that blood money must be paid for the two men whom ʿAmr had mistakenly killed."[38]

- -

17 WHY WAS THE PROPHET CAUTIOUS OF BANI NADIR?   `RAMADAN`

"Muhammad knew that since the Banu Qaynuqa's forced exile, the Banu Nadir had become suspicious, if not hostile to him, and that they had established ties with tribes hostile to the Muslims. He was therefore extremely cautious."[39]

This was not the first time **Muhammad ibn Maslamah** was involved with Bani Nadir. Recall that after Badr, he volunteered to assassinate their poet, Kaʿb ibn Ashraf. At the Conquest of Mecca, he will lead the Prophet's camel as they circle the Kaʿbah.

Soon after the incident, the Prophet sends Muhammad ibn Maslamah back to Bani Nadir conveying details of their assassination plot. For the crime of treason, the entire clan is given 10 days to leave the city.

Following ʿAbd Allah ibn Ubayy's advice, the Bani Nadir refuse to leave, and instead reach out to their old allies: Qurayzah and Ghatafan. To their dismay, their Jewish brethren refuse to break their pact with the Prophet and the Ghatafan do not bother to answer their call.

Meanwhile, the Prophet sends ʿAli with a group of men to surround the Jewish settlement. After a 10-day stand-off, the Prophet orders his Companions to send a message to Nadir by cutting down a few of their prized palm trees. Bani Nadir take the threat seriously and ask the Prophet to spare their crops. They give word that they will leave, anticipating the day they will return to their orchards once the Quraysh defeat the Prophet.

♦ **SURAH AL HASHR** (The Gathering) is a relatively short Medinan chapter named after its second verse, which mentions the gathering and exile of the Jewish clan of Bani Nadir. The last three verses provide a powerful summation of 15 divine attributes.

> Whether you had cut the palm trees or let them stand firmly, it was all by the will of God, (though He commanded them to be cut) so that the rebels could be disgraced. — *Al Hashr (The Gathering, 59:5)*

According to the new terms of their expulsion, Bani Nadir is only allowed to leave Medina with whatever their camels can carry—everything, that is, except their arms and armor. With Medina fading in the distance, Huyay ibn Akhtab leads his people to the northern Jewish stronghold of Khaybar.

18 THE EXPULSION OF BANI NADIR WATT

"Such an ultimatum seems out of proportion to the offence, or rather to the apparently flimsy grounds for supposing that treachery was meditated. Yet perhaps the grounds were not so flimsy as they appear at first sight to the Westerner of today. Both parties knew how some Muslims had treated Ka'b b. al-Ashraf, and, in accordance with the ideas of the Arabia of that day, Muhammad was bound to expect that, if he gave his opponents an opportunity, they would kill him. An-Nadir's postponement of a reply created such an opportunity, and was therefore tantamount to a hostile act.

... The expulsion of an-Nadir from Medina was not the end of their dealings with Muhammad. From Khaybar some of them continued to intrigue assiduously against Medina, and they played a considerable part in the formation of the great confederacy to besiege Medina in April 627."[40]

19 THE EXPULSION OF BANI NADIR ARMSTRONG

"In the space of two short years, Muhammad had expelled two powerful tribes from Medina, and the Muslims now managed the market vacated by Qaynuqa'. As we have seen, this was not Muhammad's intention. He had wanted to cut the cycle of violence and dispossession, not continue it. Muhammad had shown that he was still a man to be reckoned with, but he must also have reflected on the moral and political sterility of this type of success, because Nadir remained just as much of a threat in nearby Khaybar."[41]

20 THE EXPULSION OF BANI NADIR ASLAN

"The Nadir had no choice but to surrender to Muhammad, but only on the condition that they be given the same opportunity as Banu Qaynuqa to lay down their arms and leave Medina in peace. Again, to the utter disgust of his followers, many of whom had been seriously wounded in the battle, Muhammad agreed."[42]

21 HOW DID SOME OF THE PROPHET'S ENEMIES REPAY HIM FOR HIS LENIENCY? RAMADAN

"Muhammad had always been generous and lenient after battles, despite his enemies' betrayals and ungratefulness; he had found some of the captives he had spared after Badr among his fiercest enemies at Uhud. The same thing would happen this time too: several months after allowing the Banu Nadir to flee, he would find some of the tribe's leaders ... were to join against him."[43]

13
14
15
16
17
18

After settling in the northern city of Khaybar, **Bani Nadir** will continue to rally support against the Prophet and join the enemy forces that besiege Medina during the Battle of the Trench (QY 18.1). One year later, after Hudaybiyah, the Prophet will march with 1,600 men to surround the city and force the inhabitants of Khaybar to sign a treaty of surrender (QY 19.8).

After Bani Nadir's expulsion to Khaybar, the tribe's land is allotted to Emigrants to relieve the financial burden placed on the Helpers who had been supporting them since the Hijrah. Surah Al Hashr explains the transaction:

> (Also distribute something) to the poor refugees (from Mecca) who were driven from their homes and deprived of their properties in their pursuit of the grace and pleasure of God, and also because they were helping God and His Messenger. They were sincere (in their intentions).
>
> Those who already had homes here (in Medina) and who believed (in Islam), extended their heartfelt hospitality to those (Meccan refugees) who came to them seeking a safe haven. They're not inwardly jealous of the portions (that the refugees) are receiving.
>
> And even though they might be needy themselves, they give preference to others first. Whoever is saved from the greed of his own soul will be successful. —*Al Hashr (The Gathering, 59:8-9)*

---

22 **WHAT WAS THE ECONOMIC REALITY OF EMIGRANTS IN MEDINA?** ASLAN

"The problem is that the Companions [Emigrants] … are primarily traders and merchants, but Yathrib is not a city built on trade; Yathrib is not a city at all. It is a loose federation of villages inhabited by farmers and orchardists, tillers of the earth. It is nothing like the bustling, prosperous city the Emigrants left behind. Even if they could transform themselves from traders to farmers, all the best agricultural lands in Yathrib are already occupied."[44]

23 **WHAT DID THE DISTRIBUTION OF NADIR'S WEALTH SAY ABOUT ISLAMIC ECONOMIC THEORY?** SALAHI

"This type of gain is known in Islamic terminology as fay'. The established principle is that fay' belongs to the Muslim state. The way it is shared out is explained in the Qur'an (59: 7) …
The Qur'anic verse also establishes a far-reaching rule of the Islamic economic and social system: the rule which makes it absolutely clear that wealth must not be confined only to the rich. Islam allows private ownership as legitimate but qualifies it with this rule, which makes it clear that the poor have a claim to a share in the wealth of the community. Hence, any situation or system that results in money being monopolized by the rich only, or any class of society, is not in line with the Islamic economic theory and system. Financial dealings and relations within Islamic society must be so organized as not to create such a situation, or allow it to continue if it happens to exist."[45]

YEAR 17: BADR 2

17.1 THE MORAL VICTORY AT BADR

Nearly a year has passed since Uhud, and a drought in Mecca has left the Quraysh unwilling and unprepared to fight a rematch at Badr. The situation in Medina, however, is quite the opposite:

> Muhammad was able to attract military support because his was a religious movement and because he was being carried forward in the stream of emergent social forces. The Meccans, on the other hand, were attempting to retain a position of privilege that was no longer appropriate in the new circumstances. How was each side going to fare in the months ahead?[1]

Hoping to preserve his reputation by intimidating the Prophet, Abu Sufyan sends Nu'aym ibn Mas'ud of Bani Ghatafan to Medina to spread a rumor that Mecca has amassed a great army and is preparing to march to Badr. The Prophet is unfazed and, after leaving 'Abd Allah ibn 'Ubayy's son, 'Abd Allah, in charge of Medina, he leads 1,500 men to the battlefield. When the Quraysh army does not show up, news of the Muslim victory quickly spreads throughout Arabia.

This is not the last time **Nu'aym ibn Mas'ud** will be involved in espionage. One year later, at the Battle of the Trench, Nu'aym will flee to the Prophet's side and spy against the Quraysh (QY 18.3).

 WHAT HAPPENED TO THE QURAYSH AFTER UHUD?   WATT

"Divided counsels made their appearance immediately after the battle of Uhud. Safwan's [ibn Umayyah] view of the situation was that the Meccans ought to be content with the success they had achieved and not endanger it, whereas 'Amr b. al-'As and Abu Sufyan thought they ought to drive home their advantage by attacking Medina. We might conjecture that Safwan was afraid that, as Abu Sufyan was supreme commander, a successful campaign might redound too much to the latter's glory. It is also possible, however, that Abu Sufyan was more of a statesman."[2]

17.2 THE GHATAFAN EXPEDITION & THE PRAYER OF FEAR

After returning from the second Badr expedition, the Prophet leads a preemptive strike against several hostile clans of Ghatafan that had been planning to attack Medina. Although no actual fighting takes place, the expeditions are inherently dangerous and Surah An-Nisa gives the Companions a much needed reprieve in the form of the prayer of fear:

> When you travel through the open countryside, it isn't wrong if you shorten your prayers out of the fear that the faithless might ambush you, for those who cover over (their ability to have faith) are clearly your enemies. —*An-Nisa (The Women, 4:101)*

 HOW DID THE MUSLIMS PERFORM THE PRAYER OF FEAR?   SALAHI

"This method means that the army is divided into two halves and they take turns as they pray with the Prophet. He himself would pray the whole prayer while one half of his men joined him for the first part of the prayers, then they would finish their prayers individually. When they had finished, the other half would join the Prophet for the rest of his prayers. Thus everyone in the army would have joined the same prayers while one half would always be free, watching the enemy and making sure that they did not exploit the time of prayers in order to attack the Muslims. This method of prayer is outlined in verse 102 of Surah 4, entitled Women."[3]

13
14
15
16
17
18

17.3 THE DUMAT AL-JANDAL EXPEDITION

After the Ghatafan expedition, the Prophet leads 1,000 men to Dumat al-Jandal (near the Syrian border) in a surprise move to break up a group of marauders from the northern tribe of Kalb and demonstrate the growing momentum of the Prophet's mission. It is a daring move and Surah Al Anfal explains the source of the Muslims' unity:

> He united the hearts of the believers (in brotherhood, even though they came from so many diverse backgrounds). Even if you spent everything on earth, you never could've produced that kind of heartfelt (unity by your own efforts), but God brought them together, for He is powerful and wise.
>
> — *Al Anfal (The Spoils of War, 8:63)*

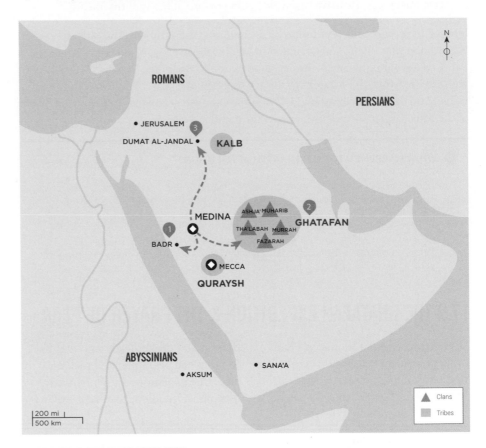

FIGURE 17A. EXPEDITIONS AFTER UHUD

The year after Uhud, the Muslims went on three separate military expeditions. The first was a rematch of Uhud that was supposed to take place at Badr. But the Quraysh never showed up and the Prophet was able to claim the victory. This was soon followed by expeditions to the hostile inland tribe of Ghatafan, followed by Bani Kalb (the tribe of Zayd ibn Harithah) near the city of Dumat al-Jandal. With little actual fighting, the three offensives broadcasted Medina's growing presence in Arabia.

17.4 UMM SALAMAH & ZAYNAB BINT JAHSH

Aside from the expeditions noted above, the year after Uhud is also marked by considerable changes in the Prophet's household. *Husayn* (little Hasan) is born to Fatimah and 'Ali. The delightful addition, however, is tempered by the death of Zaynab bint Khuzaymah—the Prophet's wife of fewer than eight months. Her passing is soon followed by the death of Abu Salamah, one of the Prophet's dearest cousins. Just before his death, Abu Salamah prayed that his wife would remarry to a man better than him. Four months later, the Prophet asks Abu Salamah's 29-year-old widow to join his household through marriage.

While 'A'ishah had no difficulty accepting Hafsah and Zaynab into the family, Umm Salamah's beauty becomes a source of mild jealousy for the Prophet's youngest wife.

---

3 **HOW DID UMM SALAMAH STAND OUT FROM THE OTHER WIVES?** ARMSTRONG

"Umm Salamah quickly became the spokesperson for Medina. Muhammad's living arrangements, which had physically positioned his wives at the epicenter of the community, had given Muslim women a new vision of their role ... Shortly after her marriage, a deputation of women asked her why they were mentioned so rarely in the Qur'an. Umm Salamah brought their questions to the Prophet ... A few days later she heard Muhammad reciting a revolutionary new surah in the mosque:

'Men and women who have surrendered,
Believing men and believing women
Obedient men and obedient women
Truthful men and truthful women
Enduring men and enduring women
[Men and women who are humble]
Men and women who give in charity
Men and women who fast,
Men and women who guard their private parts
Men and women who remember God oft—
For them God has prepared forgiveness
And a mighty wage.' [Qur'an 33:35]

In other words, there was to be complete sexual equality in Islam; both men and women had the same duties and responsibilities. When the women heard these verses, they were determined to make this vision a concrete reality in their daily lives. God seemed to be on their side.
...Qur'anic legislation insisted that the individual was free and sovereign—and that also applied to women."[4]

Abu Salamah was the son of the Prophet's aunt Barrah, and one of the Prophet's earliest supporters. He and his wife sought asylum in Abyssinia and later migrated to Medina after the death of Abu Talib. In fact, it is through **Umm Salamah bint Abi Umayyah** that many of the accounts of the Abyssinian migration have been narrated. Abu Salamah and Umm Salamah were always close to the Prophet's family. In fact, Umm Salamah and 'A'ishah both prepared Fatimah's wedding to 'Ali a few years ago. She will later accompany the Prophet to Hudaybiyah, Khaybar, and the Conquest of Mecca, where she serves as his trusted adviser.

Be sure to read Lings' description of the Prophet's role as a father, husband, adviser, and leader (p. 217-219).

With relative peace in Medina, the Prophet can focus on guiding his Companions on how to live a balanced and meaningful life. An ideal day, he teaches, should be broken into thirds: for work, worship, and family. The Prophet's daily routine includes playing with his grandsons Hasan and Husayn (through Fatimah), his granddaughter Umamah (through Zaynab), and his grandson Usamah (through Zayd). Despite his growing family responsibilities, the Prophet remains committed to serving the community and spending time with his Companions. In fact, not a day passes that he does not visit his closest friend, Abu Bakr.

---

4 WHY WAS FAMILY TIME SO IMPORTANT TO THE PROPHET? `RAMADAN`

"He was the example, the model, who lived among them and offered his love to them all, to the poor, to the old; he showed courteous regard for women and was attentive to children. He was a grandfather and would carry his children while praying in the mosque, thus conveying through his daily example that one cannot remember and be close to God without generosity and human attention."[5]

In light of the Prophet's many responsibilities as a messenger, statesman, commander, husband, father, and teacher, the Qur'an specifically grants him exclusive rights as God's prophet. In the year after Uhud, Surah Al Ahzab permits him to marry more than four wives—the limit given to other Muslims—and specifically instructs him to take Zaynab bint Jahsh's hand in marriage. Despite the social stigma attached to marrying the ex-wife of one's adopted son, the Prophet heeds the injunction and marries Zaynab four months after she divorces Zayd.

---

5 HOW DID THE PROPHET USE HIS MARRIAGES TO ADVANCE DIPLOMACY? `ASLAN`

"As Shaykh of the Ummah, it was Muhammad's responsibility to forge links within and beyond his community through the only means at his disposal: marriage. Thus, his unions with Aisha and Hafsah linked him to the two most important and influential leaders of the early Muslim community—to Abu Bakr and Umar, respectively. His marriage to Umm Salamah a year later forged an important relationship with one of Mecca's most powerful clans, the Makhzum. His union with Sawdah … served as an example to the Ummah to marry those women in need of financial support. His marriage to Rayhana, a Jew, linked him with the Banu Qurayza, while his marriage to Mariyah, a Christian and a Copt, created a significant political alliance with the ruler of Egypt.

While these scholars [who have defended Muhammad's marriages] should be commended for their work in debunking the bigoted and ignorant critiques of anti-Islamic preachers and pundits, the fact is that Muhammad needs no defense on this point.

Like the great Jewish patriarchs Abraham and Jacob, like the prophets Moses and Hosea, like the Israelite kings Saul, David, and Solomon; and like nearly all of the Christian/Byzantine and Zoroastrian/Sasanian monarchs, all Shaykhs in Arabia—Muhammad included—had either multiple wives, multiple concubines, or both. In seventh-century Arabia, a Shaykh's power and authority was in large part determined by the size of his harem. And while Muhammad's union with a nine-year-old girl may be shocking to our modern sensibilities, his betrothal to Aisha was just that: a betrothal. Aisha did not consummate her marriage to Muhammad until after reaching puberty, which is when every girl in Arabia without exception became eligible for marriage. The most shocking aspect of Muhammad's marriages is not his ten years of polygamy in Yathrib, but his twenty-five years of monogamy in Mecca, something practically unheard of at the time."[6]

"And (Muhammad, when Zayd wanted to divorce his wife Zaynab,) you had said to (your adopted son Zayd, a man) who had received God's grace and your favor, "Stay (married) to your wife and be mindful of God.""

However, you were hiding something in your heart that God was about to disclose. You were afraid of (what) people (would think if you were to marry the woman that Zayd divorced, but it's more appropriate) for you to fear God.

Then, after Zayd dissolved (his marriage) to her, following all the proper procedures, We joined her in marriage to you, so that there wouldn't be any more (confusion) among the faithful about (the permissibility) of marrying the ex-spouses of their adopted children, after all the proper procedures (of divorce) have been followed, for God's command must be fulfilled.

There shouldn't be any obstacles for the Prophet in discharging the duty that God has laid upon him. This principle of God was practiced by those who passed before, and the command of God is an irresistible decree.

— *Al Ahzab (The Allied Forces, 33:37-38)*

SURAH AL AHZAB (The Allied Forces) is named after its detailed description of the allied enemy tribes that descended on Medina for one final assault on the city (QY 18). Among other issues, the surah contains several verses that discuss family law, the rights of adopted children, and the special privileges of the Prophet and his wives.

---

6 **WAS THE PROPHET HIDING HIS LOVE FOR ZAYNAB OR HIS HESITANCE TO MARRY HER?** [SALAHI]

"Despite these clear statements by God [33:37], the enemies of Islam continued to spread rumours and make false accusations. One of the most stupid of their accusations is the one which claims that the Prophet was in love with Zaynab and tried to hide his love. When it was known, it is so claimed, he felt he should marry her. Those who maintain such an indefensible view also claim that the Qur'anic verse quoted above criticizes the Prophet for suppressing his feelings towards Zaynab. Such claims are self-contradictory, to say the least. Who could have prevented the Prophet from marrying Zaynab, his own cousin who was a devout Muslim? It was he who asked her to marry Zayd against her own wishes. He also tried repeatedly to comfort her so that she would be satisfied with her marriage. Moreover, the claim that the Prophet is criticized for not making his love to Zaynab known to people cannot stand any analysis. Suppose that a man falls in love with another man's wife — is he morally bound to speak of that love in public? Would God criticize a man who could not help his feelings if he suppressed such a love and kept it to himself? Would he be better rewarded if he were to write some love poems expressing his feelings? It is this kind of ludicrous interpretation that is advanced as the meaning of the Qur'anic verse. The Qur'anic statement admits only the incidents just related. The Prophet is being told by God that he also cannot delay the implementation of God's orders. He need not feel any worry about breaking former social traditions when he has received God's instructions to do so, for God's will must be done. Hence, the Prophet had no option but to proceed with this marriage. When Zayd divorced his wife and she had completed her waiting period, the Prophet asked Zayd to go over to Zaynab and propose to her on his behalf ... Then the Qur'anic verse which speaks of this marriage was revealed and the Prophet came to Zaynab's home and entered without waiting for permission. The Prophet's action in entering Zaynab's house without waiting for permission is, in itself, an indication that the matter was no longer in his or Zaynab's hands. This is a marriage which was ordered by God for, among other things, legislative purposes."[7]

13
14
15
16
17
18

7 DID THE PROPHET FALL IN LOVE WITH ZAYNAB? `WATT`

"Zayd's absence and being swept off his [the Prophet's] feet by her physical attractiveness must be taken with a grain of salt. It does not occur in the earliest source. Moreover, Zaynab was thirty-five or thirty-eight at the time of the marriage, and for an Arab woman of those days that was 'getting on'. All Muhammad's other wives except Khadijah were younger when he married them, and most of them very much younger ... It is most unlikely that at the age of fifty-six such a man as he should have been carried away."[8]

- -

8 HOW WAS ZAYNAB A TEST FOR THE PROPHET? `YUSUF`

"Now Allah had already told the Prophet that He was going to marry him to Zaynab. The Prophet was worried ... that the Jews and the *munafiqeen* [hypocrites] would talk because this was a taboo in jahili Arabian culture ... You could not marry your adopted son's ex-wife. ...
Obviously a revelation hadn't come, so he didn't know what to do. When the revelation came down that said, 'You fear people and Allah is more worthy to fear,' don't misconstrue that in any way. What Allah was saying was simply that, 'your concerns were unwarranted.' In other words, 'you should not be worried when Allah has decreed something.'
There was a lesson in there for the Messenger of Allah himself. He is moving up in *darajat* [degrees]. He is also a believer. Don't forget that—there were lessons for the Messenger of Allah himself."[9]

Although the Prophet is addressed, or referred to, throughout the Qur'an, this is one of only five times he is mentioned by name. (The name *Muhammad* is used in surahs Ali 'Imran, Al Ahzab, Muhammad, and Al Fet-h; and *Ahmad* is used in Surah As-Saff). After hearing the Prophet recite this verse, Zayd ibn Muhammad reverted to his birth name—Zayd ibn Harithah.

Examples of the Prophet's generosity include an instance when he collected funds for Salman al-Farisi to help him pay the exorbitant price needed to buy his freedom. That same year, he persuaded one of his poorest Companions, Jabir ibn 'Abd Allah, to sell his camel for an ounce of gold. The next day, the Prophet returned the camel to Jabir and insisted that he keep the gold as a gift so he could get married. (Remember that Jabir's father, 'Abd Allah ibn 'Amr, was a widower who was recently martyred at Uhud. Before the battle, 'Abd Allah had instructed Jabir to stay behind and take care of his seven sisters.)

Surah Al Ahzab specifically mentions the Prophet by name, and in the next few verses underscores his extraordinary position as God's final messenger:

> Muhammad is not the father of any of your men, but he is the Messenger of God and the Seal of the Prophets. Indeed, God knows about all things.
> — *Al Ahzab (The Allied Forces, 33:40)*

Regardless of his position, the Prophet's generosity and forgiving nature make him an irresistible source of comfort and strength to those around him. Even before the first revelations, his friends constantly sought his time and attention. During the Meccan period, this may not have caused a problem; however, his ever-expanding role coupled with his growing popularity in Medina create a new problem altogether. In the year after Uhud, the strain upon the Prophet is obvious, and Surah Al Ahzab addresses the issue head on:

> All you who believe! When you're coming for a meal, don't enter the Prophet's house without permission, and don't arrive so early that you're waiting around for (the food to) finish (cooking). When you're invited inside, come in. Then, when the meal is over, leave in a timely fashion without trying to engage in small talk. This annoys the Prophet, but he's too shy to ask you to leave - though God isn't too shy to tell you the truth. — *Al Ahzab (The Allied Forces, 33:53)*

Acts of kindness and generosity notwithstanding, the Prophet's greatest gift (other than the transmission of God's Word) is demonstrating how to live the Qur'an in his daily life. The surah reminds listeners of this unique blessing:

◇ God and His angels send blessings down upon the Prophet. All you who believe! Call for prayers to be sent down upon him, and wish him peace with due respect. —*Al Ahzab (The Allied Forces, 33:56)*

On more than one occasion, the Prophet explains:

"An angel came unto me and said, 'None invokes blessings upon thee once, but God invokes blessings upon him tenfold.' "[10]

"Not one of you hath faith until I am dearer to him than his son and his father and all men together."[11]

Despite his lofty station as the seal of the prophets, the Prophet emphasizes that Muslims should never differentiate between any of God's messengers. On one occasion, a quarrel breaks out between a Jew and a Muslim. When the Jew swears by Moses, the Muslim impulsively strikes him saying:

"Wilt thou swear by Him who chose Moses above all mankind when the Prophet is present in our midst?"[12]

When the incident is brought to the Prophet's attention, he sharply criticizes the Muslim for raising the Prophet above Moses.

The Messenger believes in what his Lord revealed, as do the faithful. Each of them believes in God, His angels, His books and His messengers.

◇ (The believers say), "We don't consider one of His messengers as being better than another." (They pray), "We hear, and we obey, (and we seek) Your forgiveness, Our Lord, for we (know that our) final destination is back with You." —*Al Baqarah (The Cow, 2:285)*

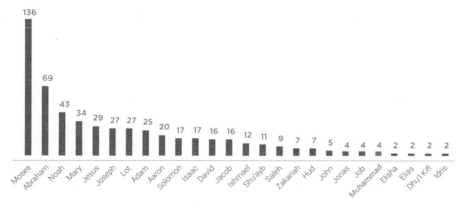

FIGURE 17B. PROPHETS MENTIONED BY NAME IN THE QUR'AN

Twenty-five prophets are mentioned by name in the Qur'an. Some scholars believe that Shu'ayb, Dhu'l Kifl, and Idris were the biblical prophets Jethro, Ezekial, and Enoch. The Prophet Muhammad is mentioned only four times by name (a fifth time as *Ahmad*) but is indirectly referred to numerous times. (Mary is also included because of her unparalleled spiritual significance in Islam.)

Not surprisingly, the Prophet's argument against differentiating between God's messengers is in accordance with several verses from the Qur'an that highlight the lofty position of the early biblical and Hebrew prophets:

> "Moses!" (God) said. "I've chosen you above other people with the message (I've sent to you) and the words (I've spoken to you). Take (the revelation) that I'm giving you, and be thankful." — *Al A'raf (The Heights, 7:144)*

> Truly, God chose Adam, Noah and the families of Abraham and Amran above all others in the world. — *Ali 'Imran (The Family of Amran, 3:33)*

---

9 ISLAM LEFT NO ROOM FOR RELIGIOUS SUPERIORITY   ARMSTRONG

"Muslims must remember that every community had its own specially revealed din [faith], so they must not take part in these pointless squabbles; if the People of the Book attacked their faith, Muslims must behave with hilm [wisdom], and courteously reply: 'God knows best what you are doing.' [Qur'an 2:74]
...Abraham, for example, had not belonged to an exclusive cult. He had simply been a Muslim, 'one who surrendered himself' and a 'man of pure faith (hanif).' [Qur'an 3:67]"[13]

- -

10 WHAT GUIDED THE PROPHET'S VIEWS ON MUSLIM-JEWISH RELATIONS?   RAMADAN

"When he settled in Medina, the Prophet did not require anybody to convert, and he made it clear that he wanted relations within the new society to be egalitarian. Later, when conflicts arose and alliances were betrayed, the situation decayed and relations with one or another of the Jewish tribes deteriorated greatly.
Those developments [betrayal of Qaynuqa, etc.] by no means affected the principles underlying the relationship between Muslims and Jews: mutual recognition and respect, as well as justice before the law or in the settlement of disputes between individuals and/or groups. For instance ... a Muslim thought he might escape responsibility for a theft he had perpetrated by laying the blame on a Jew. An eight-verse Revelation denounced the serious treachery committed by the Muslim culprit and revealed the Jew's innocence [An-Nisa (The Women, 4:108-116)]. The Muslim's culpability is explicit: 'But if anyone earns a fault or a sin and throws it onto one who is innocent, he burdens himself with a false charge and a flagrant sin.' [Qur'an 4:112] Whatever conflict may occur with other groups, the inalienable principles of respect and justice remained and transcended historical realities requiring that the Muslim conscience not yield to blinding passions and hatred...
'O you who believe! Stand out firmly for God, as witnesses to fair dealing, and let not the hatred of others to you make you depart from justice. Be just: that is next to piety; and fear God, for God is well acquainted with all that you do.' [Qur'an 5:8]"[14]

YEAR 18: THE TRENCH

18.1 THE ALLIED ENEMY FORCES

The Quraysh had been licking their wounds since the humiliating defeat at Badr. They had failed to destroy the Muslims at Uhud and had been further humiliated by the Muslims' no-contest victory at the second Badr encounter. Their only remaining hope is a final, all-out assault on Medina:

> They had made a great effort and had not succeeded. Unless they could do something much better they were faced with disaster. For the expedition of Uhud they had collected all the available men from Quraysh and the surrounding tribes friendly to them. The only possibility of raising a more powerful army was to attract the active support of some of the great nomadic tribes to the east and northeast of Medina, using propaganda about Muhammad's weakness, memories of the prestige of Quraysh, promises of booty, and even straight bribes. To this task Quraysh now devoted their energies.[2]

From the safety of their new abode in Khaybar, the exiled Bani Nadir ally with the Quraysh, telling them that the Meccan way of idolatry is closer to the truth than Islam. The Quraysh also gain help from the tribes of Hawazin and Ghatafan, and successfully assemble a force more than three times the size of Abu Sufyan's army at Uhud. The strategy is simple—amass a federation of enemy tribes and launch a unified, decisive siege on Medina.

FIGURE 18A. THE ALLIED ENEMY FORCES

Two years after Uhud, the Quraysh launched their first multilateral offensive on Medina. They had persuaded their eastern and northern allies to attack the city by guaranteeing vast spoils of war. The Quraysh had assembled 4,000 men, and were reinforced by the tribe of Ghatafan, which dispatched 2,000 soldiers, Bani Asad's 1,000 men, and Bani Sulaym's 700 mercenaries. The Jews of Khaybar joined the offensive and rounded out the total number of enemy combatants to 10,000 men—three times larger than anything the Muslims had ever seen before.

---

1 **HOW DID BANI NADIR THREATEN MEDINA'S SECURITY?** `RAMADAN`

"The Banu Nadir chief, Huyay [ibn Akhtab], went to Mecca with Jewish leaders from Khaybar to seal an alliance with the Quraysh that left no room for doubt: Muhammad and his community must be attacked and eliminated. To this end, they contacted other tribes to integrate them into the pact; the Banu Asad, Banu Ghatafan, and Banu Sulaym joined in. Only the Banu Amir, one of whose women the Prophet had married ... refused to be part of the new coalition." [1]

Of the many inland tribes invited to attack Medina, one in particular—Bani 'Amir, the clan of the Prophet's late wife Zaynab bint Khuzaymah—refuses to fight and stays behind.

Surah Al Ahzab, (The Allied Forces), takes its name from these united enemy tribes bent on destroying the Prophet's city.

> Indeed, when the believers (in the city of Medina) saw the Allied Forces (approaching in the distance to attack), they said, "This is what God and His Messenger promised us (would happen), and God and His Messenger told us the truth." (The specter of desperate battle) did no more than increase their faith and submission (to God). — *Al Ahzab (The Allied Forces, 33:22)*

18.2 DIGGING THE TRENCH

By the time the Muslims learn about the imminent attack, they have only one week to prepare their defenses. The Prophet consults his advisers, who collectively agree to Salman al-Farisi's strategy of digging a trench along the city's most vulnerable borders to hold off the enemy's cavalry.

After delegating portions of the trench to different groups in the community, the Prophet jumps into the trench alongside his Companions to help loosen up the earth and haul it away. The entire city is in danger, and the Jewish tribe of Qurayzah readily lends its excavating equipment to speed up the dig.

---

2 **WHAT DOES THE TRENCH SAY ABOUT THE PROPHET'S STYLE OF LEADERSHIP?** `RAMADAN`

"The Prophet taught his Companions both deep faith and the exploitation of intellectual creativity in all circumstances: they had not hesitated to borrow a foreign war technique, suggested by a Persian, and adapt it to their situation in Medina. The genius of peoples, the wisdom of nations, and healthy human creativity were integrated into their mode of thinking, without hesitation or timidity ... This was an invitation to study the best human thoughts and products and adopt them as part of humankind's positive heritage ... On a broader level, it meant showing curiosity, inventiveness, and creativity in the management of human affairs, and this appeared not only through his approach to war and its strategies but also, as we have seen, through his way of considering the world of ideas and culture." [3]

Everyone is helping—even children not permitted to fight in battle are allowed to assist with the excavation. Among the youth, only two 15-year-olds—Usamah ibn Zayd and 'Abd Allah ibn 'Umar—are granted special permission to join the army if fighting ensues. Although the stakes are high and the work is intense, the men sing while they work, expressing their confidence in the Prophet's leadership.

---

③ WHAT WAS THE SIGNIFICANCE OF THE MEN SINGING WHILE THEY WORKED? `RAMADAN`

"Faith needs culture. Thus, when he needed to unite his Companions' energies, Muhammad summoned up all the levels of their being in the world in order to perfect the unity of his community: deep faith in the One, the poetic phrasing of feelings, the musicality of the song of emotions. From within his community, sharing their daily lives, he attested that while he was indeed at the One's service, beyond time and space, he also experienced their history and partake [partook] of their culture: he was one of them."[4]

While digging, some Companions uncover a large rock that no one can dislodge. The Prophet approaches the boulder and crushes it with three successive blows that send a flash of lightning south, north, and east. Salman al-Farisi asks him about the significance of the flashes, and the Prophet explains that God will soon grant the Prophet control over Yemen to the south, Syria to the north, and Persia to the east.

At the end of an exhausting day of labor, Jabir ibn 'Abd Allah invites the Prophet to dinner. To Jabir's dismay, the Prophet extends the invitation to the rest of the exhausted Companions. With no way to feed everyone, Jabir exclaims:

"Verily we are for God, and verily unto Him are we returning!"[5]

When the Prophet arrives, he blesses the food and, to Jabir's surprise, there is enough to feed every guest.

Recall that **Jabir ibn 'Abd Allah** is the poor Companion who was left in charge of his seven sisters after his father's death at Uhud. Just a year ago, the Prophet had given Jabir an ounce of gold so he could afford to get married.

18.3 THE SIEGE

As commander-in-chief, Abu Sufyan leads the confederate army to the northwest Medinan valley of 'Aqiq. As with Uhud, Khalid ibn al-Walid and 'Ikrimah ibn Abi Jahl lead the left and right battalions. The Meccans had never seen a trench such as Salman's before, and their first few attacks are easily repelled by the Prophet's archers, who are lined up behind the expansive ditch.

The unexpected obstacle forces the Quraysh to regroup, and after reconsidering their options, they agree to a plan masterminded by the chief of Bani Nadir, Huyay ibn Akhtab. Huyay convinces them that he can persuade Bani Qurayzah to turn against the Prophet. By drawing the Prophet's attention to Bani Qurayzah's rebellion at the southern border, he argues that the Quraysh will be able to breach Medina's much-weakened northern defense. Huyay approaches the chief of Qurayzah, Ka'b ibn Asad, and urges him to turn on his own city. At first Ka'b is reluctant, but Huyay finally persuades him and the rest of Qurayzah to open Medina's southern border to the allied enemy's forces.

This is not the first time **Huyay ibn Akhtab** is treacherous to the Prophet. Two years ago, his plot to kill the Prophet was foiled and the entire clan of Nadir was exiled. Nonetheless, after the Conquest of Mecca and the fall of Khaybar, Huyay's own daughter Safiyyah will have a vision of marrying the Prophet and soon after become his ninth wife.

13
14
15
16
17
18

4 WHAT WERE THE QURAYZAH THINKING? `ASLAN`

"The Banu Qurayzah—now the largest Jewish clan in the oasis—openly and actively supported the forces of the Quraysh, going so far as to provide them with weapons and supplies. Why the Qurayzah would so openly have betrayed Muhammad is impossible to say. The brazenness ... indicates they may have thought this was the end of Muhammad's movement and wanted to be on the right side when the dust settled. Even if Muhammad won the battle, the Qurayzah probably assumed that at worst they would be exiled from Medina like the Qaynuqa and Nadir."[6]

5 WHAT WAS THE MAGNITUDE OF QURAYZAH'S DECISION? `RAMADAN`

"This defection meant that the whole strategy of the Medina people collapsed, since the Banu Qurayzah's alliance with the enemy opened a breach from inside and gave the enemy access to the city, which meant certain defeat and no less certain extermination for the Muslims."[7]

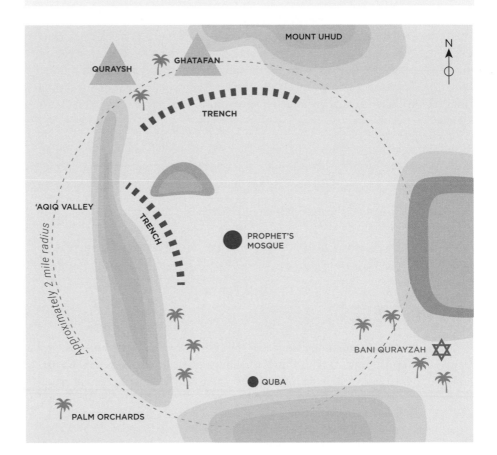

FIGURE 18B. THE BATTLE OF THE TRENCH

Medina's enemy forces stationed themselves at the northwest border of Medina, separated from the city by a series of trenches and natural barriers. Although Bani Qurayzah had lent their supplies to prepare for the siege, they later betrayed the Prophet and opened up the southeastern border of Medina to the enemy. The Quraysh planned to weaken Medina's northwest defenses by drawing the Prophet's attention to the southeast side of the city; but their plan was foiled at the last minute by Nu'aym ibn Mas'ud.

The Prophet learns about Qurayzah's treachery and, as expected, sends reinforcements to the south. With fewer men defending the northern trench, the Quraysh try to attack once more, but still cannot cross the divide.

The Muslims vigilantly hold their ranks all through the night and the next day. For the moment, the trench appears to be all that is preventing the imminent collapse of Medina. During the intense standoff, the Companions miss their obligatory prayers; only after the enemy retreats for the evening can they make up the prayers they had missed.

Surah Al Ahzab captures the dramatic moment:

> The (enemy) came upon you from above you and below you - eyes lost hope, and hearts leapt up to their throats, (as some of you) imagined all sorts of (treasonous) thoughts against God. That was traumatic for the faithful, and they were shaken with intense trembling.
>
> The hypocrites and the sick at heart (panicked and) cried out, "God and His Messenger have promised us nothing more than a fantasy." Some of them said, "People of Yathrib! You can't withstand (this assault)! Pull back now (and protect your own homes)!"
>
> A group of them even went to the Prophet and asked to be excused from the defense (of the city), saying, "Our homes are exposed and undefended." Their homes were not exposed, nor were they without defense. They only wanted to run away (from the front lines).
>
> If there had, in fact, been a way (for the enemy to slip through) from the sides (of the city), and if (those infiltrators) called to (the hypocrites) to betray (the believers) and join them, then (know that) they wouldn't have hesitated for an instant to do it! (Indeed, they would've turned on you), even though they had already made an agreement with God not to turn their backs on you, and an agreement with God must be answered for! — *Al Ahzab (The Allied Forces, 33:10-15)*
>
> The Messenger of God provides you with a beautiful example (to follow), for anyone who longs for God and the Last Day and who remembers God often.
>
> Indeed, when the believers (in the city of Medina) saw the Allied Forces (approaching in the distance to attack), they said, "This is what God and His Messenger promised us (would happen), and God and His Messenger told us the truth." (The specter of desperate battle) did no more than increase their faith and submission (to God). — *Al Ahzab (The Allied Forces, 33:21-22)*

---

6 WHAT DOES SURAH AL AHZAB TEACH ABOUT FOLLOWING THE MESSENGER WHEN TIMES ARE BLEAK?   RAMADAN

"It tells of the Prophet's role and status in and for the life of every Muslim individual, but it takes on an even more powerful dimension when one remembers the circumstances of its Revelation: a besieged community, shaken, unable within the scope of human sight and intelligence to see any way out of the impending disaster, whose ranks dwindle away through desertion and treason, and who unite around the Messenger, his faith, and his trust."[8]

13
14
15
16
17
18

Surah Al Baqarah challenges the Prophet's followers to reflect on their trial of faith:

> Did you think you could enter Paradise without experiencing what those before you did? They were tested through affliction and loss, and (some were) so shaken that even their messenger joined with them in crying, "When will God's help arrive?" (Remember) that the help of God is always near!
> —*Al Baqarah (The Cow, 2:214)*

With no end to the battle in sight, the Prophet suggests negotiating with Bani Ghatafan and tells 'Uthman ibn 'Affan to draw up a treaty. But before the plan comes to fruition, Sa'd ibn Mu'adh persuades the Prophet not to negotiate with their longtime enemies.

Meanwhile, one of the Quraysh's prominent allies, Nu'aym ibn Mas'ud, secretly defects to the Muslim camp and accepts Islam. The Prophet instructs Nu'aym to return to the enemy forces and try to turn them against themselves. He grants Nu'aym permission to lie explaining that, "war is deception."

Nu'aym advises the Bani Qurayzah to ask the Quraysh for some of their leaders as hostages. He explains that if the Quraysh lose, they will not flee back to Mecca and abandon their leaders to the Muslims. Then Nu'aym approaches the Quraysh and tells them the Bani Qurayzah have re-allied themselves with the Muslims and will ask for the Quraysh leaders as hostages, intending to hand them over to the Muslims as a token of repentance. As expected, the two parties grow suspicious of the other's request, and in little time, Abu Sufyan is convinced that Bani Qurayzah will turn on the Quraysh just as they had turned on the Prophet.

As planned Nu'aym's scheme takes full advantage of the enemy's biggest weakness:

> The Muslims had a valuable asset in their comparative unity and better discipline, which contrasted with the lack of cohesion in the confederacy and the lack of mutual confidence between the various groups. Of this disunity Muhammad's diplomacy took full advantage ... The whole was a battle of wits in which the Muslims had the best of it; without cost to themselves they weakened the enemy and increased the dissension.[9]

Remember that just one year ago, **Nu'aym ibn Mas'ud**, from the tribe of Ghatafan, had been bribed by the Quraysh to try and intimidate the Muslims from marching to the second meeting at Badr.

---

7 HOW COULD THE PROPHET JUSTIFY LYING DURING WARFARE? [YUSUF]

"The Prophet, God's peace and blessings upon him, says, 'War is trickery.' This is also how Sun Tsu's 'Art of War' begins. This is an ancient principle in warfare. The nature of war is that it's deceptive. In other words, the Prophet, God's peace and blessings upon him, is telling them that this is a time when deception is permissible. In times of war, one can lie because it is an actual part of warfare. To kill a human being is the worst thing you can do, but in war, it becomes acceptable because that's the nature of war. So things that, in normal times are completely unacceptable, in times of war, become acceptable because of the nature of war. However, Islam limits what you can do: You cannot mutilate. You cannot kill children. You cannot kill women. You cannot kill religious people. You cannot kill old people. You cannot kill livestock, or cut down fruit trees, or burn crops. There are rules of warfare in Islam."

When Quraysh's allies—Ghatafan, Sulaym, and Asad—had agreed to join the siege on Medina, they were motivated by the prospect of plundering the city's abundant resources in a relatively short period of time. However, two weeks have passed since they started their siege, and with food and supplies running dangerously low, their collective determination quickly starts to fade.

On the other side of the trench, the Muslims have also grown weary and exhausted. With no end in sight, the Prophet invokes God's help—a prayer that is answered several days later when a vicious storm descends upon the enemy clans:

> All you who believe! Remember the favor of God upon you when an overwhelming horde (of enemies) came down upon you (to attack you right at Medina). We let loose against them a fierce desert sandstorm and other forces you couldn't even see, for God is watching everything you do!
> — Al Ahzab (The Allied Forces, 33:9)

The cold, raging winds devastate the enemy campsite, ripping up tents and extinguishing fires. Their window of opportunity has passed, and the enemy clans are forced to salvage whatever is left from their camp and return home. Most importantly, the violent storm douses any flickers of hope for the Quraysh:

> The break-up of the confederacy marked the utter failure of the Meccans to deal with Muhammad. The outlook for them now was dismal. They had exerted their utmost strength to dislodge him from Medina, but he remained there, more influential than ever as a result of the fiasco of the confederacy. Their trade with Syria was gone, and much of their prestige lost. Even if Muhammad did not attack them, they had no hope of retaining their wealth and position; but he might very well use armed force against them, and try to annihilate them as they had tried to annihilate him. It would be strange if some of the Meccans–a practical people–had not begun to wonder whether it would not be best to accept Muhammad and his religion.[10]

18.4 THE EXECUTION OF BANI QURAYZAH

The enemy forces leave at dawn, and by early afternoon, Gabriel instructs the Prophet to confront Bani Qurayzah for their treachery. The Prophet sends 3,000 troops to the Jewish fortress, but instructs them not to pray the late-afternoon prayer until they arrive. However, as the sun begins to set before their arrival, the Companions are unsure if they should follow the Prophet's instructions and knowingly miss the prayer. The discussion splits the group in two—half perform the prayer in its prescribed time, the remainder postpone it until they arrive at their destination.

---

8   **HOW DID THE PROPHET REACT TO DIFFERENT SCHOOLS OF THOUGHT?**   `RAMADAN`

"It was time to pray al-Asr, and some of them, literally repeating the Prophet's order, maintained that they must not pray on the way but must wait until they reached the Banu Qurayzah … Later on they asked the Prophet which was the correct interpretation, and he accepted both. This attitude was to have major consequences for the future of the Muslim community, as after the Prophet's death, two main schools of thought appeared: the Ahl al-Hadith, who … kept to the literal meaning of the sayings reported in Prophetic tradition (sunnah), and the Ahl ar-Ray who … tried to understand the purpose of the saying, its spirit, and its occasional figurative meaning. Both approaches had been accepted by the Prophet, and both were therefore correct and legitimate ways of remaining faithful to the message."[11]

This is not the first time **Abu Lubabah ibn 'Abd al-Mundhir** disappoints the Prophet. Recall that after Badr, he refused to give his disputed palm tree to an orphan in charity even when the Prophet had offered him a reward in Paradise (QY 15.12).

Soon enough, Bani Qurayzah's entire enclave is surrounded by troops led by 'Ali ibn Abi Talib. After a 25-day standoff, the leaders of Qurayzah reach out to one of their old liaisons, Abu Lubabah ibn 'Abd al-Mundhir, and ask if surrendering to the Prophet would afford them the same leniency offered to Bani Qaynuqa and Nadir. Abu Lubabah instructs them to surrender, but as he does so, he points to his neck, implying that even if they surrender, they will not be forgiven. No sooner does he make the gesture than he is overwhelmed by a wave of guilt. Instead of returning to the Prophet, he ties himself to a pillar in the mosque and waits for God's judgment for betraying His messenger. The Prophet had been waiting for Abu Lubabah's return, and when he learns that he tied himself up in the mosque, he simply comments:

> "If he had come to me I would have prayed to God to forgive him; but seeing that he hath done what he hath done, it is not for me to free him until God shall relent unto him."[12]

---

⑨ WHY WAS THE PROPHET ORDERED TO BARRICADE BANI QURAYZAH?
RAMADAN

"His clemency, repeatedly betrayed, was seen as a sign of weakness, if not madness. Besides, the Banu Qurayzah's treason was so serious that if their plans had been successful, it would have led to the extermination of the Muslims, betrayed from within and crushed by an army of more than ten thousand."[13]

- -

⑩ WHY WOULD ABU LUBABAH DISOBEY THE PROPHET?
WATT

"There is no suggestion that Abu Lubabah was other than a faithful member of the Islamic community; he had no thought of leaving that community, but on a certain matter of policy he differed from Muhammad. This, then, is the characteristic of the Muslim opposition to Muhammad during the last few years of his life. It accepts the community as a fact but disagrees with particular lines of policy, usually for selfish reasons."[14]

In the Qurayzah enclave, one of their men, 'Amr ibn Su'da, officially disassociates himself from his people for breaking their pact with the Prophet. He suggests to his clansmen that they embrace the Prophet's religion, or at least pay the Prophet a yearly tribute. But the majority of Qurayzah refuse both ideas, stating that they would rather be killed than pay a tribute to the Arabs. Faced with no other options, 'Amr and another clansman, Rifa'ah ibn Samaw'al, escape to join 'Ali's army.

---

⑪ WHAT WAS QURAYZAH'S CRIME?
YUSUF

"This was an act of treachery in war and [this punishment] is acceptable in any civilization. Even today, treason, in times of martial law, is punishable by death. It was treason against the state, in modern terms. The Prophet, God's peace and blessings upon him, was the most compassionate of people when compassion was warranted, but when justice was warranted, an example had to be set. He is responsible for the city of Medina."[15]

The next day, Bani Qurayzah surrenders and the men are quickly separated from the rest of the group. 'Abd Allah ibn Sallam, the former rabbi of Bani Qaynuqa, is put in charge of the women and children. Just as the Khazraj had asked for leniency for Bani Qaynuqa after Badr, the Aws now send a deputation to the Prophet asking him to show clemency for their former allies. The Prophet listens to their plea and asks if they would be satisfied if he places the fate of Qurayzah in the hands of the Aws chief, Sa'd ibn Mu'adh. The Aws agree to the Prophet's proposal and beg their leader to be lenient with Qurayzah. But Sa'd's sense of justice is uncompromising—he orders that Qurayzah's fighters be executed, while their women, children, and property be spared.

12 DID THE PROPHET INFLUENCE SA'D'S DECISION TO EXECUTE QURAYZAH? [WATT]

"There is no need to suppose that Muhammad brought pressure to bear on Sa'd ibn-Mu`adh to punish Qurayzah as he did. A far-sighted man like Sa'd must have realized that to allow tribal or clan allegiance to come before Islamic allegiance would lead to a renewal of the fratricidal strife from which they hoped the coming of Muhammad had delivered Medina. As he was being led into Muhammad's presence to pronounce his sentence, Sa'd is said to have made a remark to the effect that, with death not far from him, he must consider above all doing his duty to God and the Islamic community, even at the expense of former alliances."[16]

13 WAS THE EXECUTION OF QURAYZAH AN ACT OF GENOCIDE? [ASLAN]

1) "To begin with, the Banu Qurayza were not executed for being Jews. A significant number of the Banu Kilab—Arab clients of the Qurayza ... were also executed for treason. Describing the death of only slightly more than one percent of Medina's Jewish population as a 'genocidal act' is not only a preposterous exaggeration, it is an affront to the memory of those millions of Jews who truly have suffered the horrors of genocide."

2) "The execution of the Banu Qurayzah did not in any way set a precedent for future treatment of Jews in Islamic territories ... Even during the most oppressive periods in Islamic history, Jews under Muslim rule received far better treatment and had far greater rights than when they were under Christian rule."

3) "The execution of the Banu Qurayza was not, as it has so often been presented, reflective of an intrinsic religious conflict between Muhammad and the Jews. Simply put, the Jewish clans of Medina were in no way a religiously observant group ... It would be simplistic to argue that no polemical conflict existed between Muhammad and the Jews of his time. But this conflict had far more to do with political alliances and economic ties than with a theological debate over scripture."[17]

14 DID THE EXECUTION OF QURAYZAH MARK A NEW PHASE OF ANTI-JEWISH DISCRIMINATION? [WATT]

"The continuing presence of at least a few Jews in Medina is an argument against the view sometimes put forward by European scholars that in the second year after the Hijrah Muhammad adopted a policy of clearing all Jews out of Medina just because they were Jews, and that he carried out this policy with ever-increasing severity. It was not Muhammad's way to have policies of this kind. He had a balanced view of the fundamentals of the contemporary situation and of his long-term aims, and in the light of this he moulded his day-to-day plans in accordance with the changing factors in current events. The occasions of his attacks on the first two Jewish clans were no more than occasions; but there were also deep underlying reasons. The Jews in general by their verbal criticisms of the Qur'anic revelation were trying to undermine the foundation of the whole Islamic community; and they were also giving political support to Muhammad's enemies and to opponents such as the Hypocrites. In so far as the Jews abandoned these forms of hostile activity Muhammad allowed them to live in Medina unmolested."[18]

Recall that after Badr, the fate of the Meccan captives was hotly debated. Sa'd and 'Umar felt that the captives should be killed while the Prophet and Abu Bakr sought leniency. Soon thereafter, a revelation sided with Sa'd and 'Umar's decision (Qur'an 8:67).

According to Lings, Sa'd's decision to execute the men of Qurayzah was not unexpected, as it was in accordance with Jewish law:

"When you march up to attack a city, make its people an offer of peace. If they accept and open their gates, all the people in it shall be subject to forced labor and shall work for you. If they refuse to make peace and they engage you in battle, lay siege to that city. When the Lord your God delivers it into your hand, put to the sword all the men in it. As for the women, the children, the livestock and everything else in the city, you may take these as plunder for yourselves. And you may use the plunder the Lord your God gives you from your enemies. This is how you are to treat all the cities that are at a distance from you and do not belong to the nations nearby." (Deuteronomy 20:10-15)

14 WAS THE ENTIRE CLAN OF QURAYZAH REALLY EXECUTED? SALAHI

"Reports that all adult males of the Qurayzah Jews were killed while all their women and children were enslaved are quoted in practically all books on the Prophet's life and its events ... However, a more careful examination of these reports proves that this could not have been the case. The number of those who were killed could not have been more than twenty-five, if not less...

We find two statements speaking of Sa'd's judgement. Both state that he ruled that 'their fighters were to be killed and their offspring to be taken captive'. Where Ibn Ishaq's report goes wrong is to interpret this judgement as applying to every single person of the Qurayzah Jews, thus making the death sentence applicable to all adult males and the captivity to all women and children. There is nothing in either the Qur'anic or the Hadith texts to confirm this. The Qur'an speaks of some being killed and some taken prisoner [33:26-27], while the two hadith traditions speak of executing the fighters and imprisoning their offspring.

Several points in Ibn Ishaq's report call it into question. To start with, he mentions that prior to their execution, the men were placed in Usamah ibn Zayd's house, while the women were placed in Kayyisah bint al-Harith's home. How many people could these two homes accommodate? ... The number of the Qurayzah men mentioned in these reports ranges between 600 and 900. What sort of home would take all these people?

... Al-Waqidi (130-207 H) was a prominent historian who wrote extensively about the history of Islam ... Al-Waqidi gives us the names of nine people executed as a result of Sa'd ibn Muadh's ruling ... He also mentions that two people were sent to each of several clans of the Ansar where they were executed. This brings the total number to less than 25. When we relate this information to the most reliable wording of Sa'd ibn Muadh's ruling, which condemns the Qurayzah fighters to be killed, we conclude that these were the actual fighters who took an active part in the treachery that aimed to eradicate Islam and all Muslims.

Ibn Ishaq's account of the life of the Prophet Muhammad was the main source on which later historians relied as they analysed events that took place during the Prophet's lifetime ... The first reason for rejecting this report is that meting out such a collective punishment is contrary to Islamic teachings and to the Prophet's own practice. Islam does not condone punishing a group of people for the crime of one, or punishing many for the crime of the few. It punishes all those who actually take part in a crime...

Ibn Ishaq's report suggests that all women and children were taken captive. The question arises: what happened to them after that? In the universal tradition of the time, they would have become slaves and given to those who took part in the siege of the Qurayzah forts. Yet Islam had already established a rule for the prisoners of war, requiring Muslims to set them free, either against ransom or as a gracious gesture. We have no report to suggest that they stayed in Madinah as slaves. There is not a single story on any such woman going through a problem with the family where she might have been placed. The children involved would have been raised as Muslims. We do not have a single report of any of them distinguishing himself in any field of life. Nor do we have any report of any conversation between the Prophet's Companions referring to the punishment of the Qurayzah Jews or to the fate of their families. How can this absence of reporting be explained? We note that a similar lack of reporting applies to the other two Jewish tribes that were evacuated from Madinah during the Prophet's lifetime, the Qaynuqā and the al-Nadīr. This suggests that the Prophet's Companions and the early Muslim historians did not concern themselves with tracing the fate of those evacuated Jews after they had left Madinah. The same must have applied to the Qurayzah Jews.

We therefore conclude that after the execution of the perpetrators of the treachery, the rest of the tribe were allowed to leave Madinah on similar terms to other Jewish tribes which were previously evacuated."[19]

16 **WAS QURAYZAH PUNISHED FOR BEING JEWISH?** [ARMSTRONG]

"Revolting as it seems to us today, almost everybody in Arabia would have expected Sa'd's judgment. According to the texts, not even the Qurayzah were surprised by the decision. The executions sent a grim message to the Jews of Khaybar, and the Bedouin would have noted that Muhammad did not shrink from retaliation. He had staged a defiant show of strength, which, it was hoped, would bring the conflict to an end. Change was coming to this desperate, primitive society, but for the time being, violence and killing on this scale were the norm.

It is, however, important to note that the Qurayzah were not killed on religious or racial grounds. None of the other Jewish tribes in the oasis either objected or attempted to intervene, clearly regarding it as a purely political and tribal matter ... Muhammad had no ideological quarrel with the Jewish people ... The men of Qurayzah were executed for treason. The seventeen other Jewish tribes of Medina remained in the oasis, living on friendly terms with the Muslims for many years, and the Qur'an continued to insist that Muslims remember their spiritual kinship with the people of the book." [20]

"Don't argue with the Followers of Earlier Revelation except in a better way, unless it's with those who are corrupt among them. Say to them, "We believe in the revelation that's come down to us and also in what's come down to you. Our God and your God are the same, and we surrender to His will." [Qur'an, 29:46]

17 **WERE THE PROPHET'S ACTIONS ANTI-SEMITIC?** [ASLAN]

"Bear in mind, Muhammad's biographies were written at a time when the Jewish minority in the Muslim state was Islam's only remaining theological rival. It is not surprising, therefore, that Muslim historians and theologians would have buttressed their arguments against the rabbinical authorities of their time by planting their words in Muhammad's mouth. If Muhammad's biographies reveal anything at all, it is the anti-Jewish sentiments of the Prophet's biographers, not the Prophet himself. To understand Muhammad's actual beliefs regarding the Jews and Christians of his time, one must look not into the words that chroniclers put into his mouth hundreds of years after his death, but rather to the words that God put into his mouth when he was alive."

"Say to them, 'We believe in God and in what was revealed to us, as well as in what was revealed to Abraham, Ishmael, Isaac, Jacob and the tribes (of Israel), and (we believe) in what was given to Moses and Jesus and to all other prophets from their Lord. We don't claim that one of them was better than another, and to Him we surrender.' " [Qur'an 3:84]

"Those (Muslims) who believe, along with the Jews, the Sabians and the Christians, anyone who believes in God and the Last Day and who does what's morally right, they'll have no cause for sorrow or regret." [Qur'an 5:69][21]

Many scholars suggest that the **Sabians** are an unidentified group of monotheists that predated the Prophet.

13
14
15
16
17
18

The conclusion of the Bani Qurayzah account is succinctly captured in Surah Al Ahzab:

> He brought the Followers of Previous Revelation who had joined the (enemy's) side down from their strongholds and caused their hearts to panic. You killed a portion of the (Banu Qurayzah) and took another portion (as bonded-servants).
>
> He made you inherit their lands, houses and goods. (Then, later on), you also (gained control) over (the distant city of Khaybar), a place where you had never been before, for God has power over all things.
> — *Al Ahzab (The Allied Forces, 33:26-27)*

The Bani Nadir ransom some of the women and children of Qurayzah, but many are absorbed by the community in Medina. Rayhanah bint Zayd, a woman of Bani Nadir married to a man of Qurayzah, becomes a servant in the Prophet's household and later embraces Islam.

SURAH AT-TAWBAH (Repentance) is the only chapter in the Qur'an, that does not begin with the standard opening, "In the Name of God, The Compassionate, the Merciful." (See Emerick's introduction to the surah for plausible explanations.) The surah is named after one of its central themes—that God mercifully accepts the repentance of those who turn back to Him in sincerity. Surah At-Tawbah is a must-read chapter that touches on numerous historical elements in the Sirah, including the renunciation of certain treaties after the Conquest of Mecca, the expedition to Tabuk, the Mosque of Harm, and a warning against the hypocrites.

Shortly after the Battle of the Trench, Sa'd ibn Mu'adh passes away and is buried by the Prophet. Meanwhile, about two weeks after Abu Lubabah had tied himself up in the mosque, the Prophet brings him happy news in the form of Surah At-Tawbah's latest installment:

> (There are) some other (people) who've admitted to their sins. They had mixed moral deeds with evil ones, but God may yet turn to them (in forgiveness), for God is forgiving and merciful.
>
> Take charity from their wealth so you can cleanse and purify them, and pray for them, for your prayers are truly a source of tranquility for them. God hears and knows (about all things).
>
> Don't they know that God accepts the repentance of His servants and that He accepts their charitable contributions? God is the One Who Accepts Repentance, and (He truly is) the Merciful. — *At-Tawbah (Repentance, 9:102-104)*

The Prophet personally unties Abu Lubabah from the pillar to which he had confined himself. In the spirit of the final verse, Abu Lubabah promptly gives away one-third of his property in charity.

---

18 HOW DID THE PROPHET COACH HIS FOLLOWERS? `RAMADAN`

"Forgiveness came, and the Prophet himself unfastened Abu Lubabah's ties. This individual experience shows that spiritual edification was never totally accomplished, that consciences were constantly being tried, and that the Prophet accompanied his teachings with strictness but also with benevolence."[22]

18.5 ABU L-'AS RETURNS TO MECCA

Recall that after Badr, **Safwan ibn Umayyah** (son of the slain chief of Jumah) urged his cousin 'Umayr ibn Wahb to assassinate the Prophet. After the Conquest of Mecca, Safwan is one of only three men who does not enter Islam, but is nonetheless given four months of amnesty. A few months later, after the Battle of Hunayn, the Prophet gives Safwan a very generous portion of the spoils and Safwan finally embraces Islam.

Five months after the Battle of the Trench, Zayd ibn Harithah leads an expedition that successfully intercepts a southbound caravan belonging to Safwan ibn Umayyah. While a number of Meccans are taken captive, Abu l-'As ibn ar-Rabi' somehow escapes to Medina to visit his wife Zaynab and daughter Umamah. The next morning, at the pre-dawn prayer, Zaynab surprises the congregation by announcing that she is officially protecting Abu l-'As, who is staying with her in Medina. The Prophet accepts his daughter's plea but emphasizes that their marriage is void because Abu l-'As has not yet embraced Islam.

---

19 HOW COULD ZAYNAB SPEAK UP IN THE MOSQUE? `RAMADAN`

"Zaynab often went to the mosque, which was a space open to both men and women, and nobody objected to her making a statement there, among men; in fact, it was not at all uncommon for Muslim women to speak up publicly in such a manner."[23]

Abu l-'As ibn ar-Rabi' was not only Khadijah's son-in-law but also her nephew. He marched out against the Prophet at Badr and was held captive until the Prophet let him go in exchange for Zaynab and Umamah.

A portion of the spoils taken from the caravan include a number of items that are under the care of Abu l-'As. Zaynab asks that his merchandise be returned to him so he can deliver them to their rightful owners. The Companions agree and Abu l-'As leaves for Mecca to fulfill his business obligations, before returning to Medina to embrace Islam and rejoin his family.

18.6 THE MUSTALIQ INVASION

The loss of Safwan's caravan prompts the Quraysh to rally support from their allies along the Red Sea coast to re-open their western caravan route. When the Prophet learns of their plans, he leads a group of men to the coast and preemptively encircles Bani Mustaliq, who had been planning a raid on Medina. Although the two parties exchange arrows, little actual fighting takes place and Bani Mustaliq is quickly subdued by the Prophet's army.

After Bani Mustaliq's surrender, Juwayriyah bint Harith—the daughter of their chief—approaches the Prophet and asks for help to pay her ransom. When the Prophet offers her ransom and his hand in marriage, Juwayriyah gladly accepts. Juwayriyah's father is unaware of the arrangement and when he arrives to pay for his daughter's release, the Prophet surprises him by asking why he hid two of his best camels from the ransom total. Harith ibn Abi Durar is struck by the Prophet's clairvoyance, and after embracing Islam, consents to his daughter's marriage.

The new alliance creates a strong bond between Medina and the coastal tribe. Upon the Prophet's marriage to Juwayriyah, the Companions willingly free more than 100 captive families from Juwayriyah's clan. The release of the Mustaliq captives make such an impression on 'A'ishah, that she later stated:

"I know of no woman who was a greater blessing to her people than she."[24]

Bani Mustaliq belonged to the larger tribe of Khuza'ah, which was displaced from Mecca by Qusayy several generations ago (P2.1).

Al-Mubarakpuri notes 11 other military expeditions that occurred between the Battle of the Trench and Hudaybiyah (p.287-289, 297-298).

---

20 **WHAT WAS BEHIND THE PROPHET'S MANY MARRIAGES?** | WATT |

"Though there is no reason to suppose that he disregarded the factor of physical attraction, it is practically certain that he had his feelings towards the fair sex well under control, and that he did not enter into marriages except when they were politically and socially desirable.
It is possible, too, to go further and, while restricting oneself to the standpoint of Muhammad's time, to turn the alleged instances of treachery and sensuality into matter for praise. In his day and generation Muhammad was a social reformer, indeed a reformer even in the sphere of morals. He created a new system of social security and a new family structure, both of which were a vast improvement on what went before. In this way he adapted for settled communities all that was best in the morality of the nomad, and established a religious and social framework for the life of a sixth of the human race today. That is not the work of a traitor or a lecher."[25]

- -

21 **WHAT IS THE DANGER IN RATIONALIZING ALL OF THE PROPHET'S MARRIAGES?** | SALAHI |

"It is tempting to explain most of the Prophet's marriages in terms of the political, social or religious aims which attended each one of them. One must be wary, however, of oversimplifying matters, seeking justification for things which one should accept without too much worry. The Prophet was allowed by God to marry as many women as he wished. If he therefore availed himself of this permission for no reason other than that for which people normally get married, this should be an absolutely satisfactory explanation. The fact that he made use of this concession in order to achieve beneficial results for Islam and for the Muslim community increases one's love and respect for him. One need not unduly bother with what he did in this connection. Sufficient is the fact that this permission was given to him by God and that he, God's Messenger, could judge best when to use this concession."[26]

During the return trip to Medina, a scuffle takes place between 'Umar's horseman and another Companion. In the midst of the bickering, 'Abd Allah ibn Ubayy seizes an opportunity to voice his long-simmering dissatisfaction with Emigrants living in Medina.

> *"They seek to take precedence over us, they crowd us out of our own country, and naught will fit us and these rags of Quraysh but the old saying, 'Feed thy dog and it will feed on thee.' By God, when we return to Medina, the higher and the mightier of us will drive out the lower and the weaker."*[27]

A young Khazraji named Zayd ibn Arqam witnesses the incident and relates it to the Prophet. When 'Umar suggests punishing 'Abd Allah, the Prophet gently responds:

> *"Why O 'Umar! The people will say that Muhammad kills his followers?"*[28]

When 'Abd Allah ibn Ubayy denies the allegation, the Prophet swiftly dismisses the matter, ordering everyone to break camp and hastily return to Medina. Shortly thereafter, Surah Al Munafiqun confirms Zayd's account of the incident.

SURAH AL MUNAFIQUN (The Hypocrites) is a relatively short Medinan surah that exposes the treachery of the hypocrites in Medina (and their leader, 'Abd Allah ibn Ubayy).

> (Now during the return journey from the campaign against the Banu Mustaliq), they're saying (to each other), "When we get back to the city, the affluent will throw those beggars out!"
>
> (Well, they should know that) affluence belongs only to God, His Messenger and the faithful, though the hypocrites don't know it. —*Al Munafiqun (The Hypocrites, 63:8)*

㉒ WHAT DID THE PROPHET FEAR MOST FOR HIS COMMUNITY? [SALAHI]

"It is indeed worth noting that the Prophet moved quickly to stamp out any tribal or communal division among the Muslims. Indeed, he feared nothing more than internal division in his newly formed community. This should serve as a reminder to all Muslims that their differences should at no time cause a split into separate camps which are hostile to each other, when the bond of Islam exists between them all. Muslims may have different points of view, but such differences must not be allowed to alienate any group of them from the other. They must always feel that any Muslim remains a brother with whom they have the strongest of ties. The Muslim community must always remain a single, united community, with mutual love and compassion prevailing among all its members."[29]

Al Munafiqun publicly exposes the elements of hypocrisy hiding among the Companions. 'Abd Allah ibn Ubayy's son, 'Abd Allah, anticipates that the Prophet will order his father to be punished for his insincerity and asks the Prophet for permission to carry out the punishment himself. The Companions are puzzled that a son would want to execute his father, but 'Abd Allah explains that he would harm any other man who laid a hand on his father. To 'Abd Allah's surprise, the Prophet dismisses the entire affair saying:

"Nay, but let us deal gently with him and make the best of his companionship so long as he be with us."[30]

'Abd Allah ibn Ubayy's son, **'Abd Allah,** is an ardent supporter of the Prophet, and had marched to Uhud even when his own father had abandoned the Prophet along with 300 others (QY 16.5). One year later, the Prophet left him in charge of Medina during the second Badr expedition.

㉓ WHY WAS THE PROPHET LENIENT WITH 'ABD ALLAH IBN UBAYY? [SALAHI]

"Some historians may suggest that had the Prophet adopted a strong attitude towards him right from the beginning, he was bound to think twice before he took another hostile position. This argument does not take into consideration the fact that 'Abdullāh had a large following in Madinah amongst the Arabs who viewed Islam with suspicion and hatred. 'Abdullāh was indeed a man of strong influence. Before the Prophet's emigration to Madinah, preparations were under way to crown him as king of Madinah. It was only owing to the rise of Islam in Madinah that he was deprived of that position. He, however, continued to wield great influence among all those who did not readily accept Islam. Had the Prophet taken him to task on this first occasion of insolence, many of the Arabs who considered him as leader would have been quick to defend him. There might have been a situation of polarization which could have led to a confrontation between the Muslim Arabs and the non-Muslim Arabs in Madinah. That would have meant civil war. Only the Jews and the Quraysh would have benefited from that situation. The Qaynuqā Jews would have felt much stronger and, together with 'Abdullāh ibn Ubayy and his followers, would have tried to deal a crushing blow to the Prophet and his companions. Yet the fact that the Prophet decided to take a conciliatory attitude towards 'Abdullāh did not mean that he felt himself to be weak. Indeed, it is the strong who can afford to take such an attitude."[31]

The Qur'an's examination of the hypocrites leads many Companions to reflect on their own level of sincerity. On one occasion, a well-meaning Companion approaches the Prophet fearing that he might be harboring elements of hypocrisy. He explains that his faith is strong when he is with the Prophet, yet weakens when he goes about his daily business. After listening to his concerns, the Prophet gently reassures him that his pattern of behavior is not a sign of hypocrisy, but of his humanity—by its very nature, he explains, spirituality is in a constant state of flux.

㉔ HOW DID THE PROPHET RESPOND TO THE COMPANIONS' FEELINGS OF HYPOCRISY? [RAMADAN]

"He [Muhammad] kept striving to soothe the consciences of the believers who were afraid of their own weaknesses and failings ... Their situation had nothing to do with hypocrisy: it was merely the reality of human nature, which remembers and forgets, and which needs to remember precisely because it forgets, because human beings are not angels.
He thus invited them [his Companions] to deny or despise nothing in their humanity and taught them that the core of the matter was achieving self-control. Spirituality means both accepting and mastering one's instincts: living one's natural desires in the light of one's principles is a prayer. It is never a misdeed, nor is it hypocrisy.
The Prophet hated to let his Companions nurture a pointless feeling of guilt. He kept telling them that they must never stop conversing with the One, the Most Kind, the Most Merciful, who welcomes everyone in His grace and benevolence and who loves the sincerity of hearts that regret their misdeed and return to Him."[32]

13
14
15
16
17
18

18.7 'A'ISHAH'S TRIAL

During the return march to Medina, 'A'ishah misplaces an onyx necklace her mother had given her as a wedding gift. When the entire caravan is ordered to stop, Abu Bakr chides his 14-year-old daughter for senselessly halting the caravan well before the next oasis. With no water in sight, the Companions are worried that they will not be able to wash themselves before the next prayer, but the Qur'an responds with the following verse:

> ...Don't (pray) in a state of ritual impurity, unless you're on the road traveling, until you've washed your whole body. If you're sick or on a journey or one of you has come from using the bathroom or had intimate relations and you can find no water (for your ablutions), then you can take clean sand and wipe your faces and hands with it. Indeed, God pardons (sins) and forgives.
> — *An-Nisa (The Women, 4:43)*

The revelation comes as a great relief to the Companions, one of whom comments:

"This is not the first blessing that you have brought unto us, O family of Abu Bakr."[33]

When 'A'ishah's camel arises, she finds her necklace underneath. But at the next oasis, she loses it a second time. When she goes to look for it, the caravan unknowingly leaves without her. She returns to the empty camp and falls asleep while waiting for the departed caravan to return. Meanwhile, Safwan ibn Mu'attal, a Companion who had fallen behind and was catching up with the caravan, is astonished to find the Prophet's young wife sleeping alone in the desert. He offers her his camel and escorts her to the caravan on foot.

When 'A'ishah returns to Medina, she stays with her parents to recover from an illness acquired during the journey. Unbeknownst to her, a salacious rumor has spread throughout Medina regarding her and Safwan. When her aunt accidentally leaks the gossip, 'A'ishah is devastated.

Those who spread the rumor include Mistah ibn Uthathah ('A'ishah's second cousin), Hamnah bint Jahsh, Hassan ibn Thabit, and 'Abd Allah ibn Ubayy.

Meanwhile, the Prophet seeks the opinion of his household regarding the matter, and all rush to 'A'ishah's defense. Usamah and his mother, Umm Ayman, shower 'A'ishah with praise. 'Ali, however, gives a more calculated response:

"God hath not restricted thee, and there are many women besides her. But question her maidservant and she will tell thee the truth."[34]

After much deliberation, the only fault 'A'ishah's servant can find with her is trivial—she explains that when 'A'ishah was a child, she was assigned to keep guard over kneaded dough, but sometimes she would fall asleep and her lamb would eat it.

Recall that **Hamnah bint Jahsh** is the sister of Zaynab bint Jahsh, the fourth wife of the Prophet. Zaynab was considered to be the Prophet's favorite wife after 'A'ishah. Lings notes that Hamnah publicly spread the rumor to further her sister's status at 'A'ishah's expense.

Recall that **Umm Ayman** (previously known as Barakah) used to be the servant of the Prophet's father and was one of the central members of the Prophet's household. She is the wife of Zayd ibn Harithah and mother of Usamah.

The next day the Prophet ascends his pulpit in the mosque and publicly defends his wife's honor. Usayd ibn Hudayr (of Aws) openly swears to punish anyone, from Aws or Khazraj, who spread rumors about the Prophet's family. Many of the men involved in the rumors are Khazraji, so upon hearing Usayd's announcement, Sa'd ibn 'Ubadah (of Khazraj) promptly accuses him of lying and says that no one from Aws would be allowed to punish any man of Khazraj. He swears that Usayd wouldn't be making such declarations had any of the people involved in the rumor been of Aws. Usayd condemns Sa'd as a liar and calls him a "hypocrite, striving amongst hypocrites." But before the argument can turn violent, the Prophet quickly disperses the congregation.

All this time, 'A'ishah is unaware that her husband is publicly defending her, and waits for a sign to exonerate her. When the Prophet visits her at Abu Bakr's house, he tries to comfort her, and prays to God to help resolve the matter:

> It was not enough that he should himself believe 'A'ishah and Safwan to be innocent. The situation was a grave one, and it was imperative to have evidence which would convince the whole community. To this end 'A'ishah herself had proved the least helpful. It was now time that her silence should be broken ... the Koran promised that questions asked during the period of its revelation would be answered.[35]

> All you who believe! Don't ask questions about (trivial) things that would be difficult for you if they were explained to you in detail. However, if you ask (about religious stipulations) when the Qur'an is being revealed, then they'll be clarified for you. God pardons that (kind of appropriate questioning), for God is forgiving and forbearing. Some people before you questioned (their messengers) incessantly like that, and eventually they fell into rejection (of God). — *Al Ma'idah (The Banquet Table, 5:101-102)*

The Prophet asks his inconsolable wife to declare her innocence or guilt. 'A'ishah is speechless and turns to her parents for help. But when Abu Bakr and Umm Ruman are unable to answer the Prophet, 'A'ishah cries:

> *"Should I tell you I am innocent, and Allah knows that I am surely innocent, you will not believe me; and if I were to admit something of which, Allah knows, I am innocent, you will believe me; so there is nothing for me and you except the words of the father of Prophet Yusuf (Joseph):"[37]*

 "...As for me, I can only wait with gracious patience. Only God can (help me) bear (the pain) of what you've described." — *Yusuf (Joseph, 12:18)*

'A'ishah later recalled:

> *"Then I turned to my couch and lay on it, hoping that God would declare me innocent. Not that I thought He would send down a Revelation on my account, for it seemed to me that I was too paltry for my case to be spoken of in the Qur'an. But I was hoping that the Prophet would see in his sleep a vision that would exculpate me."[38]*

This is not the first time the Prophet's most prominent Companions let their emotions get the best of them. Despite their differences, the Prophet trusted them both. A few years later at the Conquest of Mecca, Usayd will ride alongside the Prophet while Sa'd is given leadership of one of the four battalions that march into the city.

SURAH YUSUF (Joseph) relates the full story of Prophet Joseph, and is the longest surah in the Qur'an that follows a single storyline from beginning to end. When asked to relate the story of Joseph, the Prophet patiently waited for God's instruction. When it was revealed to him, he emerged in public and recited the wondrous surah (self-described as "the most beautiful story") in its entirety.

Be sure to read Salahi (p. 414-419) for an account of the entire incident in 'A'ishah's own words.

As they sit in silence, the Prophet is suddenly inspired by new verses from Surah An-Noor:

> Those who brought out the slanderous (charge of adultery against the Prophet's wife A'ishah) are nothing more than a gang among you (who tried to stir up trouble).
>
> Don't think of it as a bad thing, however, for it was ultimately a good thing for you (that this issue was dealt with openly). Every man among them will have his sin recorded, and the one who was the most involved among them will have a terrible punishment (from God).
>
> When you first heard of the situation, why didn't the men and women of faith think better (of A'ishah) to themselves and say, "This is obviously a false charge"? Why didn't they bring four witnesses to prove it? When they failed to bring witnesses, they were (proven) to be liars in the sight of God.
>
> If it wasn't for God's favor towards all of you and His mercy - both in this world and in the next - then a terrible punishment would've certainly befallen you on account of your indulgence in this affair.
>
> While you (people) were eagerly passing (this lie along) with your tongues and saying with your mouths things you knew nothing about, you thought it was just a trivial matter, but in God's sight it was a serious issue.
>
> When you (first) heard about it, why didn't you say, "It's not right for us to talk about this. Glory to You, (Our Lord), this is an awful rumor!" God is warning you seriously not to repeat this (vicious rumor-mongering), that is if you're (sincere) believers. —*An-Noor (The Light, 24:11-17)*

◈ **SURAH AN-NOOR** (The Light) is named after the illustrious verse that begins, "God is the Light of the heavens and the earth." The surah deals with a number of topics, most notably the importance of safeguarding the honor of respectable women (and in particular, the Prophet's youngest wife, 'A'ishah).

---

25 **WHAT IS THE SIGNIFICANCE OF THE QUR'AN'S MONTHLONG DELAY IN EXONERATING 'A'ISHAH?** [SALAHI]

"This was not given to him [the Prophet] for a whole month, during which the Prophet must have felt the agony of any man whose beloved wife stands accused of adultery while he is unable to prove her innocence. The fact that revelations on this matter were not vouchsafed to him for a whole month served more than one purpose. The Prophet trusted in God's wisdom and that He would do to him only what was right and good. He conducted himself with perfect dignity and forbearance until God saw fit to reveal Ā'ishah's innocence. Indeed, the delay added to the strength of her defence. It is also evidence of the truthfulness of Muhammad's message. Had he been a false prophet who invented the Qur'an, as the unbelievers alleged, he would probably have hastened to fabricate some sort of statement which gave judgement on this matter. Far was it from Prophet Muhammad to do any such thing. What should be emphasized here is that human nature could not, of its own accord, have seen the wisdom for such a delay. When people were speaking ill of the honour of the Prophet, human nature dictated that all those rumours should be stamped out immediately. The Prophet, however, realized that the decision was not his to make. He waited for guidance. This fits well with the fact that the Prophet did not have any control on matters which affected the Muslim community as a whole, or his own affairs as a human being."[36]

26 **HOW WAS 'A'ISHAH'S RESPONSE AN ACT OF DEEP FAITH?** | YUSUF |

"The *mumin* [believer] does not defend himself. Defending yourself is believing there is something to defend. For 'A'ishah, she doesn't care. This is *iman* [faith]. Allah defends the people of iman. There's a hadith that says: 'O children of Adam, you have a place with me as long as you don't have a place with your own self.'
In other words, [Yusuf paraphrasing here], God will consider you to be something as long as you don't consider yourself something. And when you consider yourself something, God will no longer have consideration for you.
And that's where 'A'ishah was. She deemed herself nothing and she said, 'I would never think that Allah would mention this issue in the Qur'an because I was too insignificant. But I was hoping that maybe Allah would show the Messenger a vision or something in his dreams that would free me from it.'
 [Yusuf citing an authentic hadith from Muslim] 'Whoever is humble for the sake of Allah, Allah raises him up.'
And so Allah completely absolves her, removes any suspicion and any doubt about that in the Book of Allah."[39]

27 **HOW WAS 'A'ISHAH'S TRIAL A NECESSARY EXPERIENCE?** | YUSUF |

"This is the wisdom of understanding that tribulations are hikmah [wisdom] for the mumin [believer]. Don't think tribulations are a bad thing. Tribulations can be a good thing. Look how much you learn. Look how much 'A'ishah learns. She had to have this experience because Allah wanted great things for 'A'ishah, and one of them is that she comes to know Allah absolutely and completely. So don't think these bad things that happen to you are evil. They're not bad things; they're good things because you're a believer."[40]

Following 'A'ishah's exoneration, Abu Bakr swears to withold charity to Mistah ibn Uthathah, but then recants his oath after hearing the next few verses from Surah An-Noor:

> Don't let those who've been endowed (with great wealth and status) among you swear that they're no longer going to help their relatives, the needy or those who've migrated in the cause of God (simply because those people might have behaved poorly). Forgive them and overlook (their faults). Don't you want God to forgive you, too? God is forgiving and merciful!
> — *An-Noor (The Light,* 24:22)

Despite his Companions' lapse in judgment, the Prophet shows great generosity to Hassan ibn Thabit and the others who repented after spreading rumors about his family. He forgives Hamnah bint Jahsh and later marries her to Talhah ibn 'Ubayd Allah.

A year later, the ruler of Egypt will send the Prophet a gift of two slave girls named Mariyah and Sirin. The Prophet will keep Mariyah in his household and give custodianship of Sirin to **Hassan ibn Thabit.**

Recall that **Hamnah bint Jahsh's** husband, Mus'ab ibn 'Umayr, was martyred at Uhud. He and Talhah were among the Prophet's closest Companions.

Disruptive as it was, the entire necklace scandal marks the end of ʿAbd Allah ibn Ubayy's longstanding opposition to the Prophet:

> He seems to have realized that his influence was now too slight for him to achieve anything, and to have taken no further active steps against Muhammad. He was too old to become an enthusiastic Muslim, and he may have sometimes grumbled … The 'affair of the lie' (together with the failure of the siege a month later) may be said to mark the end of the opposition to Muhammad by ʿAbd-Allah and his party of Hypocrites. The weakness of his position was that it had no intellectual basis. As a Jewish leader is said to have put it, he did not know what he wanted; he was whole-heartedly committed neither to Islam nor to Judaism nor to the old religion of the Arabs. What moved him was chiefly personal ambition, and he lacked both the statesmanship to see the vaster issues involved and the vision to propound a way of dealing with them that would attract men. He must have seen the need for peace in Medina, but his attempts to meet it were along conservative lines and already discredited. In opposing Muhammad he had failed to move with the times.[41]

---

28 WHY DIDN'T THE PROPHET PREEMPTIVELY PUNISH THE HYPOCRITES? SALAHI

"It may be asked here whether it would not have been easier for the Muslims had God chosen to unveil to the Prophet the identity of each of the hypocrites so that the Muslims could at least be on their guard against them. That was certainly easy for God to do, if He so wished, but He chose not to. One must not forget that the hypocrites pretended to be Muslims. Were the Prophet to take any positive action against them, he would appear, in the eyes of others, to be punishing a section of his followers for no apparent crime. This might have frightened away from Islam many people who would otherwise have decided to accept the faith. The Prophet would have also appeared to be a tyrant who passed arbitrary judgement on some of his followers. Moreover, he was setting an example for the following generations of Muslims. Since no other Muslim ruler would receive revelations from God, the identity of the hypocrites in succeeding Muslim generations could not be ascertained. These generations needed guidance on how to deal with the problem of hypocrisy. Such guidance could be provided only by the Prophet. He was therefore instructed by God to accept people as they professed to be, leaving judgement on their true intentions and their true motives to God alone. Thus the hypocrites represented a danger of an unknown quantity. The Muslims were to keep on their guard, but they were not to strike the first blow."[42]

The Prophet's age before Hudaybiyah: __58__

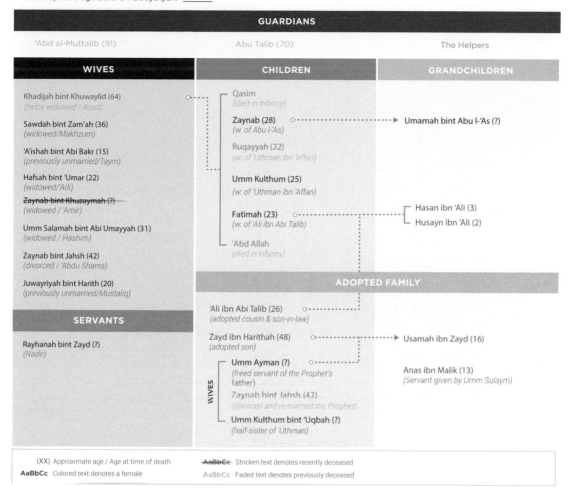

GUARDIANS		
'Abd al-Muttalib (81)	Abu Talib (70)	The Helpers

WIVES	CHILDREN	GRANDCHILDREN
Khadijah bint Khuwaylid (64) *(twice widowed / Asad)*	Qasim *(died in infancy)*	
Sawdah bint Zam'ah (36) *(widowed/Makhzum)*	Zaynab (28) *(w. of Abu l-'As)*	Umamah bint Abu l-'As (?)
'A'ishah bint Abi Bakr (15) *(previously unmarried/Taym)*	Ruqayyah (22) *(w. of 'Uthman ibn 'Affan)*	
Hafsah bint 'Umar (22) *(widowed/'Adi)*	Umm Kulthum (25) *(w. of 'Uthman ibn 'Affan)*	
~~Zaynab bint Khuzaymah (?)~~ *(widowed / 'Amir)*	Fatimah (23) *(w. of 'Ali ibn Abi Talib)*	Hasan ibn 'Ali (3) Husayn ibn 'Ali (2)
Umm Salamah bint Abi Umayyah (31) *(widowed / Hashim)*	'Abd Allah *(died in infancy)*	
Zaynab bint Jahsh (42) *(divorced / 'Abdu Shams)*		
Juwayriyah bint Harith (20) *(previously unmarried/Mustaliq)*		

ADOPTED FAMILY	
'Ali ibn Abi Talib (26) *(adopted cousin & son-in-law)*	
Zayd ibn Harithah (48) *(adopted son)*	Usamah ibn Zayd (16)
WIVES: Umm Ayman (?) *(freed servant of the Prophet's father)*	
Zaynab bint Jahsh (42) *(divorced and re-married the Prophet)*	Anas ibn Malik (13) *(Servant given by Umm Sulaym)*
Umm Kulthum bint 'Uqbah (?) *(half-sister of 'Uthman)*	

SERVANTS

Rayhanah bint Zayd (?)
(Nadir)

(XX) Approximate age / Age at time of death	~~AaBbCc~~ Stricken text denotes recently deceased
AaBbCc Colored text denotes a female	AaBbCc Faded text denotes previously deceased

FIGURE 18C. THE PROPHET'S HOUSEHOLD BEFORE HUDAYBIYAH

Zaynab bint Khuzaymah's late husband, 'Ubaydah ibn al-Harith, was the oldest man to fight at the opening duels at Badr where he was martyred. After the Battle of Uhud, the Prophet married Zaynab, who was from the Hawazin clan of 'Amir. The union prompted the chief of her clan to invite 40 scholars to teach Islam to his people. However, the party was ambushed and killed along the way. Shortly after the second Badr expedition, Fatimah and 'Ali had a second son, Husayn. The addition, however, was tempered by the death of the Prophet's newest wife, Zaynab. (Khadijah and Zaynab were the only two wives who died during the Prophet's lifetime.) Her passing was soon followed by the death of the Prophet's cousin Abu Salamah, who as he lay dying, prayed that his wife would marry a man better than him. Shortly after his death, Umm Salamah joined the Prophet's household as his sixth wife. Unlike Hafsah and Zaynab, Umm Salamah's addition to the household became a source of mild jealousy for 'A'ishah. The Prophet's marriage to Umm Salamah was soon followed by his marriage to Zayd's ex-wife, Zaynab bint Jahsh. Zaynab was the Prophet's first cousin and the oldest of the Prophet's wives (excluding Khadijah). The marriage, as commanded in Surah Al Ahzab, broke tribal customs in Arabia. The end of the Early Medinan Period saw the additions of Rayhanah bint Zayd (from Bani Nadir) and Juwayriyah bint Harith (from the clan of Mustaliq). Upon Juwayriyah's marriage to the Prophet, the Companions released more than 100 captive families from her clan.

(Refer to Figs. P25, 6b, 13f, and 16b for previous details about the Prophet's household.)

13
14
15
16
17
18

LATE MEDINA

PROPHETIC GENEROSITY

◇

Jābir ibn 'Abdullāh narrated: "The Messenger of Allāh (peace be upon him) was never asked of something to which he said 'No.'"

———

'Umar ibn al-Khattab narrated: "A man came to the Prophet (peace be upon him) asking for something. The Prophet (peace be upon him) replied, 'I do not have anything at present but go and purchase something on my name and I will pay for it when I have sufficient money.' 'Umar said, 'O Messenger of Allāh! You have already given him that which you had and Allāh did not make you responsible for that which is beyond your means.' The Messenger (peace be upon him) disliked this statement of 'Umar. A man from the Ansār said, 'O Messenger of Allāh! Spend whatever you wish , and do not fear any diminution from the Lord of the Throne.' The Messenger (peace be upon him) smiled and the happiness could be seen on his face due to the statement of the man. He (peace be upon him) then said, 'With this I have been ordered.' "

———

Taken from A Commentary on the Depiction of Prophet Muhammad,
by Imam al-Tirmidhi (#352, #355)

YEAR 19: HUDAYBIYAH

19.1 THE MARCH TO HUDAYBIYAH

Shortly after the end of Ramadan, the Prophet experiences a vivid dream instructing him to lead the 'Umrah (lesser pilgrimage). He relates the vision to his Companions and soon a group of more than 1,000 pilgrims and 70 sacrificial camels are assembled for the journey to Mecca. 'Umar suggests that the men travel fully armed, but the Prophet insists that they only travel as pilgrims. Among the Prophet's wives, Umm Salamah is chosen to join the expedition. In accordance with the pilgrimage rites, the Prophet removes his turban and exchanges his clothes for the *ihram* (pilgrim's attire consisting of two unfinished white sheets), before leading the caravan to Mecca on his favorite camel, Qaswa.

The Quraysh soon learn about the approaching pilgrims and send Khalid ibn al-Walid with 200 men to block their entry. Hoping to avoid a confrontation, the pilgrims veer off the expected route to Mecca. Along the way, however, Qaswa unexpectedly kneels to the ground. But when the Companions fault her for her stubbornness, the Prophet responds:

> *"She is not stubborn, it is not in her nature; but He holdeth her who held the elephant."*[1]

The Prophet halts the caravan in the valley of Hudaybiyah. As the men set up camp, they notice that the wells are nearly dry. They turn to the Prophet, who miraculously causes the wells to fill with enough water for all the pilgrims and animals. As 'Abd Allah ibn Ubayy is drinking his fill, a clansman pointedly asks him how many more miracles he needs to witness to become a true believer. To the Companions' frustration, 'Abd Allah glibly swears that he has seen such miracles before. Although this is not his first controversial statement, 'Abd Allah immediately apologizes to the Prophet and confesses his mistake, in an effort to avoid yet another storm.

While the pilgrims are encamped at Hudaybiyah, the local tribe of Khuza'ah provides for their daily needs. Although the Khuza'ah had not yet entered Islam, they had allied themselves with the Prophet to counterbalance a strong alliance their rival, Bani Bakr, shared with the Quraysh.

Budayl ibn Warqa', one of the Khuza'ah leaders, is visiting Mecca at this time. When he hears about the Prophet's pilgrimage, he rides to Hudaybiyah to warn him that the Quraysh will not allow the pilgrims to enter the Sanctuary under any circumstances. The Prophet instructs Budayl to return to Mecca with a message of peace:

> *"We came not here for battle; we came only to make our pilgrimal rounds about the House. He that standeth in our way, him we shall fight; but I will grant them time, if they so desire it, to take their precautions and to leave the way clear for us."*[2]

Al-Mubarakpuri numbers the expedition at 1,400 - 1,500 pilgrims.

Recall that **Umm Salamah** is the sixth wife of the Prophet. She had followed her previous husband, Abu Salamah, into Islam and migrated to Abyssinia. Less than three years ago, Abu Salamah had passed away after the battle of Uhud.

The Prophet is referring to Abraha's elephant who refused to enter Mecca's Sacred Precinct, nearly 60 years ago (P3.3).

Remember that several centuries earlier, the tribe of **Khuza'ah** used to control Mecca until they were ousted by the Quraysh (led by Qusayy). A few generations later, they formed an alliance with Hashim by helping 'Abd al-Muttalib take back control of Mecca from his uncle Nawfal (P2.3) The alliance with Khuza'ah will soon bring a huge reward to the Muslims.

Two years later at the Conquest of Mecca, **Budayl ibn Warqa'** joins Abu Sufyan ibn al-Harb in a last-minute appeal to the Prophet's advancing army outside of Mecca and testifies his faith. The Prophet will later place Budayl in charge of transporting all the captives and spoils from Hunayn to the valley of Ji'ranah.

The Quraysh ignore his message. Instead, they send a scout to Hudaybiyah by the name of Hulays ibn 'Alqamah—a powerful man who commanded all of Mecca's Bedouin allies (known collectively as the *Ahabish*). When Hulays returns to Mecca confirming Budayl's report that the pilgrims have come in peace, the Quraysh scoff at him, saying that he is a simple nomad who cannot understand the complexity of city politics. Their condescension does not sit well with Hulays, who responds with an ultimatum—either the Quraysh allow the pilgrims into the Holy Sanctuary, or the Ahabish will forgo their alliance with Mecca.

'Urwah ibn Mas'ud, a man from Bani Thaqif, also happens to be in Mecca during this time. When the Quraysh ignore the advice of their first two scouts, 'Urwah offers to meet with the Prophet and confirm what Budayl observed. After visiting the Muslim camp, 'Urwah returns to Mecca in complete awe of the Prophet. He advises the Quraysh:

> *"I have been to Chosroes, Caesar and Negus in their kingdoms, but never have I seen a king among a people like Muhammad among his Companions ... They will not abandon him for anything in any case. He now offers you a reasonable plan, so do what you please."*[3]

Eager to disrupt any chance of a truce between Mecca and Medina, a group of approximately 70 young Meccans try to ambush the pilgrims' camp. However, their plan is foiled by Muhammad ibn Maslamah, whom the Prophet had placed in charge of the camp's security. The Meccan party is taken captive, but—as described in Surah Al Fet-h—the Prophet makes a conciliatory gesture by releasing them back to the Quraysh.

> He's the One Who restrained their hands from you and your hands from them - right in the midst (of their own territory) of Mecca. Then, afterwards, He gave you victory over them (through the truce), and God is watching whatever you do. —*Al Fet-h (Victory, 48:24)*

The Prophet dispatches Khirash ibn Umayyah to negotiate on his behalf, but Khirash—after nearly being killed in Mecca—returns to Hudaybiyah instructing the Prophet to send someone better protected. When the Prophet suggests 'Umar ibn al-Khattab, 'Umar responds that 'Uthman ibn 'Affan is more powerful in Mecca and better protected than he is.

Although 'Uthman is unable to negotiate a deal, the Quraysh offer him the opportunity to perform the pilgrimage rites on his own. When 'Uthman flatly refuses, they send another messenger to 'Abd Allah ibn Ubayy with the same offer. To the Prophet's delight, 'Abd Allah also refuses to perform the pilgrimage before the Prophet is allowed to enter the Sanctuary.

19.2 THE PACT OF ALLEGIANCE

Having come to an impasse with 'Uthman and 'Abd Allah ibn Ubayy, the Quraysh send three men—Suhayl ibn 'Amr al-'Amiri, Mikraz ibn Hafs, and Huwaytib ibn 'Abd al-'Uzzah—to negotiate a treaty with the Prophet.

Suhayl ibn 'Amr al-'Amiri is the chief of the clan of Amir whose many family members became Muslims (ironically his son 'Abd Allah is one of the Muslim co-signers of the Treaty of Hudaybiyah). Recall that Suhayl refused the Prophet's request for protection after Ta'if, and was later captured at Badr. After the Conquest of Mecca, he will be one of three men who does not enter Islam, but is nonetheless given protection. He will finally embrace Islam after the Prophet gives him a generous portion of the spoils of Hunayn.

> **❶ WHY WASN'T ABU SUFYAN AT THE HUDAYBIYAH NEGOTIATIONS?** WATT
>
> "The rivalry between Abu Sufyan and Safwan b. Umayyah abated sufficiently to allow a united expedition to Badr in April 626 and the attempt to capture Medina in April 627, but the dissensions between the Meccan leaders led to delay on both occasions. Abu Sufyan had the supreme command in view of the hereditary privilege of his clan. 'Ikrimah, however, began to come into prominence at the siege of Medina, especially in negotiations with the Jews; and by the time of Muhammad's expedition to al-Hudaybiyah in March 628 we find the triumvirate of Safwan b. Umayyah, Suhayl b. 'Amr ('Amir), and 'Ikrimah b. Abi Jahl constituting the core of the resistance to the Muslims. When Muhammad suggested negotiations, however, the triumvirate was divided. 'Ikrimah was against any negotiations, and at one point maltreated Muhammad's envoy, but he was opposed by Safwan along with al-Harith b. Hisham of Makhzum. 'Ikrimah was eventually won over, and when it came to the final negotiation of the treaty, this was entrusted to the third of the triumvirate, Suhayl, assisted by two of his fellow clansmen. In all this there is no mention of Abu Sufyan; and mere absence is not enough to explain this silence, though absence if he were absent would help."[4]

Just before negotiations begin, the Prophet receives inspiration instructing him to first renew a pact of allegiance with the Companions. Sitting under the shade of an acacia tree, he shakes each pilgrim's hand as they pledge their allegiance to him, in what comes to be known as the *Pact of Ridwan* (The Pact of Allegiance).

On behalf of 'Uthman ibn 'Affan, who had not yet returned from Mecca, the Prophet takes his left hand in his right and makes the pledge for him. Surah Al Fet-h elaborates:

> God's good pleasure was upon the believers when they pledged their allegiance to you under the tree (at Hudaybiyyah, while the fate of your emissary was still in question). He knew what was in their hearts, and He sent tranquility down upon them and rewarded them with a quick victory (through the signing of the truce deal). — *Al Fet-h (Victory, 48:18)*

This verse from Surah Al Fet-h was revealed during the return trip to Medina from Hudaybiyah.

> **❷ WHAT MADE THE PACT OF RIDWAN DIFFERENT FROM THE PLEDGES OF 'AQABAH?** RAMADAN
>
> "They had all pledged their allegiance [at the Second 'Aqabah] thinking that they were expressing their fidelity in a situation of conflict, and moreover one in which they were in a weak position. Now their fidelity was going to be tested through the implementation and terms of a truce in which they held a strong position. The Muslims were demanding their right, they bore a message that they were certain was true, and they had acquired great prestige after the latest battles, so keeping a low profile was out of the question."[5]
>
> -
>
> **❸ WHY DID THE PROPHET MAKE A SYMBOLIC PACT OF ALLEGIANCE FOR 'UTHMAN?** YUSUF
>
> "This is foresight from the Messenger of Allah, God's peace and blessings upon him, about people who would try to attack 'Uthman by saying that he didn't fight at Badr, nor was he present at the Pact of Ridwan."[6]

19

20

21

22

23

19.3 THE TREATY & ITS RECEPTION

The Prophet begins dictating the terms of the treaty starting with *Bismillah ar-Rahman ar-Rahim* (In the Name of God, the Good, the Merciful). Suhayl responds that he does not know *ar-Rahman* and demands that the document simply begin with *Bismik Allahumma*, (In Thy Name, Oh God). The Prophet consents to his request and continues dictating:

> *"This is what Muhammad the Messenger of Allah, has agreed to with Suhail bin 'Amr."*

Again Suhayl insists on rephrasing the sentence explaining:

> *"If we knew thee to be the Messenger of God, we would not have barred thee from the House, neither would we have fought thee; but write Muhammad the son of 'Abd Allah."*[7]

---

4 **HOW COULD THE PROPHET STRIKE OUT HIS OWN TITLE?**   RAMADAN

"The Prophet heard his [Suhayl's] point of view and was able, at that particular moment, to shift his perspective and see things from his interlocutor's standpoint. What Suhayl was saying was perfectly true according to his outlook. It was indeed obvious that if the Quraysh had acknowledged his [Muhammad's] status as God's Messenger, they would not have fought against him; therefore, an agreement on an equal footing could not possibly state an element that would in effect acknowledge what one side held as truth while contradicting the other's position..."[8]

The Prophet again yields to Suhayl's objection and asks 'Ali to strike out the title "Messenger of God" after his name. 'Ali cannot bring himself to cross out the words, but agrees to point them out so the Prophet can strike them out himself and replace it with "Muhammad ibn 'Abd Allah."

---

5 **WHAT WAS THE PROPHET'S MINDSET AT HUDAYBIYAH?**   WATT

"The treaty was only satisfactory for the Muslims in so far as one believed in Islam and its attractive power. Had Muhammad not been able to maintain and strengthen his hold on the Muslims by the sway of the religious ideas of Islam over their imaginations, and had he not been able to attract fresh converts to Islam, the treaty would not have worked in his favour. Material reasons certainly played a large part in the conversion of many Arabs to Islam. But other factors of supreme importance were Muhammad's belief in the message of the Qur'an, his belief in the future of Islam as a religious and political system, and his unflinching devotion to the task to which, as he believed, God had called him. These attitudes underlay the policy Muhammad followed at al-Hudaybiyah."[9]

- -

6 **HOW COULD 'ALI DISOBEY THE PROPHET?**   YUSUF

"This is an important *fiqh* [jurisprudence] issue. The scholars describe this action as 'disobeying the Messenger of Allah out of *adab* [respect, courtesy] to the Messenger of Allah.' We also see an example of this in Abu Bakr when he refuses to lead the prayer in front of the Messenger."[10]

After joint deliberation, the two parties draft the terms of the treaty:

> *In Thy name, O God. This is the treaty which Muhammad b. 'Abdallah made with Suhayl b. 'Amr. They agreed to remove war from the people for ten years. During this time the people are to be in security and no one is to lay hands on another. Whoever of Quraysh comes to Muhammad without permission of his protector (or guardian), Muhammad is to send back to them; whoever of those with Muhammad comes to Quraysh is not to be sent back to him. Between us evil is to be abstained from, and there is to be no raiding or spoliation. Whoever wants to enter into a covenant and alliance with Muhammad is to do so and whoever wants to enter into a covenant and alliance with Quraysh is to do so. ... You are to withdraw from us this year and not enter Mecca against us; and when next year comes we shall go out in front of you and you shall enter it (Mecca) with your companions and remain in it three days; you shall have the arms of the rider, swords in scabbards; you shall not enter it bearing anything else.[11]*

The document is co-signed by 'Umar, Abu Bakr, 'Abd ar-Rahman ibn 'Awf, Mahmud ibn Maslamah, and 'Abd Allah ibn Suhayl (one of Suhayl's sons).

---

7 **WHY DID MUHAMMAD ACCEPT THE TREATY OF HUDAYBIYAH?** `ASLAN`

"It is difficult to say why Muhammad accepted the treaty of Hudaybiyah. He may have been hoping to regroup and wait for an opportune time to return and conquer Mecca by force. He may have been observing the Quranic mandate and jihadi doctrine to 'fight until oppression ends and God's law prevails. But if [the enemy] desists, then you must also cease hostilities' (2:193)."[12]

'Abd ar-Rahman ibn 'Awf was one of the first men to embrace Islam. A few years later, during the march to Tabuk, he leads the congregational prayer and the Prophet joins behind him, saying, *"Ye have done well, for verily a Prophet dieth not until he hath been led in prayer by a pious man of his people."*[13]

THE TRUCE

TREATY OF HUDAYBIYAH

① Both parties agree to a conditional 10-year truce.
② Any Meccans who flee to Medina must return to Mecca.
③ Any Medinans who flee to Mecca may remain in Mecca.
④ There will be no tolerance for treachery or subterfuge.
⑤ Each city is free to make pacts with third parties.
⑥ The Muslim pilgrims will not perform the pilgrimage that year.
⑦ The Muslim pilgrims may return the following year (bearing no arms, except the arms of a traveler).

FIGURE 19A. THE TERMS OF HUDAYBIYAH

19
20
21
22
23

8 **SIGNING THE TREATY REQUIRED A DEEP UNDERSTANDING** RAMADAN

"What appeared as an unacceptable compromise from the sole viewpoint of the believers' faith was fair and equitable from the double viewpoint of the respective rationalities of each of the parties drawing up the peace treaty.
Agreeing not to enter the sanctuary that year took into account the Quraysh's vulnerability and protected their prestige, and this contributed toward long-term peace ... Trust in God, allied to strict intellectual coherence and an exceptionally acute mind, had enabled the Prophet to establish a ten-year truce with the prospect of a visit to the sanctuary the following year. Most of the Companions, and particularly Umar ibn al-Khattab, considered only immediate results, however, and felt this was a humiliation that could amount to nothing but a defeat.
The signing of the pact was therefore, once again, a privileged moment of spiritual edification with, moreover, an exceptional lesson about the value of intelligence and perspicacity."[14]

9 **WHY DID THE PROPHET AGREE TO THE TREATY?** ARMSTRONG

"After defeating the Quraysh at the Battle of the Trench, the obvious plan would have been to press on and destroy them unilaterally. But this had never been Muhammad's intention. The downfall of Mecca would be an inconceivable catastrophe for Arabia, a backward region that sorely needed the commercial genius of the Quraysh, who would never see the point of Islam while the war continued to fuel destructive anger and hatred on both sides. By abandoning the economic blockade, Muhammad hoped to win them over. He could see further than anybody else at Hudaybiyah...
Muslims were not supposed to be men of war; they were characterized by the spirit of hilm, a peace and fore-bearance that allied them with the Jews and Christians, the People of the Book."[15]

10 **WHAT DOES HUDAYBIYAH TEACH ABOUT THE NATURE OF COMPROMISE?** YUSUF

"The *muminun* [believers] have to have patience with the wisdom of the Messenger of Allah, God's peace and blessings upon him. What you get from Hudaybiyah is that there was a compromise, but the compromise did not concern first principles. In other words, there was nothing that was disobedient to Allah in the compromises that the Messenger of Allah, God's peace and blessings upon him, made. And this is an indication for Muslims in situations of weakness, that sometimes circumstances necessitate compromises that are difficult for the believers to accept with the idea that you think in terms of the long-term picture.
There's a wisdom in recognizing that you have to do things that might be difficult for a greater benefit. And this is clearly what the Messenger of Allah, God's peace and blessings upon him, did."[16]

The renewal of this pre-existing alliance with Khuza'ah will be pivotal to the Prophet's success. Two years from now, some men of Bani Bakr (with the help of a few Meccans) attack the Khuza'ah. Their offensive breaks the terms of the treaty, opening up the path for the Prophet to conquer Mecca.

In addition to forming a pact with the Quraysh, the Prophet renews his alliance with Bani Khuza'ah, which have been generously caring for the pilgrims.

The Companions are frustrated over the terms of the treaty, and their patience is soon tested when Abu Jandal, Suhayl's believing son whom Suhayl had imprisoned in Mecca, enters the camp in chains seeking refuge with the Muslims. The terms of the newly signed treaty dictate that a Meccan may not defect to the Muslim side without permission from his guardian in Mecca. Although the signatures have barely dried on the document, the Prophet is forced to keep his word and gently counsels Abu Jandal:

"Be patient, resign yourself to the Will of Allah. Allah is going to provide for you and your helpless companions relief and means of escape. We have concluded a

treaty of peace with them and we have taken the pledge in the Name of Allah. We are, therefore, under no circumstances prepared to break it."[17]

The scene is too much for 'Umar, who later asks the Prophet:

"Aren't you the true Messenger of Allah? Aren't we on the path of righteousness and our enemies in the wrong? Then we shouldn't suffer any humiliation in the matter of faith ... Did you not tell us that we shall perform pilgrimage?"

The Prophet replies:

"But I have never told you that we shall do so this very year."[18]

Unsatisfied, 'Umar approaches Abu Bakr with the same questions and receives the same reply.

---

11 WHY WAS THE TREATY HARD TO ACCEPT? `ARMSTRONG`

"During the last five years, many Muslims had died for their religion; others had risked everything and given up family and friends. Yet now Muhammad had calmly handed the advantage back to the Quraysh, and the pilgrims must agree to go home meekly, without even forcing the pilgrimage issue. The treaty assaulted every single jahili instinct."[19]

- -

12 WHAT WAS 'UMAR LIKELY FEELING AT HUDAYBIYAH? `ARMSTRONG`

"He [Umar] did not understand that the values of gentleness and nonviolence were also central to the Islamic ideal. ... Faced with Muhammad's apparent about-face at Hudaybiyyah, he was bewildered and confused."[20]

- -

13 WHAT DOES HUDAYBIYAH TEACH US ABOUT ABU BAKR? `YUSUF`

[Yusuf re-enacting the scene between 'Umar and Abu Bakr]: " 'Umar goes to Abu Bakr looking for an explanation. Abu Bakr grabs 'Umar and responds, 'Where do you think he's being commanded from? Who's telling him what to do? Don't you remember who he is?' Hearing this 'Umar suddenly comes to his senses."[21]

Although the treaty forbids the Muslims from entering Mecca that year, the Prophet instructs them to complete the final rites of the pilgrimage at the campsite in Hudaybiyah. For the first time in his prophetic career, the Prophet's words fall on deaf ears; the Companions cannot bring themselves to complete the sacraments without having entered the Holy Sanctuary.

Discouraged by their inaction, the Prophet seeks Umm Salamah's advice. She suggests that he first perform the rites of shaving his head and sacrificing his camel to set an example. As she predicted, the Companions immediately follow his example.

---

14 HOW DID THE PROPHET REGARD HIS WIVES? `ARMSTRONG`

"That dialogue, that understanding and listening, expresses the very essence of the Prophet's attitude toward his wives. As with Khadijah so many years before, he never hesitated to take the time to confide in the women around him, to consult them, talk with them, and adopt their opinions. At a time when the future of the whole community was playing out through visions, pledges of allegiance, and peace covenants, he returned to his wife's side and, like a simple human being, told her of his need for love, trust, and advice—an example for all human beings."[22]

19
20
21
22
23

On their way back to Medina, 'Umar is troubled over having questioned the Prophet's judgment and worries that the Qur'an will condemn him. Instead, when the Prophet summons 'Umar to his side, he instead shares with him the wonderful news that had just been revealed to him:

(Muhammad,) We've truly granted you a clear victory (through the signing of a truce with the Meccans)! — *Al Fet-h (Victory, 48:1)*

Surah Al Fet-h goes on to explain the victory and God's promise to the Muslim community:

While the faithless had hearts filled with rage - the rage of ignorance - God was sending His tranquility down upon His Messenger and also upon the believers, helping them to obey the order to restrain themselves. They were true to it and were more entitled to it, and God has knowledge of all things.

And so God fulfilled the vision of His Messenger (when he had seen himself in a dream leading the believers on a pilgrimage to hostile Mecca). Now you can enter the Sacred Mosque, (next year) as God wills, with peace of mind, with your heads shaved or hair cut short and without fear, (on account of the truce deal). He knew what you didn't know, and He granted you an early victory besides this, as well. He's the One Who sent His Messenger with guidance and the true way of life, to proclaim it over all other ways of life, and God is enough as a witness.

Muhammad is the Messenger of God. Those who are with him are hard on the faithless but compassionate among each other. You'll see them bowing and prostrating themselves (in prayer), seeking the grace of God and (His) pleasure. On their faces are the marks of their prostrations, and this is their example in the Torah. Their example in the Gospel is like a seed that sends out its blade and then makes itself strong. It then thickens and stands on its own stem, filling the farmers with satisfaction.

However, (such firm belief) fills the faithless with rage against (the believers). God has promised those among them who believe and do what's morally right forgiveness and a great reward. — *Al Fet-h (Victory, 48:26-29)*

SURAH AL FET-H (Victory) is named after its opening verse, which describes the Muslim triumph at Hudaybiyah. The next several verses provide a spiritual commentary on those who obeyed the Prophet and attended the Pact of Ridwan, as opposed to the Bedouins and hypocrites who lagged behind. The surah ends by describing the state of true God-consciousness, a theme previously mentioned in the Torah of Moses and Gospel of Jesus.

---

15 WAS HUDAYBIYAH REALLY A CLEAR VICTORY? YUSUF

"It was not clear to the sahaba [companions]. It looked like a clear defeat. And this is one of the greatest lessons of Hudaybiyah: Don't think you understand what's going on. You have to trust in Allah. You have to give up your own intellect in trying to understand the wisdoms behind all of what Allah is doing. You have to really see that Allah is doing what is good for the believers. And that is what we are being told in Surah Fet-h.

"Abu Bakr will later say, 'There was no greater *fet-h* [victory] in Islam than the fath of Hudaybiyah.' The understanding of the Muslims was shortsighted on that day. They couldn't see the long-term benefits that came from that, because all the openings that occur later come from Hudaybiyah. All the ease and victories came from that day. It was a momentous event and they couldn't see it at that moment."[23]

19.4 ABU BASIR & HIS MEN

Shortly after the Companions returned from Hudaybiyah, a Meccan named Abu Basir ibn Asid flees Mecca to live in Medina. The Prophet learns of his escape and, in accordance with the terms of the treaty, instructs him to return home. Two Meccans arrive to escort Abu Basir back, but, he kills one of them at the first stop outside Medina. The other escort flees for his life and Abu Basir travels west, settling near the Red Sea coast along Mecca's northern caravan route to Syria.

News of the escape reaches Mecca, and soon other prisoners including Abu Jandal ibn Suhayl and Walid ibn al-Walid escape to join Abu Basir's renegade camp. Under Abu Basir's leadership, the group (numbering 70 men) begins ambushing Mecca's northbound caravans. The Quraysh are unprepared for new hostilities and approach the Prophet in search of an amicable solution. As much as they want to punish Abu Basir and his followers, they elect to surrender them to Medina so the Prophet can hold them to the terms of the treaty. It is a concession they are willing to make to safeguard their northern trade route.

Just before the men depart for Medina, however, Abu Basir passes away and his companions build a mosque beside his grave at the site of their encampment.

Abu Basir ibn Asid independently organized these raids against the Quraysh. From a political perspective, the Quraysh could not hold the Prophet responsible for the hostilities.

Remember that **Walid ibn al-Walid** fought the Prophet at Badr and was captured. His brothers ransomed their father's famous armor for him, but on the way home, Walid escaped back to Medina, where he entered Islam. He later returned to Mecca to gather some of his belongings and his family imprisoned him.

19.5 THE GROWTH OF MEDINA AFTER HUDAYBIYAH

'Uthman ibn 'Affan's half-sister Umm Kulthum also escapes Mecca to seek asylum in Medina. The Prophet permits her to stay because of Surah Al Mumtahinah's injunction which forbids believing women to remain with pagan men. Furthermore, the terms of Hudaybiyah did not explicitly mention that women were not allowed to leave Mecca. Following the Prophet's recommendation, Umm Kulthum marries his adopted son Zayd ibn Harithah.

> All you who believe! When believing women come to you as refugees (from enemy territory), interview them to establish the validity of their convictions, although God knows best their true level of faith. If you determine that they're sincere believers, then don't send them back to the faithless.
>
> (Believing women) are no longer legitimate for them (as wives,) even as (idol-worshippers) are no longer legitimate (as husbands for women of faith). Reimburse (the idol-worshippers) for what they spent (on their marriage gifts to the women who have now deserted them). Then there will be no blame if you (believing men seek to) marry (such women) after offering them a marriage gift.
>
> As for any women (who are idol-worshippers, they're no longer your responsibility), so don't play host to them. Ask for the dowry you gave to them from (the idol-worshippers), even as they may seek what they spent (on the women joining you). This is the law of God and His judgment between you. God is full of knowledge and wisdom. — *Al Mumtahinah (She Who is Interviewed, 60:10)*

In accordance to the ruling, 'Umar divorces two pagan wives he had married in Mecca. The women subsequently marry Mu'awiyah ibn Abi Sufyan and Safwan ibn Umayyah.

✎ **SURAH AL MUMTAHINAH** (She Who is Interviewed) was revealed shortly before the Conquest of Mecca and is named after a verse that explains how to judge the intentions of Meccan women who were arriving in Medina after Hudaybiyah. Among other things, the surah highlights the example of Prophet Abraham, stresses the importance of communal solidarity, and encourages kindness to non-Muslim friends..

Both **Mu'awiyah ibn Abi Sufyan** and **Safwan ibn Abi Umayyah** will become Muslims after the Conquest of Mecca. While Mu'awiyah does not play a significant role in the Sirah literature, in the years to come, he will ascend the ranks of power to become the founder of the 'Umayyad Dynasty, which followed the Caliphate of 'Ali ibn Abi Talib.

Recall that only a few years ago at Uhud, **'Abd al-Ka'bah** emerged on his horse and openly challenged the Muslim forces. Abu Bakr rose to fight his son but the Prophet bade Abu Bakr to remain by his side.

Meanwhile, Abu Bakr's wife Umm Ruman (mother of 'A'ishah) passes away. News of her death reaches her son, 'Abd al-Ka'bah, who comes to Medina to embrace Islam. The Prophet warmly accepts Abu Bakr's son and changes his name from 'Abd al-Ka'bah (servant of the Ka'bah) to *'Abd ar-Rahman* (servant of the Most Merciful).

 16 **WHAT ARE "ISLAMIC" NAMES?** `RAMADAN`

"Never did the Muslims imagine that there could be such a thing as 'Islamic names,' of exclusively Arab origin. Indeed what preoccupied them was the opposite: they were to avoid the few names with a meaning clearly contrary to Islamic teachings, and allow an unrestricted choice of all sorts of different names, from all languages and origins."[24]

'Ubayd Allah ibn Jahsh was the Prophet's first cousin through his aunt Umaymah (Fig. P28). Although originally a Christian, 'Ubayd Allah was one of the first to embrace Islam in Mecca after the first revelations. He migrated to Abyssinia and remained there with Ja'far while the majority of refugees returned after the ban on Hashim was lifted. Although 'Ubayd Allah reverted to Christianity before his death in Abyssinia, his wife Umm Habibah remained a Muslim.

Meanwhile in Abyssinia, 'Ubayd Allah ibn Jahsh passes away, leaving behind his wife Umm Habibah, the daughter of Abu Sufyan. Shortly after 'Ubayd Allah's passing, the Prophet sends a messenger to the Negus asking him to ratify the Prophet's marriage to her. He also sends word to Ja'far ibn Abi Talib requesting that he and the remaining Muslims in Abyssinia come to Medina.

During this time of relative peace, the community of Muslims nearly doubles. With so many changes happening in Medina, Surah Al Mumtahinah hints at a new breeze of reconciliation moving through Arabia:

 It just may be that God will create love between you and your opponents, for God is capable enough (to bring that about), and God is forgiving and merciful. God doesn't forbid you from being kind and fair to those who don't fight you because of your beliefs or drive you from your homes, for God loves the tolerant. — *Al Mumtahinah (She Who is Interviewed, 60:7-8)*

17 **HOW DID THE TREATY END UP FAVORING THE MUSLIMS?** `YUSUF`

"They [the believers] are quite clearly seeing that it [the treaty] really was a great victory for them. And it's interesting because at that time, the Quraysh actually believed that it was a great victory for them too, but the opposite turns out to be true. Meanwhile, because there is a truce, there is peace. There is more interchange. The Muslims are freer; the whole environment [in Mecca and Medina] is a lot easier now.

People are beginning to convert as a result of this event [Hudaybiyah] and Allah reminds them that He can place love in the hearts after there was enmity between people. And this is really one of the proofs of the entire Sirah of the Messenger of Allah, God's peace and blessings upon him. You can see that his worst enemies, such as Khalid ibn al-Walid, 'Ikrimah ibn Abu Jahl, 'Amr ibn al-'As, Abu Sufyan, Hind, Wahshi and others are going to end up becoming Muslim."[25]

19.6 LETTERS TO THE SURROUNDING POWERS

With his message spreading throughout the region, the Prophet sends letters of introduction to the surrounding empires, inviting them all to Islam. He writes to Emperor Heraclius (via the Roman governor of Syria), the Muqawqis (the Coptic ruler of Alexandria), and Chosroes II (the king of Persia) via his viceroy in Yemen. The Prophet also sends letters of diplomacy to Abyssinia, Damascus, Yamamah, Oman, and Bani Ghassan.

Replies from the north and west take months to years. The Persian king, already aware of the Prophet's growing power in Arabia, orders his Yemeni governor Badhan to gather more information. When the Yemeni envoy arrives in Medina, the Prophet informs the visitors that the Persian crown prince, Kavadh II, had just overthrown his father—Chosroes II. He invites the delegation to Islam, warning that his religion will inevitably overtake the Persian Empire. The men return to Yemen and repeat the Prophet's words to Badhan. At the same time, the governor receives word from the new shah, verifying the Prophet's news that Chosroes II was, in fact, slain by his son. The Yemeni governor immediately acknowledges the Prophet's authority and pledges his people's allegiance to Medina. In response, the Prophet grants him continued rule over Yemen.

In 628, Emperor Heraclius led the Roman forces toward the Persian capital of Ctesiphon. Fearing for his life, Chosroes II fled his throne. Later that year, his son Kavadh II (whom Chosroes had imprisoned) killed his father and assumed rule over the Persians. His reign will only last a few months before the empire begins to crumble. Within a few years, the Persian lands will ultimately succumb to the growing Muslim community under the leadership of Caliph Abu Bakr.

This is the beginning of the fulfillment of the prophecy revealed during the digging of the trench, when the Prophet told Salman al-Farisi that God would soon grant the Prophet control over Yemen to the south, Syria to the north, and Persia to the east (QY 18.2).

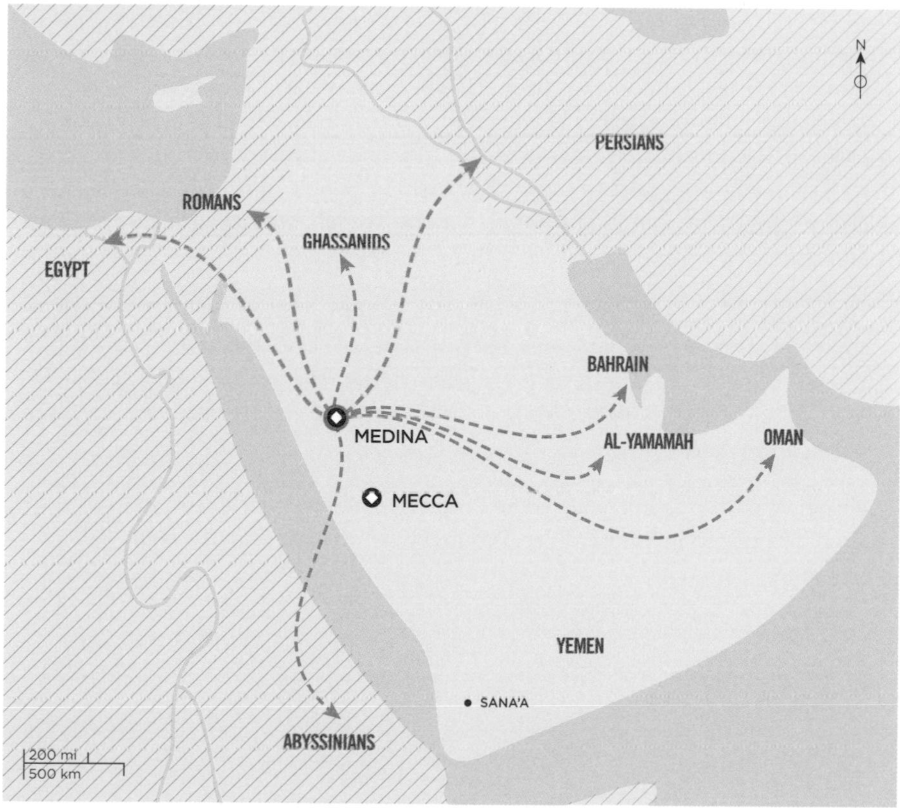

FIGURE 19B. LETTERS TO SURROUNDING RULERS

Aside from the letters sent to the Egyptians, Romans, and Persians, the Prophet also sent five letters to neighboring rulers: (1) Ashamah ibn Al-Abjar, Negus of Abyssinia, (2) Mundir ibn Sawa, governor of Bahrain, (3) Haudhah ibn 'Ali, governor of Al-Yamamah, (4) Al-Harith ibn Abi Shimir Al-Ghassani, king of Damascus (5) Jaifer ibn Julandai, king of Oman. NOTE: Some of these letters may have been sent before or after the three letters mentioned above. (See Al-Mubarakpuri, p.310-321)

19.7 LABID'S SPELL ON THE PROPHET

In the year after Hudaybiyah, the inhabitants of the northern Jewish settlement of Khaybar prompt a renowned sorcerer in Medina named Labid to cast a spell on the Prophet whereby his strength and memory are weakened. The Prophet begins to suffer from forgetfulness, weakness, and loss of appetite. When he prays for a cure, he is instructed to recite Surahs Al Falaq and An-Nas and quickly regains his health. Ultimately the Prophet forgives Labid, who explains that he was bribed by the people of Khaybar.

Lings mentions that these two surahs may have been revealed much earlier in Mecca. They are the last two chapters of the Qur'an and are often recited as a protection against evil.

Say: "I seek safety with the Lord of the Dawn from the evil (of the unknown) in creation, from the evil of approaching darkness, from the evil of spell-casters and from the evil of the envious whenever he resents."
— *Al Falaq (Daybreak, 113:1-5)*

Say: "I seek safety with the Lord of people, the Ruler of people, the God of people, from the subtle temptations of evil, whispered into the hearts of people by jinns or by other people." — *An-Naas (People, 114:1-6)*

19.8 KHAYBAR, FADAK & WADI L-QURA

While the Treaty of Hudaybiyah brings relative peace to Mecca, the city of Medina continues to face serious threats from Khaybar—about 100 miles to the north, and the eastern Bedouin tribes of Ghatafan and Hawazin. Khaybar is not a city like Mecca; it is a fertile oasis composed of hills and valleys, dotted with separate fortresses that house each of its Jewish clans. The people of Khaybar had not only instigated the Quraysh in their campaign at the Trench, but had also kept the Bani Ghatafan at odds with Medina:

> The Jews of Khaybar, especially the leaders of the clan of an-Nadir exiled from Medina, were still incensed at Muhammad. They made lavish, though no doubt judicious, use of their wealth to induce the neighbouring Arabs to take up arms against the Muslims. This was a straightforward reason for attacking Khaybar.[26]

Their persistent antagonism leads the Prophet to believe that the other "early victory" mentioned in Surah Al Fet-h could be none other than the conquest of Khaybar:

He knew what you didn't know, and He granted you an early victory besides this, as well. — *Al Fet-h (Victory, 48:27)*

As the men prepare for the northbound march, a man from Aws named Abu 'Abs ibn Jabir approaches the Prophet for help. He is too poor to provide for his family and has nothing but rags to wear on the expedition. The Prophet gives him a new cloak, but Abu 'Abs barters it for a less expensive cloak and some dates for his family. When the Prophet sees him a few days later, he laughs, saying:

> "...if ye keep safe and live yet a little while, ye shall have abundance of provisions and leave abundantly for your families. Ye shall abound in dirhams and in slaves; and it will not be good for you!"[27]

The people of Khaybar are not expecting a confrontation. In fact, only after 'Abd Allah ibn Ubayy warns them that the Prophet is about to march out of Medina, do they seek assistance from Bani Ghatafan. Kinanah ibn Abi l-Huqayq, the de facto chief of Khaybar, offers Ghatafan half his city's annual date harvest in exchange for 4,000 reinforcements. With their help, Khaybar's defenses would be boosted to 14,000 men.

In comparison, the Prophet sets out from Medina with a force of only 1,600 men. The small number is largely due to Surah Al Fet-h, which instructs the Prophet to limit the Khaybar expedition to those Companions who accompanied him to Hudaybiyah a few months earlier.

> Ah, but when it's time for you to march out and collect some gains, those who lagged behind will say, "Let us go along with you, too." They want to change the very decree of God! Tell them, "You can't follow us just like that. God has already imposed (this prohibition) before." Then they'll say, "Oh! Well, you're just jealous of us." No way! They just don't understand very much.
> —Al Fet-h (Victory, 48:15)

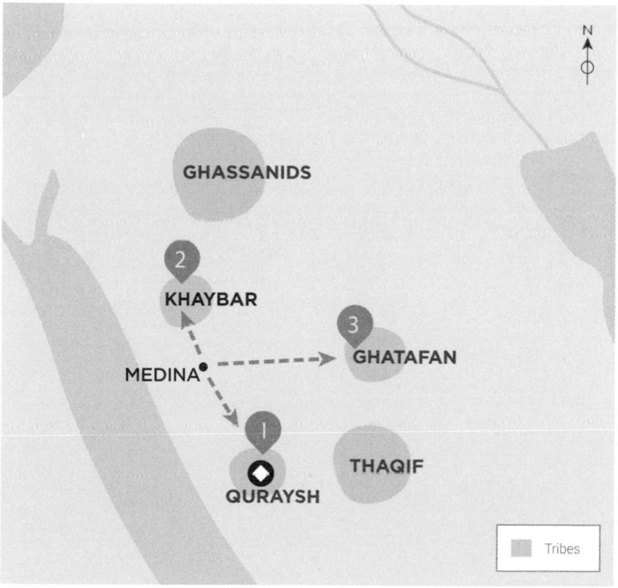

Salahi reports that the Prophet first sent 30 Companions led by 'Abd ar-Rahman ibn 'Awf to try to negotiate a peace treaty with the Jews of Khaybar. Only after they try to assassinate 'Abd ar-Rahman does the Prophet mobilize his troops (p.532-533).

FIGURE 19C. MAJOR THREATS DURING THE LATE MEDINAN PERIOD

Qur'anic Year 19 consisted of a number of diplomatic and military efforts aimed at securing Medina's borders from three outside threats: the Quraysh in Mecca, the Jews of Khaybar, and the Bedouins from Bani Ghatafan. Immediately after neutralizing the Meccan offensive through the Treaty of Hudaybiyah, the Prophet turned his attention north and, after failing to negotiate a truce with the inhabitants of Khaybar, successfully laid siege to the city. That same year, the Prophet led his men east to subdue a number of hostile Ghatafan clans that had been planning raids on Medina. The following year, the Prophet addressed more distant threats including the Ghassanids to the north and Bani Thaqif to the southeast.

≫ **SURAH AS-SAFFAT** (The Rows) is named after its opening verse, which describes how the faithful stand in straight rows, ready to serve their Lord. The surah addresses its skeptics and reminds them of the reality of final judgment. As with many other surahs, As-Saffat calls up the examples of God's prophets—Noah, Abraham, Moses, Aaron, Elijah, Lot, and Jonah—as a source of instruction and inspiration.

The Muslim army reaches the settlement's limits by the third night and, as described in Surah As-Saffat, lay seige to it at dawn.

> ...Do they really want to hurry on Our punishment? Oh, but when it does descend before them in their own front yard - how terrible will that morning be for the forewarned (and heedless)! —*As-Saffat (The Rows, 37:176-177)*

Despite their impressive numbers, the people of Khaybar are unable to mount a unified response and instead fortify themselves in their separate garrisons. Surah Al Hashr describes the scene inside:

> They'll never fight you in united front, except from behind fortified areas or mighty ramparts, and even though their bravado might make it seem as if they're strong and united, in reality their hearts are divided, for they're a people devoid of sense. —*Al Hashr (The Gathering, 59:14)*

In contrast, Surah As-Saff depicts the solidarity of the Prophet's men:

> God loves those who fight in His cause in tight formations, as if they were a brick wall, (rather than those who disobey orders, like the believers did at Uhud). —*As-Saff (The Formations, 61:4)*

Recalling the story of David and Goliath, Surah Al Baqarah reminds Muslims not to be intimidated by the enemy:

> Then after they crossed over (the stream,) the (few remaining) faithful (soldiers) lamented, "We're no match for Goliath and his army today." However, those who were certain they would meet God one day, said, "How many were the times when a small force defeated a larger one by God's will? God is with those who persevere!"
>
> As they advanced upon Goliath and his forces, they prayed, "Our Lord, pour determination down upon us, make our stance firm and help us against this nation that rejects (faith)."
>
> And so by God's will they routed them, and David killed Goliath. God also gave (David) leadership skills, wisdom and whatever else He wanted to teach him. If God didn't enable one people to deter another, then the world would be filled with turmoil, but God is infinitely bountiful to the entire universe.
>
> These are the revelations of God that We're reciting to you in all truth, for you, (Muhammad), are one of the messengers. —*Al Baqarah (The Cow, 2:249-252)*

Unlike the battles at Badr and Uhud, the siege on Khaybar grows into an extended confrontation of many smaller battles. Several days pass with varying success. Much to the dismay of Khaybar's inhabitants, the city's eastern reinforcements are nowhere to be found. Little do they know that Bani Ghatafan's 4,000 troops had been diverted by a mysterious voice in the desert that cried out to them, *"Your people! Your people!"* Fearing the worst, the troops rushed back home. Although their wives and children remained as they had left them, the soldiers decided not to march back to Khaybar, thinking that it would be too late to share in the spoils of war.

---

18 **WHY DID THE GHATAFAN RETURN TO THEIR HOMES?** SALAHI

"The Muslims encamped in an open valley called al-Raji, on the route between the Ghatafan and Khaybar. They wanted to block the route so that the Ghatafan could not come to the aid of their Jewish allies … What had probably taken place was that the Prophet had actually sent a detachment of his forces when he realized that the Ghatafan were planning to support the Jews, in order to frighten the Ghatafan away from supporting their allies. Other reports suggest that the Prophet actually asked the Ghatafan not to support the Jews of Khaybar, and he promised to give the Ghatafan a portion of what the Muslims stood to win when they achieved victory. Whichever report was true, the practical result was that the Ghatafan did not actually help the Jews, and left them to face the Muslims on their own."[28]

Starting with the least guarded fortress, the garrisons fall to the Prophet's forces over the next several days. On the sixth day, when the army encounters a particularly well-guarded stronghold, the Prophet tells his men:

"Tomorrow I will give the banner to a man who loves Allah and His Messenger and Allah and His Messenger love him."[29]

The following morning, the Prophet gives the banner to his cousin, 'Ali ibn Abi Talib. 'Ali leads a successful charge against that fortress and, one by one, the remaining strongholds fall to Muslim forces. On the advice of a Jewish spy, 'Ali's men defeat one of the strongholds by cutting off its hidden water source and forcing the inhabitants to fight.

---

19 **HOW DID 'UMAR FEEL ABOUT LEADERSHIP?** YUSUF

"Everybody that night was hoping that they would be that person. Sayidna 'Umar said, 'It was the only time in my life I wanted to have a position of authority.' Which shows that he didn't have any love of leadership."[30]

After several days of fighting, the richest fortress in Khaybar, belonging to Kinanah ibn Abi l-Huqayq's clan, is one of the few that remains intact. After a two-week standoff, Kinanah finally comes out to negotiate his people's surrender.

With Abu Bakr, 'Umar, 'Ali, and Zubayr ibn al-'Awwam standing as witnesses, Kinanah surrenders to the Prophet under the following conditions:

- None of the people of the garrison should be put to death or made captive as long as they leave Khaybar.

- The property of those leaving the garrison belongs to the victors.

- Anyone trying to hide possessions would be punished by death or captivity.

19
20
21
22
23

Having just signed the document, Kinanah nonetheless tries to conceal his wealth as he exits Khaybar. When his treasure is discovered, the Jewish leader is quickly put to death and his family is taken captive.

The Prophet was serious about protecting his Jewish allies—within a few months, he will urgently dispatch an expedition to protect the Jews of Fadak from Bani Ghatafan (QY 19.10).

After Kinanah's mistake, the two remaining clans in the oasis surrender to the Prophet on the condition that they may remain in Khaybar if they pay a yearly tribute to Medina called the *jizyah*. The Prophet also stipulates that he will retain the right to banish the clans anytime in the future. A third Jewish clan in Fadak (northeast of Khaybar) hears of this new arrangement and, with rumors swirling that the Prophet intends to march to their oasis next, reaches out to the Prophet and agrees to the same terms.

20 WHAT CAUSED THE FALL OF KHAYBAR AND THE END OF JEWISH AUTONOMY IN ARABIA? `WATT`

"The lack of fundamental unity among the Jews was a weakness which meant that it was easy for Muhammad to find Jews who were ready to help him. The Arab allies of the Jews, too, being attached to them chiefly by bribes, were easily detached, partly by fear of Muslim reprisals and partly by Muhammad's diplomatic skill. The fall of Khaybar and surrender of the other Jewish colonies marked the end of the Jewish question during Muhammad's lifetime, for the expulsion of the Jews from the Hijaz by the caliph `Umar belongs to later history. The Jews had opposed Muhammad to the utmost of their ability, and they had been utterly crushed. Many still remained in their former homes in Medina and elsewhere, but they had lost much of their wealth and had become politically quiescent."[31]

The parties in Khaybar come to an agreement and a feast of lamb is prepared for the Prophet and his Companions. The Prophet takes his first bite but immediately spits it out having received inspiration that the meat is poisoned. He asks for the cook, and a widow from Khaybar enters. She explains:

> "...thou knowest what thou hast done unto my people; and thou hast slain my father and mine uncle and my husband. So I told myself: 'If he be a king, I shall be well quit of him; and if he be a Prophet he will be informed of the poison.' "[32]

Bishr ibn Bara' is the son of Bara' ibn Mar'ur, a Khazraj chief who was present at the Second 'Aqabah six years ago. Lings suggests that the Prophet forgave the cook, while Al-Mubarakpuri says the Prophet ordered her to be killed after Bishr's death.

One of the Companions, Bishr ibn Bara', however, had already swallowed a morsel of lamb and dies shortly thereafter.

While the people of Khaybar return to their homes, Kinanah's 17-year-old widow, Safiyyah bint Huyay, approaches the Prophet and relates a dream in which she saw a brilliant moon over the city of Medina. The moon moved to Khaybar and then fell into her lap. The Prophet interprets her dream by giving her the choice of returning to her people or embracing Islam and joining his household as his 10th wife. Safiyyah readily chooses the latter.

Before returning to Medina, the Prophet turns west to confront another Khaybar ally—the predominantly Jewish tribe at Wadi l-Qura. After a three-day standoff, the tribe capitulates to the same conditions as the inhabitants of Khaybar. Its surrender induces another Jewish enclave from the settlement of Taima' to enter into a similar agreement with Medina. By securing an annual tribute from these tribes (one-fifth of which is reserved for the Prophet's family), the Muslims return to Medina wealthier than they had ever been before.

21 WHAT ARE THE ORIGINS OF THE JIZYAH TAX? WATT

"The idea of such an arrangement is probably derived from the nomadic custom whereby a strong tribe would take a weaker one under its protection; it then became a matter of honour for the stronger to make its protection effective. The excellent record of Islam in the toleration of religious minorities is largely due to this fact—once it had said it would protect a group it was a matter of honour to do so effectively. Even on the political side the system of protected minorities was highly advantageous, and many of the troubles of the Arabic-speaking world today are due to the fact that it has broken down and that no other system has been found to replace it."[33]

22 WAS IT FAIR FOR THE PROPHET TO TAKE A FIFTH OF THE SPOILS FOR HIS FAMILY? WATT

"The provision for his wives and relatives which Muhammad made out of the annual tribute from Khaybar might seem to indicate partiality. It must be remembered, however, that Muhammad stood in a special relation to the clans of Hashim and al-Muttalib; he was their leader among the Muslims. According to the principles of the Qur'an, therefore, it was above all to him that the poor and needy members of these clans must look for help. Moreover, while the leaders of other clans of the Emigrants, such as 'Abd ar-Rahman b. 'Awf, might spend their time in the market making money, some of which they would give to their relatives, Muhammad had to devote all his time to political duties, and it was thus no more than fair that he should use on their behalf some of the money that came to him."[34]

When the Prophet returns to Medina, Safiyyah joins the household and 'A'ishah (who is only one year younger) quickly grows to enjoy her company. At first Safiyyah has a difficult time with the other wives on account of her father being the treacherous leader of Bani Nadir—Huyay ibn Akhtab. But when she complains to the Prophet, he counsels her to be proud of her Jewish heritage:

"Why did you not reply to them and say: 'how can you be superior to me when Aaron is my father [meaning her lineage ended with him], and Moses is my uncle and my husband is Muhammad?' "

Safiyyah bint Huyay is not only the widow of Kinanah ibn Abi l-Huqayq, she is the daughter of Huyay ibn Akhtab, the exiled chief of Bani Nadir. Recall that several years ago, Huyay's plot to kill the Prophet was foiled and his clan of Nadir was subsequently exiled. During the Battle of the Trench, Huyay returned from Khaybar and persuaded Bani Qurayzah to break their pact with the Prophet. When Qurayzah ultimately surrendered, Huyay was put to death along with the other men of Qurayzah for treason.

23 WHY MIGHT THE PROPHET HAVE MARRIED SAFIYYAH? ARMSTRONG

"The marriage expressed the attitude of reconciliation and forgiveness that he was trying to promote; it was time to lay aside the hatred and bloodshed of the past."[35]

During the siege of Khaybar, the Prophet's beloved cousin, Ja'far ibn Abi Talib, returns from Abyssinia after 15 years. The Prophet receives him warmly and admits that Ja'far's return brings him equal if not greater joy than the victory at Khaybar.

24 HOW VALUABLE WAS THE EMIGRANTS' ROLE IN ABYSSINIA? SALAHI

"When the last of the Prophet's companions who went to Abyssinia came back, they joined the Prophet and his army at the conquest of Khaybar, when the battle was already over ... The Prophet gave the new arrivals equal shares of the spoils of the war against the Jews in Khaybar. He did not apportion any share to any one of his companions who did not take part in the battle of Khaybar, apart from those returning emigrants from Abyssinia. The Prophet would not have given them such shares had he not considered that they were on a mission which was equal to that of those who took part in the Battle of Khaybar. He valued their contribution to the welfare of Islam and considered that their stay in Abyssinia was a part of the work to establish Islam as a Divine message for all mankind."[36]

19
20
21
22
23

19.9 COMPETITION WITH 'A'ISHAH

Be sure to read Lings (p. 279-282) for a touching description of the Prophet's household and his relationship with his wives.

Upon his arrival from Khaybar, the Prophet's household includes eight wives, who all live in separate apartments beside the mosque. As the family steadily grows, several wives begin to voice their jealousy over 'A'ishah's favored status with the Prophet. Even the Companions sense 'A'ishah's effect on him and wait for his alotted day with her before asking him for favors.

Umm Salamah finally confronts the Prophet about the issue, and he responds with the observation that divine revelation only comes to him when he is with her. His explanation leaves Zaynab bint Jahsh unimpressed and she sends Fatimah to talk to her father. When Fatimah relays Zaynab's concerns, the Prophet gently reminds her to love the one whom he loves. But Zaynab remains unfazed. When she confronts the Prophet directly, he counsels her to speak with 'A'ishah and settle the issue amicably.

---

25 **DID THE PROPHET MARRY FOR POLITICAL REASONS?** WATT

"The last feature to be noted about Muhammad's marriages is that he used both his own and those of the closest Companions to further political ends. This was doubtless a continuation of older Arabian practice. All Muhammad's own marriages can be seen to have a tendency to promote friendly relations in the political sphere. Khadijah brought him wealth, and the beginnings of influence in Meccan politics. In the case of Sawdah, whom he married at Mecca, the chief aim may have been to provide for the widow of a faithful Muslim, as also in the later marriage with Zaynab bint Khuzaymah; but Sawdah's husband was the brother of a man whom Muhammad perhaps wanted to keep from becoming an extreme opponent; and Zaynab's husband belonged to the clan of al-Muttalib, for which Muhammad had a special responsibility, while he was also cultivating good relations with her own tribe of 'Amir b. Sa'sa'ah. His first wives at Medina, 'A'ishah and Hafsah, were the daughters of the men on whom he leaned most, Abu Bakr and 'Umar; and 'Umar also married Muhammad's grand-daughter, Umm Kulthum bint 'Ali [after the Prophet's death]. Umm Salamah was not merely a deserving widow, but a close relative of the leading man of the Meccan clan of Makhzum. Juwayriyah was the daughter of the chief of the tribe of al-Mustaliq, with whom Muhammad had been having special trouble. Zaynab bint Jahsh, besides being Muhammad's cousin, was a confederate of the Meccan clan of 'Abd Shams, but a social motive may have outweighed the political one in her case to demonstrate that Muhammad had broken with old taboos. Nevertheless the clan of 'Abd Shams, and Abu Sufyan b. Harb in particular, were in his thoughts, for Abu Sufyan had a Muslim daughter, Umm Habibah, married to a brother of Zaynab bint Jahsh; and when the husband died in Abyssinia, Muhammad sent a messenger there to arrange a marriage with her. The marriage with Maymunah would similarly help to cement relations with her brother-in-law, Muhammad's uncle, al-'Abbas. There may also have been political motives in the unions with the Jewesses, Safiyah and Rayhanah."[37]

Around this time, Khadijah's sister Halah came to Medina to visit her son Abu l-'As and his family (Zaynab and Umamah). 'A'ishah said that when the Prophet heard Halah speaking outside 'A'ishah's apartment, he trembled because her voice so closely resembled Khadijah's.

Ironically, while many wives are jealous of 'A'ishah, she recalls feeling envious of only one wife:

"I was not jealous of any other wife of the Prophet as I was jealous of Khadijah, for his constant mentioning of her and because God had bidden him give her good tidings of a mansion in Paradise of precious stones. And whensoever he sacrificed a sheep, he would send a goodly portion of it unto those who had been her intimate friends. Many a time said I unto him: It is as if there had never been any other woman in the world, save only Khadijah."[38]

26 **WHY WAS 'A'ISHAH JEALOUS OF KHADIJAH?** [YUSUF]

"The reason that she was jealous was the fact that the Prophet, God's peace and blessings upon him, would mention Khadijah a great deal. Also whenever he sacrificed [animals] or food was given to him, he would send food to the friends of Khadijah. When 'A'ishah asked the Prophet, God's peace and blessings upon him, 'Why do you love Khadijah better when she is long dead and now I'm your wife and I'm younger?' the Prophet, God's peace and blessings upon him, became upset and said, 'Khadijah was with me when everyone abandoned me. She gave me wealth, and supported me.' "[39]

Hoping to ease growing tension between his wives, the Prophet once teases them by saying he will give an onyx necklace to his "most beloved." Anticipation mounts until he finally sets it upon his only granddaughter Umamah (daughter of Zaynab).

Similar to the affection 'Abd al-Muttalib showered upon him, the Prophet never missed an opportunity to express affection for his grandchildren, especially Fatimah's two boys. He once said, *"The dearest unto me of the people of my house are Hasan and Husayn."*[40]

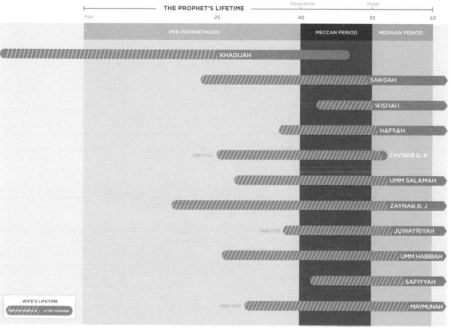

FIGURE 19D. THE PROPHET'S WIVES

The relative ages of all 11 wives are displayed in the order they married the Prophet. The eldest women are farthest to the left (Khadijah and Zaynab bint Jahsh) and the youngest are farthest to the right ('A'ishah and Safiyyah). The darker area represents the portion of their life that they were married to the Prophet.

A few notable points: (1) 'A'ishah was the only wife who had never been married before—the rest were either divorced or widowed. (2) Khadijah and Zaynab bint Khuzaymah were the only two wives who died during the Prophet's lifetime. (3) Khadijah spent far more time married to the Prophet (25 monogamous years) than any other wife. (4) After Safiyyah's addition to the household, 'A'ishah noted that the wives generally fell into two social circles. The first included Sawdah, A'ishah, Hafsah, and Safiyyah. The second included Umm Salamah, Zaynab bint Jahsh, Juwayriyah, and Umm Habibah. (5) Maymunah had not yet joined the family but will marry the Prophet in the coming year.

19.10 EASTERN EXPEDITIONS TO SUBDUE GHATAFAN

Read Al-Mubarakpuri (p. 334-336) for a description of lesser expeditions aimed at controlling the Bedouins east of Medina. He places the incident between the Prophet and Du'thur ibn al-Harith (QY 16.1) during one of these expeditions.

After securing treaties with Mecca and Khaybar, the Prophet returns to Medina and focuses his attention to the east. When he hears that Bedouin clans from Bani Ghatafan are planning to attack Medina, the Prophet, Abu Bakr, 'Umar, and several other Companions lead a number of preemptive campaigns to subdue the threat.

These include urgent expeditions to protect the Jews of Fadak against the Ghatafan clan of Murrah. During one confrontation, 17-year-old Usamah ibn Zayd chases a man of Bani Murrah into the desert and kills him just after the man hurriedly testifies his faith in Islam. When Usamah returns to camp and explains what happened, the elder Companions scold him for his poor judgment. When he reaches out to the Prophet, the Prophet pointedly asks him to reflect on his intentions:

"Would you rip open his heart to detect whether he is truthful or a liar?"[42]

Following the spirit of the Qur'an, the Prophet forbids Muslims from acting out of ego or self-interest:

> All you who believe! When you go abroad (to fight) in the cause of God, check carefully (before taking action against those whom you meet on the battlefield, and about whose intentions you're uncertain).
>
> Don't say to an (enemy soldier) who (seems to pause) to offer you the greetings of peace, "You aren't a believer," (wanting to kill him) in your greed for the temporary riches of this life.
>
> There's plenty of profits and prizes with God. You used to (kill for profit) like that before (accepting Islam), until God placed His favor upon you. So check carefully (whom it is you're confronting), for God is aware of everything you do.
> — *An-Nisa (The Women, 4:94)*

19.11 PROSPERITY AFTER HUDAYBIYAH

The months after Hudaybiyah are marked by a period of relative peace and prosperity in Medina. As wealth enters the city, the Prophet's wives begin to ask more of him. On one occasion, 'Umar approaches the Prophet's house only to hear the Prophet's wives talking loudly to each other and the Prophet regarding the fate of some garments that came to the household as part of the spoils of war. But when 'Umar enters the Prophet's house, the room immediately falls silent. The scene is all too much for the Prophet who lovingly tells 'Umar:

"Oh son of Khattab, by Him in whose hand is my soul, if Satan found that you were traveling upon a certain path, he would choose to go himself by any other path but yours."[43]

---

27 **WHAT DID THE PROPHET EXPECT FROM HIS WIVES?**   RAMADAN

"His wives could differentiate between Muhammad's role as a prophet and his life as an ordinary husband and human being. Muhammad had never demanded to be treated in any specific way and he tried to respond to his wives' many expectations."[44]

Even Zayd's wife, Umm Ayman, wants a share of the wealth coming into Medina. When she asks the Prophet for her own camel, the Prophet sternly replies that he will only give her the child of a camel. At first Umm Ayman refuses, but when she sees a smile creeping over his face, she realizes that all camels are the children of camels, and that the Prophet had intended to give her a full-grown animal.

Since the Hijrah, many Meccan men are finding themselves unaccustomed to Medinan culture, where the women tend to be more outspoken with their husbands:

> Indeed the women of Medina in general were noted for pride and for jealousy of their honour and position summarized in the word ghayr. Muhammad is said to have remarked that, because of their ghayr he would not marry a woman of the Ansar, since she would not have sufficient patience to endure fellow-wives; and, even if this is not the whole reason for Muhammad's not marrying a Medinan woman, there is doubtless something in it, and the contrast between the social attitudes in Mecca and Medina may explain why there was hardly any inter-marriage between the Emigrants and the Ansar. A saying of the caliph 'Umar's is recorded: "We of Quraysh used to dominate (our) women; but when we came among the Ansar, they proved to be a people whose women dominated them, and our women began to copy the habits of the women of the Ansar."[45]

Despite 'Umar's looming personality, he too is often tested by his wife Zaynab bint Maz'un. On one occasion, when he scolds her for her boldness, Zaynab counters that even the wives of the Prophet (including their own daughter Hafsah) are free to voice their opinions to the Messenger.

Troubled by the Prophet's wives' bold behavior, 'Umar confronts Hafsah and Umm Salamah. To his surprise, Umm Salamah defends her behavior along with the conduct of the Prophet's other wives. The sharp response sends 'Umar retreating, and he realizes it is not his place to mediate the Prophet's domestic affairs.

28 **HOW WAS THE HIJRAH A TRIAL OF INTELLIGENCE?** RAMADAN

"Medina meant new customs, new types of social relationships, a wholly different role for women, and more complex intertribal relations, as well as the influential presence of Jewish and Christian communities which was something new to Muslims. Very early on, the community of faith, following the Prophet's example, had to distinguish between what belonged to Islamic principles and what was more particularly related to Meccan culture. They were to remain faithful to the first while learning to adopt a flexible and critical approach to their original culture.

This was a difficult experience for him ['Umar], as it was for others, who might have been tempted to think that their habits and customs were in themselves Islamic: hijrah, exile, was to reveal that this was not the case and that one must question every single cultural practice, both to be faithful to Islamic principles and to open up to other cultures and gain from their wealth.

Not only did he [Muhammad] recognize a cultural feature or taste that was not in itself opposed to Islamic principles, but he integrated it as an enrichment of his own human experience. Hijrah was also, then, a trial of intelligence, spurring the need to distinguish between principles and their cultural manifestations; moreover, it implied opening up and confidently welcoming new customs, new ways of being and thinking, new tastes."[46]

----

29 **HOW DID THE PROPHET CHAMPION THE EMERGING ROLE OF WOMEN?** ARMSTRONG

" 'Umar was furious when his wife started to answer him back instead of meekly accepting his reproaches, and when he rebuked her she simply replied that the Prophet allowed his wives to argue with him. Trouble was brewing. Muhammad's deliberate conflation of private and public was a blow to male supremacy, which can only exist if this distinction is maintained...

The Qur'an was attempting to give women a legal status that most Western women would not enjoy until the nineteenth century. The emancipation of women was a dear project to the Prophet's heart, but it was resolutely opposed by many men in the Ummah, including some of his closest companions...

The Prophet did not regard his wives as chattel. They were his 'companions'—just like the men ... Muhammad's domestic arrangements gave his wives a new access to politics, and they seemed quite at home in this sphere. It would not be long before other women began to feel similarly empowered, and his enemies would use this women's movement to discredit the Prophet."[47]

----

30 **WHY DIDN'T THE PROPHET HAVE A MEDINAN WIFE?** WATT

"It is noteworthy that Muhammad had no Medinan wife ... Clearly he could only be successful in Medina if he was impartial, and his impartiality would be seriously infringed by such marriages. Abu Bakr married a woman of the Khazraj, apparently towards the end of his life ... and 'Umar had a wife from the Aws. On the whole, however, there was very little inter-marriage at Medina between the Meccans and the Medinans, perhaps because of the differences in the social systems."[48]

19.12 SURAH AT-TAHREEM: QUESTIONS OF DIVORCE

After the surrender of Khaybar, the Muqawqis of Egypt responds to the Prophet's invitation letter with many generous gifts and two servant girls named Mariyah and Sirin. The Prophet houses Mariyah in a nearby apartment and places Sirin under the custodianship of Hassan ibn Thabit. But soon enough, the Prophet's wives become displeased with Mariyah's presence:

> They well knew that he was altogether within his rights—rights which had been recognised from the time of Abraham and before. Were they not all, except Safiyyah, descended from the union of Abraham with the bondmaid Hagar? Moreover, the law revealed to Moses had corroborated such rights, and the Koran itself expressly allowed a master to take his bondmaid as concubine on condition of her free consent. But the wives also knew that the Prophet was exceedingly sensitive, and they saw to it that his whole domestic life was now penetrated by their deliberately undisguised reactions.[49]

31 **HOW WAS MARIYAH A TEST FOR THE OTHER WIVES?**   [RAMADAN]

"The slave girl Mariyah had been a trial for all the Prophet's wives … They could not try to use his status as a prophet in public life to obtain special rights or treatment from the community.
Within a couple, each spouse's responsibilities, choices, and behavior determine his or her fate. In this respect, the Prophet's wives could claim no privilege, and humility was required. The wives' trial was to be intensified by the fact that Mariyah became the mother of the only boy born to the Prophet after Qasim and Abdullah. The Prophet called his son Ibrahim, after the prophet Abraham, whom the Coptic tradition of Mariyah also recognized as the father of monotheism."[50]

With 'A'ishah's support, Hafsah approaches the Prophet and expresses the collective displeasure of the other wives. Their complaint plays on his sensitive nature, and the Prophet swears not to see Mariyah again. The renunciation of his lawful rights sets the stage for the opening verses of Surah At-Tahreem:

> O Prophet! Why would you forbid yourself from something that God has allowed for you? Are you thinking that this is what you have to do to please your spouses? God is forgiving and merciful! God has already given you a required method to cancel your (hasty) promises. God is the protector of you all, and He is the Knowing and the Wise.
>
> When the Prophet told something in confidence to one wife, she told it to another, and God made this known to him. Then he had (to tell others about the matter), while leaving some of its (details) vague. When he confronted her (about her having told the secret), she exclaimed, "Who told you that (I told someone else)?"
>
> "I was informed," he said, "by the Knowing and the Well-Informed."
>
> Both of you, (the wife who told the secret and the one to whom she told it), should turn to God in repentance, if your hearts lead you to do it. If you try to defend each other against (the Prophet, know that) his protector is God, even as is Gabriel, every righteous believer and the very angels themselves, who will all defend him.

Recall that just one year ago, **Hassan ibn Thabit** was involved in spreading rumors that falsely accused 'A'ishah of infidelity. As was his nature, the Prophet had long forgiven Hassan for his indiscretion.

☙ **SURAH AT-TAHREEM** (Prohibition) is named after its opening verse, which asks the Prophet why he had prohibited what God made permissible. The surah urges the Prophet's wives and followers to turn to God with a pure heart, just like the purest of women—the Pharaoh's wife and the Virgin Mary.

19
20
21
22
23

(Wives of the Prophet), if he were to divorce you all, it just might be that God would provide him with wives who are much better than you, who are surrendered (to God), who believe, who are devout, penitent, dedicated to (God's) service and who are outgoing (in spreading the faith), whether previously married or not. —*At-Tahreem (Prohibition, 66:1-5)*

The surah ends by mentioning the deficiencies in the wives of Noah and Lot, comparing them with the best examples of Muslim women—Mary and the wife of the Pharaoh.

For the faithless, God points out the example of the wife of Noah and the wife of Lot. They were under (the care) of two of our righteous servants; yet, each betrayed (her husband).

Their (association with their husbands) did them no good against God, for they're going to be told, "Enter the Fire along with all those who have to enter!"

For the believers, God points out the example of Pharaoh's wife who had prayed, "My Lord, prepare for me a house in the Garden near to You. Save me from the (evil) deeds of (my husband), the pharaoh, and save me from the wrongdoers."

(Yet another example) is that of Mary, daughter of (the house of) Amran, who guarded her chastity. We breathed Our spirit into her (womb), and she accepted the truth of her Lord's words and scriptures, for she was among the compliant. —*At-Tahreem (Prohibition, 66:10-12)*

The newly revealed verses spur the Prophet to seek solitude from his wives. Rumor spreads that he has divorced them, and only 'Umar has the courage to inquire about the matter. When he approaches the Prophet, the Prophet explains that he simply needs time to be apart from their company. Finally, after a full month of solitude, Surah Al Ahzab instructs him to return to his wives with a single, probing question:

O Prophet! Say to your wives, "If you want the life of this world and all its glitter, then come on! I'll set you up in style and then set you free in a fine manner. However, if you're longing for God and His Messenger and the home of the next life, (know that) God has prepared a tremendous reward for the good among you." —*Al Ahzab (The Allied Forces, 33:28-29)*

Without hesitation, each wife chooses God and His Messenger.

---

(32) WHAT DOES 'A'ISHAH'S TRIAL TELL US ABOUT OURSELVES? `YUSUF`

"In order for order to be in place, there has to be submission to Allah, the Sublime and Exalted. And this is the foundation of the successful life inside the house. If there's not submission to Allah and his Messenger, God's peace and blessings upon him, it will be trouble for your own souls and it will be trouble for the deen (religion) of Allah. If the Messenger of Allah, God's peace and blessings upon him, is troubled, we're all troubled. By extension this applies to believing women and to believing men."[51]

YEAR 20: THE CONQUEST OF MECCA

20.1 THE FIRST 'UMRAH

In the year after Hudaybiyah, the Prophet leaves Abu Dharr al-Ghifari in charge of Medina before departing for the lesser pilgrimage to Mecca. He places Abu Hurayrah, a poor emigrant from Bani Daws, in charge of the sacrificial camels, while another Companion, 'Abd Allah ibn Rawahah, is charged with leading the Prophet's camel and 2,000 pilgrims into the Sacred Precinct.

The Quraysh cleared out of the city before the pilgrims' arrival. Upon entering the Holy Sanctuary, the Prophet carefully leads his followers in the footsteps of Abraham and Hagar. The pilgrims circle the Ka'bah seven times before walking between the hills of Safa and Marwah another seven times. Watching from a distance, the locals are outraged when they see Umayyah's former Abyssinian slave, Bilal, climb atop the Ka'bah to make the call for prayer.

---

1 WHAT WAS SIGNIFICANT ABOUT BILAL'S CALL TO PRAYER? `SALAHI`

"What made Bilal's action even more offensive to the people of Makkah was the fact that he used to be a slave owned by Umayyah ibn Khalaf, who was later killed at the Battle of Badr. In the Makkan idolatrous society, which was extremely class-conscious, the fact that a former slave could rise on top of the Ka'bah, where the Quraysh put their idols, was something they could not accept. 'Ikrimah ibn Abī Jahl said: 'God has certainly been kind to my father by causing him to die before he could hear this slave saying such words.' " [1]

The Prophet's uncle 'Abbas had remained in Mecca all these years. During the 'umrah pilgrimage, 'Abbas joins his nephew and helps him take care of family affairs. He arranges the Prophet's marriage to 'Abbas' widowed sister-in-law, Maymunah (Umm al-Fadl's full sister), and also coordinates the safe passage of Hamzah's orphaned daughter 'Umarah to Medina. 'Umarah's mother Salma' bint Umays (Umm al-Fadl's half-sister) agrees to the plan and places her daughter under the care of the Prophet's daughter Fatimah.

Recall that **Abu Dharr** was a highway brigand from the rugged clan of Ghifar who embraced Islam during the Early Meccan Period and took Islam back to his people (QY 10.5).

Abu Hurayrah came to Medina during the expedition of Khaybar. He was poor and lived among the Ahl as-Suffah. Although his name was 'Abd ar-Rahman, he is famously known as *Abu Hurayrah* (father of the kitten) because he used to care for a number of kittens outside the Prophet's house. He is considered to be one of the most trustworthy and often-cited narrators of *hadith* (prophetic sayings) in the Sunni tradition.

'Abd Allah ibn Rawahah was the Companion who first stood up to 'Abd Allah ibn Ubayy when he demeaned the Prophet, shortly after the Hijrah. He was also the first to march out to duel the Meccans at Badr. In a few months, he will be martyred by the Ghassanids near Syria.

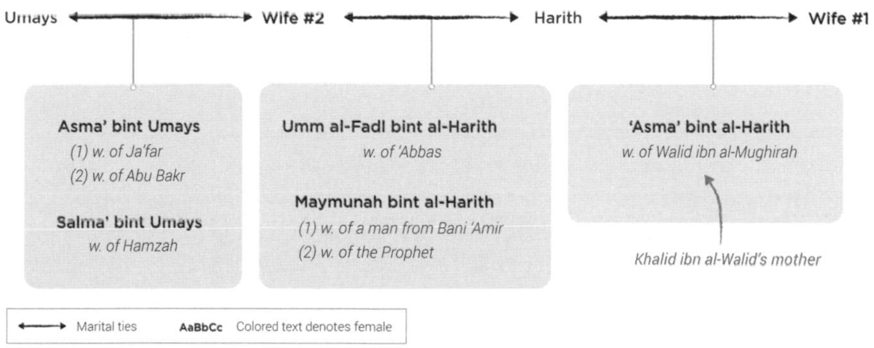

Asma' bint Umays
(1) w. of Ja'far
(2) w. of Abu Bakr

Salma' bint Umays
w. of Hamzah

Umm al-Fadl bint al-Harith
w. of 'Abbas

Maymunah bint al-Harith
(1) w. of a man from Bani 'Amir
(2) w. of the Prophet

'Asma' bint al-Harith
w. of Walid ibn al-Mughirah

Khalid ibn al-Walid's mother

⟷ Marital ties   **AaBbCc** Colored text denotes female

FIGURE 20A. THE BELIEVING SISTERS

'Abbas' wife Umm al-Fadl was the Prophet's longtime supporter. Her full-sister was Maymunah, while her paternal half-sister was 'Asma', the mother of Khalid ibn al-Walid. Both Umm al-Fadl and Maymunah were also maternal half-sisters to Asma' and Salma' bint Umays. These five "believing sisters" (as they were often called), were married to luminaries such as Abu Bakr, Ja'far ibn Abi Talib, Hamzah, 'Abbas, and the Prophet. The effect of all of these virtuous personalities clearly made an impression on Khalid ibn al-Walid, who, despite his father's longstanding enmity toward Islam, finally joined the Prophet in Medina (QY 20.3).

2 WHY MIGHT THE PROPHET HAVE MARRIED MAYMUNAH?   RAMADAN

"By marrying the widow Maymunah, the Prophet also established a kinship relationship with his fierce opponents the Makhzum, who were henceforth bound to him."[2]

20.2 ABU SUFYAN & HERACLIUS

Abu Sufyan is on a trading expedition to Syria and misses the Prophet's visit to Mecca. While traveling through Gaza, he is approached by Roman guards who escort him to meet Emperor Heraclius in Jerusalem. Heraclius has reason to believe that a mysterious Arabian prophet might soon annex Syria from the Romans, and interrogates the visiting Meccan chief about this man named Muhammad. Abu Sufyan explains:

> "Muhammad descends from a noble family. No one of his family happened to assume kingship. His followers are those considered weak, with numbers ever growing. He neither tells lies nor betrays others, we fight him and he fights us but with alternate victory. He bids people to worship Allah alone with no associate, and abandon our fathers' beliefs. He orders us to observe prayer, honesty, and abstinence; and to maintain strong family ties."

Abu Sufyan's honest appraisal strikes a cord with the emperor, who warns him:

> "You said he orders worship of Allah with no associates, observance of prayer, honesty and abstinence, and prohibition of paganism, if this is true, he will soon rule the place beneath my feet."[3]

Having confirmed Muhammad's prophethood, Heraclius returns to Homs in Syria and assembles the city's chiefs. Referring to the invitation letter that the Prophet had sent to the Roman governor in Syria, the emperor suggests the possibility of forming an alliance. Although the proposal is swiftly rejected by his advisers, Heraclius holds onto his personal conviction that the Prophet will eventually overtake Syria.

20.3 OLD ENEMIES, NEW FRIENDS

For a compelling, first-hand account of Khalid's conversion, read Salahi (p. 589-591).

'Uthman ibn Talhah is from the clan of 'Abd ad-Dar, to which the keys of the Ka'bah were traditionally entrusted (P 2.1). One year later at the Conquest of Mecca, the Prophet will preserve this tradition by giving the keys to 'Uthman.

Ever since the failed siege on Medina two years earlier, Khalid ibn al-Walid's animosity toward Islam had begun to unravel. His mother and her sisters were committed Muslims, and one of his aunts, Maymunah, had just married the Prophet. In addition, Khalid's brother, Walid, constantly wrote to him from Medina encouraging Khalid to join him. Not wanting to go to Medina alone, Khalid seeks out the company of other prominent sons of Mecca—'Amr ibn al-'As, Safwan ibn Umayyah, and 'Ikrimah ibn Abi Jahl. 'Amr is nowhere to be found, while Safwan and 'Ikrimah reiterate their dislike for the Prophet. But Khalid ultimately finds a friend in 'Uthman ibn Talhah, who joins him in his journey to Medina shortly after the Prophet returned from his lesser pilgrimage.

'Amr, meanwhile, realizes the Prophet's influence is unstoppable and flees to Abyssinia seeking asylum from the people of Mecca and Medina. To 'Amr's surprise, the Negus denies his request and instead instructs him to follow the Prophet:

> *"Do what I tell thee, O 'Amr, and follow him. His is the truth, by God, and he will triumph over every persuasion that setteth itself against him, even as Moses triumphed over Pharaoh and his hosts."*[4]

'Amr returns and meets Khalid and 'Uthman ibn Talhah along the way and together, the three men continue to Medina. Khalid worries that his past enmity will not be forgiven, but upon his arrival, the Prophet warmly embraces him and explains that submission to God washes away all past sins.

In an ironic twist, **'Amr ibn al-'As** was one of the two Qurayshi mercenaries who had traveled to Abyssinia over a decade ago hoping to persuade the Negus to deny asylum to the Muslim emigrants led by Ja'far ibn Abi Talib. Details of 'Amr's second journey to Abyssinia can be found in Salahi (p. 585-589).

---

3 **WHAT CAN WE LEARN ABOUT KHALID AND 'AMR'S CONVERSIONS TO ISLAM?** RAMADAN

"Those conversions [Khalid ibn al-Walid and 'Amr ibn al-'As] were pregnant with teachings, for not only was the past of Islam's worst enemies forgotten as soon as they recognized God's oneness, but the time these people had needed in order to follow the path of this recognition said nothing about their sincerity, their moral qualities, and their future status within the community of faith.
Thus faith—its intensity and its power to convert and transform hearts—cannot be measured on the basis of time or rationality; its very sincerity and intensity attest to its nature ... this requires people to refrain from judging others' hearts."[5]

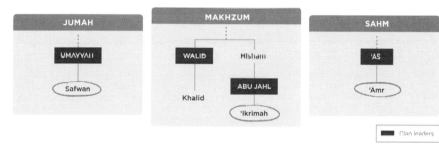

FIGURE 20B. PROMINENT SONS OF QURAYSH

Khalid's conversion to Islam did not sit well with his first cousin 'Ikrimah, who still held on to his father's enmity for the Prophet. Safwan was no different—his father Umayyah ibn Khalaf died at Uhud and Safwan was unwilling to rethink his strategy. By now, 'Amr had realized that the Prophet's influence was unstoppable and so he fled to Abyssinia in search of asylum.

The elder brother to Ja'far and 'Ali, **'Aqil ibn Abi Talib** was approximately six years younger than the Prophet. He fought the Muslims at Badr, and was captured and ransomed.

Recall that **Jubayr ibn Mut'im** had owned Wahshi and promised him his freedom if he killed Hamzah at Uhud. Jubayr's father was Mut'im ibn 'Adi, who urged the Quraysh to lift the ban on Hashim and later served as the Prophet's guardian when the Prophet returned from Ta'if.

Two years from now, Fatimah will have a baby girl whom she will name Zaynab, in honor of her eldest sister, whom she loved dearly.

Around the time of Khalid and 'Amr's emigration, 'Aqil ibn Abi Talib and Jubayr ibn Mut'im also come to Medina and enter Islam. The Prophet greets all the newcomers with open arms and specifically tells 'Aqil:

> *"I love thee with two loves, for thy near kinship unto me, and for the love that I ever saw for thee in mine uncle."*[6]

Unfortunately, the joy is tempered by the sudden loss of the Prophet's eldest daughter, Zaynab. Shortly thereafter, his sorrow is momentarily lifted by news that Mariyah is expecting her first child.

20.4 THE FIRST SYRIA EXPEDITION (MU'TAH)

Three months after the 'umrah pilgrimage, the Prophet sends a peaceful delegation of 15 men to the Syrian border to introduce Islam to the northern Arabian tribes. However, as the party nears its destination, the group is ambushed and all but one man is killed.

Remember that the **Ghassanids** were Hellenized Christian Arabs. They were originally Kahlan Arabs who left Yemen many centuries ago (Fig. P3).

Around the same time, the Prophet sends a second letter to the Roman governor in Bostra, since the first went unanswered. The message, however, is intercepted by the Ghassanids, who send a stern warning to Medina by killing the Prophet's messenger, Harith ibn 'Umayr.

When the news reaches Medina, the Prophet immediately responds with an army of 3,000 men. The expedition is led by Zayd ibn Harithah, with Ja'far ibn Abi Talib and 'Abd Allah ibn Rawahah placed second and third in command. As the men approach the Syrian border, they learn that the Romans have assembled an army of more than 100,000 men. Although the Arabs had never seen an army of that size, 'Abd Allah dismisses any notion of retreating:

> *"I swear by Allah that the very object which you are trying to avoid is the one you have set out seeking, martyrdom. In our fight, we don't count on number of soldiers or equipment but rather on the Faith that Allah has honored us with. Hasten to win either of the two, victory or martyrdom."*[7]

Despite the perceived size and grandeur of the Roman army, Zayd's forces attack at Mu'tah, near the southern part of the Dead Sea. Although the attack is unsuccessful, only Zayd, Ja'far, 'Abd Allah, and a few others are killed. The remaining Muslims narrowly escape under the skilled leadership of Khalid ibn al-Walid.

4 WAS MU'TAH A BATTLE OR A SKIRMISH? WATT

"It is unlikely that the encounter was with the whole of the opposing army. Al-Waqidi says only 8 Muslims were killed, but Ibn Hisham adds 4 other names. This is an incredibly small casualty list, however, for a pitched battle between 3,000 men on one side and, say, 20,000 or 10,000 or even 3,000 on the other unless, indeed, the Muslims completely routed the enemy ... It is possible, then, that the encounter was of the nature of a skirmish. It is difficult to conceive a skirmish in which the general and two staff officers were killed, but hardly anyone else; but, in view of Arab methods of fighting, it is not an absolute impossibility. In this encounter the Arabs may well have had the best of it; otherwise the losses would have been heavier."[8]

5 WAS THE BATTLE OF MU'TAH A SUCCESS OR FAILURE? AL-MUBARAKPURI

"The battle was a real miracle proving that the Muslims were something exceptional not then known. Moreover, it gave evidence that Allah backed them and their Prophet, Muhammad, was really Allah's Messenger. In the light of these new strategic changes, the archenemies among the desert bedouins began to reconcile themselves with the new uprising faith and several disobedient tribes like Banu Sulaim, Ashja', Ghatafan, Dhubyan, Fazarah and others came to profess Islam out of their own free will."[9]

FIGURE 20C. THE NORTHERN OFFENSIVES

The Prophet sent 3,000 men to Syria in response to recent hostilities. The attack at Mu'tah was unsuccessful and Zayd, Ja'far, and 'Abd Allah ibn Rawahah were all killed in battle. (Just a few years later, the Prophet sent Zayd's son, Usamah, at the head of 10,000 troops to finish his father's mission.)

The Mu'tah offensive was followed by another expedition of 500 men, led by 'Amr ibn al-'As to disperse the hostile tribe of Quda'ah (QY 20.5).

Shortly after Ja'far's death, his widow **Asma' bint Umays** will marry Abu Bakr, and the couple will have a child they name Muhammad.

When the army returns to Medina, the Prophet weeps over the deaths of his close Companions. He calls on Ja'far's widow, Asma' bint 'Umays, and placing his arms around her three sons, hugs the children tightly before weeping for their father. When Zayd's little daughter runs to embrace him, the Prophet begins to weep once more. Sa'd ibn 'Ubadah had never seen such an emotional display from the Prophet, and when he tries to comfort him, the Prophet replies:

"This is one who loveth yearning for his beloved."[10]

Soon after the tragic loss, the families of the departed find comfort in a prophetic vision wherein all three men are in Paradise.

---

6 **WHAT WAS THE PROPHET TRYING TO TELL SA'D?**   RAMADAN

"The Prophet had taught his Companions to express love and tenderness, and at that moment, when faced with the final parting of death, he taught them about human fragility and the dignity of tears expressing love and the suffering of those who love ... He was singular, he acted singularly, his intelligence and qualities did not resemble anyone else's, and yet he remained humble and fragile, and like them, he wept."[11]

20.5 THE EXPEDITON TO BANI QUDA'AH

Remember that **'Amr ibn al-'As** was the Qurayshi delegate who followed the earliest Muslim immigrants to Abyssinia and pleaded with the Negus to deny them asylum. He had only embraced Islam in the past year, after the Negus had refused his request for asylum from the Prophet.

Abu 'Ubaydah ibn al-Jarrah was one of the earliest men to enter Islam and fought by the Prophet's side at every battle. At Uhud, he removed the chainmail embedded in the Prophet's cheek. He achieved such a high position among the Companions that later in the year, he will lead one of four battalions at the Conquest of Mecca. In fact, after the death of the Prophet, Abu Bakr nominates Abu 'Ubaydah as the first Caliph.

Despite the recent losses, the Prophet sends out another expedition of 300 men to the Syrian border to confront the Bani Quda'ah—a northern Arabian tribe that had been provoking Medina since the Muslim victory at Khaybar. The Prophet places 'Amr ibn al-'As in charge of the expedition mostly because of 'Amr's family ties with Bani Quda'ah's ally, Bani Bali. When 'Amr sends word to Medina asking for reinforcements, the Prophet dispatches Abu 'Ubaydah ibn al-Jarrah at the head of 200 men with instructions that both parties should work as one. Although Abu 'Ubaydah has 20 years of experience over 'Amr, 'Amr demands that the senior Companion follow his lead. Abu 'Ubaydah obliges on the grounds that, while he would not disobey 'Amr, he fears that 'Amr might disobey him, and in doing so, disobey the Prophet.

The army of 500 men reaches Bani Quda'ah and successfully disperses the enemy tribe and secures the area. The crucial victory established the Prophet's influence along the Syrian border.

20.6 A BREAK IN THE TREATY OF HUDAYBIYAH

Nearly a year and a half after the Treaty of Hudaybiyah was signed, several men from the tribe of Bakr (with the help of a few men from Quraysh) attack Bani Khuza'ah. Bani Bakr was an ally of Quraysh, and their attack on Khuza'ah breaks the terms of the treaty. Abu Sufyan rushes to Medina to undo the damage, but when he arrives, the Prophet refuses to negotiate with him. Abu Sufyan desperately approaches his daughter Umm Habibah, whom he had not seen in 15 years, but before he can sit down in her apartment, she removes the Prophet's rug and asks:

> "My father, thou art lord of Quraysh and their chief. How is it that thou hast failed to enter Islam, and that thou worshippest stones which neither hear nor see?"[12]

Realizing the futility of asking for his daughter's help, Abu Sufyan approaches Abu Bakr, 'Ali, and Fatimah. No one is willing to assist him, and the discouraged Qurayshi chieftain is forced to return home without resolving the crisis.

No longer bound by the treaty, the Prophet quietly instructs Abu Bakr to prepare for an attack on the Quraysh. When Hatib ibn 'Amr, a Companion who fought at Badr, hears the news, he sends a message to his son in Mecca to warn the Quraysh about the approaching army. But Hatib's note is intercepted, and when the Prophet sends for him, Hatib explains that he only sought to win the Quraysh's favor to protect his son and family. 'Umar immediately calls for Hatib to be punished for his treachery, but the Prophet forgives him, explaining:

> "He is one of those who fought in the battle of Badr. What do you know 'Umar? Perhaps Allah has looked at the people of Badr and said: 'Do as you please, for I have forgiven you.'"[13]

Recall that **Bani Khuza'ah** had taken care of the Muslim pilgrims at Hudaybiyah. When their rival tribe Bani Bakr, allied themselves with the Quraysh, the Khuza'ah renewed their ties with the Prophet (QY 19.3). Bani Khuza'ah had an ongoing feud with Bani Bakr, which culminated with this latest attack.

Umm Habibah is the Prophet's ninth wife, and had joined the household in the past year. She had entered Islam in Mecca and went with her first husband, 'Ubayd Allah ibn Jahsh, to Abyssinia. After 'Ubayd Allah's death, the Negus married her to the Prophet before she departed for Medina.

Hatib ibn 'Amr is the brother of Suhayl ibn 'Amr al-'Amiri, clan chief of 'Amir (Fig. 5g). Much to Suhayl's dismay, Hatib entered Islam in Mecca and migrated to Abyssinia. He returned after the ban on Hashim was lifted and fought alongside the Prophet at Badr.

---

7 **WHAT CAN WE LEARN FROM THE DIFFERENT REACTIONS OF THE PROPHET AND 'UMAR?** `YUSUF`

"For 'Umar this is unacceptable, because this is war, and this is treachery, and treason is punishable by death during war.
The wisdom here is that for people who have done great good in the past, you should often overlook something that occurs to them. [Citing an Arabic proverb] 'Every steed will trip, and every sword has some cut in it.' This is the nature of human beings—they're going to make mistakes and if people are generally good, if the basic material there is good, then you should have the magnanimity in your character to overlook their faults. This was an enormity; this was not an insignificant thing, but the Prophet, God's peace and blessings upon him, believed that he was speaking the truth."[14]

- -

8 **WHAT DOES THE PROPHET'S TREATMENT OF HATIB TEACH US?** `YUSUF`

"Another very important lesson is that you don't condemn people until you understand their motives. This is something a *qari* [judge] has to do. In other words, when a situation occurs, you always want to understand the motive behind the person's actions. That's really important. So the Prophet, God's peace and blessings upon him, asked Hatib what the motive was, and he told him. And the Prophet, God's peace and blessings upon him, said, 'He has spoken the truth.'"[15]

Accompanied by his wives Umm Salamah and Maymunah, the Prophet sets out with an expedition of nearly 10,000 men but does not announce where they are heading. It is Ramadan, but the Prophet instructs his Companions not to fast for a portion of the journey.

---

9 WHY DIDN'T THE PROPHET FAST WHEN TRAVELING? `RAMADAN`

"The Prophet kept insisting on the permissions granted to the faithful, who must make the practice of their religion easy and bring good news rather than cause repulsion."[16]

Abu Sufyan ibn al-Harith is the son of the Prophet's oldest paternal uncle, Harith ibn 'Abd al-Muttalib (not Abu Sufyan ibn al-Harb, the leader of Quraysh who had just come to Medina to try to pacify the Prophet).

Named after the Prophet's father, **'Abd Allah ibn Abi Umayyah** is the Prophet's first cousin and the half-brother of Umm Salamah (Fig. 5f). Many years ago in Mecca, he had ridiculed the Prophet and said he would never believe in Islam, even if the Messenger brought down angels from Heaven.

Halfway to Mecca, they encounter the Prophet's uncle 'Abbas and his wife Umm al-Fadl. The couple recently decided it was time to live in Medina and were headed north. Instead, they join the expedition and return to Mecca with the Prophet. Several days later, the Prophet's first cousins Abu Sufyan ibn al-Harith and 'Abd Allah ibn Abi Umayyah leave Mecca to meet the Prophet and join the Muslims. At first the Prophet refuses to see them, but Umm Salamah successfully negotiates on their behalf.

---

10 WHY DID THE YOUNGER MEN OF QURAYSH ESSENTIALLY GIVE UP AFTER HUDAYBIYAH? `WATT`

"After the first breath of relief at the signing of the treaty of al-Hudaybiyah, Mecca must have felt a doomed city. The older men and those with vested interests would want to carry on, but the younger men must have seen that there was no future for them in Mecca ... Abu Sufyan b. al-Harith b. 'Abd al-Muttalib (Hashim) and 'Abdallah b. Abi Umayyah (Makhzum), the son of 'Atikah bint 'Abd al-Muttalib, joined him while he was on his way to Mecca in January 630."[17]

Ju'ayl ibn Suraqah was a man of small stature but considerable piety. He was a convert from the distant tribe of Damrah and came to live inside the mosque (as one of the People of the Bench). Ju'ayl is a popular Companion, and the men of Medina sang about him as he energetically helped dig the trench around the city. Despite his poverty, Ju'ayl will not receive any spoils after the Conquest of Mecca.

As the army continues south, the Prophet spots a dog and her puppies lying by the side of the road. Not wanting to disturb the litter, he tells Ju'ayl ibn Suraqah to guard them until the entire army has passed.

FIGURE 20D. THE ARMY THAT CONQUERED MECCA

Without announcing the details of the expedition, the Prophet set out of Medina with nearly 10,000 troops and over 800 horses. Along the way, a cavalry of 900 men from Bani Sulaym joined the Prophet's forces. News of the huge troop movement quickly spread south, putting the tribes of Quraysh and Hawazin on heightened alert.

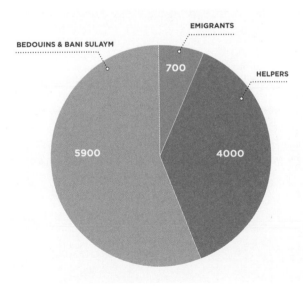

BEDOUINS & BANI SULAYM
EMIGRANTS
HELPERS
5900
700
4000

Nine hundred men from Bani Sulaym join the expedition as it progresses south toward Mecca and Ta'if. The Prophet has not yet declared the army's intentions, and as the days pass, the worried Hawazin begin to assemble troops just north of Ta'if. As the Muslim army nears the two cities, it abruptly veers southeast toward Mecca, and the Prophet orders his men to spread out over the horizon and light campfires stretching from east to west.

---

⑪ WHY DID THE PROPHET WANT TO TAKE MECCA BY SURPRISE? [SALAHI]

"As his army began to prepare, he prayed to God to enable him to take the Quraysh by surprise in their own land. The purpose of that prayer was not the launching of a surprise attack which would have resulted in mass killings among the Quraysh in return for very few casualties among the Muslims. Rather, the Prophet wanted to face the Quraysh with a situation in which they would feel themselves no match for him. In such a situation, they might choose not to put up any resistance and victory for the Muslims would be achieved without bloodshed."[18]

When the Quraysh see the horizon ablaze, they are paralyzed by the army's overwhelming presence. Hoping to avoid certain defeat, they send Abu Sufyan ibn al-Harb, Hakim ibn Hizam, and Budayl ibn Warqa' to make one last appeal to the Prophet. When Abu Sufyan arrives in the Muslim camp, the Prophet presses him:

> *"Woe to you! Isn't it time for you to bear witness to the Oneness of Allah and Prophethood of Muhammad?"*[19]

Hakim and Budayl immediately embrace Islam, but Abu Sufyan asks for a little more time to contemplate the matter. The next morning, while sitting in the Muslim camp, Abu Sufyan witnesses the fervant loyalty of the Prophet's Companions. The scene strikes a chord in him and prompts him to finally testify his faith.

Budayl ibn Warqa' of Bani Khuza'ah had acted as a messenger for the Prophet at Hudaybiyah. After the Battle of Hunayn, the Prophet will place him in charge of transporting all the captives and spoils to the valley of Ji'ranah.

Hakim ibn Hizam had always loved his aunt Khadijah and the members of her household (Fig. 5d). Though he never embraced Islam during the early days in Mecca, he provided the Muslims with supplies during the ban on Hashim. At Badr, Hakim made a last-minute appeal to persuade the Meccans to avoid fighting their kinsmen. The Prophet will give him a generous portion of the spoils from the Battle of Hunayn.

---

⑫ HOW DID THE PROPHET EARN THE RESPECT OF HIS COMPANIONS? [WATT]

"He gained men's respect and confidence by the religious basis of his activity and by qualities such as courage, resoluteness, impartiality and firmness inclining to severity but tempered by generosity. In addition to these he had a charm of manner which won their affection and secured their devotion."[20]

After Abu Sufyan's conversion, 'Abbas advises the Prophet to grant the Quraysh chieftain a level of prestige among his people. The Prophet responds with an act of unprecedented clemency—he promises amnesty to any Meccan who seeks protection in the house of Abu Sufyan as well as anyone who remains in their house or the Sacred Mosque.

19
20
21
22
23

13 **WHY DID THE PROPHET HONOR ABU SUFYAN AS THE LEADER OF MECCA?** RAMADAN

"Muhammad had turned Abu Sufyan into an ally, not only because Abu Sufyan had converted to Islam but also because the Prophet had heeded his character and personality. ... Even after Abu Sufyan had embraced Islam, the Prophet was aware that he retained an attraction for power and glory, and he took this into account when he exposed him to the strength of his army and conferred on him a specific role in the possible resolution of the conflict ... His message insisted on the principle of equality for all in justice, as well as the psychology of differences and of each person's singularity in faith."[21]

Recall that **Zubayr ibn al-'Awwam** is the Prophet's first cousin through his aunt Safiyyah. After migrating to Medina, he married Asma' bint Abi Bakr. He was one of the first to embrace Islam, and over the past 20 years, has been a constant source of support for the Prophet. Zubayr is one of the 10 to whom the Prophet promises Paradise.

Usayd ibn Hudayr was one of 12 men to represent the Helpers at the Second 'Aqabah and later carried one of the three banners at Uhud.

Sa'd ibn 'Ubadah had replaced 'Abd Allah ibn Ubayy as the de facto leader of Khazraj. A few days from now, after the Battle of Hunayn, he will approach the Prophet on behalf of the Helpers asking why the spoils were only given to the Quraysh and Hawazin tribes. After the Prophet's death, many of the Helpers will suggest that Sa'd should become the first caliph.

The Prophet positions Abu Sufyan so that he and 'Abbas can watch the Prophet's army pass by on its way to Mecca. The Quraysh chief is stunned by the sheer size and strength of the Prophet's forces and is especially amazed to see his recent ally, Khalid ibn al-Walid, leading all 10,000 men. Behind Khalid is Zubayr ibn al-'Awwam at the head of 500 Emigrants and others. The scene is too much for Abu Sufyan and when a battalion from Bani Ghatafan goes by, he turns to 'Abbas and marvels:

"Of all the Arabs, these were Muhammad's bitterest foes."

The last squadron is led by Sa'd ibn 'Ubadah, who carries the Prophet's standard. The Prophet rides behind him flanked by Abu Bakr and Usayd ibn Hudayr. As Sa'd rides by Abu Sufyan, he warns that the day will be full of slaughter. But when the Quraysh chieftain immediately complains to the Prophet, he gently allays all his fears:

"Nay, today Al-Ka'bah will be sanctified, and Quraish honored."[22]

14 **WHAT WAS THE PROPHET TRYING TO ACCOMPLISH?** ARMSTRONG

"Muhammad had never planned to overthrow the Quraysh but had simply wanted to reform the social system, which, he was convinced, would bring the city to ruin."[23]

- -

15 **HOW DID THE CONQUEST OF MECCA PREPARE THE MUSLIMS FOR FURTHER EXPANSION?** ARMSTRONG

"The true karim [Bedouin ideal of the generous hero] was no longer an aggressive chauvinist, but was filled with reverent fear. The purpose of the tribe and the nation was no longer to exalt its superiority; they must not seek to dominate, exploit, convert, conquer, or destroy other peoples, but get to know them. The experience of living in a group, coexisting with people—some of whom, despite their kinship, would inevitably be uncongenial—should prepare the tribesman or the patriot for the encounter with foreigners. It should lead to an appreciation of the unity of the human race. Muhammad had managed to redefine the concept of nobility in Arabia, replacing it with a more universal, compassionate, and self-effacing ideal."[24]

20.7 THE CONQUEST OF MECCA

The army momentarily stops at Dhu Tuwa on the outskirts of the city and the Prophet bows his head in humility. Leading the right and left wings are Khalid and Zubayr. The Prophet splits his center group into two. Sa'd leads the first half while Abu 'Ubaydah leads the remaining men along with the Prophet.

As the army approaches Mecca, Abu Bakr's elderly father Abu Quhafah ascends a nearby mountain (assisted by his daughter Quraybah) to witness the Prophet's entry into Mecca. Meanwhile 'Ikrimah ibn Abi Jahl, Safwan ibn Umayyah, and Suhayl ibn 'Amr al-'Amiri charge down from the same mountain to try to stop the advancing army. They attack Khalid's men but are quickly dispersed. Suhayl retreats to his house in Mecca while 'Ikrimah and Safwan flee to the coast.

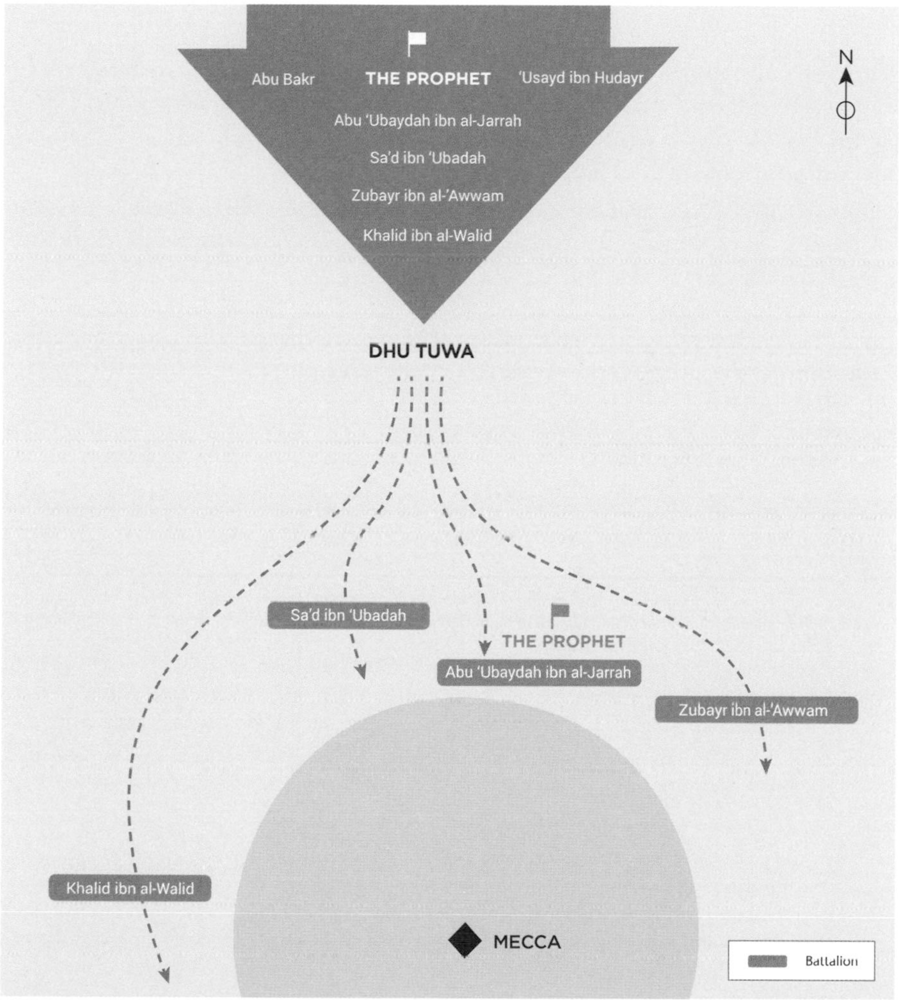

One of the earliest converts, **Abu 'Ubaydah ibn al-Jarrah** fought valiantly at every battle. After the death of the Prophet, Abu Bakr will nominate him as a successor. He is also one of the 10 to whom the Prophet promised Paradise.

Suhayl ibn 'Amr al-'Amiri was the Prophet's longtime enemy who insisted on striking out "Muhammad, the Messenger of God" on the Hudaybiyah Treaty and replacing it with "Muhammad ibn 'Abd Allah." He, 'Ikrimah, and Safwan are three of the last major leaders to enter Islam. Nonetheless, when they finally testify their faith, the Prophet generously rewards them with the spoils from the Battle of Hunayn.

FIGURE 20E. THE CONQUEST OF MECCA

Khalid ibn al-Walid led the 10,000 man march to Mecca. Sa'd ibn 'Ubadah was given the Prophet's standard and led the last squadron, with the Prophet behind him, flanked by Abu Bakr and Usayd ibn Hudayr. After momentarily stopping at Dhu Tuwa, Khalid led some of the men to the right while Zubayr and 700 Emigrants turned left. The Prophet split his center group into two. One group was led by Sa'd ibn 'Ubadah and the other by Abu 'Ubaydah ibn al-Jarrah. The Prophet entered the city with Abu 'Ubaydah's group.

The Conquest of Mecca is a very powerful moment in the story of the Prophet's life. Make sure to read Lings (p. 310-318) and listen to Yusuf (CD 21) for a very touching narration of the event.

One year ago, the honor of holding the Prophet's bridle at the Lesser Pilgrimage was given to a man of Khazraj. This time it was given to a man of Aws—Muhammad ibn Maslamah, the Helper who volunteered to kill Ka'b ibn Ashraf, the treacherous poet of Bani Nadir.

Review Surah As-Saffat (37:83-96), which describes how a young Abraham similarly knocked down the lifeless idols worshipped by his people in Iraq.

Recall that **'Uthman ibn Talhah** had just migrated to Medina with his close friend Khalid ibn al-Walid. 'Uthman is from the clan of 'Abd ad-Dar, whose traditional duty was to hold the keys to the Ka'bah (P 2.1).

The four battalions approach Mecca from all directions. After peaceably entering the city, the Prophet stops to rest in a tent just outside the Sacred Precinct. He is accompanied by Umm Salamah, Maymunah, and Fatimah. With the words *Allahu Akbar! Allahu Akbar!* (God is Great! God is Great!) resonating throughout the city, throngs of Muslims begin to settle around the Ka'bah. After a brief respite, the Prophet puts on his battle armor and mounts his camel. He approaches the Ka'bah from the southeast corner and reverently touches the Black Stone, before circling the structure seven times.

The Prophet then approaches the perimeter of the Sacred Precinct and destroys all 360 idols surrounding the Ka'bah, marking Mecca's return to the legacy of Abraham. With the destruction of each idol he recites:

> "...The truth has arrived, and falsehood will vanish, for falsehood always vanishes!" — *Al Isra' (The Night Journey, 17:81)*

The Prophet approaches the well of Zamzam where, in accordance with the traditional rights of Bani Hashim, his uncle 'Abbas provides him with water. He asks for the keys to the Ka'bah and hands them over to 'Uthman ibn Talhah, bestowing on him and his family their traditional honor of guarding the Holy Sanctuary. Then, accompanied by Bilal (who had made the call to prayer), 'Uthman ibn Talhah, and Usamah ibn Zayd, the Prophet enters the Ka'bah and destroys the idols and images inside.

---

16 **DID THE PROPHET ALLOW JESUS' IMAGE TO REMAIN IN THE KA'BAH?** `YUSUF`

"Lings, citing al-Waqidi, mentions that there was a picture of E'issa [Jesus]. However, the idea of the Prophet, God's peace and blessings upon him, leaving the picture of Jesus, peace be upon him, in the Ka'bah is just unacceptable because pictures of all prophets are prohibited in Islam."[25]

- -

17 **WHY DID THE PROPHET HAVE BILAL MAKE THE CALL TO PRAYER AT THE CONQUEST OF MECCA?** `YUSUF`

"This was an affront to the Quraysh, because everything that was related to the Ka'bah was from a family position. If you remember when the stone was placed, it was only the notables of the Quraysh who were allowed to partake in this. So taking a Habishi [black Abyssinian] slave and having him mount the Ka'bah, and actually go to the top of the Ka'bah, and call the *azaan* is a radical departure from the *jahili* understanding. This is something incredible ... [Yusuf cites Surah Hujurat, 49:13] ... The Prophet, God's peace and blessings upon him, said, 'Today Allah has played down the arrogance of the jahili days. There's no black man or white man over one or the other, except with *taqwa* [God-consciousness].'
Because Bilal is a *taqi* [a person of taqwa] Allah raised him up. This was a declaration to the Quraysh that there's a new order. The jahili days are over. There's a new order from this day on in this city."[26]

When the Prophet finally emerges from the Ka'bah, he turns to the hushed crowd and exclaims:

> "O people of Quraysh! Surely, Allah has abolished from you all pride of the pre-Islamic era and all pride in your ancestry, (because) all men are descended from Adam, and Adam was made out of dust."

He continues with a verse from Surah Al Hujurat:

> All you people! We created you from a single (pair of) a male and a female and made you into different races and tribes so you can come to know one another. The noblest among you in the sight of God is the one who is the most mindful (of his duty to Him). Truly, God knows and is aware.
> — Al Hujurat (The Inner Rooms, 49:13)

With those words, he turns to the Quraysh and asks:

> "O you people of Quraysh! What do you think of the treatment that I am about to accord you?" [27]

Then, in the words of Joseph who forgave his brothers, the Prophet continues:

> "Let there be no blame upon you this day," Joseph replied. "God will forgive you, and He's the most merciful of the merciful." — Yusuf (Joseph, 12:92)

SURAH AL HUJURAT (The Inner Rooms) is named after its opening verses, which admonish visitors to lower their voices around the Prophet, rather than shout out to him harshly while he is in his home (i.e., one of his wives' inner rooms adjoining the mosque). In many ways, the remainder of the surah is a social manifesto, urging listeners to appreciate the diversity of human creation, forgive the faults of others, and strive for mutual coexistence.

---

(18) WHAT IS THE TRUE MEANING OF FORGIVENESS IN ISLAM? [YUSUF]

"The idea of 'afu [forgiveness] in Islam is based on your ability to forgive them. For example, if an army attacks me and I say, 'Oh, I forgive them,' that's not the same as somebody who has an army that has conquered a people and really can get retribution, and yet he says, 'I forgive them.' These two are not the same. When you have the ability to get vengeance, and yet you forgive, that's greatness; that's what the Messenger of Allah, God's peace and blessings upon him, was displaying on that day." [28]

Abu Bakr leaves the mosque to find his father and escort him to the Prophet. After hearing Abu Quhafah testify his faith in Islam, the Prophet retreats to Mount Safa and receives Hind and hundreds of other Meccans, who pledge to abandon idolatry for the religion of Abraham. He then asks 'Abbas to bring the sons of Abu Lahab–'Utbah and Mu'attib—who were fearful of coming forward based on their past enmity toward the Prophet. When they arrive, the Prophet accepts their conversions and leads them hand-in-hand to the door of the Ka'bah, where he fervently prays for his cousins.

The Prophet remains in Mecca for 19 days. The keys of the Ka'bah remain with 'Uthman ibn Talhah, while responsibility for feeding the pilgrims is left to 'Abbas. Furthermore, the Prophet instructs the Quraysh to destroy every household idol and dispatches Khalid ibn al-Walid to destroy the temple of al-'Uzzah in Nakhlah (Fig. 20g).

This was not the first time the Prophet ascended Mount Safa and called his people to Islam. After the earliest revelations, he invited his family there and was ridiculed by Abu Lahab and the other elders of Hashim. Twenty years later, the Prophet lovingly welcomes Abu Lahab's two sons to Islam.

Recall that **'Utbah ibn Abi Lahab** was originally engaged to the Prophet's daughter Ruqayyah but was pressured by his father to break the engagement when the Prophet began preaching about Islam.

Of the three prominent Meccans who had not yet converted to Islam, Suhayl ibn 'Amr al-'Amiri (the chief of 'Amir) and Safwan ibn Umayyah are given temporary amnesty. The third, 'Ikrimah ibn Abi Jahl, had fled to the Red Sea coast hoping to escape to Abyssinia. But before 'Ikrimah can board the vessel, the boat's captain insists that each of his passengers testify that there is no god but God, so the ship will be protected from calamity. In that moment, 'Ikrimah recognizes that his idols have no power to save him, and when his wife sends him word that the Prophet has offered him temporary amnesty, he returns to Mecca.

The Prophet tells the Companions to be gracious to 'Ikrimah, despite his longtime enmity to the Muslims, and specifically instructs them not to malign his father, Abu Jahl. When 'Ikrimah appears before the Prophet, the Prophet welcomes him, saying:

"Thou shalt not ask me anything this day but I will give it thee."[29]

The magnaminous gesture hits its mark, and 'Ikrimah asks the Prophet to pray for his forgiveness, and promises to double his efforts in the way of Islam.

---

19 **WHY DID THE PROPHET INSTRUCT THE COMPANIONS TO BE GENTLE WITH 'IKRIMAH?**   RAMADAN

"[The Prophet] thus reminded them [the Companions] not only to forgive but also to always remember that nobody can be held responsible for someone else's mistakes, not even their father's, according to the meaning of the Quranic verse 'No bearer of burdens can bear the burden of another.' " (Qur'an 17:15)[30]

20.8 THE BATTLE OF HUNAYN

Malik ibn 'Awf is not all that different from Khalid ibn al-Walid. Both are promising young generals who, at one point, led armies against the Prophet, only to convert and lead expeditions under his command. Within days, Malik will lead his men against the Bani Thaqif at Ta'if.

To the east of Mecca lay the great inland tribe of Hawazin which had already assembled troops in case the Prophet planned to attack Ta'if. After the Conquest of Mecca and the destruction of the temple of al-'Uzzah, the Hawazin clans urgently increase their forces to 20,000 men. Leading the troops is a 30-year-old general named Malik ibn 'Awf. Despite warnings from his elder tribesmen, Malik orders his troops to bring their wives, children, and cattle with them in an effort to motivate his men to fight with all their heart.

Meanwhile, the Prophet leads his army southeast, bolstered by 2,000 new Quraysh converts as well as Meccans who have not yet entered Islam.

---

20 **WHY DID THE PAGAN MECCANS JOIN THE MARCH TO HUNAYN?**   WATT

"Muhammad, on becoming conqueror of Mecca, at once became also its champion against the threatening enemy. It was self-preservation rather than hope of booty that made the pagan Quraysh go out with him to Hunayn."[31]

From a valley north of Ta'if, Malik sends several scouts to assess the Prophet's position. Each returns more terrified than the next, and warns the young general to withdraw. But Malik mocks his scouts for their cowardice and orders the entire army to march to the valley of Hunayn, where he can ambush the Prophet's troops.

As the Prophet's men enter the valley, Malik's unseen forces descend from the surrounding ravines. At first, the Hawazin forces overwhelm Khalid's battalion. The chaos takes the Prophet's men by surprise and the Muslims begin to scatter. With Abu Sufyan by his side, the Prophet makes the order to attack, and soon, as described in Surah At-Tawbah, the momentum shifts back in the Muslims' favor.

> As it happens, God has already helped you on many battlefields. On the day of (the Battle of) Hunayn, however, when your great numbers made you feel overconfident - that by itself did nothing for you. The wide earth hemmed you in (as you passed through the narrow valley and were suddenly taken by surprise in ambush). Thus, you turned back in retreat.
>
> Then God sent His tranquility down upon the Messenger and upon the believers, and He sent forces (of angels) you couldn't even see. Thus, He punished the faithless, and that's how He repays those who cover (the light of faith within their hearts). — *At-Tawbah (Repentance, 9:25-26)*

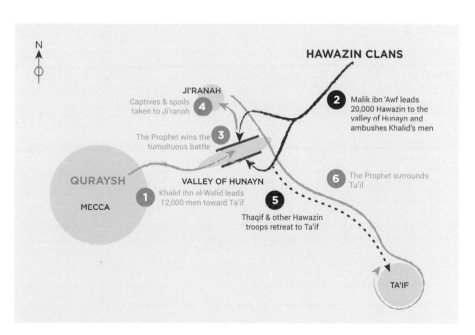

FIGURE 20F. THE AMBUSH AT HUNAYN

After the Conquest of Mecca, the Prophet marched out with 12,000 men to confront the Bani Thaqif (the Hawazin clan that inhabited the city of Ta'if) and the rest of the Hawazin tribe. Meanwhile, 30-year-old Malik ibn 'Awf had been selected to lead 20,000 Hawazin men to ambush the Prophet's forces at the valley of Hunayn. The ensuing chaos initially sent the Muslims fleeing. However, the Prophet refocused their efforts and shifted the momentum back in their favor. While most of the Hawazin clans were captured, Bani Thaqif and some additional troops managed to escape to their fortress in Ta'if. After the battle, 6,000 captives were taken with their possessions and cattle to the valley of Ji'ranah (approx. 10 miles from Mecca). The Prophet immediately ordered that all the captives be given new garments from Mecca, and later that day reunited them with their families. In return for the Prophet's generosity, Malik pledged allegiance to him and ordered his men to besiege the city of Ta'if. After a monthlong stand-off, the Prophet returned to Medina.

Recall that **Budayl ibn Warqa'** had traveled to Hudaybiyah to warn the Prophet that the Quraysh would not let the Muslim pilgrims enter Mecca. Budayl had recently embraced Islam when he and Abu Sufyan ibn al-Harb visited the Prophet's camp on the eve of the Conquest of Mecca.

The Hawazin clans begin to retreat, but many are captured by the Muslims. Several Hawazin troops, including the clan of Thaqif and Malik, escape to their fortress in Ta'if. The Prophet places Budayl ibn Warqa' in charge of transporting thousands of captives and animals to the valley of Ji'ranah approximately 10 miles from Mecca.

㉑ WHO WAS TO BLAME FOR THE SETBACK AT HUNAYN, AND WHAT CAN WE LEARN FROM IT? SALAHI

"The setback cannot be explained away by lack of courage on the part of the new soldiers. The Qur'anic admonition to the Muslims in its comment on the events of Hunayn suggests that they all shared responsibility.

One need not seek easy explanations in order to present the companions of the Prophet as free of all blame, or as having no share in the mistakes of that day. It does not help the cause of Islam in future generations to do so. The companions of the Prophet were the best Muslims; that is an absolute fact. They served the cause of Islam in such a way as to provide the best ideals for all Muslims in all generations to follow. But they must not be shown in such a light as to raise them above the level of human beings. If they are viewed as superhuman, they cease to be an example for future Muslim generations. If, on the other hand, one says that even the companions of the Prophet suffered when a feeling of complacency crept in, future generations will understand that they cannot afford to allow complacency to creep into them. Otherwise, they will suffer defeat after defeat. It is important for all Muslim generations to recognize that God will grant them victory if they themselves fulfill the requirements of victory. These include the pure motive of serving the cause of God, exerting their best efforts, coupled with a determination to make whatever sacrifice is necessary and to rely on God and trust in Him."[32]

㉒ WHAT DID HUNAYN TEACH THE QURAYSH? YUSUF

"Things completely turn around. And the amazing thing about this is that the Quraysh recognize that something divine is happening: Suddenly in the midst of all this craziness, Allah shows these people that you should not depend on your numbers, but depend on Allah because it's not your numbers that will give you victory, but it is Allah who will do so.

They came out in great numbers but Allah sent them in a completely chaotic condition where they were fleeing. At that point, the Messenger of Allah, God's peace and blessings upon him, has Abu Bakr shout at the top of his lungs 'Remember the tree!' [reminding the Companions of their oath at Hudaybiyah]. So all these people came back. They fought, and they defeated the Hawazin.

This was a great day and the Quraysh recognize this. Many of them whose *iman* [faith] was previously wavering were greatly affected; something had happened. The Battle of Hunayn was a big event."[33]

㉓ WHAT WAS THE SIGNIFICANCE OF THE HUNAYN VICTORY? WATT

"The victory, none the less, was notable and important. Hunayn was the major encounter during Muhammad's lifetime between the Muslims and the nomadic tribes. The collection and concentration of 20,000 men was a notable feat for a nomadic chief, and after Malik b. 'Awf's discomfiture none cared to repeat it against Muhammad. Instead, so long as Muhammad lived, and particularly in the year 9 of the Hijrah (April 630-April 631), deputations came to Medina from all over Arabia to make agreements and alliances."[34]

When an elderly woman named Shayma' bint al-Harith emerges from the group of captives claiming that she is the Prophet's sister, she is brought before him. She explains that she is the daughter of Harith and Halimah from the Hawazin clan of Sa'd ibn Bakr, and the Prophet's eyes fill with tears as she tells him of the death of his beloved foster-parents. Hoping to spend time and reconnect with her, he gives Shayma' a rich present and instructs her to remain in the camp while he pursues Bani Thaqif, who had already retreated to Ta'if.

Not only is Ta'if well fortified, but its inhabitants have enough provisions to last a full year. After a monthlong standoff, the Prophet ultimately decides to retreat to Ji'ranah. While departing, several Companions ask him to curse the people of Ta'if. Instead, he raises his hands and prays:

> *"O God, guide Thaqif and bring them to us as Muslims."*[35]

Recall that the Prophet lived among the people of Sa'd ibn Bakr as a young child (Fig. P19). Over 55 years had passed since then, yet he always kept a special place in his heart for the foster-parents who took him in when all others turned him away.

20.9 DISTRIBUTION OF THE SPOILS

The vast spoils from the Battle of Hunayn amount to 6,000 poorly clad women and children, 24,000 camels, and 40,000 cattle. In accordance with verses from Surah At-Tawbah which had recently identified new categories of individuals eligible to receive spoils of war, the Prophet orders that all the captives be given new garments.

> Charity is meant for the poor, for the needy, for those whose profession it is to distribute it, for encouraging (recent converts), for the (freeing) of bonded servants, for those (straining under a load) of debt, for use in the cause of God, and also (to help stranded) travelers. These are the stipulations set by God, and God is full of knowledge and wisdom. — *At-Tawbah (Repentance, 9:60)*

Before distributing the spoils, the Prophet waits in Ji'ranah for more than a week for a delegation from Hawazin to arrive to pay ransom for the captives. When they don't show up, he distributes the captives and property to his followers. He begins by heaping lavish spoils on the Quraysh who—only one month ago—were his bitterest enemies. As a conciliatory gesture, he gives 100 camels to Abu Sufyan and each of his sons—Yazid and Mu'awiyah.

---

(24) WAS THE PROPHET "BUYING" LOYALTY?   RAMADAN

"This was not meant as a means to convert people but rather was intended to strengthen, by a material gift, a faith that had already more or less expressed itself but remained fragile ... His presence was the sign of his love, while the goods he had distributed were simply evidence that he knew some hearts were still attached to the illusions of this world."[36]

19
20
21
22
23

Recall that **Safwan ibn Umayyah** is the son of Umayyah ibn Khalaf, the late chief of Jumah. At one time, Safwan urged his cousin 'Umayr ibn Wahb to assassinate the Prophet. Several years later, when Khalid ibn al-Walid asked him to come with him to Medina, Safwan replied, *"Even if every other man of Quraysh were to follow Muhammad, I would never follow him."*[38]

Be sure to listen to Yusuf (22:1-2) for a moving narration of the Prophet's speech to the Helpers.

With Safwan ibn Umayyah at his side, the Prophet rides though the valley of Ji'ranah taking stock of the vast riches they had acquired. Sensing Safwan's wonderment, the Prophet graciously offers him an entire pasture of camels, sheep, and goats. The gesture surpasses Safwan's wildest expectations, and he simply responds:

"I bear witness, that no soul could have such goodness as this, if it were not the soul of a Prophet. I bear witness that there is no god but God, and that thou art His Messenger."[37]

While the Prophet's magnanimity wins the hearts of the Quraysh, it sparks frustration among the 4,000 Helpers, many who had supported the Prophet through some of his greatest challenges. Sa'd ibn 'Ubadah voices the Helpers' concerns, and the Prophet responds by gathering them together in an exclusive assembly.

"I have been told that you are angry with me. Didn't I come to you when you were astray and Allah guided you? You were poor and Allah gave you wealth? Weren't you foes and Allah made you love one another? ... But by Allah, you might have answered and answered truly, for I would have testified to its truth myself: 'You came to us belied and rejected, and we accepted you; you came to us as helpless, and we helped you; you were a fugitive, and we took you in; you were poor and we comforted you.' You Helpers, do you feel anxious for the things of this world, wherewith I have sought to incline these people unto the Faith in which you are already established? Are you not satisfied, O group of Helpers that the people go with ewes and camels while you go along with the Messenger of Allah to your dwellings. By Him in Whose Hand is my life, had there been no migration, I would have been one of the Helpers. If the people would go through a valley and passage, and the Helpers go through another valley and passage, I would go through the valley and passage of the Helpers. Allah! Have mercy on the Helpers, their children and their children's children."

With tears flowing down their beards, the Helpers collectively respond:

"Yes, we are satisfied, O Prophet of Allah! With our lot and share."[39]

Just after the last spoils had been distributed, a delegation from Hawazin finally arrives. Several of them were already Muslim, and the rest convert after their arrival. Among the delegation is the brother of Harith ibn 'Abd al-'Uzzah, the Prophet's late foster-father, who asks him to consider forgoing the ransom and reuniting captives from the Prophet's foster clan of Sa'd ibn Bakr (and by extension all Hawazin captives) with their families. Similar to the magnanimity he showed at the Conquest of Mecca, the Prophet frees all the captives.

The Prophet did not ransom Malik ibn 'Awf's family, nor did he distribute Malik's possessions. He sends word to Ta'if promising Malik that his family and property would be returned to him if he embraced Islam. Malik secretly comes to the Prophet's camp, where he agrees to the generous proposition and promises to lead those of his troops who had already become Muslim against Bani Thaqif.

---

25 **WAS THE PROPHET CORRECT IN TRUSTING MALIK IBN 'AWF?** RAMADAN

"He had only just embraced Islam when the Prophet showed him incredible trust: he placed him in command of all the Hawazin who had already become Muslims and ordered them to go to Taif and put an end to the Banu Thaqif's resistance. ... The following days and years confirmed his intuition: Malik not only successfully carried out his mission but also remained faithful and deeply spiritual in his commitment to Islam."[40]

20.10 THE SECOND 'UMRAH & THE RETURN TO MEDINA

After leaving Ji'ranah, the Prophet performs the lesser pilgrimage before returning to Medina. On the way back, 'Urwah ibn Mas'ud catches up to the Prophet and asks for permission to return to Ta'if to summon his people to Islam. The Prophet warns him that he will be slain, but 'Urwah insists. As predicted, 'Urwah returns to Ta'if, only to be killed by his people. Upon hearing the news of his death, the Prophet comments:

> " 'Urwah is even as the man of Ya-Sin. He summoned his people unto God and they slew him."[42]

Then a man came running from a far corner of the city. He told (the gathered crowds), "My people! Obey the messengers. Obey those who ask you for no reward and who themselves have been guided. It would make no sense to me if I didn't serve the One Who created me and to Whom you will all return."

"Should I take other gods in place of Him? If the Compassionate wanted to bring some harm down upon me, (those gods) wouldn't be able to intercede for me at all, nor could they save me. If I (worshipped idols), then I'd be clearly wrong. So as for me, I believe in your Lord, so listen to me!" (Then the mob killed him in their fury, but because of his great faith) he'll be told, "Enter the Garden." Then he'll (look around and exclaim in wonderment and surprise), "Oh my! If only my people knew (about all of this), that my Lord has forgiven me and set me up among the honored." — *Ya Seen (Ya Seen, 36:20-27)*

Recall that the Quraysh sent **'Urwah ibn Mas'ud** to scout the Prophet's camp at Hudaybiyah. He returned to the Quraysh warning them, *"I have not seen a king whose men so honor him as the Companions of Muhammad honor Muhammad."*[41]

One year after 'Urwah's death, his own nephew Mughirah ibn Shu'bah will enter Ta'if and knock down the chief idol, al-Lat. At that point (11 years after they chased the Prophet out of Ta'if) the Bani Thaqif will finally enter Islam.

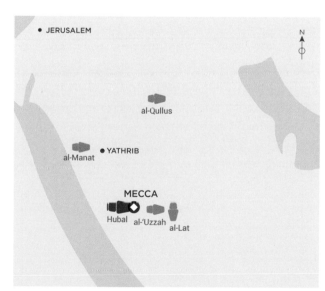

FIGURE 20G. THE FALL OF IDOLATRY

At the Conquest of Mecca, the Prophet destroyed Hubal and every other idol in the Sacred Precinct as well as in every household in Mecca. He then sent Khalid ibn al-Walid to destroy al-'Uzzah in Nakhlah, and 'Ali to destroy al-Manat and Al-Qullus. The following year, the Prophet sent Abu Sufyan ibn al-Harb and Mughirah ibn Shu'bah to destroy al-Lat in Ta'if.

19
20
21
22
23

26 **WHY DIDN'T THE PROPHET STAY IN MECCA?** ASLAN

"Yet despite the enormous power that accompanied his defeat of the Quraysh, Muhammad refused to replace the Meccan aristocracy with a Muslim monarchy. ... Muhammad did something completely unexpected: he went back home to Medina. Muhammad's return to Medina was meant to acknowledge the Ansar, who had provided him with refuge and protection when no one else would. But it was also a statement to the entire community that while Mecca was now at the heart of Islam, Medina would forever be its soul."[43]

27 **WHAT HAPPENED TO MECCA AFTER THE CONQUEST?** WATT

"It is clear that Mecca did not recover its position as a trading centre. The increase of security over a wide area was advantageous to trade, but the new restrictions, like that on usury, imposed by Muhammad stopped the old lucrative speculations in high finance. For the younger and more adaptable men, war and administration gave a better promise of a career than commerce. Almost all the people of substance had left Mecca; and even for commerce Medina was now a better centre."[44]

After the Prophet's return to Medina, Mariyah gives birth to a boy, and the next morning, the Prophet joyously announces to his Companions that he has named his son Ibrahim, in honor of his forefather.

For more information on these other expeditions, read Al-Mubarakpuri (p. 366-369).

For the next several months, the Prophet dispatches 16 expeditions to confront the remaining hostile tribes around Medina and destroy their idols. 'Ali had previously destroyed the shrine of the goddess Manat in Qudayd along the Red Sea coast. Now he is sent northeast to confront the tribe of Tayy and destroy the temple of their chief idol, al-Qullus. Bani Tayy are powerless to defend themselves—they gradually enter Islam and become valuable allies to Medina.

Shortly after the Conquest of Mecca, the Prophet receives news of the Negus' death. Fifteen years have passed since Ja'far ibn Abi Talib led the first group of emigrants to Abyssinia. Not only had the Abyssinian king provided asylum for the fragile community, but he safely restored them to Mecca and Medina. In return for his benevolence, the Prophet assembles the Companions and instructs them:

> "This day a righteous man has died. Therefore rise and pray for your brother Ashamah."[45]

YEAR 21: TABUK

21.1 TABUK

Shortly after the Battle of Hunayn, the Persians lose Jerusalem at the hands of Emperor Heraclius and the Roman army. Remarkably, the unthinkable shakeup had already been foretold in Surah Ar-Rum:

> The Romans have been defeated in the lowest place on earth, but they'll be victorious (over their Persian enemies), in spite of this defeat, in three to nine years time. Command over the past and the future belongs to God, and when that day (of victory arrives), the believers will be the ones celebrating with God's help.
>
> He helps whomever He wants, for He's the Powerful and the Merciful. (This is) God's promise, and God never backs away from His promise, but most people don't understand. — *Ar-Rum (The Romans, 30:2-6)*

With the Persians driven out of Syria and Egypt, word quickly spreads that the Romans are planning to invade Yathrib and crush the growing Arabian empire:

> Caesar could neither ignore the great benefit that the Mu'tah Battle had brought to Muslims nor disregard the Arab tribes' expectations of independence and their hopes of getting free from his influence and reign nor their alliance to the Muslims ... So, he concluded that demolition of the Muslims' power had grown an urgent necessity. [1]

Despite reports that numbered the Roman army greater than 100,000 men, the Prophet elects to confront the enemy head-on. He calls on the Quraysh and other allied tribes to unite with his men in Medina, and by October of the year 630 CE, assembles an army larger and better equipped than any the Arabs have ever seen before. While many Companions are eager to follow him into battle, the hypocrites make numerous excuses to stay behind, the three most common being:

- They are about to march out amid a drought and an unusually hot season.

- It is harvest time in Medina.

- The enemy is far greater than anything the Arabs had seen before.

SURAH AR-RUM (The Romans) also highlights countless signs of God's presence in the natural world. It concludes, "And so We've laid out in this Qur'an every kind of example for people (to learn from), but even if you brought them a miracle (that they couldn't deny), the faithless would say of it, 'You're only talking nonsense.' That's how God seals the hearts of those who won't understand. Have patience with them, for God's promise is real, and don't let the faithless shake your resolve." (30:58-60)

Lings notes that Heraclius was concerned about the Prophet's growing power and actually considered acquiescing Syria to the Arabs. His generals were so averse to the notion that he abandoned the idea altogether.

---

1 HOW OUTRAGEOUS WAS THE MARCH TO TABUK? | YUSUF |

"The Arabs, in their wildest dreams, would have never thought about going up against the Byzantines. It was not in their frame of reference. It would be the equivalent of Haitians thinking about invading America. It's actually outrageous. Only somebody who had absolute certainty with his Lord could do this. It is an outrageous thing to do. And the hypocrites knew it was outrageous."[2]

Remember that **Ka'b ibn Malik** was present at the 'Aqabah. Several years later at Uhud, he spread the news that the Prophet had not been killed but was very much alive.

Initially Abu Khaythamah ibn 'Abd Allah and Ka'b ibn Malik stay behind. Abu Khaythamah is hesitant to march out in the summer heat, but quickly joins the army when he realizes he cannot sit still in Medina while the Prophet is marching into battle. Ka'b experiences a similar change of heart, but delays his departure until the expedition is too far to join.

In contrast, seven Companions who want to join the army are left behind because the Prophet cannot find adequate transport for them. Their heartfelt disappointment is captured in Surah At-Tawbah:

> (There are also no grounds of complaint) against those who came to you for transportation and to whom you had to say, "I have no transportation for you."
>
> They turned back with tears overflowing from their eyes at their inability to spend (money to arrange their own way). — *At-Tawbah (Repentance, 9:92)*

The Tabuk expedition includes 30,000 men and 10,000 horses. 'Uthman alone purchases provisions for 10,000 men. 'Umar gives half his wealth to the cause, and Abu Bakr gives everything he owns.

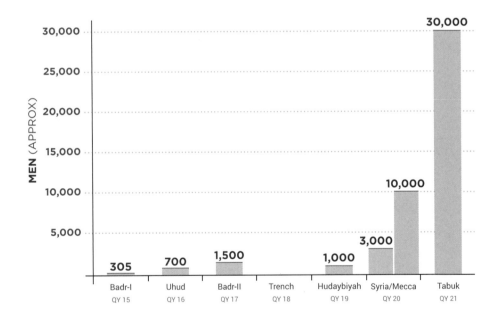

FIGURE 21A. MAJOR EXPEDITIONS LED OUT OF MEDINA

The Prophet led several major expeditions out of Medina, each approximately one year apart. (The Battle of the Trench is included in this list even though it was a defensive campaign that took place within the confines of Medina.)

❷ HOW DID TABUK COMPARE WITH PREVIOUS EXPEDITIONS? | WATT |

"An interesting measure of Muhammad's growing wealth is the number of horses on his expeditions. At Badr in 624 he had over 300 men and only 2 horses. When he returned there in 626 he had 1,500 men but still only 10 horses. Two years later at Khaybar there was about the same number of men, but 200 horses. At Hunayn after another two years 700 Emigrants had 300 horses and 4,000 Helpers another 500. Then came the great expansion. Later in the same year (630) on the expedition to Tabuk there are said to have been 30,000 men and 10,000 horses. The military significance of these figures can be seen from the fact that the Meccan cavalry, which played a decisive part at Uhud, numbered 200 in a force of 2,000. After the battle of Hunayn Muhammad was vastly stronger and richer than Mecca had ever been."[3]

---

❸ WHAT EXPLAINED THE PROPHET'S NORTHWARD MARCH? | WATT |

"If the Pax Islamica was to be permanent, the standard of living must be maintained; and for that a new source of wealth was required...It is one of the great statesmanlike insights of Muhammad that at a comparatively early period he conceived of the Pax Islamica as embracing all or most of the Arabs, and consequently being forced to expand northward. This insight governed his tribal policy. His first aim was to see that the members of his community and those in alliance with them enjoyed a high degree of security for life and property both from enemies without and enemies within. After that, however, his chief effort was to increase his influence along the road to Syria. In the closing years he also seems to have cultivated the friendship of the tribes in the direction of 'Iraq. In contrast with this he seems to have done little to spread Islam in the south and southeast of Arabia."[4]

Abu Bakr is placed in charge of the expedition at a camp outside Medina until it is time for the troops to set out. Meanwhile, the Prophet asks 'Ali to stay behind to watch after his family. But when 'Ali overhears a rumor that the Prophet is trying to exclude him from the mission, he rides out of the city to ask the Prophet himself. The Prophet reaffirms his decision and adds:

> *"Would it not suffice you to be my successor in the way that Aaron (Harun) was to Moses? But no Prophet succeeds me."*[5]

❹ WHAT CAN WE LEARN FROM THE PROPHET'S DECISION TO KEEP 'ALI IN MEDINA? | YUSUF |

"The *ishara* [lesson] in this is important because: (1) Abu Bakr is given the standard and placed in charge of the army. (2) Sayidna 'Ali is left behind. This is a clear indication that the spiritual authority of the Bani Hashim is rested on Sayidna 'Ali."[6]

Along the way to Tabuk, the Prophet is late one morning to lead the dawn prayer. With time running out before sunrise, 'Abd ar-Rahman ibn 'Awf leads the prayer and the Prophet joins behind him. After the prayer, the Prophet commends 'Abd ar-Rahman for taking charge, saying:

> *"Ye have done well, for verily a Prophet dieth not until he hath been led in prayer by a pious man of his people."*[7]

Recall that **'Abd ar-Rahman ibn 'Awf** was one of the first men to embrace Islam in Mecca. He fought in every major battle and was one of the five men to sign the Treaty of Hudaybiyah, and is one of the 10 to whom the Prophet promises Paradise.

19
20
21
22
23

The expedition passes by Al-Hijr, the native land of the Prophet Saleh and the people of Thamud (P 1.1). On numerous occasions, the Qu'ran uses Thamud as a warning to future generations. The Prophet instructs his Companions not to linger in the area, but to move on until the ancient rock carved dwellings are well behind them.

> "Remember that He let you inherit (the earth) after the people of 'Ad and gave you dwellings within the earth out of which you build palaces and fortresses for yourselves, both in the plains and in the mountains, where you carve them (from the mountainsides). Remember (all the blessings) that you've received from God, and cause no harm or chaos in the earth." — *Al A'raf (The Heights, 7:74)*

> As for the (people of) 'Ad, they acted arrogantly throughout the land against all right. They boasted, "Who is stronger in power than we are?" Didn't they see that God, the One Who created them, was infinitely mightier than they (could ever be)? They worked against Our signs with determination, so We sent a terrible sandstorm against them, causing many days of disaster, in order to give them a taste of the most degrading punishment this life can offer. The punishment of the next life will be even more degrading still, and they'll have no one to help them.
>
> As for the (people of) Thamud, We offered them guidance, but they preferred blindness over guidance, so a sudden humiliating disaster overtook them as a consequence of what they earned.   However, We saved those who believed and who were mindful (of God among both nations).
> — *Fussilat (Clear Explanation, 41:15-18)*

After several long days of marching in the desert sun, the army finally reaches the perimeter of Tabuk and camps on the outskirts of town. After 20 days of waiting for the Romans to show up, the Prophet forms alliances with Jewish and Christian tribes living at the head of the gulf of 'Aqabah and along its eastern coast.

He then asks his Companions whether they should continue north and confront the Romans in Syria. After listening to various opinions, he finally agrees to lead the army back to Medina. Four hundred men stay behind and, under the leadership of Khalid ibn al-Walid, travel northeast to the northern outpost of Dumat al-Jandal to secure the city's allegiance before returning home.

---

5 THE COMPANIONS CHALLENGED THE PROPHET'S OPINION, NOT HIS REVELATIONS　　　YUSUF

"At this point the Prophet, God's peace and blessings upon him, asks his inner sanctum, 'Should we keep going and take over Syria?' This is a man who has been promised by Allah to have Syria; he knows it is his. So he's saying, 'Should we do it now?' And 'Umar says, 'Oh Messenger of Allah, is this revelation or opinion?' Again, they're not questioning the revelation, they're questioning the personal opinion. And the Prophet, God's peace and blessings upon him, said, 'it is my opinion.' They said, 'Let's go back to Medina, and when we get stronger we'll come back.' And 'Umar will do the job.
The point is the Prophet, God's peace and blessings upon him, is a man in a complete state of *yaqin* [absolute certainty]. He has no doubts whatsoever, and history testifies that his certainty was justifiable and correct."[8]

6 **WHY IS TABUK SO IMPORTANT TO US TODAY?**   YUSUF

"Tabuk is an act of deep faith. These people had extraordinary *iman* [faith] to go out and with absolute sincerity and belief, think they were doing something intelligent and possible. The Prophet, God's peace and blessings upon him, through iman was making what was impossible to the materialist possible to the spiritualist. That is one of the greatest gifts of the Messenger of Allah, God's peace and blessings upon him. He made the impossible possible. Tabuk is making the impossible possible. That's why Tabuk is so important for us to remember. Despite incredible odds, we have to believe in the promise of our Messenger, God's peace and blessings upon him."[9]

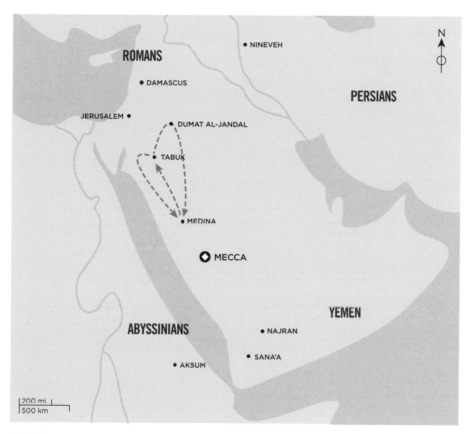

FIGURE 21B. EXPEDITIONS TO TABUK AND DUMAT AL-JANDAL

After waiting 20 days in Tabuk, the Prophet led a party west to the Gulf of 'Aqabah where he secured peace treaties with Christian and Jewish communities in the area. Meanwhile, Khalid ibn al-Walid led a party northeast to Dumat al-Jandal and secured the city's allegiance.

19
20
21
22
23

21.2 EXCUSES AFTER TABUK

During the return trip from Tabuk, a band of hypocrites in the expedition craft a plan to assassinate the Prophet. As related in Surah At-Tawbah, their scheme never comes to fruition, and the Prophet is instructed to take a firm stance against them:

> O Prophet! Strive hard against the faithless and the hypocrites. Be firm with them, for their dwelling place is in Hellfire – the worst destination!
>
> They swear to God that they've never said anything (against you), but indeed they've uttered words of rejection, and they're rejecting (God) even after (they claimed) to have submitted (to Him).
>
> They tried to (assassinate the Prophet), though they were unable to carry it out. This was their response to the bounty with which God and His Messenger had enriched them!
>
> If they repent, it would be the best for them, but if they persist (in their rebellious ways,) then God will punish them with a painful penalty, both in this life and in the next. In that case, no one on earth would be able to protect them or help them! — At-Tawbah (Repentance, 9:73-74)

Recall that Ruqayyah died six years ago when the Prophet was away at Badr. Shortly after her death, the Prophet arranged for Umm Kulthum's marriage to 'Uthman.

When the army returns from Tabuk, the Prophet learns that another of his daughters has died—Umm Kulthum. After praying at her grave, he comforts 'Uthman saying that if he had another daughter, he would have offered her to him in marriage as well.

Be sure to read Salahi (p. 711-717) for Ka'b's firsthand account of the incident.

The Prophet listens to the hypocrites' excuses and pardons them for not joining the Tabuk expedition. Aside from the hypocrites who stayed behind, three well-respected Companions come forward to greet the Prophet. The first two try to explain their absences, but the third, Ka'b ibn Malik, remains silent, feeling that it would be unbefitting to offer an excuse before the Prophet. The Prophet instructs his Companions not to speak to the three men until God decides their fate. The days slowly turn into weeks and finally, after an interminable stretch of 50 days, Surah At-Tawbah delivers God's verdict:

> ... (They were so remorseful) that the vast earth, itself, seemed to close in upon them, and their souls seemed to strangle them (with guilt), as well.
>
> They understood that there was no running away from God, unless (it was on a path) that led back to Him. So He turned towards them so they could repent, for God is the Acceptor of Repentance and the Merciful.
> — At-Tawbah (Repentance, 9:118)

---

7 **WHY DIDN'T KA'B IBN MALIK OFFER AN EXCUSE?** YUSUF

"The lesson for us as people who aspire to be like these believers is don't offer excuses. Allah will defend those who believe. You don't need to defend yourself. The Arabs say, 'The excuse is uglier than the original wrong.' Don't offer excuses. A man knows his soul; even if he throws out all his excuses, he knows that 'I'm inexcusable.' The hypocrite is one who defends himself.

The best expression of this is an event that took place with Abu Bakr when he was in a [sitting area] with the Messenger of Allah, God's peace and blessings upon him, and somebody came in and began to accuse Abu Bakr of things that Abu Bakr was not guilty of. And Abu Bakr sat very patiently listening; but finally the man said something that was so troubling to Abu Bakr that he could no longer contain himself, and he defended himself. Prior to that the Messenger, God's peace and blessings upon him, had been sitting and smiling as he was hearing these things being said about Abu Bakr. But when Abu Bakr defended himself, the Prophet, God's peace and blessings upon him, frowned and walked out.

Abu Bakr went to him after and asked him, 'Why is it that you sat there smiling when this man was saying obvious lies about me, and yet when I defended myself you got up and left?'

He said, 'Oh Abu Bakr, when you were silent, I saw the angels defending you. But the moment you began to defend yourself, they dispersed and *Shaytan* [the devil] came into the room. And a Prophet and Shaytan cannot sit in the same room.' "[10]

21.3 THE MOSQUE OF HARM

Just before the Tabuk expedition, the Prophet had been invited to pray in a newly erected mosque near Quba, on the outskirts of Medina. The urgency of the expedition, however, prompted the Prophet to delay his visit until the army returned to Medina. In the interval, however, Surah At-Tawbah informs him of the hypocrites' true intent.

Recall that Quba is also the site of the very first mosque, erected shortly after the Prophet escaped from Mecca (QY 13.4)

> There are those who built a mosque (for no other purpose) than to promote mischief and rejection (of God), seeking to divide the believers and to set up a rallying place for those who previously made war on God and His Messenger. They're going to swear that they meant nothing but good by it, but God declares that they're all liars.
>
> Never set foot within (their mosque), for there's (another) mosque (nearby in the town of Quba) whose foundations were laid from the first day upon mindfulness (of God). It's far more appropriate for you to stand within that one, for there are people inside of it who love to be purified, and God loves those who make themselves pure! — *At-Tawbah (Repentance, 9:107-108)*

Upon receiving the news of Masjid ad-Dirar (The Mosque of Harm), the Prophet orders his Companions to send a firm message to the hypocrites in Medina by razing the structure to the ground:

> The severity of the punishment shows the importance of the matter, and several Qur'anic verses indicate that about this time those now called 'Hypocrites' were practically excluded from the community; they were to be treated roughly and threatened with Hell as apostates. A little reflection makes it clear that, if the Islamic community was to engage in expeditions into Syria which would involve the absence of most of its fighting men for long periods, it could not allow a body of dissidents to ensconce themselves in a suburb of Medina.[11]

19
20
21
22
23

21.4 THE DEATH OF 'ABD ALLAH IBN UBAYY

Not long after Tabuk, 'Abd Allah ibn Ubayy falls gravely ill and dies soon after. Although he had been an outright hypocrite for most of the Medinan period, in his final hours he asks the Prophet to pray for his soul. Surah At-Tawbah had already instructed the Prophet how to deal with the disbelievers.

> Whether you ask for their forgiveness or not – even if you asked seventy times for their forgiveness, God won't forgive them because they rejected God and His Messenger. God will not guide a people who are rebellious and corrupt.
> — *At-Tawbah (Repentance, 9:80)*

Against 'Umar's advice, the Prophet leads 'Abd Allah ibn Ubayy's burial prayer and instructs the Companions to follow behind him. When 'Umar asks why the Prophet would lead a prayer over a hypocrite's funeral (given the verse from Surah At-Tawbah above), the Prophet responds:

> *"And did I know that God would forgive him if I prayed more than seventy times, I would increase the number of my supplications."*[12]

Surah At-Tawbah describes the hypocrites who remained behind during the Tabuk expedition, and orders the Prophet never to pray for them again.

Lings notes that there is disagreement over whether the prohibition for praying at the funeral of hypocrites (Qur'an 9:84) had already been revealed before 'Abd Allah ibn Ubayy's death. However, he writes, even if the Prophet was aware of the prohibition, he had acknowledged a true change in 'Abd Allah before he died.

> If God brings you back to any of them and they ask you for (permission) to venture out (with you on some future expedition), tell them, "You're never going to venture out with me, nor will you ever fight an enemy by my side, for you chose to sit and be inactive the first time, so now keep sitting with those who get left behind."
>
> Never offer a (funeral) prayer for any of them that dies, nor stand by their grave (as they're being lowered down into it), for they rejected God and His Messenger, and thus died in a state of defiant rebellion.
> — *At-Tawbah (Repentance, 9:83-84)*

---

8 **WHAT DID 'ABD ALLAH IBN UBAYY STAND FOR?** `WATT`

"Ibn Ubayy did not know what he wanted; he was whole-heartedly committed neither to Islam nor to Judaism nor to the old religion of his people. He was probably moved chiefly by personal ambition, and lacked the statesmanship to see all the vaster issues involved and the vision to propound a way of dealing with them that would attract men. He must have seen the need for peace in Medina, but his attempts to meet it were along conservative lines that were already discredited. His opposition to Muhammad may be said to be due to a failure to move with the times; and it is significant that one source remarks that there was only one young man among the Hypocrites."[13]

- -

9 **WHY DID THE PROPHET PRAY FOR 'ABD ALLAH IBN UBAYY?** `YUSUF`

"Somebody who knows the hellfire does not wish it on his worst enemy. And nobody knows this better than the Messenger of Allah."[14]

10 DID 'ABD ALLAH IBN UBAYY REALLY MAKE A COMPLETE TURNAROUND? [YUSUF]

"I think that in the book, Martin Lings deals with the death of 'Abd Allah ibn Ubayy a little strangely. He almost makes it sound like he's made a complete *tawbah* [repentance], and if you read that, it is somewhat misleading because 'Abd Allah ibn Ubayy is considered a hypocrite, as far as we know. He opposed the Prophet, God's peace and blessings upon him, and created a lot of conflict."[15]

- -

11 WHAT CAN WE LEARN FROM THE PROPHET'S TREATMENT OF THE HYPOCRITES? [RAMADAN]

"He remained cautious, sometimes wary, but he avoided any final judgment. … Nothing warrants passing a final judgment on their hypocrisy while they are still alive, and the only suitable behavior is that exemplified by the Prophet, who never allowed himself to utter a judgment about a hypocrite while that individual was still alive, since to the very end everything remained possible as far as conversion and sincerity of heart were concerned. God only enjoined him not to pray for them after they died, when the situation could no longer be reversed and it had become clear that they had lived and died in hypocrisy, treason, and lies."[16]

19
20
21
22
23

YEAR 22: THE DELEGATIONS

22.1 THE FIRST HAJJ

The Hajj is the "greater" pilgrimage that falls once a year during the month of Dhul Hijjah and is obligatory on all able-bodied Muslims at least once in their lifetime. Starting with (and including) the Hudaybiyah expedition, the Prophet has already led three 'Umrahs, or "lesser" (non-obligatory) pilgrimages with his Companions.

With the month of Dhul Hijjah fast approaching, the Prophet asks Abu Bakr to lead the first *Hajj* pilgrimage. No sooner had the pilgrims departed, but the Prophet receives a new verse from Surah At-Tawbah regarding the idolaters in Mecca:

> All you who believe! The idol-worshippers are impure, so don't let them come near the Sacred Mosque after this year of theirs has passed.] If you're afraid of becoming poor (on account of the financial losses that this ban might cause), then God will enrich you as He wills from His Own bounty, for God is full of knowledge and wisdom. —*At-Tawbah (Repentance, 9:28)*

He sends 'Ali to catch up to the pilgrims to recite the recently revealed verses in Mina and deliver an ultimatum to the remaining idolaters in Mecca: after four months, the Prophet will be under no obligation to protect them. Understandably, the verse leaves the newly converted Muslims worried about the fate of their pagan friends in the city.

22.2 THE DEATH OF IBRAHIM

By age 62, the Prophet had buried five of his six children from Khadijah. Fatimah gives birth to a baby girl she names after her eldest sister Zaynab, who had passed away two years ago. But the joyous news of Zaynab's birth is soon followed by the untimely death of the Prophet's son, Ibrahim.

Although the Prophet previously forbade loud lamentations over the departed, the tragic news brings him to tears. 'Abd ar-Rahman ibn 'Awf sees the Prophet weeping for his son and questions the seemingly unrestrained display of emotion. The Prophet explains:

> *"Not this do I forbid. These are the promptings of tenderness and mercy, and he that is not merciful, unto him shall no mercy be shown. O Ibrahim, if it were not that the promise of reunion is sure, and that this is a path which all must tread, and that the last of us shall overtake the first, verily we should grieve for thee, O Ibrahim. The eye weepeth, and the heart grieveth, nor say we aught that would offend the Lord."[1]*

After comforting Mariyah and Sirin, the Prophet·looks on as 'Abbas' son, Fadl, prepares Ibrahim's body for burial. After the funeral, the Prophet notices an uneven patch of dirt over his son's grave and smoothens it out with his hand. He turns to his Companions and explains:

> *"When one of you doeth aught, let him do it to perfection."[3]*

The difficult news coincides with a solar eclipse in Medina. When the Prophet overhears people attributing it to the sad occasion, he reminds them that the natural world is a sign from God that does not alter its course for any person's death.

22.3 PEACEFUL DELEGATIONS ENTER MEDINA

Although no actual fighting took place at Tabuk, the expedition proved to the Arabs that the Prophet is willing and able to take on the colossal Roman Empire. The impact is profound, and in the ninth year after the Hijrah, a steady stream of delegations visit Medina to pledge allegiance to him. In the remaining years after Tabuk, the Prophet cordially receives over 70 delegations and a number of repentant individuals, with the sole request that they abandon polytheism.

Read Al-Mubarakpuri (p.386-396) for a description of 16 separate delegations that visited Medina during this period.

2 **WHAT OPTIONS DID THE OTHER ARABS HAVE AFTER TABUK?**   RAMADAN

"Thus, throughout the Peninsula, the message was clear: the tribes who accepted Islam were to give up any idea of syncretism, for the Prophet did not negotiate over the fundamentals of faith. As soon as the profession of faith had been pronounced, religious statues were to be destroyed, and Islamic practices were to be fully implemented, from prayer and fasting to the payment of the purifying social tax (zakat) and pilgrimage. When tribes wanted to remain faithful to their tradition, they drew up a pact with similarly clear terms: the payment of a tax in exchange for protection."[4]

One notable arrival is Ka'b ibn Zuhayr, a treacherous poet from the coastal tribe of Muzaynah. Considered one of the greatest poets in Arabia, Ka'b has a recent change of heart which compels him to come to Medina (possibly before the Tabuk expedition) to seek the Prophet's forgiveness. His entrance into the mosque angers many Companions, but the Prophet graciously receives Ka'b and instructs his followers:

"Leave him alone! He has become a repentant Muslim after his disposal of the past."[5]

Ka'b returns the Prophet's goodwill and recites eloquent verses he had written about him and his Companions.

After years of bitter enmity, the Bani Thaqif finally send word from Ta'if that they are ready to pledge allegiance to Medina. They propose abandoning idolatry under two conditions: (1) they are exempted from daily prayers, and (2) they may keep their chief idol, al-Lat, for three more years. The Prophet firmly rejects both conditions, and when the Thaqif finally capitulate, he sends Mughirah ibn Shu'bah and Abu Sufyan ibn al-Harb to destroy Ta'if's idols.

One year ago, on the eve of the Conquest of Mecca, two of its inhabitants, Abu 'Amir ibn Sayfi and Wahshi, fled to Ta'if. With Bani Thaqif's new alliance with the Prophet, the two men have nowhere to hide. Unwilling to compromise, Abu 'Amir sets off for Syria, where he dies alone. Meanwhile, Wahshi travels to Medina hoping for the Prophet's forgiveness. The Companions bristle with anger when they see the Abyssinian, but the Prophet urges them to show mercy toward his uncle's assassin.

Mughirah ibn Shu'bah is the nephew of 'Urwah ibn Mas'ud. Recall that the Prophet had described 'Urwah as "the man of Ya Seen" because he was killed by his own people in Ta'if when he tried to call them to Islam.

Recall that before the Hijrah, **Abu 'Amir ibn Sayfi,** or "the Monk" considered himself the spiritual leader of Yathrib. When the Prophet arrived in Medina, Abu 'Amir challenged his authority, vowing, *"May God let the liar die a lonely outcast in exile!"*

Wahshi was Jubayr ibn Mut'im's Abyssinian slave who earned his freedom by killing Hamzah at Uhud. He will kill the false-prophet Musaylimah in the coming year.

19
20
21
22
23

At one of these meetings, the Prophet brings 'Ali, Fatimah, Hasan, and Husayn, and positions all of them under his cloak. From then on, 'Ali's family became known as "the People of the Cloak."

 SURAH AL MA'IDAH (The Banquet Table) is one of the final surahs to be revealed in the Qur'an. It is named after an intriguing selection of verses that describe a miraculous banquet feast sent from the sky to Jesus' hesitant disciples. The surah appeals to the sensibilities of Jews and Christians, and decries the doctrine of the trinity as an unfortunate innovation. In fact, the surah describes how Jesus will testify to God when asked if he instructed his followers to worship him and his mother in place of God. As with every revelation, it is a must-read surah that covers a wide variety of topics including (but not limited to) dietary regulations, an appeal to Jews and Christians, the story of Cain and Abel, and the wisdom of moderation.

Several Jewish and Christian delegations also arrive to meet the Prophet. In the fair-minded spirit of Surah Al Ma'idah, the Prophet forms alliances with each of them.

> Now We've sent the Book to you, (Muhammad), in all truthfulness, affirming the scriptures that came before you and safeguarding within it (the truth of the previous revelations), so judge between (the Jews and Christians) according to what God has revealed (to you). Don't follow their petty whims and thus swerve away from the truth that's come to you.
>
> We've given to each one of you (differing religious groups) a legal tradition and a clear method (for dealing with legal issues). If God had wanted, He could've made you all into one community, but He tests you in what He's given you, so forge ahead as if you were racing towards everything virtuous. Your ultimate return is back to God, and He's going to show you (the truth) of those things about which you argued. — *Al Ma'idah (The Banquet Table, 5:48)*

Among the many delegations, a party of Yemeni Christians arrive to discuss their differences with the Prophet and ask him what his religion says about Jesus. After witholding a response for an entire day, the Prophet answers with the newest revelation from Surah Ali 'Imran:

> The example of Jesus in the sight of God is like that of Adam. He created him from dust, saying, "Be," and he was. The truth is from your Lord, so don't be assailed by doubt. — *Ali 'Imran (The Family of Amran, 3:59-60)*

Even though the Christians maintain their traditional view of Jesus, the Prophet hosts them in Medina and allows them to pray in the mosque facing East. The two parties come to an amicable agreement whereby the Najran Arabs agree to pay a yearly tribute to Medina in exchange for military protection.

---

③ WHAT CAN BE LEARNED FROM THE TREATMENT OF THE NAJRAN CHRISTIANS?   `RAMADAN`

"They [Companions] were to draw from it the substance of the respect that Islam demands of its faithful, whom it invites to go beyond tolerance, to learn, listen, and recognize others' dignity ...More than tolerance (which smacks of condescension within a power relationship), the respect required by God is based on an egalitarian relationship of mutual knowledge."
'You will find the nearest among men in love to the believers [the Muslims] those who say, 'We are Christians' because among these are priests and monks, and they are not arrogant.' [Qur'an 5:82]
... With Christians, as with all other spiritual or religious traditions, the invitation to meet, share, and live together fruitfully will always remain based on these three conditions: trying to get to know the other, remaining sincere during the encounter and debates, and, finally, learning humility in regard to one's claim to possess the truth. ... As can be seen, he did not hesitate to question and even contradict the Christians' beliefs (such as the Trinity or the role of priests), but in the end his attitude was based on knowledge, sincerity, and humility, which are three conditions of respect."[6]

22.4 THE RAPID GROWTH OF THE COMMUNITY

Although the Muslim community experiences tremendous growth after the moral victory at Tabuk, the Prophet warns his Companions that the struggle over injustice is not over. In fact, surahs Al Hujurat and At-Tawbah indicate that the conversions of the newest Bedouin communities are not entirely spiritual:

> The (bedouin) Arabs (are quick) to say, "We believe!" Yet, say to them, "You have no faith, for you're only saying, 'We're surrendered to God,' but (sincere) faith hasn't yet entered your hearts. If you obey God and His Messenger, He won't decrease (the value) of any of your (good) deeds, for God is forgiving and merciful." — *Al Hujurat (The Inner Rooms, 49:14)*

> The (bedouin) Arabs are the worst when it comes to rejection and hypocrisy and are thus more likely to be ignorant of the command that God has sent down to His Messenger. God is full of knowledge and wisdom.
>
> Some of the (bedouin) Arabs consider what they spend (in charity) to be a financial penalty. They keep looking for disasters to come upon you, but let the worst disasters fall upon them, for God listens and knows (all about their treachery).
>
> Some of the (bedouin) Arabs, however, do believe in God and the Last Day. They look upon what they spend (in charity) as a way to bring themselves closer to God's presence and to (be worthy) of the Prophet's prayers (for their forgiveness and success.) They truly are brought closer (to God by their charity and sincerity), and soon God will admit them to His mercy, for God is forgiving and merciful. — *At-Tawbah (Repentance, 9:97-99)*

④ DID THE PROPHET RULE OVER ALL OF ARABIA? WATT

"The traditional Muslim view is that in the last year of his life Muhammad was the ruler of almost the whole of Arabia. The more skeptical European scholars, on the other hand, suggest that at his death he ruled only a small region round Medina and Mecca. The true state of affairs was somewhere between these two extremes, but it is difficult to determine precisely. The Islamic state in 632 was a conglomeration of tribes in alliance with Muhammad on varying terms, having as its inner core the people of Medina and perhaps also of Mecca. After the Islamic state had become an empire, every Arab tribe naturally wanted to show that it had been in alliance with Muhammad himself in his lifetime, and produced the best story it could of how it had sent a deputation and become Muslim. Even if these stories are accepted as roughly genuine, there are difficulties; the deputation may have represented not the whole tribe but only themselves ; and the terms of alliance may not have given Muhammad any say in the affairs of the tribe, and may not even have included profession of Islam.

...When due allowance has been made for all these points, we get a picture of the situation roughly as follows. The tribes in a broad region round Mecca and Medina were all firmly united to Muhammad and had all professed Islam. In a similar position were those in the centre of Arabia and along the road to `Iraq, but those nearest `Iraq had not become Muslims. In the Yemen and the rest of the south-west many groups had professed Islam, but they generally constituted only a section of each tribe, and in all were probably less than half the population; they were very dependent on support from Medina. The position in the southeast and along the Persian Gulf was similar, but the Muslims were probably much less than half the population. On the Syrian border beyond about the Gulf of Akaba there had been little success in detaching tribes from the Byzantine emperor."[7]

19
20
21
22
23

---

5 **WHAT WAS THE BIGGEST CHALLENGE FOR THE GROWING MUSLIM COMMUNITY?**   RAMADAN

"The unity in adversity that had prevailed so far had paradoxically been easier to achieve than the unity in faith, love, and respect that must henceforth be established now that there were no major enemies left in the region."[8]

Despite the rapidly growing number of converts, the Prophet often speaks fondly of his original Companions, and even promises Paradise to 10 of his closest followers:

> *"The best of my people are my generation; then they that come after them; then they that come after them."*[9]

That there are varying degrees of spirituality in the growing Muslim community is not a new concept to the original Companions. Those who strived with the Prophet, fought by his side, and were tested with their lives came to know that only after submission (*Islam*), comes deep faith (*Iman*), followed by perfection (*Ihsan*). Leading by example, the Prophet continues to coach his followers on how to perfect their character. The Qur'an teaches that only perfection in character brings lasting peace for the soul—the ultimate aim of the Muslim:

> "O soul at rest," (the righteous will be told), "return to your Lord completely satisfied, even as (He is) completely satisfied with you. Then enter now, and be among My servants. Enter now into My Paradise." —*Al Fajr (The Dawn, 89:27-30)*

 SURAH AL FAJR (The Dawn) is an early Meccan revelation named after its opening verse. Here God swears by the dawn, of the convincing message of the Qur'an. Revealed at the height of Meccan capitalism, it warns listeners against arrogance and oppression. "There's no way (you can blame God for your troubles,) when you're not even generous with orphans, nor do you urge each other to feed the poor. You waste your inheritance eagerly, and on top of that you crave wealth more than anything else!"

NAME	TRIBE (CLAN)	RELATIONSHIP TO THE PROPHET	YEARS OF SERVICE	BADR	UHUD	TRENCH	MECCA	TABUK
Abu Bakr ibn Abi Quhafah	Quraysh (Taym)	Father-in-law (through 'A'ishah)	22+	Yes	Yes	Yes	Yes	Yes
'Umar ibn al-Khattab	Quraysh ('Adi)	Father-in-law (through Hafsah)	17+	Yes	Yes	Yes	Yes	Yes
'Uthman ibn 'Affan	Quraysh ('Abdu Shams)	Son-in-law (through Ruqayyah and Umm Kulthum)	22+	No	Yes	Yes	Yes	Yes
'Ali ibn Abi Talib	Quraysh (Hashim)	First cousin, Foster-son, Son-in-law (through Fatimah)	22+	Yes	Yes	Yes	Yes	No
'Abd ar-Rahman ibn 'Awf	Quraysh (Zuhrah)		22+	Yes	Yes	Yes	Yes	Yes
Abu 'Ubaydah ibn al-Jarrah	Quraysh (Harith)		22+	Yes	Yes	Yes	Yes	Yes
Talhah ibn 'Ubayd Allah	Quraysh (Taym)		22+	No	Yes	Yes	Yes	Yes
Zubayr ibn al-'Awwam	Quraysh (Asad)	First cousin	22+	Yes	Yes	Yes	Yes	Yes
Sa'd ibn Abi Waqqas	Quraysh (Zuhrah)	Maternal relative	22+	Yes	Yes	Yes	Yes	Yes
Sa'id ibn Zayd	Quraysh ('Adi)		20+	No	Yes	Yes	Yes	Yes

FIGURE 22A. THE 10 COMPANIONS PROMISED PARADISE

Known in Arabic as al-'Ashara al-Mubasharin bi-l-Janna, these 10 Companions were promised Paradise by the Prophet. Each was from the tribe of Quraysh and had accepted Islam during the Early Meccan Period when it was a vulnerable, fledgling movement. (In fact, 'Umar was the last to convert, in the sixth year of Qur'anic revelation.) The Companions participated in every major military expedition with a few exceptions. 'Uthman did not to fight at Badr because he was taking care of his dying wife, Ruqayyah. Talhah and Sa'id did not fight at Badr because the Prophet had sent them to get news of Abu Sufyan's caravan, and when they returned to Medina, the Prophet had already left. Finally, 'Ali did not participate in Tabuk because the Prophet specifically instructed him to stay behind and look after the Prophet's family. Taken together, these Companions remained at the Prophet's side for nearly every major challenge of his 23-year career.

The Prophet's age after Tabuk: __62__

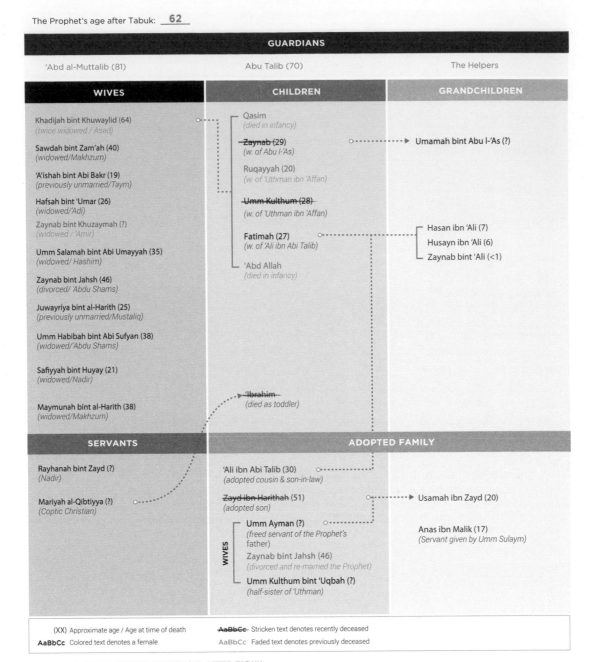

GUARDIANS		
'Abd al-Muttalib (81)	Abu Talib (70)	The Helpers

WIVES	CHILDREN	GRANDCHILDREN
Khadijah bint Khuwaylid (64) *(twice widowed / Asad)*	Qasim *(died in infancy)*	
Sawdah bint Zam'ah (40) *(widowed/Makhzum)*	~~Zaynab (29)~~ *(w. of Abu l-'As)*	Umamah bint Abu l-'As (?)
'A'ishah bint Abi Bakr (19) *(previously unmarried/Taym)*	Ruqayyah (20) *(w. of 'Uthman ibn 'Affan)*	
Hafsah bint 'Umar (26) *(widowed/'Adi)*	~~Umm Kulthum (28)~~ *(w. of 'Uthman ibn 'Affan)*	
Zaynab bint Khuzaymah (?) *(widowed / 'Amir)*	Fatimah (27) *(w. of 'Ali ibn Abi Talib)*	Hasan ibn 'Ali (7) Husayn ibn 'Ali (6) Zaynab bint 'Ali (<1)
Umm Salamah bint Abi Umayyah (35) *(widowed/ Hashim)*	'Abd Allah *(died in infancy)*	
Zaynab bint Jahsh (46) *(divorced/ 'Abdu Shams)*		
Juwayriya bint al-Harith (25) *(previously unmarried/Mustaliq)*		
Umm Habibah bint Abi Sufyan (38) *(widowed/'Abdu Shams)*		
Safiyyah bint Huyay (21) *(widowed/Nadir)*		
Maymunah bint al-Harith (38) *(widowed/Makhzum)*	~~'Ibrahim~~ *(died as toddler)*	

SERVANTS	ADOPTED FAMILY	
Rayhanah bint Zayd (?) *(Nadir)*	'Ali ibn Abi Talib (30) *(adopted cousin & son-in-law)*	
Mariyah al-Qibtiyya (?) *(Coptic Christian)*	~~Zayd ibn Harithah~~ (51) *(adopted son)*	Usamah ibn Zayd (20)
	WIVES — Umm Ayman (?) *(freed servant of the Prophet's father)*	Anas ibn Malik (17) *(Servant given by Umm Sulaym)*
	Zaynab bint Jahsh (46) *(divorced and re-married the Prophet)*	
	Umm Kulthum bint 'Uqbah (?) *(half-sister of 'Uthman)*	

(XX) Approximate age / Age at time of death	~~AaBbCc~~ Stricken text denotes recently deceased
AaBbCc Colored text denotes a female	AaBbCc Faded text denotes previously deceased

FIGURE 22B. THE PROPHET'S HOUSEHOLD AFTER TABUK

Shortly after Hudaybiyah, 'Uthman's half-sister, Umm Kulthum bint 'Uqbah, escaped to Medina. The Prophet welcomed her to the community and married her to Zayd ibn Harithah. Nearly 17 years ago, Abu Sufyan's daughter Umm Habibah had migrated to Abyssinia with her husband, 'Ubayd Allah ibn Jahsh, who reverted back to Christianity before passing away. After 'Ubayd Allah died, the Prophet sent for Umm Habibah along with the remaining Muslims still in Abyssinia. But first he asked the Negus to marry her to the Prophet before she left. That same year, the Prophet's men conquered the settlement of Khaybar. Safiyyah bint Huyay, widow of the leader of Khaybar, experienced a dream in which she married the Prophet. After the fall of Khaybar, she returned to Medina as the Prophet's 10th wife. Around this time, the Muqawqis of Egypt sent Mariyah and Sirin as gifts to the Prophet. The Prophet housed Mariyah in a nearby apartment and placed Sirin under the guardianship of Hassan ibn Thabit. One year after Hudaybiyah, 'Abbas arranged the marriage of his widowed sister-in-law, Maymunah, to the Prophet while the Prophet visited Mecca to perform 'Umrah. Shortly after, his eldest daughter, Zaynab, and one of his most beloved Companions, Zayd ibn Harithah (at the battle of Mu'tah) died. The following year, his third daughter, Umm Kulthum, also died. The many losses were somewhat alleviated by the birth of Fatimah's third child, Zaynab, whom she named after her eldest sister. Unfortunately, Zaynab's birth was soon followed by the death of Mariyah's young son, Ibrahim, who was born shortly after the Conquest of Mecca.

(Refer to Figs. P25, 6b, 13f, 16b, and 18c for previous details about the Prophet's household.)

YEAR 23: THE FAREWELL PILGRIMAGE

23.1 THE FAREWELL PILGRIMAGE

Every year in Medina, the Prophet would retreat to the Mosque during the middle 10 days of Ramadan. This year however, he remains for the last 10 days as well. He later confides in Fatimah:

> *"Gabriel reciteth the Koran unto me and I unto him once every year; but this year he hath recited it with me twice. I cannot but think that my time hath come."*[1]

As the month of Dhul-Hijjah approaches, the Prophet announces that he will lead the annual Hajj pilgrimage. Given that it is his first Hajj, 30,000 pilgrims from all over Arabia eagerly join the expedition. Along the way, Abu Bakr's wife, Asma' bint Umays, gives birth to a son whom they name Muhammad.

Shortly before the Hajj, during the month of Ramadan, 'Ali had been leading an expedition of 300 men to Yemen. On their return march to Mecca, he travels ahead of his men to complete the Hajj with the Prophet. Before leaving, he instructs his men not to divide the linen in their spoils until it is first presented to the Prophet. But when the men arrive in Mecca, 'Ali is furious to see them in new clothes and orders them to change out of their garments. The command is met with resentment, but when the men voice their case to the Prophet, he simply replies:

> *"O people, blame not 'Ali, for he is too scrupulous in the path of God to be blamed. ... Whose nearest I am, his nearest 'Ali is."*[2]

When the Prophet reaches Mecca, he leads the rites of the ancient pilgrimage, carefully following Abraham's long-forgotten example:

> Some of the Meccans expressed surprise that he had gone so far [to 'Arafah], for while the other pilgrims went on to 'Arafah, Quraysh had been accustomed to remain within the sacred precinct saying: "We are the people of God." But he [the Prophet] said that Abraham had ordained the day on 'Arafah as an essential part of the Pilgrimage, and that Quraysh had forsaken this practice in this respect. The Prophet stressed that day the antiquity of the Pilgrimage, and the words "Abraham's legacy" were often on his lips.[3]

Pilgrimages during the Prophet's lifetime:

QY 19: Hudaybiyah (although they did not enter Mecca, the Companions were instructed to complete the rites of the pilgrimage)

QY 20: 'UMRAH (often called the *compensatory 'Umrah* because it made up for the Hudaybiyah pilgrimage)

QY 21: 'UMRAH (after the Battle of Hunayn)

QY 22: HAJJ (led by Abu Bakr)

QY 23: HAJJ (led by the Prophet)

Remember that **Asma' bint Umays** was married to Ja'far ibn Abi Talib, who died in Syria two years ago. She subsequently became Abu Bakr's third wife.

Be sure to read Lings (p. 348-351) and listen to Yusuf (24:1-3) for a detailed description of the Prophet's Hajj.

Having arrived in 'Arafah, the Prophet ascends the Mount of Mercy and turns to the thousands of pilgrims below to deliver his last sermon, concluding with one of the Qur'an's final revelations:

> ...This day, those who cover over (the truth of God) have given up all hope of (destroying) your way of life. So don't be afraid of them; rather, fear only Me. This day, I have perfected your way of life for you, completed My favor upon you and have chosen for you Islam as your way of life.
> — *Al Ma'idah (The Banquet Table, 5:3)*

---

1 WHAT WAS THE RELIGION OF ISLAM CALLED ALL THIS TIME? WATT

"The name of Muhammad's religion was not always Islam. In the Meccan period one name for it seems to have been tazakki, 'righteousness', but the religion and its adherents are seldom explicitly mentioned. After the Hijrah there are many references to 'believers' (mu'minun), 'those who believe', and so forth; in some cases these terms include the Jews. On Muhammad's break with the Jews he claimed to be following the religion of Abraham, the hanif and for some time Muhammad's religion must have been known as the Hanifiyah. This word was read instead of 'Islam' by Ibn Mas'ud in Qur'an 3.19/17, and was presumably the original reading. It also occurs in sayings of Muhammad to the effect that the religion he took to Medina was the Hanifiyah."[4]

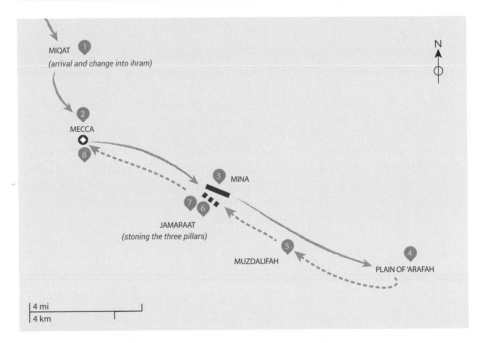

FIGURE 23A. THE RITES OF HAJJ

The pagan Arabs had been performing variations of the pilgrimage as it had been passed down from their forefathers. In 630 CE, the Prophet led 30,000 pilgrims on his first and only Hajj pilgrimage. By carefully following in the footsteps of Abraham, the Prophet reestablished the Hajj rites as follows:

(1) Don the ihram (pilgrims' attire) before entering Mecca. (2) Circumambulate the Ka'bah and run between Safa and Marwah, both seven times. (3) Spend the night in Mina. (4) Travel to the plain of 'Arafah seeking God's mercy (known as the Day of Mercy). (5) Spend the night in Muzdalifah. (6) Stone the pillars in Mina (to commemorate Abraham's refusal to heed the devil's temptation). (7) Sacrifice an animal to commemorate Abraham's unwavering obedience to God in agreeing to sacrifice his son. (8) Circumambulate the Ka'bah and run between Safa and Marwa, seven times before leaving.

◇———— THE LAST SERMON ————◇

"O People, lend me an attentive ear, for I know not whether after this year, I shall ever be amongst you again. Therefore listen to what I am saying to you very carefully and take these words to those who could not be present today.

O People, just as you regard this month, this day, this city as Sacred, so regard the life and property of every Muslim as a sacred trust. Return the goods entrusted to you to their rightful owners. Hurt no one so that no one may hurt you. Remember that you will indeed meet your Lord, and that He will indeed reckon your deeds. Allah has forbidden you to take usury (interest), therefore all interest obligation shall henceforth be waived. Your capital, however, is yours to keep. You will neither inflict nor suffer any inequity. Allah has judged that there shall be no interest and that all the interest due to 'Abbas ibn 'Abd'al Muttalib (Prophet's uncle) shall henceforth be waived...

Beware of Satan, for the safety of your religion. He has lost all hope that he will ever be able to lead you astray in big things, so beware of following him in small things.

O People, it is true that you have certain rights with regard to your women, but they also have rights over you. Remember that you have taken them as your wives only under Allah's trust and with His permission. If they abide by your right then to them belongs the right to be fed and clothed in kindness. Do treat your women well and be kind to them for they are your partners and committed helpers. And it is your right that they do not make friends with any one of whom you do not approve, as well as never to be unchaste.

O People, listen to me in earnest, worship God, say your five daily prayers, fast during the month of Ramadan, and give your wealth in Zakat. Perform Hajj if you can afford to.

All mankind is from Adam and Eve, an Arab has no superiority over a non-Arab nor a non-Arab has any superiority over an Arab; also a white has no superiority over black nor a black has any superiority over white except by piety and good action. Learn that every Muslim is a brother to every Muslim and that the Muslims constitute one brotherhood. Nothing shall be legitimate to a Muslim which belongs to a fellow Muslim unless it was given freely and willingly. Do not, therefore, do injustice to yourselves.

Remember, one day you will appear before God and answer your deeds. So beware, do not stray from the path of righteousness after I am gone.

O People, no prophet or apostle will come after me and no new faith will be born. Reason well, the Quran and my example, the sunnah and if you follow these you will never go astray.

All those who listen to me shall pass on my words to others and those to others again; and may the last ones understand my words better than those who listen to me directly. Be my witness, O Allah, that I have conveyed your message to your people."

"This day, those who cover over (the truth of God) have given up all hope of (destroying) your way of life. So don't be afraid of them; rather, fear only Me. This day, I have perfected your way of life for you, completed My favor upon you and have chosen for you Islam as your way of life."

— *Al Ma'idah (The Banquet Table, 5:3)*

FIGURE 23B. THE PROPHET'S LAST SERMON

19
20
21
22
23

With those words, the Prophet looks to the masses and asks:

"Have I not delivered the Message (of my Lord)?"

The multitude answers with a resounding affirmation, and the Prophet replies:

"Oh Allah! Bear witness."[5]

<SURAH AN-NASR (The Help (of God)) is widely considered to be the final complete revelation sent down to the Prophet. There is a minority opinion that it was revealed several years earlier after the conquest of Khaybar. According to Salahi, upon hearing the surah, 'Umar and 'Abd Allah ibn 'Abbas both realized that the Prophet would soon be leaving them.

After the momentous day at 'Arafah, the pilgrims return to Mina and spend the next three days in prayer. At this time, the Prophet receives his final complete surah:

> When God's help arrives and victory (is achieved), and when you see people coming into God's way of life in crowds, glorify your Lord and seek His forgiveness, for He is indeed the acceptor of repentance.
> — *An-Nasr (The Help (of God), 110:1-3)*

23.2 THE FALSE PROPHETS

Several months later, **Musaylimah** will be killed by Wahshi's spear.

The Prophet's last years are marked by a period of rapid growth in Arabia. During this time, several imposters emerge claiming to be prophets alongside Muhammad. When one in particular, a man by the name of Musaylimah ibn Habib (also known as Musaylimah "the Liar") from the eastern city of Yamamah, sends a letter to the Prophet proposing to divide the earth between the two leaders, the Prophet responds with a verse from Surah Al A'raf:

> ...Pray to God for help and wait patiently, for the earth belongs to God, and He gives it as an inheritance to whichever of His servants that He wills. The final result will be for those who were mindful (of Him). — *Al A'raf (The Heights, 7:128)*

Other false prophets include Aswad ibn Ka'b from Yemen and Tulayhah ibn Khuwaylid from the distant tribe of Asad. Shortly after the Prophet's death, Musaylimah is killed by Wahshi's spear, Aswad is assassinated by his own people, and Tulayhah surrenders to Khalid ibn al-Walid and becomes a valuable ally to Medina.

FIGURE 23C. THE FALSE PROPHETS

At least three different leaders made a claim to prophethood during the Prophet's lifetime. Musaylimah and Aswad were later killed, while Tulayhah converted to Islam along with his tribe of Asad.

Shortly after the Prophet's death, during the caliphate of Abu Bakr, many followers of Musaylimah, Tulayhah, and a number of other tribes in the Arabian Peninsula revolted against Medina. But Abu Bakr was able to suppress the uprisings in what became known as the Apostate Wars.

23.3 THE SECOND SYRIA EXPEDITION

Shortly after returning from Hajj, the Prophet turns his attention north. Hoping to unify all of Arabia, he dispatches an expedition of 3,000 men led by Zayd's teenage son, Usamah, to take action against the Syrian Arabs who had fought alongside the Romans at Mu'tah three years ago.

The Prophet's choice of Usamah brings a flurry of criticism that he is too young and inexperienced to lead the large military expedition. But the Prophet responds:

> *"No wonder now you contest his leadership, for you have already contested the previous leadership of his father. Yes, by Allah, his father [Zayd ibn Harithah], who was one of the most beloved people to me, was quite efficient for leadership; and this son of his is one of the most beloved individuals to me after his father."*[6]

Only three years ago, Zayd and Ja'far were among the few Muslims killed when they attacked the Roman/Arab forces at Mu'tah near the southern border of the Dead Sea.

---

2 **WHY DID THE PROPHET CHOOSE USAMAH?**   `RAMADAN`

"By confirming his choice, the Prophet informed them that neither a man's social origin nor his age should prevent him from exerting authority and power if he possessed the spiritual, intellectual, and moral qualities required. One had to show discernment by offering the most destitute in society real equality of opportunity and trusting the young so that everybody could express their skills and talents. The Prophet taught them [older Companions] that time naturally erodes one's energy, and one must be wise enough to learn to step aside, to delegate authority to those who are young and strong enough to create and build."[7]

23.4 THE FINAL DAYS

As the days pass, the word "Paradise" is ever present on the Prophet's lips. At one point, he visits the graveyard next to the Mosque and tells his Companion Abu Muwayhibah:

> *"I have been offered the keys of the treasures of this world and immortality therein followed by Paradise, and I have been given the choice between that and meeting my Lord and Paradise."*[8]

Soon thereafter, he develops a crippling headache but continues to lead the congregational prayers. At the end one of the prayers, he turns to his followers and says:

> *"Allah the Great has given a servant of His the opportunity to make a choice between whatever he desires of Allah's provisions in this world, and what He keeps for him in the [next] world, but he has opted for the latter."*[9]

19
20
21
22
23

Of all the Companions, only Abu Bakr begins to weep. The Prophet continues:

> *"I am most obliged to Abu Bakr for the favor of his company and property. If I were to make any other Khalil (friend) except Allah, I would have chosen Abu Bakr as a friend of mine. But for him I feel affection and brotherhood of Islam. No gate shall be kept open in the Mosque except that of Abu Bakr's."*[10]

Over the next two weeks, the Prophet's condition progressively deteriorates. When he is no longer able to lead the prayer standing, he instructs his followers to pray seated behind him.

With each passing day, the wives acknowledge the Prophet's desire to be near 'A'ishah. When he is too weak to lead the congregation, he tells 'A'ishah to make sure her father leads the prayers. 'A'ishah suggests that perhaps 'Umar should lead on account that it would pain her father to take the place of the Prophet. Despite her repeated protests that her father weeps too much when reciting the Qur'an, the Prophet remains steadfast. Abu Bakr then leads the congregation for the rest of the Prophet's illness.

Sensing the seriousness of his condition, several Companions visit the Prophet and his family. But whenever Fatimah visits, 'A'ishah gives her time to be alone with her father. During one of these meetings, he whispers something to Fatimah that bring her to tears, he then whispers something else, and she smiles. Fatimah later explains to 'A'ishah:

> *"The first time he disclosed to me that he would not recover from his illness and I wept. Then he told me that I would be the first of his family to join him, so I laughed."*[11]

23.5 THE DEATH OF THE PROPHET

On June 8, 632, 11 years after his migration to Medina, the Prophet joins the congregation mid-prayer but does not allow Abu Bakr to step back from leading the prayer. Afterward, the Prophet returns to his house and rests in 'A'ishah's arms. With his head in her lap, he quietly recites a verse from Surah An-Nisa:

> Whoever obeys God and the Messenger will be with those who have the favor of God upon them, (among whom are) the prophets, the true (in faith), the witnesses (who sacrificed their lives in God's cause) and the righteous. What a beautiful fellowship! — *An-Nisa (The Women, 4:69)*

Then with his final breath, he whispers:

> *"Oh Allah, with the supreme communion."*[12]

When Abu Bakr is chosen as the first Caliph, his first military decree will be to fulfill the Prophet's wishes and dispatch Usamah's army back to Syria.

After hearing the Prophet was dying, Usamah orders his men to return to Medina. Upon their arrival, however, they learn that the Prophet has already passed away. 'Umar cannot believe the news and announces that the Prophet has departed in spirit and will soon return.

Abu Bakr hears the news and quickly arrives from the northern part of Medina. After visiting 'A'ishah and seeing the Prophet's body, he approaches the restless crowd gathered outside. 'Umar refuses to believe that the Prophet could have died, but Abu Bakr immediately interrupts him and announces:

> "And now, to he who worships Muhammad, (he should know that) Muhammad is dead. But he who worships Allah, He is Ever Living and He never dies."[13]

He then recites a verse from Surah Ali 'Imran that was revealed after the Battle of Uhud seven years earlier:

> Muhammad is no more than a messenger. There were many messengers who passed away before him. If he dies or is killed, would you then turn and run away? Anyone who runs away does no harm to God in the least, and God will quickly reward (those who serve Him) in gratitude.
> — Ali 'Imran (The Family of Amran, 3:144)

Abu Bakr's words bring 'Umar back to his senses, who later acknowledges:

> "By Allah, as soon as I heard Abu Bakr say it, I fell down to the ground. I felt as if my legs had been unable to carry me so that I collapsed when I heard him say it. Only then did I realize that Muhammad had really died."[14]

---

❸ WHAT CAN BE LEARNED FROM THE REACTIONS OF ABU BAKR AND 'UMAR? `RAMADAN`

"The two men's roles were inverted, thus showing that through his departure the Prophet offered us a final teaching: in the bright depths of spirituality, sensitivity can produce a degree of strength of being that nothing can disturb. Conversely, the strongest personality, if it forgets itself for a moment, can become vulnerable and fragile. The path to wisdom and to strength in God inevitably leads through awareness and recognition of our weaknesses."[15]

- -

❹ WHY WAS THE PROPHET'S DEATH SUCH A DIFFICULT TRIAL FOR THE COMPANIONS? `YUSUF`

"The sahaba [Companions] said that there was no greater musibah [difficulty]. Of all the things they had suffered, nothing compared to the loss of the Messenger of Allah, God's peace and blessings upon him.
Umm al-Fadl said, 'It is not the death of the Messenger, God's peace and blessings upon him, that causes this mourning we feel so much because we know he's gone to be with Allah, but it is that we have lost communication.' The divine guidance stopped."[16]

23.6 THE SELECTION OF ABU BAKR AS CALIPH

Sa'd ibn 'Ubadah was the foremost man of the Helpers. The Prophet had left him in charge of Medina when the Prophet went out on his first expedition with the Emigrants. After the spoils of Hunayn were divided among the new converts from Mecca, Sa'd approached the Prophet on behalf of the Helpers to inquire about their share of the spoils. Lings notes that according to Ibn Ishaq, after the Prophet's death, Sa'd does not pledge his allegiance to Abu Bakr and eventually migrates to Syria.

The death of the Prophet leaves the community without a leader. Many of the Helpers feel that leadership should pass to Sa'd ibn 'Ubadah—a man from their own city. But Abu Bakr reminds them that the Muslim community is much larger than the city of Medina. Given the Quraysh's preeminence among the Arabs, they are the only people who can command the respect of the entire peninsula. He nominates 'Umar and Abu 'Ubaydah for the position of caliph, but 'Umar intervenes, asking the Companions if any person would dare overtake the Prophet's decision to have Abu Bakr lead the prayer. He describes Abu Bakr as "the best of you, the Companion of God's Messenger," and reminds them of the lofty position Abu Bakr held in the Qur'an:

> ...He was just one of two (men hiding out) in a cave... — *At-Tawbah (Repentance, 9:40)*

This was not the first time Abu Bakr was distinguished for his superior qualities. On a previous occasion, the Prophet explained to the others:

> *"He [Abu Bakr] surpasseth you not through much fasting and prayer but he surpasseth you in virtue of something that is fixed in his heart."*

Abu Bakr accepts the nomination, and the next day, he addresses the congregation:

> *"I have been given the authority over you, and I am not the best of you. If I do well, help me; and if I do wrong, set me right. Sincere regard for truth is loyalty and disregard for truth is treachery. The weak amongst you shall be strong with me until I have secured his rights, if God will; and the strong amongst you shall be weak with me until I have wrested from him the rights of others, if God will. Obey me so long as I obey God and His Messenger. But if I disobey God and his Messenger, ye owe me no obedience. Arise for your prayer, God have mercy upon you!"*[17]

---

⑤ WHY ABU BAKR? YUSUF

"Who else but the one who was with him in the cave, who made the Hijra with him?

The one who the Prophet, God's peace and blessings upon him, said, 'Everyone wavered in Islam except Abu Bakr.'

The one who the Prophet, God's peace and blessings upon him, appointed as the head of the army.

The one who the Prophet, God's peace and blessings upon him, gave the standard to in going to fight the Romans.

The one who gave *all* of his wealth on the expedition to Tabuk.

Who else but Abu Bakr could take that place?"[18]

Meanwhile 'Ali is busy preparing for the Prophet's funeral and is absent from any discussion about succession. In fact, he hears about Abu Bakr's election as caliph after the matter had already been decided, and does not immediately swear allegiance to him. Lings deals gently with the issue, citing a narration related by Bukhari:

> After the death of Fatimah some months later, 'Ali said to Abu Bakr: "We know well thy preeminence and what God hath bestowed upon thee, and we are not jealous of any benefit that He hath caused to come unto thee. But thou didst confront us with a thing accomplished, leaving us no choice, and we felt that we had some claim therein for our nearness of kinship unto the Messenger of God." Then Abu Bakr's eyes filled with tears and he said: "By Him in whose hand is my soul, I had rather that all should be well between me and the kindred of God's Messenger than between me and mine own kindred"; and at noon the next day in the Mosque, he publicly exonerated 'Ali for not yet having recognized him as caliph, whereupon 'Ali affirmed the right of Abu Bakr and pledged his allegiance to him.[19]

23.7 THE BURIAL

Those helping to prepare the Prophet's body for burial are 'Ali, Usamah, 'Abbas and his sons Fadl and Qitham, and a Khazraji man named Aws ibn Khawli who represents the Helpers. After careful deliberation, Abu Bakr instructs the Companions to bury the Prophet in A'ishah's room under the couch where he passed away.

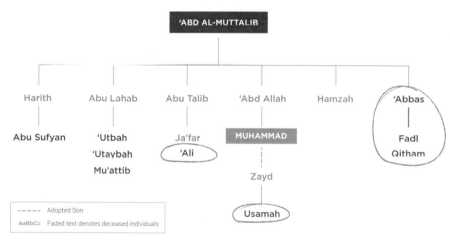

FIGURE 23D. THE PROPHET IS BURIED BY HIS CLOSEST RELATIVES

The Prophet's closest relatives (circled above) prepared and buried his body. Usamah had just left Medina with an expedition of 3,000 men, but quickly returned when he heard that the Prophet was dying.

That night, the Prophet is laid to rest by 'Ali and those who helped prepare the body. As Companions from all over Medina come to pay their respects, the Prophet's words linger in their thoughts. Jarir ibn 'Abd Allah, one of the Prophet's numerous friends later recalled:

"From the day I accepted Islam, the Messenger of Allah (peace be upon him) never prevented me from entering upon him and every time he saw me, he would smile."[20]

6 WHAT WAS BEHIND THE PROPHET'S ACCOMPLISHMENTS? WATT

"The more one reflects on the history of Muhammad and of early Islam, the more one is amazed at the vastness of his achievement. Circumstances presented him with an opportunity such as few men have had, but the man was fully matched with the hour. Had it not been for his gifts as seer, statesman, and administrator and, behind these, his trust in God and firm belief that God had sent him, a notable chapter in the history of mankind would have remained unwritten."[21]

7 WILL WE MEET THE PROPHET? YUSUF

"We have to believe with absolute certainty, insha'Allah, that we are going to meet the Messenger Allah, God's peace and blessings upon him. He said, 'The closest of you to me on that day are the best in character. I was sent to perfect human character. And so those of you who have spent your lives working on character, you are going to be the closest to me on that day.' " [22]

APPENDICES

————

APPENDIX A. A NOTE ON THE UNCERTAINTY OF DATES

While preparing this book, I kept multiple timelines to document when different scholars referenced the same events. The goal was to create a master timeline that displayed the Prophet's life according to both the Hijri (Islamic/lunar) and Gregorian (Christian/solar) calendars.

The Hijri calendar is determined by the 12-month lunar year consisting of 354 days. Unlike the Gregorian months that are fixed in their seasons, the lunar months rotate through the seasons, taking about 30 years to come full circle. Accordingly, it is nearly impossible for casual readers to assign a season to past lunar months, without first calculating their Gregorian equivalents. For example, while we know that the Prophet was chased out of Ta'if during the month of Shawwal, how do we know if this happened during the cool of winter or the peak of summer? By constructing a master timeline of the Sirah according to the Gregorian calendar, I hoped to frame the Prophet's life in a way that I was accustomed to thinking about my own.

But soon after I began the task of arranging events, I noticed that scholars were giving different dates for the same event. Some scholars differed on the Hijri dates, while others agreed on the same Hijri date but disagreed on its Gregorian equivalent. In short time, my straightforward project transformed into an awkward math puzzle.

What explains the uncertainty of Hijri dates in the Prophet's life?

I had already anticipated that historians would differ regarding the early (Meccan) events. After all, the Prophet had far fewer Companions during the Meccan period who could corroborate their experiences for the benefit of later generations. This phenomenon probably explains why it is difficult to nail down critical Meccan events like the Prophet's Night Journey, while there is little ambiguity about when the Prophet led 30,000 attentive followers on his final military expedition to Tabuk.

This difference between the Meccan and Medinan periods explained one part of the puzzle. But even if historians agree to the same Hijri date in Medina, why do they often differ on its Gregorian equivalent? Neither calendar system is terribly complicated, nor is it difficult to determine the exact Gregorian or Hijri date in any day in the past or future. What explains the dating confusion over well-documented events during the Prophet's lifetime?

The problem is not with the historians, but with the pre-Islamic Arabs who used to insert an extra month in the year to keep the lunar months in sync with the solar calendar. The worst part of this system is that they purposely tampered with the timing of the four sacred months (1, 7, 11, and 12), in which warfare and plundering were strictly forbidden. By purposely inserting extra months into their calendar, the Arabs could effectively "delay" a sacred month and attack unsuspecting tribes with impunity.

Intercalation was so widespread that Surah at-Tawbah specifically addresses the practice:

> There are twelve numbered months in God's sight, and this was recorded by Him on the day He created the heavens and the earth. Four of them have sacred restrictions, and that's the established custom, so do no wrong against yourselves within them (by violating this rule)...
>
> Arbitrarily postponing (restricted months) is an added degree of suppression (of God's truth), and those who suppress (their awareness of the truth) are led into doing wrong on account of it. They make it lawful one year (to violate a restricted month) and forbidden another year. They adjust the number of months restricted by God, so (in their eyes) restricted months become lawful! The wickedness of their actions seems good to them, but God won't guide a people who suppress (their faith). — *At-Tawbah (Repentance, 9:36-37)*

In his 1961 biography of the Prophet, Hafiz Ghulam Sarwar explains that while the intercalated system was abolished in 11 AH, a strict lunar system was not officially adopted until the caliphate of 'Umar six years later. As for the first 10 years of the Medinan period, there are no records to indicate which years had 12 months and which had 13.

> ...The difference, however, is always a question of a few months, seldom exceeding three ... In any case, there will always be the difficulty of finding out which years of the Prophet's life were intercalary years and which were not.[1]

Given these challenges, the uncertainty of dates in the Sirah has become an accepted fact among most historians. In his book, *Muhammad in Mecca*, Montgomery Watt makes an important distinction:

> The question of precise dating is not a vital one for understanding the life of Muhammad, and little is to be gained by trying to go behind the scheme explicitly or implicitly present in the standard Muslim writers on the subject ... For most purposes these dates are a sufficiently accurate guide. Their chief importance is perhaps to make us realize that, despite the meagerness of the records which causes us to feel that things happened quickly, the development of Islam at Mecca was a slow process.[2]

Giving precedence to the dates presented by Al-Mubarakpuri, Lings, and Watt, I have tried my best to construct a Gregorian timeline so Western readers can envision the Prophet's life the same way they see their own. This timeline agrees with the most established accounts of the Sirah. In the words of Hafiz Ghulam Sarwar:

> Muslim writers often forget the fact that, during the twenty-three years of the Prophet's ministry of Islam, the years were of 364 days each on the average and not 354 days and they therefore fall into error when giving the corresponding dates in English... It is now extremely difficult to give an exact calculation, and I have contented myself with as near an approximation to correctness as I could.[3]

APPENDIX B. A BRIEF HISTORY OF THE SIRAH

Throughout this book there have been numerous references to the terms "Qur'an", "Sirah," "Sunnah," and "Hadith." Because these terms are often confused by Muslims and non-Muslims alike, I have included their definitions and diagrammed their relative associations.

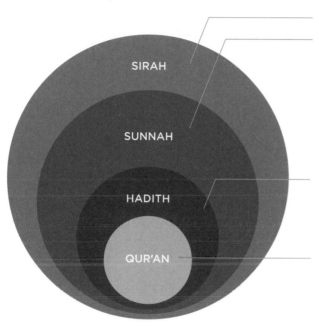

"A sira is a path through life and so by extension a biography, but the **Sira** (with a capital S, as it were) is the life of Muhammad. The Sira contains **sunna**, the latter setting out in a systematic fashion the Prophet's customary or normative behavior, that which must by and large be imitated or obeyed. The Sira narrates and charts the outward facts of his life, whereas the sunna is its ethical/legal content. The two, as stated above, are sometimes confused and spoken of in the same breath ... while the Sira of Muhammad continued over time to be an independent genre of narrative biography, the sunna of Muhammad was eventually collected in standardized **Hadith**, the name given to the "Traditions" of Muhammad, his pronouncements or his actions that have moral or legal content and that function as a guide to the believers."[4]

"[T]he **Qur'an** is God's book. The Hadith is, by and large, Muhammad's book, detailing his words and actions and organized under the main topics of Muslim ritual and belief. The first source is divine but the second is prophetic, even if divinely inspired ...most Muslim jurists down the ages have argued that the Qur'an and the Hadith are complementary texts, that the Hadith makes explicit what in the Qur'an is implicit, as for instance in its detailing of prayer, almsgiving, pilgrimage, and so forth."[5]

While the Qur'an is considered exact and immutable, and the Hadith and sunnah have been methodically standardized, the Sirah remains the most relaxed of the four disciplines. This is largely due to the organic development of Islamic scholarship in the first centuries after the Prophet's death. On the one hand, the *muhhadithun* (scholars of Hadith) recognized the spiritual and legal importance of authenticating everything before preserving anything. On the other hand, the earliest biographers attempted to paint an unabridged and unedited portrait of the Prophet by recording every anecdote they could get their hands on. The precision of the Hadith experts and the eagerness of the biographers explain why Islamic scholars rely on the Qur'an and Hadith, but not the Sirah, to formulate legal rulings.

THE HISTORICAL DEVELOPMENT OF SIRAH LITERATURE

Given Sirah literature's more relaxed standards, it has been influenced, shaped and reshaped through the ages. In his highly acclaimed book, *Images of Muhammad,* Tarif Khalidi explores how different historical periods projected an image of the Prophet that (consciously or subconsciously) responded to the needs of the time. These categories can be summarized as follows:

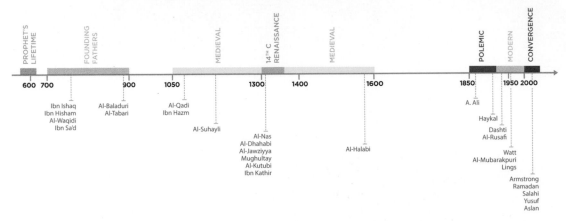

THE FOUNDING FATHERS (700S-800S)

Beginning in the eighth century, the Age of the Founding Fathers included the very first biographers, who diligently collected every available tidbit of information from the Prophet's life:

> It was a Sira so much in awe of its subject that it gathered in its net almost all the reports that fell into it, paying little attention to their consistency. The guiding principle was inclusion rather than exclusion. If any stories were found that some Muslims thought offensive or that contradicted other stories in the same narrative, it was thought better to include them rather than exclude them in the name of any pretension to piety. This is not to say that the founding fathers did not put a spin on their narrative: there can be no image without a spin. Being Sunni, the founding fathers were clearly not sympathetic, for example, to Shiite counter-narratives. But by and large the Sunni Sira preserved a great deal of historical material in a raw, unprocessed state, with little or no attempt made at establishing consistency or harmonization. [6]

The first known biographer was Muhammad ibn Ishaq, who was born about 70 years after the Prophet's death. Ibn Ishaq lived in Medina at the same time as Imam Abu Hanifa (the first of the great Sunni Islamic jurists) and interacted with the grandchildren of the Companions. Only portions of Ibn Ishaq's text, *The Life of the Messenger of God,* has survived through the works of later scholars, most notably his student, Ibn Hisham (*The Life of the Prophet*), and ibn Hisham's contemporary, Al-Waqidi.

In his *Book of History and Campaigns,* Al-Waqidi relies on Ibn Ishaq as his primary source while adding a significant amount of material about the military campaigns led out of Medina during the Prophet's lifetime. Al-Waqidi's student, Ibn Sa'd, also wrote a biography of the Prophet that did not survive through the ages.

The age of the founding fathers ended in the ninth and tenth centuries with two Persian scholars—Al-Baladhuri and Al-Tabari. Al-Baladhuri was primarily known as a historian, while Al-Tabari became a renowned Islamic scholar, best known for *Tafsir al-Tabari* (Tabari's exegesis of the Qur'an) and *The History of Prophets and Kings*, an all-encompassing examination of world history. Both scholars are often cited by Muslim historians and writers.

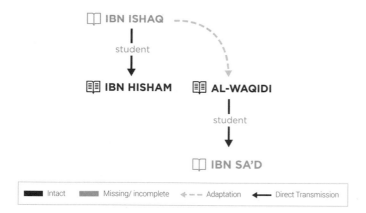

THE MEDIEVAL AGE (1000S-1600S CE)

Within just a few centuries of Ibn Ishaq, the breadth and depth of Islamic scholarship exploded (i.e., the Hadith sciences were systematized, the major schools of Islamic jurisprudence were established, and Imam al-Ghazali just produced his masterpiece, *The Revival of the Religious Sciences*). Around the turn of the 12th century, the foundational Sirah texts were eclipsed by literature from the Medieval Age. Beginning with al-Qadi 'Iyad (1083-1149), medieval Sunni scholars attempted to "clean up" the earliest biographies, transforming the Sirah from a lengthy, sometimes seemingly inconsistent narrative into a coherent and organized legal and ethical guide (often at the expense of Shiite and Mu'tazilite narratives). By highlighting the Prophet's miracles while expunging any "questionable" material, these biographers projected an image of the Prophet that was almost supernatural.

The early part of the Medieval period (1000s-1100s) was marked by three renowned Andalusian scholars al-Qadi 'Iyad, Ibn Hazm, and al-Suhayli. They were followed by what Khalidi calls a "14th-century renaissance," which included ibn Sayyid al-Nas, al-Dhahabi, al-Jawziyya, al-Hafiz Mughultay, al-Kutubi, and ending with the celebrated scholar ibn Kathir (best known for his exegesis of the Qur'an, *Tafsir ibn Kathir*).

Rounding out the Medieval period was the Syrian scholar Abu'l Faraj Nur al-Din al-Halabi, whose biography neatly integrated the work of his immediate predecessors:

> This work is in one important sense the end of the line of premodern Sira. It displays many of the features so far encountered in the later medieval period: a very thorough use of sources from diverse times, and an impressive command of theology, hadith, history, theology, natural science, philosophy, biblical literature, and Sufism, interspersed with personal memories and reflections ... Uppermost in the mind of its author is the intention to reconcile conflicting or divergent versions of the same event.[7]

THE POLEMIC AGE (1800S-EARLY 1900S)

By the late 1800s, the growth of Orientalism pushed Muslim biographers in entirely new directions. Faced with mounting criticism from the West, writers during the Polemic Age worked tirelessly to defend the Prophet from attack while figuring out how to present him as a modern hero:

> It was against this backdrop of a "scientific" European assault on Muhammad, which reached its peak in the late nineteenth and twentieth centuries, that a new breed of Islamic biographies of Muhammad began to take shape, perhaps in Muslim India and later in Egypt, Iran, and elsewhere. These works can broadly be described as defensive, polemical, and global in structure and argument. Typical of this new type of Sira is Hayat Muhammad (*The Life of Muhammad*) by the Egyptian Muhammad Husayn Haykal (d. 1956), which was addressed at least as much to the Orientalists as to the ordinary Muslim believer.[8]

While Haykal responded by projecting an image of the Prophet that might pass the test of Western standards, others like Indian scholar Ameer Ali remained unapologetic, arguing that the Prophet's legacy was a far superior alternative to Western materialism.

The Polemic period was unique in the history of Sirah because it was the first time that Muslim authors began projecting an image of the Prophet in Western languages. In her recent book, *Lives of Muhammad*, Professor Kecia Ali examines this new phenomenon and how it affected the direction of Sirah literature in the last two centuries:

> The quest for correct information about Muhammad had precedent in the work of early clerical opponents of Islam, who aimed to know Muslim doctrines the better to refute them. In this era, however, a set of questions about historical fact came to dominate Western approaches to Muhammad's life. Their preoccupations intersected with those of Muslim religious thinkers, traditional scholars, and Western-educated reformers. In a series of exchanges, mostly occurring in English, among British scholars and missionaries, Indian Muslim elites, and Hindu reformers, new visions of Muhammad were hammered out.[9]

Ali argues that as English became the lingua franca of the 20th century, the style and focus of Western-educated Muslim scholars gradually shifted away from the centuries-old, traditional Arabic narrative. Furthermore, with Muslims and non-Muslims expressing themselves in the same language, it was only a matter of time that their ideas and attitudes would begin to co-mingle.

THE MODERN AGE (1900S)

The polemic attitude continued well into the 20th century, where it merged with the Modern Age. In the years before the Second World War, biographers like the Iraqi historian Ma'ruf al-Rusafi and Iranian journalist Ali Dashti began trimming much of the Sirah's transcendental verbiage that was built up by the medieval scholars, and replaced it with descriptions of the Prophet's genius as a statesman and social activist. What prompted the modernist revisions? By removing (or altogether rejecting) the Prophet's supernatural characteristics, these authors believed they could unveil the true genius of the Prophet's humanity.

Regardless of the reasons, the Modern biographers had one goal in mind—to portray an image of the Prophet, "as a modern hero, rallying his community to the standard of reason, progress, liberty, and justice—in other words, whatever the 'modern age' demanded of its heroes."[10]

There were only a handful of authoritative biographers in the latter part of the 20th century who have enjoyed widespread support among Muslim readers. Unlike al-Rusafi and Dashti, these later scholars adopted different historical approaches to the Sirah.

In the mid-1950s W. Montgomery Watt wrote an extensive multivolume biography on the Prophet, which was the most inclusive of all the aforementioned periods of Sirah development. In the tradition of the modern period, his exhaustive research produced an image of the Prophet as a hero-statesman who could offer many valuable lessons to the West. Not surprisingly, his biographies have enjoyed a wide audience throughout the latter part of the 20th century.

Unlike Watt, Al-Mubarakpuri and Lings represent more traditional perspectives. Al-Mubarakpuri's biography is reminiscent of the Polemic Age, which unmistakably disputes Western criticism and its claim to moral authority. In contrast, Lings' strict adherence to the earliest sources is most representative of the Founding Fathers. Both Al-Mubarakpuri and Lings have garnered huge audiences and, by the turn of the millennium, were the most recognized modern biographies in the East and West respectively. Taken together, Watt, Lings, and Al-Mubarakpuri represent familiar images of the Prophet that have been projected in each of the past eras, and therefore were selected to form the backbone of the current text.

THE AGE OF CONVERGENCE (2000-PRESENT)

If Khalidi's theory of the development of Sirah can be likened to a number of separate tributaries departing from a single Prophetic source, Kecia Ali argues that since the 19th century, those rivers and streams have begun to converge once more. This rapid convergence has given rise to the most transformative period of Sirah literature since the first 200 years after the Prophet's death:

> European and American portraits of the Prophet, shaped decisively by new notions of what made a man great and what counted as merit, set the agenda for Muslim depictions. ... The considerable overlap among modern biographies illustrates the futility of appealing to a timeless clash of civilizations between Islam and the West.[11]

Citing the works of Tariq Ramadan, Karen Armstrong, and several others included in this book, Ali argues that Sirah literature is on the brink of a new age that has finally bridged the tiresome East-West divide:

> In the twenty-first century, it makes no sense to speak of Muslim views of Muhammad in opposition to Western or Christian views. Instead, the images of Muhammad that contemporary Muslims hold fervently and defend passionately arose in tandem and in tension with western European and North American intellectuals' accounts of his life. At the same time, Muslim sensibilities and beliefs have affected the way many non-Muslim authors write his life.[12]

While the Qur'an and Hadith remain unchanged, the Sirah has continued to react to the political, religious, economic, and intellectual challenges of its time. In the ever-changing world of the 21st century, where will the Sirah go next? Over a half-century ago, Watt left his readers with an interesting proposition:

> How the world answers the question about Muhammad depends to some extent on what the Muslims of today do. They still have an opportunity to give a fuller and better presentation of their case to the rest of the world. Will they be able to turn to the life of Muhammad and by sifting the universal in it from the particular discover moral principles which make a creative contribution to the present world situation?[13]

Our world is increasingly facing comprehensive issues like wealth inequality, social isolation, sex trafficking, and global warming. If Watt's prediction holds true, our biggest test will be whether we can unearth newer, more compelling truths from the Prophet's life and message that address the challenges of an increasingly uncertain world.

APPENDIX C. A TIMELINE OF CHRISTIAN THEOLOGY

The timeline to the right diagrams the various developments in Jewish, Christian, and Islamic theology since the birth of Jesus. It is important to remember that Christianity began as a collection of Jewish sects. While most Jews believed that Jesus was a heretic, the Ebionites (Hebrew for "the poor ones") accepted Jesus as the Messiah. In contrast, the Nazarenes continued to observe Mosaic Law, but regarded Jesus as the son of God.

These and other early Jewish-Christian sects never gained much traction in the Roman Empire. By the second century, several other forms of early Christianity (practiced by non-Jews) emerged with new beliefs about the divine nature of Jesus and his relationship with God ("the Father"). Adoptionists held that Jesus was a flawless human whom God adopted because of his perfect devotion. In contrast, Docetists suggested that Jesus was too perfect to be human; rather he was an apparition only appearing to exist to mankind. Neither interpretation enjoyed widespread support, and by the second and third centuries, new Christian sects began promoting the idea that Jesus was both human and divine. Despite their differences, early Christians remained a small, persecuted minority in the Roman Empire.

The major turning point in Christian theology took place in 325 CE, when the recently converted Roman emperor, Constantine I, assembled bishops from all over the Eastern Roman Empire to ratify a uniform creed. Later recognized as the first Ecumenical Council, the assembly collectively adopted the Nicene Creed, which declared Trinitarian Christianity (God as the Father, Son, and Holy Spirit) as the indisputable truth and declared all other views of Jesus as heresy. Fifty-six years later, the second Ecumenical Council (the Council of Constantinople) reaffirmed the Nicene Creed and officially rejected Arianism, which held that Jesus' divine essence was different than God's.

While the Church taught that Jesus was both human and divine, it continued
to wrestle with the nature of that relationship. Nestorians felt that Christ's
human and God-like natures were distinct entities in the same person. The Third
Ecumenical Council (in Ephesus) was convened to resolve Christ's human/divine
nature. After a politically charged theological debate, the Council declared that
Christ had a singular nature (both human and divine) and condemned Nestorian
Christianity as profane. Persecution of Nestorian Christians ultimately pushed
them east where they found refuge in Persia. Today Nestorian Christianity is
known as the Assyrian Church of the East.

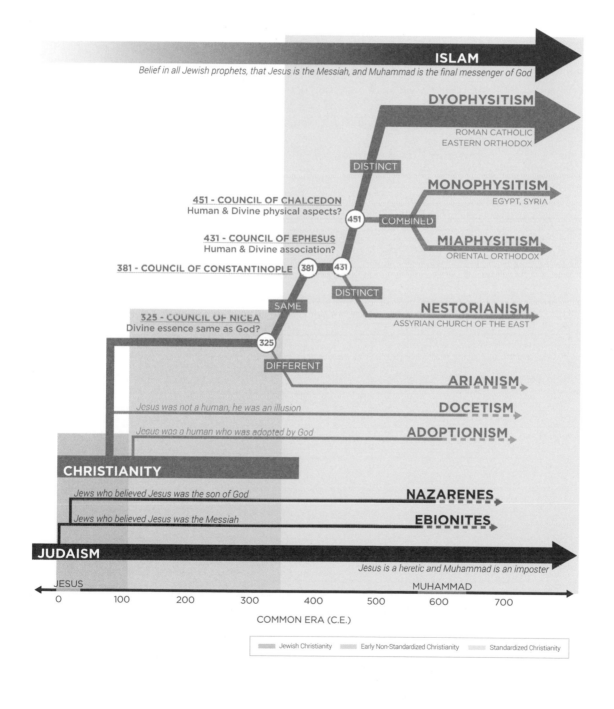

While the Church had resolved that Jesus' essence was both human and divine in the same being, it struggled to explain his physical existence. After his birth, was Jesus' nature human, divine, or both? Monophysites declared that after his incarnation, Jesus was singly divine in one nature. Miaphysites believed that his human and divine qualities were together blended in one nature. At the Fourth Ecumenical Council of Chalcedon, the Church adopted Dyophysitism, declaring that Jesus' humanity and divinity were distinct natures unified perfectly in one being. As before, they declared all alternative viewpoints as heresy. Monophysite Christians found refuge in parts of Egypt and Syria, while Miaphysite Christians established the Oriental Orthodox Church, which today includes the Coptic, Syrian, Ethiopian, Eritrean, Armenian, and Indian Churches. Dyophysitism became the accepted doctrine of the Church, and later gave rise to the Roman Catholic and Eastern Orthodox traditions that developed many centuries after the advent of Islam.

While the majority of Christians today subscribe to Trinitarian theology based on Dyophysitism, it is important to remember that Christianity was a colorful mix of beliefs and practices during Muhammad's lifetime. It is possible that the Christians who believed in the coming of Muhammad (Nestor, Bahira, Waraqah ibn Nawfal, the Negus, 'Addas) were not what we consider "mainstream" Christians of modern times, but Ebionites, Nestorians, Miaphysites, etc.

GLOSSARY

The glossary of names contains over 350 of the most salient individuals in the Sirah.

The first column denotes family ties and is limited to relevant relationships with other people in the glossary. The list includes grandparents, parents, siblings, spouses, children, and relationship to the Prophet, where applicable.

The second column is simply a quick summary of each person's role in the overall story. For the sake of brevity, these summaries may not contain well-known details that are not included in the primary sources.

The Prophet is referred to by his name in the first column, and by his title in the second. As is the convention used throughout this book, he is referred to as "Muhammad" if the pertinent event occurred before his prophethood.

USAGE NOTES:

- **IBN** means "son of." Zayd ibn Harithah signifies Zayd, the son of Harithah.
- **BINT** means "daughter of." Zaynab bint Jahsh signifies Zaynab, daughter of Jahsh.
- **ABI** is the genitive of Abu. Ali, the son of Abu Talib, is referred to as " 'Ali ibn Abi Talib." Umm Habibah, the daughter of Abu Sufyan, is referred to as "Umm Habibah bint Abi Sufyan."

A/'A

'Abbas ibn 'Abd al-Muttalib

Son of 'Abd al-Muttalib ibn Hashim
Husband of Umm al-Fadl bint al-Harith
Foster father to Ja'far ibn Abi Talib
Uncle of the Prophet
Clan of Hashim (Tribe of Quraysh)

Before revelation, 'Abbas agreed to take care of his brother's 15-year-old son, Ja'far. Although he never embraced Islam during the Meccan period, 'Abbas accompanied the Prophet to the Second 'Aqabah and arranged his meeting with the Yathrib pilgrims. A few years later, he marched with the Meccans to Badr and was captured by the Muslims. The Prophet demanded that 'Abbas pay his own ransom if he wished to return to Mecca. The following year, 'Abbas warned the Prophet that the Meccan army was marching to Uhud. Three years later, after the Prophet's first pilgrimage to Mecca after Hudaybiyah, 'Abbas arranged the Prophet's marriage to Umm al-Fadl's widowed sister Maymunah. Just before the Conquest of Mecca, 'Abbas and Umm al-Fadl joined the Muslim army, and he advised the Prophet to grant protection to Abu Sufyan and everyone in Abu Sufyan's household. After the Prophet's death, Abbas helped prepare the Prophet's body for burial.

'Abd ad-Dar ibn Qusayy

Eldest son of Qusayy ibn Kilab
(Tribe of Quraysh)

'Abd ad-Dar was the eldest, yet least impressive, of Qusayy's sons. After his father's death, he became chief of the Quraysh. When the Quraysh split into two factions, 'Abd ad-Dar led the Confederates and was given the keys to the Ka'bah.

'Abd al-Ka'bah ibn Abi Bakr (" 'Abd ar-Rahman")

Son of Abu Bakr and Umm Ruman bint Milhan
Full brother of 'A'ishah bint Abi Bakr
Clan of Taym (Tribe of Quraysh)

At first, 'Abd al-Ka'bah refused to follow his father into Islam, and fought against the Prophet at Uhud. Several years later, after the death of his mother, he came to Medina to embrace Islam and the Prophet changed his name to 'Abd ar-Rahman.

'Abd Allah ibn 'Abd Allah ibn Ubayy

Son of 'Abd Allah ibn Ubayy
Brother of Jamilah bint 'Abd Allah ibn Ubayy
Clan of Khazraj (Medina)

'Abd Allah was an ardent supporter of the Prophet and marched to Uhud even after his own father abandoned the Prophet and led 300 men back to Medina. A few years later, he offered to punish his father for his hypocrisy because he worried that he might seek revenge on anyone who harmed his father.

'Abd Allah ibn 'Abd al-Muttalib

Son of 'Abd al-Muttalib ibn Hashim
Full brother of Zubayr, Abu Talib, and Umaymah
Husband of Aminah bint Wahb
Father of Muhammad
Clan of Hashim (Tribe of Quraysh)

'Abd Allah was the 10th son of 'Abd al-Muttalib, and was chosen to be sacrificed in accordance with an oath his father had made. His father managed to spare his favorite son's life at great cost and married him to Aminah in 569 CE. 'Abd Allah died that year while on a trading caravan to the north.

'Abd Allah ibn Abi Bakr

Son of Abu Bakr and Qutaylah
Brother of Asma' bint Abi Bakr
Half-brother of 'A'ishah bint Abi Bakr
Clan of Taym (Tribe of Quraysh)

'Abd Allah entered Islam in Mecca and helped his father and the Prophet escape to Medina. Later that year, Abu Bakr asked him to escort the rest of his family—Umm Ruman, Asma' and 'A'ishah—to Medina.

'Abd Allah ibn Abi Umayyah

Son of Abu Umayyah and 'Atikah bint 'Abd al-Muttalib
Brother of Zuhayr ibn Abi Umayyah
First cousin of Muhammad
Clan of Makhzum (Tribe of Quraysh)

Although 'Abd Allah was named after the Prophet's father, he told the Prophet he would never believe in Islam, even if the Prophet brought angels down from Heaven. Just before the Prophet's army entered Mecca, however, he rushed out of the city and testified his faith to the Prophet. Several days later, he was killed during the siege of Ta'if.

'Abd Allah ibn 'Amr ibn al-'As

Grandson of al-'As ibn Wa'il (Chief of Sahm)
Son of 'Amr ibn al-'As
Clan of Sahm (Tribe of Quraysh)

'Abd Allah embraced Islam well before his father's conversion. The Prophet granted him special permission to record the Prophet's sayings, and 'Abd Allah eventually became one of the most learned Companions of his generation. 'Abd Allah's father followed a more circuitous route to Islam.

'Abd Allah ibn 'Amr ibn Haram

Father of Jabir ibn 'Abd Allah
Clan of Khazraj (Medina)

'Abd Allah pledged his loyalty to the Prophet at the Second 'Aqabah. Several years later, he had a dream about martyrdom and was subsequently killed on the Uhud battlefield.

'Abd Allah ibn Jahsh

Son of Jahsh ibn Ri'ab and Umaymah bint 'Abd al-Muttalib
First cousin of Muhammad
Clan of 'Abdu Shams* (Tribe of Quraysh)

'Abd Allah was 12 years younger than the Prophet and was one of the first in his family to embrace Islam. He migrated to Abyssinia and returned after the ban on Hashim was lifted. Just before Badr, he led eight Emigrants on a reconnaissance mission and ended up attacking a northbound Quraysh caravan from Yemen. The Prophet was upset that they carried out the attack during the sacred month of Rajab, however the Qur'an (2:217) absolved them. 'Abd Allah died two years later at Uhud and was buried next to the Prophet's beloved uncle Hamzah.

*His father was from the distant tribe of Asad and was given honorary membership in 'Abdu Shams

---

'Abd Allah ibn Jubayr

Clan of Aws (Medina)

'Abd Allah was placed in charge of 50 archers at Uhud, but was only left with nine of them when the others abandoned him to chase after the spoils of battle. Khalid ibn al-Walid spotted the weakness in the archers' line of defense and killed all 10 of them.

'Abd Allah ibn Jud'an

Chief of Taym (Tribe of Quraysh)

Years before the first revelation, 'Abd Allah initiated the Pact of Chivalry in an attempt to establish a Qurayshi code of ethics.

'Abd Allah ibn Mas'ud

Shepherd of 'Uqbah ibn Abi Mu'ayt
Confederate of the clan of Zuhrah

'Abd Allah was not a Qurayshi by blood but rather a confederate of the Quraysh clan of Zuhrah. He was a humble shepherd in Mecca, and was one of the first to embrace Islam. During the Early Meccan Period, Abu Jahl struck him on the face for publicly reciting the Qur'an at the Ka'bah (according to Lings, 'Abd Allah was the first to do this). At Badr, 'Abd Allah stood over an injured Abu Jahl and finished him. 'Abd Allah was a close member of the Prophet's household and eventually became one of the most authoritative reciters of the Qur'an.

'Abd Allah ibn Muhammad

Sixth child of Muhammad and Khadijah
bint Khuwaylid
Clan of Hashim (Tribe of Quraysh)

'Abd Allah was born after Fatimah and was Muhammad and Khadijah's second son. He died in infancy, and the Prophet adopted 'Ali soon after.

'Abd Allah ibn Rawahah

Clan of Khazraj (Medina)

'Abd Allah, a renowned poet, confronted 'Abd Allah ibn Ubayy when ibn Ubayy told the Prophet to limit his preaching to his own house. 'Abd Allah was the first to march out to fight the Meccans at Badr, and later led the Prophet's camel into Mecca for the 'Umrah in 629 CE. A few months later, the Prophet placed 'Abd Allah as third in command of the expedition sent to Bani Ghassan in Syria (after Zayd and Ja'far), where he was martyred.

'Abd Allah ibn Sallam ("Husayn")

Bani Qaynuqa (Medina)

'Abd Allah was the chief rabbi of Bani Qaynuqa, but was quickly disowned by his people when he announced his conversion to Islam. After Badr, he informed the Prophet about Qaynuqa's treachery. After the Battle of the Trench, the Prophet placed him in charge of the women and children of Qurayzah, while Sa'd ibn Mu'adh punished their men for sedition.

'Abd Allah ibn Suhayl

Son of Suhayl ibn 'Amr al-'Amiri (chief of 'Amir)
Clan of 'Amir (Tribe of Quraysh)

Like many of Suhayl's children, 'Abd Allah was a devout follower of the Prophet. During the Meccan period, his father kept a close eye on him so he could not escape to Medina like his sister and brother-in-law (Sahlah and Abu Hudayfah). When Suhayl brought him to Badr to fight alongside the Quraysh, 'Abd Allah escaped to join the Prophet's army. Five years later, he was one of five Companions who signed the Treaty of Hudaybiyah. Despite his father's constant enmity, the Prophet agreed to forgive Suhayl after the Conquest of Mecca.

'Abd Allah ibn Ubayy

Father of 'Abd Allah and Jamilah
Father-in-law to Hanzalah ibn Abi 'Amir
Clan of Khazraj (Medina)

Before the Hijrah, 'Abd Allah was the de facto political leader of Yathrib. Despite a few glimpses of sincerity, he was generally considered to be the leader of the hypocrites (he is often referred to simply as ibn Ubayy). After Badr, he begged the Prophet to forgive the Bani Qaynuqa for breaking their covenant. Before Uhud, he suggested staying fortified in the city rather than marching out to meet the Quraysh. When the Prophet decided to take the offensive, 'Abd Allah withdrew his 300 men from the Muslim army. After the battle, Bani Nadir was found guilty of treachery, and

'Abd Allah ibn Ubayy (cont.)

'Abd Allah tried to come to their rescue. A few months later, he publicly criticized the Emigrants; when confronted, he vehemently denied doing so. Surah al-Munafiqun (The Hypocrites) was revealed shortly thereafter and confirmed his behavior. 'Abd Allah died after Tabuk, and the Prophet prayed for him at his burial, which upset 'Umar. The Prophet responded, "...did I know that God would forgive him if I prayed more than seventy times, I would increase the number of my supplications."

'Abd Allah ibn 'Umar

*Son of 'Umar ibn al-Khattab and Zaynab
   bint Maz'un*
Brother of Hafsah bint 'Umar
Clan of 'Adi (Tribe of Quraysh)

At age 13, 'Abd Allah tried to join the Muslim army at Uhud but was sent home because he was too young to fight. At 15, he was permitted to join the forces at the Battle of the Trench. He is widely considered one of the most authentic narrators of hadith.

'Abd Allah ibn Umm Makhtum

Clan unspecified (Mecca)

'Abd Allah was a blind man that Surah 'Abasa (He Frowned) refers to. The Prophet ignored him when he sought guidance while the Prophet was meeting with a Qurayshi leader. Several years later, the Prophet appointed him to lead the prayers in Medina when the Muslim army marched out to Badr and Uhud.

'Abd Allah ibn Unays

Clan of Khazraj (Medina)

The Prophet sent 'Abd Allah to kill the leader of Bani Hudayl for inciting hostilities against Medina.

'Abd Allah ibn Uraiqit

Clan unspecified (Mecca)

Although 'Abd Allah was a non-Muslim at the time of the Hijrah, he was entrusted to safely guide the Prophet and Abu Bakr to Medina by avoiding the usual caravan route.

'Abd Allah ibn Zayd

Clan of Khazraj (Medina)

'Abd Allah was present at the Second 'Aqabah, and later experienced a dream that established the Adhaan as the official call to prayer.

'Abd al-Muttalib ibn Hashim ("Shaybah")

*Son of Hashim ibn 'Abdi Manaf and Salma'
   bint 'Amr*
Foster-son of Muttalib ibn 'Abdi Manaf
Married to Fatimah bint 'Amr
*Father of Abu Lahab, Abu Talib, Hamzah,
   'Abd Allah, and many others*
Grandfather of Muhammad
Clan of Hashim (Tribe of Quraysh)

Shaybah grew up in Yathrib with his mother. After his father's death, he was adopted by his uncle Muttalib and taken back to Mecca. When the Quraysh saw him riding behind his uncle as the two entered the city, they called him " 'Abd al-Muttalib," or "slave of Muttalib." 'Abd al-Muttalib was highly esteemed in Mecca and was selected to lead the Scented Ones after Muttalib's death. He dreamt of the well of Zamzam and rediscovered it with his son Harith. He arranged the marriage of his son 'Abd Allah to Aminah and married Aminah's cousin Halah the same day. When Muhammad's mother died, 'Abd al-Muttalib opened his house to the orphan and remained inseparable from him until he died two years later.

'Abd al-'Uzzah ibn 'Abd al-Muttalib

See Abu Lahab

'Abd ar-Rahman ibn 'Awf

Son of 'Awf (distant kinsman to Muhammad's mother)
Clan of Zuhrah (Tribe of Quraysh)

'Abd ar-Rahman was one of the first people to embrace Islam. The Prophet changed his name from 'Abdu 'Amr, a pagan name, to 'Abd ar-Rahman. After Badr, he dropped the spoils of armor he had collected to take his old friend Umayyah ibn Khalaf captive. However, when Bilal saw Umayyah, who was his old master, he slew him and left 'Abd ar-Rahman without his spoils or his captive. Four years later, 'Abd ar-Rahman was one of the five Companions who signed the Treaty of Hudaybiyah. On the march to Tabuk, he led the one of the congregational prayers and the Prophet joined behind him. The Prophet said, "Ye have done well, for verily a Prophet dieth not until he hath been led in prayer by a pious man of his people." 'Abd ar-Rahman was one of 10 Companions to whom the Prophet promised Paradise.

'Abdu 'Amr ibn 'Awf

See 'Abd ar-Rahman ibn 'Awf

'Abdu Manaf ibn Qusayy

Second son of Qusayy ibn Kilab
Father to 'Abdu Shams, Hashim, Muttalib, and Nawfal
Tribe of Quraysh

Although 'Abdu Manaf was the most promising of Qusayy's sons, he accepted his father's wish that his older brother, 'Abd ad-Dar, lead the Quraysh. However, in the next generation, 'Abdu Manaf's son Hashim was recognized for his exceptional qualities and was supported by half the Quraysh clans as the leader of the Scented Ones.

'Abdu Shams ibn 'Abdi Manaf

Son of 'Abdu Manaf ibn Qusayy
Brother of Hashim ibn 'Abdi Manaf
Paternal uncle of 'Abd al-Muttalib ibn Hashim
Great uncle of Muhammad
Father of Umayyah (Umayyad branch)
Clan of 'Abdu Shams (Tribe of Quraysh)

'Abdu Shams was the founder of a separate clan of Quraysh. His son Umayyah founded the Umayyad branch of his clan. 'Abdu Shams was too busy as a merchant to take leadership after his brother Hashim died. His descendants included 'Uthman ibn 'Affan and Abu Sufyan ibn al-Harb.

'Abdu Shams ibn 'Affan

See 'Uthman ibn 'Affan

Abraha

Abyssinian governor of Yemen

Abraha was an Abyssinian general who helped re-conquer Yemen from the Himyarites in 525 CE. Soon thereafter, he quickly maneuvered into leadership as the governor of Yemen. Many years later, he led an army of soldiers and elephants to destroy the Ka'bah, but his forces were miraculously turned away ("Year of the Elephant").

Abraham

Husband of Sarah
Father of Isaac (through Sarah)
Husband of Hagar
Father of Ishmael (through Hagar)
Direct forefather of Muhammad

Abraham was the founder of the three Abrahamic faiths and is considered to be the archetypal Muslim. He left Hagar and Ishmael in the valley of Becca but returned often to visit and later erect the Ka'bah. During his prophecy, he established the foundations of Islam and the rituals of prayer.

Abu 'Abs ibn Jabr

Clan of Aws (Medina)

Before the expedition to Khaybar, Abu 'Abs had nothing but rags to wear and was too poor to leave his family. The Prophet gave him a new cloak, which Abu 'Abs barters for dates and a less expensive cloak. The Prophet laughed and said, "…if ye keep safe and live yet a little while, ye shall have abundance of provisions and leave abundantly for your families. Ye shall abound in dirhams and in slaves; and it will not be good for you!"

Abu 'Amir ibn Sayfi ("the Monk")

Cousin of 'Abd Allah ibn Ubayy
Father of Hanzalah ibn Abi 'Amir
Clan of Aws (Medina)

Abu 'Amir lived as an ascetic, and considered himself the spiritual leader of Yathrib. He challenged the Prophet's message, vowing that whoever was defeated would live in exile. He was in the front ranks of the Meccan army at Uhud and afterward asked Hind not to mutilate his son's body. After the Conquest of Mecca, he sought refuge in Ta'if. When the people of Ta'if entered Islam, he fled to Syria and died in exile (thus fulfilling his own prophesy).

Abu Ayyub ibn Zayd ("Abu Ayyub al-Ansari")

Clan of Khazraj (Medina)

Abu Ayyub was one of the 12 representatives who pledged themselves at the second 'Aqabah. He later housed the Prophet in Medina until the Prophet's own house was erected.

Abu 'Aziz ibn 'Umayr

Brother of Mus'ab ibn 'Umayr
Clan of 'Abd ad-Dar (Tribe of Quraysh)

Abu 'Aziz fought against the Prophet and was captured at Badr. His brother Mus'ab told the others to bind him tightly because their mother was rich and would pay a heavy ransom.

Abu Bakr ibn Abi Quhafah ("Atiq")

Son of Abu Quhafah ibn 'Amir
Husband of Qutaylah
Father of 'Abd Allah, Asma' (through Qutaylah)
Husband of Umm Ruman bint Milhan
Father of 'Abd al-Ka'bah, 'A'ishah
  (through Umm Ruman)
Husband of Asma' bint Umays (widow of Ja'far).
Father of Muhammad (through Asma')
Father-in-law to Zubayr ibn al-'Awwam
  (through Asma')
Father-in-law to Muhammad (through 'A'ishah)
Clan of Taym (Tribe of Quraysh)

Abu Bakr was a year or two younger than the Prophet. As a boy, he and Muhammad were present at the Pact of Chivalry. Many years later, Abu Bakr was one of the first to embrace Islam, and became the Prophet's closest Companion. He was instrumental in many early conversions including those of 'Uthman, Talhah, Bilal, and 'Amir ibn Fuhayrah. On one occasion, his unflinching faith left him (and Talhah) beaten and bound on the side of the road. Without any protection, he fled the city but returned under the guardianship of Ibn ad-Dughannah. Abu Bakr spent a majority of his wealth supporting the Muslims during the ban on Hashim. A few years later, he was one of the first Companions to endorse the Prophet's narration of the Night Journey. For this, the Prophet bestowed him with the title "as-Siddiq" (the great witness of truth). Abu Bakr built a mosque in front of his house and released Ibn ad-Dughannah as his guardian saying, "I am content with the protection of God." Prior to the Hijrah, he agreed to marry his daughter 'A'ishah to the Prophet. He cried with joy when the Prophet asked him to join him on the Hijrah.

GLOSSARY

Abu Bakr ibn Abi Quhafah (cont.)

With the help of Abu Bakr's children, Asma' and 'Abd Allah, the two men narrowly escaped Mecca. He is one of the few Companions referenced in the Qur'an (Surah At-Tawbah, 9:40).

After the Hijrah, the Prophet continued to consult Abu Bakr on a daily basis. Abu Bakr and 'Umar urged the Prophet to march to Badr, and helped him don his armor for the Battle of Uhud. 'Umar considered Abu Bakr his best friend and was hurt when Abu Bakr turned down 'Umar's request that he marry Hafsah, 'Umar's recently widowed daughter. But Abu Bakr later explained that the Prophet had confided interest in marrying 'Umar's daughter. Abu Bakr was one of the five Companions to sign the Treaty of Hudaybiyah, and rode next to the Prophet during the Conquest of Mecca. The Prophet placed Abu Bakr in charge of the vast army that set out for Tabuk until he could join a few days later. The Prophet also asked Abu Bakr to lead the first Hajj pilgrimage. The Prophet was clear about Abu Bakr's superior position among the Companions, saying: "He surpasseth you not through much fasting and prayer but he surpasseth you in virtue of something that is fixed in his heart." Upon the Prophet's insistence, Abu Bakr led the congregational prayers when the Prophet was too weak to attend. In fact, the Prophet prayed his final prayer seated next to Abu Bakr. In the Prophet's last days, he said, "O people, the most beneficent of men unto me in his companionship and in that which his hand bestoweth is Abu Bakr; and if I were to take from all mankind an inseparable friend, he would be Abu Bakr..."

After the Prophet's death, Abu Bakr reminded the Companions that the Prophet was only mortal, and that Allah is Ever-Living. He was quickly nominated to be the first Caliph, and was one of the 10 Companions to whom the Prophet promised Paradise.

Abu Bara ibn Malik

Chief of the clan of 'Amir (Tribe of Hawazin)

After the Prophet married Zaynab bint Khuzaymah (of Bani 'Amir), Abu Bara invited a delegation of Muslims to speak to his people. All 40 scholars were attacked by the neighboring hostile clan of Sulaym in the Ma'unah ambush, and only one survived.

Abu Basir ibn Asid

Clan unspecified

Abu Basir was a Muslim who escaped Mecca just after the Prophet signed the Treaty of Hudaybiyah, and was forced to return in accordance with the pact. He killed one of his two escorts on the way back, and ended up settling along the Red Sea coast. Soon other prisoners in Mecca (like Walid bin al-Walid) escaped and joined his camp. Abu Basir led his men in ambushes against several Meccan caravans. Unhappy with the threat to their trade route, the Quraysh told the Prophet that they would prefer that Abu Basir and his men enter Medina and abide by the Treaty of Hudaybiyah. He died before leaving for Medina, and the men erected a mosque at the campsite where he is buried.

Abu Dharr ibn Junadah ("al-Ghifari")

Brother of Unays ibn Junadah
Tribe of Ghifar (northwest of Mecca by the
  Red Sea)

Abu Dharr was a highway robber who heard of the Prophet through his brother Unays. He came to Mecca to embrace Islam and carried the Prophet's message back to his tribe. The Prophet left him in charge of Medina during the first 'Umrah.

Abu Dujanah ibn Kharashah

Clan of Khazraj (Medina)

On the morning of Uhud, the Prophet gave a sword to Abu Dujanah, which he wielded mightily and swaggers in front of the Muslim army. The Prophet said, "This is a sort of walking that Allah hates except in such a situation." He wrought havoc in the battle with his sword, and almost killed Hind before realizing she was a woman.

Abu Hudhayfah ibn 'Utbah

Son of 'Utbah ibn Rabi'ah (Shamsite leader)
Married to Sahlah bint Suhayl
  (daughter of the chief of 'Amir)
Clan of 'Abdu Shams (Tribe of Quraysh)

Abu Hudhayfah entered Islam with his wife Sahlah in Mecca. They sought asylum in Abyssinia, and returned when the ban on Hashim was lifted. When he saw his father 'Utbah killed at Badr, he felt remorse that heis father hadn't entered Islam before dying.

Abu Hurayrah ad-Dawsi (" 'Abd ar-Rahman")

Tribe of Daws (southeast of Mecca)

Abu Hurayrah arrived in Medina during the campaign at Khaybar, and was one of the poorest of the Ahl as-Suffah (People of the Bench). A year after Hudaybiyah, the Prophet placed him in charge of the sacrificial camels during the 'Umrah. Abu Hurayrah later became one of the most commonly referenced narrators of hadith in the Sunni tradition. Though his real name was 'Abd ar-Rahman, he was fond of kittens and thus earned his nickname as the "father of kittens."

Abu Jahl ibn Hisham ("Abu l-Hakam")

Grandson of Mughirah ibn 'Abd Allah
  (late chief of Makhzum)
Nephew of Walid ibn al-Mughirah
  (chief of Makhzum)
Full brother of Harith
Half-brother (maternal) of 'Ayyash ibn
  Abi Rabi'ah
Brother of 'Umar ibn al-Khattab's mother
Son of Hisham ibn al-Mughirah
Father of 'Ikrimah ibn Abi Jahl
Clan of Makhzum (Tribe of Quraysh)

Known for his wealth and ruthlessness, Abu Jahl was the most tireless opponent of the Prophet. He eventually succeeded his uncle as chief of Makhzum. His public assault on the Prophet led to Hamzah's conversion to Islam. Just before the Hijrah, he persuaded the Quraysh to assassinate the Prophet. Two year later, he led the Quraysh at Badr, where he was killed. Though his real name was Abu l-Hakam, the Muslims called him Abu Jahl, "Father of Ignorance."

Abu Jandal ibn Suhayl

Son of Suhayl ibn 'Amr al-'Amiri (chief of 'Amir)
Clan of 'Amir (Tribe of Quraysh)

As soon as the Treaty of Hudaybiyah was signed, the Quraysh brought Abu Jandal out in chains. Rather than break the treaty, the Prophet advised Abu Jandal to be patient and wait for Allah's help.

Abu Khaythamah ibn 'Abd Allah

Clan of Khazraj (Medina)

When the Prophet's army set out for Tabuk, Abu Khaythamah initially stayed at home. After several days, he felt guilty and caught up with the northward expedition.

Abu Lahab ibn 'Abd al-Muttalib (" 'Abd al-'Uzzah")

Son of 'Abd al-Muttalib ibn Hashim (the only son through his mother)
Father of 'Utbah, 'Utaybah, Mu'attib
Half-uncle of Muhammad
Clan of Hashim (Tribe of Quraysh)

Abu Lahab was the richest of 'Abd al-Muttalib's sons. He ridiculed the Prophet when the Prophet gathered the clan of Hashim together to invite them to Islam, and later was the only member of the clan exempted from the ban on Hashim. He succeeded Abu Talib as the chief of his clan and purposely excused himself from the meeting where the chiefs of Quraysh strategized the Prophet's assassination. Abu Lahab sent a proxy soldier to Badr to fight in Abu Lahab's place. After the Meccan defeat, Umm al-Fadl struck his head when she saw him beat her slave for rejoicing at the news of the Muslim victory. He died a week later.

Abu l-'As ibn ar-Rabi'

Son of Halah bint Khuwaylid (sister of Khadijah)
Husband of Zaynab bint Muhammad
Father of Umamah and 'Ali ibn ar-Rabi'
Son-in-law of Muhammad
Clan of 'Abdu Shams (Tribe of Quraysh)

Abu l-'As married Zaynab before the Prophet's first revelation. He loved Zaynab deeply but did not at first embrace Islam. He marched out against the Prophet at Badr and was captured. The Prophet forwent his ransom, but asked that he send Zaynab to Medina. Five months after the Battle of the Trench, Abu l-'As secretly entered Medina to visit Zaynab and his daughter Umamah. He returned to fulfill his business obligations, then returned to Medina, embraced Islam and rejoined his family.

Abu l-Bakhtari ibn Hisham

Clan of Asad (Tribe of Quraysh)

Abu l-Bakhtari struck Abu Jahl on the head with a camel bone when Abu Jahl tried to stop Hakim (Abu l-Bakhtari's clansman from Bani Asad) from taking food to Hakim's aunt Khadijah during the ban on Hashim. Abu l-Bakhtari was one of the five men who persuaded the Quraysh to end the ban.

Abu Lubabah ibn 'Abd al-Mundhir

Clan of Aws (Medina)

Abu Lubabah was left in charge of Medina when the Prophet set out to confront Bani Qaynuqa. On one occasion, Abu Lubabah refused the Prophet's request to donate his palm tree to an orphan after a dispute over ownership. A few years later, when Bani Qurayzah was surrounded by 'Ali's forces, Abu Lubabah was sent to discuss matters with them. He instructed them to surrender, but pointed to his neck to warn them of their punishment for treachery. He was overwhelmed by guilt and tied himself to a pillar in the mosque awaiting God's judgment. Two weeks later, he was expiated for his mistake and he gave away a third of his property in charity.

Abu Muwayhibah

Clan unspecified

In the final year of his life, the Prophet asked Abu Muwayhibah to accompany him to the graves at Baqi', where he told him of his choice to move on to the Afterlife and meet his Lord.

THE STORY OF MUHAMMAD *peace & blessings be upon him* ◇ 367

Abu Qays ibn Abi Anas

Indirect uncle of Waraqah and Khadijah
(through marriage)
Clan of Aws (Medina)

Abu Qays was indirectly related to Waraqah and respected his opinion of the Prophet. He was married to Khadijah's aunt, thereby forming an indirect link between the Aws and the Prophet.

Abu Quhafah ibn 'Amir

Father of Abu Bakr and Quraybah
Clan of Taym (Tribe of Quraysh)

Before the prophethood, Abu Quhafah brought his son Abu Bakr to the meeting of the "Pact of Chivalry." After the Conquest of Mecca, Abu Bakr brought his father to the Prophet so Abu Quhafah could finally enter Islam.

Abu Rafi'

Slave of 'Abbas and Umm al-Fadl

Abu Rafi' rejoiced in Mecca when he heard Abu Sufyan discuss the Meccan defeat at Badr, and was beaten by Abu Lahab. Later in Medina, 'Abbas gave him to the Prophet, who set him free.

Abu Sabrah ibn Abi Ruhm

Son of Barrah bint 'Abd al-Muttalib and Abu Ruhm
(a man from 'Amir)
Husband of Umm Kulthum bint Suhayl
Cousin of the Prophet
Clan of 'Amir (Tribe of Quraysh)

Abu Sabrah entered Islam in Mecca and migrated to Abyssinia with his wife. He returned when the ban on Hashim was lifted.

Abu Salamah ibn 'Abd al-Asad

Son of Barrah bint 'Abd al-Muttalib
Husband of Umm Salamah (later the sixth wife of
the Prophet)
Cousin of Muhammad
Clan of Makhzum (Tribe of Quraysh)

Abu Salamah was a dear cousin of the Prophet, and one of the first to embrace his message. He sought asylum in Abyssinia with his wife Umm Salamah, but returned under the protection of Abu Talib when the ban on Hashim was lifted. When Abu Talib died, Abu Salamah became the first person to leave for Medina before the official Hijrah. His wife and child were taken back to Mecca, but later came to Medina with the help of 'Uthman ibn Talhah. Shortly after Uhud, Abu Salamah successfully led an expedition to disperse the northwest tribe of Asad, which was planning to raid Medina. Just before his death (shortly after the expedition), he expressed his desire that Umm Salamah remarry a man better than him. She later married the Prophet.

Abu Sufyan ibn al-Harb

Grandson of Umayyah (namesake of the
Umayyad subclan)
Son of Harb ibn Umayyah
Husband of Hind bint 'Utbah
Father of Umm Habibah, Hanzalah, 'Amr, Yazid,
and Mu'awiyah
Clan of 'Abdu Shams (Tribe of Quraysh)

Abu Sufyan was the chief of the powerful Quraysh clan of 'Abdu Shams. His caravan was threatened by Muslim forces and became the driving force behind the Battle of Badr. His son 'Amr was held captive, but in an act of public demonstration, Abu Sufyan refused to pay his ransom. He led the Meccan army at Uhud, and did not stop other Qurayshis from mutilating Muslim bodies of the battlefield. Before leaving the battlefield, Abu Sufyan challenged the Prophet to a rematch at Badr, but failed to show up. He commanded the Meccan armies at Uhud and the Trench. After the Meccan breach of the Treaty of Hudaybiyah, he unsuccessfully tried to soothe things over with the Prophet and later made a last-minute appeal to the Prophet's advancing army outside Mecca. Abu Sufyan testified his faith at the Prophet's camp. After the Battle of Hunayn, he received a generous portion of the spoils. When the people of Ta'if entered Islam, the Prophet sent him there (along with Mughirah ibn Shu'bah) to destroy the statue of al-Lat.

Abu Sufyan ibn al-Harith

Son of Harith ibn 'Abd al-Muttalib
Cousin of the Prophet
Clan of Hashim (Tribe of Quraysh)

Abu Sufyan was the same age and physical likeness of the Prophet. Both were nursed by Halimah and grew up as close friends. He became an enemy of the Muslims and satirized the Prophet in his poetry. Just before the Conquest of Mecca, Abu Sufyan rode out to meet the Prophet and convert to Islam.

Abu Talib ibn 'Abd al-Muttalib

Son of 'Abd al-Muttalib ibn Hashim
Full brother of Zubayr, Umaymah, and 'Abd Allah
Husband of Fatimah bint Asad
Father of 'Aqil, Ja'far, Umm Hani (Fakhitah)
*   and 'Ali*
Full uncle of Muhammad
Clan of Hashim (Tribe of Quraysh)

Abu Talib was the Prophet's uncle and became his guardian after the death of 'Abd al-Muttalib. He raised the Prophet in his house and protected him and his followers from Quraysh persecution until Abu Talib died in 619 CE. His sons Ja'far and 'Ali were adopted by 'Abbas and the Prophet. In his final hours, Abu Talib was too proud to convert to Islam, yet the Prophet prayed for his forgiveness.

Abu 'Ubaydah ibn al-Jarrah

Clan of Harith (Tribe of Quraysh)

Abu 'Ubaydah was one of the earliest converts and fought at every battle. At Uhud, he removed chainmail embedded in the Prophet's cheek. He joined forces with Amr ibn l-'As for the Bani Quda'ah expedition and shortly after, led one of the four battalions at the Conquest of Mecca. After the death of the Prophet, Abu Bakr nominated him to be the first Caliph. He was one of the 10 to whom the Prophet promised Paradise.

Abu Wahb ibn 'Amr

Brother of Fatimah bint 'Amr (grandmother
*   of Muhammad)*
Clan of Makhzum (Tribe of Quraysh)

Abu Wahb was the first person to remove a stone from the Ka'bah when the Quraysh decided to rebuild the sanctuary.

'Addas

Christian slave of 'Utbah and 'Shaybah
*   ibn Rabiah*
Clan unspecified (from Nineveh, near present day
*   Mosul, Iraq)*

Originally from Nineveh, 'Addas was a Christian servant in Ta'if who offered grapes to the Prophet when he was mercilessly chased out of the city. 'Addas inadvertently reminded the Prophet about the Prophet Jonah, who was also tested with extraordinary difficulties during his prophetic career.

'Adi ibn Hatim

Tribe of Tayy

After the Battle of Hunayn, 'Adi avoided capture by the forces of 'Ali, who had led an expedition against the Bani Tayy. Soon after, 'Adi traveled to Medina to embrace Islam and forged an alliance between the Prophet and his tribe.

'A'ishah bint Abi Bakr

Daughter of Abu Bakr ibn Abi Quhafah and
Umm Ruman bint Milhan
Full sister of 'Abd al-Ka'bah
Half-sister of 'Abd Allah and Asma'
Third wife of the Prophet
Clan of Taym (Tribe of Quraysh)

'A'ishah was one of the first children to be born into Islam. She was approximately seven years old at time of Hijrah. At nine, she married the Prophet and later became his favorite wife. She developed close friendships with some of his other wives — Hafsah, Sawdah, and Safiyyah. After the Battle of the Trench, 'A'ishah was at the center of the "Necklace" scandal — gossip spread throughout Medina that she had been unfaithful to the Prophet. She was exonerated by verses in Surah An-Noor (The Light). Safiyyah was nearest in age to 'A'ishah, and her addition to the household became a temporary source of jealousy until the two grew to become close companions. Several years later, when the Prophet began spending time with Mariyah, Hafsah and 'A'ishah vented the wives' dissatisfaction to him. The Qur'an responds to all the wives in Surah At-Tahreem (The Prohibition). During the Prophet's last days, his wives recognized his desire to be with 'A'ishah and allowed him to spend all his time with her. He died in her arms, and the Companions agreed to bury him in 'A'ishah's room where he passed away.

Akhnas ibn Shariq

Confederate of Zuhrah (Tribe of Quraysh)

When the Prophet returned from Ta'if, Akhnas denied his request for protection. Four years later, he marched out to Badr, but at Juhfa, urged his clan of Zuhrah to return to Mecca. After Uhud, he witnessed the death of Zayd ibn ad-Dathinnah, who was killed after he refused to renounce Islam, and commented, "No father so loveth his son as the Companions of Muhammad love Muhammad."

'Ali ibn Abi Talib

Son of Abu Talib ibn 'Abd al-Muttalib
Full brother of Ja'far and Umm Hani
Husband of Fatimah bint Muhammad
Father of Hasan, Husayn, and Zaynab
First cousin, foster-son, and son-in-law
of Muhammad
Clan of Hashim (Tribe of Quraysh)

Shortly after Muhammad lost his second son, 'Abd Allah, he adopted 'Ali (4) to alleviate Abu Talib's financial stress. 'Ali was around the same age as the Muhammad's daughters Ruqayyah and Umm Kulthum, and a few years older than Fatimah. When 'Ali was 10, he was the second person to embrace Islam after Khadijah and the only one who spoke up in support of the Prophet when he introduced Islam to his extended family. 'Ali lay in the Prophet's bed, thus allowing the Prophet to escape Mecca under the nose of assassins sent to kill him. 'Ali fought in the opening duels of Badr and Uhud. He married Fatimah. After the Battle of the Trench, 'Ali led a successful campaign against Bani Qurayzah. He was one of the five Companions who signed the Treaty of Hudaybiyah. The Prophet spoke highly of 'Ali on many occasions; prior to the battle at Khaybar, he said, "Tomorrow I will give the banner to a man who loves Allah and His Messenger and Allah and His Messenger love him." After the Prophet's death, 'Ali helped prepare the Prophet's body for burial and was not present for the discussion of succession. He was one of 10 Companions to whom the Prophet promised Paradise.

Aminah bint Wahb

Daughter of Wahb bint 'Abdi Manaf az-Zuhri
(the late chief of Zuhrah)
Wife of 'Abd Allah ibn 'Abd al-Muttalib
Mother of Muhammad
Clan of Zuhrah (Tribe of Quraysh)

Aminah was married to 'Abd Allah at the same time that her first cousin Halah married 'Abd Allah's father 'Abd al-Muttalib. She took her 6-year-old son to Yathrib but died in Abwa' on the return journey.

'Amir ibn al-Hadrami

Brother of 'Amr ibn al-Hadrami
Tribe of Kindah (confederate of 'Abdu Shams)

At Badr, 'Amir goaded the Quraysh to seek revenge for the death of his brother 'Amr, who was killed at Nakhlah by nine Emigrants during the sacred month of Rajab.

'Amir ibn Fuhayrah

Clan unspecified (Mecca)

'Amir was an indentured shepherd who embraced Islam early on in Mecca. He was freed by Abu Bakr and subsequently took care of Abu Bakr's flock. He covered the tracks of the Prophet and Abu Bakr when they escaped Mecca. After Uhud, the Prophet sent him with a delegation of 40 men to teach Islam to the Hawazin clan of 'Amir, but the party was ambushed and massacred. When 'Amir's body was not found among the dead, the Prophet confirmed that 'Amir had been physically lifted up to heaven.

'Ammar ibn Yasir

Son of Yasir ibn 'Amir and Sumayyah bint Khubbat
Clan of Makhzum (Tribe of Quraysh)

During the early Meccan period, 'Ammar and his family refused to renounce their belief in Islam, even under torture by Abu Jahl and his clansmen. His mother Sumayyah was tortured to death, and the Prophet later referred to 'Ammar as one of three Companions for whom Paradise longs.

'Amr ibn Abi Sufyan

Son of Abu Sufyan ibn al-Harb
Brother of Hanzalah ibn Abi Sufyan
Clan of 'Abdu Shams (Tribe of Quraysh)

'Amr and his brother Hanzalah fought against the Prophet at Badr. Hanzalah was killed and 'Amr was taken captive. His father, Abu Sufyan, managed to bring him back to Mecca.

'Amr ibn al-'As

Son of al-'As ibn Wa'il (chief of Sahm)
Half-brother of Hisham ibn al-'As
Father of 'Abd Allah ibn 'Amr al-'As
Clan of Sahm (Tribe of Quraysh)

The Quraysh sent 'Amr to Abyssinia to persuade the Negus to deny asylum to the Muslim emigrants. 'Amr challenged Ja'far to explain Islam's view of Jesus, but the ploy backfired and he returned to Mecca empty-handed. Ironically, 'Amr fled to Abyssinia to seek asylum from the Muslims as they conquered Mecca. The Negus advised him to return to Medina and accept the Prophet's message. When 'Amr finally embraced Islam, he was unable to look at the Prophet's face out of reverence. The Prophet chose him to lead an army of 500 men to the Syrian border.

'Amr ibn al-Hadrami

Brother of 'Amir ibn al-Hadrami
Tribe of Kindah (confederate of 'Abdu Shams, tribe of Quraysh)

'Amr was killed at Nakhlah when his caravan was raided by nine Emigrants during the sacred month of Rajab. His brother 'Amir sought his revenge, and urged the Meccans to attack the Prophet at Badr.

'Amr ibn Asad

Brother of Khuwaylid ibn Asad (Khadijah's father)
Uncle of Khadijah bint Khuwaylid
Clan of Asad (Tribe of Quraysh)

'Amr consented to his niece Khadijah's marriage to Muhammad.

'Amr ibn Jamuh

Clan unspecified (Medina)

After 'Amr was martyred at Uhud, his sister tried to take his body back to Medina. The Prophet intervened and ordered that he be buried at Uhud with the other martyrs.

'Amr ibn Nufayl

*Half-brother of Khattab ibn Nufayl
(through different mothers)
Uncle of 'Umar ibn al-Khattab
Father of Zayd ibn 'Amr
Clan of 'Adi (Tribe of Quraysh)*

'Amr was the half-brother of Khattab. When his father died, 'Amr married his father's other wife (Khattab's mother) and had a son named Zayd ibn 'Amr.

'Amr ibn Su'da

Tribe of Qurayzah

During the Battle of the Trench, 'Amr opposed his tribe when they broke their pact with the Prophet. After the battle, the Qurayzah were surrounded, and he suggested they pay a tribute to avoid punishment. They replied that they would rather die than pay a tax, and 'Amr left the fortress to join the Muslims.

'Amr ibn Umayyah ad-Damri

Clan of Damrah (Tribe of Kinanah)

After Uhud, 'Amr joined the delegation of 40 men headed to the Hawazin clan of 'Amir that was ambushed by Bani Sulaym. As the only survivor, 'Amr was responsible for identifying the bodies of his companions before returning to Medina. On the way back, he wrongfully killed two men from Bani 'Amir, thinking they were responsible for the attack.

'Amr ibn Umayyah ath-Thaqifi

Chief of the clan of Thaqif (Tribe of Hawazin)

'Amr was the chief of Ta'if during the leadership of Walid ibn al-Mughirah in Mecca. When the Prophet visited Ta'if, he was ridiculed by 'Amr's three sons, who had become the city's leaders.

Anas ibn Malik

*Son of Umm Sulaym bint Milhan
Clan unspecified (Medina)*

Anas was named after his uncle Anas ibn Nadir. At the age of 10, his mother gave him to the Prophet as a servant. He dutifully served in the household until the Prophet's death about eight years later. Given his close relationship with the Prophet, he later becomes one of the most authoritative scholars on Qur'an and hadith.

Anas ibn Nadr

*Brother of Rubayyi' bint an-Nadr
Uncle of Anas ibn Malik
Uncle of Harithah ibn Suraqah
Clan unspecified (Medina)*

When morale plummeted at Uhud after rumors of the Prophet's death began to circulate, Anas cried out, "What are you waiting for? What do you live for after Muhammad? Come on and die for what Allah's Messenger has died for." He fought so fiercely that after the battle, his body was found with more than 80 wounds, and was only recognizable by his fingers.

'Aqil ibn Abi Talib

Son of Abu Talib ibn 'Abd al-Muttalib
Brother of Talib, Ja'far, Ali, and Umm Hani
First cousin of Muhammad
Clan of Hashim (Tribe of Quraysh)

At first, 'Aqil and his brother Talib did not join their younger brothers Ja'far and 'Ali in support of the Prophet. 'Aqil marched alongside the Meccans at Badr and was captured. Five years later, he embraced Islam and the Prophet said to him, "I love thee with two loves, for thy near kinship unto me, and for the love that I ever saw for thee in mine uncle."

Arqam ibn 'Abdi Manaf

Second cousin of Abu Salamah
Clan of Makhzum (Tribe of Quraysh)

Arqam was a wealthy Makhzumi who donated his house at the foot of Mount Safa to the service of Islam during the Early Meccan Period.

Arwa bint 'Abd al-Muttalib

Daughter of 'Abd al-Muttalib ibn Hashim
Mother of Tulayb ibn 'Umayr
Paternal aunt of Muhammad
Clan of Hashim (Tribe of Quraysh)

Initially, Arwa held out for a while before embracing Islam, saying she wanted to see what the rest of her sisters planned to do. Ultimately she was challenged by her 15-year-old son Tulayb and she accepted Islam.

As'ad ibn Zurahah

First cousin of Sa'd ibn Mu'adh
Clan of Khazraj (Medina)

As'ad was the first of six Khazraj pilgrims from Yathrib to pledge themselves to the Prophet (before the First 'Aqabah) and later housed Mus'ab ibn 'Umayr when Mus'ab arrived in Medina before the Hijrah. When the Prophet arrived one year later, As'ad arranged the sale of the orphans' (Sahl and Suhayl) courtyard to the Prophet. As'ad died shortly after the Hijrah. At his funeral, Salman al-Farisi entered Islam.

Ashamah

See "Negus"

Asma' bint Abi Bakr

Daughter of Abu Bakr and Qutaylah
Full sister to 'Abd Allah ibn Abi Bakr
Half-sister to 'A'ishah bint Abi Bakr
Wife of Zubayr ibn al-'Awwam (Prophet's cousin)
Clan of Taym (Tribe of Quraysh)

Asma' entered Islam in Mecca and helped her father and the Prophet escape to Medina. She tore her girdle in half to lash provisions for the two men and came to be known as "she of the two girdles." She married the Prophet's first cousin Zubayr ibn al-'Awwam.

'Asma' bint al-Harith

Half-sister of Umm al-Fadl and Maymunah
 bint al-Harith
Wife of Walid ibn al-Mughirah
Mother of Khalid ibn al-Walid
Clan of Makhzum (Tribe of Quraysh)

'Asma' entered Islam before her son Khalid, which left a lasting impression on him.

Asma' bint Umays

Half-sister (maternal) of Umm al-Fadl bint al-Harith
Wife of Ja'far ibn Abi Talib
Wife of Abu Bakr ibn Abi Quhafah
 (after the death of Ja'far)
Mother of Muhammad ibn Abi Bakr
Clan unspecified (Tribe of Quraysh)

Asma' followed her sister Umm al-Fadl into Islam. She migrated to Abyssinia with Ja'far and returned 13 years later. After Ja'far's death on an expedition in Syria, she married Abu Bakr and they had a child whom they named Muhammad.

Aswad ibn ʿAbd al-Asad

Clan of Makhzum (Tribe of Quraysh)

ʿAswad was killed by Hamzah at Badr. He was the first Meccan to be slain when he tried to drink at the Badri wells controlled by the Muslims.

Aswad ibn Kaʿb

Clan unspecified (Yemen)

Aswad was a false prophet who emerged after the Conquest of Mecca. His pride got the best of him and his own people assassinated him.

Aswad ibn Nawfal

Son of Nawfal ibn Khuwaylid
Nephew of Khadijah bint Khuwaylid
Clan of Asad (Tribe of Quraysh)

Nawfal first heard about Islam through Abu Bakr and Talhah. His father Nawfal (the half-brother of Khadijah) attacked the two men for talking to his son about Islam. Aswad embraced Islam in Mecca.

ʿAtikah bint ʿAbd al-Muttalib

Daughter of ʿAbd al-Muttalib ibn Hashim
Wife of Abu Umayyah (Makhzumi)
Mother of ʿAbd Allah and Zuhayr ibn ʿAbi Umayyah
Aunt of Muhammad
Clan of Hashim (Tribe of Quraysh)

ʿAtika was one of the Prophet's paternal aunts who married a man from Makhzum. Although her son ʿAbd Allah was named after the Prophet's father, he was a bitter enemy of the Prophet. Before Badr, ʿAtikah dreamt that the Quraysh would be destroyed. She later entered Islam prior to her two sons.

ʿAwf ibn al-Harith

Brother of Muʿadh and Muʿawwidh ibn al-Harith
Clan of Khazraj (Sub-clan of Najjar, Medina)

ʿAwf was one of the Khazraj pilgrims present at the First ʿAqabah. At the opening duels of Badr, he sought to answer ʿUtbah ibn Rabiʿah's challenge, but was held back by the Prophet, who sent his own family to fight. ʿAwf fought without his chainmail and was martyred.

ʿAwwam ibn Khuwaylid

Brother of Khadijah bint Khuwaylid
First cousin of Waraqah and Qutaylah bint Nawfal
Husband of Safiyyah bint ʿAbd al-Muttalib
Father to Zubayr ibn al-ʿAwwam
Clan of Asad (Tribe of Quraysh)

ʿAwwam married Safiyyah, the Prophet's paternal aunt.

ʿAyyash ibn Abi Rabiʿah

Half-brother of Abu Jahl and Harith ibn Hisham
Clan of Makhzum (Tribe of Quraysh)

ʿAyyash migrated to Medina with ʿUmar ibn al-Khattab but Abu Jahl and Harith persuaded him to return by informing him that his mother had taken an oath of self-neglect if he did not return. When he entered Mecca, his half-brothers bound him up and forced him to renounce his faith. Despite their efforts, ʿAyyash returned to Islam.

Ayman ibn ʿUbayd

Son of Umm Ayman (aka Barakah)
Half-brother of Usamah ibn Zayd
Clan unspecified

At the Battle of Hunayn, Ayman rode by the Prophet's side and was killed by the enemy.

B

Bahira

Clan unspecified

Bahira was a Christian monk in Syria who recognized young Muhammad as a future prophet. He instructed Abu Talib to guard over his special nephew.

Bara' ibn Mar'ur

Father of Bishr ibn Bara'
Tribe of Khazraj (Medina)

Bara' was the chief of a Khazraj clan. On his way south to meet the Prophet at the Second 'Aqabah, he was inspired to pray toward Mecca while the other pilgrims prayed toward Jerusalem.

Barakah

See Umm Ayman

Barrah bint 'Abd al-Muttalib

Daughter of 'Abd al-Muttalib ibn Hashim
Wife of 'Abd al-Asad (Makhzumi)
Mother of Abu Salamah and Abu Sabrah
(half-brothers)
Aunt of Muhammad
Clan of Hashim (Tribe of Quraysh)

Barrah was first married to a man of Makhzum and gave birth to Abu Salamah. After her husband's death, she married a man from the clan of 'Amir and gave birth to Abu Sabrah. Both her sons migrated to Abyssinia. Later her widowed daughter-in-law Umm Salamah married the Prophet in Medina.

Bilal

Abyssinian slave of Umayyah ibn Khalaf
(chief of Jumah clan)

Bilal was tortured by Umayyah ibn Khalaf for converting to Islam. Abu Bakr bought Bilal's freedom, and he later became the first muezzin (person who delivers the call to prayer). He slew Umayyah after Badr. Upon entering Mecca for the first full pilgrimage in 629 CE, he stood atop the Ka'bah and gave the call to prayer. Later that year, during the Conquest of Mecca, the Prophet entered the Ka'bah with Usamah, Bilal, and 'Uthman ibn Talhah by his side.

Bishr ibn Bara'

Son of Bara' ibn Mar'ur
Clan of Khazraj (Medina)

After the fall of Khaybar, Bishr died when he ate poisoned food that was intended for the Prophet.

Budayl ibn Warqa'

Clan of Khuza'ah

Budayl, a Khuza'ite, was in Mecca when the Prophet arrived at Hudaybiyah for the pilgrimage. Budayl went to Hudaybiyah to warn the Prophet that the Quraysh would not let him enter Mecca for the pilgrimage. After the dissolution of the Hudaybiyah Pact, Budayl joined Abu Sufyan ibn al-Harb in a last-minute appeal to stop the Prophet's army outside Mecca. At the Prophet's camp, Budayl testified his faith. Soon after, at the Battle of Hunayn, he was placed in charge of transporting all the captives and spoils from Hunayn to the Valley of Ji'ranah.

C

Chosroes II
Persian ruler

Chosroes II was the Persian emperor who was killed by his own son shortly after the Treaty of Hudaybiyah. His son Kavadh II ripped up the Prophet's letter of invitation to Islam.

D

Damdam al-Ghifari
Tribe of Ghifar

Damdam was hired by Abu Sufyan to urgently call the Meccans to Badr to protect his southbound caravan from the Muslims.

Du'thur ibn al-Harith
Chief of the clan of Muharib, sub-clan of Sulaym (Tribe of Hawazin)

During the Prophet's expedition against Bani Muharib, Du'thur crept up on the Prophet while he was asleep and raised his sword to kill him. When Du'thur was abruptly thrust back by the Angel Gabriel, he recognized it was a miraculous force and he embraced Islam.

F

Fadl ibn al-'Abbas
Eldest son of 'Abbas ibn 'Abd al-Muttalib and Umm al-Fadl bint al-Harith
First cousin of the Prophet
Clan of Hashim (Tribe of Quraysh)

Fadl was a beloved cousin of the Prophet and would visit him when the Prophet stayed with Fadl's maternal aunt Maymunah, the Prophet's aunt. When Fadl and his parents decided to join the Prophet before the Conquest of Mecca, they met the southward marching army and joined in. Two years later, Fadl and Usamah prepared Ibrahim's body for burial (the Prophet's son with Mariyah). Fadl later helped prepare the Prophet's body for burial.

Fakhitah bint Abi Talib
See Umm Hani Bint Abi Talib

Fatimah bint ʿAmr

Wife of ʿAbd al-Muttalib ibn Hashim
Mother of Zubayr, Abu Talib, Umaymah and
*   ʿAbd Allah*
Grandmother of Muhammad
Clan of Makhzum (Tribe of Quraysh)

Fatimah was from the powerful clan of Makhzum and was the most influential of ʿAbd al-Muttalib's wives.

Fatimah bint Asad

Wife of Abu Talib ibn ʿAbd al-Muttalib
Mother of Talib, ʿAqil, Jaʿfar, ʿAli, and Umm Hani
Clan unspecified (Tribe of Quraysh)

Fatimah served as a second mother to the Prophet after the death of Aminah and ʿAbd al-Muttalib. Many years later, the Prophet would say that Fatimah would feed him, even if it meant not feeding her own children.

Fatimah bint Khattab

Daughter of Khattab ibn Nufayl
Sister of ʿUmar ibn al-Khattab
Wife of Saʿid ibn Zayd
Clan of ʿAdi (Tribe of Quraysh)

Fatimah and her husband Saʿid were early converts in Mecca. When her brother ʿUmar heard of their conversion, he stormed into their house and hit her while attacking her husband.

Fatimah bint Muhammad

Fourth daughter of Muhammad and Khadijah
*   bint Khuwaylid*
Wife of ʿAli ibn Abi Talib
Mother of Hasan, Husayn, and Zaynab bint ʿAli
Clan of Hashim (Tribe of Quraysh)

After moving to Medina, Fatimah dedicated her time to caring for the People of the Bench. Abu Bakr and ʿUmar asked to marry her when she was in her 20s, but the Prophet instead arranged her marriage to ʿAli. The couple asked the Prophet for a servant, but he turned down their request and instead taught them how to increase their remembrance of God after every prayer, which he said was better than what they requested. Fatimah had a unique relationship with her father, and was by his side during much of his life. For this reason, Zaynab bint Jahsh and his other wives asked her to tell her father to remain impartial toward ʿAʾishah. Fatimah was with the Prophet after Uhud and dressed his many wounds. During the Prophet's last Ramadan, he told Fatimah that Gabriel had recited the Qurʾan twice with him, signifying that it was the last time they would review it together. Just before his death, he whispered to her that he would not recover from his illness, and then told her that she would be the first from his family to follow him. The Prophet once told Fatimah, she was the best of women, second to Mary, mother of Jesus.

G

Gabriel

The angel Gabriel transmitted the Qurʾan to the Prophet over a 23-year period. He is recognized as an archangel in Judaism, Christianity, and Islam.

H

Habbar ibn al-Asad

Tribe of Quraysh (clan unspecified)

Habbar rode out of Mecca to stop Kinanah ibn ar-Rabi' from escorting the Prophet's pregnant daughter Zaynab and granddaughter 'Umamah to Medina. He frightened Zaynab and she later miscarried.

Hafsah bint 'Umar

Daughter of 'Umar ibn al-Khattab and Zaynab bint Maz'un
Wife of Khunays ibn Hudhafah (Sahmi)
Fourth wife of the Prophet
Clan of 'Adi (Tribe of Quraysh)

Hafsah migrated to Medina with her husband, but was widowed at age 18 when Khunays died shortly after Badr. Known for her beauty and intelligence, she could read and write like her father. When 'Umar tried to get her remarried, he was turned down by Abu Bakr and 'Uthman, but found a son-in-law in Prophet. Hafsah joined the household before Uhud, and became good friends with 'A'ishah and Sawdah, and later Safiyyah. Several years later, when the Prophet began spending time with Mariyah, Hafsah and 'A'ishah vented the wives' dissatisfaction to him. The Qur'an responded to all the wives in Surah At-Tahreem (Prohibition).

Hagar

Wife of Abraham
Mother of Ishmael

According to God's command, Abraham left Hagar in the barren valley of Becca with her son Ishmael. She desperately searched for water by running seven times between the hills of Safa and Marwah, before the water miraculously sprang up at th baby's feet. The pre-Islamic Arabs and later the Prophet commemorated her footsteps as one of the rites of the annual Hajj pilgrimage.

Hakam

(last name unspecified)

Hakam was captured during the caravan raid at Nakhlah by 'Abd Allah ibn Jahsh. When he was brought to Medina, he embraced Islam and did not return to Mecca.

Hakim ibn Hizam

Son of Hizam ibn Khuwaylid (brother of Khadijah)
Brother of Khalid ibn Hizam
Nephew of Khadijah and Muhammad
Clan of Asad (Tribe of Quraysh)

Hakim loved Khadijah and her family but did not embrace Islam in the early days in Mecca. He purchased Zayd at a market in Ukaz (near Ta'if) and gave him to Khadijah. He supplied the Muslims with necessities during the ban on Hashim. At Badr, he made a last-minute attempt to persuade the Meccans to avoid fighting. Nearly six years later, he joined Abu Sufyan and made a last-minute appeal to the Prophet's advancing army outside Mecca. At the Prophet's camp, he converted to Islam. Soon after, the Prophet awarded him a generous portion of the spoils after Hunayn.

Halah bint Khuwaylid

Sister of Khadijah bint Khuwaylid
Mother of Abu l-'As ibn ar-Rabi'
Clan of Asad (Tribe of Quraysh)

Halah was Khadijah's beloved sister who agreed to marry her son Abu l-'As to Khadijah's eldest daughter Zaynab. After Khaybar, she visited her son's family. When the Prophet heard her voice, he trembled because of its close resemblance to his late beloved wife.

Halah bint Wuhayb

Daughter of Wuhayb ibn Abi Wahb
First cousin of Aminah bint Wahb
Wife of 'Abd al-Muttalib ibn Hashim
Mother of Hamzah and Safiyyah
Clan of Zuhrah (Tribe of Quraysh)

Halah married 'Abd al-Muttalib at the same ceremony that her first cousin Aminah married 'Abd al-Muttalib's son 'Abd Allah. Her children became close friends and confidants to the Prophet.

Halimah bint Abi Dhu'ayb

Daughter of Abu Dhu'ayb
Wife of Harith ibn 'Abd al-'Uzzah
Nursemaid of Muhammad
Clan of Sa'd ibn Bakr (Tribe of Hawazin)

Unable to find a suitable nursling, Halimah finally agreed to take Aminah's orphaned son Muhammad into her care. She was also the nursemaid to the Prophet's first cousin Abu Sufyan ibn al-Harith.

Hamnah bint Jahsh

Daughter of Jahsh ibn Ri'ab and Umaymah bint
* 'Abd al-Muttalib*
Sister of 'Ubayd Allah, 'Abd Allah, and Zaynab
Wife of Mus'ab ibn 'Umayr
Wife of Talhah ibn 'Ubayd Allah
First cousin of Muhammad
Clan of 'Abdu Shams (Tribe of Quraysh)*

Hamnah was a beloved cousin of the Prophet who lost her uncle (Hamzah), husband (Mus'ab), and brother ('Abd Allah) at Uhud. One year later, she spread rumors about 'A'ishah in Medina, but was later forgiven by the Prophet. He subsequently arranged her marriage to Talhah ibn 'Ubayd Allah.

*Hamnah's father was from the distant tribe of Asad and was given honorary membership in 'Abdu Shams.

Hamzah ibn 'Abd al-Muttalib

Son of 'Abd al-Muttalib ibn Hashim and Halah
* bint Wuhayb*
Husband of Salma' bint 'Umays
Father of 'Umarah bint Hamzah
Paternal uncle and maternal cousin of Muhammad
Clan of Hashim (Tribe of Quraysh)

Hamzah was the Prophet's youngest uncle and one of his closest Companions. The two played together as children and later, Hamzah escorted the Prophet to the house of 'Amr ibn Asad to ask for Khadijah's hand in marriage. He defended the Prophet against Abu Jahl's verbal assault and testified to his nephew's religion on the spot. At the Pact of Brotherhood, the Prophet linked Hamzah with Zayd ibn Harithah. Hamzah won the opening duels at Badr and Uhud. He was killed at Uhud by Wahshi, and his body was mutilated by Hind. The Prophet buried his uncle on the battlefield next to 'Abd Allah ibn Jahsh.

Hanzalah at-Tamimi

Tribe of Tamim

Hanzalah was from the distant tribe of Tamim but had settled in Medina. He approached Abu Bakr worried that his inconsistent faith was a sign of hypocrisy. The two approached the Prophet, who assured them it was human nature for one's faith to wax and wane.

Hanzalah ibn Abi 'Amir

Son of Abu 'Amir ibn Sayfi (the monk)
Husband of Jamilah bint 'Abd Allah ibn Ubayy
Clan of Aws (Medina)

Hanzalah married Jamilah, the daughter of 'Abd Allah ibn Ubayy, the night before Uhud. He set out to catch up with the army the next day and was martyred on the battlefield.

Hanzalah ibn Abi Sufyan

Son of Abu Sufyan ibn al-Harb
Brother of 'Amr ibn Abi Sufyan
Clan of 'Abdu Shams (Tribe of Quraysh)

Hanzalah and his brother 'Amr fought against the Prophet at Badr. Hanzalah was killed and his brother was taken captive. His death was one of many reasons his father led the Meccan army at Uhud.

Harb ibn Umayyah

Grandson of 'Abdu Shams ibn 'Abdi Manaf
Son of Umayyah ibn 'Abdu Shams
Father of Abu Sufyan ibn al-Harb
Clan of 'Abdu Shams (Tribe of Quraysh)

After his father's death, Harb became the chief of the Umayyad branch of the clan of 'Abdu Shams. He granted clan membership to Jahsh ibn Ri'ab, the husband of the Prophet's paternal aunt Umaymah.

Harith al-Muzani

Tribe of Muzaynah (Bedouin tribe)

Harith was a Bedouin convert who valiantly defended the Prophet at Uhud.

Harith ibn 'Abd al-Muttalib

Eldest son of 'Abd al-Muttalib ibn Hashim
Father of Abu Sufyan ibn al-Harith
Half-uncle of Muhammad
Clan of Hashim (Tribe of Quraysh)

Harith was the Prophet's eldest uncle. In the early years, he helped his father, 'Abd al-Muttalib, uncover the well of Zamzam. He died before the Prophet received his first revelation. Harith's son Abu Sufyan was the Prophet's foster-brother but resisted Islam for most of his life.

Harith ibn 'Abd al-'Uzzah

Husband of Halimah bint Abi Dh'ayb
   (nursemaid of Muhammad)
Father of Shayma' bint al-Harith
Clan of Sa'd ibn Bakr (Tribe of Hawazin)

Harith and his wife agreed to take young Muhammad under their foster-care. Harith died sometime thereafter. After Hunayn, Harith's brother approached the Prophet and asked him if he would release all the captives held in Ji'ranah.

Harith ibn Abi Durar

Father of Juwayriyah bint al-Harith
   (eighth wife of the Prophet)
Chief of Bani Mustaliq (Tribe of Khuza'ah)

When Harith's clan was captured, he came to pay his daughter's ransom, and the Prophet asked him why he hid two of his best camels from the ransom total. The Prophet's insight led him to embrace Islam. He approved Juwayriyah's marriage to the Prophet, and upon their wedding, the Muslims released over 100 families of Bani Mustaliq.

Harith ibn as-Simmah

Clan of Khazraj (Medina)

The Prophet used Harith's spear to kill Ubayy ibn Khalaf at Uhud. After the battle, Harith found Hamzah's mutilated body and was aghast. He was sent with a peaceful delegation of 40 men to teach Islam the Hawazin clan of 'Amir. The group was ambushed by Bani Sulaym while Harith and another Companion were away herding the animals. When he returned and found his companions slaughtered, he refused to be taken captive but asked to be given a sword to fight the men of Bani Sulaym until his death.

Harith ibn Hisham

Nephew of Walid ibn al-Mughirah (chief of Makhzum)
Son of Hisham ibn al-Mughirah
Full brother of Abu Jahl
Uncle of 'Ikrimah ibn Abi Jahl
Clan of Makhzum (Tribe of Quraysh)

Harith and his brother Abu Jahl tricked their maternal half-brother 'Ayyash, into returning from Medina to release their mother from her oath of self-neglect. When 'Ayyash arrived in Mecca, his brother imprisoned him.

Harith ibn 'Umayr

Clan unspecified

The Prophet sent Harith as a messenger to the Roman governor of Syria with an invitation to Islam. He was murdered by the Ghassanids, who had intercepted him along his route. His death prompted the Prophet to dispatch Zayd at the head of 3,000 men to the Syrian border (Mu'tah expedition).

Harithah ibn Nu'man

Clan of Khazraj (Medina)

After Fatimah's marriage to 'Ali, Harithah gave his house to the newlyweds so they could live closer to the Prophet.

Harithah ibn Sharahil

Brother of Ka'b ibn Sharahil
Father of Zayd ibn Harithah
  (adopted son of Muhammad)
Tribe of Kalb (between Syria and Iraq)

When Harithah heard that his son Zayd was a slave in Mecca, he visited Muhammad, prepared to pay for his son's release. Muhammad acknowledged Harithah's right to be reunited with his son and gave Zayd the option to leave. Zayd chose to stay with Muhammad, who publicly declared Zayd his son in front of his father and uncle.

Harithah ibn Suraqah

Son of Rubayyi' bint an-Nadr
Clan of Khazraj (Medina)

Harithah was the first person killed before the Battle of Badr when he was hit by an enemy arrow while drinking from a well. The Prophet reassured Harithah's mother that he was a martyr, telling her that all deeds are counted according to their intention.

Hasan ibn 'Ali

First son of 'Ali ibn Abi Talib and Fatimah
  bint Muhammad
Brother of Husayn and Zaynab bint 'Ali
Grandson of Muhammad
Clan of Hashim (Tribe of Quraysh)

Hasan was born between the Badr and Uhud. He was the beloved grandson of the Prophet, who once said, "The dearest unto me of the people of my house are Hasan and Husayn." Hasan was 8 when the Prophet died.

Hashim ibn 'Abdi Manaf

Son of 'Abdu Manaf ibn Qusayy
Husband of Salma' bint 'Amr
Father of 'Abd al-Muttalib (aka Shaybah)
Great-grandfather of Muhammad
Clan of Hashim (Tribe of Quraysh)

Hashim was an exceptional man of his generation and was chosen by his peers (the Scented Ones) to take control of Quraysh leadership from the clan of 'Abd ad-Dar. He was credited for establishing the summer and winter caravan routes that transformed Mecca into a commercial trading center. Hashim died while on a caravan trip in Gaza, leaving his wife and son Shaybah behind. His brother Muttalib succeeded him as leader of the Scented Ones.

Hassan ibn Thabit

Clan unspecified

Hassan was a poet from Medina who spread false rumors about 'A'ishah after the Battle of the Trench. After the incident was resolved, the Prophet forgave him. In fact, when the Prophet later received Mariyah and Sirin as gifts from the Muqawqis, he gave Sirin to Hassan.

Hatib ibn 'Amr

Brother of Suhay, Salit, Sakran, and Hatib ibn 'Amr
Clan of 'Amir (Tribe of Quraysh)

Much to his brother Suhayl's dismay, Hatib embraced Islam in Mecca. He migrated to Abyssinia and returned after the ban on Hashim was lifted. Just before the Conquest of Mecca, Hatib sent a message to his son warning him about the impending invasion. His message was intercepted, but the Prophet instructed the Companions to forgive him because he fought with them at Badr.

Heraclius

Roman emperor

Heraclius ruled the Roman emperor from 610-641 CE, spanning the entire period of Qur'anic revelation. He defeated the Persian army in 627 CE, and later regained control of Jerusalem. Just before the Conquest of Mecca, Heraclius questioned Abu Sufyan about the Prophet's mission. He was inclined to Muhammad's prophethood but could not persuade his chiefs to form an alliance with Medina.

Hisham ibn al-'As

Son of al-'As ibn Wa'il (chief of Sahm)
Half-brother of 'Amr ibn al-'As
Clan of Sahm (Tribe of Quraysh)

Hisham migrated to Abyssinia and watched his half-brother 'Amr ibn al-'As fail to persuade the Negus to return the Muslims to Mecca. He returned after the ban on Hashim was lifted. Hisham agreed to migrate to Medina with 'Umar ibn al-Khattab and 'Ayyash ibn Abi Rabi'ah, but his father and brother forced him to stay and renounce his Islam. He later renewed his faith and joined the Emigrants in Medina. Many years later, he rejoiced when his brother 'Amr finally embraced Islam.

Hisham ibn al-Walid

Son of Walid ibn al-Mughirah (late chief of Makhzum)
Full brother of Walid and half-brother of Khalid
Clan of Makhzum (Tribe of Quraysh)

After Badr, Hisham and Khalid ransomed their father's famous armor for their captive brother Walid. But when they were returning to Mecca with Walid, Walid escaped back to Medina and entered Islam. Several years later, Hisham entered Islam at Ji'ranah after Hunayn.

Hisham ibn 'Amr

Clan of 'Amir (Tribe of Quraysh)

During the ban on Hashim, Hisham regularly sent supplies to Abu Talib's house. Nearly thre years later, he led the push to end the sanctions.

Hind bint 'Utbah

Daughter of 'Utbah ibn Rabi'ah
Sister of Walid ibn 'Utbah
Wife of Abu Sufyan ibn al-Harb
Clan of 'Abdu Shams (Tribe of Quraysh)

Hind lost her father 'Utbah, uncle Shaybah, and brother Walid at Badr. She vowed to eat the raw liver of Hamzah who killed her father and uncle in the battle. After Uhud, she and several others mutilate the bodies of the martyred. After the Conquest of Mecca, she sought the Prophet's forgiveness and entered Islam.

Hizam ibn Khuwaylid

Brother of Khadijah bint Khuwaylid
Father of Hakim and Khalid
Clan of Asad (Tribe of Quraysh)

Hizam's son Hakim purchased Zayd ibn Harithah at a market in Ukaz (near Ta'if) and gave him to Khadijah.

Hubab ibn al-Mundhir

Clan of Khazraj (Medina)

As the Prophet's army approached Badr, Hubab made a tactical suggestion to the Prophet that they continue marching to the farthest well, nearest the Meccan army, and take control of all the wells. He later carried one of three banners at Uhud.

Hubal (idol)

Chief idol of the Quraysh
Associated with sister idols Al-Lat, Al-Manat,
and al-'Uzzah

Hubal was a Moabite idol brought to Mecca by the tribe of Khuza'ah. It was later destroyed by the Prophet at the Conquest of Mecca.

Hubayrah ibn Abi Wahb

Husband of Umm Hani bint Abi Talib
Clan of Makhzum (Tribe of Quraysh)

Abu Talib preferred Hubayrah to Muhammad as a son-in-law for his daughter Umm Hani. Hubayrah was a gifted poet who left his wife in Mecca (before the Conquest) to live in Najran.

Hudhayfah ibn al-Yaman

Clan unspecified

As the standoff at the Trench neared its end, the Prophet asked Hudhayfah to venture out into the bitter rain and howling winds to obtain news about the Meccan army's movements. He reported that Abu Sufyan had ordered the weary Quraysh army to return home.

Hulayl ibn Hubshiyah

Father-in-law of Qusayy ibn Kilab
Chief of the tribe of Khuza'ah

Hulayl married his daughter to Qusayy ibn Kilab and later favored him over his own sons as a successor and keeper of the Ka'bah. After Hulayl's death, Qusayy established himself and his tribe of Quraysh as rulers of Mecca.

Hulays ibn 'Alqamah

Clan of Harith (Tribe of Kinanah)

Hulays fought on the Meccan side at Uhud but rebuked Abu Sufyan for allowing the mutilation of Muslim bodies. Four years later, the Quraysh sent Hulays to scout the enemy position at Hudaybiyah. However, when he returned to tell them that the Prophet had come in peace, the Quraysh dismissed his opinion as that of an outsider. Hulays responded by threatening to break the Quraysh's valuable alliance with all the Ahabish (Bedouin tribes of the desert).

Husayn ibn 'Ali

*Second son of 'Ali ibn 'Abi Talib and Fatimah
bint Muhammad
Brother of Hasan and Zaynab bint 'Ali
Grandson of Muhammad
Clan of Hashim (Tribe of Quraysh)*

Husayn was born after Uhud. He was the beloved grandson of the Prophet, who once said, "The dearest unto me of the people of my house are Hasan and Husayn." Husayn was 7when the Prophet died.

Huwaytib ibn 'Abd al-'Uzzah

Clan unspecified (Tribe of Quraysh)

The Quraysh sent Huwaytib with Suhayl ibn 'Amr al-'Amiri to negotiate the Treaty of Hudaybiyah with the Prophet.

Huyay ibn Akhtab

*Father of Safiyyah bint Huyay (10th wife of
the Prophet)
Father-in-law of Kinanah ibn Abi l-Huqayq
Chief of the Tribe of Nadir (Medina)*

After Uhud, Huyay's plot to kill the Prophet was foiled and his clan of Nadir was exiled from Medina. He sought refuge in Khaybar, but returned to Medina during the Battle of the Trench to persuade Bani Qurayzah to break their pact with the Prophet. Huyay's plan backfired when Nu'aym ibn Mas'ud planted seeds of doubt between the Qurayzah and Quraysh. When the Qurayzah were defeated, Huyay was executed along with the men of Qurayzah for treason.

I/'I

Ibn ad-Dughannah

Confederate of Qurayzah (Medina)

Ibn ad-Dughannah was the leader of a small group of confederate tribes near the Red Sea. Prior to the Hijrah, he encountered Abu Bakr—who was migrating to Abyssinia—and promised to protect him if Abu Bakr returned to Mecca.

Ibn al-Hayyaban

Confederate of Tribe of Qurayzah (Medina)

Ibn al-Hayyaban was a saintly Jew who had migrated from Syria to Yathrib and foretold the coming of a prophet. He died before the Prophet arrived in Medina.

Ibn Qami'ah

Clan unspecified (Quraysh of the Outskirts)

During Uhud, Ibn Qami'ah tried to deliver a deathblow to the Prophet, but his strike was deflected by Talhah ibn 'Ubayd Allah. The impact still momentarily stunnned the Prophet and he fell to the ground. Ibn Qami'ah then announced that Muhammad had been killed. It is believed that Ibn Qami'ah killed Mus'ab ibn 'Umayr during the battle.

Ibrahim ibn Muhammad

*Son of Muhammad and Mariyah
Clan of Hashim (Tribe of Quraysh)*

As a toddler, Ibrahim fell ill and died. According to Lings, he could walk and was just starting to talk. The Prophet wept at his grave and instructed his Companions to bury him in the perfect manner.

'Ikrimah ibn Abi Jahl

Great-grandson of Mughirah ibn 'Abd Allah
(late chief of Makhzum)
Son of Abu Jahl ibn Hisham
Husband of Umm Hakim bint al-Harith
Clan of Makhzum (Tribe of Quraysh)

For most of the Prophet's life, 'Ikrimah followed the example of his father, the fiercest of the Prophet's enemies. After the Hijrah, he watched over the imprisoned Muslims in Mecca, and later led a Meccan battalion at Uhud and the Trench. He turned down Khalid ibn al-Walid's request to join him when Khalid decided to migrate to Medina. A few years later, 'Ikrimah unsuccessfully attacked Khalid's forces at the Conquest of Mecca. With nowhere else to go, he fled to the coast but was told to testify his faith in God before boarding a boat to Abyssinia. The incident forced him to reconsider his beliefs, and when his wife sent word to him that the Prophet offered him amnesty, he returned to Mecca to ask the Prophet for forgiveness. He entered Islam and promised to double his efforts toward justice and against oppression.

Isaac

Son of Abraham and Sarah
Half-brother of Ishmael
Father of Jacob
Grandfather of Joseph

Isaac was the forefather of the Hebrew prophets. He and his brother Ishmael buried their father in Hebron.

Ishmael

Son of Abraham and Hagar
Half-brother of Isaac
Father of Nabet, Qidar, and 10 other sons

When he was a baby, Ishmael was taken to the valley of Becca, where he grew up as an archer. He later built the Ka'bah with his father. He married into the clan of Jurhum and had 12 sons who settled throughout Arabia. He and his brother Isaac buried their father in Hebron. Ishmael is buried in the Hijr next to his mother, Hagar.

Iyas ibn Mu'adh

Brother of Sa'd ibn Mu'adh
Clan of Aws (Medina)

Iyas was among a delegation of Aws pilgrims in Mecca when the Prophet invited them to Islam. Iyas was the only one to accept his invitation, and was berated by his elders. He died shortly thereafter and was considered the first Muslim from Yathrib.

J

Jabbar ibn Salma

Clan of Sulaym (Tribe of Hawazin)

Jabbar was one of the men of Bani Sulaym who ambushed 40 Muslims at Ma'unah who were on their way to visit the rival clan of 'Amir to teach them Islam. He later related to the Prophet how 'Amir ibn Fuhayrah declared victory the moment Jabbar's spear pierced his chest. Jabbar described seeing 'Amir's body being lifted up to heaven, and the Prophet confirmed that 'Amir had in fact been raised to Paradise. Jabbar then entered Islam, along with many of his tribesmen who had attacked the envoy.

Jabir ibn 'Abd Allah

Son of 'Abd Allah ibn 'Amr
Clan of Khazraj (Medina)

Before Uhud, Jabir's father sent him home to care for his many sisters, in case he died in battle. The next day, the Prophet allowed Jabir to help the Muslim army chase away the retreating Quraysh army. Jabir was very poor, and on the way back from the second march to Badr, the Prophet "purchased" Jabir's camel from him, only to give it back as a wedding gift. During the digging of the trench, Jabir invited the Prophet to dinner, and the Prophet opened the invitation to all the Companions. With little means to provide for the entire army, Jabir exclaimed, "Verily we are for God, and verily unto Him are we returning!" At the dinner, Prophet blessed the food and there was more than enough for all the guests.

Jadd ibn Qays

Clan unspecified (Medina)

Jadd was the only Companion at Hudaybiyah who did not pledge allegiance to the Prophet at the Pact of Ridwan.

Ja'far ibn Abi Talib

Son of Abu Talib ibn 'Abd al-Muttalib
Foster-son of 'Abbas ibn 'Abd al-Muttalib
Husband of Asma' bint Umays
Father of 'Abd Allah, Muhammad, and 'Awn
First cousin of Muhammad
Clan of Hashim (Tribe of Quraysh)

At 15, Ja'far was adopted by his uncle 'Abbas. He was about 16 years younger than the Prophet, and was one of the first to embrace Islam. The Prophet once said to him, "Thou art like me in looks and in character." At 27, he led a group of emigrants to Abyssinia. He arrived in Medina 15 years later. The Prophet placed him as second-in-command (after Zayd) of the army sent to confront Bani Ghassan near Syria. He was martyred during that confrontation.

Jahsh ibn Ri'ab

Husband of Umaymah bint 'Abd al-Muttalib
Father of 'Abd Allah, 'Ubayd Allah, Zaynab,
*   and Hamnah*
Clan of 'Abdu Shams (Tribe of Quraysh)

Originally from the northern clan of Asad (not the Quraysh clan of Asad), Jahsh settled in Mecca and was given honorary membership by the Quraysh clan of 'Abdu Shams. His children were the Prophet's first cousins and his most loyal supporters.

Jamilah bint 'Abd Allah ibn Ubayy

Daughter of 'Abd Allah ibn Ubayy
Sister of 'Abd Allah ibn 'Abd Allah ibn Ubayy
Wife of Hanzalah ibn Abi 'Amir
Clan of Khazraj (Medina)

Although Jamilah was the daughter of 'Abd Allah ibn Ubayy, she was an ardent supporter of the Prophet. She married Hanzalah ibn Abi 'Amir the day before Uhud, where he was martyred.

Ju'ayl ibn Suraqah

Tribe of Damrah

Ju'ayl was among the Ahl as-Suffa (People of the Bench), and was known for his small stature and considerable piety. As they dug around Medina before the Battle of the Trench, the Companions joyfully sang about Ju'ayl's enthusiastic digging, and the Prophet joined the merriment. Three years later, during the march to Mecca, the Prophet asked Ju'ayl to protect a stray dog and her pups as the army passed by. Despite his considerable poverty, Ju'ayl did not receive any spoils after the Conquest of Mecca.

Jubayr ibn Mut'im

Son of Mut'im ibn 'Adi (chief of Nawfal)
Clan of Nawfal (Tribe of Quraysh)

Jubayr conceded his engagement to 'A'ishah bint Abi Bakr when the Prophet asked to marry her. After Badr, he came to Medina to ransom a few captives. During his visit, he heard a few versus from Surah At-Tur (Mount Tur) and developed a fleeting inclination toward Islam. Still, Jubayr instructed his slave Wahshi to avenge the death of Jubayr's uncle by killing Hamzah at Uhud. Four years later, after the prophet's 'Umrah, Jubayr came to Medina to embrace Islam.

Juhaym ibn as-Salt

Clan of Muttalib (Tribe of Quraysh)

On the eve of Badr, Juhaym dreamed that the Quraysh would be defeated. He dismissed the significance of his dream when his companions mocked him.

Juwayriyah bint Harith

Daughter of Harith ibn Abi Durar (Chief of Mustaliq)
Eighth wife of the Prophet
Clan of Mustaliq (Tribe of Khuza'ah)

After the surrender of her clan of Mustaliq, Juwayriyah approached the Prophet and asked for help paying her ransom. The Prophet offered to pay her ransom and proposed to her as well. Juwayriyah gladly accepted, and the marriage created a strong tie between the Muslims and Bani Mustaliq. After the wedding, the Companions agreed to free more than 100 captive families of her clan. 'A'ishah later said, "I know of no woman who was a greater blessing to her people than she."

K

Ka'b ibn Asad

Tribe of Qurayzah (Medina)

As the chief of Qurayzah, Ka'b agreed to Huyay ibn Akhtab's plan to open the southern border of Medina to the Quraysh, during the Battle of the Trench.

Ka'b ibn Ashraf

Half Arab-half Jewish
Tribe of Nadir (Medina)

Ka'b was a prominent poet who relentlessly slandered the Prophet. He left Medina after the Hijrah and returned shortly after Badr. Upon his arrival, the Prophet instructed Muhammad ibn Maslamah to lure Ka'b out of his house and kill him. The Prophet explained to his Companions that deception was a military tactic in warfare.

Ka'b ibn Malik

Clan of Khazraj (Medina)

Ka'b was present at the 2nd 'Aqabah and pledged to protect the Prophet if under attack. At Uhud, when rumors spread that the Prophet was killed, Ka'b saw that he was still alive and spread the good news. Five years later, the Prophet led an expedition to Tabuk, but Ka'b stayed behind. After 50 days of solitude, he was absolved of his mistake (Quran 9:118).

Ka'b ibn Sharahil

Brother of Harithah ibn Sharahil
Uncle of Zayd ibn Harithah
Tribe of Kalb (between Syria and Iraq)

When Ka'b heard that his nephew Zayd was in Mecca, he accompanied his brother Harithah to bring Zayd home.

Ka'b ibn Zuhayr

Tribe of Muzaynah

Ka'b was one of the two most famous poets in Arabia and lived with the tribe of Ghatafan. He wrote scathing lyrics about the Prophet until the Conquest of Mecca. After Hunayn, he came to Medina, professed his faith and recited an eloquent poem he wrote for the occasion. The Prophet forgave Ka'b and praised his poetry.

Khabbab ibn al-Aratt

Confederate of Zuhrah (Tribe of Quraysh)

Like Zayd, Khabbab was kidnapped and brought to Mecca as a child. He was one of the earliest converts and was abused more than most of his peers. Khabbab was reciting Surah Ta-Ha to 'Umar's sister and her husband, Sa'id, when 'Umar stormed into their house.

Khadijah bint Khuwaylid

Daughter of Khuwaylid ibn Asad
Cousin of Waraqah and Qutaylah bint Nawfal
Aunt of Zubayr ibn al-'Awwam, Abu l-'As ibn
*   ar-Rabi', Aswad ibn Nawfal, and Hakim*
*   and Khalid ibn Hizam*
First wife of the Prophet
Mother of Qasim, Zaynab, Ruqayyah, Umm
Kulthum, Fatimah, and 'Abd Allah
Clan of Asad (Tribe of Quraysh)

Khadijah was the first wife of the Prophet and the very first person to enter Islam. She was his closest Companion and greatest source of strength in the early years of his prophethood. The two were married for 25 years, during which the Prophet did not take any other wife. Many years after Khadijah's death, 'A'ishah noted that the Prophet always regarded Khadijah at a higher level than the rest of his wives.

Khalid ibn al-Walid

Son of Walid ibn al-Mughirah (late chief of
*   Makhzum) and 'Asma' bint al-Harith*
Nephew of Maymunah bint al-Harith
Half-brother to Walid and Hisham ibn al-Walid
First cousin of Abu Jahl ibn Hisham
Nephew-in-law of the Prophet
Clan of Makhzum (Tribe of Quraysh)

After Badr, Khalid and Hisham ransomed their father's famous armor to free their captive brother Walid. However, when they were returning to Mecca, Walid escaped back to Medina and entered Islam. Khalid was a natural leader and commanded Meccan battalions at Uhud and at the Trench. Despite Khalid's animosity toward the Prophet, several of his close family members were devout Muslims including his mother ('Asma'), aunt (Maymunah), and brother (Walid). On several occasions, Walid wrote to Khalid from Medina imploring him to join them. One year after Hudaybiyah, Khalid traveled to Medina with 'Uthman ibn Talhah and 'Amr ibn al-'As. When he testified his faith to the Prophet, he was troubled that his past enmity would not be forgiven. The Prophet warmly embraces him and explains that submission to God washes away all past sins.

GLOSSARY

Khalid ibn al-Walid (cont.)

The Prophet immediately entrusted Khalid to lead the Muslim army. Khalid took part in the Syrian expedition led by Zayd ibn Harithah, and successfully maneuvered the defeated army back home. Khalid led one of four battalions at the Conquest of Mecca and earned the name Saifullah (sword of Allah).

Khalid ibn Hizam

Son of Hizam ibn Khuwaylid
Brother of Hakim ibn Hizam
Nephew of Khadijah bint Khuwaylid
Clan of Asad (Tribe of Quraysh)

Khalid cared for his aunt Khadijah's family yet did not embrace Islam in Mecca.

Khalid ibn Sa'id

Son of Sa'id ibn al-'As
Clan of 'Abdu Shams (Tribe of Quraysh)

Khalid embraced Islam in Mecca after having a vivid dream in which the Prophet saved him from a pit of fire.

Khallad ibn 'Amr

Clan unspecified (Medina)

When Khallad was martyred at Uhud, his mother tried to take his body back to Medina. However, the Prophet instructed her to bury him at Uhud with the rest of the martyrs.

Khattab ibn Nufayl

Half-brother of Zayd ibn 'Amr and 'Amr ibn Nufayl
Husband of Abu Jahl's sister
Father of 'Umar ibn al-Khattab
Clan of 'Adi (Tribe of Quraysh)

Khattab was a staunch polytheist who persecuted his half-brother Zayd ibn 'Amr, forcing him to leave Mecca for Iraq. Khattab raised his son 'Umar to hold fast to the pagan ways of their ancestors.

Khawlah bint al-Hakim

Wife of 'Uthman ibn Maz'un
Clan unspecified (Tribe of Quraysh)

After the death of Khadijah, Khawlah attended to the daily needs of the Prophet's household, and suggested A'ishah and Sawdah as suitable wives for him.

Khaythamah Abu Sa'd

Father of Sa'd ibn Khaythamah
Clan of Aws (Medina)

Before Uhud, Khaythamah saw his martyred son in a dream, beckoning him to Paradise. When the Prophet was debating whether to wait for the enemy in Medina or march to Uhud, Khaythamah argued to take the offensive so he could die and join his son. Khaythamah was martyred at Uhud.

Khirash ibn Umayyah

Tribe of Khuza'ah

From his camp at Hudaybiyah, the Prophet sent Khirash to Mecca as an envoy to the Quraysh. Khirash was unable to negotiate with them and was nearly killed. He returned and advised the Prophet to send a man better protected than he. The Prophet sent 'Uthman ibn 'Affan. Once the treaty was signed, Khirash ritually shaved the Prophet's head to signify the completion of the pilgrimage. The Companions followed the Prophet's example.

Khubayb ibn 'Adi

Clan of Aws (Medina)

Shortly after Uhud, Khubayb and Zayd ibn ad-Dathinah were captured by Bani Hudayl at Raji and sold to the Quraysh. Khubayb was tied up and attacked by 40 boys with spears. During the assault, he made sure to send a message of peace to the Prophet. He died an hour later, reciting the words, "There is no god but God. And Muhammad is the Messenger of God."

Khunays ibn Hudhafah

Husband of Hafsah bint 'Umar
Clan of Sahm (Tribe of Quraysh)

Khunays migrated to Abyssinia and returned after the ban on Hashim was lifted. He married Hafsah in Mecca but died a few years later.

Kinanah ibn Abi l-Huqayq

Husband of Safiyyah bint Huyay
Clan unspecified

Kinanah was the de facto chief of the Jewish fortresses at Khaybar. When his own fortress was surrounded, he agreed that that his people would surrender their property in exchange for safe passage out of Khaybar. Despite the favorable agreement, Kinanah tried to conceal his wealth as he exited the settlement. When his plan was foiled, he was killed for breaking the terms of surrender.

Kinanah ibn ar-Rabi'

Brother of Abu l-'As ibn ar-Rabi'
(husband of Zaynab bint Muhammad)
Clan of 'Abdu Shams (Tribe of Quraysh)

After Badr, Kinanah escorted Zaynab and her daughter Umamah from Mecca to Medina.

Kulthum ibn Hidm

Clan of Aws (Medina)

Kulthum was an elderly man from Quba who housed the Prophet during the Hijrah. He had previously housed Hamzah and Zayd when they had migrated to Medina.

L

Labid ibn al-A'sam

Clan unspecified

Labid was a Jewish mystic who was bribed by the people of Khaybar to place a spell on the Prophet that temporarily affected his memory and strength. Nonetheless, the Prophet ultimately forgave him.

Labid ibn Rabi'ah

Clan unspecified

Labid was widely considered to be one of the two most famous poets in Arabia during the early seventh century. He converted to Islam after the expedition to Tabuk.

Lat, al- (idol)

Sister idol to al-'Uzzah and al-Manat

Al-Lat was the chief idol of Ta'if, several miles east of Mecca. It was destroyed after the Conquest of Mecca by Abu Sufyan ibn al-Harb and Mughirah ibn Shu'bah.

M

Mahmud ibn Maslamah
Clan unspecified

Mahmud was one of the five Companions to sign the Treaty of Hudaybiyah.

Malik ibn 'Awf
Clan of Nasr (Tribe of Hawazin)

Malik a 30-year-old general of the Hawazin army that ambushed the Prophet's men at the Valley of Hunayn. When the Hawazin ultimately lost the battle, Malik pledged his allegiance to the Prophet and redirected his men to besiege the city of Ta'if.

Malik ibn Sinan
Clan of Khazraj (Medina)

When arguing for why the Muslims should march to Uhud, Malik told the Prophet, "O Messenger of God, we have before us one of the two good things: either Allah will grant us mastery of them, and that is what we would have; or else Allah will grant us martyrdom. I care not which it may be, for verily there is good in both." Malik fought valiantly at Uhud and was too wounded to chase the Quraysh back to Mecca. During the battle, when the Prophet's cheek was bleeding, Malik sucked on the blood to stem the flow. Though he died a few days later, the Prophet ordered that his body be returned to the battlefield and buried alongside the other martyrs.

Manat, al- (idol)
Sister idol to al-Lat and al-'Uzzah

Al-Manat was the chief idol of Qudayd, northwest of Mecca. It was destroyed after the Conquest of Mecca by 'Ali ibn Abi Talib.

Mariyah
Coptic Egyptian servant
Sister of Sirin
Mother of Ibrahim ibn Muhammad
(died in childhood)

Mariyah was sent as a gift to the Prophet by the Muqawqis of Egypt. Her arrival caused much jealousy among the Prophet's wives and ultimately led to the revelation of Surah At-Tahreem (Prohibition). In 629 CE, she gave birth to Ibrahim, who died as a toddler.

Maymunah bint al-Harith
Full sister of Umm al-Fadl bint al-Harith
  (wife of 'Abbas)
Maternal half-sister to Salma' and Asma'
  bint Umays
Paternal half-sister to 'Asma' bint al-Harith
Paternal aunt of Khalid ibn al-Walid
Eleventh and last wife of the Prophet
Clan of Makhzum (Tribe of Quraysh)

Maymunah followed her sister Umm al-Fadl into Islam during the Early Meccan Period. She was a widow, and shortly after the 'Umrah (after Hudaybiyah), became the last woman to marry the Prophet. The union made Khalid ibn al-Walid the Prophet's nephew by marriage. Maymunah and Umm Salamah traveled with the Prophet during the Conquest of Mecca.

Maysarah
Clan unspecified

Maysarah was Khadijah's servant who accompanied 25-year-old Muhammad on his caravan journey to Syria. When they arrived in Bostra, the Christian monk Nestor told Maysarah that Muhammad was destined to become a prophet.

Mikraz ibn Hafs
Clan unspecified (Tribe of Quraysh)

The Quraysh sent Mikraz with Suhayl ibn ʿAmr al-ʿAmiri to negotiate the Treaty of Hudaybiyah with the Prophet.

Miqdad ibn ʿAmr
Clan unspecified (Tribe of Quraysh)

When the Prophet consulted his men about whether to attack or retreat at Badr, Miqdad swore on behalf of the Companions that they would never leave his side.

Mistah ibn Uthathah
Cousin of ʿAʾishah bint Abi Bakr

After the Battle of the Trench, Mistah spread rumors about ʿAʾishah. When ʿAʾishah was exonerated of infidelity, at first Abu Bakr refused to give alms to Mistah. However, upon hearing Surah An-Noor (The Light, 24:22): "…Do you not love that God should forgive you?" Abu Bakr swore never to withhold charity from Mistah again.

Muʾadh ibn al Harith
Brother of ʿAwf and Muʾawwidh ibn al-Harith
Clan of Khazraj (Sub-clan of Najjar, Medina)

At Badr, Muʾadh's arm was almost completely severed by ʿIkrimah ibn Abi Jahl. Muʾadh jerked off the dangling extremity and continued to fight until he was martyred.

Muʾadh ibn Jabal
Clan of Khazraj (Medina)

Before leaving for Hunayn, the Prophet put Muʾadh in charge of teaching Islam to the new Meccan converts.

Muʾattib ibn Abi Lahab
Son of Abu Lahab ibn ʿAbd al-Muttalib
Brother of ʿUtbah and ʿUtaybah ibn Abi Lahab
Cousin of the Prophet
Clan of Hashim (Tribe of Quraysh)

Muʾattib and his brothers inherited their father's disdain of his nephew. At the Conquest of Mecca, he and his brother ʿUtbah were too scared to approach the Prophet. The Prophet sent for them, and after they testified their faith in Islam, he walked with them hand-in-hand to pray at the Kaʾbah.

Muʾawiyah ibn Abi Sufyan
Son of Abu Sufyan and Hind bint ʿUtbah
Brother of Yazid, Hanzalah, ʿAmr, and
  Umm Habibah
Clan of ʿAbdu Shams (Tribe of Quraysh)

Muʾawiyah supported his parents against the Prophet until the Conquest of Mecca. Thereafter he rose up through the administrative ranks under the leadership of the Prophet, Abu Bakr, and ʿUmar. He later became the first Caliph of the ʿUmayyad Dynasty.

Muʾawwidh ibn al-Harith
Brother of ʿAwf and Muʾadh ibn al-Harith
Clan of Khazraj (Sub-clan of Najjar, Medina)

At Badr, Muʾawwidh nearly killed Abu Jahl but was martyred.

Mubashshir ibn ʿAbd al-Mudhir
Clan unspecified (Medina)

Mubashshir was martyred at Badr, and later appeared in ʿAbd Allah ibn ʿAmr ibn Haram's dream, where he beckoned his friend ʿAbd Allah to Paradise. Soon after, ʿAbd Allah was martyred at Uhud.

Mughirah ibn 'Abd Allah

Father of Walid and Hisham ibn al-Mughirah
Grandfather of Abu Jahl and Khalid ibn al-Walid
Chief of the clan of Makhzum (Tribe of Quraysh)

Mughirah dissuaded 'Abd al-Muttalib from fulfilling his oath to sacrifice his son 'Abd Allah, whose mother was from Mughirah's clan of Makhzum. Mughirah died well before the Prophet's first revelation.

Mughirah ibn Shu'bah

Nephew of 'Urwah ibn Mas'ud
Clan of Thaqif (Tribe of Hawazin)

Mughirah accompanied the Prophet to Hudaybiyah and warned his uncle 'Urwah not to tug on the Prophet's beard when he was talking to him (out of familiarity). After the people of Ta'if entered Islam, the Prophet sent Mughirah and Abu Sufyan ibn al-Harb to Ta'if to destroy their chief ido, al-Lat.

Muhammad ibn Abi Bakr

Son of Abu Bakr ibn Abi Quhafah and Asma'
bint Umays
Clan of Taym (Tribe of Quraysh)

Muhammad was born to Abu Bakr and Asma' on the way to Mecca during the Farewell Hajj.

Muhammad ibn Maslamah

Clan of Aws (Medina)

After Badr, Muhammad was the first to volunteer to assassinate Ka'b ibn Ashraf, the treacherous poet of Bani Nadir. The Prophet condoned his plan stating that deception was a military tactic in warfare. After Uhud, he returned to the Bani Nadir as a messenger telling them that the Prophet had ordered his tribe to leave on account of their treachery. Five years later at the Conquest of Mecca, he led the Prophet's camel as they circled the Ka'bah.

Mukhayriq

Rabbi of the clan of Tha'labah

The morning of Uhud, Mukhayriq urged his people to fulfill their covenant with the Prophet and defend Medina from the confederated enemy tribes. They did not listen, and he set out alone, leaving his inheritance for the Prophet. Mukhayriq was martyred on the battlefield, and the Prophet later referred to him as "the best of the Jews."

Mundhir ibn 'Amr

Clan of Khazraj (Medina)

After Uhud, Mundhir led a delegation of 40 scholars to the Hawazin clan of 'Amir. The group was ambushed by Bani Sulaym, and only one Companion survived the massacre.

Muqawqis

Coptic Ruler (Egypt)

The Muqawqis accepted the Prophet's letter of invitation to Islam and responded by sending Mariyah and Sirin to Medina, in addition to many generous gifts.

Mus'ab ibn 'Umayr

Brother of Abu 'Aziz ibn 'Umayr
Husband of Hamnah bint Jahsh
Clan of 'Abd ad-Dar (Tribe of Quraysh)

Mus'ab migrated to Abyssinia and returned after the ban on Hashim was lifted. Prior to the Hijrah, the Prophet sent Mus'ab to Yathrib to introduce Islam to Aws and Khazraj, and prepare the city for his arrival. After the Hijrah, Mus'ab married the Prophet's cousin Hamnah bint Jahsh. The Prophet relied on him heavily and gave him the honor of carrying one of the three banners at Badr and Uhud. After the Badr, Mus'ab told his companions to bind his captive brother tightly because their mother was rich and would pay a nice ransom.

Musaylimah ibn Habib

Tribe of Haifah

Musaylimah was a false prophet from the eastern city of Yamamah who wrote a letter to the Prophet and asked to split his dominion between the two leaders. The Prophet responded by telling him that the earth was the dominion of God alone. Musaylimah was killed a few months later by Wahshi.

Mut'im ibn 'Adi

Grandson of Nawfal ibn 'Abdi Manaf
Father of Jubayr ibn Mut'im
Chief of Nawfal Clan (Tribe of Quraysh)

Mut'im was one of five men who persuaded the Quraysh to end the ban against the clan of Hashim. He pledged to guard the Prophet when the Prophet returned from Ta'if, and kept him well protected until his death—at which point the Quraysh decided to assassinate the Prophet. Originally, Abu Bakr had arranged for his daughter 'A'ishah to marry Mut'im's son Jubayr. Mut'im later agreed to dissolve the engagement so 'A'ishah could marry the Prophet.

Muttalib ibn 'Abdi Manaf

Full brother of Hashim ibn 'Abdi Manaf
Foster-father of 'Abd al-Muttalib ibn Hashim
Great-uncle of Muhammad
Clan of Muttalib (Tribe of Quraysh)

Muttalib assumed leadership of the Scented Ones when his brother Hashim died, and was the namesake of the Quraysh clan most closely related to the clan of Hashim. He preferred his nephew Shaybah ('Abd al-Muttalib) as a successor over his own sons and persuaded Shaybah's mother to let her son leave Yathrib and come to Mecca. When Shaybah was seen entering Mecca next to Muttalib, he was given the name 'Abd al-Muttalib (the servant of Muttalib).

N

Nawfal ibn 'Abd Allah

Clan of Makhzum (Tribe of Quraysh)

Shortly after the Hijrah, Nawfal was captured during a caravan raid led by 'Abd Allah ibn Jahsh. He managed to escape and later fought alongside the Quraysh at Badr. Three years later, he faced off against the Muslims at the Battle of the Trench and was killed when his horse failed to clear the expansive ditch.

Nawfal ibn 'Abdi Manaf

Half-brother of Hashim ibn 'Abdi Manaf
Great-uncle of Muhammad
Clan of Nawfal (Tribe of Quraysh)

Nawfal was too busy with his commercial ventures to take leadership of the Scented Ones after Hashim's death.

Nawfal ibn al-Harith

Son of Harith ibn 'Abd al-Muttalib
Brother of Abu Sufyan ibn al-Harith
First cousin of Muhammad
Clan of Hashim (Tribe of Quraysh)

Like his brother, Nawfal was a bitter enemy of the Prophet and fought against him at Badr, where he was captured. After the battle, he was ransomed by his uncle 'Abbas ibn 'Abd al-Muttalib.

Nawfal ibn Khuwaylid

Half-brother of Khadijah bint Khuwaylid
Father of Aswad ibn Nawfal
Clan of Asad (Tribe of Quraysh)

Nawfal was one of the Prophet's most violent enemies and attacked Abu Bakr and Talhah for exposing his son Aswad to Islam. He later marched out to fight the Prophet at Badr.

Negus (aka Ashamah)

Ruler of Abyssinia

The Negus granted asylum to the Muslim from Mecca emigrants, and later solemnized the marriage of the Prophet to Umm Habibah, who had become a widow in Abyssinia. He passed away shortly after the Conquest of Mecca (Rajab of 630 CE), and the Prophet held a funeral prayer for him in Medina.

Nestor

Christian monk

Nestor was a Christian monk in Syria who observed Muhammad as a child and predicted that he would become a prophet.

Nu'aym ibn 'Abd Allah

Clan of 'Adi (Tribe of Quraysh)

Toward the end of the early Meccan years, Nu'aym prevented 'Umar ibn al-Khattab from trying to kill the Prophet by telling him to first confront his sister, who had recently embraced Islam.

Nu'aym ibn Mas'ud

Tribe of Ghatafan (Clan of Bani Ashja')

One year after Uhud, Abu Sufyan sent Nu'aym to Medina with a contrived story that the Meccan army was armed and ready to march to Badr for a 3rd and final battle. Undeterred, the Prophet led 1,500 men to Badr, only to find an empty battlefield. One year later at the Battle of the Trench, Nu'aym escaped to join the Muslim army, and the Prophet used him to turn the Quraysh and Bani Qurayzah against each other.

Nufayl ibn 'Abd Allah

Father of Khattab ibn Nufayl
Grandfather of 'Umar ibn al-Khattab
Clan of 'Adi (Tribe of Quraysh)

Nufayl had two wives and several grandsons including Zayd "the Haneef" and 'Umar ibn al-Khattab.

Nufayl ibn Habib

Chief of the tribe of Khath'am (north of Yemen)

Nufayl was captured by Abraha and forced to guide the Abyssinian army to Mecca. Just before entering the city, he secretly commanded the lead elephant of the army to kneel.

Nufaysah

Clan unspecified (Tribe of Quraysh)

Nufaysah relayed her friend Khadijah's marriage proposal to Muhammad.

Nusaybah bint Ka'b

Wife of Ghaziyyah ibn 'Amr
Clan of Khazraj (Medina)

Nusaybah was one of the few women present at the Second 'Aqabah. Having pledged to protect the Prophet, she insisted on marching to Uhud to support the Muslim forces that included her husband and two sons. Several years later, she joined the expeditions to Hudaybiyah and Khaybar.

Q

Qasim ibn Muhammad

First child of Muhammad and Khadijah
bint Khuwaylid
Clan of Hashim (Tribe of Quraysh)

Qasim died before he was two. After his birth, the Prophet was called Abu l-Qasim.

Qaylah

Mother of Aws and Khazraj (Medina)

Qaylah was the Arab ancestress of Yathrib whose sons founded the main clans of the city.

Qitham ibn al-'Abbas

Son of 'Abbas ibn 'Abd al-Muttalib
First cousin of Muhammad
Clan of Hashim (Tribe of Quraysh)

Qitham was a late convert who marched behind the Prophet at Hunayn and later helped 'Ali prepare the Prophet's body for burial.

Qullus, Al- (idol)

Al-Qullus was the chief idol of Bani Tayy, to the northeast of Mecca. It was destroyed by 'Ali ibn Abi Talib after the Conquest of Mecca.

Quraybah bint Abi Quhafah

Daughter of Abu Quhafah
Sister of Abu Bakr
Clan of Taym (Tribe of Quraysh)

Quraybah converted to Islam during the Meccan period, but stayed there to care for her elderly father.

Qusayy ibn Kilab

Married to daughter of Hulayl ibn Hubshiyah
(chief of Khuza'ah)
Forefather of Muhammad
Tribe of Quraysh

Qusayy was a prominent Qurayshi who took control of Mecca after the death of his father-in-law. He settled in the heart of Mecca with his close relatives (Quraysh of the Hollow), while his distant relatives moved to the surrounding areas (Quraysh of the Outskirts).

Qutaylah bint Nawfal

Daughter of Nawfal ibn Asad
Sister of Waraqah ibn Nawfal
Clan of Asad (Tribe of Quraysh)

Qutaylah's brother Waraqah, a Chritian Haneef, informed her of the coming of a prophet. When she saw a radiance emanating from 'Abd Allah ibn 'Abd al-Muttalib, she asked to marry him on the spot. 'Abd Allah turned her down as he was on his way to marry Aminah bint Wahb.

R

Rafi' ibn Khadij

Clan of Aws (Medina)

Rafi' was a young boy who convinced the Prophet that he was strong enough to fight at Uhud.

Rayhanah bint Zayd

Wife of a man from Bani Qurayzah
Servant of Muhammad
Tribe of Nadir (Medina)

Although she was originally from Bani Nadir, Rayhanah was married to a man from Bani Qurayzah. After the Battle of the Trench, she joined the Prophet's household as a servant and later entered Islam. She died five years after the Battle of the Trench.

Rifa'ah ibn Samaw'al

Tribe of Qurayzah (Medina)

After the Battle of the Trench, Rifa'ah escaped the besieged fortress of Bani Qurayzah and entered Islam.

Rubayyi' bint an-Nadr

Mother of Harithah ibn Suraqah
Sister of Anas ibn Nadr
Clan of Khazraj (Medina)

When Rubayyi' heard of her son's death at Badr, the Prophet reminded her that Harithah would be rewarded for his intentions.

Ruqayyah bint Muhammad

Second daughter of Muhammad and Khadijah
bint Khuwaylid
First wife of 'Uthman ibn 'Affan
Clan of Hashim (Tribe of Quraysh)

Ruqayyah was originally engaged to 'Utbah ibn Abi Lahab but the engagement was anulled. She instead married 'Uthman ibn 'Affan. The couple sought asylum in Abyssinia, and returned when the ban on Hashim was lifted. She fell gravely ill before the Badr, and 'Uthman stayed behind to care for her. She died soon after and was buried while the Prophet was away at battle.

S

Sa'd ibn Abi Waqqas (aka Sa'd of Zuhrah)

Son of Abu Waqqas
Brother of 'Umayr ibn Abi Waqqas
Maternal cousin of Muhammad
Clan of Zuhrah (Tribe of Quraysh)

Sa'd was one of the first Meccans to embrace Islam. He and a few other Companions got into a public scuffle with the Quraysh during the early Meccan years. He fought at Badr and later killed one of the first soldiers at Uhud. He was one of the 10 Companions to whom the Prophet promised Paradise.

Sa'd ibn Khaythamah

Son of Khaythamah Abu Sa'd
Clan of Aws (Medina)

Sa'd was martyred at Badr. His father later had a dream about joining him in Paradise and urged the Muslims to take the offensive at Uhud so he too could become a martyr.

Sa'd ibn Mu'adh

Brother of Iyas ibn Mu'adh
Clan of Aws (Medina)

After the First 'Aqabah, Sa'd was angry that his cousin As'ad had lodged Mus'ab ibn 'Umayr, and sent his clansman Usayd ibn Hudayr to drive Mus'ab out of Yathrib. When 'Usayd returned a Muslim, Sa'd confronted Mus'ab directly and ended up also accepting Islam. He invited his clan to the new religion, and they converted the same day. Sa'd and 'Ali carried the two black pennants to Badr. On the eve of the battle, the Prophet asked if the Helpers would support him beyond what they had pledged at the Second 'Aqabah, and Sa'd eloquently voiced the Helpers' unanimous support. After the battle, Sa'd and 'Umar felt that the captives at Badr should be executed, while the Prophet and Abu Bakr sought leniency. The Qur'an later supported Sa'd's opinion. During the Battle of the Trench, he advised the Prophet not to make a peace treaty with the Bani Ghatafan. After the battle, the Prophet placed the fate of Bani Qurayzah in Sa'd's hands. In accordance with Jewish law, Sa'd decreed that the men should be executed for their treachery and the Prophet agreed. Sa'd died shortly after the Trench, and the Prophet eloquently prayed for him.

Sa'd ibn 'Ubadah

Clan of Khazraj (Medina)

Soon after the Hijrah, Sa'd quickly emerged as one of the preeminent leaders of Khazraj. When the Prophet left Medina on his first military expedition, he placed Sa'd in charge of the city. As one of the Prophet's closest Companions, Sa'd personally guarded the Prophet the night before Uhud. Several years later, he led one of the four battalions at the Conquest of Mecca. Shortly after, when the spoils of Hunayn were divided generously among the Quraysh and Hawazin tribes, Sa'd approached the Prophet on behalf of the Helpers, asking for their share of the spoils. After the Prophet's death, many of the Companions nominated Sa'd as the first caliph. According to Lings, when Abu Bakr got the position, Sa'd did not pledge his allegiance and eventually migrated to Syria.

Safiyyah bint 'Abd al-Muttalib

Daughter of Abd al-Muttalib ibn Hashim and
  Halah bint Wuhayb
Wife of 'Awwam ibn Khuwaylid (Khadijah's brother)
Mother of Zubayr ibn al-'Awwam
Paternal aunt and maternal cousin of Muhammad
Clan of Hashim (Tribe of Quraysh)

Safiyyah was a few years younger than Muhammad, and grew up as his playmate. She was a constant presence in the Prophet's household. She married Khadijah's brother and entered Islam when the Prophet invited his family to hear his message. After Uhud, Safiyyah's son Zubayr warned her not to look upon the mutilated body of her brother Hamzah. Safiyyah insisted on seeing him, and prayed beside the Prophet for the martyred. Several years later, she joined the expedition to Khaybar.

Safiyyah bint Huyay

Daughter of Huyay ibn Akhtab
  (Chief of Bani Nadir)
Wife of Kinanah ibn Abi l-Huqayq
10th wife of Muhammad
Tribe of Nadir (Medina)

After the conquest of Khaybar, Safiyyah, a widow, was given the choice of returning to her people or embracing Islam and marrying the Prophet. She replied, "I choose God and His Messenger." When the other wives teased her because of her Jewish heritage, the Prophet counseled her to be proud of her ancestry.

Safwan ibn Mu'attal

Tribe of Hawazin (clan of Sulaym)

On the return journey to Medina (from the Bani Mustaliq expedition) Safwan finds 'A'ishah bint Abi Bakr sleeping alone in the desert. When he escorts her back to Medina, salacious rumors begin to circulate about Safwan and 'A'ishah.

Safwan ibn Umayyah

Son of Umayyah ibn Khalaf
  (chief of Jumah)
Clan of Jumah (Tribe of Quraysh)

After Badr, Safwan urged his cousin 'Umayr ibn Wahb to assassinate the Prophet in Medina, a plan that backfired when 'Umayr instead embraced Islam. Just before Uhud, Zayd ibn Harithah ambushed Safwan's summer caravan. After the battle, Safwan joined Abu Sufyan in signing a pact with the Jews of Khaybar to unite against the Prophet. Despite the pact, Zayd still managed to ambush another one of Safwan's caravans after the Battle of the Trench. Soon after, when Khalid ibn al-Walid invited Safwan to embrace Islam, he answered, "Even if every other man of Quraysh were to follow Muhammad, I would never follow him." After the Conquest of Mecca, he was one of only three notable Quraysh who did not pledge allegiance to the Prophet. Nonetheless, the Prophet gave him four months of amnesty. Safwan fought alongside the Prophet at Hunayn, and when the Prophet rewarded him with 100 camels and an entire ravine filled with cattle, Safwan testified his faith.

Sahl ibn 'Amr

Orphan under the guardianship of As'ad
  ibn Zurahah
Clan unspecified (Medina)

Sahl and his brother Suhayl owned the courtyard in Medina that was purchased by the Prophet when he entered the city.

Sahlah bint Suhayl

Daughter of Suhayl, Salit, and Hatib ibn 'Amr
Wife of Abu Hudhayfah ibn 'Utbah
Clan of 'Amir (Tribe of Quraysh)

After entering Islam with her husband in Mecca, Sahlah migrated to Abyssinia and returned a few years later when the ban on Hashim ended.

Sa'id ibn al-'As

Father of Khalid ibn Sa'id
Clan of 'Abdu Shams (Tribe of Quraysh)

Sa'id was a powerful man in Mecca who beat his son for embracing Islam. Several days later when Khalid escaped, Sa'id publicly disowned him.

Sa'id ibn Zayd

Son of Zayd ibn 'Amr (aka Zayd "the Haneef")
Cousin and brother-in-law of 'Umar ibn al-Khattab
Husband of Fatimah bint al-Khattab
Clan of 'Adi (Tribe of Quraysh)

Sa'id was a childhood friend of 'Umar, yet unlike 'Umar, he had monotheistic tendencies like his father, Zayd. Prior to Badr, he was sent with his cousin Talhah to the coast to get information about Abu Sufyan's caravan. They returned after the army's departure. He was one of 10 Companions to whom the Prophet promised Paradise.

Sakran ibn 'Amr

Brother of Suhayl, Salit, and Hatib ibn 'Amr
Husband of Sawdah bint Zam'ah
Clan of 'Amir (Tribe of Quraysh)

After entering Islam with his wife in Mecca, they migrated to Abyssinia and returned a few years later when the ban on Hashim was lifted. He died shortly thereafter.

Salamah ibn Abi Salamah

Grandson of Barra bint 'Abd al-Muttalib
Son of Abu Salamah ibn 'Abd al-Asad and Umm Salamah bint Abi Umayyah
Husband of 'Umarah bint Hamzah
Clan of Makhzum (Tribe of Quraysh)

The Prophet arranged Salamah's marriage to 'Umarah shortly after the expedition to Khaybar.

Salit ibn 'Amr

Brother of Suhayl, Sakran, and Hatib ibn 'Amr
Clan of 'Amir (Tribe of Quraysh)

Salit entered Islam in Mecca, much to his brother Suhayl's dismay.

Salma' bint 'Amr

Wife of Hashim ibn 'Abdi Manaf
Mother of 'Abd al-Muttalib ibn Hashim (aka Shaybah)
Great-grandmother of Muhammad
Najjar Clan of Khazraj (Medina)

Salma' agreed to marry Hashim as long as she could keep their future child (Shaybah) in Yathrib. When Hashim died, she agreed to let her son go to Mecca with his uncle Muttalib.

Salma' bint Umays

Maternal half-sister of Umm al-Fadl bint al-Harith
Wife of Hamzah ibn 'Abd al-Muttalib
Mother of 'Umarah bint Hamzah
Clan unspecified (Tribe of Quraysh)

Salma' followed her sister Umm al-Fadl into Islam during the Early Meccan Period. She was widowed after Hamzah was slain at Uhud.

Salma' (last name unspecified)

Clan unspecified

Salma' was the servant of Safiyyah bint 'Abd al-Muttalib and delivered all of Khadijah's children. She was a constant fixture in the Prophet's house, and many years later, delivered the Prophet's last son Ibrahim.

Salman al-Farisi

Persian slave from Nineveh
Owned by a man from Qurayzah (Medina)

Although Salman was born to Zoroastrian parents, he converted to Christianity and dedicated his youth to searching for a much-anticipated Arabian prophet. From his birthplace in Iran, he ended up in Medina as a slave, and finally encountered the Prophet in Quba. After Uhud, the Prophet and his Companions bought Salman's freedom. Two years later, when enemy forces were enroute to surround Medina, Salman suggested digging a trench around the most vulnerable parts of the city, as was the custom in Persia. He was admired for his work ethic, and the Emigrants and Helpers started a friendly rivalry to claim Salman as one of theirs. In response, the Prophet said, that Salman belonged to his family.

Samurah ibn Jundub

Clan unspecified

Samurah was a young orphan from one of the inland Nejd tribes who convinced the Prophet that he was strong enough to fight at Uhud despite his youth.

Sarah

Wife of Abraham
Mother of Isaac
Grandmother of Jacob (Israel)

As mentioned in the Bible and Qur'an, Sarah was blessed with a son despite her old age. According to Biblical tradition (unlike Islamic tradition), she asked Abraham to send Hagar and Ishmael away.

Sawad ibn Ghaziyyah

Clan unspecified (Medina)

Before Badr, the Prophet inspected his fledgling army and while aligning the ranks, poked Sawad in the abdomen with his arrow. Sawad feigned pain and asked for retribution. When the Prophet bared his own abdomen, Sawad kissed him saying, "I desired that at my last moment with thee—if so be it—my skin should touch thy skin."

Sawdah bint Zam'ah

Daughter of Zam'ah ibn Qays
Widow of Sakran ibn 'Amr al-'Amiri
Second wife of Muhammad
Clan of 'Amir (Tribe of Quraysh)

Sawdah migrated to Abyssinia with her husband, Sakran, but was widowed shortly after they returned to Mecca. At age 30, she married the Prophet (after the death of Khadijah, but before the Hijrah). She was a maternal figure to 'A'ishah and Hafsah. In her later years, she volunteered her allotted time with the Prophet to 'A'ishah. She was a central figure in the household, and helped Umm Ayman and Umm Salamah prepare the Prophet's daughter Zaynab's body for burial.

Shammas ibn 'Uthman (aka Zubayr)

Maternal nephew of 'Utbah ibn Rabi'ah
Clan of Makhzum (Tribe of Quraysh)

Shammas' name means "deacon," and he was known for his exceedingly good looks. He immigrated to Abyssinia and returned a few years later. At Uhud, he protected the Prophet and was later described as a human shield. After the battle, he was too wounded to chase the Quraysh back to Mecca. He died soon after and the Prophet ordered that Shammas be buried on the battlefield with the other martyrs.

Shas ibn Qais

Tribe of Qaynuqa

In an attempt to break the pact between the Aws and Khazraj before Badr, Shas ibn Qais instructed a young clansman to recite poems about the Battle of Bu'ath, the most recent skirmish between the two sides. The Prophet dissipated the situation before the Companions came to blows over their past differences.

Shaybah ibn Rabi'ah

Grandson of 'Abdu Shams ibn 'Abdi Manaf
Brother of 'Utbah ibn Rabi'ah
Uncle of Hind bint 'Utbah
Clan of 'Abdu Shams (Tribe of Quraysh)

Shaybah and his brother 'Utbah were vacationing in Ta'if when they saw the Prophet and sent him grapes through their servant 'Addas. Hamzah killed Shaybah in the opening duels of Badr.

Shayma' bint al-Harith

Daughter of Harith ibn 'Abd al-'Uzzah and
*   Halimah bint Abi Dh'ayb*
Foster-sister of Muhammad
Clan of Sa'd ibn Bakr (Tribe of Hawazin)

After the Hunayn, Shayma' approached the Prophet and informed him of the death of his beloved foster-parents, Harith and Halimah.

Sirin

Coptic Egyptian servant
Sister to Mariyah

The Muqawqis of Egypt sent Sirin as a gift to the Prophet, who gave her to Hassan ibn Thabit.

Suhayl ibn 'Amr

Orphan under the guardianship of As'ad ibn Zurahah
Clan unspecified (Medina)

Suhayl and his brother Sahl owned the courtyard in Medina that the Prophet purchased when he entered the city.

Suhayl ibn 'Amr al-'Amiri

Brother of Hatib, Sakran, and Salit ibn
*   'Amr al-'Amiri*
Father of 'Abd Allah, Abu Jandal, Sahlah,
*   and Umm Kulthum*
Clan of 'Amir (Tribe of Quraysh)

As chief of the clan of 'Amir, Suhayl was incensed to see so many of his family (siblings, sons, sons-in-law, and daughters) enter Islam during the early Meccan years. Not surprisingly, he declined the Prophet's request for protection after the Prophet returned from Ta'if. Several years later, Suhayl was captured at Badr. After the Battle of Uhud, he conspired with Abu Sufyan to send a messenger to Medina hoping to intimidate the Prophet into not showing up for a second meeting at Badr. Two years later, the Quraysh sent him to negotiate the Treaty of Hudaybiyah, where he insisted on striking out "Muhammad, the Messenger of God" and replacing it with "Muhammad ibn 'Abd Allah." After the Conquest of Mecca, Suhayl was one of three notable men of Quraysh who did not enter Islam. Nonetheless, the Prophet granted him protection. Suhayl embraced Islam after the Prophet gifted him a generous portion of the spoils after the Battle of Hunayn.

Sumayyah bint Khubbat

Wife of Yasir ibn 'Amir
Mother of 'Ammar ibn Yasir
Confederate of Makhzum (Tribe of Quraysh)

Sumayyah was an early Muslim convert who was tortured to death by Abu Jahl and her fellow Makhzumis for not renouncing her faith. She is considered the first female martyr in Islam.

T

Talhah ibn 'Abd Allah

Clan of 'Abd ad-Dar (Tribe of Quraysh)

Talhah carried the Meccan banner at Uhud and was killed by 'Ali ibn Abi Talib in the opening duel.

Talhah ibn 'Ubayd Allah

Cousin of Abu Bakr ibn Abi Quhafah
Husband of Hamnah bint Jahsh
Clan of Taym (Tribe of Quraysh)

While returning from Syria, Talhah encountered 'Uthman ibn 'Affan and told him that a Syrian monk had recently asked him about the coming of "Ahmed." The two approached Abu Bakr who directed them to the Prophet. Soon after Talhah embraced Islam, he and Abu Bakr were ambushed by Khadijah's half-brother Nawfal. When they were left bound and tattersed on the side of the road, their clan of Taym turned a blind eye. Several years later, Talhah was returning from another trip to Syria, when he ran into the Prophet and Abu Bakr (who were escaping north to Medina) and supplied them with fresh garments before he continued on to Mecca. Before Badr, he was sent with his cousin Sa'id ibn Zayd to Hawra' on the coast to get information about Abu Sufyan's caravan. They returned but missed the march to Badr. One year later, Talhah fought gloriously at Uhud where he deflected a deathblow meant for the Prophet. The Prophet became too weak to climb to higher ground, and Talhah carried him on his back. Later the Prophet remarked, "He that would behold a martyr walking the face of the earth, let him look on Talhah the son of 'Ubayd Allah." Talhah married Hamnah bint Jahsh after she was widowed by her husband Mus'ab. Talhah was one of 10 Companions to whom the Prophet promised Paradise.

Talib ibn Abi Talib

Son of Abu Talib ibn 'Abd al-Muttalib
Brother of 'Aqil, Ja'far, Umm Hani, and 'Ali
First cousin of Muhammad
Clan of Hashim (Tribe of Quraysh)

Talib was the same age as the Prophet. Like his father, Talib resisted becoming a Muslim yet remained tolerant to the cause. Although he marched out against the Prophet at Badr, he turned around before the battle and returned to Mecca with many of his clansmen.

Thabit ibn ad-Dahdahah

Clan unspecified (Medina)

When Thabit overheard that Abu Lubabah had refused to give one of his palm trees to a needy orphan (despite the Prophet's urging), Thabit traded his entire orchard for the single palm tree so he could give it in charity to the boy. When Thabit was martyred at Uhud, the Prophet remarked that Thabit would have date palms in Paradise.

Tufayl ibn 'Amr

Tribe of Daws (southeast of Mecca)

Tufayl was a prominent poet from the southeast tribe of Daws. When he visited Mecca, the Quraysh warned him of a local sorcerer named Muhammad. At first Tufayl stuffed his ears with cotton to avoid his "spell." But when he saw the Prophet praying, he decided to listen to the recitation and subsequently embraced Islam. When Tufayl was unable to persuade his people to embrace Islam, he returned to Mecca and asked the Prophet to condemn them. Instead, the Prophet prayed for their guidance and instructed him to return to his people and call them gently to Islam.

Tulayb ibn 'Umayr

Son of Arwa bint 'Abd al-Muttalib
First cousin of Muhammad
Clan of Hashim (Tribe of Quraysh)

As a 15-year-old, Tulayb successfully persuaded his mother to enter Islam. He migrated to Abyssinia and returned after the ban on Hashim was lifted. Tulayb migrated to Medina before the Hijrah.

Tulayhah ibn Khuwaylid

Tribe of Asad (not the Asad clan of Quraysh)

Tulayhah was a false prophet who emerged after the Conquest of Mecca. When he was surrounded by Khalid ibn al-Walid's army, he converted to Islam and became a source of strength for the community.

U/'U

'Ubadah ibn Samit

Clan of Khazraj (Medina)

When Bani Qaynuqa broke their covenant with the Prophet, they sought help from 'Ubadah and 'Abd Allah ibn Ubayy. 'Ubadah, however, stuck to his covenant with the Prophet and refused to uphold the old Qaynuqa-Khazraj alliance.

'Ubayd Allah ibn Jahsh

Son of Jahsh ibn Ri'ab and Umaymah bint
'Abd al-Muttalib
Husband of Umm Habibah bint Abi Sufyan
(ninth wife of the Prophet)
Cousin of Muhammad
Clan of 'Abdu Shams* (Tribe of Quraysh)

'Ubayd Allah was a Christian who became one of the first to embrace Islam before the Prophet's open invitation to Hashim. He migrated to Abyssinia with his wife and remained there with Ja'far, even though most of the emigrants returned after the ban on Hashim ended. He reverted back to Christianity and died in Abyssinia. His widow, Umm Habibah, subsequently married the Prophet.

*'Ubayd Allah's father was from the distant tribe of Asad and was given honorary membership among 'Abdu Shams.

'Ubaydah ibn al-Harith

Grandson of 'Abd al-Muttalib ibn Hashim
Brother of Abu Sufyan and Nawfal
Husband of Zaynab bint Khuzaymah
(fifth wife of Muhammad)
First cousin of Muhammad
Clan of Hashim (Tribe of Quraysh)

'Ubaydah fought 'Utbah ibn Rabi'ah in the opening duels of Badr, but later died of his wounds. His widow, Zaynab, married the Prophet a year later, after Uhud.

Ubayy ibn Khalaf

Brother of Umayyah ibn Khalaf (chief of Jumah)
Clan of Jumah (Tribe of Quraysh)

During the Early Meccan Period, Ubayy confronted the Prophet by crumbling a dry bone and blowing it into his face (see Qur'an 36:77-79). After Badr, he came to Medina to ransom his captive son. As Ubayy was leaving, he vowed to train his horse for the next battle with the Muslims, where he promised to ride up to the Prophet and slay him. One year later at Uhud, he charged at the Prophet, who struck him down with a single blow from a spear.

Umamah bint Abi l-'As

Daughter of Zaynab bint Muhammad and
*   Abu l-'As ibn ar-Rabi'*
Granddaughter of Muhammad
Clan of 'Abdu Shams (Tribe of Quraysh)

Umamah was the Prophet's beloved granddaughter who was escorted to Medina with her mother after Badr. The Prophet adored her, and in one instance, teased his wives saying he would give a necklace to the one whom he loved most. They waited in eager anticipation only to discover that he was referring to Zaynab's daughter. Umamah's mother died shortly before the Conquest of Mecca.

'Umar ibn al-Khattab

Son of Khattab ibn Nufayl and the sister of
*   Abu Jahl ibn Hisham*
Cousin and brother-in-law of Sa'id ibn Zayd
Brother-in-law to 'Uthman ibn Maz'un
Husband of Zaynab bint Maz'un
Father of 'Abd Allah and Hafsah
Father-in-law of Muhammad
Clan of 'Adi (Tribe of Quraysh)

Growing up, 'Umar inherited his father's fierce loyalty to the pagan traditions in Mecca. On one occasion, Abu Bakr freed one of 'Umar's slaves when he saw 'Umar beating her for entering Islam. Meanwhile, 'Umar's wife, Zaynab, was the sister of 'Uthman ibn Maz'un, one of the earliest converts. 'Umar was about 19 years younger than the Prophet, and his hatred for the Prophet finally drove him to try to assassinate him. However, he was re-directed to his sister's house, where he heard a recitation of Surah Ta Ha, and embraced Islam. He immediately confronted his uncle Abu Jahl with news of his conversion, and started publicly praying at the Ka'bah. His conversion at age 26 marked a turning point for the Muslims in Mecca, and led the Quraysh to draft formal sanctions against the clan of Hashim.

After the Hijrah, he fought alongside the Prophet at every battle. After Badr, 'Umar and Sa'd ibn Mu'adh said that the captives should be killed, but the Prophet and Abu Bakr decided otherwise. Surah Al Anfal (The Spoils of War) supported 'Umar's view but accepted the Prophet's decision. 'Umar was known for his outspoken personality and stern demeanor. On more than one occasion (the mourners at Badr, the capture of Hatib ibn 'Amr, the death of 'Abd Allah ibn Ubayy), the Prophet urged him toward gentleness. On on occasion, the Prophet laughed when 'Umar entered his house and the Prophet's wives quickly hushed. The Prophet said: "Oh son of Khattab, by Him in whose hand is my soul, if Satan found that you were traveling upon a certain path, he would choose to go himself by any other path but yours."

When the Prophet agreed to the Treaty of Hudaybiyah, 'Umar was unable to control his frustration. Soon after, the Prophet shared with him the good news of Surah Al Fet-h (Victory). When it appeared that the Prophet had divorced his wives, 'Umar did not hesitate to approach the him to inquire abou the matter. A few years later, he was unable to reconcile the news of the Prophet's death. He adamantly told the community that the Prophet would return, but was quickly silenced by Abu Bakr, who reminded the community that the Prophet was a mortal like everyone else. Abu Bakr nominated 'Umar as the first Caliph. He was one of 10 Companions to whom the Prophet promised Paradise.

'Umarah bint Hamzah

Daughter of Hamzah ibn 'Abd al-Muttalib and
*   Salma' bint Umays*
Wife of Salamah ibn Abi Salamah
Cousin of Muhammad
Clan of Hashim (Tribe of Quraysh)

'Umarah remained in Mecca with her widowed mother and came to meet the Prophet when he arrived for 'Umrah, a year after Hudaybiyah. Fatimah brought her back to Medina and 'Umarah lived in her house. When 'Ali, Zayd, and Ja'far got into a heated conversation about who had more right to take care of Hamzah's orphaned daughter, the Prophet awarded guardianship to Ja'far. The Prophet later arranged 'Umarah's marriage to her cousin Salamah (the grandson of Hamzah's half-sister Barrah).

Umaymah bint 'Abd al-Muttalib

Daughter of 'Abd al-Muttalib ibn Hashim
Full sister of Zubayr, Abu Talib, 'Abd Allah
Half-sister of Abu Lahab ibn 'Abd al-Muttalib
Wife of Jahsh ibn Ri'ab
Mother of 'Abd Allah, 'Ubayd Allah, Zaynab,
*   and Hamnah*
Aunt of Muhammad
Clan of Hashim (Tribe of Quraysh)

Although all four of her children were teh Prophet's earliest supporters, Umaymah herself resisted her nephew's invitation to Islam until after the Hijrah. She came to Medina to pledge allegiance to the Prophet after her daughter Zaynab married Zayd ibn Harithah.

'Umayr ibn Abi Waqqas

Brother of Sa'd ibn Abi Waqqas
Maternal cousin of Muhammad
Clan of Zuhrah (Tribe of Quraysh)

'Umayr was one of the youngest Companions to enter Islam in Mecca. Although he was only 15, he begged the Prophet to let him fight at Badr, where he was martyred.

'Umayr ibn Wahb

Clan of Jumah (Tribe of Quraysh)

On the eve of Badr, 'Umayr rode out to the Muslim camp to spy on the Prophet's army. He returned and warned the Meccans to prepare for significant losses if they went to battle. After Badr, his son was captured in Medina and 'Umayr could not afford to pay his ransom. 'Umayr's cousin Safwan ibn Umayyah promised to care for his family should something happen to him, and then urged 'Umayr to assassinate the Prophet. When 'Umayr approached the Prophet, the Prophet recounted the exact conversation 'Umayr had with Safwan. Upon hearing the Prophet's words, 'Umayr embraced Islam. At the Conquest of Mecca, 'Umayr approached the Prophet and secured a four-month respite for Safwan.

Umayyah ibn 'Abdu Shams

Son of 'Abdu Shams ibn 'Abdi Manaf
Father of Harb and Abu l-'As ibn Umayyah
Grandfather of Abu Sufyan ibn al-Harb
Clan of 'Abdu Shams (Tribe of Quraysh)

Umayyah was the founder of the Umayyad branch of the Quraysh clan of 'Abdu Shams. (The Umayyads took control of the Muslim empire after the caliphate of 'Ali ibn Abi Talib.) Notable Umayyads included 'Uthman ibn 'Affan, Abu Sufyan ibn al-Harb, and Umm Habibah bint Abi Sufyan.

Umayyah ibn Khalaf

Brother of Ubayy ibn Khalaf
Father of 'Ali and Safwan
Clan of Jumah (Tribe of Quraysh)

Umayyah was the overweight chief of Jumah who tortured his slave Bilal for converting to Islam. Many years later, Umayyah tried to avoid marching to Badr, but was eventually goaded into fighting by 'Uqbah ibn Abi Mu'ayt. He was captured, but before he could be ransomed, Bilal killed him.

Umm al-Fadl bint al-Harith

Full sister to Maymunah bint al-Harith
Wife of 'Abbas ibn 'Abd al-Muttalib
Mother of Fadl and Qitham ibn 'Abbas
Clan of Makhzum (Tribe of Quraysh)

Umm al-Fadl was particularly dear to the Prophet, and was the second woman to enter Islam after Khadijah (well before her husband, 'Abbas). After Badr, Abu Lahab beat one of her servants for rejoicing in the Prophet's victory. Umm al-Fadl struck Abu Lahab over the head, and he died a week later. She and 'Abbas decided to migrate to Medina eight years after the Hijrah. But along the way, they ended up joining the Prophet who was marching south to conquer Mecca.

Umm Ayman (aka Barakah)

Wife of a man of Yathrib
Wife of Zayd ibn Harithah
Mother of Usamah ibn Zayd
Clan unspecified

Also known as Barakah, she served the Prophet's father before his death. The Prophet freed her at his wedding to Khadijah. Barakah then married a man from Yathrib, and had a son named Ayman (for whom she was then called Umm Ayman). She later returned to the Prophet's household for unclear reasons, and—with the Prophet's encouragement—married Zayd ibn Harithah. Together they had a son named Usamah. Umm Ayman remained an integral part of the Prophet's household and later participated in the expedition to Khaybar. Before the Conquest of Mecca, the Prophet asked her, Sawdah, and Umm Salamah to prepare his daughter Zaynab's body for burial.

Umm Habibah bint Abi Sufyan

Daughter of Abu Sufyan ibn al-Harb (Umayyad chief)
Sister of Mu'awiyah, Yazid, Hanzalah, and 'Amr
Wife of 'Ubayd Allah ibn Jahsh
Ninth wife of Muhammad
Clan of 'Abdu Shams (Tribe of Quraysh)

Much to her father's dismay, Umm Habibah entered Islam in Mecca and migrated to Abyssinia with her husband. The couple remained in Abyssinia much longer than the others. 'Ubayd Allah eventually reverted to Christianity and died there. When the Prophet heard the news, just after Hudaybiyah, he asked the Negus to officiate the Prophet's marriage with Umm Habibah while she was still in Abyssinia. At the age of 35, she came to Medina and joined the Prophet's household.

Umm Hani bint Abi Talib (aka Fakhitah)

Daughter of Abu Talib ibn 'Abd al-Muttalib
Wife of Hubayrah ibn Abi Wahb
Cousin of Muhammad
Clan of Hashim (Tribe of Quraysh)

The Prophet originally asked to marry Fakhitah, but Abu Talib refused. She was married to a man from Makhzum named Hubayrah. The Prophet visited her in Mecca and on one occasion, left her house to sleep by the Ka'bah. He returned to Umm Hani's house before dawn and related to her his miraculous Night Journey ('Isra and Mi'raj). She was the first to hear the news and discouraged the Prophet from telling others. Hubayrah remained a pagan and left her to live in Najran. She nonetheless remained a close family member of the Prophet.

Umm Jamil bint al-Harb

Sister of Abu Sufyan ibn al-Harb
Wife of Abu Lahab ibn 'Abd al-Muttalib
Mother of 'Utbah,'Utaybah, and Mu'attib ibn
*   Abi Lahab*
Clan of 'Abdu Shams (Tribe of Quraysh)

Umm Jamil was openly hostile to the Prophet. When he started inviting people to Islam, she retracted her sons' engagements to his daughters Ruqayyah and Umm Kulthum. When she heard that a surah had been revealed condemning her and her husband (111:1-5), she flew into a rage and confronted Abu Bakr, demanding to know where the Prophet was. Abu Bakr did not respond, but was amazed she could not see the Prophet sitting next to him. She stormed out, referring to the Prophet as "mudhammam" (the blameworthy). The Prophet later commented, "Is it not wondrous how God turneth away from me the injuries of Quraysh? They revile Mudhammam, whereas I am Muhammad."

Umm Kulthum bint Muhammad

Third daughter of Muhammad and Khadijah
*   bint Khuwaylid*
Second wife of 'Uthman ibn 'Affan
Clan of Hashim (Tribe of Quraysh)

Umm Kulthum was originally engaged to 'Utaybah ibn Abi Lahab, but the engagement was annulled. She married 'Uthman after the death of her sister Ruqayyah, who was also married to him. Umm Kulthum died a few years later while her father and 'Uthman were away at Tabuk. The Prophet prayed at her grave and told 'Uthman that if he had another daughter, he would have given her to him in marriage as well.

Umm Kulthum bint Suhayl

Daughter of Suhayl ibn 'Amr al-'Amiri (chief of 'Amir)
Wife of Abu Sabrah ibn Abi Ruhm
Clan of 'Amir (Tribe of Quraysh)

Umm Kulthum entered Islam and migrated to Abyssinia with her husband, Abu Sabrah. They returned after the ban on Hashim was lifted, and later migrated to Medina just before the Prophet's Hijrah.

Umm Kulthum bint 'Uqbah

Half-sister of 'Uthman ibn 'Affan
Wife of Zayd ibn Harithah
Clan of 'Abdu Shams (Tribe of Quraysh)

Umm Kulthum was the only Meccan woman to flee to Medina after the Treaty of Hudaybiyah. The Prophet refused to return her, as the terms of the pact only specified that male escapees be sent back. Umm Kulthum followed the Prophet's advice and married Zayd ibn Harithah.

Umm Mani' bint 'Amr

Clan unspecified — likely Khazraj (Medina)

Umm Mani' was one of two women present at the Second 'Aqabah. Both women later joined the expedition to Hudaybiyah.

Umm Ruman bint 'Amir

Wife of Abu Bakr ibn Abi Quhafah
Mother of 'A'ishah and 'Abd al-Ka'bah ibn 'Abi Bakr
Mother-in-law of the Prophet
Clan unspecified (Tribe of Quraysh)

Beautiful and devout, Umm Ruman followed her husband into Islam. She died shortly after the Treaty of Hudaybiyah and was buried by the Prophet.

Umm Salamah bint Abi Umayyah

Daughter of Abu Umayyah and 'Atikah (not 'Atikah bint 'Abd al-Muttalib, but Abu Umayyah's second wife by the same name)
Wife of Abu Salamah ibn 'Abd al-Asad
Mother of Salamah ibn Abi Salamah
Sixth wife of Muhammad
Clan of Makhzum (Tribe of Quraysh)

Much to the dismay of Makhzum, Umm Salamah followed her husband into Islam and both migrated to Abyssinia. She returned when the ban on Hashim was lifted. It was through her that many of the accounts of the Abyssinian migration were narrated. They tried to leave for Medina before the Prophet's Hijrah, but she and their son were taken back to Mecca. The two finally went north with the help of 'Uthman ibn Talhah. Her husband died in the year after Uhud, and Umm Salamah (29) married the Prophet. Her beauty became a source of mild jealousy for 'A'ishah. Umm Salamah later accompanied the Prophet to Hudaybiyah, and advised the Prophet to shave his head and sacrifice his camel so others might follow his example. She also accompanied the Prophet to Khaybar and was with him at the Conquest of Mecca. Just before leaving for the conquest, the Prophet asked her, Umm Ayman, and Sawdah to prepare his daughter Zaynab's body for burial.

Umm Sulaym bint Milhan

Mother of Anas ibn Malik
Clan unspecified (Medina)

Umm Sulaym gave her 10-year-old son Anas to the Prophet as a servant for his household. She was one of two women who joined the Companions at the Battle of Uhud, and later took part in the expedition to Khaybar.

Unays ibn Junadah

Brother of Abu Dharr ibn Junadah
Tribe of Ghifar (northwest of Mecca by the Red Sea)

On a trip to Mecca, Unays heard about an Arabian prophet and told his brother the news. Abu Dharr came to meet the Prophet, became a Musim, and conveyed the Prophet's message back to his tribe.

'Uqbah ibn Abi Mu'ayt

Second husband of Arwa (mother of 'Uthman)
Father of Umm Kulthum bint 'Uqbah (the half-sister of 'Uthman)
Stepfather of 'Uthman ibn 'Affan
Clan of 'Abdu Shams (Tribe of Quraysh)

'Uqbah owned a flock of sheep that were tended by 'Abd Allah ibn Mas'ud. After the death of Abu Talib, 'Uqbah heaped entrails, blood, and excrement on the Prophet. He goaded Umayyah ibn Khalaf to fight at Badr, where both men were captured and put to death.

'Urwah ibn Mas'ud

Uncle of Mughirah ibn Shu'bah
Clan of Thaqif (Tribe of Hawazin)

The Meccans sent 'Urwah to assess the Prophet's intentions at Hudaybiyah. When he tugged the Prophet's beard out of familiarity, his own nephew Mughirah ibn Shu'bah slapped 'Urwah's hand with his sword, telling him to show respect for the Prophet. 'Urwah returned to Mecca describing a man who garnered more admiration from his people than a king. He entered Islam after Hunayn and asked the Prophet if he could return to Ta'if and summon his people to Islam. When he was slain by his kinfolk, the Prophet commented, "'Urwah is even as the man of Ya-Sin. He summoned his people unto God and they slew him." A year later, the Prophet sent Mughirah to Ta'if to destroy the temple of al-Lat.

Usamah ibn Zayd

Son of Zayd ibn Harithah and Umm Ayman
"Grandson" of Muhammad
Tribe of Kalb (adopted into the clan of Hashim, tribe of Quraysh)

Usamah was one of the first children to be born into Islam, and the Prophet considered him his own grandson. When he was 13, Usamah tried to join the army at Uhud but was sent home because he was too young. He was about the same age as 'A'ishah and vigorously defended her during the infidelity scandal. On one occasion, the Prophet rebuked Usamah for chasing a combatant and killing him even though the man surrendered and hastily testified his faith. He and Fadl ibn 'Abbas laid the Prophet's son Ibrahim in his grave. Usamah, Bilal, and 'Uthman ibn Talhah entered the Ka'bah with the Prophet during the Farewell Hajj Pilgrimage. Three years after his father Zayd was martyred in Syria, the Prophet dispatched Usamah at the head of 10,000 men to establish control over the area. However, when Usamah heard of the Prophet's worsening condition, he immediately returned to Medina. A few days later, he helped 'Ali prepare the Prophet's body for burial.

Usayd ibn Hudayr

Clan of Aws (Medina)

Just before the Hijrah, Usayd was sent by his clansman Sa'd ibn Mu'adh to drive Mus'ab ibn 'Umayr out of Yathrib. When Usayd embraced Islam, Sa'd approached Mus'ab directly and ended up embracing Islam as well. Usayd was one of 12 to pledge his allegiance to the Prophet at the Second 'Aqabah and carried one of the three banners at Uhud. Four years later, he rode alongside the Prophet during the Conquest of Mecca.

Usayrim ibn Thabit

Clan of Aws (Medina)

Usayrim converted to Islam on the morning of Uhud, where he was martyred. Thereafter, he was known as the man who entered Paradise without ever having prayed one of the obligatory daily prayers.

‘Utaybah ibn Abi Lahab

Son of Abu Lahab ibn ‘Abd al-Muttalib
Brother of ‘Utbah and Mu’attib
Engaged to Umm Kulthum bint Muhammad
First cousin of Muhammad
Clan of Hashim (Tribe of Quraysh)

‘Utaybah was arranged to be married to the Prophet's daughter Umm Kulthurm, but the engagement was broken by his parents when the Prophet began to preach about Islam.

‘Utbah ibn Abi Lahab

Son of Abu Lahab ibn ‘Abd al-Muttalib
Brother of ‘Utaybah and Mu’attib ibn Abi Lahab
Engaged to Ruqayyah bint Muhammad
First cousin of Muhammad
Clan of Hashim (Tribe of Quraysh)

‘Utbah was arranged to be married to the Prophet's daughter Ruqayyah, but the engagement was broken by his parents when the Prophet began to preach about Islam. At the Conquest of Mecca, ‘Utbah and his brother Mu’attib were too scared to ask the Prophet for forgiveness. Nonetheless, the Prophet sent for them and they testified their faith in Islam. Afterward, the Prophet led the two brothers, hand-in-hand, to the Ka’bah to pray.

‘Utbah ibn Rabi’ah

Grandson of ‘Abdu Shams ibn ‘Abdi Manaf
Brother of Shaybah ibn Rabi’ah
Father of Walid, Abu Hudhayfah, and Hind
Father-in-law of Abu Sufyan ibn al-Harb
Clan of ‘Abdu Shams (Tribe of Quraysh)

‘Utbah was the first Meccan to suggest making conciliatory offers to the Prophet. He approached the Prophet, but when the Prophet replied with verses from Surah Fussilat (Clear Explanation), ‘Utbah returned warning the others to leave him alone. He and his brother Shaybah were vacationing in Ta’if when they saw the Prophet and sent him grapes with their servant ‘Addas. ‘Utbah fought ‘Ubaydah ibn al-Harith in the opening duels of Badr, and was killed.

‘Uthman ibn ‘Abd Allah

Clan of Makhzum (Tribe of Quraysh)

‘Uthman was captured during a caravan raid led by ‘Abd Allah ibn Jahsh. He was held captive in Medina until his clansmen paid his ransom.

‘Uthman ibn ‘Affan (aka ‘Abdu Shams)

Maternal great-grandson of ‘Abd al-Muttalib
   ibn Hashim
Son of ‘Affan ibn Abi l-‘As
Half-brother of Umm Kulthum bint ‘Uqbah
Husband of Ruqayyah and Umm Kulthum
   bint Muhammad
Son-in-law of Muhammad (twice)
Clan of ‘Abdu Shams (Tribe of Quraysh)

‘Uthman was a successful merchant who was returning to Mecca when he heard a voice in the desert that said, "Sleepers, awake, for verily Ahmad has come forth in Mecca." After consulting Abu Bakr, he became one of the first men to embrace Islam. He was remarkably handsome, and when he married the Prophet's daughter Ruqayyah, the Prophet and Khadijah were especially pleased with the beautiful couple. A few years later, the couple sought asylum in Abyssinia, but returned when the ban on Hashim was lifted. During Badr, ‘Uthman stayed behind to care for his gravely ill wife. Soon after Ruqayyah's death, he turned down ‘Umar's proposal on behalf oh his daughter, Hafsah, but later agreed to marry Ruqayyah's younger sister, Umm Kulthum. At the Battle of the Trench, ‘Uthman was charged with negotiating a ceasefire with Ghatafan, but the plan did not come to fruition. At Hudaybiyah, the Prophet sent him to assess the situation in Mecca. Although he was well received by his clan of ‘Abdu Shams, they refused to allow the Muslims into the city to complete their pilgrimage. They allowed ‘Uthman to perform his pilgrimage, but he declined. While ‘Uthman was away at Tabuk, his wife, Umm Kulthum ,died. The Prophet consoled him saying that if he had another daughter, he would have given her to ‘Uthman in marriage as well. ‘Uthman was one of 10 Companions to whom the Prophet promised Paradise.

'Uthman ibn Maz'un

Brother of Zaynab bint Maz'un
  (wife of 'Umar)
Cousin of Umayyah and Ubayy ibn Khalaf
Husband of Khawlah bint al-Hakim
Clan of Jumah (Tribe of Quraysh)

'Uthman migrated to Abyssinia, but returned when the ban on Hashim was lifted. He sought protection under Walid ibn al-Mughirah, the chief of Makhzum, but later renounced it when he saw others being persecuted. He was an ascetic by nature and on several occasions, the Prophet had to counsel him toward moderation. When 'Uthman died shortly after Badr, the Prophet kissed him and wept. At first, 'Umar was surprised that such an eminent Companion did not die a martyr's death, but later changed his stance after the deaths of the Prophet and Abu Bakr. 'Uthman's widow, Khawlah, was an integral member of the Prophet's extended household.

'Uthman ibn Talhah

Clan of 'Abd ad-Dar (Tribe of Quraysh)

Although 'Uthman was not yet a Muslim, he helped Umm Salamah and her son migrate to Medina to join Abu Salamah. After the second 'Umrah, he and Khalid ibn al-Walid traveled to Medina to embrace Islam. At the Conquest of Mecca, the Prophet honored the clan of 'Abd ad-Dar by giving 'Uthman the keys to the Ka'bah. 'Uthman entered the Ka'bah alongside the Prophet, Usamah, and Bilal, and they destroyed the idols and images inside.

'Uzzah, Al- (idol)

Sister idol to Al-Lat and Al-Manat

Al-'Uzzah was the chief idol of Nakhlah, several miles south of Mecca. It was destroyed after the Conquest of Mecca by Khalid ibn al-Walid.

W

Wahb al-Muzani

Tribe of Muzaynah (Bedouin tribe)

Wahb was a Bedouin convert who defended the Prophet at Uhud and fought so valiantly that 'Umar later commented, "Of all deaths, the one I would most fain have died was the Muzaynite's death."

Wahb ibn 'Abdi Manaf

Father of Aminah bint Wahb
Maternal grandfather of the Muhammad
Clan of Zuhrah (Tribe of Quraysh)

Wahb was the chief of Zuhrah, but had died before his daughter Aminah married the 'Abd Allah ibn 'Abd al-Muttalib.

Wahshi

Slave of Jubayr ibn Mut'im
Abyssinian

Goaded by his master and Hind, Wahshi killed Hamzah with his javelin at Uhud and earned his freedom. After the Conquest of Mecca, he sought refuge in Ta'if. When the people of Ta'if also entered Islam, he came to Medina to testify his faith to the Prophet. Wahshi later killed Musaylimah ibn Habib, a false prophet from Yamamah.

Walid ibn al-Mughirah

Son of Mughirah ibn 'Abd Allah (late chief
*   of Makhzum)*
Husband of 'Asma bint al-Harith
Father of Khalid, Hisham, and Walid ibn al-Walid
Clan of Makhzum (Tribe of Quraysh)

As the chief of Makhzum and de facto leader of Quraysh, Walid was one of the first to take part in rebuilding the Ka'bah. During the Early Meccan Period, he accused the Prophet of being a sorcerer and warned anyone visiting the city to steer clear of him. On one occasion, the Prophet was trying to invite Walid to Islam when a blind man, 'Abd Allah ibn Umm Makhtum, approached the Prophet asking for guidance. The Prophet ignored 'Abd Allah and Surah 'Abasa (He Frowned) was immediately revealed. Later, Walid suggested that the Quraysh would consider incorporating Islam into their pagan practices, and the Prophet responded by reciting Surah Al Kafirun (The Faithless).

Walid ibn al-Walid

Son of Walid ibn al-Mughirah (chief of Makhzum)
Full brother to Hisham ibn al-Walid
Half-brother to Khalid ibn al-Walid
Clan of Makhzum (Tribe of Quraysh)

Walid fought against the Prophet at Badr and was captured. His brothers ransomed their father's famous armor for him, but when they were returning to Mecca, Walid escaped and returned to Medina. He explained that he did not want people to think he was entering Islam to help his family avoid paying his ransom. When Walid returned to Mecca to gather his belongings, his family imprisoned him. After Hudaybiyah, Walid managed to escape Mecca and join Abu Basir's camp along the Red Sea coast. He died before reaching Medina. However just before his death, he wrote to his brother Khalid telling him that the Prophet sometimes asked about him.

Walid ibn 'Utbah

Great-grandson of 'Abdu Shams ibn 'Abdi Manaf
Son of 'Utbah ibn Rabi'ah
Brother of Hind bint 'Utbah
Brother-in-law of Abu Sufyan ibn al-Harb
Clan of 'Abdu Shams (Tribe of Quraysh)

Walid was killed by 'Ali ibn Abi Talib in the opening duels of Badr. His death helped fuel Hind's hatred for the Prophet and Hamzah and desire for revenge.

Waraqah ibn Nawfal

Son of Nawfal ibn Asad
Brother of Qutaylah bint Nawfal
Cousin of Khadijah bint Khuwaylid
Clan of Asad (Tribe of Quraysh)

Waraqah was a Christian Haneef who anticipated the coming of an Arabian prophet. Before Khadijah's marriage, he confirmed her instincts about young Muhammad. Fifteen years later, Waraqah confirmed his prophethood and told the Prophet, "Anyone who came with something similar to what you have brought was treated with hostility: and if I should be alive till that day, then I would support you strongly."

Wuhayb ibn 'Abdi Manaf

Father of Halah bint Wuhayb
Uncle of Aminah bint Wahb
Father-in-law of 'Abd al-Muttalib
Clan of Zuhrah (Tribe of Quraysh)

Wuhayb was the guardian of his orphaned niece, Aminah. He agreed to marry her to 'Abd Allah ibn 'Abd al-Muttalib. That same day, Wuhayb also consented to his daughter's marriage (Halah) to 'Abd Allah's father, 'Abd al-Muttalib.

Y

Yasir ibn 'Amir

Husband of Sumayyah bint Khubbat
Father of 'Ammar ibn Yasir
Clan of Makhzum (Tribe of Quraysh)

During the early Meccan period, Abu Jahl abused Yasir and his family for their unshakeable conviction in Islam. Ultimately, Yasir's wife, Sumayyah, died from the torture.

Yusuf Dhu Nawas

Himyarite King

Yusuf was a sixth century Himyarite king who attempted to force Christians in Najran to convert to Judaism. When they refused, he exterminated tens of thousands of faithful Christians. They were thrown into a ditch of fire—a massacre that scholars believe is referenced in Surah Al Buruj.

Z

Zabir ibn Bata

Tribe of Qurayzah (Medina)

When the men of Bani Qurayzah were found guilty of treason, the Prophet showed leniency toward Zabir. The elderly Jew nonetheless decided to join his executed clansmen rather than live alone with his family and property.

Zam'ah ibn al-Aswad

Clan of Asad (Tribe of Quraysh)

Zam'ah was one of five men who persuade the Quraysh to end the ban on Hashim.

Zayd ibn ad-Dathinnah

Clan of Khazraj (Medina)

After Uhud, Zayd and Khubab ibn 'Adi were captured by Bani Hudayl at Raji and sold to the Meccans. They killed Zayd when he refused to renounce his faith. Both men's dramatic refusal and deaths displayed their extraordinary love for the Prophet which left a lasting impression on their captors.

Zayd ibn 'Amr (aka Zayd the Haneef)

Son of 'Amr ibn Nufayl
Half-brother of Khattab ibn Nufayl (maternal)
Father of Sa'id ibn Zayd
Clan of 'Adi (Tribe of Quraysh)

Before Islam, Zayd was a Haneef who was persecuted by his half-brother Khattab. He migrated to Iraq and Syria, where he ultimately died. The Prophet later said commented that Zayd worth was equivalent to an entire nation of people. Zayd's son, Sa'id, was an ardent supporter of the Prophet and one of 10 Companions to whom the Prophet promised Paradise.

Zayd ibn Arqam

Clan of Khazraj (Medina)

Zayd overheard 'Abd Allah ibn Ubayy disparage the Emigrants and told the Prophet of the incident. Ibn Ubayy denied the accusation, but his actions were later confirmed by verses in Surah Al Munafiqun (The Hypocrites).

Zayd ibn Harithah

Son of Harithah ibn Sharahil
Husband of Umm Ayman, Zaynab bint Jahsh, and Umm Kulthum bint 'Uqbah
Father of Usamah ibn Zayd (through Umm Ayman)
Adopted son of Muhammad
Tribe of Kalb (adopted into clan of Hashim, Tribe of Quraysh)

As a boy, Zayd was kidnapped from his northern tribe of Kalb and subsequently purchased by Hakim ibn Hizam. Hakim gave Zayd to his aunt Khadijah, who gifted the boy to the Prophet on their wedding day. When Zayd's father heard where his son was, he traveled to Mecca to buy his freedom. However Zayd chose to stay with the Prophet, who adopted him as his own son. Years later, Zayd became one of the first men to embrace Islam, and one of the Prophet's most trusted Companions. He followed the Prophet's advice and married Umm Ayman, and they had a son named Usamah. After the Hijrah, the Prophet linked Zayd with Hamzah at the Pact of Brotherhood, and entrusted him to retrieve Sawdah, Umm Kulthum, and Fatimah from Mecca. The Prophet also encouraged him to marry Zaynab bint Jahsh (a marriage that lasted just three years). After Uhud, Zayd was instructed to take back his original name, Zayd ibn Harithah. During the Battle of the Trench, Zayd was placed at the head of a large force to patrol the southern border of Medina. He led a successful caravan raid after the Trench, and another much larger expedition of 3,000 men to fight the Bani Ghassan near the Syrian border, where he was martyred.

Zaynab bint 'Ali

Third child of 'Ali ibn Abi Talib and Fatimah bint Muhammad
Clan of Hashim (Tribe of Quraysh)

Zaynab was born to Fatimah the same year that the Prophet's son Ibrahim died. She was named after Fatimah's eldest sister, who died two years earlier.

Zaynab bint Jahsh

Daughter of Jahsh ibn Ri'ab and Umaymah bint 'Abd al-Muttalib
Sister of 'Abd Allah, 'Ubayd Allah, and Hamnah bint Jahsh
First cousin of Muhammad
Seventh wife of Muhammad
Clan of 'Abdu Shams* (Tribe of Quraysh)

Known for her beauty, Zaynab was a dear cousin of the Prophet. She agreed to marry Zayd ibn Harithah at the Prophet's behest, but they divorced three years later. She married the Prophet after Uhud. When it became apparent that the Prophet was especially fond of 'A'ishah, Zaynab sent Fatimah to the Prophet to ask him to remain impartial to his wives. When Fatimah returned unsuccessful, Zaynab approached him directly. Like her predecessor, Zaynab bint Khuzaymah, Zaynab bint Jahsh was also known for her generosity. On one occasion, the Prophet told his wives that the first to follow him into Paradise would be "she of the longest reach." All the wives set out to measure their arms, but some 10 years later, Zaynab was the first to pass away. Her reach was measured by her generosity.

*Zaynab's father was from the distant tribe of Asad and was given honorary membership in 'Abdu Shams.

Zaynab bint Khuzaymah

Wife of 'Ubaydah ibn al-Harith (martyred at Badr)
Fifth wife of Muhammad
Clan of 'Amir (Tribe of Hawazin)

Zaynab was widowed after Badr when 'Ubaydah was killed in battle. She married the Prophet after Uhud, and earned the title "mother of the poor," for her endless generosity. After the wedding, Abu Bara (the chief of her clan of 'Amir) requested that the Prophet send scholars to teach Islam and promised their protection. A group of 40 teachers was sent and all but one were killed by a neighboring clan. Zaynab died eight months after her marriage to the Prophet and was buried near Ruqayyah's grave.

Zaynab bint Maz'un

Sister of 'Uthman ibn Maz'un
Wife of 'Umar ibn al-Khattab
Mother of Hafsah and 'Abd Allah ibn 'Umar
Clan of Jumah (Tribe of Quraysh)

Zaynab was the wife of 'Umar and sister of 'Uthman ibn Maz'un, one of the first responders to the Prophet's call.

Zaynab bint Muhammad

First daughter of Muhammad and Khadijah
Wife of Abu l-'As ibn ar-Rabi'
Mother of Umamah and 'Ali ibn Abi l-'As (he died in infancy)
Clan of Hashim (Tribe of Quraysh)

Zaynab was the eldest daughter of Muhammad, and was married to Abu l-'As before revelation began. When Abu l-'As was captured after Badr, Zaynab tried to ransom him from Mecca, but was requested to leave her husband and come to Medina with her daughter Umamah. Along the way, she miscarried her third child. Abu l-'As returned to Mecca, but several years later, he rejoined his family in Medina and embraced Islam. After the 'Umrah, a year after Hudaybiyah, Zaynab died. Two years later, her sister Fatimah gave birth to a baby girl whom she named Zaynab after her late aunt.

Zubayr ibn 'Abd al-Muttalib

Son of 'Abd al-Muttalib ibn Hashim
Full brother of Umaymah, Abu Talib, and 'Abd Allah
Half-brother of Abu Lahab ibn 'Abd al-Muttalib
Full uncle of Muhammad
Clan of Hashim (Tribe of Quraysh)

Zubayr was the Prophet's full uncle and became the chief of Hashim at the time of the Sacrilegious Wars. He was one of the organizers of the Pact of Chivalry, and brought his young nephew Muhammad along as a witness. Zubayr's younger half-sister, Safiyyah, named her son Zubayr ibn al-'Awwam after him.

Zubayr ibn al-'Awwam

Son of 'Awwam ibn Khuwaylid and Safiyyah bint 'Abd al-Muttalib
Husband of Asma' bint Abi Bakr
First cousin of Muhammad
Clan of Asad (Tribe of Quraysh)

Zubayr was named after his maternal uncle Zubayr ibn 'Abd al-Muttalib, and was one of the first family members to embrace Islam. He later migrated to Abyssinia and returned before the Hijrah. After settling in Medina, he married Asma' bint Abi Bakr. On the eve of Uhud, Zubayr was disappointed when the Prophet gave a special sword to Abu Dujanah ibn Kharashah, but later understood why, when he watched Abu Dujanah wreak havoc on the battlefield. After Hudaybiyah, he asked to marry Umm Kulthum bint 'Uqbah, 'Uthman's half-sister, but she ultimately married to Zayd ibn Harithah. Zubayr led one of four battalions at the Conquest of Mecca. Zubayr and Talhah retreated to Ali's house during the discussion of succession after the Prophet's death and were not present when Abu Bakr was nominated as the first Caliph. He was one of 10 Companions to whom the Prophet promised Paradise.

Zuhayr ibn Abi Umayyah

Son of Abu Umayyah and 'Atikah bint 'Abd al-Muttalib
Brother of 'Abd Allah ibn Abi Umayyah
Clan of Makhzum (Clan of Quraysh)

Although Zuhayr was one of the five men who encouraged the Quraysh to lift the ban on Hashim, he did not become a Muslim for most of the Prophet's life. He finally embraced Islam at Ji'ranah, after Hunayn.

ENDNOTES

P 1

1	Al-Mubarakpuri, 23
2	Yusuf, 3:2
3	Yusuf, 3:2
4	Yusuf, 3:2
5	Ramadan, 5-6
6	Ramadan, 1
7	Aslan, 27-28
8	Al-Mubarakpuri, 44

P 2

1	Aslan, 29
2	Yusuf, 3:9
3	Ibn Ishaq, 93 (via Lings, 10)

P 3

1	Armstrong, 31
2	Armstrong, 22
3	Aslan, 9
4	Lings, 16
5	Aslan, 13
6	Aslan, 13, 15
7	Yusuf, 4:3
8	Armstrong, 32
9	Aslan, 28
10	Lings, 20
11	Watt(1), 14
12	Lings, 21
13	Yusuf, 4:6
14	Yusuf, 4:7
15	Aslan, 23

P 4

1	Watt(1), 23
2	Ramadan, 12
3	Ramadan, 13-14
4	Aslan, 6
5	Yusuf, 4:8
6	Watt(1), 36
7	Watt(3), 8
8	Aslan, 23
9	Ramadan, 16-17
10	Aslan, 30
11	Armstrong, 12-13
12	Yusuf, 5:1
13	Aslan, 30-31
14	Armstrong, 22-23
15	Ibn Hisham 1/113,135 (via Al-Mubarakpuri, 61)
16	Watt(3), 9
17	Watt(3), 9
18	Aslan, 31
19	Ramadan, 21-22
20	Yusuf, 5:3
21	Yusuf, 5:5
22	Ibn Ishaq, 120 (via Lings, 35)
23	Watt(1), 38
24	Watt(2), 293-294
25	Ibn Sa'd 3/1,28 (via Lings, 38)
26	Watt(2), 295
27	Yusuf, 5:7
28	Al-Mubarakpuri, 28
29	Ramadan, 25

QY 1

1	Al-Mubarakpuri, 67
2	Watt(1), 44
3	Ramadan, 27
4	Aslan, 34
5	Armstrong, 27
6	Ibn Ishaq I.I, 151 (via Lings, 44)
7	Salahi, 65
8	Aslan, 37
9	Aslan, 35
10	Al-Mubarakpuri, 69
11	Armstrong, 34
12	Yusuf, 5:8
13	Armstrong, 37
14	Yusuf, 5:8
15	Al-Mubarakpuri, 69
16	Aslan, 38
17	Watt(3), 116
18	Ramadan, 31
19	Aslan, 38
20	Ramadan, 33
21	Ibn Hisham 156 (via Lings, 50)
22	Ramadan, 12
23	Armstrong, 53
24	Watt(1), 78
25	Watt, (1), 3
26	Al-Mubarakpuri, 74
27	Armstrong, 62
28	Ramadan, 32
29	Watt (1), 86
30	Ibn Sa'd, 3/1, 37 (via Lings, 48)
31	Armstrong, 49
32	Watt(3), 37-39
33	Armstrong, 43-44

QY 2

1	Lings, 47-48
2	Ramadan, 17
3	Armstrong, 52

QY 3

1	Ibn Al-Athir 1/584,585 (via Al-Mubarakpuri, 78)
2	Aslan, 41
3	Armstrong, 55-56
4	Al-Bukhari 2/702 (via Al-Mubarakpuri, 78)
5	Al-Bukhari 2/702 (via Al-Mubarakpuri, 78)
6	Ibn Ishaq, 234 (via Lings, 92)
7	Watt(3), 49
8	Watt(1), 75-76
9	Watt(3), 23, 26

QY 4

1	Aslan, 44
2	Armstrong, 68
3	Ibn Hisham 1/265-266 (via Al-Mubarakpuri, 86)
4	Watt(3), 51
5	Lings, 69
6	Lings, 70
7	Watt(3), 52-53
8	Watt(3), 22
9	Armstrong, 66-67
10	Watt(1), 72

11	Armstrong, 63
12	Watt(1), 78
13	Aslan, 44
14	Aslan, 40
15	Armstrong, 65-66

QY 5

1	Watt(1), 210
2	Salahi, 132-133
3	Ibn Hisham, 1/334-338 (via Al-Mubarakpuri, 94)
4	Ibn Hisham, 1/334-338 (via Al-Mubarakpuri, 95)
5	Salahi, 131
6	Salahi, 135
7	Watt(1), 19
8	Lings, 72
9	Armstrong, 67
10	Ibn Ishaq, 239 (via Lings, 76)

QY 6

1	Yusuf, 6:3
2	Ibn Hisham, 1/289-90 (via Al-Mubarakpuri, 97)
3	Armstrong, 66
4	Ibn Hisham, 1/289-90 (via Al-Mubarakpuri, 98)
5	Watt(3), 59
6	Ramadan, 65
7	Tarikh 'Umar bin Khattab, 13 (via Al-Mubarakpuri, 102)
8	Al-Mubarakpuri, 101
9	Ibn Hisham, 1/293-294 (via Al-Mubarakpuri, 103)
10	Aslan, 44
11	Armstrong, 48
12	Ibn Hisham, 1/293-294 (via Al-Mubarakpuri, 104)
13	Armstrong, 51
14	Ibn Hisham, 188 (via Lings, 64)
15	Yusuf, 7:4
16	Ibn Ishaq, 188 (via Lings, 65)
17	Watt(1), 136
18	Ibn Hisham, 1/362 (via Al-Mubarakpuri, 106)
19	Watt(1), 109
20	Ibn Hisha, 1/299-301 (via Al-Mubarakpuri, 107)
21	Ramadan, 57
22	Lings, 79-80
23	Lings, 80

QY 7

1	Aslan, 46-47
2	Watt(1), 121
3	Ramadan, 72-73

QY 8

1	Al-Mubarakpuri, 109

QY 9

1	Watt(1), 122
2	Lings, 95

QY 10

1	Ibn Hisham, 1/417-419 (via Al-Mubarakpuri, 113)
2	Yusuf, 9:3
3	Lings, 99
4	Musnad Imam Ahmad, 6/116 (via Al-Mubarakpuri, 115)
5	Ramadan, 35
6	Lings, 99
7	Yusuf, 9:4
8	Armstrong, 63
9	Ibn Hisham, 416 (via Al-Mubarakpuri, 116)
10	Ibn Hisham, 1/419-421 (via Al-Mubarakpuri, 124)

11	Yusuf, 9:6
12	Ramadan, 7
13	Ibn Hisham, 1/419-421 (via Al-Mubarakpuri, 125)
14	Yusuf, 9:6
15	Ramadan, 70
16	Watt(1), 137
17	Al-Bukhari 2,573 (via Al-Mubarakpuri, 128)
18	Ibn Sa'd, 4/164 (via Lings, 56
19	Ibn Ishaq, 252-254 (via Lings, 57)
20	Watt(3), 88
21	Armstrong, 89
22	Watt(2), 193
23	Armstrong, 90

QY 11

1	Watt(1), 143
2	Watt(1), 138
3	Ibn Hisham, 1/428-430 (via Al-Mubarakpuri, 134)
4	Watt(2), 176
5	Yusuf, 10:6-7
6	Salahi, 808-818
7	Armstrong, 92-93
8	Yusuf, 9:3
9	Armstrong, 84
10	Ibn Ishaq, 271 (via Al-Mubarakpuri, 137)
11	Ramadan, 86-87
12	Yusuf, 10:4
13	Ibn Ishaq, 265 (via Lings, 106)
14	Al-Mubarakpuri, 139

QY 12

1	Al-Bukhari, 1/550, 2/1003 (via Al-Mubarakpuri, 141)
2	Yusuf, 10:8-9
3	Yusuf, 10:8
4	Armstrong, 94

QY 13

1	Ibn Hisham, 1/442 (via Al-Mubarakpuri, 143)
2	Armstrong, 99
3	Salahi, 213-214
4	Al-Bukhari, 3905 (via Al-Mubarakpuri, 151)
5	Ramadan, 77-78
6	Lings, 120
7	Watt(1), 150
8	Aslan, 49
9	Armstrong, 96-97
10	Ramadan, 82-83
11	Armstrong, 102
12	Ramadan, 81
13	Al-Bukhari, 1/516,558 (via Al-Mubarakpuri, 157)
14	Yusuf, 11:1
15	Ramadan, 85
16	Ibn Sa'd, 1/1,159 (via Lings, 124)
17	Ramadan, 88
18	Watt(2), 301
19	Armstrong, 105-106
20	Watt(3), 100-101
21	Yusuf, 11:5
22	Al-Mubarakpuri, 167-168
23	Armstrong, 108
24	Ramadan, 88
25	Watt(3), 99
26	Armstrong, 96
27	Aslan, 57-59
28	Armstrong, 109-110
29	Al-Mubarakpuri, 173
30	Yusuf, 11:7
31	Ramadan, 93
32	Ibn Ishaq, 411-412 (via Lings, 131)

33   Lings, 132
34   Aslan, 55
35   Watt(3), 114-118
36   Ibn Hisham, 571 (via Lings, 193)

QY 14

1   Armstrong, 114
2   Yusuf, 12:2
3   Ramadan, 96
4   Watt(3), 105-106
5   Armstrong, 116
6   Ramadan, 98
7   Watt(2), 8-9
8   Salahi, 249
9   Al-Mubarakpuri, 188
10   Salahi, 251-252

QY 15

1   Aslan, 82
2   Yusuf, 12:9
3   Yusuf, 12:6
4   Salahi, 260
5   Al-Mubarakpuri, 193
6   Ramadan, 102-103
7   Al-Mubarakpuri, 194
8   Aslan, 83
9   Al-Mubarakpuri, 198
10   Lings, 149
11   Yusuf, 12:7
12   Ramadan, 104
13   Armstrong, 124
14   Al-Bukhari, 64:10; Ibn Ishaq, 444 (via Lings, 149)
15   Lings, 151
16   Yusuf, 12:8
17   Al-Mubarakpuri, 199
18   Aslan, 84
19   Aslan, 84
20   Watt(3),124
21   Watt(2), 18
22   Lings, 153
23   Yusuf, 5:10
24   Watt(2), 13
25   Armstrong, 124
26   Watt(2), 232
27   Al-Mubarakpuri, 210
28   Watt(3), 125-126
29   Ibn Sa'd, 8:24 (via Lings, 167)
30   Ramadan, 111-113
31   Watt(2), 14
32   Lings, 145
33   at-Tabari, 1344 (via Lings, 160)
34   Al-Waqidi, 251 (via Lings, 161)
35   Ibn Sa'd, 4:415; Ibn Ishaq, 472-473 (via Lings, 162)
36   Al-Mubarakpuri, 214
37   Ramadan, 108
38   Aslan, 60
39   Lings, 165
40   Watt(3),193-194
41   Aslan, 89
42   Salahi, 308
43   Armstrong, 130
44   Aslan, 90
45   Ramadan, 91
46   Ibn Sa'd, 3/1,289 (via Lings, 169)
47   Yusuf, 12:9
48   Ramadan, 133
49   Ramadan, 114
50   Aslan, 60
51   Ramadan, 150

QY 16

1   Al-Mubarakpuri, 354
2   Lings, 176
3   Yusuf, 12:6
4   Watt(3), 128-129
5   Lings, 169
6   Al-Mubarakpuri, 219
7   Al-Waqidi, 212-214 (via Lings, 179)
8   Ramadan, 122
9   Al-Waqidi, 214 (via Al-Mubarakpuri, 223)
10   Yusuf, 13:3
11   Al-Waqidi, 221 (via Lings, 183)
12   Ahmad "Fathul Bari", 7/350 (Al-Mubarakpuri, 226)
13   Al-Bukhari, 1/426 (via Al-Mubarakpuri, 227)
14   Ibn Ishaq, 561 (via Al-Mubarakpuri, 228)
15   Yusuf, 13:3
16   Ramadan, 125-127
17   Al-Waqidi, 275 (via Lings, 189)
18   Al-Bukhari, 2/579 (via Al-Mubarakpuri, 236)
19   Al-Bukhari, 2/582 (via Al-Mubarakpuri, 239)
20   Muslim, 2/108 (via Al-Mubarakpuri, 239)
21   Al-Waqidi, 247 (via Lings, 129)
22   Ibn Hisham, 2/284 (via Al-Mubarakpuri, 246)
23   Lings, 193
24   Aslan, 59
25   Lings, 197
26   Al-Waqidi, 256 (via Lings,190)
27   Watt(3), 140-141
28   Ramadan, 126
29   Aslan, 63
30   Armstrong, 133-136
31   Aslan, 61-62
32   Watt(2), 274-276
33   Watt(2), 277
34   Ramadan, 126
35   Watt(3), 143-144
36   Watt(2), 26
37   Lings, 207
38   Ramadan, 130
39   Ramadan, 131
40   Watt(2), 211-212
41   Armstrong, 139
42   Aslan, 90
43   Ramadan, 132
44   Aslan, 51

QY 17

1   Watt(3), 142
2   Watt(2), 57-58
3   Salahi, 390
4   Armstrong, 143-144
5   Ramadan, 136
6   Aslan, 64-65
7   Salahi, 490-491
8   Watt(3), 159-160
9   Yusuf, 16:1
10   Ad-Darimi, 20:58 (via Lings, 221)
11   Muslim, 1:16 (via li 217)
12   Al-Bukhari, 65 (via Lings, 218)
13   Armstrong, 109
14   Ramadan, 90

QY 18

1   Ramadan, 136-137
2   Watt(2), 29-30
3   Ramadan, 138
4   Ramadan, 139
5   Ibn Ishaq, 672 (via Lings, 226)
6   Yusuf, 18:3

6	Aslan, 90
7	Ramadan, 140
8	Ramadan, 141
9	Watt(3), 170-171
10	Watt(2), 39
11	Ramadan, 144-145
12	Al-Waqidi, 507 (via Lings, 238)
13	Ramadan, 146
14	Watt(2), 189
15	Yusuf, 16:1
16	Watt(3), 173-174
17	Aslan, 93-98
18	Watt(3), 175
19	Salahi, 467-473
20	Armstrong, 149-151
21	Aslan, 99
22	Ramadan, 133
23	Ramadan, 148
24	Ibn Ishaq, 729 (via Lings, 250)
25	Watt(2), 332
26	Salahi, 407
27	Ibn Ishaq, 726-728 (via Lings, 246)
28	Al-Mubarakpuri, 293
29	Salahi, 408
30	Ibn Ishaq, 726-728 (via Lings, 246)
31	Salahi, 310
32	Ramadan, 112
33	Lings, 248
34	Lings, 252
35	Lings, 253
36	Salahi, 424-425
37	Al-Bukhari, 1/364, 2/696-698; Ibn Hisham 2/297-307 (via Al-Mubarakpuri, 295)
38	Al-Bukhari, 52,15 (via Lings, 253)
39	Yusuf, 17:7
40	Yusuf, 17:7
41	Watt(3), 165-166
42	Salahi, 377

QY 19

1	Ibn Ishaq, 741 (via Lings, 256)
2	Lings, 257
3	Al-Mubarakpuri, 301
4	Watt(2), 58-59
5	Ramadan, 154
6	Yusuf, 18:3
7	Ibn Ishaq, 747-748 (via Lings, 260)
8	Ramadan, 157
9	Watt(3), 188
10	Yusuf, 18:4
11	Ibn Hisham (via Watt(2), 47-48)
12	Aslan, 105
13	Al-Waqidi, 1012 (via Lings, 332)
14	Ramadan, 157-159
15	Armstrong, 173
16	Yusuf, 19:1
17	Al-Mubarakpuri, 304
18	Al-Bukhari, 1/378-381 (via Al-Mubarakpuri, 307)
19	Armstrong, 173
20	Yusuf, 18:5
21	Armstrong, 172
22	Ramadan, 159
23	Yusuf, 18:5
24	Ramadan, 159-60
25	Yusuf, 19:2
26	Watt(1), 189
27	Al-Waqidi, 636 (via Lings, 272)
28	Salahi, 534-535
29	Yusuf, 20:2
30	Watt(3), 191

31	Watt(3), 220
32	Al-Bukhari, 51:28 (via Lings, 276)
33	Watt(2), 261
34	Salahi, 548
35	Armstrong, 180
36	Salahi, 139-140
37	Watt(2), 287-288
38	Al-Bukhari, 63:20 (via Lings, 281)
39	Yusuf, 20:5
40	Ibn Sa'd 4/1, 43 (via Lings, 282)
41	Fathul-Bari, 7/416 (via Al-Mubarakpuri, 355)
42	Al-Waqidi, 725 (via Al-Mubarakpuri, 336)
43	Al-Bukhari, 62:6 (via Lings, 285)
44	Ramadan, 169
45	Watt(2), 381-382
46	Ramadan, 85
47	Armstrong, 128, 135-137
48	Watt(2), 288
49	Lings, 286
50	Ramadan, 168-169
51	Yusuf, 20:10

QY 20

1	Salahi, 581
2	Ramadan, 171
3	At-Tabari, 1564 (via mu 316)
4	Al-Waqidi, 742 (via Lings, 295)
5	Ramadan, 171
6	Ibn Sa'd, 4:2, 30 (via Lings, 296)
7	Al-Mubarakpuri, 340
8	Watt(2), 54-55
9	Al-Mubarakpuri, 341
10	Ibn Sa'd, 3:1, 32 (via Lings, 299)
11	Ramadan, 172
12	Lings, 304
13	Al-Bukhari, 1/422, 2/612 (via Al-Mubarakpuri, 345)
14	Yusuf, 21:3
15	Yusuf, 21:2
16	Ramadan, 104
17	Watt(2), 59
18	Salahi, 634-635
19	Al-Mubarakpuri, 346
20	Watt(3), 231
21	Ramadan, 176
22	Al-Mubarakpuri, 347
23	Armstrong, 166
24	Armstrong, 189
25	Yusuf, 21:6
26	Yusuf, 21:6
27	Al-Mubarakpuri, 349
28	Yusuf, 21:9
29	Al-Waqidi, 850-853 (via Lings, 316)
30	Ramadan, 178
31	Watt(2), 71
32	Salahi, 656-657
33	Yusuf, 21:11
34	Watt(2), 72-73
35	Al-Mubarakpuri, 362
36	Ramadan, 184, 186
37	Lings, 322
38	Lings, 294
39	Ibn Hisham, 2/499,500; Al-Bukhari, 2/620,621 (via Al-Mubarakpuri, 364)
40	Ramadan, 185
41	Al-Bukhari 54, 15 (via Lings, 258)
42	Al-Waqidi, 961 (Lings, 326)
43	Aslan, 108
44	Watt(2), 76
45	Al-Bukhari, 63:37 (Lings, 329)

QY 21

1	Al-Mubarakpuri, 370
2	Yusuf, 23:2
3	Watt(3), 214
4	Watt(2), 145-146
5	Al-Mubarakpuri, 374
6	Yusuf, 23:4
7	Al-Waqidi, 1012 (via Lings, 332)
8	Yusuf, 23:4
9	Yusuf, 23:3
10	Yusuf, 23:6
11	Watt(2), 190
12	Watt(2), 18
13	Ibn Ishaq, 927 (via Lings, 336)
14	Yusuf, 23:10
15	Yusuf, 23:10
16	Ramadan, 167

QY 22

1	Ibn Sa'd, 1/1, 88-89 (via Lings, 339)
2	Ramadan, 192
3	Ibn Sa'd, 1/1, 88-89 (via Lings, 340)
4	Ramadan, 190
5	Al-Mubarakpuri, 387
6	Ramadan, 116
7	Watt(3), 222-223
8	Al-Bukhari, 62:1 (via Lings, 345)

QY 23

1	Al-Bukhari, 61:25 (via Lings, 348)
2	Ibn Kathir, al-Bidayahwa n-nihayah, V, 209 (via Lings, 351)
3	Lings, 349
4	Watt(3), 303-304
5	Muslim, 1/397 (via Al-Mubarakpuri, 403)
6	Al-Bukhari, 2/612 (via Al-Mubarakpuri, 407)
7	Ramadan, 200
8	Ibn Ishaq, 1000 (via Lings, 345)
9	Mishkatul-Masabih, 2/546 (via Al-Mubarakpuri, 410)
10	Al-Bukhari, 1/22 (via Al-Mubarakpuri, 411)
11	Al-Bukhari, 2/638 (via Al-Mubarakpuri, 413)
12	Ibn Ishaq, 2/2,27 (via Lings, 358)
13	Al-Bukhari, 2/640 (Al-Mubarakpuri, 416)
14	Al-Bukhari, 1/169 (Al-Mubarakpuri, 416)
15	Ramadan, 210
16	Yusuf, 24:6
17	Ibn Ishaq, 1017 (via Lings, 361)
18	Yusuf, 24:8
19	Al-Bukhari, 64:38 (via Lings, 361)
20	At-Tirmidhi, #231
21	Watt(3), 237
22	Yusuf, 24:8

APPENDICES

1	Sarwar, xxii
2	Watt(1), 8
3	Sarwar, xx
4	Khalidi, 15
5	Khalidi, 36-37
6	Khalidi, 175
7	Khalidi, 238
8	Khalidi, 335
9	Ali, 43
10	Khalidi, 262
11	Ali, 231
12	Ali, 2
13	Watt2, 333

ENDNOTES

WORKS CONSULTED

Abu Khalil, Shawqi. *Atlas on the Prophet's Biography: Places, Nations, Landmarks.*
    Riyadh, KSA: Darussalam, 2003.

Al-Tirmidhi. *A Commentary on the Depiction of Muhammad.*
    Birmingham, UK: Dar al-Arqam, 2015

Ali, Kecia. *The Lives of Muhammad.*
    President and Fellows of Harvard College, 2014

Al-Mubarakpuri, Safiur-Rehman. *The Sealed Nectar (Ar-Raheequl-Makhtum).*
    Riyadh, KSA: Darussalam, 2002

Armstrong, Karen. *Muhammad: A Prophet for our Time.*
    New York, NY: HarperCollins, 2007.

Aslan, Reza. *No God but God.*
    New York, NY: Random House, 2006

Emerick, Yahiyah. *The Meaning of the Holy Qur'an in Today's English.*
    CreateSpace, 2000.

Khalidi, Tarif. *Images of Muhammad: Narratives of the Prophet in Islam Across the Centuries.*
    New York, NY: Doubleday, 2009.

Lings, Martin. *Muhammad: His Life Based on the Earliest Sources.*
    Rochester, VT: Inner Traditions, 2006.

Ramadan, Tariq. *In the Footsteps of the Prophet.*
    New York, NY: Oxford University Press, 2007.

Robinson, Neal. *Discovering the Quran.*
    Great Britain: SCM Press, 2003.

Salahi, Adil. *Muhammad: Man and Prophet.*
    United Kingdom: The Islamic Foundation, 2002

Sarwar, Hafiz Ghulam. *Muhammad: The Holy Prophet.*
    Lahore, Pakistan: Sh. Muhammad Ashraf, 1961.

Watt, Montgomery. *Muhammad in Mecca.*
    Great Britain: Oxford University Press, 1953

Watt, Montgomery. *Muhammad in Medina.*
    Great Britain: Oxford University Press, 1956

Watt, Montgomery. *Muhammad: Prophet and Statesman.*
    Great Britain: Oxford University Press, 1961

Yusuf, Hamza. *The Life of the Prophet Muhammad.* CD
    Hayward, CA: Alhambra Productions, 1998.

NOTE   Watt citations in the text have been annotated as follows: Watt(1)—Muhammad in Mecca; Watt(2)—Muhammad in Medina; Watt(3)—Muhammad Prophet and Statesman

INDEX

INDEX

T

U/'U

ACKNOWLEDGMENTS

In the course of the past 13 years, this book has been shaped, discussed, debated, and polished by a number of family members, friends, and scholars. Each one of them has been far more instrumental than they realize, and deserves to be recognized for their unique contributions.

First and foremost, I'd like to begin with my wife, Hafsa Farooqui, not only for solving the book's difficult layout challenges and rendering my sketches into professional diagrams, but more importantly, for embracing my dreams and making the personal sacrifices to see them through. After an exhausting day of being mom, few wives allow their husbands to come home from work and spend the next six hours behind a laptop.

A very special thanks goes out to my tireless editor, Arifa Chaudhry, who cheerfully and meticulously edited and fact-checked three complete versions of this book without ever complaining about my consistent misuse, of commas. I have come to trust her implicitly, and without a doubt, she is the unsung hero of this project. I'd like to thank my multi-talented graphic designer, Nermin Moufti, for developing the sophisticated look and feel of this book. When I challenged Nermin to help me design a cover that reflects the beauty of its subject matter, I had no idea it would feel this special. I'd also like to thank my trusted friend Shehla Syed, at Westhill Technology Counsel, whose resourceful legal work allowed me to incorporate the diverse scholarship presented herein. Thank you to Omman Hussain for his revisions of the first edition, and of course, Rana Barbour, for helping us bring this product to the public.

Thank you Yahiya Emerick, for graciously providing such an accessible translation of the Qur'an. I'd also like to thank the scholars whose work was used in this book, and their publishers (HarperCollins, Random House, Oxford University Press, Darrusalam, The Islamic Foundation, and Zaytuna College) for granting permission to use their materials.

Dr. Sherman Jackson came into this project when I needed him most, and despite an unbelievable work schedule, he carefully reviewed my manuscript and delivered a powerful foreword that is both urgent and essential. I feel deeply blessed every time we share a meal, or even a quick phone call. Truly some of the greatest minds don't know how empowering their words can be.

The same can be said for matters of the heart. For this, I am grateful to Dr. Umar Faruq Abd-Allah, and the long list of scholars who have influenced me along the way.

Special thanks to my entire family, most notably Majid and Imraan. Ever since I began this project, the two of you have been by my side during the hardest parts of my journey. Because of you, I'm finally beginning to learn how to think smarter and write clearer.

Finally, I'd like to take a moment to thank my parents. From the very beginning, my mother instilled in me a tireless work ethic, while my father endowed me with a wonderful disregard for what others think is possible. Together they have taught me more about the Prophet than a roomful of books could ever achieve. While *Revelation* is dedicated to my readers, its reward belongs to my parents. May they receive each and every blessing that comes out of this project. *Ameen.*